PRESENTED TO

_____

FROM

_____

DATE

_____

Walk Through the Word: A New Testament Devotional
© 2012 by Thomas Nelson, Inc.

Published in Nashville, Tennessee, by Thomas Nelson®. Thomas Nelson is a registered trademark of Thomas Nelson, Inc.

Thomas Nelson, Inc., titles may be purchased in bulk for educational, business, fund-raising, or sales promotional use. For information, please e-mail SpecialMarkets@ThomasNelson.com.

Scripture quotations are taken from THE NEW KING JAMES VERSION. © 1982 by Thomas Nelson, Inc. Used by permission. All rights reserved.

ISBN-13: 978-1-4041-7467-2

Printed in China

12 13 14 15 16 RRD 5 4 3 2 1

www.thomasnelson.com

Walk
THROUGH
THE WORD

A New Testament Devotional

A Division of Thomas Nelson Publishers

THOMAS NELSON
Since 1798

NASHVILLE   DALLAS   MEXICO CITY   RIO DE JANEIRO

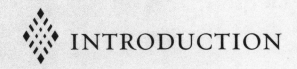# INTRODUCTION

Fifty-one other pastors have joined me in contributing time and expertise in order to bring Scripture alive for each day of *Walk Through the Word*. We invite you to embark on a meaningful journey of reading through the New Testament in a year. It is our prayer that you will grow in your faith and deepen your walk with God along the way.

Each week you will be encouraged to journal your thoughts on the scriptures and commentary you have read. As you continue your walk through God's Word, your knowledge of Him will grow, and you will find yourself becoming more like Christ.

"The word of God is living and powerful, and sharper than any two-edged sword, piercing even to the division of soul and spirit, and of joints and marrow, and is a discerner of the thoughts and intents of the heart" (Hebrews 4:12). Praise God His message is alive and active for all of us when we spend time in His Word. May your life be changed as you walk through God's Word this year.

Johnny M. Hunt

Dr. Johnny M. Hunt
Pastor, First Baptist Church of Woodstock
Woodstock, Georgia

◆ CONTENTS

Walk

THROUGH
THE WORD

A New Testament Devotional

WEEK I, DAY I

The Savior of God's
People Is Born

Matthew 1:1–25

The Genealogy of Jesus Christ

1 The book of the genealogy of Jesus Christ, the Son of David, the Son of Abraham:

²Abraham begot Isaac, Isaac begot Jacob, and Jacob begot Judah and his brothers. ³Judah begot Perez and Zerah by Tamar, Perez begot Hezron, and Hezron begot Ram. ⁴Ram begot Amminadab, Amminadab begot Nahshon, and Nahshon begot Salmon. ⁵Salmon begot Boaz by Rahab, Boaz begot Obed by Ruth, Obed begot Jesse, ⁶and Jesse begot David the king.

David the king begot Solomon by her who had been the wife of Uriah. ⁷Solomon begot Rehoboam, Rehoboam begot Abijah, and Abijah begot Asa. ⁸Asa begot Jehoshaphat, Jehoshaphat begot Joram, and Joram begot Uzziah. ⁹Uzziah begot Jotham, Jotham begot Ahaz, and Ahaz begot Hezekiah. ¹⁰Hezekiah begot Manasseh, Manasseh begot Amon, and Amon begot Josiah. ¹¹Josiah begot Jeconiah and his brothers about the time they were carried away to Babylon.

¹²And after they were brought to Babylon, Jeconiah begot Shealtiel, and Shealtiel begot Zerubbabel. ¹³Zerubbabel begot Abiud, Abiud begot Eliakim, and Eliakim begot Azor. ¹⁴Azor begot Zadok, Zadok begot Achim, and Achim begot Eliud. ¹⁵Eliud begot Eleazar, Eleazar begot Matthan, and Matthan begot Jacob. ¹⁶And Jacob begot Joseph the husband of Mary, of whom was born Jesus who is called Christ.

¹⁷So all the generations from Abraham to David are fourteen generations, from David until the captivity in Babylon are fourteen generations, and from the captivity in Babylon until the Christ are fourteen generations.

Christ Born of Mary

¹⁸Now the birth of Jesus Christ was as follows: After His mother Mary was betrothed to Joseph, before they came together, she was found with child of the Holy Spirit. ¹⁹Then Joseph her husband, being a just man, and not wanting to make her a public example, was minded to put her away secretly. ²⁰But while he thought about these things, behold, an angel of the Lord appeared to him in a dream, saying, "Joseph, son of David, do not be afraid to take to you Mary your wife, for that which is conceived in her is of the Holy Spirit. ²¹And she will bring forth a Son, and you shall call His name Jesus, for He will save His people from their sins."

²²So all this was done that it might be fulfilled which was spoken by the Lord through the prophet, saying: ²³"Behold, the virgin shall be with child, and bear a Son, and they shall call His name Immanuel," which is translated, "God with us."

²⁴Then Joseph, being aroused from sleep, did as the angel of the Lord commanded him and took to him his wife, ²⁵and did not know her till she had brought forth her firstborn Son. And he called His name Jesus.

DEVOTIONAL

The Incarnation is here, presented for all to see our heavenly Father's deep love for the world. He cared enough to clothe Himself in flesh and come to us. This is the true picture of our Immanuel, God with us. The promise of Isaiah 7:14 is now a reality: "The virgin shall conceive and bear a Son." Oswald Chambers, in My Utmost for His Highest, *said, "The whole meaning of the Incarnation is the cross. Beware of separating God manifest in the flesh from the Son becoming sin. The Incarnation was for the purpose of Redemption.... The centre of salvation is the cross of Jesus, and the reason it is so easy to obtain salvation is because it cost God so much."[1]*

After four hundred years of silence, the Lord wasted no time in speaking through His servant Matthew, sharing the good news—that He had made a way for humanity to be forgiven of sin by His only Son. This first chapter of Matthew prompts a believer not only to celebrate Christmas, but also to foresee the cross and the hope for celebration come Easter.

Think back to the garden of Eden, where the first couple sinned against a holy God. They were separated from Him and cast out of the Garden. Yet in Genesis 3:15 the Scriptures promise a deliverer. Now, after years of waiting, God Himself had come in the flesh in the Person of His Son. As you consider God's divine rescue plan today, express your gratitude to the Babe in the manger who paid the ultimate price for you.

—Dr. Johnny Hunt
First Baptist Church, Woodstock, GA

WEEK I, DAY 2

The Wise Will Seek God

Matthew 2:1–23

Wise Men from the East

2 Now after Jesus was born in Bethlehem of Judea in the days of Herod the king, behold, wise men from the East came to Jerusalem, ²saying, "Where is He who has been born King of the Jews? For we have seen His star in the East and have come to worship Him."

³When Herod the king heard this, he was troubled, and all Jerusalem with him. ⁴And when he had gathered all the chief priests and scribes of the people together, he inquired of them where the Christ was to be born.

⁵So they said to him, "In Bethlehem of Judea, for thus it is written by the prophet:

6   'But you, Bethlehem, in the land of Judah,
     Are not the least among the rulers of Judah;
     For out of you shall come a Ruler
     Who will shepherd My people Israel.'"

⁷Then Herod, when he had secretly called the wise men, determined from them what time the star appeared. ⁸And he sent them to Bethlehem and said, "Go and search carefully for the young Child, and when you have found Him, bring back word to me, that I may come and worship Him also."

⁹When they heard the king, they departed; and behold, the star which they had seen in the East went before them, till it came and stood over where the young Child was. ¹⁰When they saw the star, they rejoiced with exceedingly great joy. ¹¹And when they had come into the house, they saw the young Child with Mary His mother, and fell down and worshiped Him. And when they had opened their treasures, they presented gifts to Him: gold, frankincense, and myrrh.

¹²Then, being divinely warned in a dream that they should not return to Herod, they departed for their own country another way.

The Flight into Egypt

¹³Now when they had departed, behold, an angel of the Lord appeared to Joseph in a dream, saying, "Arise, take the young Child and His mother, flee to Egypt, and stay there until I bring you word; for Herod will seek the young Child to destroy Him."

¹⁴When he arose, he took the young Child and His mother by night and departed for Egypt, ¹⁵and was there until the death of Herod, that it might be fulfilled which was spoken by the Lord through the prophet, saying, "Out of Egypt I called My Son."

Massacre of the Innocents

¹⁶Then Herod, when he saw that he was deceived by the wise men, was exceedingly angry; and he sent forth and put to death all the male children who were in Bethlehem and in all its districts, from two years old and under, according to the time which he had determined from the wise men. ¹⁷Then was fulfilled what was spoken by Jeremiah the prophet, saying:

18   "A voice was heard in Ramah,
     Lamentation, weeping, and great mourning,
     Rachel weeping for her children,
     Refusing to be comforted,
     Because they are no more."

The Home in Nazareth

¹⁹Now when Herod was dead, behold, an angel of the Lord appeared in a dream to Joseph in Egypt, ²⁰saying, "Arise, take the young Child and His mother, and go to the land of Israel, for those who sought the young Child's life are dead." ²¹Then he arose took the young Child and His mother, and came into the land of Israel.

²²But when he heard that Archelaus was reigning over Judea instead of his father Herod, he was afraid to go there. And being warned by God in a dream, he turned aside into the region of Galilee. ²³And he came and dwelt in a city called Nazareth, that it might be fulfilled which was spoken by the prophets, "He shall be called a Nazarene."

DEVOTIONAL

M atthew chapter 2 introduces three different characters: King Herod, the chief priests and scribes, and the wise men. Each of them depicts a different attitude. Herod's attitude was one of indignation, hatred, and hostility. The chief priests and scribes were indifferent. The wise men, however, declared, "If there is a God, and we can know Him, we will seek Him with all of our hearts," which is what our attitude should be. If Jesus Christ is who He says He is, we must lay at His feet our lives as offerings that will rebound to His glory. Wise men still seek Him today!

—Dr. Johnny Hunt
First Baptist Church, Woodstock, GA

WEEK I, DAY 3

Jesus, Our Example

Matthew 3:1–4:11

John the Baptist Prepares the Way

3 In those days John the Baptist came preaching in the wilderness of Judea, ²and saying, "Repent, for the kingdom of heaven is at hand!" ³For this is he who was spoken of by the prophet Isaiah, saying:

"The voice of one crying in the wilderness:
 'Prepare the way of the LORD;
 Make His paths straight.'"

⁴Now John himself was clothed in camel's hair, with a leather belt around his waist; and his food was locusts and wild honey. ⁵Then Jerusalem, all Judea, and all the region around the Jordan went out to him ⁶and were baptized by him in the Jordan, confessing their sins.

⁷But when he saw many of the Pharisees and Sadducees coming to his baptism, he said to them, "Brood of vipers! Who warned you to flee from the wrath to come? ⁸Therefore bear fruits worthy of repentance, ⁹and do not think to say to yourselves, 'We have Abraham as our father.' For I say to you that God is able to raise up children to Abraham from these stones. ¹⁰And even now the ax is laid to the root of the trees. Therefore every tree which does not bear good fruit is cut down and thrown into the fire. ¹¹I indeed baptize you with water unto repentance, but He who is coming after me is mightier than I, whose sandals I am not worthy to carry. He will baptize you with the Holy Spirit and fire. ¹²His winnowing fan is in His hand, and He will thoroughly clean out His threshing floor, and gather His wheat into the barn; but He will burn up the chaff with unquenchable fire."

John Baptizes Jesus

¹³Then Jesus came from Galilee to John at the Jordan to be baptized by him. ¹⁴And John tried to prevent Him, saying, "I need to be baptized by You, and are You coming to me?"

¹⁵But Jesus answered and said to him, "Permit it to be so now, for thus it is fitting for us to fulfill all righteousness." Then he allowed Him.

¹⁶When He had been baptized, Jesus came up immediately from the water; and behold, the heavens were opened to Him, and He saw the Spirit of God descending like a dove and alighting upon Him. ¹⁷And suddenly a voice came from heaven, saying, "This is My beloved Son, in whom I am well pleased."

Satan Tempts Jesus

4 Then Jesus was led up by the Spirit into the wilderness to be tempted by the devil. ²And when He had fasted forty days and forty nights, afterward He was hungry. ³Now when the tempter came to Him, he said, "If You are the Son of God, command that these stones become bread."

⁴But He answered and said, "It is written, 'Man shall not live by bread alone, but by every word that proceeds from the mouth of God.'"

⁵Then the devil took Him up into the holy city, set Him on the pinnacle of the temple, ⁶and said to Him, "If You are the Son of God, throw Yourself down. For it is written:

'He shall give His angels charge over you,'

and,

In their hands they shall bear you up,
 Lest you dash your foot against a stone.'"

⁷Jesus said to him, "It is written again, 'You shall not tempt the Lord your God.'"

⁸Again, the devil took Him up on an exceedingly high mountain, and showed Him all the kingdoms of the world and their glory. ⁹And he said to Him, "All these things I will give You if You will fall down and worship me."

¹⁰Then Jesus said to him, "Away with you, Satan! For it is written, 'You shall worship the Lord your God, and Him only you shall serve.'"

¹¹Then the devil left Him, and behold, angels came and ministered to Him.

DEVOTIONAL

P age after page of the New Testament shows us how Jesus is our ultimate example. In Matthew 3, we see Him submit to baptism to fulfill all righteousness and to identify with all those He came to save. We're called to submit to baptism, just like Jesus did. Here we also see Him overcome Satan's temptations by putting faith in specific truths from God's Word. We can do the same! The next time you face temptation, remember that Jesus overcame the world, He is in you, and He gave you an example to follow of allowing God's Word to defeat temptation. Ask Him to help you, empower you, and make you more like Him.

—Dr. Johnny Hunt
First Baptist Church, Woodstock, GA

WEEK I, DAY 4

"Come, Follow Me"

Matthew 4:12–5:12

Jesus Begins His Galilean Ministry

Now when Jesus heard that John had been put in prison, He departed to Galilee. 13And leaving Nazareth, He came and dwelt in Capernaum, which is by the sea, in the regions of Zebulun and Naphtali, 14that it might be fulfilled which was spoken by Isaiah the prophet, saying:

15 "The land of Zebulun and the land of Naphtali,
By the way of the sea, beyond the Jordan,
Galilee of the Gentiles:

16 The people who sat in darkness have seen a
great light,
And upon those who sat in the region and
shadow of death
Light has dawned."

17From that time Jesus began to preach and to say, "Repent, for the kingdom of heaven is at hand."

Four Fishermen Called as Disciples

18And Jesus, walking by the Sea of Galilee, saw two brothers, Simon called Peter, and Andrew his brother, casting a net into the sea; for they were fishermen. 19Then He said to them, "Follow Me, and I will make you fishers of men." 20They immediately left their nets and followed Him.

21Going on from there, He saw two other brothers, James the son of Zebedee, and John his brother, in the boat with Zebedee their father, mending their nets. He called them, 22and immediately they left the boat and their father, and followed Him.

Jesus Heals a Great Multitude

23And Jesus went about all Galilee, teaching in their synagogues, preaching the gospel of the kingdom, and healing all kinds of sickness and all kinds of disease among the people. 24Then His fame went throughout all Syria; and they brought to Him all sick people who were afflicted with various diseases and torments, and those who were demon-possessed, epileptics, and paralytics; and He healed them. 25Great multitudes followed Him—from Galilee, and from Decapolis, Jerusalem, Judea, and beyond the Jordan.

The Beatitudes

5And seeing the multitudes, He went up on a mountain, and when He was seated His disciples came to Him. 2Then He opened His mouth and taught them, saying:

3 "Blessed are the poor in spirit,
For theirs is the kingdom of heaven.

4 Blessed are those who mourn,
For they shall be comforted.

5 Blessed are the meek,
For they shall inherit the earth.

6 Blessed are those who hunger and thirst for
righteousness,
For they shall be filled.

7 Blessed are the merciful,
For they shall obtain mercy.

8 Blessed are the pure in heart,
For they shall see God.

9 Blessed are the peacemakers,
For they shall be called sons of God.

10 Blessed are those who are persecuted for
righteousness' sake,
For theirs is the kingdom of heaven.

11"Blessed are you when they revile and persecute you, and say all kinds of evil against you falsely for My sake. 12Rejoice and be exceedingly glad, for great is your reward in heaven, for so they persecuted the prophets who were before you."

DEVOTIONAL

*A*fter John the Baptist was arrested, Jesus took up John's message and began preaching repentance to the people. He also called His first disciples. If you listen today, you may hear His still, small voice calling you from whatever you are doing to make Him the major focus of your life and, in particular, of your day.

Chapter 5 provides a list called the Beatitudes that help us to do just that and be kingdom-minded as we go about our daily lives. As Christ followers, these are the attitudes that ought to be prominent in our lives. One day we will rule with the Lord Jesus, but we can reign in this life if He reigns in us and we allow Him to change our attitudes to be like His. Pray that your attitude would be one that brings Him glory today.

—Dr. Johnny Hunt
First Baptist Church, Woodstock, GA

WEEK I, DAY 5

Take God's Light into the World

Matthew 5:13–37

Believers Are Salt and Light

"You are the salt of the earth; but if the salt loses its flavor, how shall it be seasoned? It is then good for nothing but to be thrown out and trampled underfoot by men.

14"You are the light of the world. A city that is set on a hill cannot be hidden. 15Nor do they light a lamp and put it under a basket, but on a lampstand, and it gives light to all who are in the house. 16Let your light so shine before men, that they may see your good works and glorify your Father in heaven.

Jesus Fulfills the Law

17"Do not think that I came to destroy the Law or the Prophets. I did not come to destroy but to fulfill. 18For assuredly, I say to you, till heaven and earth pass away, one jot or one tittle will by no means pass from the law till all is fulfilled. 19Whoever therefore breaks one of the least of these commandments, and teaches men so, shall be called least in the kingdom of heaven; but whoever does and teaches them, he shall be called great in the kingdom of heaven. 20For I say to you, that unless your righteousness exceeds the righteousness of the scribes and Pharisees, you will by no means enter the kingdom of heaven.

Murder Begins in the Heart

21"You have heard that it was said to those of old, 'You shall not murder, and whoever murders will be in danger of the judgment.' 22But I say to you that whoever is angry with his brother without a cause shall be in danger of the judgment. And whoever says to his brother, 'Raca!' shall be in danger of the council. But whoever says, 'You fool!' shall be in danger of hell fire. 23Therefore if you bring your gift to the altar, and there remember that your brother has something against you, 24leave your gift there before the altar, and go your way. First be reconciled to your brother, and then come and offer your gift. 25Agree with your adversary quickly, while you are on the way with him, lest your adversary deliver you to the judge, the judge hand you over to the officer, and you be thrown into prison. 26Assuredly, I say to you, you will by no means get out of there till you have paid the last penny.

Adultery in the Heart

27"You have heard that it was said to those of old, 'You shall not commit adultery.' 28But I say to you that whoever looks at a woman to lust for her has already committed adultery with her in his heart. 29If your right eye causes you to sin, pluck it out and cast it from you; for it is more profitable for you that one of your members perish, than for your whole body to be cast into hell. 30And if your right hand causes you to sin, cut it off and cast it from you; for it is more profitable for you that one of your members perish, than for your whole body to be cast into hell.

Marriage Is Sacred and Binding

31"Furthermore it has been said, 'Whoever divorces his wife, let him give her a certificate of divorce.' 32But I say to you that whoever divorces his wife for any reason except sexual immorality causes her to commit adultery; and whoever marries a woman who is divorced commits adultery.

Jesus Forbids Oaths

33"Again you have heard that it was said to those of old, 'You shall not swear falsely, but shall perform your oaths to the Lord.' 34But I say to you, do not swear at all: neither by heaven, for it is God's throne; 35nor by the earth, for it is His footstool; nor by Jerusalem, for it is the city of the great King. 36Nor shall you swear by your head, because you cannot make one hair white or black. 37But let your 'Yes' be 'Yes,' and your 'No,' 'No.' For whatever is more than these is from the evil one."

DEVOTIONAL

Did you know God sees you as salt and light in this fallen world we live in? As we are faithful to the Lord, He uses us as lights that penetrate darkness and as salt that preserves and causes others to desire a fresh drink of living water from Jesus' well. What a wonderful reminder that it is His righteousness, not our goodness, that allows us to make a difference—to be the light and salt. We must examine our own hearts, as many times it is not our actions as much as our attitudes that keep us from walking in the light as He is in the light. We must have fellowship with God to renew our stores of salt and light, so draw near to Him. Give someone a taste of Jesus today and shine His light on every dark corner of your world!

—Dr. Johnny Hunt
First Baptist Church, Woodstock, GA

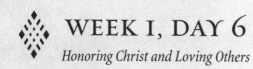

WEEK I, DAY 6

Honoring Christ and Loving Others

Matthew 5:38–6:15

Go the Second Mile

"You have heard that it was said, 'An eye for an eye and a tooth for a tooth.' 39But I tell you not to resist an evil person. But whoever slaps you on your right cheek, turn the other to him also. 40If anyone wants to sue you and take away your tunic, let him have your cloak also. 41And whoever compels you to go one mile, go with him two. 42Give to him who asks you, and from him who wants to borrow from you do not turn away.

Love Your Enemies

43"You have heard that it was said, 'You shall love your neighbor and hate your enemy.' 44But I say to you, love your enemies, bless those who curse you, do good to those who hate you, and pray for those who spitefully use you and persecute you, 45that you may be sons of your Father in heaven; for He makes His sun rise on the evil and on the good, and sends rain on the just and on the unjust. 46For if you love those who love you, what reward have you? Do not even the tax collectors do the same? 47And if you greet your brethren only, what do you do more than others? Do not even the tax collectors do so? 48Therefore you shall be perfect, just as your Father in heaven is perfect.

Do Good to Please God

6"Take heed that you do not do your charitable deeds before men, to be seen by them. Otherwise you have no reward from your Father in heaven. 2Therefore, when you do a charitable deed, do not sound a trumpet before you as the hypocrites do in the synagogues and in the streets, that they may have glory from men. Assuredly, I say to you, they have their reward. 3But when you do a charitable deed, do not let your left hand know what your right hand is doing, 4that your charitable deed may be in secret; and your Father who sees in secret will Himself reward you openly.

The Model Prayer

5"And when you pray, you shall not be like the hypocrites. For they love to pray standing in the synagogues and on the corners of the streets, that they may be seen by men. Assuredly, I say to you, they have their reward. 6But you, when you pray, go into your room, and when you have shut your door, pray to your Father who is in the secret place; and your Father who sees in secret will reward you openly. 7And when you pray, do not use vain repetitions as the heathen do. For they think that they will be heard for their many words.

8"Therefore do not be like them. For your Father knows the things you have need of before you ask Him. 9In this manner, therefore, pray:

> Our Father in heaven,
> Hallowed be Your name.
> 10 Your kingdom come.
> Your will be done
> On earth as it is in heaven.
> 11 Give us this day our daily bread.
> 12 And forgive us our debts,
> As we forgive our debtors.
> 13 And do not lead us into temptation,
> But deliver us from the evil one.
> For Yours is the kingdom and the power and the
> glory forever. Amen.

14"For if you forgive men their trespasses, your heavenly Father will also forgive you. 15But if you do not forgive men their trespasses, neither will your Father forgive your trespasses."

DEVOTIONAL

It has been said that more of us should travel on the "second mile" because there are so few people there. It is more and more difficult to be not only a second-miler but also to find others who will join us on the journey. The Bible teaches us to love our enemies—even those who spitefully use us, persecute us, and hate us. But without God's constant help, this kind of living is not just difficult—it is simply impossible. We must be yielded to Christ, who enables us to love our enemies.

Spend time with Him today. Find a secret place, close the door behind you, and make your needs known to Him. You will learn intimacy, submission, dependence, forgiveness, and obedience, all of which are absolutely necessary as you seek to develop the endurance it takes to get up on the high road and go that second mile. And as you have opportunity to do good today to those who cross your path, do it as unto the Lord!

—Dr. Johnny Hunt
First Baptist Church, Woodstock, GA

WEEK I, DAY 7

Lord, may the motives of my heart be those that please You. May they be love for You and not desire for recognition from others. Lord, who can I be salt and light to today?

List those who need to see Jesus in your life and draw close to Him.

_____

_____

_____

_____

_____

_____

_____

_____

It is in these passages that we see Christ's coming, baptism, and temptation. If Christ as the Son of God was tempted and resisted, to whom else can you look to help you overcome temptation and sin? Write a prayer asking God to help you overcome specific temptations and sins in your life.

_____

_____

_____

_____

_____

_____

_____

_____

WEEK 2, DAY 1

Truly Trusting God

Matthew 6:16–7:6

Fasting to Be Seen Only by God

"Moreover, when you fast, do not be like the hypocrites, with a sad countenance. For they disfigure their faces that they may appear to men to be fasting. Assuredly, I say to you, they have their reward. 17But you, when you fast, anoint your head and wash your face, 18so that you do not appear to men to be fasting, but to your Father who is in the secret place; and your Father who sees in secret will reward you openly.

Lay Up Treasures in Heaven

19"Do not lay up for yourselves treasures on earth, where moth and rust destroy and where thieves break in and steal; 20but lay up for yourselves treasures in heaven, where neither moth nor rust destroys and where thieves do not break in and steal. 21For where your treasure is, there your heart will be also.

The Lamp of the Body

22 "The lamp of the body is the eye. If therefore your eye is good, your whole body will be full of light. 23But if your eye is bad, your whole body will be full of darkness. If therefore the light that is in you is darkness, how great is that darkness!

You Cannot Serve God and Riches

24"No one can serve two masters; for either he will hate the one and love the other, or else he will be loyal to the one and despise the other. You cannot serve God and mammon.

Do Not Worry

25"Therefore I say to you, do not worry about your life, what you will eat or what you will drink; nor about your body, what you will put on. Is not life more than food and the body more than clothing? 26Look at the birds of the air, for they neither sow nor reap nor gather into barns; yet your heavenly Father feeds them. Are you not of more value than they? 27Which of you by worrying can add one cubit to his stature?

28"So why do you worry about clothing? Consider the lilies of the field, how they grow: they neither toil nor spin;

29and yet I say to you that even Solomon in all his glory was not arrayed like one of these. 30Now if God so clothes the grass of the field, which today is, and tomorrow is thrown into the oven, will He not much more clothe you, O you of little faith?

31"Therefore do not worry, saying, 'What shall we eat?' or 'What shall we drink?' or 'What shall we wear?' 32For after all these things the Gentiles seek. For your heavenly Father knows that you need all these things. 33But seek first the kingdom of God and His righteousness, and all these things shall be added to you. 34Therefore do not worry about tomorrow, for tomorrow will worry about its own things. Sufficient for the day is its own trouble.

Do Not Judge

7 "Judge not, that you be not judged. 2For with what judgment you judge, you will be judged; and with the measure you use, it will be measured back to you. 3And why do you look at the speck in your brother's eye, but do not consider the plank in your own eye? 4Or how can you say to your brother, 'Let me remove the speck from your eye'; and look, a plank is in your own eye? 5Hypocrite! First remove the plank from your own eye, and then you will see clearly to remove the speck from your brother's eye.

6"Do not give what is holy to the dogs; nor cast your pearls before swine, lest they trample them under their feet, and turn and tear you in pieces."

DEVOTIONAL

Do you really trust God? Or is that something you just tell yourself and others? This portion of the Sermon on the Mount reminds us that religion, wealth, and the challenges of life often undermine our most basic commitments to God.

Broadcasting our piety before others, such as with fasting, only demonstrates our dependence on people rather than God for ultimate approval. Pursuing wealth to the detriment of our faith reveals that we draw more security from our possessions than the Father who gives us all things to enjoy. Worrying about the future insults the Creator, who meticulously meets needs for every part of creation. Judging others prematurely without first examining our motives and integrity elevates us to a place that only God deserves.

Trust Him for the affirmation you seek. Rely on Him for the security you need. Rest in Him for the relief that anxiety steals. Wait on Him for the justice you long for. Only then will trust become more than a slogan.

—Dr. Adam Dooley
Dauphin Way Baptist Church, Mobile, AL

WEEK 2, DAY 2

The Ways of Righteousness

Matthew 7:7–8:4

Keep Asking, Seeking, Knocking

"Ask, and it will be given to you; seek, and you will find; knock, and it will be opened to you. 8For everyone who asks receives, and he who seeks finds, and to him who knocks it will be opened. 9Or what man is there among you who, if his son asks for bread, will give him a stone? 10Or if he asks for a fish, will he give him a serpent? 11If you then, being evil, know how to give good gifts to your children, how much more will your Father who is in heaven give good things to those who ask Him! 12Therefore, whatever you want men to do to you, do also to them, for this is the Law and the Prophets.

The Narrow Way

13"Enter by the narrow gate; for wide is the gate and broad is the way that leads to destruction, and there are many who go in by it. 14Because narrow is the gate and difficult is the way which leads to life, and there are few who find it.

You Will Know Them by Their Fruits

15"Beware of false prophets, who come to you in sheep's clothing, but inwardly they are ravenous wolves. 16You will know them by their fruits. Do men gather grapes from thornbushes or figs from thistles? 17Even so, every good tree bears good fruit, but a bad tree bears bad fruit. 18A good tree cannot bear bad fruit, nor can a bad tree bear good fruit. 19Every tree that does not bear good fruit is cut down and thrown into the fire. 20Therefore by their fruits you will know them.

I Never Knew You

21"Not everyone who says to Me, 'Lord, Lord,' shall enter the kingdom of heaven, but he who does the will of My Father in heaven. 22Many will say to Me in that day, 'Lord, Lord, have we not prophesied in Your name, cast out demons in Your name, and done many wonders in Your name?' 23And then I will declare to them, 'I never knew you; depart from Me, you who practice lawlessness!'

Build on the Rock

24"Therefore whoever hears these sayings of Mine, and does them, I will liken him to a wise man who built his house on the rock: 25and the rain descended, the floods came, and the winds blew and beat on that house; and it did not fall, for it was founded on the rock.

26"But everyone who hears these sayings of Mine, and does not do them, will be like a foolish man who built his house on the sand: 27and the rain descended, the floods came, and the winds blew and beat on that house; and it fell. And great was its fall."

28And so it was, when Jesus had ended these sayings, that the people were astonished at His teaching, 29for He taught them as one having authority, and not as the scribes.

Jesus Cleanses a Leper

8 When He had come down from the mountain, great multitudes followed Him. 2And behold, a leper came and worshiped Him, saying, "Lord, if You are willing, You can make me clean."

3Then Jesus put out His hand and touched him, saying, "I am willing; be cleansed." Immediately his leprosy was cleansed.

4And Jesus said to him, "See that you tell no one; but go your way, show yourself to the priest, and offer the gift that Moses commanded, as a testimony to them."

DEVOTIONAL

The Sermon on the Mount illustrates the practical righteousness that characterizes true believers. As the ethical implications of faith in the beginning of His sermon draw to a conclusion, Jesus encourages us to ask, seek, and knock with full assurance that God is willing to empower us for the Christian life. Jesus teaches that by His grace, He transforms us into a good tree that bears good fruit. Lest anyone think that inward and outward change is optional, Jesus reminds us that God will judge those who appear religious but are inwardly rebellious. The abundance of religious activity is no substitute for a daily, transforming walk with God.

These warnings challenge us to be doers rather than mere hearers of the Word. Failure to do so reflects a "broad way" commitment that is indicative of the passive majority (Matthew 7:13). How would you describe your walk with God? Does your life reflect the gracious fruit of salvation or the hypocritical efforts of empty religion?

—Dr. Adam Dooley
Dauphin Way Baptist Church, Mobile, AL

WEEK 2, DAY 3

Jesus' Amazing Authority

Matthew 8:5–27

Jesus Heals a Centurion's Servant

Now when Jesus had entered Capernaum, a centurion came to Him, pleading with Him, 6saying, "Lord, my servant is lying at home paralyzed, dreadfully tormented."

7And Jesus said to him, "I will come and heal him."

8The centurion answered and said, "Lord, I am not worthy that You should come under my roof. But only speak a word, and my servant will be healed. 9For I also am a man under authority, having soldiers under me. And I say to this one, 'Go,' and he goes; and to another, 'Come,' and he comes; and to my servant, 'Do this,' and he does it."

10When Jesus heard it, He marveled, and said to those who followed, "Assuredly, I say to you, I have not found such great faith, not even in Israel! 11And I say to you that many will come from east and west, and sit down with Abraham, Isaac, and Jacob in the kingdom of heaven. 12But the sons of the kingdom will be cast out into outer darkness. There will be weeping and gnashing of teeth." 13Then Jesus said to the centurion, "Go your way; and as you have believed, so let it be done for you." And his servant was healed that same hour.

Peter's Mother-in-Law Healed

14Now when Jesus had come into Peter's house, He saw his wife's mother lying sick with a fever. 15So He touched her hand, and the fever left her. And she arose and served them.

Many Healed in the Evening

16When evening had come, they brought to Him many who were demon-possessed. And He cast out the spirits with a word, and healed all who were sick, 17that it might be fulfilled which was spoken by Isaiah the prophet, saying:

"He Himself took our infirmities
And bore our sicknesses."

The Cost of Discipleship

18And when Jesus saw great multitudes about Him, He gave a command to depart to the other side. 19Then a certain scribe came and said to Him, "Teacher, I will follow You wherever You go."

20And Jesus said to him, "Foxes have holes and birds of the air have nests, but the Son of Man has nowhere to lay His head."

21Then another of His disciples said to Him, "Lord, let me first go and bury my father."

22But Jesus said to him, "Follow Me, and let the dead bury their own dead."

Wind and Wave Obey Jesus

23Now when He got into a boat, His disciples followed Him. 24And suddenly a great tempest arose on the sea, so that the boat was covered with the waves. But He was asleep. 25Then His disciples came to Him and awoke Him, saying, "Lord, save us! We are perishing!"

26But He said to them, "Why are you fearful, O you of little faith?" Then He arose and rebuked the winds and the sea, and there was a great calm. 27So the men marveled, saying, "Who can this be, that even the winds and the sea obey Him?"

DEVOTIONAL

Matthew's ultimate goal in this section of his gospel was to present Jesus as the promised Messiah. Having already demonstrated that Jesus had teaching authority, these verses reveal His authority over sickness and nature. He was the Savior of whom the prophets spoke.

Because this is true, the difficulty that comes with following Christ should not deter us. Radical commitment is the only correct response to Jesus. His sovereignty over our circumstances and life's surprises leaves little room for half-hearted faith. The supposed followers of Jesus in Matthew 8:19 and 21 promised more than they were willing to deliver and less than the Lord required. Though contemporary spectators would have applauded their ambitions, Jesus abruptly exposed their shallow pledge against the backdrop of His glorious identity.

Why do we suppose that jubilant abandonment to God's Messiah is fanatical when the touch of His hand or the sound of His voice causes disease and sickness to disappear? Do we really expect the God who controls the wind to be impressed when we tip our hat to Him? Jesus' absolute authority requires our total submission and obedience. Is this how you respond to God?

—Dr. Adam Dooley
Dauphin Way Baptist Church, Mobile, AL

WEEK 2, DAY 4

God Forgives and Saves

Matthew 8:28–9:17

Two Demon-Possessed Men Healed

When He had come to the other side, to the country of the Gergesenes, there met Him two demon-possessed men, coming out of the tombs, exceedingly fierce, so that no one could pass that way. 29And suddenly they cried out, saying, "What have we to do with You, Jesus, You Son of God? Have You come here to torment us before the time?"

30Now a good way off from them there was a herd of many swine feeding. 31So the demons begged Him, saying, "If You cast us out, permit us to go away into the herd of swine."

32And He said to them, "Go." So when they had come out, they went into the herd of swine. And suddenly the whole herd of swine ran violently down the steep place into the sea, and perished in the water.

33Then those who kept them fled; and they went away into the city and told everything, including what had happened to the demon-possessed men. 34And behold, the whole city came out to meet Jesus. And when they saw Him, they begged Him to depart from their region.

Jesus Forgives and Heals a Paralytic

9 So He got into a boat, crossed over, and came to His own city. 2Then behold, they brought to Him a paralytic lying on a bed. When Jesus saw their faith, He said to the paralytic, "Son, be of good cheer; your sins are forgiven you."

3And at once some of the scribes said within themselves, "This Man blasphemes!"

4But Jesus, knowing their thoughts, said, "Why do you think evil in your hearts? 5For which is easier, to say, 'Your sins are forgiven you,' or to say, 'Arise and walk'? 6But that you may know that the Son of Man has power on earth to forgive sins"—then He said to the paralytic, "Arise, take up your bed, and go to your house." 7And he arose and departed to his house.

8Now when the multitudes saw it, they marveled and glorified God, who had given such power to men.

Matthew the Tax Collector

9As Jesus passed on from there, He saw a man named Matthew sitting at the tax office. And He said to him, "Follow Me." So he arose and followed Him.

10Now it happened, as Jesus sat at the table in the house, that behold, many tax collectors and sinners came and sat down with Him and His disciples. 11And when the Pharisees saw it, they said to His disciples, "Why does your Teacher eat with tax collectors and sinners?"

12When Jesus heard that, He said to them, "Those who are well have no need of a physician, but those who are sick. 13But go and learn what this means: 'I desire mercy and not sacrifice.' For I did not come to call the righteous, but sinners, to repentance."

Jesus Is Questioned About Fasting

14Then the disciples of John came to Him, saying, "Why do we and the Pharisees fast often, but Your disciples do not fast?"

15And Jesus said to them, "Can the friends of the bridegroom mourn as long as the bridegroom is with them? But the days will come when the bridegroom will be taken away from them, and then they will fast. 16No one puts a piece of unshrunk cloth on an old garment; for the patch pulls away from the garment, and the tear is made worse. 17Nor do they put new wine into old wineskins, or else the wineskins break, the wine is spilled, and the wineskins are ruined. But they put new wine into new wineskins, and both are preserved."

DEVOTIONAL

Continuing to emphasize that Jesus is the Messiah, Matthew reveals that Christ has the authority to drive out demons and cure physical infirmities. A new theme emerges, however, when Jesus forgives the paralytic before healing him. Here, we discover that the purpose of these miracles is spiritual rather than physical. The signs and wonders of Jesus' ministry were never meant to distract from His identity, but to confirm it. Miraculous activity compels us to worship Jesus so that we will cling to Him for the forgiveness of sins. Celebrating what God does without acknowledging who He is will ultimately not meet our greatest need. The call of Matthew illustrates that while physical miracles are not always available to everyone, the supernatural work of forgiveness is! The worst of sinners can be forgiven through repentance and faith. Put your faith in the One who forgives and saves!

—Dr. Adam Dooley
Dauphin Way Baptist Church, Mobile, AL

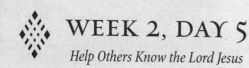

WEEK 2, DAY 5

Help Others Know the Lord Jesus

Matthew 9:18–10:10

A Girl Restored to Life and a Woman Healed

While He spoke these things to them, behold, a ruler came and worshiped Him, saying, "My daughter has just died, but come and lay Your hand on her and she will live." 19So Jesus arose and followed him, and so did His disciples.

20And suddenly, a woman who had a flow of blood for twelve years came from behind and touched the hem of His garment. 21For she said to herself, "If only I may touch His garment, I shall be made well." 22But Jesus turned around, and when He saw her He said, "Be of good cheer, daughter; your faith has made you well." And the woman was made well from that hour.

23When Jesus came into the ruler's house, and saw the flute players and the noisy crowd wailing, 24He said to them, "Make room, for the girl is not dead, but sleeping." And they ridiculed Him. 25But when the crowd was put outside, He went in and took her by the hand, and the girl arose. 26And the report of this went out into all that land.

Two Blind Men Healed

27When Jesus departed from there, two blind men followed Him, crying out and saying, "Son of David, have mercy on us!"

28And when He had come into the house, the blind men came to Him. And Jesus said to them, "Do you believe that I am able to do this?"

They said to Him, "Yes, Lord."

29Then He touched their eyes, saying, "According to your faith let it be to you." 30And their eyes were opened. And Jesus sternly warned them, saying, "See that no one knows it." 31But when they had departed, they spread the news about Him in all that country.

A Mute Man Speaks

32As they went out, behold, they brought to Him a man, mute and demon-possessed. 33And when the demon was cast out, the mute spoke. And the multitudes marveled, saying, "It was never seen like this in Israel!"

34But the Pharisees said, "He casts out demons by the ruler of the demons."

The Compassion of Jesus

35Then Jesus went about all the cities and villages, teaching in their synagogues, preaching the gospel of the kingdom, and healing every sickness and every disease among the people. 36But when He saw the multitudes, He was moved with compassion for them, because they were weary and scattered, like sheep having no shepherd. 37Then He said to His disciples, "The harvest truly is plentiful, but the laborers are few. 38Therefore pray the Lord of the harvest to send out laborers into His harvest."

The Twelve Apostles

10 And when He had called His twelve disciples to Him, He gave them power over unclean spirits, to cast them out, and to heal all kinds of sickness and all kinds of disease. 2Now the names of the twelve apostles are these: first, Simon, who is called Peter, and Andrew his brother; James the son of Zebedee, and John his brother; 3Philip and Bartholomew; Thomas and Matthew the tax collector; James the son of Alphaeus, and Lebbaeus, whose surname was Thaddaeus; 4Simon the Cananite, and Judas Iscariot, who also betrayed Him.

Sending Out the Twelve

5These twelve Jesus sent out and commanded them, saying: "Do not go into the way of the Gentiles, and do not enter a city of the Samaritans. 6But go rather to the lost sheep of the house of Israel. 7And as you go, preach, saying, 'The kingdom of heaven is at hand.' 8Heal the sick, cleanse the lepers, raise the dead, cast out demons. Freely you have received, freely give. 9Provide neither gold nor silver nor copper in your money belts, 10nor bag for your journey, nor two tunics, nor sandals, nor staffs; for a worker is worthy of his food."

DEVOTIONAL

In Matthew 8:1–9:34, we see ten miracles that demonstrate the divine identity of Jesus. By raising the dead and healing the blind (no blind man had ever been healed before at this point), the theme of messianic authority reaches a climax with the greatest miracles of all. The inclusion of a mute man speaking marks the fulfillment of Isaiah 35:5–6. Immediately following this crescendo, the emphasis turns toward sharing Jesus with others. Those who accept His identity will also embrace this important mission. Leading others to accept Jesus as their Savior and Lord is the greatest expression that we really understand who He is. With whom will you share Jesus today?

—Dr. Adam Dooley
Dauphin Way Baptist Church, Mobile, AL

WEEK 2, DAY 6

The Price of Following Jesus

Matthew 10:11–39

"Now whatever city or town you enter, inquire who in it is worthy, and stay there till you go out. 12And when you go into a household, greet it. 13If the household is worthy, let your peace come upon it. But if it is not worthy, let your peace return to you. 14And whoever will not receive you nor hear your words, when you depart from that house or city, shake off the dust from your feet. 15Assuredly, I say to you, it will be more tolerable for the land of Sodom and Gomorrah in the day of judgment than for that city!

Persecutions Are Coming

16"Behold, I send you out as sheep in the midst of wolves. Therefore be wise as serpents and harmless as doves. 17But beware of men, for they will deliver you up to councils and scourge you in their synagogues. 18You will be brought before governors and kings for My sake, as a testimony to them and to the Gentiles. 19But when they deliver you up, do not worry about how or what you should speak. For it will be given to you in that hour what you should speak; 20for it is not you who speak, but the Spirit of your Father who speaks in you.

21"Now brother will deliver up brother to death, and a father his child; and children will rise up against parents and cause them to be put to death. 22And you will be hated by all for My name's sake. But he who endures to the end will be saved. 23When they persecute you in this city, flee to another. For assuredly, I say to you, you will not have gone through the cities of Israel before the Son of Man comes.

24"A disciple is not above his teacher, nor a servant above his master. 25It is enough for a disciple that he be like his teacher, and a servant like his master. If they have called the master of the house Beelzebub, how much more will they call those of his household! 26Therefore do not fear them. For there is nothing covered that will not be revealed, and hidden that will not be known.

Jesus Teaches the Fear of God

27"Whatever I tell you in the dark, speak in the light; and what you hear in the ear, preach on the housetops. 28And do not fear those who kill the body but cannot kill the soul. But rather fear Him who is able to destroy both soul and body in hell. 29Are not two sparrows sold for a copper coin? And not one of them falls to the ground apart from your Father's will. 30But the very hairs of your head are all numbered. 31Do not fear therefore; you are of more value than many sparrows.

Confess Christ Before Men

32"Therefore whoever confesses Me before men, him I will also confess before My Father who is in heaven. 33But whoever denies Me before men, him I will also deny before My Father who is in heaven.

Christ Brings Division

34"Do not think that I came to bring peace on earth. I did not come to bring peace but a sword. 35For I have come to 'set a man against his father, a daughter against her mother, and a daughter-in-law against her mother-in-law'; 36and 'a man's enemies will be those of his own household.' 37He who loves father or mother more than Me is not worthy of Me. And he who loves son or daughter more than Me is not worthy of Me. 38And he who does not take his cross and follow after Me is not worthy of Me. 39He who finds his life will lose it, and he who loses his life for My sake will find it."

DEVOTIONAL

Opposition and difficulty are words that contemporary believers hear little about. For many, ease and prosperity are the chief characteristics of modern Christianity. Jesus' perspective, however, was just the opposite. Though we often soften the abrasiveness of these words, our general lack of persecution usually says more about the insufficiency of our commitment than the toleration of society. Our people-centered theology props up the values of acceptance, comfort, and popularity while diminishing the imperative of a crucified life. Rather than taking up our cross, we completely put it down to avoid the scorn that it invites. This is not salvation.

Confessing Christ before men is more than voicing words. It is paying any price, forsaking any person, and enduring any pain to follow Jesus. Our Savior did not break under the weight of rejection, and neither should we. Though God does not require that we seek persecution, He does insist that we refuse to run from it.

—Dr. Adam Dooley
Dauphin Way Baptist Church, Mobile, AL

WEEK 2, DAY 7

How has the authority of Jesus changed the way you worship Him or how you live your life?

_____

_____

_____

_____

_____

_____

_____

_____

_____

_____

_____

_____

What relationships, goals, or dreams do you have that will need to die in order for you to follow Jesus? What price have you paid already for being a Christian?

_____

_____

_____

_____

_____

_____

_____

_____

_____

_____

WEEK 3, DAY I

Preparing the Way of the Lord

Matthew 10:40–11:24

A Cup of Cold Water

"He who receives you receives Me, and he who receives Me receives Him who sent Me. 41He who receives a prophet in the name of a prophet shall receive a prophet's reward. And he who receives a righteous man in the name of a righteous man shall receive a righteous man's reward. 42And whoever gives one of these little ones only a cup of cold water in the name of a disciple, assuredly, I say to you, he shall by no means lose his reward."

John the Baptist Sends Messengers to Jesus

11 Now it came to pass, when Jesus finished commanding His twelve disciples, that He departed from there to teach and to preach in their cities.

2And when John had heard in prison about the works of Christ, he sent two of his disciples 3and said to Him, "Are You the Coming One, or do we look for another?"

4Jesus answered and said to them, "Go and tell John the things which you hear and see: 5The blind see and the lame walk; the lepers are cleansed and the deaf hear; the dead are raised up and the poor have the gospel preached to them. 6And blessed is he who is not offended because of Me."

7As they departed, Jesus began to say to the multitudes concerning John: "What did you go out into the wilderness to see? A reed shaken by the wind? 8But what did you go out to see? A man clothed in soft garments? Indeed, those who wear soft clothing are in kings' houses. 9But what did you go out to see? A prophet? Yes, I say to you, and more than a prophet. 10For this is he of whom it is written:

'Behold, I send My messenger before Your face,
  Who will prepare Your way before You.'

11"Assuredly, I say to you, among those born of women there has not risen one greater than John the Baptist; but he who is least in the kingdom of heaven is greater than he. 12And from the days of John the Baptist until now the kingdom of heaven suffers violence, and the violent take it by force. 13For all the prophets and the law prophesied until John. 14And if you are willing to receive it, he is Elijah who is to come. 15He who has ears to hear, let him hear!

16"But to what shall I liken this generation? It is like children sitting in the marketplaces and calling to their companions, 17and saying:

'We played the flute for you,
  And you did not dance;
We mourned to you,
  And you did not lament.'

18For John came neither eating nor drinking, and they say, 'He has a demon.' 19The Son of Man came eating and drinking, and they say, 'Look, a glutton and a winebibber, a friend of tax collectors and sinners!' But wisdom is justified by her children."

Woe to the Impenitent Cities

20Then He began to rebuke the cities in which most of His mighty works had been done, because they did not repent: 21"Woe to you, Chorazin! Woe to you, Bethsaida! For if the mighty works which were done in you had been done in Tyre and Sidon, they would have repented long ago in sackcloth and ashes. 22But I say to you, it will be more tolerable for Tyre and Sidon in the day of judgment than for you. 23And you, Capernaum, who are exalted to heaven, will be brought down to Hades; for if the mighty works which were done in you had been done in Sodom, it would have remained until this day. 24But I say to you that it shall be more tolerable for the land of Sodom in the day of judgment than for you."

DEVOTIONAL

God sent John the Baptist to the Jews with an important message: "Get ready, for your long-awaited Messiah is here!" Today's reading tells us that as John the Baptist illuminated the way to Jesus, he was really making a way to the Father. Jesus said, "He who receives Me receives Him who sent Me" (Matthew 10:40). What a promise!

Will you come in contact with those who need to receive Jesus today? Will you invite them to receive Him? When you introduce people to Jesus, you are preparing the way for them to know the Father, just like John the Baptist. Ask God to help you fulfill your purpose in Him and to be the "way maker" in someone's life today. And ask God to give those you will share Jesus with ears to hear!

—Dr. Alex Himaya
theChurch.at, Tulsa, OK

WEEK 3, DAY 2

Jesus Blesses a Childlike Faith

Matthew 11:25–12:21

Jesus Gives True Rest

At that time Jesus answered and said, "I thank You, Father, Lord of heaven and earth, that You have hidden these things from the wise and prudent and have revealed them to babes. 26Even so, Father, for so it seemed good in Your sight. 27All things have been delivered to Me by My Father, and no one knows the Son except the Father. Nor does anyone know the Father except the Son, and the one to whom the Son wills to reveal Him. 28Come to Me, all you who labor and are heavy laden, and I will give you rest. 29Take My yoke upon you and learn from Me, for I am gentle and lowly in heart, and you will find rest for your souls. 30For My yoke is easy and My burden is light."

Jesus Is Lord of the Sabbath

12 At that time Jesus went through the grainfields on the Sabbath. And His disciples were hungry, and began to pluck heads of grain and to eat. 2And when the Pharisees saw it, they said to Him, "Look, Your disciples are doing what is not lawful to do on the Sabbath!"

3But He said to them, "Have you not read what David did when he was hungry, he and those who were with him: 4how he entered the house of God and ate the showbread which was not lawful for him to eat, nor for those who were with him, but only for the priests? 5Or have you not read in the law that on the Sabbath the priests in the temple profane the Sabbath, and are blameless? 6Yet I say to you that in this place there is One greater than the temple. 7But if you had known what this means, 'I desire mercy and not sacrifice,' you would not have condemned the guiltless. 8For the Son of Man is Lord even of the Sabbath."

Healing on the Sabbath

9Now when He had departed from there, He went into their synagogue. 10And behold, there was a man who had a withered hand. And they asked Him, saying, "Is it lawful to heal on the Sabbath?"—that they might accuse Him. 11Then He said to them, "What man is there among you who has one sheep, and if it falls into a pit on the Sabbath, will not lay hold of it and lift it out? 12Of how much more value then is a man than a sheep? Therefore it is lawful to do good on the Sabbath." 13Then He said to the man, "Stretch out your hand." And he stretched it out, and it was restored as whole as the other. 14Then the Pharisees went out and plotted against Him, how they might destroy Him.

Behold, My Servant

15But when Jesus knew it, He withdrew from there. And great multitudes followed Him, and He healed them all. 16Yet He warned them not to make Him known, 17that it might be fulfilled which was spoken by Isaiah the prophet, saying:

18   "Behold! My Servant whom I have chosen,
    My Beloved in whom My soul is well pleased!
    I will put My Spirit upon Him,
    And He will declare justice to the Gentiles.
19   He will not quarrel nor cry out,
    Nor will anyone hear His voice in the streets.
20   A bruised reed He will not break,
    And smoking flax He will not quench,
    Till He sends forth justice to victory;
21   And in His name Gentiles will trust."

DEVOTIONAL

When we put our trust in Jesus, He blesses us with many things. We see one of them in Matthew 11:25 when Jesus thanked God the Father for revealing heavenly truth to those with childlike faith. Praise God that we don't have to be wise and clever! He simply reveals truth to us.

In the parallel passage in Luke, a blessing available to those with childlike faith includes authority over the Enemy (10:19). He makes us able to "put on the whole armor of God" and "stand against the wiles of the devil" (Ephesians 6:11).

Jesus invites all who are heavy laden to come to Him for rest. What a great invitation! Don't we all need rest today? If we have childlike faith, we'll receive it.

Part of our rest comes from knowing and understanding that Jesus is Lord of all. Jesus demonstrated His authority over the Sabbath and the temple in chapter 12, which tells us He is greater than religion and all of its rules and regulations. As we put our faith in Him, we find freedom!

Ask God to give you childlike faith and the revelation, rest, authority, and freedom that come from having Jesus Christ as your Lord.

—Dr. Alex Himaya
theChurch.at, Tulsa, OK

WEEK 3, DAY 3

Resisting the Enemy

Matthew 12:22–45

A House Divided Cannot Stand

Then one was brought to Him who was demon-possessed, blind and mute; and He healed him, so that the blind and mute man both spoke and saw. 23And all the multitudes were amazed and said, "Could this be the Son of David?"

24Now when the Pharisees heard it they said, "This fellow does not cast out demons except by Beelzebub, the ruler of the demons."

25But Jesus knew their thoughts, and said to them: "Every kingdom divided against itself is brought to desolation, and every city or house divided against itself will not stand. 26If Satan casts out Satan, he is divided against himself. How then will his kingdom stand? 27And if I cast out demons by Beelzebub, by whom do your sons cast them out? Therefore they shall be your judges. 28But if I cast out demons by the Spirit of God, surely the kingdom of God has come upon you. 29Or how can one enter a strong man's house and plunder his goods, unless he first binds the strong man? And then he will plunder his house. 30He who is not with Me is against Me, and he who does not gather with Me scatters abroad.

The Unpardonable Sin

31"Therefore I say to you, every sin and blasphemy will be forgiven men, but the blasphemy against the Spirit will not be forgiven men. 32Anyone who speaks a word against the Son of Man, it will be forgiven him; but whoever speaks against the Holy Spirit, it will not be forgiven him, either in this age or in the age to come.

A Tree Known by Its Fruit

33"Either make the tree good and its fruit good, or else make the tree bad and its fruit bad; for a tree is known by its fruit. 34Brood of vipers! How can you, being evil, speak good things? For out of the abundance of the heart the mouth speaks. 35A good man out of the good treasure of his heart brings forth good things, and an evil man out of the evil treasure brings forth evil things. 36But I say to you that for every idle word men may speak, they will give account of it in the day of judgment. 37For by your words you will be justified, and by your words you will be condemned."

The Scribes and Pharisees Ask for a Sign

38Then some of the scribes and Pharisees answered, saying, "Teacher, we want to see a sign from You."

39But He answered and said to them, "An evil and adulterous generation seeks after a sign, and no sign will be given to it except the sign of the prophet Jonah. 40For as Jonah was three days and three nights in the belly of the great fish, so will the Son of Man be three days and three nights in the heart of the earth. 41The men of Nineveh will rise up in the judgment with this generation and condemn it, because they repented at the preaching of Jonah; and indeed a greater than Jonah is here. 42The queen of the South will rise up in the judgment with this generation and condemn it, for she came from the ends of the earth to hear the wisdom of Solomon; and indeed a greater than Solomon is here.

An Unclean Spirit Returns

43"When an unclean spirit goes out of a man, he goes through dry places, seeking rest, and finds none. 44Then he says, 'I will return to my house from which I came.' And when he comes, he finds it empty, swept, and put in order. 45Then he goes and takes with him seven other spirits more wicked than himself, and they enter and dwell there; and the last state of that man is worse than the first. So shall it also be with this wicked generation."

DEVOTIONAL

The bookends of today's reading help us understand Satan and his demons. In Matthew 12:29, Jesus asked how one can enter a house inhabited by Satan without first binding him. This is the picture of salvation, deliverance, and freedom. Each believer is the dwelling place, or house, of God and should have undivided loyalty to Jesus. If we are double-minded, having divided loyalties, we'll be unstable *(James 1:8)*.

The reading concludes with the teaching on what happens when unclean spirits, or demons, go out and come back. They're able to return with more unclean spirits if the person is clean but empty—not full of God's Spirit to reject them. We need to ask Jesus not only to clean us but also to fill us with His Spirit.

Pray for protection from the attacks of our very real Enemy. Stay loyal to Jesus, fill up with the Word and the Spirit, and you will resist the Enemy and be strong in the Lord.

—Dr. Alex Himaya
theChurch.at, Tulsa, OK

WEEK 3, DAY 4

Eyes to See and Ears to Hear

Matthew 12:46–13:17

Jesus' Mother and Brothers Send for Him

While He was still talking to the multitudes, behold, His mother and brothers stood outside, seeking to speak with Him. 47Then one said to Him, "Look, Your mother and Your brothers are standing outside, seeking to speak with You."

48But He answered and said to the one who told Him, "Who is My mother and who are My brothers?" 49And He stretched out His hand toward His disciples and said, "Here are My mother and My brothers! 50For whoever does the will of My Father in heaven is My brother and sister and mother."

The Parable of the Sower

13 On the same day Jesus went out of the house and sat by the sea. 2And great multitudes were gathered together to Him, so that He got into a boat and sat; and the whole multitude stood on the shore.

3Then He spoke many things to them in parables, saying: "Behold, a sower went out to sow. 4And as he sowed, some seed fell by the wayside; and the birds came and devoured them. 5Some fell on stony places, where they did not have much earth; and they immediately sprang up because they had no depth of earth. 6But when the sun was up they were scorched, and because they had no root they withered away. 7And some fell among thorns, and the thorns sprang up and choked them. 8But others fell on good ground and yielded a crop: some a hundredfold, some sixty, some thirty. 9He who has ears to hear, let him hear!"

The Purpose of Parables

10And the disciples came and said to Him, "Why do You speak to them in parables?"

11He answered and said to them, "Because it has been given to you to know the mysteries of the kingdom of heaven, but to them it has not been given. 12For whoever has, to him more will be given, and he will have abundance; but whoever does not have, even what he has will be taken away from him. 13Therefore I speak to them in parables, because seeing they do not see, and hearing they do not hear, nor do they understand. 14And in them the prophecy of Isaiah is fulfilled, which says:

'Hearing you will hear and shall not understand,
And seeing you will see and not perceive;
15 For the hearts of this people have grown dull.
Their ears are hard of hearing,
And their eyes they have closed,
Lest they should see with their eyes and hear
with their ears,
Lest they should understand with their hearts
and turn,
So that I should heal them.'

16But blessed are your eyes for they see, and your ears for they hear; 17for assuredly, I say to you that many prophets and righteous men desired to see what you see, and did not see it, and to hear what you hear, and did not hear it."

DEVOTIONAL

Jesus often made a distinction between eyes that see and eyes that do not see. He was not referring to physical blindness; He was concerned about people having spiritual eyes to recognize the Holy Spirit. "Eyes to see" and "ears to hear" are phrases that refer to listening to God and obeying Him.

Jesus said whoever does the will of the Father is related to Him (Matthew 12:50). When we listen to His teaching, He will give us more understanding and an abundance of knowledge (13:12). In order to have eyes, we have to look, and in order to have ears, we have to listen. This teaching seems backward to our understanding, doesn't it? But remember, this is not an earthly principle. It is spiritual. We are not human beings with temporary spiritual experiences. We are spiritual beings with temporary human experiences. The Bible is a spiritual Book. And Jesus taught that if we really want to understand more, we have to listen and obey what we understand, and then more understanding will be given. We shouldn't expect God to give us new marching orders until we obey in the areas He's given us understanding.

What is the last thing God told you to do? Did you do it? Ask God to give you courage to obey Him today, and may the Father be able to say this to you: "Blessed are your eyes for they see, and your ears for they hear" (Matthew 13:16).

—Dr. Alex Himaya
theChurch.at, Tulsa, OK

WEEK 3, DAY 5

Protect Your Walk with God

Matthew 13:18–43

The Parable of the Sower Explained

"Therefore hear the parable of the sower: ¹⁹When anyone hears the word of the kingdom, and does not understand it, then the wicked one comes and snatches away what was sown in his heart. This is he who received seed by the wayside. ²⁰But he who received the seed on stony places, this is he who hears the word and immediately receives it with joy; ²¹yet he has no root in himself, but endures only for a while. For when tribulation or persecution arises because of the word, immediately he stumbles. ²²Now he who received seed among the thorns is he who hears the word, and the cares of this world and the deceitfulness of riches choke the word, and he becomes unfruitful. ²³But he who received seed on the good ground is he who hears the word and understands it, who indeed bears fruit and produces: some a hundredfold, some sixty, some thirty."

The Parable of the Wheat and the Tares

²⁴Another parable He put forth to them, saying: "The kingdom of heaven is like a man who sowed good seed in his field; ²⁵but while men slept, his enemy came and sowed tares among the wheat and went his way. ²⁶But when the grain had sprouted and produced a crop, then the tares also appeared. ²⁷So the servants of the owner came and said to him, 'Sir, did you not sow good seed in your field? How then does it have tares?' ²⁸He said to them, 'An enemy has done this.' The servants said to him, 'Do you want us then to go and gather them up?' ²⁹But he said, 'No, lest while you gather up the tares you also uproot the wheat with them. ³⁰Let both grow together until the harvest, and at the time of harvest I will say to the reapers, "First gather together the tares and bind them in bundles to burn them, but gather the wheat into my barn."'"

The Parable of the Mustard Seed

³¹Another parable He put forth to them, saying: "The kingdom of heaven is like a mustard seed, which a man took and sowed in his field, ³²which indeed is the least of all the seeds; but when it is grown it is greater than the herbs and becomes a tree, so that the birds of the air come and nest in its branches."

The Parable of the Leaven

³³Another parable He spoke to them: "The kingdom of heaven is like leaven, which a woman took and hid in three measures of meal till it was all leavened."

Prophecy and the Parables

³⁴All these things Jesus spoke to the multitude in parables; and without a parable He did not speak to them, ³⁵that it might be fulfilled which was spoken by the prophet, saying:

"I will open My mouth in parables;
I will utter things kept secret from the foundation
of the world."

The Parable of the Tares Explained

³⁶Then Jesus sent the multitude away and went into the house. And His disciples came to Him, saying, "Explain to us the parable of the tares of the field."

³⁷He answered and said to them: "He who sows the good seed is the Son of Man. ³⁸The field is the world, the good seeds are the sons of the kingdom, but the tares are the sons of the wicked one. ³⁹The enemy who sowed them is the devil, the harvest is the end of the age, and the reapers are the angels. ⁴⁰Therefore as the tares are gathered and burned in the fire, so it will be at the end of this age. ⁴¹The Son of Man will send out His angels, and they will gather out of His kingdom all things that offend, and those who practice lawlessness, ⁴²and will cast them into the furnace of fire. There will be wailing and gnashing of teeth. ⁴³Then the righteous will shine forth as the sun in the kingdom of their Father. He who has ears to hear, let him hear!"

DEVOTIONAL

Jesus indicated in His explanation of the parable of the sower that the seed represents the Word of God, the soil represents those receiving it, and the bird is the devil. He made it clear that when the seed is being sown, there is an enemy who attempts to steal it away. How does the Enemy distract you from receiving God's Word or other blessings He wants to give you? Ask God to give you understanding— eyes to see and ears to hear—of any and all attacks on your life. Submit yourself to God and throw off every hindrance in your walk with Him. "Resist the devil and he will flee from you" (James 4:7).

—Dr. Alex Himaya
theChurch.at, Tulsa, OK

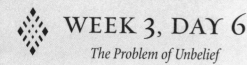

WEEK 3, DAY 6

The Problem of Unbelief

Matthew 13:44–14:12

The Parable of the Hidden Treasure

"Again, the kingdom of heaven is like treasure hidden in a field, which a man found and hid; and for joy over it he goes and sells all that he has and buys that field.

The Parable of the Pearl of Great Price

45"Again, the kingdom of heaven is like a merchant seeking beautiful pearls, 46who, when he had found one pearl of great price, went and sold all that he had and bought it.

The Parable of the Dragnet

47"Again, the kingdom of heaven is like a dragnet that was cast into the sea and gathered some of every kind, 48which, when it was full, they drew to shore; and they sat down and gathered the good into vessels, but threw the bad away. 49So it will be at the end of the age. The angels will come forth, separate the wicked from among the just, 50and cast them into the furnace of fire. There will be wailing and gnashing of teeth."

51Jesus said to them, "Have you understood all these things?"

They said to Him, "Yes, Lord."

52Then He said to them, "Therefore every scribe instructed concerning the kingdom of heaven is like a householder who brings out of his treasure things new and old."

Jesus Rejected at Nazareth

53Now it came to pass, when Jesus had finished these parables, that He departed from there. 54When He had come to His own country, He taught them in their synagogue, so that they were astonished and said, "Where did this Man get this wisdom and these mighty works? 55Is this not the carpenter's son? Is not His mother called Mary? And His brothers James, Joses, Simon, and Judas? 56And His sisters, are they not all with us? Where then did this Man get all these things?" 57So they were offended at Him.

But Jesus said to them, "A prophet is not without honor except in his own country and in his own house." 58Now He did not do many mighty works there because of their unbelief.

John the Baptist Beheaded

14At that time Herod the tetrarch heard the report about Jesus 2and said to his servants, "This is John the Baptist; he is risen from the dead, and therefore these powers are at work in him." 3For Herod had laid hold of John and bound him, and put him in prison for the sake of Herodias, his brother Philip's wife. 4Because John had said to him, "It is not lawful for you to have her." 5And although he wanted to put him to death, he feared the multitude, because they counted him as a prophet.

6But when Herod's birthday was celebrated, the daughter of Herodias danced before them and pleased Herod. 7Therefore he promised with an oath to give her whatever she might ask.

8So she, having been prompted by her mother, said, "Give me John the Baptist's head here on a platter."

9And the king was sorry; nevertheless, because of the oaths and because of those who sat with him, he commanded it to be given to her. 10So he sent and had John beheaded in prison. 11And his head was brought on a platter and given to the girl, and she brought it to her mother. 12Then his disciples came and took away the body and buried it, and went and told Jesus.

DEVOTIONAL

The crowds of Jesus' day were amazed by His teaching, for He taught as one with authority. As they heard Him teach, they would whisper to each other, "Is that not Joseph's boy? Isn't He a carpenter? I think He built our table." Their familiarity bred contempt, so much so that Matthew 13:57 says, "They were offended at Him."

Jesus did amazing miracles in many places, but in the area where He grew up, He performed only small miracles. Why? Matthew 13:58 tells us it was because of the people's unbelief. These people who had watched Jesus grow, who knew His stellar character firsthand, who should have been the first to believe His claims of deity, were one of Jesus' toughest crowds. They were curious about Jesus, but as soon as He touched on a nerve, they quickly yanked back the welcome mat.

Is there an area of unbelief in your life that is unwelcoming to the mighty power of God? Confess it to Him today, and ask Him to help you with your lack of faith.

—Dr. Alex Himaya
theChurch.at, Tulsa, OK

WEEK 3, DAY 7

Jesus said that when we are empty, we are vulnerable to an attack by the Enemy. How will you strive to fill your life with God's Word and Holy Spirit?

_____

_____

_____

_____

_____

_____

_____

_____

_____

_____

How will you make an effort to listen to God so that you may obey Him when He calls?

_____

_____

_____

_____

_____

_____

_____

_____

_____

WEEK 4, DAY 1

God Ministers to Us
and Through Us

Matthew 14:13–36

Feeding the Five Thousand

When Jesus heard it, He departed from there by boat to a deserted place by Himself. But when the multitudes heard it, they followed Him on foot from the cities. 14And when Jesus went out He saw a great multitude; and He was moved with compassion for them, and healed their sick. 15When it was evening, His disciples came to Him, saying, "This is a deserted place, and the hour is already late. Send the multitudes away, that they may go into the villages and buy themselves food."

16But Jesus said to them, "They do not need to go away. You give them something to eat."

17And they said to Him, "We have here only five loaves and two fish."

18He said, "Bring them here to Me." 19Then He commanded the multitudes to sit down on the grass. And He took the five loaves and the two fish, and looking up to heaven, He blessed and broke and gave the loaves to the disciples; and the disciples gave to the multitudes. 20So they all ate and were filled, and they took up twelve baskets full of the fragments that remained. 21Now those who had eaten were about five thousand men, besides women and children.

Jesus Walks on the Sea

22Immediately Jesus made His disciples get into the boat and go before Him to the other side, while He sent the multitudes away. 23And when He had sent the multitudes away, He went up on the mountain by Himself to pray. Now when evening came, He was alone there. 24But the boat was now in the middle of the sea, tossed by the waves, for the wind was contrary.

25Now in the fourth watch of the night Jesus went to them, walking on the sea. 26And when the disciples saw Him walking on the sea, they were troubled, saying, "It is a ghost!" And they cried out for fear.

27But immediately Jesus spoke to them, saying, "Be of good cheer! It is I; do not be afraid."

28And Peter answered Him and said, "Lord, if it is You, command me to come to You on the water."

29So He said, "Come." And when Peter had come down out of the boat, he walked on the water to go to Jesus. 30But when he saw that the wind was boisterous, he was afraid; and beginning to sink he cried out, saying, "Lord, save me!"

31And immediately Jesus stretched out His hand and caught him, and said to him, "O you of little faith, why did you doubt?" 32And when they got into the boat, the wind ceased.

33Then those who were in the boat came and worshiped Him, saying, "Truly You are the Son of God."

Many Touch Him and Are Made Well

34When they had crossed over, they came to the land of Gennesaret. 35And when the men of that place recognized Him, they sent out into all that surrounding region, brought to Him all who were sick, 36and begged Him that they might only touch the hem of His garment. And as many as touched it were made perfectly well.

DEVOTIONAL

After hearing the devastating news of John the Baptist's death, Jesus withdrew to a deserted place to be alone with the Father. He also knew the time to go to the cross was drawing near. When He saw the great multitude of people who were following Him to that deserted place, He could have sent them away. Instead, He "was moved with compassion for them, and healed their sick" (Matthew 14:14). He told the disciples to give the people something to eat, and taking their meager five loaves and two fish, He provided enough food for everyone, with plenty left over. People in a deserted place, as the disciples called it (v. 15), were blessed with abundance.

Did you notice that Jesus also fed the disciples as they served the multitude? God wants to minister through you whenever He ministers to you. How many people are in a "deserted place" because they won't bring what they have—time, talents, and treasures—to Jesus and let Him multiply it?

Remember Jesus' compassion on the crowd and that He has a heart of love and compassion for you today. And like the disciples, be willing to let God minister through you. Offer whatever you have to the Lord, and He'll use it to bless others abundantly.

—Brian Fossett
Fossett Evangelistic Ministries, Dalton, GA

WEEK 4, DAY 2

Keeping Rules Versus
Trusting in Jesus

Matthew 15:1–31

Defilement Comes from Within

15 Then the scribes and Pharisees who were from Jerusalem came to Jesus, saying, [2]"Why do Your disciples transgress the tradition of the elders? For they do not wash their hands when they eat bread."

[3]He answered and said to them, "Why do you also transgress the commandment of God because of your tradition? [4]For God commanded, saying, 'Honor your father and your mother'; and, 'He who curses father or mother, let him be put to death.' [5]But you say, 'Whoever says to his father or mother, "Whatever profit you might have received from me is a gift to God"— [6]then he need not honor his father or mother.' Thus you have made the commandment of God of no effect by your tradition. [7]Hypocrites! Well did Isaiah prophesy about you, saying:

[8] 'These people draw near to Me with their mouth,
     And honor Me with their lips,
     But their heart is far from Me.
[9]   And in vain they worship Me,
     Teaching as doctrines the commandments
          of men.'"

[10]When He had called the multitude to Himself, He said to them, "Hear and understand: [11]Not what goes into the mouth defiles a man; but what comes out of the mouth, this defiles a man."

[12]Then His disciples came and said to Him, "Do You know that the Pharisees were offended when they heard this saying?"

[13]But He answered and said, "Every plant which My heavenly Father has not planted will be uprooted. [14]Let them alone. They are blind leaders of the blind. And if the blind leads the blind, both will fall into a ditch."

[15]Then Peter answered and said to Him, "Explain this parable to us."

[16]So Jesus said, "Are you also still without understanding? [17]Do you not yet understand that whatever enters the mouth goes into the stomach and is eliminated? [18]But those things which proceed out of the mouth come from the heart, and they defile a man. [19]For out of the heart proceed evil thoughts, murders, adulteries, fornications, thefts, false witness, blasphemies. [20]These are the things which defile a man, but to eat with unwashed hands does not defile a man."

A Gentile Shows Her Faith

[21]Then Jesus went out from there and departed to the region of Tyre and Sidon. [22]And behold, a woman of Canaan came from that region and cried out to Him, saying, "Have mercy on me, O Lord, Son of David! My daughter is severely demon-possessed."

[23]But He answered her not a word.

And His disciples came and urged Him, saying, "Send her away, for she cries out after us."

[24]But He answered and said, "I was not sent except to the lost sheep of the house of Israel."

[25]Then she came and worshiped Him, saying, "Lord, help me!"

[26]But He answered and said, "It is not good to take the children's bread and throw it to the little dogs."

[27]And she said, "Yes, Lord, yet even the little dogs eat the crumbs which fall from their masters' table."

[28]Then Jesus answered and said to her, "O woman, great is your faith! Let it be to you as you desire." And her daughter was healed from that very hour.

Jesus Heals Great Multitudes

[29]Jesus departed from there, skirted the Sea of Galilee, and went up on the mountain and sat down there. [30]Then great multitudes came to Him, having with them the lame, blind, mute, maimed, and many others; and they laid them down at Jesus' feet, and He healed them. [31]So the multitude marveled when they saw the mute speaking, the maimed made whole, the lame walking, and the blind seeing; and they glorified the God of Israel.

DEVOTIONAL

N *one of us are living 100 percent of what we know 100 percent of the time. That means there are times all of us qualify as hypocrites! We're all in need of God's grace, and no matter how many rules of a religion we manage to keep, it'll never be enough to make us right with God. We cannot get to heaven by doing good works, earning titles or degrees, or keeping rules and regulations. Even church membership can't get us to heaven. Only our faith in the finished work at Calvary can save us. Jesus is the only Way, so be sure your faith is in Christ alone today!*

—Brian Fossett
Fossett Evangelistic Ministries, Dalton, GA

WEEK 4, DAY 3

The Christ, the Son of the Living God

Matthew 15:32–16:20

Feeding the Four Thousand

Now Jesus called His disciples to Himself and said, "I have compassion on the multitude, because they have now continued with Me three days and have nothing to eat. And I do not want to send them away hungry, lest they faint on the way."

33Then His disciples said to Him, "Where could we get enough bread in the wilderness to fill such a great multitude?"

34Jesus said to them, "How many loaves do you have?" And they said, "Seven, and a few little fish."

35So He commanded the multitude to sit down on the ground. 36And He took the seven loaves and the fish and gave thanks, broke them and gave them to His disciples; and the disciples gave to the multitude. 37So they all ate and were filled, and they took up seven large baskets full of the fragments that were left. 38Now those who ate were four thousand men, besides women and children. 39And He sent away the multitude, got into the boat, and came to the region of Magdala.

The Pharisees and Sadducees Seek a Sign

16Then the Pharisees and Sadducees came, and testing Him asked that He would show them a sign from heaven. 2He answered and said to them, "When it is evening you say, 'It will be fair weather, for the sky is red'; 3and in the morning, 'It will be foul weather today, for the sky is red and threatening.' Hypocrites! You know how to discern the face of the sky, but you cannot discern the signs of the times. 4A wicked and adulterous generation seeks after a sign, and no sign shall be given to it except the sign of the prophet Jonah." And He left them and departed.

The Leaven of the Pharisees and Sadducees

5Now when His disciples had come to the other side, they had forgotten to take bread. 6Then Jesus said to them, "Take heed and beware of the leaven of the Pharisees and the Sadducees."

7And they reasoned among themselves, saying, "It is because we have taken no bread."

8But Jesus, being aware of it, said to them, "O you of little faith, why do you reason among yourselves because you have brought no bread? 9Do you not yet understand, or remember the five loaves of the five thousand and how many baskets you took up? 10Nor the seven loaves of the four thousand and how many large baskets you took up? 11How is it you do not understand that I did not speak to you concerning bread?—but to beware of the leaven of the Pharisees and Sadducees." 12Then they understood that He did not tell them to beware of the leaven of bread, but of the doctrine of the Pharisees and Sadducees.

Peter Confesses Jesus as the Christ

13When Jesus came into the region of Caesarea Philippi, He asked His disciples, saying, "Who do men say that I, the Son of Man, am?"

14So they said, "Some say John the Baptist, some Elijah, and others Jeremiah or one of the prophets."

15He said to them, "But who do you say that I am?"

16Simon Peter answered and said, "You are the Christ, the Son of the living God."

17Jesus answered and said to him, "Blessed are you, Simon Bar-Jonah, for flesh and blood has not revealed this to you, but My Father who is in heaven. 18And I also say to you that you are Peter, and on this rock I will build My church, and the gates of Hades shall not prevail against it. 19And I will give you the keys of the kingdom of heaven, and whatever you bind on earth will be bound in heaven, and whatever you loose on earth will be loose in heaven."

20Then He commanded His disciples that they should tell no one that He was Jesus the Christ.

DEVOTIONAL

There is a God-sized void in all of our hearts. So many people try to fill that void with drugs, alcohol, sex, adulation from others, or money, but the truth is, only a right relationship with Jesus will fill it. Only He can bring us peace, make us whole, and satisfy that nagging sense of longing.

Matthew 16:15 tells us that Jesus asked His disciples, "Who do you say that I am?" Peter answered, "You are the Christ, the Son of the living God" (v. 16). Jesus is still asking this question two thousand years later. Who do you say that He is? If you do not have an answer, do not waste another precious day. Recognize Jesus as the Christ, the Son of the living God. Accept Him today and make Him the Lord of your life. The void will be filled, and you will be whole.

—Brian Fossett
Fossett Evangelistic Ministries, Dalton, GA

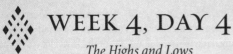

WEEK 4, DAY 4

The Highs and Lows of the Christian Journey

Matthew 16:21–17:13

Jesus Predicts His Death and Resurrection

From that time Jesus began to show to His disciples that He must go to Jerusalem, and suffer many things from the elders and chief priests and scribes, and be killed, and be raised the third day.

22Then Peter took Him aside and began to rebuke Him, saying, "Far be it from You, Lord; this shall not happen to You!"

23But He turned and said to Peter, "Get behind Me, Satan! You are an offense to Me, for you are not mindful of the things of God, but the things of men."

Take Up the Cross and Follow Him

24Then Jesus said to His disciples, "If anyone desires to come after Me, let him deny himself, and take up his cross, and follow Me. 25For whoever desires to save his life will lose it, but whoever loses his life for My sake will find it. 26For what profit is it to a man if he gains the whole world, and loses his own soul? Or what will a man give in exchange for his soul? 27For the Son of Man will come in the glory of His Father with His angels, and then He will reward each according to his works.

Jesus Transfigured on the Mount

28"Assuredly, I say to you, there are some standing here who shall not taste death till they see the Son of Man coming in His kingdom."

17Now after six days Jesus took Peter, James, and John his brother, led them up on a high mountain by themselves; 2and He was transfigured before them. His face shone like the sun, and His clothes became as white as the light. 3And behold, Moses and Elijah appeared to them, talking with Him. 4Then Peter answered and said to Jesus, "Lord, it is good for us to be here; if You wish, let us make here three tabernacles: one for You, one for Moses, and one for Elijah."

5While he was still speaking, behold, a bright cloud overshadowed them; and suddenly a voice came out of the cloud, saying, "This is My beloved Son, in whom I am well pleased. Hear Him!" 6And when the disciples heard it, they fell on their faces and were greatly afraid. 7But Jesus came and touched them and said, "Arise, and do not be afraid." 8When they had lifted up their eyes, they saw no one but Jesus only.

9Now as they came down from the mountain, Jesus commanded them, saying, "Tell the vision to no one until the Son of Man is risen from the dead."

10And His disciples asked Him, saying, "Why then do the scribes say that Elijah must come first?"

11Jesus answered and said to them, "Indeed, Elijah is coming first and will restore all things. 12But I say to you that Elijah has come already, and they did not know him but did to him whatever they wished. Likewise the Son of Man is also about to suffer at their hands." 13Then the disciples understood that He spoke to them of John the Baptist.

DEVOTIONAL

Right after Peter's great confession that Jesus was the Christ, the Son of the living God, he was called "Satan" by Jesus Himself (Matthew 16:16, 23). You can bet he was surprised at how rapidly he had descended in Jesus' eyes! Wasn't he Jesus' right-hand man with all the right answers? Peter thought he knew how Jesus would accomplish His mission here on earth, but Jesus knew Peter's heart and knew He needed to redirect him, because his thoughts and desires were not aligned with the will of God.

If Peter, a man mentored by Jesus Himself, could experience that kind of inconsistency in his spiritual life, we certainly can expect to experience the same. Whether we find ourselves at a low point or in a mountaintop moment, we need to keep striving toward the things of God and Christlikeness.

We are in a constant battle with our flesh every day. Human desires often skew our judgment and blur our vision. Just like Peter, it's easy for us to adopt an earthly perspective rather than a heavenly one. But Jesus wants us to be His followers. He calls us to become like Him, to see things His way—and it is indeed a process. Praise God that He has provided us with His Spirit to help us and guide us along the way.

The Christian life is a journey. Stay on the path toward God by continually striving to follow Christ in your words and actions, desiring each day to be closer to Him than the one before.

—Brian Fossett
Fossett Evangelistic Ministries, Dalton, GA

WEEK 4, DAY 5

*Greatness in God's Kingdom
Begins with Humility*

Matthew 17:14–18:9

A Boy Is Healed

And when they had come to the multitude, a man came to Him, kneeling down to Him and saying, 15"Lord, have mercy on my son, for he is an epileptic and suffers severely; for he often falls into the fire and often into the water. 16So I brought him to Your disciples, but they could not cure him."

17Then Jesus answered and said, "O faithless and perverse generation, how long shall I be with you? How long shall I bear with you? Bring him here to Me." 18And Jesus rebuked the demon, and it came out of him; and the child was cured from that very hour.

19Then the disciples came to Jesus privately and said, "Why could we not cast it out?"

20So Jesus said to them, "Because of your unbelief; for assuredly, I say to you, if you have faith as a mustard seed, you will say to this mountain, 'Move from here to there,' and it will move; and nothing will be impossible for you. 21However, this kind does not go out except by prayer and fasting."

Jesus Again Predicts His Death and Resurrection

22Now while they were staying in Galilee, Jesus said to them, "The Son of Man is about to be betrayed into the hands of men, 23and they will kill Him, and the third day He will be raised up." And they were exceedingly sorrowful.

Peter and His Master Pay Their Taxes

24When they had come to Capernaum, those who received the temple tax came to Peter and said, "Does your Teacher not pay the temple tax?"

25He said, "Yes."

And when he had come into the house, Jesus anticipated him, saying, "What do you think, Simon? From whom do the kings of the earth take customs or taxes, from their sons or from strangers?"

26Peter said to Him, "From strangers."

Jesus said to him, "Then the sons are free. 27Nevertheless, lest we offend them, go to the sea, cast in a hook, and take the fish that comes up first. And when you have opened its mouth, you will find a piece of money; take that and give it to them for Me and you."

Who Is the Greatest?

18At that time the disciples came to Jesus, saying, "Who then is greatest in the kingdom of heaven?"

2Then Jesus called a little child to Him, set him in the midst of them, 3and said, "Assuredly, I say to you, unless you are converted and become as little children, you will by no means enter the kingdom of heaven. 4Therefore whoever humbles himself as this little child is the greatest in the kingdom of heaven. 5Whoever receives one little child like this in My name receives Me.

Jesus Warns of Offenses

6"Whoever causes one of these little ones who believe in Me to sin, it would be better for him if a millstone were hung around his neck, and he were drowned in the depth of the sea. 7Woe to the world because of offenses! For offenses must come, but woe to that man by whom the offense comes!

8"If your hand or foot causes you to sin, cut it off and cast it from you. It is better for you to enter into life lame or maimed, rather than having two hands or two feet, to be cast into the everlasting fire. 9And if your eye causes you to sin, pluck it out and cast it from you. It is better for you to enter into life with one eye, rather than having two eyes, to be cast into hell fire."

DEVOTIONAL

A faithful man who preached the gospel for fifty years was once honored by a great gathering of people—the building was packed with hundreds who had been touched by his ministry. Because of his love for Jesus, he had added great value to the lives of others for the cause of Christ. His ministry had helped to mold and shape families, churches, and his community. This faithful man understood that worldly greatness is measured by the riches one attains, but greatness in the kingdom is about how much one gives.

That kind of greatness all begins with humility. James 4:6 says God resists the proud but gives grace to the humble. Throughout Scripture God calls us to cultivate a humble spirit, telling us not to be driven by selfish ambition or conceit, but to look out for others' needs and interests and to consider them better than ourselves (Philippians 2:3–4). Aim to have such a heart—it is beautiful in God's eyes!

—Brian Fossett
Fossett Evangelistic Ministries, Dalton, GA

WEEK 4, DAY 6

The Magnitude of God's Forgiveness

Matthew 18:10–35

The Parable of the Lost Sheep

"Take heed that you do not despise one of these little ones, for I say to you that in heaven their angels always see the face of My Father who is in heaven. [11]For the Son of Man has come to save that which was lost.

[12]"What do you think? If a man has a hundred sheep, and one of them goes astray, does he not leave the ninety-nine and go to the mountains to seek the one that is straying? [13]And if he should find it, assuredly, I say to you, he rejoices more over that sheep than over the ninety-nine that did not go astray. [14]Even so it is not the will of your Father who is in heaven that one of these little ones should perish.

Dealing with a Sinning Brother

[15]"Moreover if your brother sins against you, go and tell him his fault between you and him alone. If he hears you, you have gained your brother. [16]But if he will not hear, take with you one or two more, that 'by the mouth of two or three witnesses every word may be established.' [17]And if he refuses to hear them, tell it to the church. But if he refuses even to hear the church, let him be to you like a heathen and a tax collector.

[18]"Assuredly, I say to you, whatever you bind on earth will be bound in heaven, and whatever you loose on earth will be loosed in heaven.

[19]"Again I say to you that if two of you agree on earth concerning anything that they ask, it will be done for them by My Father in heaven. [20]For where two or three are gathered together in My name, I am there in the midst of them."

The Parable of the Unforgiving Servant

[21]Then Peter came to Him and said, "Lord, how often shall my brother sin against me, and I forgive him? Up to seven times?"

[22]Jesus said to him, "I do not say to you, up to seven times, but up to seventy times seven. [23]Therefore the kingdom of heaven is like a certain king who wanted to settle accounts with his servants. [24]And when he had begun to settle accounts, one was brought to him who owed him ten thousand talents. [25]But as he was not able to pay, his master commanded that he be sold, with his wife and children and all that he had, and that payment be made. [26]The servant therefore fell down before him, saying, 'Master, have patience with me, and I will pay you all.' [27]Then the master of that servant was moved with compassion, released him, and forgave him the debt.

[28]"But that servant went out and found one of his fellow servants who owed him a hundred denarii; and he laid hands on him and took him by the throat, saying, 'Pay me what you owe!' [29]So his fellow servant fell down at his feet and begged him, saying, 'Have patience with me, and I will pay you all.' [30]And he would not, but went and threw him into prison till he should pay the debt. [31]So when his fellow servants saw what had been done, they were very grieved, and came and told their master all that had been done. [32]Then his master, after he had called him, said to him, 'You wicked servant! I forgave you all that debt because you begged me. [33]Should you not also have had compassion on your fellow servant, just as I had pity on you?' [34]And his master was angry, and delivered him to the torturers until he should pay all that was due to him.

[35]"So My heavenly Father also will do to you if each of you, from his heart, does not forgive his brother his trespasses."

DEVOTIONAL

Christians are notorious for shooting wounded brothers instead of spending time restoring them. We tend to be quicker to forgive the people we like, but God does not condone selective forgiveness.

If you seek forgiveness from others and do not receive it, don't give up. Be generous and patient in giving grace, as God is. And instead of living with the weight of your guilt, let God's forgiveness give you peace. He is ultimately the One who matters most. Hear God's heart of compassion toward you: "They may not forgive you, but I have."

When you're the one having trouble extending forgiveness, remember that God has compassion on those who show compassion toward others. Also, take a walk down memory lane. Think back to all the times God has forgiven you—not for the purpose of reliving the guilt and pain, but to remember the experience of true forgiveness, the forgiveness that is possible because of the cross. Jesus' finished work at Calvary covers a multitude of sins. Keep praising Him for His forgiveness and extending it to others!

—Brian Fossett
Fossett Evangelistic Ministries, Dalton, GA

WEEK 4, DAY 7

Life is a precious gift from God. What are you doing with your life and the gifts (time, talents, and treasures) God has given you? Name three ways your life blesses others.

_____

_____

_____

_____

_____

_____

_____

_____

_____

_____

_____

We are not promised tomorrow. If this were your last day on earth, what would you do? From whom would you seek forgiveness? With whom would you make things right? With whom would you share the love of Jesus?

_____

_____

_____

_____

_____

_____

_____

_____

_____

WEEK 5, DAY 1

Jesus Talks About Marriage and Divorce

Matthew 19:1–26

Marriage and Divorce

19Now it came to pass, when Jesus had finished these sayings, that He departed from Galilee and came to the region of Judea beyond the Jordan. 2And great multitudes followed Him, and He healed them there.

3The Pharisees also came to Him, testing Him, and saying to Him, "Is it lawful for a man to divorce his wife for just any reason?"

4And He answered and said to them, "Have you not read that He who made them at the beginning 'made them male and female,' 5and said, 'For this reason a man shall leave his father and mother and be joined to his wife, and the two shall become one flesh'? 6So then, they are no longer two but one flesh. Therefore what God has joined together, let not man separate."

7They said to Him, "Why then did Moses command to give a certificate of divorce, and to put her away?"

8He said to them, "Moses, because of the hardness of your hearts, permitted you to divorce your wives, but from the beginning it was not so. 9And I say to you, whoever divorces his wife, except for sexual immorality, and marries another, commits adultery; and whoever marries her who is divorced commits adultery."

10His disciples said to Him, "If such is the case of the man with his wife, it is better not to marry."

Jesus Teaches on Celibacy

11But He said to them, "All cannot accept this saying, but only those to whom it has been given: 12For there are eunuchs who were born thus from their mother's womb, and there are eunuchs who were made eunuchs by men, and there are eunuchs who have made themselves eunuchs for the kingdom of heaven's sake. He who is able to accept it, let him accept it."

Jesus Blesses Little Children

13Then little children were brought to Him that He might put His hands on them and pray, but the disciples rebuked them. 14But Jesus said, "Let the little children come to Me, and do not forbid them; for of such is the kingdom of heaven." 15And He laid His hands on them and departed from there.

Jesus Counsels the Rich Young Ruler

16Now behold, one came and said to Him, "Good Teacher, what good thing shall I do that I may have eternal life?"

17So He said to him, "Why do you call Me good? No one is good but One, that is, God. But if you want to enter into life, keep the commandments."

18He said to Him, "Which ones?"

Jesus said, "'You shall not murder,' 'You shall not commit adultery,' 'You shall not steal,' 'You shall not bear false witness,' 19'Honor your father and your mother,' and, 'You shall love your neighbor as yourself.'"

20The young man said to Him, "All these things I have kept from my youth. What do I still lack?"

21Jesus said to him, "If you want to be perfect, go, sell what you have and give to the poor, and you will have treasure in heaven; and come, follow Me."

22But when the young man heard that saying, he went away sorrowful, for he had great possessions.

With God All Things Are Possible

23Then Jesus said to His disciples, "Assuredly, I say to you that it is hard for a rich man to enter the kingdom of heaven. 24And again I say to you, it is easier for a camel to go through the eye of a needle than for a rich man to enter the kingdom of God."

25When His disciples heard it, they were greatly astonished, saying, "Who then can be saved?"

26But Jesus looked at them and said to them, "With men this is impossible, but with God all things are possible."

DEVOTIONAL

Marriage is the first covenant relationship God established between man and woman. It is the foundational relationship of civilization. Since the first union in the garden of Eden, fallen humans have sought to change the priority, nature, and definition of marriage. God's standard has not changed. Marriage is between one man and one woman. The goal of marriage is a "one flesh" relationship. That means an intimacy of heart, mind, and body.

Marriage is to be honored, upheld, prized, and protected. If you are married, remain married. If you are divorced, seek reconciliation if possible. If you are going to get married, resolve to make it a lifelong commitment.

—Craig Bowers
First Baptist Church, Locust Grove, GA

WEEK 5, DAY 2

God's View of Fairness

Matthew 19:27–20:19

Then Peter answered and said to Him, "See, we have left all and followed You. Therefore what shall we have?" 28So Jesus said to them, "Assuredly I say to you, that in the regeneration, when the Son of Man sits on the throne of His glory, you who have followed Me will also sit on twelve thrones, judging the twelve tribes of Israel. 29And everyone who has left houses or brothers or sisters or father or mother or wife or children or lands, for My name's sake, shall receive a hundredfold, and inherit eternal life. 30But many who are first will be last, and the last first.

The Parable of the Workers in the Vineyard

20"For the kingdom of heaven is like a landowner who went out early in the morning to hire laborers for his vineyard. 2Now when he had agreed with the laborers for a denarius a day, he sent them into his vineyard. 3And he went out about the third hour and saw others standing idle in the marketplace, 4and said to them, 'You also go into the vineyard, and whatever is right I will give you.' So they went. 5Again he went out about the sixth and the ninth hour, and did likewise. 6And about the eleventh hour he went out and found others standing idle, and said to them, 'Why have you been standing here idle all day?' 7They said to him, 'Because no one hired us.' He said to them, 'You also go into the vineyard, and whatever is right you will receive.'

8"So when evening had come, the owner of the vineyard said to his steward, 'Call the laborers and give them their wages, beginning with the last to the first.' 9And when those came who were hired about the eleventh hour, they each received a denarius. 10But when the first came, they supposed that they would receive more; and they likewise received each a denarius. 11And when they had received it, they complained against the landowner, 12saying, 'These last men have worked only one hour, and you made them equal to us who have borne the burden and the heat of the day.' 13But he answered one of them and said, 'Friend, I am doing you no wrong. Did you not agree with me for a denarius? 14Take what is yours and go your way. I wish to give to this last man the same as to you. 15Is it not lawful for me to do what I wish with my own things? Or is your eye evil because I am good?' 16So the last will be first, and the first last. For many are called, but few chosen."

Jesus a Third Time Predicts His Death and Resurrection

17Now Jesus, going up to Jerusalem took the twelve disciples aside on the road and said to them, 18"Behold, we are going up to Jerusalem, and the Son of Man will be betrayed to the chief priests and to the scribes; and they will condemn Him to death, 19and deliver Him to the Gentiles to mock and to scourge and to crucify. And the third day He will rise again."

DEVOTIONAL

Followers of Christ make sacrifices. But the truth is, sacrifices made on earth pale in comparison to the rewards that heaven holds. In Matthew 19:27, Peter pointed out the sacrifices he and the other disciples had made for Jesus, and then he asked, "What shall we have?" Peter was really concerned about being treated fairly. Jesus responded by saying that any sacrifices made on earth will be rewarded in heaven a hundredfold, along with eternal life (v. 29). That's a great return!

A kingdom paradox follows His promise: "Many who are first will be last, and the last first" (v. 30). Jesus explained the paradox by telling a story about a typical workday in which people are hired five different times during the day. At pay time, they all receive the same compensation. That doesn't seem fair at all! Those hired early received the identical pay as those hired at the end of the day. What was Christ teaching? He was illustrating the paradox of grace. The kingdom is all about grace. Those who came to work at the end of the day represent those who become followers of Christ at the end of their lives. Those hired at the beginning of the day represent those who come to Christ early in life. All receive the same gift of eternal life. Will there be rewards in heaven? Certainly! But even a hundredfold reward pales in comparison to the inheritance of eternal life.

Grace is never free or fair. Jesus, the Righteous One, paid for our sin so that we who are unrighteous could receive eternal life. That doesn't seem fair, and it isn't. Grace isn't fair. Justice is fair. God could justly condemn us to hell, but He instead offers His grace, which Jesus paid for with His blood. Thank God for His grace!

—Craig Bowers
First Baptist Church, Locust Grove, GA

WEEK 5, DAY 3

Honoring Jesus as King

Matthew 20:20–21:11

Greatness Is Serving

Then the mother of Zebedee's sons came to Him with her sons, kneeling down and asking something from Him.

21And He said to her, "What do you wish?"

She said to Him, "Grant that these two sons of mine may sit, one on Your right hand and the other on the left, in Your kingdom."

22But Jesus answered and said, "You do not know what you ask. Are you able to drink the cup that I am about to drink, and be baptized with the baptism that I am baptized with?"

They said to Him, "We are able."

23So He said to them, "You will indeed drink My cup, and be baptized with the baptism that I am baptized with; but to sit on My right hand and on My left is not Mine to give, but it is for those for whom it is prepared by My Father."

24And when the ten heard it, they were greatly displeased with the two brothers. 25But Jesus called them to Himself and said, "You know that the rulers of the Gentiles lord it over them, and those who are great exercise authority over them. 26Yet it shall not be so among you; but whoever desires to become great among you, let him be your servant. 27And whoever desires to be first among you, let him be your slave—28just as the Son of Man did not come to be served, but to serve, and to give His life a ransom for many."

Two Blind Men Receive Their Sight

29Now as they went out of Jericho, a great multitude followed Him. 30And behold, two blind men sitting by the road, when they heard that Jesus was passing by, cried out, saying, "Have mercy on us, O Lord, Son of David!"

31Then the multitude warned them that they should be quiet; but they cried out all the more, saying, "Have mercy on us, O Lord, Son of David!"

32So Jesus stood still and called them, and said, "What do you want Me to do for you?"

33They said to Him, "Lord, that our eyes may be opened." 34So Jesus had compassion and touched their eyes. And immediately their eyes received sight, and they followed Him.

The Triumphal Entry

21 Now when they drew near Jerusalem, and came to Bethphage, at the Mount of Olives, then Jesus sent two disciples, 2saying to them, "Go into the village opposite you, and immediately you will find a donkey tied, and a colt with her. Loose them and bring them to Me. 3And if anyone says anything to you, you shall say, 'The Lord has need of them,' and immediately he will send them."

4All this was done that it might be fulfilled which was spoken by the prophet, saying:

5 "Tell the daughter of Zion,
  'Behold, your King is coming to you,
  Lowly, and sitting on a donkey,
  A colt, the foal of a donkey.'"

6So the disciples went and did as Jesus commanded them. 7They brought the donkey and the colt, laid their clothes on them, and set Him on them. 8And a very great multitude spread their clothes on the road; others cut down branches from the trees and spread them on the road. 9Then the multitudes who went before and those who followed cried out, saying:

"Hosanna to the Son of David!
  'Blessed is He who comes in the
      name of the Lord!'
  Hosanna in the highest!"

10And when He had come into Jerusalem, all the city was moved, saying, "Who is this?"

11So the multitudes said, "This is Jesus, the prophet from Nazareth of Galilee."

DEVOTIONAL

Jerusalem welcomed Jesus as King on Palm Sunday, and then rejected Him on Good Friday. Why? Because they sought one who would bring them deliverance from the oppressive yoke of Rome. They saw Him as the miracle worker who could deliver them. When it became apparent that Jesus was not as interested in bringing temporal deliverance as He was eternal salvation, the people rejected Him.

Today, so many have made Jesus into a personal ATM that gives them everything they want. Will you allow Him to be King of your life, even if it means sacrifice and submission to His purpose, knowing that He may not remove your temporal oppression?

—Craig Bowers
First Baptist Church, Locust Grove, GA

WEEK 5, DAY 4

God Seeks Sincere Worship

Matthew 21:12–32

Jesus Cleanses the Temple

Then Jesus went into the temple of God and drove out all those who bought and sold in the temple, and overturned the tables of the money changers and the seats of those who sold doves. 13And He said to them, "It is written, 'My house shall be called a house of prayer,' but you have made it a 'den of thieves.'"

14Then the blind and the lame came to Him in the temple, and He healed them. 15But when the chief priests and scribes saw the wonderful things that He did, and the children crying out in the temple and saying, "Hosanna to the Son of David!" they were indignant 16and said to Him, "Do You hear what these are saying?"

And Jesus said to them, "Yes. Have you never read,

'Out of the mouth of babes and nursing infants
  You have perfected praise'?"

17Then He left them and went out of the city to Bethany, and He lodged there.

The Fig Tree Withered

18Now in the morning, as He returned to the city, He was hungry. 19And seeing a fig tree by the road, He came to it and found nothing on it but leaves, and said to it, "Let no fruit grow on you ever again." Immediately the fig tree withered away.

The Lesson of the Withered Fig Tree

20And when the disciples saw it, they marveled, saying, "How did the fig tree wither away so soon?"

21So Jesus answered and said to them, "Assuredly, I say to you, if you have faith and do not doubt, you will not only do what was done to the fig tree, but also if you say to this mountain, 'Be removed and be cast into the sea,' it will be done. 22And whatever things you ask in prayer, believing, you will receive."

Jesus' Authority Questioned

23Now when He came into the temple, the chief priests and the elders of the people confronted Him as He was teaching, and said, "By what authority are You doing these things? And who gave You this authority?"

24But Jesus answered and said to them, "I also will ask you one thing, which if you tell Me, I likewise will tell you by what authority I do these things: 25The baptism of John—where was it from? From heaven or from men?"

And they reasoned among themselves, saying, "If we say, 'From heaven,' He will say to us, 'Why then did you not believe him?' 26But if we say, 'From men,' we fear the multitude, for all count John as a prophet." 27So they answered Jesus and said, "We do not know."

And He said to them, "Neither will I tell you by what authority I do these things.

The Parable of the Two Sons

28"But what do you think? A man had two sons, and he came to the first and said, 'Son, go, work today in my vineyard.' 29He answered and said, 'I will not,' but afterward he regretted it and went. 30Then he came to the second and said likewise. And he answered and said, 'I go, sir,' but he did not go. 31Which of the two did the will of his father?"

They said to Him, "The first."

Jesus said to them, "Assuredly, I say to you that tax collectors and harlots enter the kingdom of God before you. 32For John came to you in the way of righteousness, and you did not believe him; but tax collectors and harlots believed him; and when you saw it, you did not afterward relent and believe him."

DEVOTIONAL

During Old Testament times, the Jewish place of worship was the temple. When Jesus saw the temple compromised by competing agendas, He did not stand by and allow it to be abused. He conducted a house-cleaning crusade!

Since New Testament times, the center of worship has not been a particular place, but the position of our hearts. Christ is to be first in our hearts. Our lives are to reflect our total commitment to Him. If our Lord sees competing agendas moving into the center of our hearts, He conducts a house-cleaning crusade!

When Jesus cleansed the Jewish temple, people experienced discomfort. Similarly, He cleanses the temple of our hearts by creating discomfort in our lives. He wants to remove competing allegiances. Welcome Jesus to cleanse you so you may worship Him in spirit and in truth, and honor Him as Lord over all.

—Craig Bowers
First Baptist Church, Locust Grove, GA

WEEK 5, DAY 5

The Kingdom of Heaven
Is for All Who Obey

Matthew 21:33–22:14

The Parable of the Wicked Vinedressers

"Hear another parable: There was a certain land-owner who planted a vineyard and set a hedge around it, dug a winepress in it and built a tower. And he leased it to vinedressers and went into a far country. 34Now when vintage-time drew near, he sent his servants to the vinedressers, that they might receive its fruit. 35And the vinedressers took his servants, beat one, killed one, and stoned another. 36Again he sent other servants, more than the first, and they did likewise to them. 37Then last of all he sent his son to them, saying, 'They will respect my son.' 38But when the vinedressers saw the son, they said among themselves, 'This is the heir. Come, let us kill him and seize his inheritance.' 39So they took him and cast him out of the vineyard and killed him.

40"Therefore, when the owner of the vineyard comes, what will he do to those vinedressers?"

41They said to Him, "He will destroy those wicked men miserably, and lease his vineyard to other vinedressers who will render to him the fruits in their seasons."

42Jesus said to them, "Have you never read in the Scriptures:

'The stone which the builders rejected
Has become the chief cornerstone.
This was the Lord's doing,
And it is marvelous in our eyes'?

43"Therefore I say to you, the kingdom of God will be taken from you and given to a nation bearing the fruits of it. 44And whoever falls on this stone will be broken; but on whomever it falls, it will grind him to powder."

45Now when the chief priests and Pharisees heard His parables, they perceived that He was speaking of them. 46But when they sought to lay hands on Him, they feared the multitudes, because they took Him for a prophet.

The Parable of the Wedding Feast

22And Jesus answered and spoke to them again by parables and said: 2"The kingdom of heaven is like a certain king who arranged a marriage for his son, 3and sent out his servants to call those who were invited to the wedding; and they were not willing to come. 4Again, he sent out other servants, saying, 'Tell those who are invited, "See, I have prepared my dinner; my oxen and fatted cattle are killed, and all things are ready. Come to the wedding."' 5But they made light of it and went their ways, one to his own farm, another to his business. 6And the rest seized his servants, treated them spitefully, and killed them. 7But when the king heard about it, he was furious. And he sent out his armies, destroyed those murderers, and burned up their city. 8Then he said to his servants, 'The wedding is ready, but those who were invited were not worthy. 9Therefore go into the highways, and as many as you find, invite to the wedding.' 10So those servants went out into the highways and gathered together all whom they found, both bad and good. And the wedding hall was filled with guests.

11"But when the king came in to see the guests, he saw a man there who did not have on a wedding garment. 12So he said to him, 'Friend, how did you come in here without a wedding garment?' And he was speechless. 13Then the king said to the servants, 'Bind him hand and foot, take him away, and cast him into outer darkness; there will be weeping and gnashing of teeth.'

14"For many are called, but few are chosen."

DEVOTIONAL

Both parables in this passage teach us about the kingdom of heaven. The wicked vinedressers teach us that those who reject the Son will be rejected by the Father. The wedding feast teaches us that many are invited into the kingdom, but few will respond to the invitation. The kingdom of heaven is only for those who respond to God's initiative with a repentant, obedient heart.

The religious leaders of Israel were offended by the parable of the vinedressers. They understood Jesus was saying that they had rejected God's Messiah just as their fathers had rejected the prophets, and that even though they were very religious, they were condemned.

Could this parable relate to the religious of our day? Could it be that when those who reject a messenger of God who proclaims His truth from His Word, they are really rejecting the One who sent the messenger? Christ teaches that the kingdom of God is not for those who are religious, but for those who are responsive to His truth with a submissive, obedient heart. Seek to have such a heart for Christ today.

—Craig Bowers
First Baptist Church, Locust Grove, GA

WEEK 5, DAY 6

The Most Important Command

Matthew 22:15–40

The Pharisees: Is It Lawful to Pay Taxes to Caesar?

Then the Pharisees went and plotted how they might entangle Him in His talk. 16And they sent to Him their disciples with the Herodians, saying, "Teacher, we know that You are true, and teach the way of God in truth; nor do You care about anyone, for You do not regard the person of men. 17Tell us, therefore, what do You think? Is it lawful to pay taxes to Caesar, or not?"

18But Jesus perceived their wickedness, and said, "Why do you test Me, you hypocrites? 19Show Me the tax money."

So they brought Him a denarius.

20And He said to them, "Whose image and inscription is this?"

21They said to Him, "Caesar's."

And He said to them, "Render therefore to Caesar the things that are Caesar's, and to God the things that are God's." 22When they had heard these words, they marveled, and left Him and went their way.

The Sadducees: What About the Resurrection?

23The same day the Sadducees, who say there is no resurrection, came to Him and asked Him, 24saying: "Teacher, Moses said that if a man dies, having no children, his brother shall marry his wife and raise up offspring for his brother. 25Now there were with us seven brothers. The first died after he had married, and having no offspring, left his wife to his brother. 26Likewise the second also, and the third, even to the seventh. 27Last of all the woman died also. 28Therefore, in the resurrection, whose wife of the seven will she be? For they all had her."

29Jesus answered and said to them, "You are mistaken, not knowing the Scriptures nor the power of God. 30For in the resurrection they neither marry nor are given in marriage, but are like angels of God in heaven. 31But concerning the resurrection of the dead, have you not read what was spoken to you by God, saying, 32'I am the God of Abraham, the God of Isaac, and the God of Jacob'? God is not the God of the dead, but of the living." 33And when the multitudes heard this, they were astonished at His teaching.

The Scribes: Which Is the First Commandment of All?

34But when the Pharisees heard that He had silenced the Sadducees, they gathered together. 35Then one of them, a lawyer, asked Him a question, testing Him, and saying, 36"Teacher, which is the great commandment in the law?"

37Jesus said to him, "'You shall love the LORD your God with all your heart, with all your soul, and with all your mind.' 38This is the first and great commandment. 39And the second is like it: 'You shall love your neighbor as yourself.' 40On these two commandments hang all the Law and the Prophets."

DEVOTIONAL

Have you ever heard someone ask a question and thought, I wish I had asked that? Perhaps after you heard the answer, you were just grateful someone was insightful enough to ask the question. Regardless of the lawyer's motive, he asked one of the most important questions ever posed (Matthew 22:36).

We have many questions for God. There are many things we do not understand. Bad things happen. People suffer. We are left with a boatload of questions and few answers. Our questions flow from our desire to understand. When we can't figure it out, we feel empty and perplexed. But then we hear the one question that ushers in the one answer that disarms us: What is the greatest commandment? Love the Lord your God with all your heart, soul, and mind. The human response God is looking for most—the one at the top of His list—is love.

When we have a love relationship with Him, we know we can trust Him even when we do not understand His ways. We know and experience His love. Love trumps all explanations. When people are grieving or suffering, their primary need is not an explanation. Their hearts cry out for compassion . . . genuine, authentic love. The warm, caring embrace of a friend. The shoulder of a family member to cry on.

The most important thing you need from God is not His explanations, but His love. He loves you. Will you respond to His love by loving Him with all your heart, soul, and mind?

—Craig Bowers
First Baptist Church, Locust Grove, GA

WEEK 5, DAY 7

If the Lord did some "house cleaning" in your heart, what would be removed?

_____

_____

_____

_____

_____

_____

_____

_____

_____

_____

_____

How does your life reflect what is most important to God?

_____

_____

_____

_____

_____

_____

_____

_____

_____

WEEK 6, DAY 1

Judgment Against
False Spiritual Leaders

Matthew 22:41–23:22

Jesus: How Can David Call His Descendant Lord?

While the Pharisees were gathered together, Jesus asked them, ⁴²saying, "What do you think about the Christ? Whose Son is He?"

They said to Him, "The Son of David."

⁴³He said to them, "How then does David in the Spirit call Him 'Lord,' saying:

⁴⁴ 'The LORD said to my Lord,
"Sit at My right hand,
Till I make Your enemies Your footstool"'?

⁴⁵"If David then calls Him 'Lord,' how is He his Son?" ⁴⁶And no one was able to answer Him a word, nor from that day on did anyone dare question Him anymore.

Woe to the Scribes and Pharisees

23 Then Jesus spoke to the multitudes and to His disciples, ²saying: "The scribes and the Pharisees sit in Moses' seat. ³Therefore whatever they tell you to observe, that observe and do, but do not do according to their works; for they say, and do not do. ⁴For they bind heavy burdens, hard to bear, and lay them on men's shoulders; but they themselves will not move them with one of their fingers. ⁵But all their works they do to be seen by men. They make their phylacteries broad and enlarge the borders of their garments. ⁶They love the best places at feasts, the best seats in the synagogues, ⁷greetings in the marketplaces, and to be called by men, 'Rabbi, Rabbi.' ⁸But you, do not be called 'Rabbi'; for One is your Teacher, the Christ, and you are all brethren. ⁹Do not call anyone on earth your father; for One is your Father, He who is in heaven. ¹⁰And do not be called teachers; for One is your Teacher, the Christ. ¹¹But he who is greatest among you shall be your servant. ¹²And whoever exalts himself will be humbled, and he who humbles himself will be exalted.

¹³"But woe to you, scribes and Pharisees, hypocrites! For you shut up the kingdom of heaven against men; for you neither go in yourselves, nor do you allow those who are entering to go in. ¹⁴Woe to you, scribes and Pharisees, hypocrites! For you devour widows' houses, and for a pretense make long prayers. Therefore you will receive greater condemnation.

¹⁵"Woe to you, scribes and Pharisees, hypocrites! For you travel land and sea to win one proselyte, and when he is won, you make him twice as much a son of hell as yourselves.

¹⁶"Woe to you, blind guides, who say, 'Whoever swears by the temple, it is nothing; but whoever swears by the gold of the temple, he is obliged to perform it.' ¹⁷Fools and blind! For which is greater, the gold or the temple that sanctifies the gold? ¹⁸And, 'Whoever swears by the altar, it is nothing; but whoever swears by the gift that is on it, he is obliged to perform it.' ¹⁹Fools and blind! For which is greater, the gift or the altar that sanctifies the gift? ²⁰Therefore he who swears by the altar, swears by it and by all things on it. ²¹He who swears by the temple, swears by it and by Him who dwells in it. ²²And he who swears by heaven, swears by the throne of God and by Him who sits on it."

DEVOTIONAL

Throughout Christ's earthly ministry, Jewish leaders hounded Him, monitoring His every move. They were threatened by His message and His authority, and they were furious with envy as great crowds followed Him. The scribes and Pharisees plotted how they might destroy Jesus, and their first scheme was to try to trap Him in a series of loaded questions (Matthew 22:15). In His infinite wisdom, Jesus answered all of them perfectly and then asked, "What do you think about the Christ? Whose Son is He?" (v. 42).

These Jewish leaders recognized the humanity of the Messiah and that He descended from David, but they certainly didn't acknowledge His divinity. Answering correctly would have validated Jesus' claim to be the Son of God, and they didn't want to do that. Jesus explained that He Himself was David's Lord. He existed before David and gave David life!

Jesus exposed His antagonists' evil intentions and warned them they were only asking for judgment. His scathing rebuke of the scribes and Pharisees in chapter 23 describes how false religion parades itself under the mask of truth. Our society promotes tolerance at any cost, but Jesus was unwilling to compromise the truth of the gospel. Are you willing to compromise? Be sure you are not believing in a false and self-serving version of the gospel. Stay committed to the truth of God's Word.

—Dusty McLemore
Lindsay Lane Baptist Church, Athens, AL

WEEK 6, DAY 2

*Woe to the Self-Righteous
and Hard-Hearted*

Matthew 23:23–24:8

"Woe to you, scribes and Pharisees, hypocrites! For you pay tithe of mint and anise and cummin, and have neglected the weightier matters of the law: justice and mercy and faith. These you ought to have done, without leaving the others undone. 24Blind guides, who strain out a gnat and swallow a camel!

25"Woe to you, scribes and Pharisees, hypocrites! For you cleanse the outside of the cup and dish, but inside they are full of extortion and self-indulgence. 26Blind Pharisee, first cleanse the inside of the cup and dish, that the outside of them may be clean also.

27"Woe to you, scribes and Pharisees, hypocrites! For you are like whitewashed tombs which indeed appear beautiful outwardly, but inside are full of dead men's bones and all uncleanness. 28Even so you also outwardly appear righteous to men, but inside you are full of hypocrisy and lawlessness.

29"Woe to you, scribes and Pharisees, hypocrites! Because you build the tombs of the prophets and adorn the monuments of the righteous, 30and say, 'If we had lived in the days of our fathers, we would not have been partakers with them in the blood of the prophets.'

31"Therefore you are witnesses against yourselves that you are sons of those who murdered the prophets. 32Fill up, then, the measure of your fathers' guilt. 33Serpents, brood of vipers! How can you escape the condemnation of hell? 34Therefore, indeed, I send you prophets, wise men, and scribes: some of them you will kill and crucify, and some of them you will scourge in your synagogues and persecute from city to city, 35that on you may come all the righteous blood shed on the earth, from the blood of righteous Abel to the blood of Zechariah, son of Berechiah, whom you murdered between the temple and the altar. 36Assuredly, I say to you, all these things will come upon this generation.

Jesus Laments over Jerusalem

37"O Jerusalem, Jerusalem, the one who kills the prophets and stones those who are sent to her! How often I wanted to gather your children together, as a hen gathers her chicks under her wings, but you were not willing! 38See! Your house is left to you desolate; 39for I say to you,

you shall see Me no more till you say, 'Blessed is He who comes in the name of the Lord!'"

Jesus Predicts the Destruction of the Temple

24 Then Jesus went out and departed from the temple, and His disciples came up to show Him the buildings of the temple. 2And Jesus said to them, "Do you not see all these things? Assuredly, I say to you, not one stone shall be left here upon another, that shall not be thrown down."

The Signs of the Times and the End of the Age

3Now as He sat on the Mount of Olives, the disciples came to Him privately, saying, "Tell us, when will these things be? And what will be the sign of Your coming, and of the end of the age?"

4And Jesus answered and said to them: "Take heed that no one deceives you. 5For many will come in My name, saying, 'I am the Christ,' and will deceive many. 6And you will hear of wars and rumors of wars. See that you are not troubled; for all these things must come to pass, but the end is not yet. 7For nation will rise against nation, and kingdom against kingdom. And there will be famines, pestilences, and earthquakes in various places. 8All these are the beginning of sorrows."

DEVOTIONAL

No doubt some of Jesus' listeners were shocked by His words concerning the scribes and Pharisees. It wasn't every day they heard their religious leaders called a "brood of vipers" (Matthew 23:33)! In no uncertain terms, Jesus condemned their sinful hearts.

The scribes and Pharisees claimed if they had been in their ancestors' positions, they would not have rejected and killed God's prophets (Matthew 23:30). They said this even while they were plotting to kill Jesus! Even in His righteous anger at their self-righteousness, Jesus grieved over their lostness. The Jews had turned Him away, yet He still spoke of His longing to gather and care for them, "as a hen gathers her chicks under her wings" (v. 37). Sadly, they just hadn't let Him.

Jesus has the same heart toward you today. He pursues you with His love and longs to pull you close. The Jews were not willing to soften their hearts, repent, and humbly submit themselves to God in obedience. Learn from their example and do just the opposite!

—Dusty McLemore
Lindsay Lane Baptist Church, Athens, AL

WEEK 6, DAY 3

Signs of the End Times

Matthew 24:9–35

"Then they will deliver you up to tribulation and kill you, and you will be hated by all nations for My name's sake. [10]And then many will be offended, will betray one another, and will hate one another. [11]Then many false prophets will rise up and deceive many. [12]And because lawlessness will abound, the love of many will grow cold. [13]But he who endures to the end shall be saved. [14]And this gospel of the kingdom will be preached in all the world as a witness to all the nations, and then the end will come.

The Great Tribulation

[15]"Therefore when you see the 'abomination of desolation,' spoken of by Daniel the prophet, standing in the holy place" (whoever reads, let him understand), [16]"then let those who are in Judea flee to the mountains. [17]Let him who is on the housetop not go down to take anything out of his house. [18]And let him who is in the field not go back to get his clothes. [19]But woe to those who are pregnant and to those who are nursing babies in those days! [20]And pray that your flight may not be in winter or on the Sabbath. [21]For then there will be great tribulation, such as has not been since the beginning of the world until this time, no, nor ever shall be. [22]And unless those days were shortened, no flesh would be saved; but for the elect's sake those days will be shortened.

[23]"Then if anyone says to you, 'Look, here is the Christ!' or 'There!' do not believe it. [24]For false christs and false prophets will rise and show great signs and wonders to deceive, if possible, even the elect. [25]See, I have told you beforehand.

[26]"Therefore if they say to you, 'Look, He is in the desert!' do not go out; or 'Look, He is in the inner rooms!' do not believe it. [27]For as the lightning comes from the east and flashes to the west, so also will the coming of the Son of Man be. [28]For wherever the carcass is, there the eagles will be gathered together.

The Coming of the Son of Man

[29]"Immediately after the tribulation of those days the sun will be darkened, and the moon will not give its light; the stars will fall from heaven, and the powers of the heavens will be shaken. [30]Then the sign of the Son of Man will appear in heaven, and then all the tribes of the earth will mourn, and they will see the Son of Man coming on the clouds of heaven with power and great glory. [31]And He will send His angels with a great sound of a trumpet, and they will gather together His elect from the four winds, from one end of heaven to the other.

The Parable of the Fig Tree

[32]"Now learn this parable from the fig tree: When its branch has already become tender and puts forth leaves, you know that summer is near. [33]So you also, when you see all these things, know that it is near—at the doors! [34]Assuredly, I say to you, this generation will by no means pass away till all these things take place. [35]Heaven and earth will pass away, but My words will by no means pass away."

DEVOTIONAL

Jesus described the events leading up to His return. He told of a time of tribulation preceding His Second Coming and connected these events with Daniel's Seventieth Week (Daniel 9:27). After giving this brief overview of the tribulation, Jesus also described the abomination of desolation, which refers to a terrible desecration involving idolatrous worship in the temple.

There's a variety of views among Christians about end times and how to interpret Matthew 24. Those with a pre-tribulation view believe that people of the church age will have already been raptured by the time the tribulation begins and that the Second Coming will occur directly afterward. In other words, they believe Jesus will come for His church and later return triumphantly with His church and enter into the Millennium.

Different views of end times aside, we can all agree that Jesus is indeed coming and that we are called to be faithful. He told His disciples, "It is not for you to know times or seasons which the Father has put in His own authority," and then He went on to say they would receive the Spirit's power and be His witnesses in the world (Acts 1:7–8). We see something similar in Matthew. After Jesus described signs of the end times, He stressed the importance of living in obedient anticipation (Matthew 24:36–25:30). May we conduct our daily lives with the expectation that He could return at any moment!

—Dusty McLemore
Lindsay Lane Baptist Church, Athens, AL

WEEK 6, DAY 4

Always Be Ready for the Lord's Coming

Matthew 24:36–25:13

No One Knows the Day or Hour

"But of that day and hour no one knows, not even the angels of heaven, but My Father only. 37But as the days of Noah were, so also will the coming of the Son of Man be. 38For as in the days before the flood, they were eating and drinking, marrying and giving in marriage, until the day that Noah entered the ark, 39and did not know until the flood came and took them all away, so also will the coming of the Son of Man be. 40Then two men will be in the field: one will be taken and the other left. 41Two women will be grinding at the mill: one will be taken and the other left. 42Watch therefore, for you do not know what hour your Lord is coming. 43But know this, that if the master of the house had known what hour the thief would come, he would have watched and not allowed his house to be broken into. 44Therefore you also be ready, for the Son of Man is coming at an hour you do not expect.

The Faithful Servant and the Evil Servant

45"Who then is a faithful and wise servant, whom his master made ruler over his household, to give them food in due season? 46Blessed is that servant whom his master, when he comes, will find so doing. 47Assuredly, I say to you that he will make him ruler over all his goods. 48But if that evil servant says in his heart, 'My master is delaying his coming,' 49and begins to beat his fellow servants, and to eat and drink with the drunkards, 50the master of that servant will come on a day when he is not looking for him and at an hour that he is not aware of, 51and will cut him in two and appoint him his portion with the hypocrites. There shall be weeping and gnashing of teeth.

The Parable of the Wise and Foolish Virgins

25"Then the kingdom of heaven shall be likened to ten virgins who took their lamps and went out to meet the bridegroom. 2Now five of them were wise, and five were foolish. 3Those who were foolish took their lamps and took no oil with them, 4but the wise took oil in their vessels with their lamps. 5But while the bridegroom was delayed, they all slumbered and slept.

6"And at midnight a cry was heard: 'Behold, the bridegroom is coming; go out to meet him!' 7Then all those virgins arose and trimmed their lamps. 8And the foolish said to the wise, 'Give us some of your oil, for our lamps are going out.' 9But the wise answered, saying, 'No, lest there should not be enough for us and you; but go rather to those who sell, and buy for yourselves.' 10And while they went to buy, the bridegroom came, and those who were ready went in with him to the wedding; and the door was shut.

11"Afterward the other virgins came also, saying, 'Lord, Lord, open to us!' 12But he answered and said, 'Assuredly, I say to you, I do not know you.'

13"Watch therefore, for you know neither the day nor the hour in which the Son of Man is coming."

DEVOTIONAL

Jesus gave an indication of what the world will be like in the period before His coming, comparing it to the days of Noah (Matthew 24:37–39). At that time people were enjoying the normal pursuits of life, eating, drinking, and marrying—unaware of imminent judgment. But then the Flood came and took them all away. It came very suddenly, and the people were unprepared. They lost the best by living for the good!

Jesus emphasized the necessity of being ready for His coming. He described faithful and evil servants of a master who was away from his house. When the master returned with no notice, he expected to find his servants faithfully doing the work of the household, not behaving like lazy drunkards and mistreating fellow servants. Jesus also told a parable in which ten virgins were waiting for a delayed bridegroom so they could join the wedding procession. When the bridegroom finally arrived, only half of the virgins were prepared with lamps and oil to go meet him. So it is today, as so many are oblivious to our Lord's Second Coming. Once He returns, there will be no more time to make things right.

God's Word gives us many clear warnings not to be found unfaithful or unprepared when He returns. Jesus said, "Watch therefore, for you know neither the day nor the hour in which the Son of Man is coming" (Matthew 25:13). Jesus wants us to spend our lives keeping His Word, doing His work, and loving Him and others. He wants us to remain patient, alert, productive, and worshipful as we anticipate His coming. Are you "watching," living in readiness for Jesus' return?

—Dusty McLemore
Lindsay Lane Baptist Church, Athens, AL

WEEK 6, DAY 5

Be Faithful with What You've Been Given

Matthew 25:14–40

The Parable of the Talents

"For the kingdom of heaven is like a man traveling to a far country, who called his own servants and delivered his goods to them. ¹⁵And to one he gave five talents, to another two, and to another one, to each according to his own ability; and immediately he went on a journey. ¹⁶Then he who had received the five talents went and traded with them, and made another five talents. ¹⁷And likewise he who had received two gained two more also. ¹⁸But he who had received one went and dug in the ground, and hid his lord's money. ¹⁹After a long time the lord of those servants came and settled accounts with them.

²⁰"So he who had received five talents came and brought five other talents, saying, 'Lord, you delivered to me five talents; look, I have gained five more talents besides them.' ²¹His lord said to him, 'Well done, good and faithful servant; you were faithful over a few things, I will make you ruler over many things. Enter into the joy of your lord.' ²²He also who had received two talents came and said, 'Lord, you delivered to me two talents; look, I have gained two more talents besides them.' ²³His lord said to him, 'Well done, good and faithful servant; you have been faithful over a few things, I will make you ruler over many things. Enter into the joy of your lord.'

²⁴"Then he who had received the one talent came and said, 'Lord, I knew you to be a hard man, reaping where you have not sown, and gathering where you have not scattered seed. ²⁵And I was afraid, and went and hid your talent in the ground. Look, there you have what is yours.'

²⁶"But his lord answered and said to him, 'You wicked and lazy servant, you knew that I reap where I have not sown, and gather where I have not scattered seed. ²⁷So you ought to have deposited my money with the bankers, and at my coming I would have received back my own with interest. ²⁸Therefore take the talent from him, and give it to him who has ten talents.

²⁹'For to everyone who has, more will be given, and he will have abundance; but from him who does not have, even what he has will be taken away. ³⁰And cast the unprofitable servant into the outer darkness. There will be weeping and gnashing of teeth.'

The Son of Man Will Judge the Nations

³¹"When the Son of Man comes in His glory, and all the holy angels with Him, then He will sit on the throne of His glory. ³²All the nations will be gathered before Him, and He will separate them one from another, as a shepherd divides his sheep from the goats. ³³And He will set the sheep on His right hand, but the goats on the left. ³⁴Then the King will say to those on His right hand, 'Come, you blessed of My Father, inherit the kingdom prepared for you from the foundation of the world: ³⁵for I was hungry and you gave Me food; I was thirsty and you gave Me drink; I was a stranger and you took Me in; ³⁶I was naked and you clothed Me; I was sick and you visited Me; I was in prison and you came to Me.'

³⁷"Then the righteous will answer Him, saying, 'Lord, when did we see You hungry and feed You, or thirsty and give You drink? ³⁸When did we see You a stranger and take You in, or naked and clothe You? ³⁹Or when did we see You sick, or in prison, and come to You?' ⁴⁰And the King will answer and say to them, 'Assuredly, I say to you, inasmuch as you did it to one of the least of these My brethren, you did it to Me.'"

DEVOTIONAL

The parable of the talents illustrates that God's people are to use the abilities and opportunities He's given them to do His work. Each man in the parable received an amount of talents that suited him best. No one was overwhelmed. All of them were expected to be faithful and fruitful.

Each of us has been blessed with certain abilities and opportunities to be used for God's kingdom work (Ephesians 4:11–16). It is our privilege, not simply our duty, to serve the Lord and multiply what He has given. In other words, we get to serve our Lord! We get to edify the body of Christ and reach the world with the gospel!

Notice that two of the three men in the parable were commended for utilizing their opportunities in faithful service, while the third wasted his. Jesus' parable warns us not to waste what we've been given and teaches us that as God's children, we should be watching, witnessing, and working until He returns. What resources has God given you to do His work? How are you using what you've been given to be faithful and fruitful?

—Dusty McLemore
Lindsay Lane Baptist Church, Athens, AL

WEEK 6, DAY 6

The Long Road to the Cross

Matthew 25:41–26:19

"Then He will also say to those on the left hand, 'Depart from Me, you cursed, into the everlasting fire prepared for the devil and his angels: 42for I was hungry and you gave Me no food; I was thirsty and you gave Me no drink; 43I was a stranger and you did not take Me in, naked and you did not clothe Me, sick and in prison and you did not visit Me.'

44"Then they also will answer Him, saying, 'Lord, when did we see You hungry or thirsty or a stranger or naked or sick or in prison, and did not minister to You?' 45Then He will answer them, saying, 'Assuredly, I say to you, inasmuch as you did not do it to one of the least of these, you did not do it to Me.' 46And these will go away into everlasting punishment, but the righteous into eternal life."

The Plot to Kill Jesus

26Now it came to pass, when Jesus had finished all these sayings, that He said to His disciples, 2"You know that after two days is the Passover, and the Son of Man will be delivered up to be crucified."

3Then the chief priests, the scribes, and the elders of the people assembled at the palace of the high priest, who was called Caiaphas, 4and plotted to take Jesus by trickery and kill Him. 5But they said, "Not during the feast, lest there be an uproar among the people."

The Anointing at Bethany

6And when Jesus was in Bethany at the house of Simon the leper, 7a woman came to Him having an alabaster flask of very costly fragrant oil, and she poured it on His head as He sat at the table. 8But when His disciples saw it, they were indignant, saying, "Why this waste? 9For this fragrant oil might have been sold for much and given to the poor."

10But when Jesus was aware of it, He said to them, "Why do you trouble the woman? For she has done a good work for Me. 11For you have the poor with you always, but Me you do not have always. 12For in pouring this fragrant oil on My body, she did it for My burial. 13Assuredly, I say to you, wherever this gospel is preached in the whole world, what this woman has done will also be told as a memorial to her."

Judas Agrees to Betray Jesus

14Then one of the twelve, called Judas Iscariot, went to the chief priests 15and said, "What are you willing to give me if I deliver Him to you?" And they counted out to him thirty pieces of silver. 16So from that time he sought opportunity to betray Him.

Jesus Celebrates Passover with His Disciples

17Now on the first day of the Feast of Unleavened Bread the disciples came to Jesus, saying to Him, "Where do You want us to prepare for You to eat the Passover?"

18And He said, "Go into the city to a certain man, and say to him, 'The Teacher says, "My time is at hand; I will keep the Passover at your house with My disciples."'"

19So the disciples did as Jesus had directed them; and they prepared the Passover.

DEVOTIONAL

In Matthew 26, Jesus' last days on earth were moving toward a climax. The King was preparing to suffer and die. He explicitly told the disciples He would soon be handed over to be crucified. A beautiful scene unfolded in Simon's house when a woman (whom we know from John 12:3 was Mary, Lazarus' sister) poured expensive perfume on Jesus' head to prepare Him for burial. Meanwhile, the religious leaders plotted to kill Jesus, and Judas agreed to betray Jesus by helping them. Jesus was coming to the end of the long road to the cross.

That long road began when He gave up heavenly glory. He, "being in the form of God . . . made Himself of no reputation, taking the form of a bondservant" (Philippians 2:6–7). It continued through decades of obedience—resisting temptation and serving others—and the inescapable highs and lows of the human experience—rejoicing and grieving, depending on the day.

Jesus must have experienced a wide range of human emotions during His last days on earth . . . love, hatred, betrayal, rejection. But He remained obedient and kept moving forward in the Father's plan of redemption. "He humbled Himself and became obedient to the point of death, even the death of the cross" (Philippians 2:8). May we also be so committed to obedience in the midst of our emotions and daily praise Jesus Christ for triumphantly completing the long road to the cross!

—Dusty McLemore
Lindsay Lane Baptist Church, Athens, AL

WEEK 6, DAY 7

In Matthew 23, Jesus rebuked the scribes and Pharisees. How could the religious leaders of Jesus' day be so blind to recognizing and accepting Jesus as their Messiah?

_____

_____

_____

_____

_____

_____

_____

_____

_____

_____

_____

In Matthew 24–25, Jesus described the signs of His Second Coming. Do you see any of these signs or other prophecies from Scripture being fulfilled in our world today? Do you believe we're living in the last days? If so, why?

_____

_____

_____

_____

_____

_____

_____

_____

_____

WEEK 7, DAY 1

Staying Committed to God

Matthew 26:20–46

When evening had come, He sat down with the twelve. 21Now as they were eating, He said, "Assuredly, I say to you, one of you will betray Me."

22And they were exceedingly sorrowful, and each of them began to say to Him, "Lord, is it I?"

23He answered and said, "He who dipped his hand with Me in the dish will betray Me. 24The Son of Man indeed goes just as it is written of Him, but woe to that man by whom the Son of Man is betrayed! It would have been good for that man if he had not been born."

25Then Judas, who was betraying Him, answered and said, "Rabbi, is it I?" He said to him, "You have said it."

Jesus Institutes the Lord's Supper

26And as they were eating, Jesus took bread, blessed and broke it, and gave it to the disciples and said, "Take, eat; this is My body."

27Then He took the cup, and gave thanks, and gave it to them, saying, "Drink from it, all of you. 28For this is My blood of the new covenant, which is shed for many for the remission of sins. 29But I say to you, I will not drink of this fruit of the vine from now on until that day when I drink it new with you in My Father's kingdom."

30And when they had sung a hymn, they went out to the Mount of Olives.

Jesus Predicts Peter's Denial

31Then Jesus said to them, "All of you will be made to stumble because of Me this night, for it is written:

'I will strike the Shepherd,
And the sheep of the flock will be scattered.'

32But after I have been raised, I will go before you to Galilee."

33Peter answered and said to Him, "Even if all are made to stumble because of You, I will never be made to stumble."

34Jesus said to him, "Assuredly, I say to you that this night, before the rooster crows, you will deny Me three times."

35Peter said to Him, "Even if I have to die with You, I will not deny You!" And so said all the disciples.

The Prayer in the Garden

36Then Jesus came with them to a place called Gethsemane, and said to the disciples, "Sit here while I go and pray over there." 37And He took with Him Peter and the two sons of Zebedee, and He began to be sorrowful and deeply distressed. 38Then He said to them, "My soul is exceedingly sorrowful, even to death. Stay here and watch with Me."

39He went a little farther and fell on His face, and prayed, saying, "O My Father, if it is possible, let this cup pass from Me; nevertheless, not as I will, but as You will."

40Then He came to the disciples and found them sleeping, and said to Peter, "What! Could you not watch with Me one hour? 41Watch and pray, lest you enter into temptation. The spirit indeed is willing, but the flesh is weak."

42Again, a second time, He went away and prayed, saying, "O My Father, if this cup cannot pass away from Me unless I drink it, Your will be done." 43And He came and found them asleep again, for their eyes were heavy.

44So He left them, went away again, and prayed the third time, saying the same words. 45Then He came to His disciples and said to them, "Are you still sleeping and resting? Behold, the hour is at hand, and the Son of Man is being betrayed into the hands of sinners. 46Rise, let us be going. See, My betrayer is at hand."

DEVOTIONAL

The last thing Peter expected to do was deny our Lord. When Jesus predicted that he would, he said, "Even if I have to die with You, I will not deny you!" (Matthew 26:35). Before he knew it, he was telling people he didn't even know Jesus, and weeping bitterly over his unfaithfulness.

No one falls suddenly. It happened to Peter in stages: pride, prayerlessness, and peer pressure. Peter could have given in to his discouragement and sadness. He could have given up the faith and turned away from God in shame. Instead, he repented, and God used him mightily!

Have you experienced anything like Peter did? Remember that failure need not be final. God wants to forgive and use you again. Success is surrendering to God's will.

—Dr. Grant Ethridge
Liberty Baptist Church, Hampton, VA

WEEK 7, DAY 2

The Pain of Being Betrayed by Friends

Matthew 26:47–68

Betrayal and Arrest in Gethsemane

And while He was still speaking, behold, Judas, one of the twelve, with a great multitude with swords and clubs, came from the chief priests and elders of the people. 48Now His betrayer had given them a sign, saying, "Whomever I kiss, He is the One; seize Him." 49Immediately he went up to Jesus and said, "Greetings, Rabbi!" and kissed Him.

50But Jesus said to him, "Friend, why have you come?" Then they came and laid hands on Jesus and took Him. 51And suddenly, one of those who were with Jesus stretched out his hand and drew his sword, struck the servant of the high priest, and cut off his ear.

52But Jesus said to him, "Put your sword in its place, for all who take the sword will perish by the sword. 53Or do you think that I cannot now pray to My Father, and He will provide Me with more than twelve legions of angels? 54How then could the Scriptures be fulfilled, that it must happen thus?"

55In that hour Jesus said to the multitudes, "Have you come out, as against a robber, with swords and clubs to take Me? I sat daily with you, teaching in the temple, and you did not seize Me. 56But all this was done that the Scriptures of the prophets might be fulfilled." Then all the disciples forsook Him and fled.

Jesus Faces the Sanhedrin

57And those who had laid hold of Jesus led Him away to Caiaphas the high priest, where the scribes and the elders were assembled. 58But Peter followed Him at a distance to the high priest's courtyard. And he went in and sat with the servants to see the end.

59Now the chief priests, the elders, and all the council sought false testimony against Jesus to put Him to death, 60but found none. Even though many false witnesses came forward, they found none. But at last two false witnesses came forward 61and said, "This fellow said, 'I am able to destroy the temple of God and to build it in three days.'"

62And the high priest arose and said to Him, "Do You answer nothing? What is it these men testify against You?"

63But Jesus kept silent. And the high priest answered and said to Him, "I put You under oath by the living God: Tell us if You are the Christ, the Son of God!"

64Jesus said to him, "It is as you said. Nevertheless, I say to you, hereafter you will see the Son of Man sitting at the right hand of the Power, and coming on the clouds of heaven."

65Then the high priest tore his clothes, saying, "He has spoken blasphemy! What further need do we have of witnesses? Look, now you have heard His blasphemy! 66What do you think?"

They answered and said, "He is deserving of death."

67Then they spat in His face and beat Him; and others struck Him with the palms of their hands, 68saying, "Prophesy to us, Christ! Who is the one who struck You?"

DEVOTIONAL

The betrayal of Judas was one of Jesus' greatest hurts. Did He know it was coming? Yes. Did He stop the hurt? No. Judas was His friend. They had spent time together. People who are close enough to help us are also close enough to hurt us. All of us know what it's like to be hurt by a family member or close friend. When we're hurting, we must remember what a Friend we have in Jesus! Jesus has gone before us, and He knows how we feel when we hurt.

While relationships do involve the possibility of pain, we shouldn't keep people at arm's length. Remember, Jesus called Judas "friend." We love because God loved us first, and His love is greater than we can comprehend. Jesus leads us to love others sincerely, even when we've been betrayed. He asks us to follow Him in choosing not to repay evil for evil and in blessing those who hurt us (Romans 12:14, 17). It won't always be easy, but God will always enable you to obey. He will fill your heart with His love so it can overflow to others. Be willing to allow others to receive Jesus' love through you.

—Dr. Grant Ethridge
Liberty Baptist Church, Hampton, VA

WEEK 7, DAY 3

Repentance Is the Answer

Matthew 26:69–27:19

Peter Denies Jesus, and Weeps Bitterly

Now Peter sat outside in the courtyard. And a servant girl came to him, saying, "You also were with Jesus of Galilee."

70But he denied it before them all, saying, "I do not know what you are saying."

71And when he had gone out to the gateway, another girl saw him and said to those who were there, "This fellow also was with Jesus of Nazareth."

72But again he denied with an oath, "I do not know the Man!"

73And a little later those who stood by came up and said to Peter, "Surely you also are one of them, for your speech betrays you."

74Then he began to curse and swear, saying, "I do not know the Man!"

Immediately a rooster crowed. 75And Peter remembered the word of Jesus who had said to him, "Before the rooster crows, you will deny Me three times." So he went out and wept bitterly.

Jesus Handed Over to Pontius Pilate

27When morning came, all the chief priests and elders of the people plotted against Jesus to put Him to death. 2And when they had bound Him, they led Him away and delivered Him to Pontius Pilate the governor.

Judas Hangs Himself

3Then Judas, His betrayer, seeing that He had been condemned, was remorseful and brought back the thirty pieces of silver to the chief priests and elders, 4saying, "I have sinned by betraying innocent blood."

And they said, "What is that to us? You see to it!"

5Then he threw down the pieces of silver in the temple and departed, and went and hanged himself.

6But the chief priests took the silver pieces and said, "It is not lawful to put them into the treasury, because they are the price of blood." 7And they consulted together and bought with them the potter's field, to bury strangers in. 8Therefore that field has been called the Field of Blood to this day.

9Then was fulfilled what was spoken by Jeremiah the prophet, saying, "And they took the thirty pieces of silver, the value of Him who was priced, whom they of the children of Israel priced, 10and gave them for the potter's field, as the LORD directed me."

Jesus Faces Pilate

11Now Jesus stood before the governor. And the governor asked Him, saying, "Are You the King of the Jews?"

Jesus said to him, "It is as you say." 12And while He was being accused by the chief priests and elders, He answered nothing.

13Then Pilate said to Him, "Do You not hear how many things they testify against You?" 14But He answered him not one word, so that the governor marveled greatly.

Taking the Place of Barabbas

15Now at the feast the governor was accustomed to releasing to the multitude one prisoner whom they wished. 16And at that time they had a notorious prisoner called Barabbas. 17Therefore, when they had gathered together, Pilate said to them, "Whom do you want me to release to you? Barabbas, or Jesus who is called Christ?" 18For he knew that they had handed Him over because of envy.

19While he was sitting on the judgment seat, his wife sent to him, saying, "Have nothing to do with that just Man, for I have suffered many things today in a dream because of Him."

DEVOTIONAL

Judas was lost and filled with regret. Things had not turned out the way he had planned. He thought he could keep the money and Jesus would go free. It's so easy for us to think we can sin without facing consequences, but the truth is that sin always kills—relationships, marriages, families, businesses, nations. When Judas faced the consequences of his sin, he was so overcome with shame, he took his own life.

Are you overwhelmed by the guilt of your sin? Suicide is not the solution. Repentance is the answer. God wants you to draw near to Him so He can make you right with Him. No matter what you've done, He still loves you! Read through Psalm 51 and confess your sins. Ask Him to create in you a clean heart and set you on a new path with Him. Jesus offers you forgiveness and a fresh start today.

—Dr. Grant Ethridge
Liberty Baptist Church, Hampton, VA

WEEK 7, DAY 4

Jesus, the King of Kings

Matthew 27:20–44

But the chief priests and elders persuaded the multitudes that they should ask for Barabbas and destroy Jesus. 21The governor answered and said to them, "Which of the two do you want me to release to you?"

They said, "Barabbas!"

22Pilate said to them, "What then shall I do with Jesus who is called Christ?"

They all said to him, "Let Him be crucified!"

23Then the governor said, "Why, what evil has He done?"

But they cried out all the more, saying, "Let Him be crucified!"

24When Pilate saw that he could not prevail at all, but rather that a tumult was rising, he took water and washed his hands before the multitude, saying, "I am innocent of the blood of this just Person. You see to it."

25And all the people answered and said, "His blood be on us and on our children."

26Then he released Barabbas to them; and when he had scourged Jesus, he delivered Him to be crucified.

The Soldiers Mock Jesus

27Then the soldiers of the governor took Jesus into the Praetorium and gathered the whole garrison around Him. 28And they stripped Him and put a scarlet robe on Him. 29When they had twisted a crown of thorns, they put it on His head, and a reed in His right hand. And they bowed the knee before Him and mocked Him, saying, "Hail, King of the Jews!" 30Then they spat on Him, and took the reed and struck Him on the head. 31And when they had mocked Him, they took the robe off Him, put His own clothes on Him, and led Him away to be crucified.

The King on a Cross

32Now as they came out, they found a man of Cyrene, Simon by name. Him they compelled to bear His cross. 33And when they had come to a place called Golgotha, that is to say, Place of a Skull, 34they gave Him sour wine mingled with gall to drink. But when He had tasted it, He would not drink.

35Then they crucified Him, and divided His garments, casting lots, that it might be fulfilled which was spoken by the prophet:

"They divided My garments among them,
And for My clothing they cast lots."

36Sitting down, they kept watch over Him there. 37And they put up over His head the accusation written against Him:

THIS IS JESUS THE KING OF THE JEWS.

38Then two robbers were crucified with Him, one on the right and another on the left.

39And those who passed by blasphemed Him, wagging their heads 40and saying, "You who destroy the temple and build it in three days, save Yourself! If You are the Son of God, come down from the cross."

41Likewise the chief priests also, mocking with the scribes and elders, said, 42"He saved others; Himself He cannot save. If He is the King of Israel, let Him now come down from the cross, and we will believe Him. 43He trusted in God; let Him deliver Him now if He will have Him; for He said, 'I am the Son of God.'"

44Even the robbers who were crucified with Him reviled Him with the same thing.

DEVOTIONAL

People have to decide for themselves who Jesus is and what they'll do with Him. They cannot remain neutral. He is either a liar, a lunatic, or Lord.

Consider what the people in Matthew 27 did with Jesus. The crowd mocked Him. They thought He should prove He was the Son of God by coming down from the cross, not understanding He would prove it by coming out of the tomb. Pilate made the mistake of listening to public opinion. He wanted to wash his hands of the matter and find an easy way out. Instead of doing the right thing, he did the expedient thing. Two thieves were crucified that day; one rejected Jesus and one repented (Luke 23:42).

Everyone will either accept Jesus or reject Him, confess Him or deny Him. Those are the only two choices people have. No one can make the decision for you. Put your faith in the truth of Scripture: Jesus is the Son of God, the Redeemer of all humanity, and the King of kings! He was wounded for our transgressions. He endured the cross so we could be forgiven. Repent and confess Him as King of your life. Take up your cross and follow Him.

—Dr. Grant Ethridge
Liberty Baptist Church, Hampton, VA

WEEK 7, DAY 5

He Is Big Enough

Matthew 27:45–28:10

Jesus Dies on the Cross

Now from the sixth hour until the ninth hour there was darkness over all the land. 46And about the ninth hour Jesus cried out with a loud voice, saying, "Eli, Eli, lama sabachthani?" that is, "My God, My God, why have You forsaken Me?"

47Some of those who stood there, when they heard that, said, "This Man is calling for Elijah!" 48Immediately one of them ran and took a sponge, filled it with sour wine and put it on a reed, and offered it to Him to drink. 49The rest said, "Let Him alone; let us see if Elijah will come to save Him."

50And Jesus cried out again with a loud voice, and yielded up His spirit.

51Then, behold, the veil of the temple was torn in two from top to bottom; and the earth quaked, and the rocks were split, 52and the graves were opened; and many bodies of the saints who had fallen asleep were raised; 53and coming out of the graves after His resurrection, they went into the holy city and appeared to many.

54So when the centurion and those with him, who were guarding Jesus, saw the earthquake and the things that had happened, they feared greatly, saying, "Truly this was the Son of God!"

55And many women who followed Jesus from Galilee, ministering to Him, were there looking on from afar, 56among whom were Mary Magdalene, Mary the mother of James and Joses, and the mother of Zebedee's sons.

Jesus Buried in Joseph's Tomb

57Now when evening had come, there came a rich man from Arimathea, named Joseph, who himself had also become a disciple of Jesus. 58This man went to Pilate and asked for the body of Jesus. Then Pilate commanded the body to be given to him. 59When Joseph had taken the body, he wrapped it in a clean linen cloth, 60and laid it in his new tomb which he had hewn out of the rock; and he rolled a large stone against the door of the tomb, and departed. 61And Mary Magdalene was there, and the other Mary, sitting opposite the tomb.

Pilate Sets a Guard

62On the next day, which followed the Day of Prepa-ration, the chief priests and Pharisees gathered together to Pilate, 63saying, "Sir, we remember, while He was still alive, how that deceiver said, 'After three days I will rise.' 64Therefore command that the tomb be made secure until the third day, lest His disciples come by night and steal Him away, and say to the people, 'He has risen from the dead.' So the last deception will be worse than the first."

65Pilate said to them, "You have a guard; go your way, make it as secure as you know how." 66So they went and made the tomb secure, sealing the stone and setting the guard.

He Is Risen

28 Now after the Sabbath, as the first day of the week began to dawn, Mary Magdalene and the other Mary came to see the tomb. 2And behold, there was a great earthquake; for an angel of the Lord descended from heaven, and came and rolled back the stone from the door, and sat on it. 3His countenance was like lightning, and his clothing as white as snow. 4And the guards shook for fear of him, and became like dead men.

5But the angel answered and said to the women, "Do not be afraid, for I know that you seek Jesus who was crucified. 6He is not here; for He is risen, as He said. Come, see the place where the Lord lay. 7And go quickly and tell His disciples that He is risen from the dead, and indeed He is going before you into Galilee; there you will see Him. Behold, I have told you."

8So they went out quickly from the tomb with fear and great joy, and ran to bring His disciples word.

The Women Worship the Risen Lord

9And as they went to tell His disciples, behold, Jesus met them, saying, "Rejoice!" So they came and held Him by the feet and worshiped Him. 10Then Jesus said to them, "Do not be afraid. Go and tell My brethren to go to Galilee, and there they will see Me."

DEVOTIONAL

Jesus cried out to His Father from the cross, asking, "Why?" Have you ever asked God the same question? You can take your questions, concerns, and pain to God. He is big enough to handle anything you bring Him. God has promised to never leave us, and He wants you to "come boldly to the throne of grace" (Hebrews 4:16). Cast your cares on Him, because He cares for you (1 Peter 5:7)!

—Dr. Grant Ethridge
Liberty Baptist Church, Hampton, VA

WEEK 7, DAY 6

Tell the Good News

Matthew 28:11–Mark 1:20

The Soldiers Are Bribed

N ow while they were going, behold, some of the guard came into the city and reported to the chief priests all the things that had happened. 12When they had assembled with the elders and consulted together, they gave a large sum of money to the soldiers, 13saying, "Tell them, 'His disciples came at night and stole Him away while we slept.' 14And if this comes to the governor's ears, we will appease him and make you secure." 15So they took the money and did as they were instructed; and this saying is commonly reported among the Jews until this day.

The Great Commission

16Then the eleven disciples went away into Galilee, to the mountain which Jesus had appointed for them. 17When they saw Him, they worshiped Him; but some doubted.

18And Jesus came and spoke to them, saying, "All authority has been given to Me in heaven and on earth. 19Go therefore and make disciples of all the nations, baptizing them in the name of the Father and of the Son and of the Holy Spirit, 20teaching them to observe all things that I have commanded you; and lo, I am with you always, even to the end of the age." Amen.

John the Baptist Prepares the Way

1 The beginning of the gospel of Jesus Christ, the Son of God. 2As it is written in the Prophets:

"Behold, I send My messenger before Your face,
Who will prepare Your way before You."
3 "The voice of one crying in the wilderness:
'Prepare the way of the Lord;
Make His paths straight.'"

4John came baptizing in the wilderness and preaching a baptism of repentance for the remission of sins. 5Then all the land of Judea, and those from Jerusalem, went out to him and were all baptized by him in the Jordan River, confessing their sins.

6Now John was clothed with camel's hair and with a leather belt around his waist, and he ate locusts and wild honey. 7And he preached, saying, "There comes One after me who is mightier than I, whose sandal strap I am not worthy to stoop down and loose. 8I indeed baptized you with water, but He will baptize you with the Holy Spirit."

John Baptizes Jesus

9It came to pass in those days that Jesus came from Nazareth of Galilee, and was baptized by John in the Jordan. 10And immediately, coming up from the water, He saw the heavens parting and the Spirit descending upon Him like a dove. 11Then a voice came from heaven, "You are My beloved Son, in whom I am well pleased."

Satan Tempts Jesus

12Immediately the Spirit drove Him into the wilderness. 13And He was there in the wilderness forty days, tempted by Satan, and was with the wild beasts; and the angels ministered to Him.

Jesus Begins His Galilean Ministry

14Now after John was put in prison, Jesus came to Galilee, preaching the gospel of the kingdom of God, 15and saying, "The time is fulfilled, and the kingdom of God is at hand. Repent, and believe in the gospel."

Four Fishermen Called as Disciples

16And as He walked by the Sea of Galilee, He saw Simon and Andrew his brother casting a net into the sea; for they were fishermen. 17Then Jesus said to them, "Follow Me, and I will make you become fishers of men." 18They immediately left their nets and followed Him.

19When He had gone a little farther from there, He saw James the son of Zebedee, and John his brother, who also were in the boat mending their nets. 20And immediately He called them, and they left their father Zebedee in the boat with the hired servants, and went after Him.

DEVOTIONAL

J esus commissioned His followers to make disciples of all nations. Being mission-minded starts at home. The light that shines the farthest shines the brightest at home. How can you help grow your local church or encourage someone to come closer to Christ?

Anything God gives you the authority to do, He will give you the ability to do. He goes before you, behind you, and beside you, so what are you waiting for? Jesus is alive. The Bible is true. Heaven and hell are real. People need what you can give . . . so give it!

*—Dr. Grant Ethridge
Liberty Baptist Church, Hampton, VA*

WEEK 7, DAY 7

The same Jesus who called the disciples to be fishers of men has called us. What are you willing to forsake today to follow the risen Christ?

_____

_____

_____

_____

_____

_____

_____

_____

_____

_____

_____

_____

In what areas of your life do you need to pray as Jesus did in the Garden of Gethsemane: "Not as I will, but as You will" (Matthew 26:39)?

_____

_____

_____

_____

_____

_____

_____

_____

_____

_____

_____

WEEK 8, DAY I

The God Who Can Heal Us

Mark 1:21–45

Jesus Casts Out an Unclean Spirit

Then they went into Capernaum, and immediately on the Sabbath He entered the synagogue and taught. 22And they were astonished at His teaching, for He taught them as one having authority, and not as the scribes.

23Now there was a man in their synagogue with an unclean spirit. And he cried out, 24saying, "Let us alone! What have we to do with You, Jesus of Nazareth? Did You come to destroy us? I know who You are—the Holy One of God!"

25But Jesus rebuked him, saying, "Be quiet, and come out of him!" 26And when the unclean spirit had convulsed him and cried out with a loud voice, he came out of him. 27Then they were all amazed, so that they questioned among themselves, saying, "What is this? What new doctrine is this? For with authority He commands even the unclean spirits, and they obey Him." 28And immediately His fame spread throughout all the region around Galilee.

Peter's Mother-in-Law Healed

29Now as soon as they had come out of the synagogue, they entered the house of Simon and Andrew, with James and John. 30But Simon's wife's mother lay sick with a fever, and they told Him about her at once. 31So He came and took her by the hand and lifted her up, and immediately the fever left her. And she served them.

Many Healed After Sabbath Sunset

32At evening, when the sun had set, they brought to Him all who were sick and those who were demon-possessed. 33And the whole city was gathered together at the door. 34Then He healed many who were sick with various diseases, and cast out many demons; and He did not allow the demons to speak, because they knew Him.

Preaching in Galilee

35Now in the morning, having risen a long while before daylight, He went out and departed to a solitary place; and there He prayed. 36And Simon and those who were with Him searched for Him. 37When they found Him, they said to Him, "Everyone is looking for You."

38But He said to them, "Let us go into the next towns, that I may preach there also, because for this purpose I have come forth."

39And He was preaching in their synagogues throughout all Galilee, and casting out demons.

Jesus Cleanses a Leper

40Now a leper came to Him, imploring Him, kneeling down to Him and saying to Him, "If You are willing, You can make me clean."

41Then Jesus, moved with compassion, stretched out His hand and touched him, and said to him, "I am willing; be cleansed." 42As soon as He had spoken, immediately the leprosy left him, and he was cleansed. 43And He strictly warned him and sent him away at once, 44and said to him, "See that you say nothing to anyone; but go your way, show yourself to the priest, and offer for your cleansing those things which Moses commanded, as a testimony to them."

45However, he went out and began to proclaim it freely, and to spread the matter, so that Jesus could no longer openly enter the city, but was outside in deserted places; and they came to Him from every direction.

DEVOTIONAL

Years ago Time *magazine published the results of a survey that asked over a thousand adults about their beliefs regarding prayer and illness. The survey found that 82 percent of participants believe in the healing power of personal prayer, and 73 percent believe praying for someone else can help cure that person's illness. When asked about God's role in healing, 77 percent said they believe God sometimes intervenes to cure people who have a serious illness.[2]*

How would you answer? Scripture tells us that Jesus healed many sick people (Matthew 4:23) and empowered His disciples to do the same (10:8). It also says God works powerfully through our prayers (James 5:16). Bring your needs to God in prayer with confidence, but also express willingness to submit to His perfect will. Norwegian theologian Ole Hallesby once prayed: "Lord, if it will be to Your glory, heal suddenly; if it will glorify You more, heal gradually; if it will glorify You even more, may Your servant remain sick awhile; and if it will glorify Your name still more, take him to Yourself in Heaven!"[3] Amen!

—Dr. James Merritt
Cross Pointe Church, Duluth, GA

WEEK 8, DAY 2

The Joy of Forgiveness

Mark 2:1–22

Jesus Forgives and Heals a Paralytic

2 And again He entered Capernaum after some days, and it was heard that He was in the house. ²Immediately many gathered together, so that there was no longer room to receive them, not even near the door. And He preached the word to them. ³Then they came to Him, bringing a paralytic who was carried by four men. ⁴And when they could not come near Him because of the crowd, they uncovered the roof where He was. So when they had broken through, they let down the bed on which the paralytic was lying.

⁵When Jesus saw their faith, He said to the paralytic, "Son, your sins are forgiven you."

⁶And some of the scribes were sitting there and reasoning in their hearts, ⁷"Why does this Man speak blasphemies like this? Who can forgive sins but God alone?"

⁸But immediately, when Jesus perceived in His spirit that they reasoned thus within themselves, He said to them, "Why do you reason about these things in your hearts? ⁹Which is easier, to say to the paralytic, 'Your sins are forgiven you,' or to say, 'Arise, take up your bed and walk'? ¹⁰But that you may know that the Son of Man has power on earth to forgive sins"—He said to the paralytic, ¹¹"I say to you, arise, take up your bed, and go to your house." ¹²Immediately he arose took up the bed, and went out in the presence of them all, so that all were amazed and glorified God, saying, "We never saw anything like this!"

Matthew the Tax Collector

¹³Then He went out again by the sea; and all the multitude came to Him, and He taught them. ¹⁴As He passed by, He saw Levi the son of Alphaeus sitting at the tax office. And He said to him, "Follow Me." So he arose and followed Him.

¹⁵Now it happened, as He was dining in Levi's house, that many tax collectors and sinners also sat together with Jesus and His disciples; for there were many, and they followed Him. ¹⁶And when the scribes and Pharisees saw Him eating with the tax collectors and sinners, they said to His disciples, "How is it that He eats and drinks with tax collectors and sinners?"

¹⁷When Jesus heard it, He said to them, "Those who are well have no need of a physician, but those who are sick. I did not come to call the righteous, but sinners, to repentance."

Jesus Is Questioned About Fasting

¹⁸The disciples of John and of the Pharisees were fasting. Then they came and said to Him, "Why do the disciples of John and of the Pharisees fast, but Your disciples do not fast?"

¹⁹And Jesus said to them, "Can the friends of the bridegroom fast while the bridegroom is with them? As long as they have the bridegroom with them they cannot fast. ²⁰But the days will come when the bridegroom will be taken away from them, and then they will fast in those days. ²¹No one sews a piece of unshrunk cloth on an old garment; or else the new piece pulls away from the old, and the tear is made worse. ²²And no one puts new wine into old wineskins; or else the new wine bursts the wineskins, the wine is spilled, and the wineskins are ruined. But new wine must be put into new wineskins."

DEVOTIONAL

*W*hat are the things in life that get you really excited? Maybe it's breaking ninety on the golf course or going on a romantic getaway with your spouse. Maybe it's eating warm, homemade chocolate chip cookies or spending time with your grandchildren. Maybe it's knowing that God loves you unconditionally and that you are going to heaven.

What gets God excited? Mark 2:1–12 tells us of three things. First, He loves to see our faith. Jesus was excited to see the paralytic's friends' belief that He could heal. He was so moved by their faith that He healed their friend—both spiritually and physically. Second, God gets excited about sharing His forgiveness. Jesus' favorite thing to say to anyone is, "Your sins are forgiven!" Third, He loves to show His faithfulness. God is always able to heal, to meet our needs, and to reach us with His faithfulness. May we never forget that it cost Him His Son for Him to be faithful to His character and forgive us of our sins.

If you are forgiven and know it, get excited!

—Dr. James Merritt
Cross Pointe Church, Duluth, GA

WEEK 8, DAY 3

Jesus Teaches About the Rules of the Sabbath

Mark 2:23–3:27

Jesus Is Lord of the Sabbath

Now it happened that He went through the grainfields on the Sabbath; and as they went His disciples began to pluck the heads of grain. 24And the Pharisees said to Him, "Look, why do they do what is not lawful on the Sabbath?"

25But He said to them, "Have you never read what David did when he was in need and hungry, he and those with him: 26how he went into the house of God in the days of Abiathar the high priest, and ate the showbread, which is not lawful to eat except for the priests, and also gave some to those who were with him?"

27And He said to them, "The Sabbath was made for man, and not man for the Sabbath. 28Therefore the Son of Man is also Lord of the Sabbath."

Healing on the Sabbath

3 And He entered the synagogue again, and a man was there who had a withered hand. 2So they watched Him closely, whether He would heal him on the Sabbath, so that they might accuse Him. 3And He said to the man who had the withered hand, "Step forward." 4Then He said to them, "Is it lawful on the Sabbath to do good or to do evil, to save life or to kill?" But they kept silent. 5And when He had looked around at them with anger, being grieved by the hardness of their hearts, He said to the man, "Stretch out your hand." And he stretched it out, and his hand was restored as whole as the other. 6Then the Pharisees went out and immediately plotted with the Herodians against Him, how they might destroy Him.

A Great Multitude Follows Jesus

7But Jesus withdrew with His disciples to the sea. And a great multitude from Galilee followed Him, and from Judea 8and Jerusalem and Idumea and beyond the Jordan; and those from Tyre and Sidon, a great multitude, when they heard how many things He was doing, came to Him. 9So He told His disciples that a small boat should be kept ready for Him because of the multitude, lest they should crush Him. 10For He healed many, so that as many as had afflictions pressed about Him to touch Him. 11And the unclean spirits, whenever they saw Him, fell down before Him and cried out, saying, "You are the Son of God." 12But He sternly warned them that they should not make Him known.

The Twelve Apostles

13And He went up on the mountain and called to Him those He Himself wanted. And they came to Him. 14Then He appointed twelve, that they might be with Him and that He might send them out to preach, 15and to have power to heal sicknesses and to cast out demons: 16Simon, to whom He gave the name Peter; 17James the son of Zebedee and John the brother of James, to whom He gave the name Boanerges, that is, "Sons of Thunder"; 18Andrew, Philip, Bartholomew, Matthew, Thomas, James the son of Alphaeus, Thaddaeus, Simon the Cananite; 19and Judas Iscariot, who also betrayed Him. And they went into a house.

A House Divided Cannot Stand

20Then the multitude came together again, so that they could not so much as eat bread. 21But when His own people heard about this, they went out to lay hold of Him, for they said, "He is out of His mind."

22And the scribes who came down from Jerusalem said, "He has Beelzebub," and, "By the ruler of the demons He casts out demons."

23So He called them to Himself and said to them in parables: "How can Satan cast out Satan? 24If a kingdom is divided against itself, that kingdom cannot stand. 25And if a house is divided against itself, that house cannot stand. 26And if Satan has risen up against himself, and is divided, he cannot stand, but has an end. 27No one can enter a strong man's house and plunder his goods, unless he first binds the strong man. And then he will plunder his house."

DEVOTIONAL

In God's created world, even dirt needs to rest (Exodus 23:10–11). It's in keeping with His command to keep the Sabbath and devote one day out of seven to rest.

But some things never get to rest—and shouldn't. Obeying God never takes a break. Loving others never takes a vacation. Ministering to others' needs never takes a hiatus. The Lord of the Sabbath plucked grain and healed a man on the Sabbath, and we are to love our neighbor as ourselves every day of the week! The best way to honor the Sabbath is to follow Jesus' lead.

—Dr. James Merritt
Cross Pointe Church, Duluth, GA

WEEK 8, DAY 4

*Those Who Obey God
Belong to God*

Mark 3:28–4:20

The Unpardonable Sin

"Assuredly, I say to you, all sins will be forgiven the sons of men, and whatever blasphemies they may utter; 29but he who blasphemes against the Holy Spirit never has forgiveness, but is subject to eternal condemnation"— 30because they said, "He has an unclean spirit."

Jesus' Mother and Brothers Send for Him

31Then His brothers and His mother came, and standing outside they sent to Him, calling Him. 32And a multitude was sitting around Him; and they said to Him, "Look, Your mother and Your brothers are outside seeking You." 33But He answered them, saying, "Who is My mother, or My brothers?" 34And He looked around in a circle at those who sat about Him, and said, "Here are My mother and My brothers! 35For whoever does the will of God is My brother and My sister and mother."

The Parable of the Sower

4And again He began to teach by the sea. And a great multitude was gathered to Him, so that He got into a boat and sat in it on the sea; and the whole multitude was on the land facing the sea. 2Then He taught them many things by parables, and said to them in His teaching:

3"Listen! Behold, a sower went out to sow. 4And it happened, as he sowed, that some seed fell by the wayside; and the birds of the air came and devoured it. 5Some fell on stony ground, where it did not have much earth; and immediately it sprang up because it had no depth of earth. 6But when the sun was up it was scorched, and because it had no root it withered away. 7And some seed fell among thorns; and the thorns grew up and choked it, and it yielded no crop. 8But other seed fell on good ground and yielded a crop that sprang up, increased and produced: some thirtyfold, some sixty, and some a hundred."

9And He said to them, "He who has ears to hear, let him hear!"

The Purpose of Parables

10But when He was alone, those around Him with the twelve asked Him about the parable. 11And He said to them, "To you it has been given to know the mystery of the kingdom of God; but to those who are outside, all things come in parables, 12so that

'Seeing they may see and not perceive,
And hearing they may hear and not understand;
Lest they should turn,
And their sins be forgiven them.'"

The Parable of the Sower Explained

13And He said to them, "Do you not understand this parable? How then will you understand all the parables? 14The sower sows the word. 15And these are the ones by the wayside where the word is sown. When they hear, Satan comes immediately and takes away the word that was sown in their hearts. 16These likewise are the ones sown on stony ground who, when they hear the word, immediately receive it with gladness; 17and they have no root in themselves, and so endure only for a time. Afterward, when tribulation or persecution arises for the word's sake, immediately they stumble. 18Now these are the ones sown among thorns; they are the ones who hear the word, 19and the cares of this world, the deceitfulness of riches, and the desires for other things entering in choke the word, and it becomes unfruitful. 20But these are the ones sown on good ground, those who hear the word, accept it, and bear fruit: some thirtyfold, some sixty, and some a hundred."

DEVOTIONAL

God is more anxious for you to know His will than you are to find it. In fact, it's not really your responsibility to find the will of God. It is your responsibility to **do** the will of God. If God wants you to know His will, it is His responsibility to reveal it. It is your responsibility to obey it. Scripture is clear in saying that obedience is a birthmark of the believer.

A store that was having a going-out-of-business sale hung a huge sign that said, "No refunds. No returns. All transactions final." That describes the kind of no-excuses, sold-out obedience God wants from us, the kind Jesus described in Mark 3:35. Trust and obey God as He reveals His will to you—it's the only way God's children truly live!

—Dr. James Merritt
Cross Pointe Church, Duluth, GA

WEEK 8, DAY 5

*Jesus Demonstrates His
Power over All*

Mark 4:21–5:10

Light Under a Basket

Also He said to them, "Is a lamp brought to be put under a basket or under a bed? Is it not to be set on a lampstand? 22For there is nothing hidden which will not be revealed, nor has anything been kept secret but that it should come to light. 23If anyone has ears to hear, let him hear."

24Then He said to them, "Take heed what you hear. With the same measure you use, it will be measured to you; and to you who hear, more will be given. 25For whoever has, to him more will be given; but whoever does not have, even what he has will be taken away from him."

The Parable of the Growing Seed

26And He said, "The kingdom of God is as if a man should scatter seed on the ground, 27and should sleep by night and rise by day, and the seed should sprout and grow, he himself does not know how. 28For the earth yields crops by itself: first the blade, then the head, after that the full grain in the head. 29But when the grain ripens, immediately he puts in the sickle, because the harvest has come."

The Parable of the Mustard Seed

30Then He said, "To what shall we liken the kingdom of God? Or with what parable shall we picture it? 31It is like a mustard seed which, when it is sown on the ground, is smaller than all the seeds on earth; 32but when it is sown, it grows up and becomes greater than all herbs, and shoots out large branches, so that the birds of the air may nest under its shade."

Jesus' Use of Parables

33And with many such parables He spoke the word to them as they were able to hear it. 34But without a parable He did not speak to them. And when they were alone, He explained all things to His disciples.

Wind and Wave Obey Jesus

35On the same day, when evening had come, He said to them, "Let us cross over to the other side." 36Now when they had left the multitude, they took Him along in the boat as He was. And other little boats were also with Him. 37And a great windstorm arose, and the waves beat into the boat, so that it was already filling. 38But He was in the stern, asleep on a pillow. And they awoke Him and said to Him, "Teacher, do You not care that we are perishing?"

39Then He arose and rebuked the wind, and said to the sea, "Peace, be still!" And the wind ceased and there was a great calm. 40But He said to them, "Why are you so fearful? How is it that you have no faith?" 41And they feared exceedingly, and said to one another, "Who can this be, that even the wind and the sea obey Him!"

A Demon-Possessed Man Healed

5Then they came to the other side of the sea, to the country of the Gadarenes. 2And when He had come out of the boat, immediately there met Him out of the tombs a man with an unclean spirit, 3who had his dwelling among the tombs; and no one could bind him, not even with chains, 4because he had often been bound with shackles and chains. And the chains had been pulled apart by him, and the shackles broken in pieces; neither could anyone tame him. 5And always, night and day, he was in the mountains and in the tombs, crying out and cutting himself with stones.

6When he saw Jesus from afar, he ran and worshiped Him. 7And he cried out with a loud voice and said, "What have I to do with You, Jesus, Son of the Most High God? I implore You by God that You do not torment me." 8For He said to him, "Come out of the man, unclean spirit!" 9Then He asked him, "What is your name?"

And he answered, saying, "My name is Legion; for we are many." 10Also he begged Him earnestly that He would not send them out of the country.

DEVOTIONAL

We all face storms of some kind in life—storms of illness, unemployment, unfaithfulness, betrayal. They are real, and they play no favorites. In every storm there's a lesson we need to learn about fear and faith, and it is rooted in Jesus' question to the disciples: "Why are you so fearful? How is it that you have no faith?" (Mark 4:40). They had a choice. They didn't have to be controlled by fear, and in fact, they had every reason not to be. Every time you face a storm in your life, you can face it with fear or you can face it with faith. The One who stills the storms says, "Trust Me!"

—Dr. James Merritt
Cross Pointe Church, Duluth, GA

WEEK 8, DAY 6

The Power of Faith

Mark 5:11–36

Now a large herd of swine was feeding there near the mountains. 12So all the demons begged Him, saying, "Send us to the swine, that we may enter them." 13And at once Jesus gave them permission. Then the unclean spirits went out and entered the swine (there were about two thousand); and the herd ran violently down the steep place into the sea, and drowned in the sea.

14So those who fed the swine fled, and they told it in the city and in the country. And they went out to see what it was that had happened. 15Then they came to Jesus, and saw the one who had been demon-possessed and had the legion, sitting and clothed and in his right mind. And they were afraid. 16And those who saw it told them how it happened to him who had been demon-possessed, and about the swine. 17Then they began to plead with Him to depart from their region.

18And when He got into the boat, he who had been demon-possessed begged Him that he might be with Him. 19However, Jesus did not permit him, but said to him, "Go home to your friends, and tell them what great things the Lord has done for you, and how He has had compassion on you." 20And he departed and began to proclaim in Decapolis all that Jesus had done for him; and all marveled.

A Girl Restored to Life and a Woman Healed

21Now when Jesus had crossed over again by boat to the other side, a great multitude gathered to Him; and He was by the sea. 22And behold, one of the rulers of the synagogue came, Jairus by name. And when he saw Him, he fell at His feet 23and begged Him earnestly, saying, "My little daughter lies at the point of death. Come and lay Your hands on her, that she may be healed, and she will live." 24So Jesus went with him, and a great multitude followed Him and thronged Him.

25Now a certain woman had a flow of blood for twelve years, 26and had suffered many things from many physicians. She had spent all that she had and was no better, but rather grew worse. 27When she heard about Jesus, she came behind Him in the crowd and touched His garment. 28For she said, "If only I may touch His clothes, I shall be made well."

29Immediately the fountain of her blood was dried up, and she felt in her body that she was healed of the affliction. 30And Jesus, immediately knowing in Himself that power had gone out of Him, turned around in the crowd and said, "Who touched My clothes?"

31But His disciples said to Him, "You see the multitude thronging You, and You say, 'Who touched Me?'"

32And He looked around to see her who had done this thing. 33But the woman, fearing and trembling, knowing what had happened to her, came and fell down before Him and told Him the whole truth. 34And He said to her, "Daughter, your faith has made you well. Go in peace, and be healed of your affliction."

35While He was still speaking, some came from the ruler of the synagogue's house who said, "Your daughter is dead. Why trouble the Teacher any further?"

36As soon as Jesus heard the word that was spoken, He said to the ruler of the synagogue, "Do not be afraid; only believe."

DEVOTIONAL

Mark 5 gives an account of the only incident in Scripture when Jesus directly addressed a woman as "daughter" (v. 34). Can you imagine how that made her feel? As someone who was considered unclean by her community because of her health condition, she probably couldn't remember the last time anyone had a kind word for her or used a term of affection for her. More than likely, she couldn't remember the last time anyone looked at her with anything but disgust. She was an outcast—poor, lonely, and desperate.

Yet, with a look of love that only He could give, Jesus tenderly called her "daughter." Why did He refer to her that way? Because our kinship with Christ is not established by blood but by faith. This woman had touched the hem of Jesus' garment thinking, "If only I may touch His garment, I shall be made well" (verses 27–28). She believed Jesus could heal her, and He made mention of her great faith, saying it had made her well.

Every time we place our faith in the risen Christ, we activate God's power, we elevate God's purpose, and we celebrate God's presence. In every difficulty, God is always asking this one question: "Do you trust Me or not?" May your answer always be yes!

—Dr. James Merritt
Cross Pointe Church, Duluth, GA

WEEK 8, DAY 7

How do you need Christ—the One who heals the sick, calms the storms, and rules the Sabbath—to intervene in your life today?

_____

_____

_____

_____

_____

_____

_____

_____

_____

_____

_____

_____

In what areas of your life do you need to start fully obeying God, which will bring the most honor and glory to Him?

_____

_____

_____

_____

_____

_____

_____

_____

_____

_____

_____

WEEK 9, DAY I

Believing Is Seeing

Mark 5:37–6:20

And He permitted no one to follow Him except Peter, James, and John the brother of James. 38Then He came to the house of the ruler of the synagogue, and saw a tumult and those who wept and wailed loudly. 39When He came in, He said to them, "Why make this commotion and weep? The child is not dead, but sleeping."

40And they ridiculed Him. But when He had put them all outside, He took the father and the mother of the child, and those who were with Him, and entered where the child was lying. 41Then He took the child by the hand, and said to her, "Talitha, cumi," which is translated, "Little girl, I say to you, arise." 42Immediately the girl arose and walked, for she was twelve years of age. And they were overcome with great amazement. 43But He commanded them strictly that no one should know it, and said that something should be given her to eat.

Jesus Rejected at Nazareth

6Then He went out from there and came to His own country, and His disciples followed Him. 2And when the Sabbath had come, He began to teach in the synagogue. And many hearing Him were astonished, saying, "Where did this Man get these things? And what wisdom is this which is given to Him, that such mighty works are performed by His hands! 3Is this not the carpenter, the Son of Mary, and brother of James, Joses, Judas, and Simon? And are not His sisters here with us?" So they were offended at Him.

4But Jesus said to them, "A prophet is not without honor except in his own country, among his own relatives, and in his own house." 5Now He could do no mighty work there, except that He laid His hands on a few sick people and healed them. 6And He marveled because of their unbelief. Then He went about the villages in a circuit, teaching.

Sending Out the Twelve

7And He called the twelve to Himself, and began to send them out two by two, and gave them power over unclean spirits. 8He commanded them to take nothing for the journey except a staff—no bag, no bread, no copper in their money belts— 9but to wear sandals, and not to put on two tunics. 10Also He said to them, "In whatever place you enter a house, stay there till you depart from that place. 11And whoever will not receive you nor hear you, when you depart from there, shake off the dust under your feet as a testimony against them. Assuredly, I say to you, it will be more tolerable for Sodom and Gomorrah in the day of judgment than for that city!"

12So they went out and preached that people should repent. 13And they cast out many demons, and anointed with oil many who were sick, and healed them.

John the Baptist Beheaded

14Now King Herod heard of Him, for His name had become well known. And he said, "John the Baptist is risen from the dead, and therefore these powers are at work in him."

15Others said, "It is Elijah."

And others said, "It is the Prophet, or like one of the prophets."

16But when Herod heard, he said, "This is John, whom I beheaded; he has been raised from the dead!" 17For Herod himself had sent and laid hold of John, and bound him in prison for the sake of Herodias, his brother Philip's wife; for he had married her. 18Because John had said to Herod, "It is not lawful for you to have your brother's wife."

19Therefore Herodias held it against him and wanted to kill him, but she could not; 20for Herod feared John, knowing that he was a just and holy man, and he protected him. And when he heard him, he did many things, and heard him gladly.

DEVOTIONAL

Do you believe the Lord can do anything? That is exactly what He says in His Word: "With God all things are possible" (Mark 10:27). Intellectual atheists say there is no God. Practical atheists say God is real, but they live as if God is not really involved in their lives. They believe in Him, but you would never know it by the way they live.

There is a stark contrast seen in today's reading: a dad and mom who believed Jesus in a desperate situation (Mark 5:38–43), and a cynical crowd of unbelievers who had no clue who was standing before them (6:1–6). The unbelieving crowd in Nazareth proves that the tragic consequence of unbelief is seeing nothing. Today, choose to believe God and watch Him work. It is true that believing is seeing!

—Jeff Crook
Blackshear Place Baptist Church, Flowery Branch, GA

WEEK 9, DAY 2

Trust God for His Provision

Mark 6:21–44

Then an opportune day came when Herod on his birthday gave a feast for his nobles, the high officers, and the chief men of Galilee. 22And when Herodias' daughter herself came in and danced, and pleased Herod and those who sat with him, the king said to the girl, "Ask me whatever you want, and I will give it to you." 23He also swore to her, "Whatever you ask me, I will give you, up to half my kingdom."

24So she went out and said to her mother, "What shall I ask?"

And she said, "The head of John the Baptist!"

25Immediately she came in with haste to the king and asked, saying, "I want you to give me at once the head of John the Baptist on a platter."

26And the king was exceedingly sorry; yet, because of the oaths and because of those who sat with him, he did not want to refuse her. 27Immediately the king sent an executioner and commanded his head to be brought. And he went and beheaded him in prison, 28brought his head on a platter, and gave it to the girl; and the girl gave it to her mother. 29When his disciples heard of it, they came and took away his corpse and laid it in a tomb.

Feeding the Five Thousand

30Then the apostles gathered to Jesus and told Him all things, both what they had done and what they had taught. 31And He said to them, "Come aside by yourselves to a deserted place and rest a while." For there were many coming and going, and they did not even have time to eat. 32So they departed to a deserted place in the boat by themselves.

33But the multitudes saw them departing, and many knew Him and ran there on foot from all the cities. They arrived before them and came together to Him. 34And Jesus, when He came out, saw a great multitude and was moved with compassion for them, because they were like sheep not having a shepherd. So He began to teach them many things. 35When the day was now far spent, His disciples came to Him and said, "This is a deserted place, and already the hour is late. 36Send them away, that they may go into the surrounding country and villages and buy themselves bread; for they have nothing to eat."

37But He answered and said to them, "You give them something to eat."

And they said to Him, "Shall we go and buy two hundred denarii worth of bread and give them something to eat?"

38But He said to them, "How many loaves do you have? Go and see."

And when they found out they said, "Five, and two fish."

39Then He commanded them to make them all sit down in groups on the green grass. 40So they sat down in ranks, in hundreds and in fifties. 41And when He had taken the five loaves and the two fish, He looked up to heaven, blessed and broke the loaves, and gave them to His disciples to set before them; and the two fish He divided among them all. 42So they all ate and were filled. 43And they took up twelve baskets full of fragments and of the fish. 44Now those who had eaten the loaves were about five thousand men.

DEVOTIONAL

It was the miracle everyone talked about. Jesus affected more people at this event than in any of His other miracles. It's called the feeding of five thousand, but some suggest the crowd was actually close to twenty thousand.

What is everyone talking about today? Bad economy. Debt crisis. Home foreclosures. Gas prices. Problems are on people's minds, and they're talking about them endlessly. Our problems should turn us to Jesus.

God uses problems to bring us face-to-face with our deficiencies so that we might view His sufficiency as our only alternative. Every problem we have is an opportunity for us to believe in His power and goodness and to watch Him work in a miraculous way. What we need to recognize is something Vance Havner expressed well: "We are shipwrecked on God and stranded on omnipotence!"4

The day Jesus fed the multitudes, the need was great—thousands had nothing to eat. When Jesus took the bread and fish in His hands, "they all ate and were filled" (Mark 6:42). What do you need to put in His hands? There's no need too big and no concern too small. You can trust your loving Savior to provide for any need.

—Jeff Crook
Blackshear Place Baptist Church, Flowery Branch, GA

WEEK 9, DAY 3

Faith-Building Tests

Mark 6:45–7:13

Jesus Walks on the Sea

Immediately He made His disciples get into the boat and go before Him to the other side, to Bethsaida, while He sent the multitude away. ⁴⁶And when He had sent them away, He departed to the mountain to pray. ⁴⁷Now when evening came, the boat was in the middle of the sea; and He was alone on the land. ⁴⁸Then He saw them straining at rowing, for the wind was against them. Now about the fourth watch of the night He came to them, walking on the sea, and would have passed them by. ⁴⁹And when they saw Him walking on the sea, they supposed it was a ghost, and cried out; ⁵⁰for they all saw Him and were troubled. But immediately He talked with them and said to them, "Be of good cheer! It is I; do not be afraid." ⁵¹Then He went up into the boat to them, and the wind ceased. And they were greatly amazed in themselves beyond measure, and marveled. ⁵²For they had not understood about the loaves, because their heart was hardened.

Many Touch Him and Are Made Well

⁵³When they had crossed over, they came to the land of Gennesaret and anchored there. ⁵⁴And when they came out of the boat, immediately the people recognized Him, ⁵⁵ran through that whole surrounding region, and began to carry about on beds those who were sick to wherever they heard He was. ⁵⁶Wherever He entered, into villages, cities, or the country, they laid the sick in the marketplaces, and begged Him that they might just touch the hem of His garment. And as many as touched Him were made well.

Defilement Comes from Within

7 Then the Pharisees and some of the scribes came together to Him, having come from Jerusalem. ²Now when they saw some of His disciples eat bread with defiled, that is, with unwashed hands, they found fault. ³For the Pharisees and all the Jews do not eat unless they wash their hands in a special way, holding the tradition of the elders. ⁴When they come from the marketplace, they do not eat unless they wash. And there are many other things which they have received and hold, like the washing of cups, pitchers, copper vessels, and couches. ⁵Then the Pharisees and scribes asked Him, "Why do Your disciples not walk according to the tradition of the elders, but eat bread with unwashed hands?"

⁶He answered and said to them, "Well did Isaiah prophesy of you hypocrites, as it is written:

'This people honors Me with their lips,
But their heart is far from Me.
7   And in vain they worship Me,
Teaching as doctrines the commandments
of men.'

⁸For laying aside the commandment of God, you hold the tradition of men—the washing of pitchers and cups, and many other such things you do."

⁹He said to them, "All too well you reject the commandment of God, that you may keep your tradition. ¹⁰For Moses said, 'Honor your father and your mother'; and, 'He who curses father or mother, let him be put to death.' ¹¹But you say, 'If a man says to his father or mother, "Whatever profit you might have received from me is Corban"—' (that is, a gift to God), ¹²then you no longer let him do anything for his father or his mother, ¹³making the word of God of no effect through your tradition which you have handed down. And many such things you do."

DEVOTIONAL

Does anyone enjoy exams? In school, exams are necessary to reveal what we know and what we still need to learn. As followers of Christ, many tests are given to us for the same reason.

Jesus often gave His disciples "exams" to see whether they understood what He was teaching them. The disciples were slow learners. The Lord knew how short their memories were, so He arranged a test: He sent them into a storm. They didn't do too well.

The Lord is so merciful that even in our failures, He is still faithful. He was faithful to pray for the disciples while they were in the boat and He was on land. They were never really alone, and neither are we. He was faithful to come to them, right where they were. He walked on top of the troubled waters. What was over their heads was under His feet! He was faithful to calm their fears by calming the storm. He was faithful to step into their boat and patiently continue to develop and perfect their faith. There would be more tests, but in each one, Jesus would prove His faithfulness and grow their faith.

—Jeff Crook
Blackshear Place Baptist Church, Flowery Branch, GA

WEEK 9, DAY 4

Our Hearts Need Jesus' Cleansing

Mark 7:14–37

When He had called all the multitude to Himself, He said to them, "Hear Me, everyone, and understand: 15There is nothing that enters a man from outside which can defile him; but the things which come out of him, those are the things that defile a man. 16If anyone has ears to hear, let him hear!"

17When He had entered a house away from the crowd, His disciples asked Him concerning the parable. 18So He said to them, "Are you thus without understanding also? Do you not perceive that whatever enters a man from outside cannot defile him, 19because it does not enter his heart but his stomach, and is eliminated, thus purifying all foods?" 20And He said, "What comes out of a man, that defiles a man. 21For from within, out of the heart of men, proceed evil thoughts, adulteries, fornications, murders, 22thefts, covetousness, wickedness, deceit, lewdness, an evil eye, blasphemy, pride, foolishness. 23All these evil things come from within and defile a man."

A Gentile Shows Her Faith

24From there He arose and went to the region of Tyre and Sidon. And He entered a house and wanted no one to know it, but He could not be hidden. 25For a woman whose young daughter had an unclean spirit heard about Him, and she came and fell at His feet. 26The woman was a Greek, a Syro-Phoenician by birth, and she kept asking Him to cast the demon out of her daughter. 27But Jesus said to her, "Let the children be filled first, for it is not good to take the children's bread and throw it to the little dogs."

28And she answered and said to Him, "Yes, Lord, yet even the little dogs under the table eat from the children's crumbs."

29Then He said to her, "For this saying go your way; the demon has gone out of your daughter."

30And when she had come to her house, she found the demon gone out, and her daughter lying on the bed.

Jesus Heals a Deaf-Mute

31Again, departing from the region of Tyre and Sidon, He came through the midst of the region of Decapolis to the Sea of Galilee. 32Then they brought to Him one who was deaf and had an impediment in his speech, and they begged Him to put His hand on him. 33And He took him aside from the multitude, and put His fingers in his ears, and He spat and touched his tongue. 34Then, looking up to heaven, He sighed, and said to him, "Ephphatha," that is, "Be opened."

35Immediately his ears were opened, and the impediment of his tongue was loosed, and he spoke plainly. 36Then He commanded them that they should tell no one; but the more He commanded them, the more widely they proclaimed it. 37And they were astonished beyond measure, saying, "He has done all things well. He makes both the deaf to hear and the mute to speak."

DEVOTIONAL

*A*re you aware of what's in your heart? The prophet Jeremiah wrote, "The heart is deceitful above all things, and desperately wicked; who can know it?" (Jeremiah 17:9). Jesus echoed Jeremiah in Mark 7:1–23, teaching that defilement comes from within. The Pharisees professed to have righteous hearts, but Jesus, like a skilled physician reporting to a patient about an unfavorable X-ray, said their hearts were not healthy. He indicated that their hearts were sick, even contaminated. More than that, their hearts were far from God and outright evil! You can be sure that it wasn't a report they enjoyed receiving!

You can also be certain that any or all of the things listed in Mark 7:21–22 are capable of rising up in our hearts. But the Pharisees did not see the deadly enemy lurking within. Martin Luther once said, "I am more afraid of my own heart than of the pope and all his cardinals. I have within me the greatest pope, self." Our self-righteousness will always condemn us. Human goodness will never be good enough. The heart must be under constant surveillance (Proverbs 4:23). We must daily ask Jesus to search and cleanse our hearts. We have His faithful promise that He will make our hearts clean: "If we confess our sins, He is faithful and just to forgive us our sins and to cleanse us from all unrighteousness" (1 John 1:9).

Give the Lord praise for cleansing your heart. Ask Him to keep your heart close to Him. Pray for others this day that their hearts would be converted by Christ's transforming power.

—Jeff Crook
Blackshear Place Baptist Church, Flowery Branch, GA

WEEK 9, DAY 5

Miracles Won't Soften
Hard Hearts

Mark 8:1–26

Feeding the Four Thousand

8 In those days, the multitude being very great and having nothing to eat, Jesus called His disciples to Him and said to them, 2"I have compassion on the multitude, because they have now continued with Me three days and have nothing to eat. 3And if I send them away hungry to their own houses, they will faint on the way; for some of them have come from afar."

4Then His disciples answered Him, "How can one satisfy these people with bread here in the wilderness?"

5He asked them, "How many loaves do you have?"

And they said, "Seven."

6So He commanded the multitude to sit down on the ground. And He took the seven loaves and gave thanks, broke them and gave them to His disciples to set before them; and they set them before the multitude. 7They also had a few small fish; and having blessed them, He said to set them also before them. 8So they ate and were filled, and they took up seven large baskets of leftover fragments. 9Now those who had eaten were about four thousand. And He sent them away, 10immediately got into the boat with His disciples, and came to the region of Dalmanutha.

The Pharisees Seek a Sign

11Then the Pharisees came out and began to dispute with Him, seeking from Him a sign from heaven, testing Him. 12But He sighed deeply in His spirit, and said, "Why does this generation seek a sign? Assuredly, I say to you, no sign shall be given to this generation."

Beware of the Leaven of the Pharisees and Herod

13And He left them, and getting into the boat again, departed to the other side. 14Now the disciples had forgotten to take bread, and they did not have more than one loaf with them in the boat. 15Then He charged them, saying, "Take heed, beware of the leaven of the Pharisees and the leaven of Herod."

16And they reasoned among themselves, saying, "It is because we have no bread."

17But Jesus, being aware of it, said to them, "Why do you reason because you have no bread? Do you not yet perceive nor understand? Is your heart still hardened? 18Having eyes, do you not see? And having ears, do you not hear? And do you not remember? 19When I broke the five loaves for the five thousand, how many baskets full of fragments did you take up?"

They said to Him, "Twelve."

20"Also, when I broke the seven for the four thousand, how many large baskets full of fragments did you take up?"

And they said, "Seven."

21So He said to them, "How is it you do not understand?"

A Blind Man Healed at Bethsaida

22Then He came to Bethsaida; and they brought a blind man to Him, and begged Him to touch him. 23So He took the blind man by the hand and led him out of the town. And when He had spit on his eyes and put His hands on him, He asked him if he saw anything.

24And he looked up and said, "I see men like trees, walking."

25Then He put His hands on his eyes again and made him look up. And he was restored and saw everyone clearly. 26Then He sent him away to his house, saying, "Neither go into the town, nor tell anyone in the town."

DEVOTIONAL

Jesus was direct and clear when He said, "No sign shall be given" (Mark 8:12). The Pharisees were demanding signs. Where had they been? Earlier, when Jesus performed a double miracle by healing the deaf and mute man, the crowd responded, "He has done all things well" (Mark 7:37). The second miraculous feeding of the multitudes followed, and His fame spread. Did the Pharisees not see or hear what Jesus was doing? They were truly spiritually sick, being both blind and deaf. They were looking for more, and Jesus was saying, "I am the sign."

The greatest sign of all would be the miracle of the resurrection. And the Pharisees would miss it. Jesus was the sign and the great miracle; however, their blind eyes, closed ears, and hard hearts did not recognize Him.

What happened next? "He left them" (Mark 8:13). It was an act of judgment when Jesus turned and walked away. Miracles won't soften hard hearts. The miracle needed in every heart is the new birth that results when the living Christ comes to live in our hearts.

—Jeff Crook
Blackshear Place Baptist Church, Flowery Branch, GA

WEEK 9, DAY 6
Made for Eternity

Mark 8:27–9:13

Peter Confesses Jesus as the Christ

Now Jesus and His disciples went out to the towns of Caesarea Philippi; and on the road He asked His disciples, saying to them, "Who do men say that I am?" 28So they answered, "John the Baptist; but some say, Elijah; and others, one of the prophets." 29He said to them, "But who do you say that I am?" Peter answered and said to Him, "You are the Christ." 30Then He strictly warned them that they should tell no one about Him.

Jesus Predicts His Death and Resurrection

31And He began to teach them that the Son of Man must suffer many things, and be rejected by the elders and chief priests and scribes, and be killed, and after three days rise again. 32He spoke this word openly. Then Peter took Him aside and began to rebuke Him. 33But when He had turned around and looked at His disciples, He rebuked Peter, saying, "Get behind Me, Satan! For you are not mindful of the things of God, but the things of men."

Take Up the Cross and Follow Him

34When He had called the people to Himself, with His disciples also, He said to them, "Whoever desires to come after Me, let him deny himself, and take up his cross, and follow Me. 35For whoever desires to save his life will lose it, but whoever loses his life for My sake and the gospel's will save it. 36For what will it profit a man if he gains the whole world, and loses his own soul? 37Or what will a man give in exchange for his soul? 38For whoever is ashamed of Me and My words in this adulterous and sinful generation, of him the Son of Man also will be ashamed when He comes in the glory of His Father with the holy angels."

Jesus Transfigured on the Mount

9And He said to them, "Assuredly, I say to you that there are some standing here who will not taste death till they see the kingdom of God present with power." 2Now after six days Jesus took Peter, James, and John, and led them up on a high mountain apart by themselves; and He was transfigured before them. 3His clothes became shining, exceedingly white, like snow, such as no launderer on earth can whiten them. 4And Elijah appeared to them with Moses, and they were talking with Jesus. 5Then Peter answered and said to Jesus, "Rabbi, it is good for us to be here; and let us make three tabernacles: one for You, one for Moses, and one for Elijah"— 6because he did not know what to say, for they were greatly afraid.

7And a cloud came and overshadowed them; and a voice came out of the cloud, saying, "This is My beloved Son. Hear Him!" 8Suddenly, when they had looked around, they saw no one anymore, but only Jesus with themselves.

9Now as they came down from the mountain, He commanded them that they should tell no one the things they had seen, till the Son of Man had risen from the dead. 10So they kept this word to themselves, questioning what the rising from the dead meant.

11And they asked Him, saying, "Why do the scribes say that Elijah must come first?"

12Then He answered and told them, "Indeed, Elijah is coming first and restores all things. And how is it written concerning the Son of Man, that He must suffer many things and be treated with contempt? 13But I say to you that Elijah has also come, and they did to him whatever they wished, as it is written of him."

DEVOTIONAL

Jesus asked a soul-searching question: "What will it profit a man if he gains the whole world, and loses his own soul?" (Mark 8:36). When God created man, He breathed into his nostrils "the breath of life," and he became a living soul (Genesis 2:7). You are a soul, and you have a body. The body is the house in which your soul lives. The body will one day die, but your soul will live forever in eternity. There was a time when you were not, but there will never be a time when you will not be. Your soul is eternal, which makes it very valuable.

Jesus asked the crowd, "What will a man give in exchange for his soul?" (Mark 8:37). There is no greater or even equal exchange. What about exchanging your soul for the world? Even if you could gain the whole world, you couldn't keep it. We were not made for this world. We were made for eternity. This world is not filling; it's fading. Hear the Word of God speak into your soul today: "The world is passing away . . . but he who does the will of God abides forever" (1 John 2:17). These are "priceless" words.

—Jeff Crook
Blackshear Place Baptist Church, Flowery Branch, GA

WEEK 9, DAY 7

___

In Mark 6, Jesus was rejected by His hometown. Why is it difficult to be a witness to our closest friends and family? List some ways you can be salt and light as the Lord gives you opportunities.

___

___

___

___

___

___

___

___

___

___

___

In Mark 8, we see the first of three statements Jesus made in Mark's gospel concerning His impending death (Mark 8:31; 9:31; 10:33–34). Why were the disciples upset and ashamed? Do you ever feel or act ashamed of your Lord?

___

___

___

___

___

___

___

___

WEEK 10, DAY 1

Grace for the Humble
and Faithful

Mark 9:14–37

A Boy Is Healed

And when He came to the disciples, He saw a great multitude around them, and scribes disputing with them. 15Immediately, when they saw Him, all the people were greatly amazed, and running to Him, greeted Him. 16And He asked the scribes, "What are you discussing with them?"

17Then one of the crowd answered and said, "Teacher, I brought You my son, who has a mute spirit. 18And wherever it seizes him, it throws him down; he foams at the mouth, gnashes his teeth, and becomes rigid. So I spoke to Your disciples, that they should cast it out, but they could not."

19He answered him and said, "O faithless generation, how long shall I be with you? How long shall I bear with you? Bring him to Me." 20Then they brought him to Him. And when he saw Him, immediately the spirit convulsed him, and he fell on the ground and wallowed, foaming at the mouth.

21So He asked his father, "How long has this been happening to him?"

And he said, "From childhood. 22And often he has thrown him both into the fire and into the water to destroy him. But if You can do anything, have compassion on us and help us."

23Jesus said to him, "If you can believe, all things are possible to him who believes."

24Immediately the father of the child cried out and said with tears, "Lord, I believe; help my unbelief!"

25When Jesus saw that the people came running together, He rebuked the unclean spirit, saying to it: "Deaf and dumb spirit, I command you, come out of him and enter him no more!" 26Then the spirit cried out, convulsed him greatly, and came out of him. And he became as one dead, so that many said, "He is dead." 27But Jesus took him by the hand and lifted him up, and he arose.

28And when He had come into the house, His disciples asked Him privately, "Why could we not cast it out?"

29So He said to them, "This kind can come out by nothing but prayer and fasting."

Jesus Again Predicts His Death and Resurrection

30Then they departed from there and passed through Galilee, and He did not want anyone to know it. 31For He taught His disciples and said to them, "The Son of Man is being betrayed into the hands of men, and they will kill Him. And after He is killed, He will rise the third day." 32But they did not understand this saying, and were afraid to ask Him.

Who Is the Greatest?

33Then He came to Capernaum. And when He was in the house He asked them, "What was it you disputed among yourselves on the road?" 34But they kept silent, for on the road they had disputed among themselves who would be the greatest. 35And He sat down, called the twelve, and said to them, "If anyone desires to be first, he shall be last of all and servant of all." 36Then He took a little child and set him in the midst of them. And when He had taken him in His arms, He said to them, 37"Whoever receives one of these little children in My name receives Me; and whoever receives Me, receives not Me but Him who sent Me."

DEVOTIONAL

Humility and faith go hand in hand. It is hard to put your trust in God if you are filled with self-centeredness, self-reliance, and self-importance. Who is the greatest? Jesus, and Jesus alone. All the rest of us are just unworthy slaves who should be crying out in brokenness and humility, "Lord, I am so weak, frail, and prone to fear and faithlessness. I do believe in You and Your power to do miracles in my life, but I need You to help my unbelief."

The Lord is good, kind, and patient. He opposes the proud, but He gives grace to the humble (James 4:6). He graciously answers us in our time of need, even when our faith is weak. Search your heart today. Is there some pride lurking in the shadows? Do you tend to compare yourself with others and feel puffed up when you sense you are greater? Confess it as sin. Ask God to make you a person of great humility, thinking not of yourself and your accomplishments, and make you a person of great faith, putting all your confidence in Him because He is able.

—Jeff Schreve
First Baptist Church, Texarkana, TX

WEEK 10, DAY 2

Flee All Evil

Mark 9:38–10:16

Jesus Forbids Sectarianism

Now John answered Him, saying, "Teacher, we saw someone who does not follow us casting out demons in Your name, and we forbade him because he does not follow us."

39But Jesus said, "Do not forbid him, for no one who works a miracle in My name can soon afterward speak evil of Me. 40For he who is not against us is on our side. 41For whoever gives you a cup of water to drink in My name, because you belong to Christ, assuredly, I say to you, he will by no means lose his reward.

Jesus Warns of Offenses

42"But whoever causes one of these little ones who believe in Me to stumble, it would be better for him if a millstone were hung around his neck, and he were thrown into the sea. 43If your hand causes you to sin, cut it off. It is better for you to enter into life maimed, rather than having two hands, to go to hell, into the fire that shall never be quenched— 44where

'Their worm does not die,
And the fire is not quenched.'

45And if your foot causes you to sin, cut it off. It is better for you to enter life lame, rather than having two feet, to be cast into hell, into the fire that shall never be quenched— 46where

'Their worm does not die,
And the fire is not quenched.'

47And if your eye causes you to sin, pluck it out. It is better for you to enter the kingdom of God with one eye, rather than having two eyes, to be cast into hell fire— 48where

'Their worm does not die,
And the fire is not quenched.'

Tasteless Salt Is Worthless

49"For everyone will be seasoned with fire, and every sacrifice will be seasoned with salt. 50Salt is good, but if the salt loses its flavor, how will you season it? Have salt in yourselves, and have peace with one another."

Marriage and Divorce

10Then He arose from there and came to the region of Judea by the other side of the Jordan. And multitudes gathered to Him again, and as He was accustomed, He taught them again.

2The Pharisees came and asked Him, "Is it lawful for a man to divorce his wife?" testing Him.

3And He answered and said to them, "What did Moses command you?"

4They said, "Moses permitted a man to write a certificate of divorce, and to dismiss her."

5And Jesus answered and said to them, "Because of the hardness of your heart he wrote you this precept. 6But from the beginning of the creation, God 'made them male and female.' 7For this reason a man shall leave his father and mother and be joined to his wife, 8and the two shall become one flesh'; so then they are no longer two, but one flesh. 9Therefore what God has joined together, let not man separate."

10In the house His disciples also asked Him again about the same matter. 11So He said to them, "Whoever divorces his wife and marries another commits adultery against her. 12And if a woman divorces her husband and marries another, she commits adultery."

Jesus Blesses Little Children

13Then they brought little children to Him, that He might touch them; but the disciples rebuked those who brought them. 14But when Jesus saw it, He was greatly displeased and said to them, "Let the little children come to Me, and do not forbid them; for of such is the kingdom of God. 15Assuredly, I say to you, whoever does not receive the kingdom of God as a little child will by no means enter it." 16And He took them up in His arms, laid His hands on them, and blessed them.

DEVOTIONAL

Sin is not your friend. Compromising with sin is like drinking "a little" poison. Even a little will hurt you and may kill you. By exaggeration, Jesus said sin is so bad and its ultimate effects so terrible (eternal hell) that it is better to perform radical amputation surgery than it is to compromise with sin (Mark 9:43–48). Watch out for the things you allow your eyes to see, the activities you allow your hands to engage in, and the places you allow your feet to go. Be faithful. Every little decision matters!

—Jeff Schreve
First Baptist Church, Texarkana, TX

WEEK 10, DAY 3

Serve the One True God

Mark 10:17–41

Jesus Counsels the Rich Young Ruler

Now as He was going out on the road, one came running, knelt before Him, and asked Him, "Good Teacher, what shall I do that I may inherit eternal life?"

18So Jesus said to him, "Why do you call Me good? No one is good but One, that is, God. 19You know the commandments: 'Do not commit adultery,' 'Do not murder,' 'Do not steal,' 'Do not bear false witness,' 'Do not defraud,' 'Honor your father and your mother.'"

20And he answered and said to Him, "Teacher, all these things I have kept from my youth."

21Then Jesus, looking at him, loved him, and said to him, "One thing you lack: Go your way, sell whatever you have and give to the poor, and you will have treasure in heaven; and come, take up the cross, and follow Me."

22But he was sad at this word, and went away sorrowful, for he had great possessions.

With God All Things Are Possible

23Then Jesus looked around and said to His disciples, "How hard it is for those who have riches to enter the kingdom of God!" 24And the disciples were astonished at His words. But Jesus answered again and said to them, "Children, how hard it is for those who trust in riches to enter the kingdom of God! 25It is easier for a camel to go through the eye of a needle than for a rich man to enter the kingdom of God."

26And they were greatly astonished, saying among themselves, "Who then can be saved?"

27But Jesus looked at them and said, "With men it is impossible, but not with God; for with God all things are possible."

28Then Peter began to say to Him, "See, we have left all and followed You."

29So Jesus answered and said, "Assuredly, I say to you, there is no one who has left house or brothers or sisters or father or mother or wife or children or lands, for My sake and the gospel's, 30who shall not receive a hundredfold now in this time—houses and brothers and sisters and mothers and children and lands, with persecutions—and in the age to come, eternal life. 31But many who are first will be last, and the last first."

Jesus a Third Time Predicts His Death and Resurrection

32Now they were on the road, going up to Jerusalem, and Jesus was going before them; and they were amazed. And as they followed they were afraid. Then He took the twelve aside again and began to tell them the things that would happen to Him: 33"Behold, we are going up to Jerusalem, and the Son of Man will be betrayed to the chief priests and to the scribes; and they will condemn Him to death and deliver Him to the Gentiles; 34and they will mock Him, and scourge Him, and spit on Him, and kill Him. And the third day He will rise again."

Greatness Is Serving

35Then James and John, the sons of Zebedee, came to Him, saying, "Teacher, we want You to do for us whatever we ask."

36And He said to them, "What do you want Me to do for you?"

37They said to Him, "Grant us that we may sit, one on Your right hand and the other on Your left, in Your glory."

38But Jesus said to them, "You do not know what you ask. Are you able to drink the cup that I drink, and be baptized with the baptism that I am baptized with?"

39They said to Him, "We are able."

So Jesus said to them, "You will indeed drink the cup that I drink, and with the baptism I am baptized with you will be baptized; 40but to sit on My right hand and on My left is not Mine to give, but it is for those for whom it is prepared."

41And when the ten heard it, they began to be greatly displeased with James and John.

DEVOTIONAL

Money is a wonderful servant but a terrible master. You can't serve God and money, but that is what the rich young ruler tried to do . . . and Jesus wouldn't give him that option.

If we choose to serve any false gods (money, pleasure, power, fame, family, sports) above the one true God, we are trading gold for garbage and eternal glory for passing, momentary pleasures. It is a terrible choice that so many people still make today. The rich young ruler chose his riches over redemption, and now, in hell, he has neither. If we choose Jesus over all else, we will certainly endure hardships on earth, but someday we will enjoy Jesus' presence and eternal rewards in heaven. Mark it down: it pays to serve Jesus!

—Jeff Schreve
First Baptist Church, Texarkana, TX

WEEK 10, DAY 4

Greatness for God's Glory

Mark 10:42–11:14

But Jesus called them to Himself and said to them, "You know that those who are considered rulers over the Gentiles lord it over them, and their great ones exercise authority over them. ⁴³Yet it shall not be so among you; but whoever desires to become great among you shall be your servant. ⁴⁴And whoever of you desires to be first shall be slave of all. ⁴⁵For even the Son of Man did not come to be served, but to serve, and to give His life a ransom for many."

Jesus Heals Blind Bartimaeus

⁴⁶Now they came to Jericho. As He went out of Jericho with His disciples and a great multitude, blind Bartimaeus, the son of Timaeus, sat by the road begging. ⁴⁷And when he heard that it was Jesus of Nazareth, he began to cry out and say, "Jesus, Son of David, have mercy on me!"

⁴⁸Then many warned him to be quiet; but he cried out all the more, "Son of David, have mercy on me!"

⁴⁹So Jesus stood still and commanded him to be called.

Then they called the blind man, saying to him, "Be of good cheer. Rise, He is calling you."

⁵⁰And throwing aside his garment, he rose and came to Jesus.

⁵¹So Jesus answered and said to him, "What do you want Me to do for you?"

The blind man said to Him, "Rabboni, that I may receive my sight."

⁵²Then Jesus said to him, "Go your way; your faith has made you well." And immediately he received his sight and followed Jesus on the road.

The Triumphal Entry

11 Now when they drew near Jerusalem, to Bethphage and Bethany, at the Mount of Olives, He sent two of His disciples; ²and He said to them, "Go into the village opposite you; and as soon as you have entered it you will find a colt tied, on which no one has sat. Loose it and bring it. ³And if anyone says to you, 'Why are you doing this?' say, 'The Lord has need of it,' and immediately he will send it here."

⁴So they went their way, and found the colt tied by the door outside on the street, and they loosed it. ⁵But some of those who stood there said to them, "What are you doing, loosing the colt?"

⁶And they spoke to them just as Jesus had commanded. So they let them go. ⁷Then they brought the colt to Jesus and threw their clothes on it, and He sat on it. ⁸And many spread their clothes on the road, and others cut down leafy branches from the trees and spread them on the road. ⁹Then those who went before and those who followed cried out, saying:

"Hosanna!
'Blessed is He who comes in the name of
the Lᴏʀᴅ!'
10 Blessed is the kingdom of our father David
That comes in the name of the Lord!
Hosanna in the highest!"

¹¹And Jesus went into Jerusalem and into the temple. So when He had looked around at all things, as the hour was already late, He went out to Bethany with the twelve.

The Fig Tree Withered

¹²Now the next day, when they had come out from Bethany, He was hungry. ¹³And seeing from afar a fig tree having leaves, He went to see if perhaps He would find something on it. When He came to it, He found nothing but leaves, for it was not the season for figs. ¹⁴In response Jesus said to it, "Let no one eat fruit from you ever again."

And His disciples heard it.

DEVOTIONAL

Do you want to be great? God wants that for you. He wants your life to make a great impact for Him. What are some keys to greatness? One key is humility and having an others-first attitude. The Lord hates pride, but gives grace to those who are humble and serve others.

Another key is having bold faith. Blind Bartimaeus would not keep quiet (Mark 10:48). Jesus was passing by, and Bartimaeus was not going to let the stern warnings of the faithless keep him from encountering the Savior and bringing his needs to Him.

A third key is having a heart of praise. The Lord is worthy of our praise. God loves it when we praise Him for His goodness and grace. If things are going well for you today, praise Him. If they are going badly, praise Him anyway. He is a good God who loves you and will work all things together for your good and His glory.

—Jeff Schreve
First Baptist Church, Texarkana, TX

WEEK 10, DAY 5

Jesus Values Humility

Mark 11:15–12:12

Jesus Cleanses the Temple

So they came to Jerusalem. Then Jesus went into the temple and began to drive out those who bought and sold in the temple, and overturned the tables of the money changers and the seats of those who sold doves. 16And He would not allow anyone to carry wares through the temple. 17Then He taught, saying to them, "Is it not written, 'My house shall be called a house of prayer for all nations'? But you have made it a 'den of thieves.'"

18And the scribes and chief priests heard it and sought how they might destroy Him; for they feared Him, because all the people were astonished at His teaching. 19When evening had come, He went out of the city.

The Lesson of the Withered Fig Tree

20Now in the morning, as they passed by, they saw the fig tree dried up from the roots. 21And Peter, remembering, said to Him, "Rabbi, look! The fig tree which You cursed has withered away."

22So Jesus answered and said to them, "Have faith in God. 23For assuredly, I say to you, whoever says to this mountain, 'Be removed and be cast into the sea,' and does not doubt in his heart, but believes that those things he says will be done, he will have whatever he says. 24Therefore I say to you, whatever things you ask when you pray, believe that you receive them, and you will have them.

Forgiveness and Prayer

25"And whenever you stand praying, if you have anything against anyone, forgive him, that your Father in heaven may also forgive you your trespasses. 26But if you do not forgive, neither will your Father in heaven forgive your trespasses."

Jesus' Authority Questioned

27Then they came again to Jerusalem. And as He was walking in the temple, the chief priests, the scribes, and the elders came to Him. 28And they said to Him, "By what authority are You doing these things? And who gave You this authority to do these things?"

29But Jesus answered and said to them, "I also will ask you one question; then answer Me, and I will tell you by what authority I do these things: 30The baptism of John—was it from heaven or from men? Answer Me."

31And they reasoned among themselves, saying, "If we say, 'From heaven,' He will say, 'Why then did you not believe him?' 32But if we say, 'From men' "—they feared the people, for all counted John to have been a prophet indeed. 33So they answered and said to Jesus, "We do not know." And Jesus answered and said to them, "Neither will I tell you by what authority I do these things."

The Parable of the Wicked Vinedressers

12 Then He began to speak to them in parables: "A man planted a vineyard and set a hedge around it, dug a place for the wine vat and built a tower. And he leased it to vinedressers and went into a far country. 2Now at vintage-time he sent a servant to the vinedressers, that he might receive some of the fruit of the vineyard from the vinedressers. 3And they took him and beat him and sent him away empty-handed. 4Again he sent them another servant, and at him they threw stones, wounded him in the head, and sent him away shamefully treated. 5And again he sent another, and him they killed; and many others, beating some and killing some. 6Therefore still having one son, his beloved, he also sent him to them last, saying, 'They will respect my son.' 7But those vinedressers said among themselves, 'This is the heir. Come, let us kill him, and the inheritance will be ours.' 8So they took him and killed him and cast him out of the vineyard.

9"Therefore what will the owner of the vineyard do? He will come and destroy the vinedressers, and give the vineyard to others. 10Have you not even read this Scripture:

'The stone which the builders rejected
  Has become the chief cornerstone.
11 This was the LORD's doing,
  And it is marvelous in our eyes'?"

12And they sought to lay hands on Him, but feared the multitude, for they knew He had spoken the parable against them. So they left Him and went away.

DEVOTIONAL

Jesus was tough on the religious leaders of His day. He spoke cutting parables against them and disrupted their system of religion. But He treated repentant sinners much differently. Why? Because Jesus hates pride and self-righteousness. May you walk today in humility and in awe of His amazing grace.

—Jeff Schreve
First Baptist Church, Texarkana, TX

WEEK 10, DAY 6

To Know Him Is to Love Him

Mark 12:13–31

The Pharisees: Is It Lawful to Pay Taxes to Caesar?

Then they sent to Him some of the Pharisees and the Herodians, to catch Him in His words. 14When they had come, they said to Him, "Teacher, we know that You are true, and care about no one; for You do not regard the person of men, but teach the way of God in truth. Is it lawful to pay taxes to Caesar, or not? 15Shall we pay, or shall we not pay?"

But He, knowing their hypocrisy, said to them, "Why do you test Me? Bring Me a denarius that I may see it." 16So they brought it.

And He said to them, "Whose image and inscription is this?" They said to Him, "Caesar's."

17And Jesus answered and said to them, "Render to Caesar the things that are Caesar's, and to God the things that are God's."

And they marveled at Him.

The Sadducees: What About the Resurrection?

18Then some Sadducees, who say there is no resurrection, came to Him; and they asked Him, saying: 19"Teacher, Moses wrote to us that if a man's brother dies, and leaves his wife behind, and leaves no children, his brother should take his wife and raise up offspring for his brother. 20Now there were seven brothers. The first took a wife; and dying, he left no offspring. 21And the second took her, and he died; nor did he leave any offspring. And the third likewise. 22So the seven had her and left no offspring. Last of all the woman died also. 23Therefore, in the resurrection, when they rise, whose wife will she be? For all seven had her as wife."

24Jesus answered and said to them, "Are you not therefore mistaken, because you do not know the Scriptures nor the power of God? 25For when they rise from the dead, they neither marry nor are given in marriage, but are like angels in heaven. 26But concerning the dead, that they rise, have you not read in the book of Moses, in the burning bush passage, how God spoke to him, saying, 'I am the God of Abraham, the God of Isaac, and the God of Jacob'? 27He is not the God of the dead, but the God of the living. You are therefore greatly mistaken."

The Scribes: Which Is the First Commandment of All?

28Then one of the scribes came, and having heard them reasoning together, perceiving that He had answered them well, asked Him, "Which is the first commandment of all?"

29Jesus answered him, "The first of all the commandments is: 'Hear, O Israel, the Lord our God, the Lord is one. 30And you shall love the Lord your God with all your heart, with all your soul, with all your mind, and with all your strength.' This is the first commandment. 31And the second, like it, is this: 'You shall love your neighbor as yourself.' There is no other commandment greater than these."

DEVOTIONAL

What a righteous rebuke! Jesus told the religious Sadducees they did not know the Scriptures or the power of God (Mark 12:24). They who prided themselves in knowing both were told in no uncertain terms that they didn't know squat about either.

God wants us to know His Word and believe He has almighty power to make a difference in our lives. When you read the Bible, remember that it is true . . . every miracle, story, and promise. You can trust God's Word and cling to His promises, because it is impossible for Him to lie (Hebrews 6:18).

And what does God's Word say He wants from you more than anything else? Your love. He wants you to love Him with all you have. That is the greatest commandment. And how do you fulfill it? How do you really love God supremely and completely? Contrary to natural tendencies, you don't do it by gritting your teeth and trying harder. You do it by simply focusing on His love for you. "We love Him because He first loved us" (1 John 4:19).

If you are having trouble with your all-out love for God (as evidenced by disobedience, spiritual compromise, and a loss of passion in your walk with Jesus), do this to remedy the problem: meditate on the cross. See and experience anew and afresh His unfathomable love for you. Regardless of what is going on in your life today, you can be certain God loves you because the blood-stained cross of Calvary proves it. He gave His all for you. Will you give your all for Him?

—Jeff Schreve
First Baptist Church, Texarkana, TX

WEEK 10, DAY 7

Praise is something we cannot do too much. God loves it when we praise Him, especially when life is hard. Are you a fair-weather Christian? Do you only praise Him in the sunshine . . . and grumble in the storms? Write down the good things and bad things going on in your life today, and praise Him for it all. He was worthy of praise on Palm Sunday, and He is worthy of praise today.

_____

_____

_____

_____

_____

_____

_____

_____

_____

_____

Many Christians struggle with the love of God. They tend to evaluate God's love for them based on current circumstances ("If things are going badly, He must not love me."). Or they feel so guilty over past sins they think there is no way God could really love them. How do you feel about the love of God for you? He loves you beyond words . . . but do you believe it and act like it?

_____

_____

_____

_____

_____

_____

_____

WEEK II, DAY I

Give Generously to God

Mark 12:32–13:10

So the scribe said to Him, "Well said, Teacher. You have spoken the truth, for there is one God, and there is no other but He. 33And to love Him with all the heart, with all the understanding, with all the soul, and with all the strength, and to love one's neighbor as oneself, is more than all the whole burnt offerings and sacrifices."

34Now when Jesus saw that he answered wisely, He said to him, "You are not far from the kingdom of God."

But after that no one dared question Him.

Jesus: How Can David Call His Descendant Lord?

35Then Jesus answered and said, while He taught in the temple, "How is it that the scribes say that the Christ is the Son of David? 36For David himself said by the Holy Spirit:

'The LORD said to my Lord,
"Sit at My right hand,
Till I make Your enemies Your footstool." '

37Therefore David himself calls Him 'Lord'; how is He then his Son?"

And the common people heard Him gladly.

Beware of the Scribes

38Then He said to them in His teaching, "Beware of the scribes, who desire to go around in long robes, love greetings in the marketplaces, 39the best seats in the synagogues, and the best places at feasts, 40who devour widows' houses, and for a pretense make long prayers. These will receive greater condemnation."

The Widow's Two Mites

41Now Jesus sat opposite the treasury and saw how the people put money into the treasury. And many who were rich put in much. 42Then one poor widow came and threw in two mites, which make a quadrans. 43So He called His disciples to Himself and said to them, "Assuredly, I say to you that this poor widow has put in more than all those who have given to the treasury; 44for they all put in out of their abundance, but she out of her poverty put in all that she had, her whole livelihood."

Jesus Predicts the Destruction of the Temple

13 Then as He went out of the temple, one of His disciples said to Him, "Teacher, see what manner of stones and what buildings are here!"

2And Jesus answered and said to him, "Do you see these great buildings? Not one stone shall be left upon another, that shall not be thrown down."

The Signs of the Times and the End of the Age

3Now as He sat on the Mount of Olives opposite the temple, Peter, James, John, and Andrew asked Him privately, 4"Tell us, when will these things be? And what will be the sign when all these things will be fulfilled?"

5And Jesus, answering them, began to say: "Take heed that no one deceives you. 6For many will come in My name, saying, 'I am He,' and will deceive many. 7But when you hear of wars and rumors of wars, do not be troubled; for such things must happen, but the end is not yet. 8For nation will rise against nation, and kingdom against kingdom. And there will be earthquakes in various places, and there will be famines and troubles. These are the beginnings of sorrows.

9"But watch out for yourselves, for they will deliver you up to councils, and you will be beaten in the synagogues. You will be brought before rulers and kings for My sake, for a testimony to them. 10And the gospel must first be preached to all the nations."

DEVOTIONAL

As Christians, we probably all agree that greed is not good. But we also probably struggle with greed more than we think we do. It's possible to give to others and still be greedy. After all, Jesus' point in Mark 12:43–44 is not about how much we give as much as it is about how much we keep for ourselves. He said the poor widow gave more to the treasury with her two mites than the rich who put in a larger quantity of money, "for they all put in out of their abundance, but she out of her poverty put in all that she had, her whole livelihood" (verse 44).

So, let's be extravagantly generous. Let's not store up treasures for ourselves; let's be rich toward God. Let's give until it hurts. Let's intentionally and strategically give more of our money away. Let's give sacrificially.

The only way to become less greedy is to become more generous. Look around you—who has unmet needs? Pray for God's guidance, and then let the heart of Christ reign in you as you offer what you have to bless others in His name.

—Dr. Jerry Walls
Southside Baptist Church, Warner Robins, GA

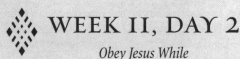

WEEK 11, DAY 2

*Obey Jesus While
Anticipating His Return*

Mark 13:11–37

"But when they arrest you and deliver you up, do not worry beforehand, or premeditate what you will speak. But whatever is given you in that hour, speak that; for it is not you who speak, but the Holy Spirit. ¹²Now brother will betray brother to death, and a father his child; and children will rise up against parents and cause them to be put to death. ¹³And you will be hated by all for My name's sake. But he who endures to the end shall be saved.

The Great Tribulation

¹⁴"So when you see the 'abomination of desolation,' spoken of by Daniel the prophet, standing where it ought not" (let the reader understand), "then let those who are in Judea flee to the mountains. ¹⁵Let him who is on the housetop not go down into the house, nor enter to take anything out of his house. ¹⁶And let him who is in the field not go back to get his clothes. ¹⁷But woe to those who are pregnant and to those who are nursing babies in those days! ¹⁸And pray that your flight may not be in winter. ¹⁹For in those days there will be tribulation, such as has not been since the beginning of the creation which God created until this time, nor ever shall be. ²⁰And unless the Lord had shortened those days, no flesh would be saved; but for the elect's sake, whom He chose, He shortened the days.

²¹"Then if anyone says to you, 'Look, here is the Christ!' or, 'Look, He is there!' do not believe it. ²²For false christs and false prophets will rise and show signs and wonders to deceive, if possible, even the elect. ²³But take heed; see, I have told you all things beforehand.

The Coming of the Son of Man

²⁴"But in those days, after that tribulation, the sun will be darkened, and the moon will not give its light; ²⁵the stars of heaven will fall, and the powers in the heavens will be shaken. ²⁶Then they will see the Son of Man coming in the clouds with great power and glory. ²⁷And then He will send His angels, and gather together His elect from the four winds, from the farthest part of earth to the farthest part of heaven.

The Parable of the Fig Tree

²⁸"Now learn this parable from the fig tree: When its branch has already become tender, and puts forth leaves, you know that summer is near. ²⁹So you also, when you see these things happening, know that it is near—at the doors! ³⁰Assuredly, I say to you, this generation will by no means pass away till all these things take place. ³¹Heaven and earth will pass away, but My words will by no means pass away.

No One Knows the Day or Hour

³²"But of that day and hour no one knows, not even the angels in heaven, nor the Son, but only the Father. ³³Take heed, watch and pray; for you do not know when the time is. ³⁴It is like a man going to a far country, who left his house and gave authority to his servants, and to each his work, and commanded the doorkeeper to watch. ³⁵Watch therefore, for you do not know when the master of the house is coming—in the evening, at midnight, at the crowing of the rooster, or in the morning— ³⁶lest, coming suddenly, he find you sleeping. ³⁷And what I say to you, I say to all: Watch!"

DEVOTIONAL

Many Christians are so concerned about reigning with Christ in the future that they're not living for Christ in the present. They're so busy speculating about the Second Coming of Jesus that they neglect to tell people about the first time He came. They're so caught up in trying to decipher and decode certain prophetic passages that they never get around to applying basic Christian principles and virtues.

Jesus doesn't ask us to crack some mysterious code. He doesn't want us to spend our days on earth making guesses about the future. He wants us to take the gospel to every nation and to anticipate His Second Coming in a watchful, prayerful way (Mark 13:10, 33). He wants us to fulfill the two greatest commandments of God—to love the Lord our God with all our heart, mind, and soul and to love our neighbors as ourselves.

The angels don't know when Jesus will return. Neither does Jesus Himself. Only the Father does. Honor His will and His wisdom, and be content with knowing what He's revealed. Don't get distracted from what's most important—fulfilling Jesus' explicit commands—and lovingly encourage others to do the same.

—Dr. Jerry Walls
Southside Baptist Church, Warner Robins, GA

WEEK II, DAY 3
The Lord's Supper

Mark 14:1–26

The Plot to Kill Jesus

14 After two days it was the Passover and the Feast of Unleavened Bread. And the chief priests and the scribes sought how they might take Him by trickery and put Him to death. 2But they said, "Not during the feast, lest there be an uproar of the people."

The Anointing at Bethany

3And being in Bethany at the house of Simon the leper, as He sat at the table, a woman came having an alabaster flask of very costly oil of spikenard. Then she broke the flask and poured it on His head. 4But there were some who were indignant among themselves, and said, "Why was this fragrant oil wasted? 5For it might have been sold for more than three hundred denarii and given to the poor." And they criticized her sharply.

6But Jesus said, "Let her alone. Why do you trouble her? She has done a good work for Me. 7For you have the poor with you always, and whenever you wish you may do them good; but Me you do not have always. 8She has done what she could. She has come beforehand to anoint My body for burial. 9Assuredly, I say to you, wherever this gospel is preached in the whole world, what this woman has done will also be told as a memorial to her."

Judas Agrees to Betray Jesus

10Then Judas Iscariot, one of the twelve, went to the chief priests to betray Him to them. 11And when they heard it, they were glad, and promised to give him money. So he sought how he might conveniently betray Him.

Jesus Celebrates the Passover with His Disciples

12Now on the first day of Unleavened Bread, when they killed the Passover lamb, His disciples said to Him, "Where do You want us to go and prepare, that You may eat the Passover?"

13And He sent out two of His disciples and said to them, "Go into the city, and a man will meet you carrying a pitcher of water; follow him. 14Wherever he goes in, say to the master of the house, 'The Teacher says, "Where is the guest room in which I may eat the Passover with My disciples?" ' 15Then he will show you a large upper room, furnished and prepared; there make ready for us."

16So His disciples went out, and came into the city, and found it just as He had said to them; and they prepared the Passover.

17In the evening He came with the twelve. 18Now as they sat and ate, Jesus said, "Assuredly, I say to you, one of you who eats with Me will betray Me."

19And they began to be sorrowful, and to say to Him one by one, "Is it I?" And another said, "Is it I?"

20He answered and said to them, "It is one of the twelve, who dips with Me in the dish. 21The Son of Man indeed goes just as it is written of Him, but woe to that man by whom the Son of Man is betrayed! It would have been good for that man if he had never been born."

Jesus Institutes the Lord's Supper

22And as they were eating, Jesus took bread, blessed and broke it, and gave it to them and said, "Take, eat; this is My body."

23Then He took the cup, and when He had given thanks He gave it to them, and they all drank from it. 24And He said to them, "This is My blood of the new covenant, which is shed for many. 25Assuredly, I say to you, I will no longer drink of the fruit of the vine until that day when I drink it new in the kingdom of God."

26And when they had sung a hymn, they went out to the Mount of Olives.

DEVOTIONAL

*M*ost people need reminders. Many doctor's appointments, lunch meetings, and project deadlines would be missed without them! Jesus gave us something to help us remember Him. Some call it the Lord's Supper; some call it communion. Whatever it's called, it's a time for us to stop whatever we're doing and remember what Jesus did for us.

Jesus established this ordinance for us because He knows our tendency to let the pace and pressures of life distract us from our relationship with God. He knows our affinity for things that don't matter, so He established a reminder of what matters most.

Through communion, Jesus calls out to us: "Remember My love. Don't forget what I accomplished or the price I paid. Remember who I am. Don't forget what I did, what I am doing, and what I promised to do for you." Respond to Him with grateful worship and loving reverence.

—Dr. Jerry Walls
Southside Baptist Church, Warner Robins, GA

WEEK II, DAY 4

Opening Our Hearts in Prayer

Mark 14:27–52

Jesus Predicts Peter's Denial

Then Jesus said to them, "All of you will be made to stumble because of Me this night, for it is written:

'I will strike the Shepherd,
And the sheep will be scattered.'

28"But after I have been raised, I will go before you to Galilee."

29Peter said to Him, "Even if all are made to stumble, yet I will not be."

30Jesus said to him, "Assuredly, I say to you that today, even this night, before the rooster crows twice, you will deny Me three times."

31But he spoke more vehemently, "If I have to die with You, I will not deny You!"

And they all said likewise.

The Prayer in the Garden

32Then they came to a place which was named Gethsemane; and He said to His disciples, "Sit here while I pray." 33And He took Peter, James, and John with Him, and He began to be troubled and deeply distressed. 34Then He said to them, "My soul is exceedingly sorrowful, even to death. Stay here and watch."

35He went a little farther, and fell on the ground, and prayed that if it were possible, the hour might pass from Him. 36And He said, "Abba, Father, all things are possible for You. Take this cup away from Me; nevertheless, not what I will, but what You will."

37Then He came and found them sleeping, and said to Peter, "Simon, are you sleeping? Could you not watch one hour? 38Watch and pray, lest you enter into temptation. The spirit indeed is willing, but the flesh is weak."

39Again He went away and prayed, and spoke the same words. 40And when He returned, He found them asleep again, for their eyes were heavy; and they did not know what to answer Him.

41Then He came the third time and said to them, "Are you still sleeping and resting? It is enough! The hour has come; behold, the Son of Man is being betrayed into the hands of sinners. 42Rise, let us be going. See, My betrayer is at hand."

Betrayal and Arrest in Gethsemane

43And immediately, while He was still speaking, Judas, one of the twelve, with a great multitude with swords and clubs, came from the chief priests and the scribes and the elders. 44Now His betrayer had given them a signal, saying, "Whomever I kiss, He is the One; seize Him and lead Him away safely."

45As soon as he had come, immediately he went up to Him and said to Him, "Rabbi, Rabbi!" and kissed Him.

46Then they laid their hands on Him and took Him. 47And one of those who stood by drew his sword and struck the servant of the high priest, and cut off his ear.

48Then Jesus answered and said to them, "Have you come out, as against a robber, with swords and clubs to take Me? 49I was daily with you in the temple teaching, and you did not seize Me. But the Scriptures must be fulfilled."

50Then they all forsook Him and fled.

A Young Man Flees Naked

51Now a certain young man followed Him, having a linen cloth thrown around his naked body. And the young men laid hold of him, 52and he left the linen cloth and fled from them naked.

DEVOTIONAL

There is a difference between simply saying prayers and actually praying. A lot of us are guilty of saying prayers without thinking about what we're saying. We just go through the motions, saying the same things we usually say in the same way we always say them. It's like we put our prayers on autopilot. We're good at saying prayers. We're not so good at actually praying.

Praying should involve truly opening our hearts to God and nurturing a close, honest relationship with Him. He wants us to come to Him, talk to Him, and be real with Him. He welcomes us to spill out whatever may be on our hearts. So, if you're frustrated, you can share your frustrations with Him. If you're thankful, express thanks. If you're worried, take your anxiety to Him. Whatever you're feeling, go to Him about it, and be real with Him.

Make sure you're not praying the same old prayer without thinking about what you're actually saying. His mercies are new every morning . . . your prayers should be too!

—Dr. Jerry Walls
Southside Baptist Church, Warner Robins, GA

WEEK II, DAY 5

Blameless Jesus
Endured the Cross

Mark 14:53–15:5

Jesus Faces the Sanhedrin

And they led Jesus away to the high priest; and with him were assembled all the chief priests, the elders, and the scribes. 54But Peter followed Him at a distance, right into the courtyard of the high priest. And he sat with the servants and warmed himself at the fire.

55Now the chief priests and all the council sought testimony against Jesus to put Him to death, but found none. 56For many bore false witness against Him, but their testimonies did not agree.

57Then some rose up and bore false witness against Him, saying, 58"We heard Him say, 'I will destroy this temple made with hands, and within three days I will build another made without hands.'" 59But not even then did their testimony agree.

60And the high priest stood up in the midst and asked Jesus, saying, "Do You answer nothing? What is it these men testify against You?" 61But He kept silent and answered nothing.

Again the high priest asked Him, saying to Him, "Are You the Christ, the Son of the Blessed?"

62Jesus said, "I am. And you will see the Son of Man sitting at the right hand of the Power, and coming with the clouds of heaven."

63Then the high priest tore his clothes and said, "What further need do we have of witnesses? 64You have heard the blasphemy! What do you think?"

And they all condemned Him to be deserving of death.

65Then some began to spit on Him, and to blindfold Him, and to beat Him, and to say to Him, "Prophesy!" And the officers struck Him with the palms of their hands.

Peter Denies Jesus, and Weeps

66Now as Peter was below in the courtyard, one of the servant girls of the high priest came. 67And when she saw Peter warming himself, she looked at him and said, "You also were with Jesus of Nazareth."

68But he denied it, saying, "I neither know nor understand what you are saying." And he went out on the porch, and a rooster crowed.

69And the servant girl saw him again, and began to say to those who stood by, "This is one of them." 70But he denied it again.

And a little later those who stood by said to Peter again, "Surely you are one of them; for you are a Galilean, and your speech shows it."

71Then he began to curse and swear, "I do not know this Man of whom you speak!"

72A second time the rooster crowed. Then Peter called to mind the word that Jesus had said to him, "Before the rooster crows twice, you will deny Me three times." And when he thought about it, he wept.

Jesus Faces Pilate

15 Immediately, in the morning, the chief priests held a consultation with the elders and scribes and the whole council; and they bound Jesus, led Him away, and delivered Him to Pilate. 2Then Pilate asked Him, "Are You the King of the Jews?"

He answered and said to him, "It is as you say."

3And the chief priests accused Him of many things, but He answered nothing. 4Then Pilate asked Him again, saying, "Do You answer nothing? See how many things they testify against You!" 5But Jesus still answered nothing, so that Pilate marveled.

DEVOTIONAL

In Jesus' darkest hour, no one stood up for Him. Judas was guilty of handing Him over to the authorities. The disciples were guilty of leaving Jesus in His most desperate hour. The Sanhedrin was guilty of falsely accusing Him. Peter was guilty of denying Him. Pilate was guilty of ignoring the obvious about Him. The crowd was guilty of shouting out, "Crucify Him!" All of them were guilty, and so are we. After all, our sin is the only reason He had to go to the cross in the first place.

The only truly innocent Person in all of human history had to give His life for those who were far from innocent. But Jesus didn't run from His responsibility. He embraced the cross. He endured its pain. He did it all for you and me, and He did it for the Father's glory.

Take time to meditate on these staggering realities of Jesus. Read through Isaiah 53. Remember that you have been redeemed "with the precious blood of Christ, as of a lamb without blemish and without spot" (1 Peter 1:19). Honor your Savior. Love and thank Him every way you can. Live for Him today.

—Dr. Jerry Walls
Southside Baptist Church, Warner Robins, GA

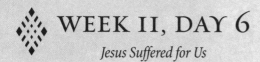

WEEK II, DAY 6

Jesus Suffered for Us

Mark 15:6–32

Taking the Place of Barabbas

Now at the feast he was accustomed to releasing one prisoner to them, whomever they requested. 7And there was one named Barabbas, who was chained with his fellow rebels; they had committed murder in the rebellion. 8Then the multitude, crying aloud, began to ask him to do just as he had always done for them. 9But Pilate answered them, saying, "Do you want me to release to you the King of the Jews?" 10For he knew that the chief priests had handed Him over because of envy.

11But the chief priests stirred up the crowd, so that he should rather release Barabbas to them. 12Pilate answered and said to them again, "What then do you want me to do with Him whom you call the King of the Jews?"

13So they cried out again, "Crucify Him!"

14Then Pilate said to them, "Why, what evil has He done?"

But they cried out all the more, "Crucify Him!"

15So Pilate, wanting to gratify the crowd, released Barabbas to them; and he delivered Jesus, after he had scourged Him, to be crucified.

The Soldiers Mock Jesus

16Then the soldiers led Him away into the hall called Praetorium, and they called together the whole garrison. 17And they clothed Him with purple; and they twisted a crown of thorns, put it on His head, 18and began to salute Him, "Hail, King of the Jews!" 19Then they struck Him on the head with a reed and spat on Him; and bowing the knee, they worshiped Him. 20And when they had mocked Him, they took the purple off Him, put His own clothes on Him, and led Him out to crucify Him.

The King on a Cross

21Then they compelled a certain man, Simon a Cyrenian, the father of Alexander and Rufus, as he was coming out of the country and passing by, to bear His cross. 22And they brought Him to the place Golgotha, which is translated, Place of a Skull. 23Then they gave Him wine mingled with myrrh to drink, but He did not take it. 24And when they crucified Him, they divided His garments, casting lots for them to determine what every man should take.

25Now it was the third hour, and they crucified Him. 26And the inscription of His accusation was written above:

THE KING OF THE JEWS.

27With Him they also crucified two robbers, one on His right and the other on His left. 28So the Scripture was fulfilled which says, "And He was numbered with the transgressors."

29And those who passed by blasphemed Him, wagging their heads and saying, "Aha! You who destroy the temple and build it in three days, 30save Yourself, and come down from the cross!"

31Likewise the chief priests also, mocking among themselves with the scribes, said, "He saved others; Himself He cannot save. 32Let the Christ, the King of Israel, descend now from the cross, that we may see and believe."

Even those who were crucified with Him reviled Him.

DEVOTIONAL

When you think of the final week of Jesus' life and ministry, there is a unique and strange contrast at work. In one sense, it was the worst week ever. In another sense, it was without a doubt the best week ever.

From the disciples' perspective, it was the worst week ever. The man they believed to be the Messiah was ridiculed, tortured, and murdered. Their hopes and dreams were put to death right along with Jesus. It seemed like the most horrible thing imaginable had happened.

But on this side of history, we know what came after the agony of the cross. We know that even when Jesus was put to death, God's loving rescue plan was still in motion. When He died and rose again, He paid for our sins, and salvation became possible for us! Left to ourselves, we are dead in our sins, but because of the events of that week, we can become alive in Christ. We can be forgiven, made right with God, and freed from the bondage of sin. We can receive the Holy Spirit and live a life of purpose and worship. We can share in Jesus' triumph over the grave and look forward to our own resurrection and eternal life in heaven. From our perspective, what in history can top that? We hate that our Savior suffered, bled, and died on the cross, but at the same time, we're so thankful for what He accomplished when He did!

How will you regularly celebrate and give thanks to God for the best week in history?

—Dr. Jerry Walls
Southside Baptist Church, Warner Robins, GA

WEEK 11, DAY 7

Are you in the habit of simply saying prayers . . . or actually praying? What can you do to make sure you don't just say a prayer but truly pray?

_____

_____

_____

_____

_____

_____

_____

_____

_____

_____

_____

We know Jesus died for us, so what can you do to make sure you live for Him?

_____

_____

_____

_____

_____

_____

_____

_____

_____

_____

WEEK 12, DAY 1
The Heart of Redemption

Mark 15:33–16:8

Jesus Dies on the Cross

Now when the sixth hour had come, there was darkness over the whole land until the ninth hour. ³⁴And at the ninth hour Jesus cried out with a loud voice, saying, "Eloi, Eloi, lama sabachthani?" which is translated, "My God, My God, why have You forsaken Me?"

³⁵Some of those who stood by, when they heard that, said, "Look, He is calling for Elijah!" ³⁶Then someone ran and filled a sponge full of sour wine, put it on a reed, and offered it to Him to drink, saying, "Let Him alone; let us see if Elijah will come to take Him down."

³⁷And Jesus cried out with a loud voice, and breathed His last.

³⁸Then the veil of the temple was torn in two from top to bottom. ³⁹So when the centurion, who stood opposite Him, saw that He cried out like this and breathed His last, he said, "Truly this Man was the Son of God!"

⁴⁰There were also women looking on from afar, among whom were Mary Magdalene, Mary the mother of James the Less and of Joses, and Salome, ⁴¹who also followed Him and ministered to Him when He was in Galilee, and many other women who came up with Him to Jerusalem.

Jesus Buried in Joseph's Tomb

⁴²Now when evening had come, because it was the Preparation Day, that is, the day before the Sabbath, ⁴³Joseph of Arimathea, a prominent council member, who was himself waiting for the kingdom of God, coming and taking courage, went in to Pilate and asked for the body of Jesus. ⁴⁴Pilate marveled that He was already dead; and summoning the centurion, he asked him if He had been dead for some time. ⁴⁵So when he found out from the centurion, he granted the body to Joseph. ⁴⁶Then he bought fine linen, took Him down, and wrapped Him in the linen. And he laid Him in a tomb which had been hewn out of the rock, and rolled a stone against the door of the tomb. ⁴⁷And Mary Magdalene and Mary the mother of Joses observed where He was laid.

He Is Risen

16 Now when the Sabbath was past, Mary Magdalene, Mary the mother of James, and Salome bought spices, that they might come and anoint Him. ²Very early in the morning, on the first day of the week, they came to the tomb when the sun had risen. ³And they said among themselves, "Who will roll away the stone from the door of the tomb for us?" ⁴But when they looked up, they saw that the stone had been rolled away—for it was very large. ⁵And entering the tomb, they saw a young man clothed in a long white robe sitting on the right side; and they were alarmed.

⁶But he said to them, "Do not be alarmed. You seek Jesus of Nazareth, who was crucified. He is risen! He is not here. See the place where they laid Him. ⁷But go, tell His disciples—and Peter—that He is going before you into Galilee; there you will see Him, as He said to you."

⁸So they went out quickly and fled from the tomb, for they trembled and were amazed. And they said nothing to anyone, for they were afraid.

DEVOTIONAL

In today's passage we find the heart of redemption and hope. When Jesus cried out to the Father, "Why have You forsaken Me?" (Mark 15:34), He indicated the precise moment He took our sins upon Himself and the Father responded accordingly. The Father, who is so holy He cannot look upon sin, turned away from His Son, who had been made sin on our behalf (2 Corinthians 5:21). Jesus went through the darkness so that we might be brought into the light. He became sin so that we might become righteousness. Jesus' last words on the cross stand as a clear testimony of God's love for you, both now and forever.

In those moments that rocked the world, the veil of the temple was torn from top to bottom by divine hands to indicate that now, once and for all, we who come to Jesus may come into the Most Holy Place through His blood.

There's more. Jesus not only conquered sin, but also death! His resurrection paralyzed the death grip Satan once had on us, and it gives us hope as nothing else can.

Scripture documents the facts, details, eyewitnesses, and even the adversaries of Christ's resurrection. These things were recorded so we may believe and be transformed!

—John Meador
First Baptist Church, Euless, TX

WEEK 12, DAY 2

Signs of Belief

Mark 16:9–Luke 1:13

Mary Magdalene Sees the Risen Lord

Now when He rose early on the first day of the week, He appeared first to Mary Magdalene, out of whom He had cast seven demons. 10She went and told those who had been with Him, as they mourned and wept. 11And when they heard that He was alive and had been seen by her, they did not believe.

Jesus Appears to Two Disciples

12After that, He appeared in another form to two of them as they walked and went into the country. 13And they went and told it to the rest, but they did not believe them either.

The Great Commission

14Later He appeared to the eleven as they sat at the table; and He rebuked their unbelief and hardness of heart, because they did not believe those who had seen Him after He had risen. 15And He said to them, "Go into all the world and preach the gospel to every creature. 16He who believes and is baptized will be saved; but he who does not believe will be condemned. 17And these signs will follow those who believe: In My name they will cast out demons; they will speak with new tongues; 18they will take up serpents; and if they drink anything deadly, it will by no means hurt them; they will lay hands on the sick, and they will recover."

Christ Ascends to God's Right Hand

19So then, after the Lord had spoken to them, He was received up into heaven, and sat down at the right hand of God. 20And they went out and preached everywhere, the Lord working with them and confirming the word through the accompanying signs. Amen.

Dedication to Theophilus

1Inasmuch as many have taken in hand to set in order a narrative of those things which have been fulfilled among us, 2just as those who from the beginning were eyewitnesses and ministers of the word delivered them to us, 3it seemed good to me also, having had perfect understanding of all things from the very first, to write to you an orderly account, most excellent Theophilus, 4that you may know the certainty of those things in which you were instructed.

John's Birth Announced to Zacharias

5There was in the days of Herod, the king of Judea, a certain priest named Zacharias, of the division of Abijah. His wife was of the daughters of Aaron, and her name was Elizabeth. 6And they were both righteous before God, walking in all the commandments and ordinances of the Lord blameless. 7But they had no child, because Elizabeth was barren, and they were both well advanced in years.

8So it was, that while he was serving as priest before God in the order of his division, 9according to the custom of the priesthood, his lot fell to burn incense when he went into the temple of the Lord. 10And the whole multitude of the people was praying outside at the hour of incense. 11Then an angel of the Lord appeared to him, standing on the right side of the altar of incense. 12And when Zacharias saw him, he was troubled, and fear fell upon him.

13But the angel said to him, "Do not be afraid, Zacharias, for your prayer is heard; and your wife Elizabeth will bear you a son, and you shall call his name John."

DEVOTIONAL

It seems amazing that Jesus' followers had such a difficult time believing He had risen from the dead, and yet Mark's account makes it plain. Those who did not see simply did not believe. Jesus' resurrection was so astounding and so supernatural that people couldn't grasp the reality of its occurrence.

Perhaps it is unfair to be hard on them. After all, we often walk in unbelief as well. We who know the whole story of Jesus—even how it ends—often struggle to live as though He is alive today.

The fact that the disciples eventually professed belief in Christ and went out and preached about the truth of Jesus everywhere shows that they became fully convinced of His resurrection. Their eyewitness accounts should help us believe and tell others too.

What signs of belief accompany your everyday life? Do you minister to people through prayer and intervention? Do you walk with boldness and confidence? Do you go out and, in some sense, preach everywhere? Start walking in obedience today by praying, "Lord, I believe! Help me live as though I do."

—John Meador
First Baptist Church, Euless, TX

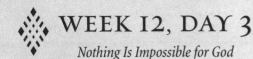

WEEK 12, DAY 3

Nothing Is Impossible for God

Luke 1:14–45

"And you will have joy and gladness, and many will rejoice at his birth. ¹⁵For he will be great in the sight of the Lord, and shall drink neither wine nor strong drink. He will also be filled with the Holy Spirit, even from his mother's womb. ¹⁶And he will turn many of the children of Israel to the Lord their God. ¹⁷He will also go before Him in the spirit and power of Elijah, 'to turn the hearts of the fathers to the children,' and the disobedient to the wisdom of the just, to make ready a people prepared for the Lord."

¹⁸And Zacharias said to the angel, "How shall I know this? For I am an old man, and my wife is well advanced in years."

¹⁹And the angel answered and said to him, "I am Gabriel, who stands in the presence of God, and was sent to speak to you and bring you these glad tidings. ²⁰But behold, you will be mute and not able to speak until the day these things take place, because you did not believe my words which will be fulfilled in their own time."

²¹And the people waited for Zacharias, and marveled that he lingered so long in the temple. ²²But when he came out, he could not speak to them; and they perceived that he had seen a vision in the temple, for he beckoned to them and remained speechless.

²³So it was, as soon as the days of his service were completed, that he departed to his own house. ²⁴Now after those days his wife Elizabeth conceived; and she hid herself five months, saying, ²⁵"Thus the Lord has dealt with me, in the days when He looked on me, to take away my reproach among people."

Christ's Birth Announced to Mary

²⁶Now in the sixth month the angel Gabriel was sent by God to a city of Galilee named Nazareth, ²⁷to a virgin betrothed to a man whose name was Joseph, of the house of David. The virgin's name was Mary. ²⁸And having come in, the angel said to her, "Rejoice, highly favored one, the Lord is with you; blessed are you among women!"

²⁹But when she saw him, she was troubled at his saying, and considered what manner of greeting this was. ³⁰Then the angel said to her, "Do not be afraid, Mary, for you have found favor with God. ³¹And behold, you will conceive in your womb and bring forth a Son, and shall call His name JESUS. ³²He will be great, and will be called the Son of the Highest; and the Lord God will give Him the throne of His father David. ³³And He will reign over the house of Jacob forever, and of His kingdom there will be no end."

³⁴Then Mary said to the angel, "How can this be, since I do not know a man?"

³⁵And the angel answered and said to her, "The Holy Spirit will come upon you, and the power of the Highest will overshadow you; therefore, also, that Holy One who is to be born will be called the Son of God. ³⁶Now indeed, Elizabeth your relative has also conceived a son in her old age; and this is now the sixth month for her who was called barren. ³⁷For with God nothing will be impossible."

³⁸Then Mary said, "Behold the maidservant of the Lord! Let it be to me according to your word." And the angel departed from her.

Mary Visits Elizabeth

³⁹Now Mary arose in those days and went into the hill country with haste, to a city of Judah, ⁴⁰and entered the house of Zacharias and greeted Elizabeth. ⁴¹And it happened, when Elizabeth heard the greeting of Mary, that the babe leaped in her womb; and Elizabeth was filled with the Holy Spirit. ⁴²Then she spoke out with a loud voice and said, "Blessed are you among women, and blessed is the fruit of your womb! ⁴³But why is this granted to me, that the mother of my Lord should come to me? ⁴⁴For indeed, as soon as the voice of your greeting sounded in my ears, the babe leaped in my womb for joy. ⁴⁵Blessed is she who believed, for there will be a fulfillment of those things which were told her from the Lord."

DEVOTIONAL

When God acts in human lives, He always seems to use the unlikeliest people at the unlikeliest times of their lives. God ordained that a barren Elizabeth and her older husband would have a son who would be known as John, and that a teenage virgin named Mary would bear a Son and call Him Jesus. Understandably, Mary asked, "How can this be?" The angel answered her well by saying, "With God nothing will be impossible" (Luke 1:34, 37).

Today, God may choose to use you in a powerful way in His kingdom or lead you to speak simple words of truth to someone in need. When you wonder how God can use you, remember the answer of the angel.

—John Meador
First Baptist Church, Euless, TX

WEEK 12, DAY 4

Rejoice and Magnify the Lord

Luke 1:46–77

The Song of Mary

And Mary said:

"My soul magnifies the Lord,
47 And my spirit has rejoiced in God my Savior.
48 For He has regarded the lowly state of His
    maidservant;
    For behold, henceforth all generations will call
    me blessed.
49 For He who is mighty has done great things for me,
    And holy is His name.
50 And His mercy is on those who fear Him
    From generation to generation.
51 He has shown strength with His arm;
    He has scattered the proud in the imagination
        of their hearts.
52 He has put down the mighty from their thrones,
    And exalted the lowly.
53 He has filled the hungry with good things,
    And the rich He has sent away empty.
54 He has helped His servant Israel,
    In remembrance of His mercy,
55 As He spoke to our fathers,
    To Abraham and to his seed forever."

56And Mary remained with her about three months, and returned to her house.

Birth of John the Baptist

57Now Elizabeth's full time came for her to be delivered, and she brought forth a son. 58When her neighbors and relatives heard how the Lord had shown great mercy to her, they rejoiced with her.

Circumcision of John the Baptist

59So it was, on the eighth day, that they came to circumcise the child; and they would have called him by the name of his father, Zacharias. 60His mother answered and said, "No; he shall be called John."

61But they said to her, "There is no one among your relatives who is called by this name." 62So they made signs to his father—what he would have him called.

63And he asked for a writing tablet, and wrote, saying, "His name is John." So they all marveled. 64Immediately his mouth was opened and his tongue loosed, and he spoke, praising God. 65Then fear came on all who dwelt around them; and all these sayings were discussed throughout all the hill country of Judea. 66And all those who heard them kept them in their hearts, saying, "What kind of child will this be?" And the hand of the Lord was with him.

Zacharias' Prophecy

67Now his father Zacharias was filled with the Holy Spirit, and prophesied, saying:

68 "Blessed is the Lord God of Israel,
    For He has visited and redeemed His people,
69 And has raised up a horn of salvation for us
    In the house of His servant David,
70 As He spoke by the mouth of His holy prophets,
    Who have been since the world began,
71 That we should be saved from our enemies
    And from the hand of all who hate us,
72 To perform the mercy promised to our fathers
    And to remember His holy covenant,
73 The oath which He swore to our father Abraham:
74 To grant us that we,
    Being delivered from the hand of our enemies,
    Might serve Him without fear,
75 In holiness and righteousness before Him all the
        days of our life.

76 "And you, child, will be called the prophet of
        the Highest;
    For you will go before the face of the Lord to
        prepare His ways,
77 To give knowledge of salvation to His people
    By the remission of their sins."

DEVOTIONAL

When God spoke to Mary, and when God fulfilled His prophecy to Zacharias and Elizabeth, they rejoiced! These passages are full of the joyful responses of people who saw the Lord at work. Zacharias rejoiced in what had already happened. Mary rejoiced in what was yet to come. Both lifted up their voices to magnify the Lord! We exist to bring glory and honor to the Lord. If humanity's "chief end" is "to glorify God and enjoy Him forever," as the famous catechism teaches, how will you advance that in your life today?

—John Meador
First Baptist Church, Euless, TX

LUKE

WEEK 12, DAY 5
The Spectacular Versus the Significant

Luke 1:78–2:26

"Through the tender mercy of our God,
With which the Dayspring from on high has visited us;
79 To give light to those who sit in darkness and the shadow of death,
To guide our feet into the way of peace."

80So the child grew and became strong in spirit, and was in the deserts till the day of his manifestation to Israel.

Christ Born of Mary

2 And it came to pass in those days that a decree went out from Caesar Augustus that all the world should be registered. 2This census first took place while Quirinius was governing Syria. 3So all went to be registered, everyone to his own city.

4Joseph also went up from Galilee, out of the city of Nazareth, into Judea, to the city of David, which is called Bethlehem, because he was of the house and lineage of David, 5to be registered with Mary, his betrothed wife, who was with child. 6So it was, that while they were there, the days were completed for her to be delivered. 7And she brought forth her firstborn Son, and wrapped Him in swaddling cloths, and laid Him in a manger, because there was no room for them in the inn.

Glory in the Highest

8Now there were in the same country shepherds living out in the fields, keeping watch over their flock by night. 9And behold, an angel of the Lord stood before them, and the glory of the Lord shone around them, and they were greatly afraid. 10Then the angel said to them, "Do not be afraid, for behold, I bring you good tidings of great joy which will be to all people. 11For there is born to you this day in the city of David a Savior, who is Christ the Lord. 12And this will be the sign to you: You will find a Babe wrapped in swaddling cloths, lying in a manger."

13And suddenly there was with the angel a multitude of the heavenly host praising God and saying:

14 "Glory to God in the highest,
And on earth peace, goodwill toward men!"

15So it was, when the angels had gone away from them into heaven, that the shepherds said to one another, "Let us now go to Bethlehem and see this thing that has come to pass, which the Lord has made known to us." 16And they came with haste and found Mary and Joseph, and the Babe lying in a manger. 17Now when they had seen Him, they made widely known the saying which was told them concerning this Child. 18And all those who heard it marveled at those things which were told them by the shepherds. 19But Mary kept all these things and pondered them in her heart. 20Then the shepherds returned, glorifying and praising God for all the things that they had heard and seen, as it was told them.

Circumcision of Jesus

21And when eight days were completed for the circumcision of the Child, His name was called Jesus, the name given by the angel before He was conceived in the womb.

Jesus Presented in the Temple

22Now when the days of her purification according to the law of Moses were completed, they brought Him to Jerusalem to present Him to the Lord 23(as it is written in the law of the Lord, "Every male who opens the womb shall be called holy to the Lord"), 24and to offer a sacrifice according to what is said in the law of the Lord, "A pair of turtledoves or two young pigeons."

Simeon Sees God's Salvation

25And behold, there was a man in Jerusalem whose name was Simeon, and this man was just and devout, waiting for the Consolation of Israel, and the Holy Spirit was upon him. 26And it had been revealed to him by the Holy Spirit that he would not see death before he had seen the Lord's Christ.

DEVOTIONAL

What an unexpected entrance! While the world expected the arrival of a Messiah, they did not expect Him to come this way. It's a humble picture: a virgin mother, a smelly stable, an obscure location. Even the shepherds who were the first to hear the announcement were the humblest of means and standing. No wonder Mary pondered in her heart. It seemed nothing like what one would suppose. And yet, it was clearly divine.

How often have you looked for the spectacular, and missed the significant?

—John Meador
First Baptist Church, Euless, TX

83

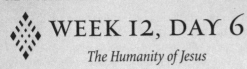

WEEK 12, DAY 6

The Humanity of Jesus

Luke 2:27–52

So he came by the Spirit into the temple. And when the parents brought in the Child Jesus, to do for Him according to the custom of the law, 28he took Him up in his arms and blessed God and said:

29 "Lord, now You are letting Your servant depart
     in peace,
     According to Your word;
30 For my eyes have seen Your salvation
31 Which You have prepared before the face of
     all peoples,
32 A light to bring revelation to the Gentiles,
     And the glory of Your people Israel."

33And Joseph and His mother marveled at those things which were spoken of Him. 34Then Simeon blessed them, and said to Mary His mother, "Behold, this Child is destined for the fall and rising of many in Israel, and for a sign which will be spoken against 35(yes, a sword will pierce through your own soul also), that the thoughts of many hearts may be revealed."

Anna Bears Witness to the Redeemer

36Now there was one, Anna, a prophetess, the daughter of Phanuel, of the tribe of Asher. She was of a great age, and had lived with a husband seven years from her virginity; 37and this woman was a widow of about eighty-four years, who did not depart from the temple, but served God with fastings and prayers night and day. 38And coming in that instant she gave thanks to the Lord, and spoke of Him to all those who looked for redemption in Jerusalem.

The Family Returns to Nazareth

39So when they had performed all things according to the law of the Lord, they returned to Galilee, to their own city, Nazareth. 40And the Child grew and became strong in spirit, filled with wisdom; and the grace of God was upon Him.

The Boy Jesus Amazes the Scholars

41His parents went to Jerusalem every year at the Feast of the Passover. 42And when He was twelve years old, they went up to Jerusalem according to the custom of the feast. 43When they had finished the days, as they returned, the Boy Jesus lingered behind in Jerusalem. And Joseph and His mother did not know it; 44but supposing Him to have been in the company, they went a day's journey, and sought Him among their relatives and acquaintances. 45So when they did not find Him, they returned to Jerusalem, seeking Him. 46Now so it was that after three days they found Him in the temple, sitting in the midst of the teachers, both listening to them and asking them questions. 47And all who heard Him were astonished at His understanding and answers. 48So when they saw Him, they were amazed; and His mother said to Him, "Son, why have You done this to us? Look, Your father and I have sought You anxiously."

49And He said to them, "Why did you seek Me? Did you not know that I must be about My Father's business?" 50But they did not understand the statement which He spoke to them.

Jesus Advances in Wisdom and Favor

51Then He went down with them and came to Nazareth, and was subject to them, but His mother kept all these things in her heart. 52And Jesus increased in wisdom and stature, and in favor with God and men.

DEVOTIONAL

This passage contains some of the few words we have about Jesus' childhood. They reveal the amazing process of the infinite God-Man becoming mature. He grew, became strong, and was filled with wisdom. He increased in stature and favor with both God and people (Luke 2:52). These words could describe anyone. Yet they describe Jesus, the Son of God, in His younger years in human flesh.

What a powerful reminder that we have a Savior and Lord who has walked with us through literally every step of life. He was at one point young and inexperienced. He grew and matured. He was misunderstood by His parents and others. He gained His maturity by carefully walking with His heavenly Father, something we are also called to do.

Be encouraged by the reality that "we do not have a High Priest who cannot sympathize with our weaknesses, but was in all points tempted as we are, yet without sin" (Hebrews 4:15). Jesus understands your struggles. Let Him lead you and empower you to obey the Father today.

—John Meador
First Baptist Church, Euless, TX

WEEK 12, DAY 7

In what way does your life reflect a heart of belief in Jesus? If the signs that accompanied the early believers were so radical, what signs accompany your life today?

Have you missed the significant while searching for the sensational and spectacular? How are you tempted to lay aside the eternal in order to experience the temporal, and how are you responding to that temptation?

WEEK 13, DAY I

Fulfilling a Role in God's Plan

Luke 3:1–22

John the Baptist Prepares the Way

3 Now in the fifteenth year of the reign of Tiberius Caesar, Pontius Pilate being governor of Judea, Herod being tetrarch of Galilee, his brother Philip tetrarch of Iturea and the region of Trachonitis, and Lysanias tetrarch of Abilene, 2while Annas and Caiaphas were high priests, the word of God came to John the son of Zacharias in the wilderness. 3And he went into all the region around the Jordan, preaching a baptism of repentance for the remission of sins, 4as it is written in the book of the words of Isaiah the prophet, saying:

> "The voice of one crying in the wilderness:
> 'Prepare the way of the LORD;
> Make His paths straight.
> 5 Every valley shall be filled
> And every mountain and hill brought low;
> The crooked places shall be made straight
> And the rough ways smooth;
> 6 And all flesh shall see the salvation of God.'"

John Preaches to the People

7Then he said to the multitudes that came out to be baptized by him, "Brood of vipers! Who warned you to flee from the wrath to come? 8Therefore bear fruits worthy of repentance, and do not begin to say to yourselves, 'We have Abraham as our father.' For I say to you that God is able to raise up children to Abraham from these stones. 9And even now the ax is laid to the root of the trees. Therefore every tree which does not bear good fruit is cut down and thrown into the fire."

10So the people asked him, saying, "What shall we do then?"

11He answered and said to them, "He who has two tunics, let him give to him who has none; and he who has food, let him do likewise."

12Then tax collectors also came to be baptized, and said to him, "Teacher, what shall we do?"

13And he said to them, "Collect no more than what is appointed for you."

14Likewise the soldiers asked him, saying, "And what shall we do?"

So he said to them, "Do not intimidate anyone or accuse falsely, and be content with your wages."

15Now as the people were in expectation, and all reasoned in their hearts about John, whether he was the Christ or not, 16John answered, saying to all, "I indeed baptize you with water; but One mightier than I is coming, whose sandal strap I am not worthy to loose. He will baptize you with the Holy Spirit and fire. 17His winnowing fan is in His hand, and He will thoroughly clean out His threshing floor, and gather the wheat into His barn; but the chaff He will burn with unquenchable fire."

18And with many other exhortations he preached to the people. 19But Herod the tetrarch, being rebuked by him concerning Herodias, his brother Philip's wife, and for all the evils which Herod had done, 20also added this, above all, that he shut John up in prison.

John Baptizes Jesus

21When all the people were baptized, it came to pass that Jesus also was baptized; and while He prayed, the heaven was opened. 22And the Holy Spirit descended in bodily form like a dove upon Him, and a voice came from heaven which said, "You are My beloved Son; in You I am well pleased."

DEVOTIONAL

In commenting upon the life and ministry of John the Baptist, the apostle John simply declared, "There was a man sent from God, whose name was John" (John 1:6). He appeared on the public scene, accomplished what God sent him to do, and then moved away from view, quickly slipping into the shadows of obscurity.

Unimpressive in appearance but bold in proclamation, this unique man from the wilderness harbored no vain illusions of grandeur. John was wise enough to know who he was and who he wasn't, and he was perfectly content to fulfill his significant yet limited role. His will was aligned with the will of God. He wanted to see Jesus at work, exalted and glorified, saying, "He must increase, but I must decrease" (John 3:30).

That's a worthy life aim for the child of God. Wherever you find yourself today, keep John's attitude of submission and love for Jesus in your heart. Carry out your role in God's will, and lift up the name of Christ.

—Junior Hill
Junior Hill Ministries, Hartselle, AL

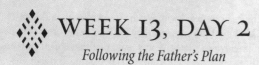

WEEK 13, DAY 2

Following the Father's Plan

Luke 3:23–4:13

The Genealogy of Jesus Christ

Now Jesus Himself began His ministry at about thirty years of age, being (as was supposed) the son of Joseph, the son of Heli, 24the son of Matthat, the son of Levi, the son of Melchi, the son of Janna, the son of Joseph, 25the son of Mattathiah, the son of Amos, the son of Nahum, the son of Esli, the son of Naggai, 26the son of Maath, the son of Mattathiah, the son of Semei, the son of Joseph, the son of Judah, 27the son of Joannas, the son of Rhesa, the son of Zerubbabel, the son of Shealtiel, the son of Neri, 28the son of Melchi, the son of Addi, the son of Cosam, the son of Elmodam, the son of Er, 29the son of Jose, the son of Eliezer, the son of Jorim, the son of Matthat, the son of Levi, 30the son of Simeon, the son of Judah, the son of Joseph, the son of Jonan, the son of Eliakim, 31the son of Melea, the son of Menan, the son of Mattathah, the son of Nathan, the son of David, 32the son of Jesse, the son of Obed, the son of Boaz, the son of Salmon, the son of Nahshon, 33the son of Amminadab, the son of Ram, the son of Hezron, the son of Perez, the son of Judah, 34the son of Jacob, the son of Isaac, the son of Abraham, the son of Terah, the son of Nahor, 35the son of Serug, the son of Reu, the son of Peleg, the son of Eber, the son of Shelah, 36the son of Cainan, the son of Arphaxad, the son of Shem, the son of Noah, the son of Lamech, 37the son of Methuselah, the son of Enoch, the son of Jared, the son of Mahalalel, the son of Cainan, 38the son of Enosh, the son of Seth, the son of Adam, the son of God.

Satan Tempts Jesus

4Then Jesus, being filled with the Holy Spirit, returned from the Jordan and was led by the Spirit into the wilderness, 2being tempted for forty days by the devil. And in those days He ate nothing, and afterward, when they had ended, He was hungry.

3And the devil said to Him, "If You are the Son of God, command this stone to become bread."

4But Jesus answered him, saying, "It is written, 'Man shall not live by bread alone, but by every word of God.'"

5Then the devil, taking Him up on a high mountain, showed Him all the kingdoms of the world in a moment of time. 6And the devil said to Him, "All this authority I will give You, and their glory; for this has been delivered to me, and I give it to whomever I wish. 7Therefore, if You will worship before me, all will be Yours."

8And Jesus answered and said to him, "Get behind Me, Satan! For it is written, 'You shall worship the LORD your God, and Him only you shall serve.'"

9Then he brought Him to Jerusalem, set Him on the pinnacle of the temple, and said to Him, "If You are the Son of God, throw Yourself down from here. 10For it is written:

'He shall give His angels charge over you,
To keep you,'

11and,

'In their hands they shall bear you up,
Lest you dash your foot against a stone.'"

12And Jesus answered and said to him, "It has been said, 'You shall not tempt the LORD your God.'"

13Now when the devil had ended every temptation, he departed from Him until an opportune time.

DEVOTIONAL

When the devil tempted Jesus, he already knew who He was, what He could do, and who protected Him. Yet he challenged Him to turn stone into bread, to worship him, and to throw Himself down from the top of the temple. The most sinister part about Satan's temptations was that he attempted to make Jesus prove His divinity on command. Satan opened two of his challenges with the phrase, "If You are the Son of God . . ." (Luke 4:3, 9). It was clearly a call for authentication by demonstration, suggesting, "If You can't show it, then you don't have it."

T. S. Eliot wrote, "The last temptation is the greatest treason: to do the right deed for the wrong reason."5 Jesus could have shown His divine power that day. He certainly put it on display later in His public ministry through His miracles. But He served one Master—His Father. He was very clear that He only did what the Father led Him to do (John 5:19).

Following the Father's plan means doing the right thing at the right time for the right reason. Is there anything you're considering doing for the wrong reason? Be honest about your motivations, and ask God for wisdom and guidance. Make the Father your Master.

—Junior Hill
Junior Hill Ministries, Hartselle, AL

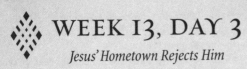

WEEK 13, DAY 3

Jesus' Hometown Rejects Him

Luke 4:14–30

Jesus Begins His Galilean Ministry

Then Jesus returned in the power of the Spirit to Galilee, and news of Him went out through all the surrounding region. 15And He taught in their synagogues, being glorified by all.

Jesus Rejected at Nazareth

16So He came to Nazareth, where He had been brought up. And as His custom was, He went into the synagogue on the Sabbath day, and stood up to read. 17And He was handed the book of the prophet Isaiah. And when He had opened the book, He found the place where it was written:

18   "The Spirit of the LORD is upon Me,
     Because He has anointed Me
     To preach the gospel to the poor;
     He has sent Me to heal the brokenhearted,
     To proclaim liberty to the captives
     And recovery of sight to the blind,
     To set at liberty those who are oppressed;
19   To proclaim the acceptable year of the LORD."

20Then He closed the book, and gave it back to the attendant and sat down. And the eyes of all who were in the synagogue were fixed on Him. 21And He began to say to them, "Today this Scripture is fulfilled in your hearing." 22So all bore witness to Him, and marveled at the gracious words which proceeded out of His mouth. And they said, "Is this not Joseph's son?"

23He said to them, "You will surely say this proverb to Me, 'Physician, heal yourself! Whatever we have heard done in Capernaum, do also here in Your country.'" 24Then He said, "Assuredly, I say to you, no prophet is accepted in his own country. 25But I tell you truly, many widows were in Israel in the days of Elijah, when the heaven was shut up three years and six months, and there was a great famine throughout all the land; 26but to none of them was Elijah sent except to Zarephath, in the region of Sidon, to a woman who was a widow. 27And many lepers were in Israel in the time of Elisha the prophet, and none of them was cleansed except Naaman the Syrian."

28So all those in the synagogue, when they heard these things, were filled with wrath, 29and rose up and thrust Him out of the city; and they led Him to the brow of the hill on which their city was built, that they might throw Him down over the cliff. 30Then passing through the midst of them, He went His way.

DEVOTIONAL

The warm welcome Jesus received in His hometown of Nazareth was short-lived. At first, His audience in the synagogue was open and respectful to His preaching—so much so that they "marveled at the gracious words which proceeded out of His mouth" (Luke 4:22). They could hardly believe their ears! They were absolutely astounded that a local young man, the son of a common citizen like Joseph, could speak such wonderful and prophetic words.

But while Jesus' listeners loved His mention of the poor, the brokenhearted, the captives, and the oppressed, they were incensed when He dared to suggest that God was also interested in showing favor to the Gentiles. Jesus reminded them of several times when God had chosen to bless or heal a Gentile in the past, when there were plenty of Israelites He could have blessed instead. Jesus was subtly telling His listeners that if Nazareth, and all of Israel, did not accept Him as Messiah, He would extend His grace to the Gentiles. At these words, the people were filled with wrath, and they kicked Him out of the city and even came close to killing Him. This scene is an illustration of something Havelock Ellis wrote: "When love is suppressed, hate takes its place."

Jesus' message was not just unpopular but spitefully, violently rejected. Jesus told His disciples they could expect to be hated by the world just like He was (John 15:18). Following Jesus often involves going against the grain of the crowd—maybe our friends or family—and things can get ugly fast. When it is painful, remember what an honor it is to belong to God in Christ. Paul described believers as "children of God without fault in the midst of a crooked and perverse generation, among whom you shine as lights in the world" (Philippians 2:15). Remember this description of God's will for you as His child and inhabit it. Stay true to Jesus and keep on the path of life.

—Junior Hill
Junior Hill Ministries, Hartselle, AL

WEEK 13, DAY 4

Trust God's Leading

Luke 4:31–5:11

Jesus Casts Out an Unclean Spirit

Then He went down to Capernaum, a city of Galilee, and was teaching them on the Sabbaths. ³²And they were astonished at His teaching, for His word was with authority. ³³Now in the synagogue there was a man who had a spirit of an unclean demon. And he cried out with a loud voice, ³⁴saying, "Let us alone! What have we to do with You, Jesus of Nazareth? Did You come to destroy us? I know who You are—the Holy One of God!"

³⁵But Jesus rebuked him, saying, "Be quiet, and come out of him!" And when the demon had thrown him in their midst, it came out of him and did not hurt him. ³⁶Then they were all amazed and spoke among themselves, saying, "What a word this is! For with authority and power He commands the unclean spirits, and they come out." ³⁷And the report about Him went out into every place in the surrounding region.

Peter's Mother-in-Law Healed

³⁸Now He arose from the synagogue and entered Simon's house. But Simon's wife's mother was sick with a high fever, and they made request of Him concerning her. ³⁹So He stood over her and rebuked the fever, and it left her. And immediately she arose and served them.

Many Healed After Sabbath Sunset

⁴⁰When the sun was setting, all those who had any that were sick with various diseases brought them to Him; and He laid His hands on every one of them and healed them. ⁴¹And demons also came out of many, crying out and saying, "You are the Christ, the Son of God!" And He, rebuking them, did not allow them to speak, for they knew that He was the Christ.

Jesus Preaches in Galilee

⁴²Now when it was day, He departed and went into a deserted place. And the crowd sought Him and came to Him, and tried to keep Him from leaving them; ⁴³but He said to them, "I must preach the kingdom of God to the other cities also, because for this purpose I have been sent." ⁴⁴And He was preaching in the synagogues of Galilee.

Four Fishermen Called as Disciples

5 So it was, as the multitude pressed about Him to hear the word of God, that He stood by the Lake of Gennesaret, ²and saw two boats standing by the lake; but the fishermen had gone from them and were washing their nets. ³Then He got into one of the boats, which was Simon's, and asked him to put out a little from the land. And He sat down and taught the multitudes from the boat.

⁴When He had stopped speaking, He said to Simon, "Launch out into the deep and let down your nets for a catch."

⁵But Simon answered and said to Him, "Master, we have toiled all night and caught nothing; nevertheless at Your word I will let down the net." ⁶And when they had done this, they caught a great number of fish, and their net was breaking. ⁷So they signaled to their partners in the other boat to come and help them. And they came and filled both the boats, so that they began to sink. ⁸When Simon Peter saw it, he fell down at Jesus' knees, saying, "Depart from me, for I am a sinful man, O Lord!"

⁹For he and all who were with him were astonished at the catch of fish which they had taken; ¹⁰and so also were James and John, the sons of Zebedee, who were partners with Simon. And Jesus said to Simon, "Do not be afraid. From now on you will catch men." ¹¹So when they had brought their boats to land, they forsook all and followed Him.

DEVOTIONAL

Being told what to do is not always easy, especially when you think you know more than your instructor. When Jesus commanded Peter to "launch out into the deep and let down your nets for a catch" (Luke 5:4), Peter challenged the idea. His initial response to Jesus' command could be read as having an air of cockiness: "Master, we have toiled all night and caught nothing" (v. 5). He seemed to infer that as a professional fisherman, he knew more about catching fish than Jesus did. However, he then said, "Nevertheless at Your word I will let down the net" (v. 5).

Praise God that Peter was a "nevertheless" disciple! His first duty as a follower of Jesus was to obey Him. Wouldn't it be wonderful if we all would confess that Jesus knows more than we do? He is God and we are not. "Trust in the LORD with all your heart, and lean not on your own understanding" (Proverbs 3:5). Like Peter, put faith in Christ by saying, "Nevertheless . . . I will do as You say, Lord."

—Junior Hill
Junior Hill Ministries, Hartselle, AL

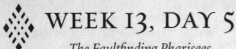

WEEK 13, DAY 5

The Faultfinding Pharisees

Luke 5:12–35

Jesus Cleanses a Leper

And it happened when He was in a certain city, that behold, a man who was full of leprosy saw Jesus; and he fell on his face and implored Him, saying, "Lord, if You are willing, You can make me clean."

¹³Then He put out His hand and touched him, saying, "I am willing; be cleansed." Immediately the leprosy left him. ¹⁴And He charged him to tell no one, "But go and show yourself to the priest, and make an offering for your cleansing, as a testimony to them, just as Moses commanded."

¹⁵However, the report went around concerning Him all the more; and great multitudes came together to hear, and to be healed by Him of their infirmities. ¹⁶So He Himself often withdrew into the wilderness and prayed.

Jesus Forgives and Heals a Paralytic

¹⁷Now it happened on a certain day, as He was teaching, that there were Pharisees and teachers of the law sitting by, who had come out of every town of Galilee, Judea, and Jerusalem. And the power of the Lord was present to heal them. ¹⁸Then behold, men brought on a bed a man who was paralyzed, whom they sought to bring in and lay before Him. ¹⁹And when they could not find how they might bring him in, because of the crowd, they went up on the housetop and let him down with his bed through the tiling into the midst before Jesus.

²⁰When He saw their faith, He said to him, "Man, your sins are forgiven you."

²¹And the scribes and the Pharisees began to reason, saying, "Who is this who speaks blasphemies? Who can forgive sins but God alone?"

²²But when Jesus perceived their thoughts, He answered and said to them, "Why are you reasoning in your hearts? ²³Which is easier, to say, 'Your sins are forgiven you,' or to say, 'Rise up and walk'? ²⁴But that you may know that the Son of Man has power on earth to forgive sins"—He said to the man who was paralyzed, "I say to you, arise, take up your bed, and go to your house."

²⁵Immediately he rose up before them, took up what he had been lying on, and departed to his own house, glorifying God. ²⁶And they were all amazed, and they glorified God and were filled with fear, saying, "We have seen strange things today!"

Matthew the Tax Collector

²⁷After these things He went out and saw a tax collector named Levi, sitting at the tax office. And He said to him, "Follow Me." ²⁸So he left all, rose up, and followed Him.

²⁹Then Levi gave Him a great feast in his own house. And there were a great number of tax collectors and others who sat down with them. ³⁰And their scribes and the Pharisees complained against His disciples, saying, "Why do You eat and drink with tax collectors and sinners?"

³¹Jesus answered and said to them, "Those who are well have no need of a physician, but those who are sick. ³²I have not come to call the righteous, but sinners, to repentance."

Jesus Is Questioned About Fasting

³³Then they said to Him, "Why do the disciples of John fast often and make prayers, and likewise those of the Pharisees, but Yours eat and drink?"

³⁴And He said to them, "Can you make the friends of the bridegroom fast while the bridegroom is with them? ³⁵But the days will come when the bridegroom will be taken away from them; then they will fast in those days."

DEVOTIONAL

No matter what Jesus did, the Pharisees never liked Him. They accused Him of doing things for the wrong reason, on the wrong day, or to the wrong person. They said He did too much or too little. The Pharisees' usual response to Jesus' good deeds or miracles was to "reason" among themselves (Luke 5:21), which is just a polite way of saying that they vainly searched for a way to condemn Him. They always found it—they were determined to find faults in Jesus. Talk about misplaced priorities! Is it any wonder that Jesus told them, "Woe to you, scribes and Pharisees, hypocrites! For you are like whitewashed tombs which appear beautiful outwardly, but inside are full of dead men's bones and all uncleanness" (Matthew 23:27)?

Don't let faultfinding become a way of life like the Pharisees did. Pray for God to rid you of self-righteousness and to help you keep a humble, repentant heart that is loving, gracious, and generous toward others.

—Junior Hill
Junior Hill Ministries, Hartselle, AL

WEEK 13, DAY 6

Having a Heart Full of Hope

Luke 5:36–6:23

Then He spoke a parable to them: "No one puts a piece from a new garment on an old one; otherwise the new makes a tear, and also the piece that was taken out of the new does not match the old. ³⁷And no one puts new wine into old wineskins; or else the new wine will burst the wineskins and be spilled, and the wineskins will be ruined. ³⁸But new wine must be put into new wineskins, and both are preserved. ³⁹And no one, having drunk old wine, immediately desires new; for he says, 'The old is better.'"

Jesus Is Lord of the Sabbath

6Now it happened on the second Sabbath after the first that He went through the grainfields. And His disciples plucked the heads of grain and ate them, rubbing them in their hands. ²And some of the Pharisees said to them, "Why are you doing what is not lawful to do on the Sabbath?"

³But Jesus answering them said, "Have you not even read this, what David did when he was hungry, he and those who were with him: ⁴how he went into the house of God, took and ate the showbread, and also gave some to those with him, which is not lawful for any but the priests to eat?" ⁵And He said to them, "The Son of Man is also Lord of the Sabbath."

Healing on the Sabbath

⁶Now it happened on another Sabbath, also, that He entered the synagogue and taught. And a man was there whose right hand was withered. ⁷So the scribes and Pharisees watched Him closely, whether He would heal on the Sabbath, that they might find an accusation against Him. ⁸But He knew their thoughts, and said to the man who had the withered hand, "Arise and stand here." And he arose and stood. ⁹Then Jesus said to them, "I will ask you one thing: Is it lawful on the Sabbath to do good or to do evil, to save life or to destroy?" ¹⁰And when He had looked around at them all, He said to the man, "Stretch out your hand." And he did so, and his hand was restored as whole as the other. ¹¹But they were filled with rage, and discussed with one another what they might do to Jesus.

The Twelve Apostles

¹²Now it came to pass in those days that He went out to the mountain to pray, and continued all night in prayer to God. ¹³And when it was day, He called His disciples to Himself; and from them He chose twelve whom He also named apostles: ¹⁴Simon, whom He also named Peter, and Andrew his brother; James and John; Philip and Bartholomew; ¹⁵Matthew and Thomas; James the son of Alphaeus, and Simon called the Zealot; ¹⁶Judas the son of James, and Judas Iscariot who also became a traitor.

Jesus Heals a Great Multitude

¹⁷And He came down with them and stood on a level place with a crowd of His disciples and a great multitude of people from all Judea and Jerusalem, and from the seacoast of Tyre and Sidon, who came to hear Him and be healed of their diseases, ¹⁸as well as those who were tormented with unclean spirits. And they were healed. ¹⁹And the whole multitude sought to touch Him, for power went out from Him and healed them all.

The Beatitudes

²⁰Then He lifted up His eyes toward His disciples, and said:

"Blessed are you poor,
For yours is the kingdom of God.
²¹ Blessed are you who hunger now,
For you shall be filled.
Blessed are you who weep now,
For you shall laugh.
²² Blessed are you when men hate you,
And when they exclude you,
And revile you, and cast out your name as evil,
For the Son of Man's sake.
²³ Rejoice in that day and leap for joy!
For indeed your reward is great in heaven,
For in like manner their fathers did to the prophets."

DEVOTIONAL

Jesus lived in the world, but He was never bound to it. He lived fully in the present, but He could see far beyond it. He told people who they could be and where they could go. He was a future-tense Savior living in a present-tense culture. His words gave people hope and a new direction for their lives.

When your soul is troubled, turn to Jesus' "shall be" statements. Remember, "weeping may endure for a night, but joy comes in the morning" (Psalm 30:5). Dwell on the good to come, and let your heart be full of hope!

—Junior Hill
Junior Hill Ministries, Hartselle, AL

WEEK 13, DAY 7

What is the number one thing that keeps you from being your best for Christ? What can you do to remove that hindrance?

_____

_____

_____

_____

_____

_____

_____

_____

_____

_____

_____

If you knew this would be your last year to live, what would you want to do with your remaining time? Make a list of your top ten goals.

_____

_____

_____

_____

_____

_____

_____

_____

_____

WEEK 14, DAY 1

Having the Father's Heart of Love

Luke 6:24–45

Jesus Pronounces Woes

24 "But woe to you who are rich,
For you have received your consolation.
25 Woe to you who are full,
For you shall hunger.
Woe to you who laugh now,
For you shall mourn and weep.
26 Woe to you when all men speak well of you,
For so did their fathers to the false prophets.

Love Your Enemies

27"But I say to you who hear: Love your enemies, do good to those who hate you, 28bless those who curse you, and pray for those who spitefully use you. 29To him who strikes you on the one cheek, offer the other also. And from him who takes away your cloak, do not withhold your tunic either. 30Give to everyone who asks of you. And from him who takes away your goods do not ask them back. 31And just as you want men to do to you, you also do to them likewise.

32"But if you love those who love you, what credit is that to you? For even sinners love those who love them. 33And if you do good to those who do good to you, what credit is that to you? For even sinners do the same. 34And if you lend to those from whom you hope to receive back, what credit is that to you? For even sinners lend to sinners to receive as much back. 35But love your enemies, do good, and lend, hoping for nothing in return; and your reward will be great, and you will be sons of the Most High. For He is kind to the unthankful and evil. 36Therefore be merciful, just as your Father also is merciful.

Do Not Judge

37"Judge not, and you shall not be judged. Condemn not, and you shall not be condemned. Forgive, and you will be forgiven. 38Give, and it will be given to you: good measure, pressed down, shaken together, and running over will be put into your bosom. For with the same measure that you use, it will be measured back to you."

39And He spoke a parable to them: "Can the blind lead the blind? Will they not both fall into the ditch? 40A disciple is not above his teacher, but everyone who is perfectly trained will be like his teacher. 41And why do you look at the speck in your brother's eye, but do not perceive the plank in your own eye? 42Or how can you say to your brother, 'Brother, let me remove the speck that is in your eye,' when you yourself do not see the plank that is in your own eye? Hypocrite! First remove the plank from your own eye, and then you will see clearly to remove the speck that is in your brother's eye.

A Tree Is Known by Its Fruit

43"For a good tree does not bear bad fruit, nor does a bad tree bear good fruit. 44For every tree is known by its own fruit. For men do not gather figs from thorns, nor do they gather grapes from a bramble bush. 45A good man out of the good treasure of his heart brings forth good; and an evil man out of the evil treasure of his heart brings forth evil. For out of the abundance of the heart his mouth speaks."

DEVOTIONAL

*J*esus came to earth to give us a new heart. He declared that one day His Father would write His law upon our hearts, and today we can experience that. It's different than the law written on tablets of stone because it no longer works from the outside in, but rather, the inside out. This new heart is in fact His heart.

However, if we're not careful, we may believe we have moved forward in our relationship with Christ only to find we have simply changed to a new set of rules. These new mandates from Jesus are no more possible to keep than those received from Mount Sinai. Our only chance at obedience comes from having a redeemed and renewed heart.

One of Jesus' mandates for us is to love our enemies. When Jesus saves us, He gives us life and the ability to give that life to others. Look for ways you can be a distributor of this great life. Who are your enemies? Who has brought you pain, difficulty, or frustration? Rather than responding to your human enemies with judgment, respond with love. Do whatever is good for them, bless them, pray for them, and give them the grace they need. Live out the new heart of love the Father has given you.

—Kenny Chinn
Northside Baptist Church, Wilmington, NC

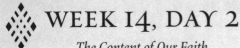

WEEK 14, DAY 2

The Content of Our Faith

Luke 6:46–7:23

Build on the Rock

"But why do you call Me 'Lord, Lord,' and not do the things which I say? 47Whoever comes to Me, and hears My sayings and does them, I will show you whom he is like: 48He is like a man building a house, who dug deep and laid the foundation on the rock. And when the flood arose, the stream beat vehemently against that house, and could not shake it, for it was founded on the rock. 49But he who heard and did nothing is like a man who built a house on the earth without a foundation, against which the stream beat vehemently; and immediately it fell. And the ruin of that house was great."

Jesus Heals a Centurion's Servant

7 Now when He concluded all His sayings in the hearing of the people, He entered Capernaum. 2And a certain centurion's servant, who was dear to him, was sick and ready to die. 3So when he heard about Jesus, he sent elders of the Jews to Him, pleading with Him to come and heal his servant. 4And when they came to Jesus, they begged Him earnestly, saying that the one for whom He should do this was deserving, 5"for he loves our nation, and has built us a synagogue."

6Then Jesus went with them. And when He was already not far from the house, the centurion sent friends to Him, saying to Him, "Lord, do not trouble Yourself, for I am not worthy that You should enter under my roof. 7Therefore I did not even think myself worthy to come to You. But say the word, and my servant will be healed. 8For I also am a man placed under authority, having soldiers under me. And I say to one, 'Go,' and he goes; and to another, 'Come,' and he comes; and to my servant, 'Do this,' and he does it."

9When Jesus heard these things, He marveled at him, and turned around and said to the crowd that followed Him, "I say to you, I have not found such great faith, not even in Israel!" 10And those who were sent, returning to the house, found the servant well who had been sick.

Jesus Raises the Son of the Widow of Nain

11Now it happened, the day after, that He went into a city called Nain; and many of His disciples went with Him, and a large crowd. 12And when He came near the gate of the city, behold, a dead man was being carried out, the only son of his mother; and she was a widow. And a large crowd from the city was with her. 13When the Lord saw her, He had compassion on her and said to her, "Do not weep." 14Then He came and touched the open coffin, and those who carried him stood still. And He said, "Young man, I say to you, arise." 15So he who was dead sat up and began to speak. And He presented him to his mother.

16Then fear came upon all, and they glorified God, saying, "A great prophet has risen up among us"; and, "God has visited His people." 17And this report about Him went throughout all Judea and all the surrounding region.

John the Baptist Sends Messengers to Jesus

18Then the disciples of John reported to him concerning all these things. 19And John, calling two of his disciples to him, sent them to Jesus, saying, "Are You the Coming One, or do we look for another?"

20When the men had come to Him, they said, "John the Baptist has sent us to You, saying, 'Are You the Coming One, or do we look for another?'" 21And that very hour He cured many of infirmities, afflictions, and evil spirits; and to many blind He gave sight.

22Jesus answered and said to them, "Go and tell John the things you have seen and heard: that the blind see, the lame walk, the lepers are cleansed, the deaf hear, the dead are raised, the poor have the gospel preached to them. 23And blessed is he who is not offended because of Me."

DEVOTIONAL

Belief is sometimes defined by the intensity with which someone accepts or trusts something, but the Bible teaches that belief is defined by its content. In whom or what do we believe? A biblical faith is believing in Jesus and in His Word.

Focusing on the words and actions of Jesus in the New Testament can help cultivate such a faith. Jesus identified Himself clearly, saying He is the Way, the Truth, and the Life, among other things. He explained God's truth in sermons and parables, and He verified His identity through miracles. When John the Baptist questioned Jesus' identity, Jesus pointed to things He'd been doing: He'd healed the sick, raised the dead, and taught the multitudes the principles of life (Luke 7:18–22).

Study God's Word, and let it instruct the content of your faith and give you confidence to trust Him today.

—Kenny Chinn
Northside Baptist Church, Wilmington, NC

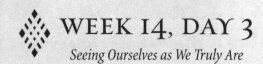

WEEK 14, DAY 3

Seeing Ourselves as We Truly Are

Luke 7:24–50

When the messengers of John had departed, He began to speak to the multitudes concerning John: "What did you go out into the wilderness to see? A reed shaken by the wind? 25But what did you go out to see? A man clothed in soft garments? Indeed those who are gorgeously apparreled and live in luxury are in kings' courts. 26But what did you go out to see? A prophet? Yes, I say to you, and more than a prophet. 27This is he of whom it is written:

'Behold, I send My messenger before Your face,
Who will prepare Your way before You.'

28For I say to you, among those born of women there is not a greater prophet than John the Baptist; but he who is least in the kingdom of God is greater than he."

29And when all the people heard Him, even the tax collectors justified God, having been baptized with the baptism of John. 30But the Pharisees and lawyers rejected the will of God for themselves, not having been baptized by him.

31And the Lord said, "To what then shall I liken the men of this generation, and what are they like? 32They are like children sitting in the marketplace and calling to one another, saying:

'We played the flute for you,
And you did not dance;
We mourned to you,
And you did not weep.'

33For John the Baptist came neither eating bread nor drinking wine, and you say, 'He has a demon.' 34The Son of Man has come eating and drinking, and you say, 'Look, a glutton and a winebibber, a friend of tax collectors and sinners!' 35But wisdom is justified by all her children."

A Sinful Woman Forgiven

36Then one of the Pharisees asked Him to eat with him. And He went to the Pharisee's house, and sat down to eat. 37And behold, a woman in the city who was a sinner, when she knew that Jesus sat at the table in the Pharisee's house, brought an alabaster flask of fragrant oil, 38and stood at His feet behind Him weeping; and she began to wash His feet with her tears, and wiped them with the hair of her head; and she kissed His feet and anointed them with the fragrant oil. 39Now when the Pharisee who had invited Him saw this, he spoke to himself, saying, "This Man, if He were a prophet, would know who and what manner of woman this is who is touching Him, for she is a sinner."

40And Jesus answered and said to him, "Simon, I have something to say to you."

So he said, "Teacher, say it."

41"There was a certain creditor who had two debtors. One owed five hundred denarii, and the other fifty. 42And when they had nothing with which to repay, he freely forgave them both. Tell Me, therefore, which of them will love him more?"

43Simon answered and said, "I suppose the *one* whom he forgave more."

And He said to him, "You have rightly judged." 44Then He turned to the woman and said to Simon, "Do you see this woman? I entered your house; you gave Me no water for My feet, but she has washed My feet with her tears and wiped them with the hair of her head. 45You gave Me no kiss, but this woman has not ceased to kiss My feet since the time I came in. 46You did not anoint My head with oil, but this woman has anointed My feet with fragrant oil. 47Therefore I say to you, her sins, which are many, are forgiven, for she loved much. But to whom little is forgiven, the same loves little."

48Then He said to her, "Your sins are forgiven."

49And those who sat at the table with Him began to say to themselves, "Who is this who even forgives sins?"

50Then He said to the woman, "Your faith has saved you. Go in peace."

DEVOTIONAL

The human eye is a marvel of the human anatomy. Its ability to distinguish the millions of colors in nature or calculate the depth of a meadow is beyond comprehension. It can see up close or to the far reaches of space. But it cannot see itself. All any of us will ever see of ourselves in this life is a mere reflection in a mirror. And what we do see of ourselves we do not believe. Think of a time when you have seen yourself in a photo or heard yourself on a recording. Were you surprised? Our ability to see the faults in others is seemingly flawless, but our ability to see ourselves is certainly flawed. Ask God for the grace to see yourself as you truly are, and He will lead you to have genuine remorse for your sin.

—Kenny Chinn
Northside Baptist Church, Wilmington, NC

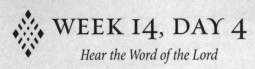

WEEK 14, DAY 4

Hear the Word of the Lord

Luke 8:1–21

Many Women Minister to Jesus

8 Now it came to pass, afterward, that He went through every city and village, preaching and bringing the glad tidings of the kingdom of God. And the twelve were with Him, 2and certain women who had been healed of evil spirits and infirmities—Mary called Magdalene, out of whom had come seven demons, 3and Joanna the wife of Chuza, Herod's steward, and Susanna, and many others who provided for Him from their substance.

The Parable of the Sower

4And when a great multitude had gathered, and they had come to Him from every city, He spoke by a parable: 5"A sower went out to sow his seed. And as he sowed, some fell by the wayside; and it was trampled down, and the birds of the air devoured it. 6Some fell on rock; and as soon as it sprang up, it withered away because it lacked moisture. 7And some fell among thorns, and the thorns sprang up with it and choked it. 8But others fell on good ground, sprang up, and yielded a crop a hundredfold." When He had said these things He cried, "He who has ears to hear, let him hear!"

The Purpose of Parables

9Then His disciples asked Him, saying, "What does this parable mean?"

10And He said, "To you it has been given to know the mysteries of the kingdom of God, but to the rest it is given in parables, that

'Seeing they may not see,
And hearing they may not understand.'

The Parable of the Sower Explained

11"Now the parable is this: The seed is the word of God. 12Those by the wayside are the ones who hear; then the devil comes and takes away the word out of their hearts, lest they should believe and be saved. 13But the ones on the rock are those who, when they hear, receive the word with joy; and these have no root, who believe for a while and in time of temptation fall away. 14Now the ones that fell among thorns are those who, when they have heard, go out and are choked with cares, riches, and pleasures of life, and bring no fruit to maturity. 15But the ones that fell on the good ground are those who, having heard the word with a noble and good heart, keep it and bear fruit with patience.

The Parable of the Revealed Light

16"No one, when he has lit a lamp, covers it with a vessel or puts it under a bed, but sets it on a lampstand, that those who enter may see the light. 17For nothing is secret that will not be revealed, nor anything hidden that will not be known and come to light. 18Therefore take heed how you hear. For whoever has, to him more will be given; and whoever does not have, even what he seems to have will be taken from him."

Jesus' Mother and Brothers Come to Him

19Then His mother and brothers came to Him, and could not approach Him because of the crowd. 20And it was told Him by some, who said, "Your mother and Your brothers are standing outside, desiring to see You."

21But He answered and said to them, "My mother and My brothers are these who hear the word of God and do it."

DEVOTIONAL

One of the reasons Jesus spoke in parables was to keep our minds from wandering into foolish speculation. He spoke of things that were easy to understand—common things with heavenly meanings—in order to teach the deep things of God.

Jesus used the parable of the sower to explain unbelief and shallow faith. Jesus used four different kinds of soil to represent four classes of hearers. Those by the wayside are shallow people who live by the easiest path, avoiding the difficult things. Those in the rocky soil represent people who have become hardened to anything that may require them to feel. Because of their pain, they erect a stone wall to the world and to God. Those in the thorny soil are people who are so attached to the wonders of the world that anything less than a thrill is dismissed. Those in the good soil are people who remain sensitive to the still, small voice of God.

Jesus admonished, "He who has ears to hear, let him hear!" (Luke 8:8). Hear Him today. Trust His wisdom. He hears you, so speak to Him right now—He cares for you!

—Kenny Chinn
Northside Baptist Church, Wilmington, NC

WEEK 14, DAY 5

God Meets Us in Our Suffering

Luke 8:22–48

Wind and Wave Obey Jesus

Now it happened, on a certain day, that He got into a boat with His disciples. And He said to them, "Let us cross over to the other side of the lake." And they launched out. 23But as they sailed He fell asleep. And a windstorm came down on the lake, and they were filling with water, and were in jeopardy. 24And they came to Him and awoke Him, saying, "Master, Master, we are perishing!"

Then He arose and rebuked the wind and the raging of the water. And they ceased, and there was a calm. 25But He said to them, "Where is your faith?"

And they were afraid, and marveled, saying to one another, "Who can this be? For He commands even the winds and water, and they obey Him!"

A Demon-Possessed Man Healed

26Then they sailed to the country of the Gadarenes, which is opposite Galilee. 27And when He stepped out on the land, there met Him a certain man from the city who had demons for a long time. And he wore no clothes, nor did he live in a house but in the tombs. 28When he saw Jesus, he cried out, fell down before Him, and with a loud voice said, "What have I to do with You, Jesus, Son of the Most High God? I beg You, do not torment me!" 29For He had commanded the unclean spirit to come out of the man. For it had often seized him, and he was kept under guard, bound with chains and shackles; and he broke the bonds and was driven by the demon into the wilderness.

30Jesus asked him, saying, "What is your name?"

And he said, "Legion," because many demons had entered him. 31And they begged Him that He would not command them to go out into the abyss.

32Now a herd of many swine was feeding there on the mountain. So they begged Him that He would permit them to enter them. And He permitted them. 33Then the demons went out of the man and entered the swine, and the herd ran violently down the steep place into the lake and drowned.

34When those who fed them saw what had happened, they fled and told it in the city and in the country. 35Then they went out to see what had happened, and came to Jesus, and found the man from whom the demons had departed, sitting at the feet of Jesus, clothed and in his right mind. And they were afraid. 36They also who had seen it told them by what means he who had been demon-possessed was healed. 37Then the whole multitude of the surrounding region of the Gadarenes asked Him to depart from them, for they were seized with great fear. And He got into the boat and returned.

38Now the man from whom the demons had departed begged Him that he might be with Him. But Jesus sent him away, saying, 39"Return to your own house, and tell what great things God has done for you." And he went his way and proclaimed throughout the whole city what great things Jesus had done for him.

A Girl Restored to Life and a Woman Healed

40So it was, when Jesus returned, that the multitude welcomed Him, for they were all waiting for Him. 41And behold, there came a man named Jairus, and he was a ruler of the synagogue. And he fell down at Jesus' feet and begged Him to come to his house, 42for he had an only daughter about twelve years of age, and she was dying.

But as He went, the multitudes thronged Him. 43Now a woman, having a flow of blood for twelve years, who had spent all her livelihood on physicians and could not be healed by any, 44came from behind and touched the border of His garment. And immediately her flow of blood stopped.

45And Jesus said, "Who touched Me?"

When all denied it, Peter and those with him said, "Master, the multitudes throng and press You, and You say, 'Who touched Me?'"

46But Jesus said, "Somebody touched Me, for I perceived power going out from Me." 47Now when the woman saw that she was not hidden, she came trembling; and falling down before Him, she declared to Him in the presence of all the people the reason she had touched Him and how she was healed immediately.

48And He said to her, "Daughter, be of good cheer; your faith has made you well. Go in peace."

DEVOTIONAL

Many people are consumed with anger toward God when they suffer, and they blame Him for things for which He is not responsible. The people Jesus healed in Luke 8 knew He was the answer to their suffering. Pursue Jesus, even when you suffer. Whether He heals you or strengthens you as you struggle, you will be blessed.

—Kenny Chinn
Northside Baptist Church, Wilmington, NC

WEEK 14, DAY 6

God Is in Control

Luke 8:49–9:17

While He was still speaking, someone came from the ruler of the synagogue's house, saying to him, "Your daughter is dead. Do not trouble the Teacher."

50But when Jesus heard it, He answered him, saying, "Do not be afraid; only believe, and she will be made well." 51When He came into the house, He permitted no one to go in except Peter, James, and John, and the father and mother of the girl. 52Now all wept and mourned for her; but He said, "Do not weep; she is not dead, but sleeping." 53And they ridiculed Him, knowing that she was dead.

54But He put them all outside, took her by the hand and called, saying, "Little girl, arise." 55Then her spirit returned, and she arose immediately. And He commanded that she be given something to eat. 56And her parents were astonished, but He charged them to tell no one what had happened.

Sending Out the Twelve

9 Then He called His twelve disciples together and gave them power and authority over all demons, and to cure diseases. 2He sent them to preach the kingdom of God and to heal the sick. 3And He said to them, "Take nothing for the journey, neither staffs nor bag nor bread nor money; and do not have two tunics apiece.

4"Whatever house you enter, stay there, and from there depart. 5And whoever will not receive you, when you go out of that city, shake off the very dust from your feet as a testimony against them."

6So they departed and went through the towns, preaching the gospel and healing everywhere.

Herod Seeks to See Jesus

7Now Herod the tetrarch heard of all that was done by Him; and he was perplexed, because it was said by some that John had risen from the dead, 8and by some that Elijah had appeared, and by others that one of the old prophets had risen again. 9Herod said, "John I have beheaded, but who is this of whom I hear such things?" So he sought to see Him.

Feeding the Five Thousand

10And the apostles, when they had returned, told Him all that they had done. Then He took them and went aside privately into a deserted place belonging to the city called Bethsaida. 11But when the multitudes knew it, they followed Him; and He received them and spoke to them about the kingdom of God, and healed those who had need of healing. 12When the day began to wear away, the twelve came and said to Him, "Send the multitude away, that they may go into the surrounding towns and country, and lodge and get provisions; for we are in a deserted place here."

13But He said to them, "You give them something to eat."

And they said, "We have no more than five loaves and two fish, unless we go and buy food for all these people." 14For there were about five thousand men.

Then He said to His disciples, "Make them sit down in groups of fifty." 15And they did so, and made them all sit down.

16Then He took the five loaves and the two fish, and looking up to heaven, He blessed and broke them, and gave them to the disciples to set before the multitude. 17So they all ate and were filled, and twelve baskets of the leftover fragments were taken up by them.

DEVOTIONAL

When God created man and woman, He gave them a mandate: "Be fruitful and multiply; fill the earth and subdue it; have dominion . . . over every living thing" (Genesis 1:28). Briefly stated, God said, "Take control." Today, we are prone to a sinful version of having dominion, one in which we refuse to call Jesus Lord. Each of us spends our days taking control of our lives. In any typical home, the battle over who will hold the TV remote illustrates the ongoing need for control.

Jesus is in control of the entire universe and of every age of history—He most certainly can and should be Lord of our lives! Yet we struggle to relinquish control to Him. You will never find true life until you give total control over to the One who holds life. Do not depend solely on your abilities or your plans. Depend on the One who is present, the Lord Jesus Christ. He can call into existence things that are not and lead you in wisdom. He is almighty and good. Praise Him and rely on Him, for He is God!

The only antidote to resisting God's control is what Jesus seeks from us: trust. Focus on His trustworthy character and put your trust in Him.

—Kenny Chinn
Northside Baptist Church, Wilmington, NC

WEEK 14, DAY 7

Have you allowed God to change the way you think? Describe a thought process that Christ has completely transformed, and consider what other thought processes might need His healing touch.

_____

_____

_____

_____

_____

_____

_____

_____

_____

_____

_____

_____

_____

How has your personal relationship with Christ imparted to someone else that which Christ has imparted to you?

_____

_____

_____

_____

_____

_____

_____

_____

_____

_____

WEEK 15, DAY 1

Worship the One True God

Luke 9:18–43a

Peter Confesses Jesus as the Christ

And it happened, as He was alone praying, that His disciples joined Him, and He asked them, saying, "Who do the crowds say that I am?"

19So they answered and said, "John the Baptist, but some say Elijah; and others say that one of the old prophets has risen again."

20He said to them, "But who do you say that I am?"

Peter answered and said, "The Christ of God."

Jesus Predicts His Death and Resurrection

21And He strictly warned and commanded them to tell this to no one, 22saying, "The Son of Man must suffer many things, and be rejected by the elders and chief priests and scribes, and be killed, and be raised the third day."

Take Up the Cross and Follow Him

23Then He said to them all, "If anyone desires to come after Me, let him deny himself, and take up his cross daily, and follow Me. 24For whoever desires to save his life will lose it, but whoever loses his life for My sake will save it. 25For what profit is it to a man if he gains the whole world, and is himself destroyed or lost? 26For whoever is ashamed of Me and My words, of him the Son of Man will be ashamed when He comes in His own glory, and in His Father's, and of the holy angels. 27But I tell you truly, there are some standing here who shall not taste death till they see the kingdom of God."

Jesus Transfigured on the Mount

28Now it came to pass, about eight days after these sayings, that He took Peter, John, and James and went up on the mountain to pray. 29As He prayed, the appearance of His face was altered, and His robe became white and glistening. 30And behold, two men talked with Him, who were Moses and Elijah, 31who appeared in glory and spoke of His decease which He was about to accomplish at Jerusalem. 32But Peter and those with him were heavy with sleep; and when they were fully awake, they saw His glory and the two men who stood with Him. 33Then it happened, as they were parting from Him, that Peter said to Jesus, "Master, it is good for us to be here; and let us make three tabernacles: one for You, one for Moses, and one for Elijah"—not knowing what he said.

34While he was saying this, a cloud came and overshadowed them; and they were fearful as they entered the cloud. 35And a voice came out of the cloud, saying, "This is My beloved Son. Hear Him!" 36When the voice had ceased, Jesus was found alone. But they kept quiet, and told no one in those days any of the things they had seen.

A Boy Is Healed

37Now it happened on the next day, when they had come down from the mountain, that a great multitude met Him. 38Suddenly a man from the multitude cried out, saying, "Teacher, I implore You, look on my son, for he is my only child. 39And behold, a spirit seizes him, and he suddenly cries out; it convulses him so that he foams at the mouth; and it departs from him with great difficulty, bruising him. 40So I implored Your disciples to cast it out, but they could not."

41Then Jesus answered and said, "O faithless and perverse generation, how long shall I be with you and bear with you? Bring your son here." 42And as he was still coming, the demon threw him down and convulsed him. Then Jesus rebuked the unclean spirit, healed the child, and gave him back to his father.

Jesus Again Predicts His Death

43And they were all amazed at the majesty of God.

DEVOTIONAL

In today's passage we read that Jesus asked the disciples who the crowds said He was. We know from Matthew 16:13 that at this time they were in the region of Caesarea Philippi, surrounded by a culture in which people worshiped various gods at various altars. There was an altar for Pan (the god of nature), a shrine to Baalism, and even an altar to worship the great Caesar of Rome.

*It's easy to repeat what others have said about Jesus, as the disciples did (Luke 9:19). Jesus, however, always makes it personal. "He said to them, 'But who do you say that I am?' Peter answered and said, 'The Christ of God'" (v. 20). Our world is filled with altars to other gods today, and our God continues to ask this personal question: "Who do **you** think I am?" Your answer will reveal the true altar of your worship.*

—Dr. Larry Thompson
First Baptist Church, Ft. Lauderdale, FL

WEEK 15, DAY 2

The High Value of Love

Luke 9:43b–10:7

But while everyone marveled at all the things which Jesus did, He said to His disciples, [44]"Let these words sink down into your ears, for the Son of Man is about to be betrayed into the hands of men." [45]But they did not understand this saying, and it was hidden from them so that they did not perceive it; and they were afraid to ask Him about this saying.

Who Is the Greatest?

[46]Then a dispute arose among them as to which of them would be greatest. [47]And Jesus, perceiving the thought of their heart, took a little child and set him by Him, [48]and said to them, "Whoever receives this little child in My name receives Me; and whoever receives Me receives Him who sent Me. For he who is least among you all will be great."

Jesus Forbids Sectarianism

[49]Now John answered and said, "Master, we saw someone casting out demons in Your name, and we forbade him because he does not follow with us."

[50]But Jesus said to him, "Do not forbid him, for he who is not against us is on our side."

A Samaritan Village Rejects the Savior

[51]Now it came to pass, when the time had come for Him to be received up, that He steadfastly set His face to go to Jerusalem, [52]and sent messengers before His face. And as they went, they entered a village of the Samaritans, to prepare for Him. [53]But they did not receive Him, because His face was set for the journey to Jerusalem. [54]And when His disciples James and John saw this, they said, "Lord, do You want us to command fire to come down from heaven and consume them, just as Elijah did?"

[55]But He turned and rebuked them, and said, "You do not know what manner of spirit you are of. [56]For the Son of Man did not come to destroy men's lives but to save them." And they went to another village.

The Cost of Discipleship

[57]Now it happened as they journeyed on the road, that someone said to Him, "Lord, I will follow You wherever You go."

[58]And Jesus said to him, "Foxes have holes and birds of the air have nests, but the Son of Man has nowhere to lay His head."

[59]Then He said to another, "Follow Me."

But he said, "Lord, let me first go and bury my father."

[60]Jesus said to him, "Let the dead bury their own dead, but you go and preach the kingdom of God."

[61]And another also said, "Lord, I will follow You, but let me first go and bid them farewell who are at my house."

[62]But Jesus said to him, "No one, having put his hand to the plow, and looking back, is fit for the kingdom of God."

The Seventy Sent Out

10 After these things the Lord appointed seventy others also, and sent them two by two before His face into every city and place where He Himself was about to go. [2]Then He said to them, "The harvest truly is great, but the laborers are few; therefore pray the Lord of the harvest to send out laborers into His harvest. [3]Go your way; behold, I send you out as lambs among wolves. [4]Carry neither money bag, knapsack, nor sandals; and greet no one along the road. [5]But whatever house you enter, first say, 'Peace to this house.' [6]And if a son of peace is there, your peace will rest on it; if not, it will return to you. [7]And remain in the same house, eating and drinking such things as they give, for the laborer is worthy of his wages. Do not go from house to house."

DEVOTIONAL

Talk about insensitivity! Jesus explained He would be betrayed, and the very next moment the disciples were arguing about who was the greatest among them!

Isn't that just like human nature? We live in a world that values status and demands we declare our rank. The idea of rank means we compare ourselves to and compete with others. The higher we go, the lower others go. It is our nature to continue overcoming more people so we may achieve an increasingly higher status in this world.

Tragically, the drive for status ultimately leaves us spiritually dry. Jesus provided us with the recipe for greatness: "Whoever receives this little child in My name receives Me" (Luke 9:48). The child cannot provide you status nor give you rank. There is only one reason to receive the child: love. In loving unconditionally you begin to see true greatness by following the great example of our Savior.

—Dr. Larry Thompson
First Baptist Church, Ft. Lauderdale, FL

WEEK 15, DAY 3

Follow Jesus' Commands

Luke 10:8–29

"Whatever city you enter, and they receive you, eat such things as are set before you. 9And heal the sick there, and say to them, 'The kingdom of God has come near to you.' 10But whatever city you enter, and they do not receive you, go out into its streets and say, 11'The very dust of your city which clings to us we wipe off against you. Nevertheless know this, that the kingdom of God has come near you.' 12But I say to you that it will be more tolerable in that Day for Sodom than for that city.

Woe to the Impenitent Cities

13"Woe to you, Chorazin! Woe to you, Bethsaida! For if the mighty works which were done in you had been done in Tyre and Sidon, they would have repented long ago, sitting in sackcloth and ashes. 14But it will be more tolerable for Tyre and Sidon at the judgment than for you. 15And you, Capernaum, who are exalted to heaven, will be brought down to Hades. 16He who hears you hears Me, he who rejects you rejects Me, and he who rejects Me rejects Him who sent Me."

The Seventy Return with Joy

17Then the seventy returned with joy, saying, "Lord, even the demons are subject to us in Your name."

18And He said to them, "I saw Satan fall like lightning from heaven. 19Behold, I give you the authority to trample on serpents and scorpions, and over all the power of the enemy, and nothing shall by any means hurt you. 20Nevertheless do not rejoice in this, that the spirits are subject to you, but rather rejoice because your names are written in heaven."

Jesus Rejoices in the Spirit

21In that hour Jesus rejoiced in the Spirit and said, "I thank You, Father, Lord of heaven and earth, that You have hidden these things from the wise and prudent and revealed them to babes. Even so, Father, for so it seemed good in Your sight. 22All things have been delivered to Me by My Father, and no one knows who the Son is except the Father, and who the Father is except the Son, and the one to whom the Son wills to reveal Him."

23Then He turned to His disciples and said privately, "Blessed are the eyes which see the things you see; 24for I tell you that many prophets and kings have desired to see what you see, and have not seen it, and to hear what you hear, and have not heard it."

The Parable of the Good Samaritan

25And behold, a certain lawyer stood up and tested Him, saying, "Teacher, what shall I do to inherit eternal life?"

26He said to him, "What is written in the law? What is your reading of it?"

27So he answered and said, "'You shall love the LORD your God with all your heart, with all your soul, with all your strength, and with all your mind,' and 'your neighbor as yourself.'"

28And He said to him, "You have answered rightly; do this and you will live."

29But he, wanting to justify himself, said to Jesus, "And who is my neighbor?"

DEVOTIONAL

Wouldn't it be easier to follow Jesus' command to love "your neighbor as yourself" (Luke 10:27) if we could redefine a few of His words? First, we might change the word love to tolerate. That way, we could even avoid interaction with the guy next door altogether! Second, we could replace the word neighbor with acquaintance. "Neighbor" sounds too much like "friend" and requires attention to that person's needs. Third, we might drop the phrase as yourself. There is no way the guy next door should be loved as much as the person we see in the mirror each morning! Finally, we could assume Jesus meant to say we should love our "neighbors"—that is, plural. We could focus on how loving we are to those who are easy to love and let ourselves off the hook for being unloving toward just one guy next door. We'd feel better about our tendency to pick and choose whom we love.

With a few simple changes, Jesus' command is pretty easy. But obviously keeping a "version" of His command that we have reformed to our tastes isn't obedience. It's catering to our selfishness—living by the flesh—not following Jesus or pleasing the Father—living by the Spirit. Godly love is sacrificial, seeks the lost, and serves others selflessly.

Aim to build relationships with your neighbors, know their spiritual condition, and meet their needs. We'll never take strides toward reaching our neighbors for Christ until we let God's love fill and direct our lives!

—Dr. Larry Thompson
First Baptist Church, Ft. Lauderdale, FL

WEEK 15, DAY 4

Balancing Worship and Service

Luke 10:30–11:13

Then Jesus answered and said: "A certain man went down from Jerusalem to Jericho, and fell among thieves, who stripped him of his clothing, wounded him, and departed, leaving him half dead. ³¹Now by chance a certain priest came down that road. And when he saw him, he passed by on the other side. ³²Likewise a Levite, when he arrived at the place, came and looked, and passed by on the other side. ³³But a certain Samaritan, as he journeyed, came where he was. And when he saw him, he had compassion. ³⁴So he went to him and bandaged his wounds, pouring on oil and wine; and he set him on his own animal, brought him to an inn, and took care of him. ³⁵On the next day, when he departed, he took out two denarii, gave them to the innkeeper, and said to him, 'Take care of him; and whatever more you spend, when I come again, I will repay you.' ³⁶So which of these three do you think was neighbor to him who fell among the thieves?"

³⁷And he said, "He who showed mercy on him."

Then Jesus said to him, "Go and do likewise."

Mary and Martha Worship and Serve

³⁸Now it happened as they went that He entered a certain village; and a certain woman named Martha welcomed Him into her house. ³⁹And she had a sister called Mary, who also sat at Jesus' feet and heard His word. ⁴⁰But Martha was distracted with much serving, and she approached Him and said, "Lord, do You not care that my sister has left me to serve alone? Therefore tell her to help me."

⁴¹And Jesus answered and said to her, "Martha, Martha, you are worried and troubled about many things. ⁴²But one thing is needed, and Mary has chosen that good part, which will not be taken away from her."

The Model Prayer

11 Now it came to pass, as He was praying in a certain place, when He ceased, that one of His disciples said to Him, "Lord, teach us to pray, as John also taught his disciples."

²So He said to them, "When you pray, say:

Our Father in heaven,
Hallowed be Your name.
Your kingdom come.

Your will be done
On earth as it is in heaven.
³ Give us day by day our daily bread.
⁴ And forgive us our sins,
For we also forgive everyone who is indebted to us.
And do not lead us into temptation,
But deliver us from the evil one."

A Friend Comes at Midnight

⁵And He said to them, "Which of you shall have a friend, and go to him at midnight and say to him, 'Friend, lend me three loaves; ⁶for a friend of mine has come to me on his journey, and I have nothing to set before him'; ⁷and he will answer from within and say, 'Do not trouble me; the door is now shut, and my children are with me in bed; I cannot rise and give to you'? ⁸I say to you, though he will not rise and give to him because he is his friend, yet because of his persistence he will rise and give him as many as he needs.

Keep Asking, Seeking, Knocking

⁹"So I say to you, ask, and it will be given to you; seek, and you will find; knock, and it will be opened to you. ¹⁰For everyone who asks receives, and he who seeks finds, and to him who knocks it will be opened. ¹¹If a son asks for bread from any father among you, will he give him a stone? Or if he asks for a fish, will he give him a serpent instead of a fish? ¹²Or if he asks for an egg, will he offer him a scorpion? ¹³If you then, being evil, know how to give good gifts to your children, how much more will your heavenly Father give the Holy Spirit to those who ask Him!"

DEVOTIONAL

Mary and Martha provide two excellent models of worship and service. Instead of valuing one over the other, we should have a balance of both. You simply cannot divorce the two and be an effective follower of Christ.

Many have criticized Martha for failing to sit with Mary at Jesus' feet. However, churches are full of Christians who "sit and soak" and never prioritize serving and applying what they have learned. Many Christians pride themselves on their faithful attendance, but the statistics have not changed for decades. Eighty percent of the work is done by twenty percent of the people.

What changes do you need to make to balance worship and service in your life?

—Dr. Larry Thompson
First Baptist Church, Ft. Lauderdale, FL

WEEK 15, DAY 5

Hear the Word of God

Luke 11:14–36

A House Divided Cannot Stand

And He was casting out a demon, and it was mute. So it was, when the demon had gone out, that the mute spoke; and the multitudes marveled. 15But some of them said, "He casts out demons by Beelzebub, the ruler of the demons."

16Others, testing Him, sought from Him a sign from heaven. 17But He, knowing their thoughts, said to them: "Every kingdom divided against itself is brought to desolation, and a house divided against a house falls. 18If Satan also is divided against himself, how will his kingdom stand? Because you say I cast out demons by Beelzebub. 19And if I cast out demons by Beelzebub, by whom do your sons cast them out? Therefore they will be your judges. 20But if I cast out demons with the finger of God, surely the kingdom of God has come upon you. 21When a strong man, fully armed, guards his own palace, his goods are in peace. 22But when a stronger than he comes upon him and overcomes him, he takes from him all his armor in which he trusted, and divides his spoils. 23He who is not with Me is against Me, and he who does not gather with Me scatters.

An Unclean Spirit Returns

24"When an unclean spirit goes out of a man, he goes through dry places, seeking rest; and finding none, he says, 'I will return to my house from which I came.' 25And when he comes, he finds it swept and put in order. 26Then he goes and takes with him seven other spirits more wicked than himself, and they enter and dwell there; and the last state of that man is worse than the first."

Keeping the Word

27And it happened, as He spoke these things, that a certain woman from the crowd raised her voice and said to Him, "Blessed is the womb that bore You, and the breasts which nursed You!"

28But He said, "More than that, blessed are those who hear the word of God and keep it!"

Seeking a Sign

29And while the crowds were thickly gathered together, He began to say, "This is an evil generation. It seeks a sign, and no sign will be given to it except the sign of Jonah the prophet. 30For as Jonah became a sign to the Ninevites, so also the Son of Man will be to this generation. 31The queen of the South will rise up in the judgment with the men of this generation and condemn them, for she came from the ends of the earth to hear the wisdom of Solomon; and indeed a greater than Solomon is here. 32The men of Nineveh will rise up in the judgment with this generation and condemn it, for they repented at the preaching of Jonah; and indeed a greater than Jonah is here.

The Lamp of the Body

33"No one, when he has lit a lamp, puts *it* in a secret place or under a basket, but on a lampstand, that those who come in may see the light. 34The lamp of the body is the eye. Therefore, when your eye is good, your whole body also is full of light. But when your eye is bad, your body also is full of darkness. 35Therefore take heed that the light which is in you is not darkness. 36If then your whole body is full of light, having no part dark, the whole body will be full of light, as when the bright shining of a lamp gives you light."

DEVOTIONAL

Many faithful Christians stay committed to reading God's Word first thing every morning. It is a holy habit that transforms their spiritual lives as much as any other discipline. They will complete their morning devotional reading, take a moment to jot a few notes in a journal, and move on to their day's work. However, if they are not careful, the Spirit of the Lord will stop them with one simple statement: "You are more proud of your daily discipline than you are of practical devotion!"

It is easy—and worthwhile—to develop a habit of reading God's Word. The great difficulty we have is not in reading God's Word but in hearing God's Word (Luke 11:28). During your quiet time of reading and prayer, ask, "What is the Spirit of God saying to me this morning as I open the Scriptures? What does He want me to do as I leave this place of quiet solitude?"

Commit to reading God's Word daily. Draw close to the Father and listen for His voice. Remember, it is by sight we read and by sound we receive. Don't walk away from reading His Word without also hearing His Word!

—Dr. Larry Thompson
First Baptist Church, Ft. Lauderdale, FL

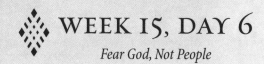

WEEK 15, DAY 6

Fear God, Not People

Luke 11:37–12:7

Woe to the Pharisees and Lawyers

And as He spoke, a certain Pharisee asked Him to dine with him. So He went in and sat down to eat. 38When the Pharisee saw it, he marveled that He had not first washed before dinner.

39Then the Lord said to him, "Now you Pharisees make the outside of the cup and dish clean, but your inward part is full of greed and wickedness. 40Foolish ones! Did not He who made the outside make the inside also? 41But rather give alms of such things as you have; then indeed all things are clean to you.

42"But woe to you Pharisees! For you tithe mint and rue and all manner of herbs, and pass by justice and the love of God. These you ought to have done, without leaving the others undone. 43Woe to you Pharisees! For you love the best seats in the synagogues and greetings in the marketplaces. 44Woe to you, scribes and Pharisees, hypocrites! For you are like graves which are not seen, and the men who walk over them are not aware of them."

45Then one of the lawyers answered and said to Him, "Teacher, by saying these things You reproach us also."

46And He said, "Woe to you also, lawyers! For you load men with burdens hard to bear, and you yourselves do not touch the burdens with one of your fingers. 47Woe to you! For you build the tombs of the prophets, and your fathers killed them. 48In fact, you bear witness that you approve the deeds of your fathers; for they indeed killed them, and you build their tombs. 49Therefore the wisdom of God also said, 'I will send them prophets and apostles, and some of them they will kill and persecute,' 50that the blood of all the prophets which was shed from the foundation of the world may be required of this generation, 51from the blood of Abel to the blood of Zechariah who perished between the altar and the temple. Yes, I say to you, it shall be required of this generation.

52"Woe to you lawyers! For you have taken away the key of knowledge. You did not enter in yourselves, and those who were entering in you hindered."

53And as He said these things to them, the scribes and the Pharisees began to assail Him vehemently, and to cross-examine Him about many things, 54lying in wait for Him, and seeking to catch Him in something He might say, that they might accuse Him.

Beware of Hypocrisy

12In the meantime, when an innumerable multitude of people had gathered together, so that they trampled one another, He began to say to His disciples first of all, "Beware of the leaven of the Pharisees, which is hypocrisy. 2For there is nothing covered that will not be revealed, nor hidden that will not be known. 3Therefore whatever you have spoken in the dark will be heard in the light, and what you have spoken in the ear in inner rooms will be proclaimed on the housetops.

Jesus Teaches the Fear of God

4"And I say to you, My friends, do not be afraid of those who kill the body, and after that have no more that they can do. 5But I will show you whom you should fear: Fear Him who, after He has killed, has power to cast into hell; yes, I say to you, fear Him! 6Are not five sparrows sold for two copper coins? And not one of them is forgotten before God. 7But the very hairs of your head are all numbered. Do not fear therefore; you are of more value than many sparrows."

DEVOTIONAL

Secrets are things we know and most other people do not know. But nothing is secret when it comes to the Lord. Jesus said, "Whatever you have spoken in the dark will be heard in the light" (Luke 12:3).

Hypocrisy is just another secret. It is the secret that results from the fear of people. We think, In order to be accepted, I must live a secret life. I will put on display a life that appears to be one thing while the truth is hidden within. When we live for the approval of people, we will do whatever it takes to maintain that approval. We will lie, cheat, and steal.

A faithful pastor once came to a breaking point in ministry. He was trying so hard to please others that he was failing in his objective and calling. One morning he read Galatians 1:10, and a powerful reality dawned on him. He thought, I am a servant of God, not people. If I live to please people, I cannot serve God. God's Word reminded him to avoid the hypocrisy of trying to be something he was not and to be who God called him to be.

Today, which is stronger in your heart: the fear of people or the fear of God? Whom are you serving, and what is your motivation?

—Dr. Larry Thompson
First Baptist Church, Ft. Lauderdale, FL

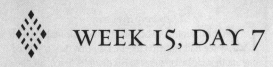

WEEK 15, DAY 7

How have you connected to a neighbor in a way that reveals you are a follower of Christ? Is there a neighbor in your circle of influence who has a need you can meet and, in doing so, bring honor to Christ and His command?

_____

_____

_____

_____

_____

_____

_____

_____

_____

_____

_____

_____

Consider your motivation for serving Christ. If your motivation is anything other than to bring honor and glory to His name as you continue to be a faithful follower of Christ, then your spiritual life will never be satisfying or productive for eternity. What has God taught you about serving Him this week?

_____

_____

_____

_____

_____

_____

_____

_____

WEEK 16, DAY 1

Our Father Knows Our Needs

Luke 12:8–34

Confess Christ Before Men

"Also I say to you, whoever confesses Me before men, him the Son of Man also will confess before the angels of God. ⁹But he who denies Me before men will be denied before the angels of God.

¹⁰"And anyone who speaks a word against the Son of Man, it will be forgiven him; but to him who blasphemes against the Holy Spirit, it will not be forgiven.

¹¹"Now when they bring you to the synagogues and magistrates and authorities, do not worry about how or what you should answer, or what you should say. ¹²For the Holy Spirit will teach you in that very hour what you ought to say."

The Parable of the Rich Fool

¹³Then one from the crowd said to Him, "Teacher, tell my brother to divide the inheritance with me."

¹⁴But He said to him, "Man, who made Me a judge or an arbitrator over you?" ¹⁵And He said to them, "Take heed and beware of covetousness, for one's life does not consist in the abundance of the things he possesses."

¹⁶Then He spoke a parable to them, saying: "The ground of a certain rich man yielded plentifully. ¹⁷And he thought within himself, saying, 'What shall I do, since I have no room to store my crops?' ¹⁸So he said, 'I will do this: I will pull down my barns and build greater, and there I will store all my crops and my goods. ¹⁹And I will say to my soul, "Soul, you have many goods laid up for many years; take your ease; eat, drink, and be merry."' ²⁰But God said to him, 'Fool! This night your soul will be required of you; then whose will those things be which you have provided?'

²¹"So is he who lays up treasure for himself, and is not rich toward God."

Do Not Worry

²²Then He said to His disciples, "Therefore I say to you, do not worry about your life, what you will eat; nor about the body, what you will put on. ²³Life is more than food, and the body is more than clothing. ²⁴Consider the ravens, for they neither sow nor reap, which have neither storehouse nor barn; and God feeds them. Of how much more value are you than the birds? ²⁵And which of you by worrying can add one cubit to his stature? ²⁶If you then are not able to do the least, why are you anxious for the rest? ²⁷Consider the lilies, how they grow: they neither toil nor spin; and yet I say to you, even Solomon in all his glory was not arrayed like one of these. ²⁸If then God so clothes the grass, which today is in the field and tomorrow is thrown into the oven, how much more will He clothe you, O you of little faith?

²⁹"And do not seek what you should eat or what you should drink, nor have an anxious mind. ³⁰For all these things the nations of the world seek after, and your Father knows that you need these things. ³¹But seek the kingdom of God, and all these things shall be added to you.

³²"Do not fear, little flock, for it is your Father's good pleasure to give you the kingdom. ³³Sell what you have and give alms; provide yourselves money bags which do not grow old, a treasure in the heavens that does not fail, where no thief approaches nor moth destroys. ³⁴For where your treasure is, there your heart will be also."

DEVOTIONAL

It's natural to be concerned about finances, especially when it comes to personal security. Who doesn't spend time thinking about things like upcoming bills, college tuition, and retirement down the road? While there's nothing wrong with prudent preparation, something goes wrong when we begin to stress out over these things. After all, in the context of a discussion on relying on God to meet our needs, Jesus said, "Do not . . . have an anxious mind" (Luke 12:29). That is stressing out!

Jesus challenged His followers to think about ravens and lilies (Luke 12:24, 27). Though they are incapable of our kind of thought processes, they depend on their Creator to supply their needs. Jesus' point is simple. If a bird and a flower can depend on God, how much more can we who are His children? He is our loving Father. He is good and He is able.

Whenever you find yourself stressed about money issues, meditate on a couple of things Jesus said in this chapter. First, look at verse 30: "Your Father knows that you need these things." Let that sink in. Then turn your focus to verse 31: "Seek the kingdom of God, and all these things shall be added to you."

—Mark Hoover
NewSpring Church, Wichita, KS

WEEK 16, DAY 2

*Living in Readiness
for Our Master*

Luke 12:35–56

The Faithful Servant and the Evil Servant

"Let your waist be girded and your lamps burning; 36and you yourselves be like men who wait for their master, when he will return from the wedding, that when he comes and knocks they may open to him immediately. 37Blessed are those servants whom the master, when he comes, will find watching. Assuredly, I say to you that he will gird himself and have them sit down to eat, and will come and serve them. 38And if he should come in the second watch, or come in the third watch, and find them so, blessed are those servants. 39But know this, that if the master of the house had known what hour the thief would come, he would have watched and not allowed his house to be broken into. 40Therefore you also be ready, for the Son of Man is coming at an hour you do not expect."

41Then Peter said to Him, "Lord, do You speak this parable only to us, or to all people?"

42And the Lord said, "Who then is that faithful and wise steward, whom his master will make ruler over his household, to give them their portion of food in due season? 43Blessed is that servant whom his master will find so doing when he comes. 44Truly, I say to you that he will make him ruler over all that he has. 45But if that servant says in his heart, 'My master is delaying his coming,' and begins to beat the male and female servants, and to eat and drink and be drunk, 46the master of that servant will come on a day when he is not looking for him, and at an hour when he is not aware, and will cut him in two and appoint him his portion with the unbelievers. 47And that servant who knew his master's will, and did not prepare himself or do according to his will, shall be beaten with many stripes. 48But he who did not know, yet committed things deserving of stripes, shall be beaten with few. For everyone to whom much is given, from him much will be required; and to whom much has been committed, of him they will ask the more.

Christ Brings Division

49"I came to send fire on the earth, and how I wish it were already kindled! 50But I have a baptism to be baptized with, and how distressed I am till it is accomplished! 51Do you suppose that I came to give peace on earth? I tell you, not at all, but rather division. 52For from now on five in one house will be divided: three against two, and two against three. 53Father will be divided against son and son against father, mother against daughter and daughter against mother, mother-in-law against her daughter-in-law and daughter-in-law against her mother-in-law."

Discern the Time

54Then He also said to the multitudes, "Whenever you see a cloud rising out of the west, immediately you say, 'A shower is coming'; and so it is. 55And when you see the south wind blow, you say, 'There will be hot weather'; and there is. 56Hypocrites! You can discern the face of the sky and of the earth, but how is it you do not discern this time?"

DEVOTIONAL

The scenario of a servant waiting for his master's return is a frequent theme in Jesus' teaching. This particular teaching in Luke 12 portrays the servants in a household waiting for their newlywed master to return from the wedding. It was expected in such situations for the servants to be waiting at attention for the unscheduled, unannounced arrival, poised and ready to spring into action to minister to their master in any way he required.

Jesus' story depicts the master returning in the middle of the night. He's immediately greeted at the door by his servants. They expect him to be hungry, and are ready to serve him dinner. But the master, delighted to see such loyalty and devotion, does the unthinkable—he takes on the role of the domestic help and serves his faithful servants dinner!

When we, who represent the waiting servants, grasp the impact of what Jesus was saying, we are faced with a serious reality: it is very important to Jesus that we obediently anticipate His arrival with joy. It is that very anticipation that keeps us from forgetting who we've been called to be. Remember, the unfaithful servants in Jesus' parable became cruel, self-indulgent, and careless. May we guard ourselves from developing harmful habits that would disappoint our Master and live in eager readiness for His return.

—Mark Hoover
NewSpring Church, Wichita, KS

WEEK 16, DAY 3

God's Patient Grace

Luke 12:57–13:21

Make Peace with Your Adversary

"Yes, and why, even of yourselves, do you not judge what is right? 58When you go with your adversary to the magistrate, make every effort along the way to settle with him, lest he drag you to the judge, the judge deliver you to the officer, and the officer throw you into prison. 59I tell you, you shall not depart from there till you have paid the very last mite."

Repent or Perish

13 There were present at that season some who told Him about the Galileans whose blood Pilate had mingled with their sacrifices. 2And Jesus answered and said to them, "Do you suppose that these Galileans were worse sinners than all other Galileans, because they suffered such things? 3I tell you, no; but unless you repent you will all likewise perish. 4Or those eighteen on whom the tower in Siloam fell and killed them, do you think that they were worse sinners than all other men who dwelt in Jerusalem? 5I tell you, no; but unless you repent you will all likewise perish."

The Parable of the Barren Fig Tree

6He also spoke this parable: "A certain man had a fig tree planted in his vineyard, and he came seeking fruit on it and found none. 7Then he said to the keeper of his vineyard, 'Look, for three years I have come seeking fruit on this fig tree and find none. Cut it down; why does it use up the ground?' 8But he answered and said to him, 'Sir, let it alone this year also, until I dig around it and fertilize it. 9And if it bears fruit, well. But if not, after that you can cut it down.'"

A Spirit of Infirmity

10Now He was teaching in one of the synagogues on the Sabbath. 11And behold, there was a woman who had a spirit of infirmity eighteen years, and was bent over and could in no way raise herself up. 12But when Jesus saw her, He called her to Him and said to her, "Woman, you are loosed from your infirmity." 13And He laid His hands on her, and immediately she was made straight, and glorified God.

14But the ruler of the synagogue answered with indignation, because Jesus had healed on the Sabbath; and he said to the crowd, "There are six days on which men ought to work; therefore come and be healed on them, and not on the Sabbath day."

15The Lord then answered him and said, "Hypocrite! Does not each one of you on the Sabbath loose his ox or donkey from the stall, and lead it away to water it? 16So ought not this woman, being a daughter of Abraham, whom Satan has bound—think of it—for eighteen years, be loosed from this bond on the Sabbath?" 17And when He said these things, all His adversaries were put to shame; and all the multitude rejoiced for all the glorious things that were done by Him.

The Parable of the Mustard Seed

18Then He said, "What is the kingdom of God like? And to what shall I compare it? 19It is like a mustard seed, which a man took and put in his garden; and it grew and became a large tree, and the birds of the air nested in its branches."

The Parable of the Leaven

20And again He said, "To what shall I liken the kingdom of God? 21It is like leaven, which a woman took and hid in three measures of meal till it was all leavened."

DEVOTIONAL

Jesus wants us to understand that while God is patient, He holds everyone accountable to His standards of holiness. When some self-righteous people hinted that certain Galileans were murdered by Pilate because of their sinfulness, Jesus confronted them with their own personal need for repentance and salvation. No one should assume that bad things happen to people because they deserve it. Every human being is a sinner who needs to turn to Christ to receive redemption and forgiveness.

The story of the fig tree reminds us that God is not eager to bring judgment on the unsaved, or chastening in the life of a wayward child. He has repeatedly proved Himself to be long-suffering throughout the history of the world. But no one should respond to His kindness with rebellious presumption. Let your heart turn fully toward Him today in complete surrender. If you do, you'll find His patient grace.

—Mark Hoover
NewSpring Church, Wichita, KS

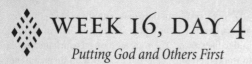

WEEK 16, DAY 4

Putting God and Others First

Luke 13:22–14:14

The Narrow Way

And He went through the cities and villages, teaching, and journeying toward Jerusalem. ²³Then one said to Him, "Lord, are there few who are saved?"

And He said to them, ²⁴"Strive to enter through the narrow gate, for many, I say to you, will seek to enter and will not be able. ²⁵When once the Master of the house has risen up and shut the door, and you begin to stand outside and knock at the door, saying, 'Lord, Lord, open for us,' and He will answer and say to you, 'I do not know you, where you are from,' ²⁶then you will begin to say, 'We ate and drank in Your presence, and You taught in our streets.' ²⁷But He will say, 'I tell you I do not know you, where you are from. Depart from Me, all you workers of iniquity.' ²⁸There will be weeping and gnashing of teeth, when you see Abraham and Isaac and Jacob and all the prophets in the kingdom of God, and yourselves thrust out. ²⁹They will come from the east and the west, from the north and the south, and sit down in the kingdom of God. ³⁰And indeed there are last who will be first, and there are first who will be last."

³¹On that very day some Pharisees came, saying to Him, "Get out and depart from here, for Herod wants to kill You."

³²And He said to them, "Go, tell that fox, 'Behold, I cast out demons and perform cures today and tomorrow, and the third day I shall be perfected.' ³³Nevertheless I must journey today, tomorrow, and the day following; for it cannot be that a prophet should perish outside of Jerusalem.

Jesus Laments over Jerusalem

³⁴"O Jerusalem, Jerusalem, the one who kills the prophets and stones those who are sent to her! How often I wanted to gather your children together, as a hen gathers her brood under her wings, but you were not willing! ³⁵See! Your house is left to you desolate; and assuredly, I say to you, you shall not see Me until the time comes when you say, 'Blessed is He who comes in the name of the LORD!'"

A Man with Dropsy Healed on the Sabbath

14 Now it happened, as He went into the house of one of the rulers of the Pharisees to eat bread on the Sabbath, that they watched Him closely. ²And behold, there was a certain man before Him who had dropsy. ³And Jesus, answering, spoke to the lawyers and Pharisees, saying, "Is it lawful to heal on the Sabbath?"

⁴But they kept silent. And He took him and healed him, and let him go. ⁵Then He answered them, saying, "Which of you, having a donkey or an ox that has fallen into a pit, will not immediately pull him out on the Sabbath day?" ⁶And they could not answer Him regarding these things.

Take the Lowly Place

⁷So He told a parable to those who were invited, when He noted how they chose the best places, saying to them: ⁸"When you are invited by anyone to a wedding feast, do not sit down in the best place, lest one more honorable than you be invited by him; ⁹and he who invited you and him come and say to you, 'Give place to this man,' and then you begin with shame to take the lowest place. ¹⁰But when you are invited, go and sit down in the lowest place, so that when he who invited you comes he may say to you, 'Friend, go up higher.' Then you will have glory in the presence of those who sit at the table with you. ¹¹For whoever exalts himself will be humbled, and he who humbles himself will be exalted."

¹²Then He also said to him who invited Him, "When you give a dinner or a supper, do not ask your friends, your brothers, your relatives, nor rich neighbors, lest they also invite you back, and you be repaid. ¹³But when you give a feast, invite the poor, the maimed, the lame, the blind. ¹⁴And you will be blessed, because they cannot repay you; for you shall be repaid at the resurrection of the just."

DEVOTIONAL

The prophet Isaiah reminds us that God's ways are not our ways, and His thoughts are beyond ours (Isaiah 55:8). This means that we may think we understand how life works, but we get it backward. In no area is this more true than our quest for personal importance. It's part of human nature to try to impress others to gain approval, status, and favor. Unfortunately, these attempts often result in embarrassing missteps, as with the Pharisee's houseguests who sat in the best seats (Luke 14:7–14). What Jesus wants us to grasp is that this is more than just human clumsiness. God actually sabotages our prideful grabs for the spotlight. He loves us too much to let us be unlike Jesus. When we put Him and others first, He loves to give us surprising favor. How can you make serving God and others a priority today?

—Mark Hoover
NewSpring Church, Wichita, KS

WEEK 16, DAY 5

Giving God Our Complete Focus

Luke 14:15–15:10

The Parable of the Great Supper

Now when one of those who sat at the table with Him heard these things, he said to Him, "Blessed is he who shall eat bread in the kingdom of God!"

16Then He said to him, "A certain man gave a great supper and invited many, 17and sent his servant at supper time to say to those who were invited, 'Come, for all things are now ready.' 18But they all with one accord began to make excuses. The first said to him, 'I have bought a piece of ground, and I must go and see it. I ask you to have me excused.' 19And another said, 'I have bought five yoke of oxen, and I am going to test them. I ask you to have me excused.' 20Still another said, 'I have married a wife, and therefore I cannot come.' 21So that servant came and reported these things to his master. Then the master of the house, being angry, said to his servant, 'Go out quickly into the streets and lanes of the city, and bring in here the poor and the maimed and the lame and the blind.' 22And the servant said, 'Master, it is done as you commanded, and still there is room.' 23Then the master said to the servant, 'Go out into the highways and hedges, and compel them to come in, that my house may be filled. 24For I say to you that none of those men who were invited shall taste my supper.'"

Leaving All to Follow Christ

25Now great multitudes went with Him. And He turned and said to them, 26"If anyone comes to Me and does not hate his father and mother, wife and children, brothers and sisters, yes, and his own life also, he cannot be My disciple. 27And whoever does not bear his cross and come after Me cannot be My disciple. 28For which of you, intending to build a tower, does not sit down first and count the cost, whether he has enough to finish it— 29lest, after he has laid the foundation, and is not able to finish, all who see it begin to mock him, 30saying, 'This man began to build and was not able to finish'? 31Or what king, going to make war against another king, does not sit down first and consider whether he is able with ten thousand to meet him who comes against him with twenty thousand? 32Or else, while the other is still a great way off, he sends a delegation and asks conditions of peace. 33So likewise,

whoever of you does not forsake all that he has cannot be My disciple.

Tasteless Salt Is Worthless

34"Salt *is* good; but if the salt has lost its flavor, how shall it be seasoned? 35It is neither fit for the land nor for the dunghill, but men throw it out. He who has ears to hear, let him hear!"

The Parable of the Lost Sheep

15Then all the tax collectors and the sinners drew near to Him to hear Him. 2And the Pharisees and scribes complained, saying, "This Man receives sinners and eats with them." 3So He spoke this parable to them, saying:

4"What man of you, having a hundred sheep, if he loses one of them, does not leave the ninety-nine in the wilderness, and go after the one which is lost until he finds it? 5And when he has found it, he lays it on his shoulders, rejoicing. 6And when he comes home, he calls together his friends and neighbors, saying to them, 'Rejoice with me, for I have found my sheep which was lost!' 7I say to you that likewise there will be more joy in heaven over one sinner who repents than over ninety-nine just persons who need no repentance.

The Parable of the Lost Coin

8"Or what woman, having ten silver coins, if she loses one coin, does not light a lamp, sweep the house, and search carefully until she finds it? 9And when she has found it, she calls her friends and neighbors together, saying, 'Rejoice with me, for I have found the piece which I lost!' 10Likewise, I say to you, there is joy in the presence of the angels of God over one sinner who repents."

DEVOTIONAL

In the age of information overload, perhaps the commodity in shortest supply is personal focus. Most people know how it feels to be with someone who's constantly checking and sending messages. They're there, but not really there!

In Luke 14, Jesus conveyed how deeply God cares about the quality of attention we give Him. The master, who represents God, invites guests to enjoy his grace. He's not asking the guests to contribute, but he does expect them to take him seriously and give him their wholehearted attention. Their thinly veiled excuses prove their focus is elsewhere.

Where is your focus? Remember how amazing it is that the God of the universe desires your complete focus today. Give it to Him—He is worthy to receive it!

—Mark Hoover
NewSpring Church, Wichita, KS

WEEK 16, DAY 6

Our Loving Heavenly Father

Luke 15:11–16:8

The Parable of the Lost Son

Then He said: "A certain man had two sons. ¹²And the younger of them said to his father, 'Father, give me the portion of goods that falls to me.' So he divided to them his livelihood. ¹³And not many days after, the younger son gathered all together, journeyed to a far country, and there wasted his possessions with prodigal living. ¹⁴But when he had spent all, there arose a severe famine in that land, and he began to be in want. ¹⁵Then he went and joined himself to a citizen of that country, and he sent him into his fields to feed swine. ¹⁶And he would gladly have filled his stomach with the pods that the swine ate, and no one gave him anything.

¹⁷"But when he came to himself, he said, 'How many of my father's hired servants have bread enough and to spare, and I perish with hunger! ¹⁸I will arise and go to my father, and will say to him, "Father, I have sinned against heaven and before you, ¹⁹and I am no longer worthy to be called your son. Make me like one of your hired servants."'

²⁰"And he arose and came to his father. But when he was still a great way off, his father saw him and had compassion, and ran and fell on his neck and kissed him. ²¹And the son said to him, 'Father, I have sinned against heaven and in your sight, and am no longer worthy to be called your son.'

²²"But the father said to his servants, 'Bring out the best robe and put it on him, and put a ring on his hand and sandals on his feet. ²³And bring the fatted calf here and kill it, and let us eat and be merry; ²⁴for this my son was dead and is alive again; he was lost and is found.' And they began to be merry.

²⁵"Now his older son was in the field. And as he came and drew near to the house, he heard music and dancing. ²⁶So he called one of the servants and asked what these things meant. ²⁷And he said to him, 'Your brother has come, and because he has received him safe and sound, your father has killed the fatted calf.'

²⁸"But he was angry and would not go in. Therefore his father came out and pleaded with him. ²⁹So he answered and said to his father, 'Lo, these many years I have been serving you; I never transgressed your commandment at any time; and yet you never gave me a young goat, that I might make merry with my friends. ³⁰But as soon as this son of yours came, who has devoured your livelihood with harlots, you killed the fatted calf for him.'

³¹"And he said to him, 'Son, you are always with me, and all that I have is yours. ³²It was right that we should make merry and be glad, for your brother was dead and is alive again, and was lost and is found.'"

The Parable of the Unjust Steward

16 He also said to His disciples: "There was a certain rich man who had a steward, and an accusation was brought to him that this man was wasting his goods. ²So he called him and said to him, 'What is this I hear about you? Give an account of your stewardship, for you can no longer be steward.'

³"Then the steward said within himself, 'What shall I do? For my master is taking the stewardship away from me. I cannot dig; I am ashamed to beg. ⁴I have resolved what to do, that when I am put out of the stewardship, they may receive me into their houses.'

⁵"So he called every one of his master's debtors to him, and said to the first, 'How much do you owe my master?' ⁶And he said, 'A hundred measures of oil.' So he said to him, 'Take your bill, and sit down quickly and write fifty.' ⁷Then he said to another, 'And how much do you owe?' So he said, 'A hundred measures of wheat.' And he said to him, 'Take your bill, and write eighty.' ⁸So the master commended the unjust steward because he had dealt shrewdly. For the sons of this world are more shrewd in their generation than the sons of light."

DEVOTIONAL

The tragic descent of the lost son began with a bad atti-tude. He had gotten it in his head that his dad was unfair, strict, and difficult to please. This part of the story can hit close to home. Within our broken natures is a predisposition to react to God the same way. Just as with the young man, the moment we question God's goodness, the bottom can drop out of our lives. So what then? Does God give up on us?

In the hog pen, the son probably thought there was no chance his father would ever love him again. When he humbly returned home, he discovered what he failed to recognize in the first place: his dad was filled with grace. The father hadn't changed, but the boy's heart had. Today, thank God that He is such a good Father and that He never gives up on you!

—Mark Hoover
NewSpring Church, Wichita, KS

WEEK 16, DAY 7

Recall times in your life when God has demonstrated remarkable love to you in response to your humble repentance.

_____

_____

_____

_____

_____

_____

_____

_____

_____

_____

_____

_____

What things in your life could be distracting you from having a close, personal relationship with the Lord?

_____

_____

_____

_____

_____

_____

_____

_____

_____

WEEK 17, DAY 1

Putting Our Trust in Christ Alone

Luke 16:9–17:4

"And I say to you, make friends for yourselves by unrighteous mammon, that when you fail, they may receive you into an everlasting home. 10He who is faithful in what is least is faithful also in much; and he who is unjust in what is least is unjust also in much. 11Therefore if you have not been faithful in the unrighteous mammon, who will commit to your trust the true riches? 12And if you have not been faithful in what is another man's, who will give you what is your own?

13"No servant can serve two masters; for either he will hate the one and love the other, or else he will be loyal to the one and despise the other. You cannot serve God and mammon."

The Law, the Prophets, and the Kingdom

14Now the Pharisees, who were lovers of money, also heard all these things, and they derided Him. 15And He said to them, "You are those who justify yourselves before men, but God knows your hearts. For what is highly esteemed among men is an abomination in the sight of God.

16"The law and the prophets were until John. Since that time the kingdom of God has been preached, and everyone is pressing into it. 17And it is easier for heaven and earth to pass away than for one tittle of the law to fail.

18"Whoever divorces his wife and marries another commits adultery; and whoever marries her who is divorced from her husband commits adultery.

The Rich Man and Lazarus

19"There was a certain rich man who was clothed in purple and fine linen and fared sumptuously every day. 20But there was a certain beggar named Lazarus, full of sores, who was laid at his gate, 21desiring to be fed with the crumbs which fell from the rich man's table. Moreover the dogs came and licked his sores. 22So it was that the beggar died, and was carried by the angels to Abraham's bosom. The rich man also died and was buried. 23And being in torments in Hades, he lifted up his eyes and saw Abraham afar off, and Lazarus in his bosom.

24"Then he cried and said, 'Father Abraham, have mercy on me, and send Lazarus that he may dip the tip of his finger in water and cool my tongue; for I am tormented in this flame.' 25But Abraham said, 'Son, remember that in your lifetime you received your good things, and likewise Lazarus evil things; but now he is comforted and you are tormented. 26And besides all this, between us and you there is a great gulf fixed, so that those who want to pass from here to you cannot, nor can those from there pass to us.'

27"Then he said, 'I beg you therefore, father, that you would send him to my father's house, 28for I have five brothers, that he may testify to them, lest they also come to this place of torment.' 29Abraham said to him, 'They have Moses and the prophets; let them hear them.' 30And he said, 'No, father Abraham; but if one goes to them from the dead, they will repent.' 31But he said to him, 'If they do not hear Moses and the prophets, neither will they be persuaded though one rise from the dead.'"

Jesus Warns of Offenses

17Then He said to the disciples, "It is impossible that no offenses should come, but woe to him through whom they do come! 2It would be better for him if a millstone were hung around his neck, and he were thrown into the sea, than that he should offend one of these little ones. 3Take heed to yourselves. If your brother sins against you, rebuke him; and if he repents, forgive him. 4And if he sins against you seven times in a day, and seven times in a day returns to you, saying, 'I repent,' you shall forgive him."

DEVOTIONAL

What are you trusting in today? Some people trust in their riches, accomplishments, or position, much like the rich man in Luke 16. These individuals believe that if they just have enough money, possessions, or influential friends, they have all they will ever need.

The rich man appeared to be blessed with all he needed and wanted in life, but at the moment of his death, it became apparent that he did not possess the most important thing—faith in Jesus Christ. Ironically, this one thing is all that Lazarus did possess during his life, and in the end, it was all he really needed. As the one who seemed to have everything entered into an eternity separated from God in constant torment, he realized he had placed his trust in the wrong things. Lazarus entered into his eternal reward, having gained it all through his trust in Jesus Christ.

Today is the day to choose whether your trust will be in the things of this world or in Christ alone.

—Dr. Marty Jacumin
Bay Leaf Baptist Church, Raleigh, NC

WEEK 17, DAY 2

Having a Thankful Heart

Luke 17:5–37

Faith and Duty

And the apostles said to the Lord, "Increase our faith." ⁶So the Lord said, "If you have faith as a mustard seed, you can say to this mulberry tree, 'Be pulled up by the roots and be planted in the sea,' and it would obey you. ⁷And which of you, having a servant plowing or tending sheep, will say to him when he has come in from the field, 'Come at once and sit down to eat'? ⁸But will he not rather say to him, 'Prepare something for my supper, and gird yourself and serve me till I have eaten and drunk, and afterward you will eat and drink'? ⁹Does he thank that servant because he did the things that were commanded him? I think not. ¹⁰So likewise you, when you have done all those things which you are commanded, say, 'We are unprofitable servants. We have done what was our duty to do.'"

Ten Lepers Cleansed

¹¹Now it happened as He went to Jerusalem that He passed through the midst of Samaria and Galilee. ¹²Then as He entered a certain village, there met Him ten men who were lepers, who stood afar off. ¹³And they lifted up their voices and said, "Jesus, Master, have mercy on us!"

¹⁴So when He saw them, He said to them, "Go, show yourselves to the priests." And so it was that as they went, they were cleansed.

¹⁵And one of them, when he saw that he was healed, returned, and with a loud voice glorified God, ¹⁶and fell down on his face at His feet, giving Him thanks. And he was a Samaritan.

¹⁷So Jesus answered and said, "Were there not ten cleansed? But where are the nine? ¹⁸Were there not any found who returned to give glory to God except this foreigner?" ¹⁹And He said to him, "Arise, go your way. Your faith has made you well."

The Coming of the Kingdom

²⁰Now when He was asked by the Pharisees when the kingdom of God would come, He answered them and said, "The kingdom of God does not come with observation; ²¹nor will they say, 'See here!' or 'See there!' For indeed, the kingdom of God is within you."

²²Then He said to the disciples, "The days will come when you will desire to see one of the days of the Son of Man, and you will not see it. ²³And they will say to you, 'Look here!' or 'Look there!' Do not go after them or follow them. ²⁴For as the lightning that flashes out of one part under heaven shines to the other part under heaven, so also the Son of Man will be in His day. ²⁵But first He must suffer many things and be rejected by this generation. ²⁶And as it was in the days of Noah, so it will be also in the days of the Son of Man: ²⁷They ate, they drank, they married wives, they were given in marriage, until the day that Noah entered the ark, and the flood came and destroyed them all. ²⁸Likewise as it was also in the days of Lot: They ate, they drank, they bought, they sold, they planted, they built; ²⁹but on the day that Lot went out of Sodom it rained fire and brimstone from heaven and destroyed them all. ³⁰Even so will it be in the day when the Son of Man is revealed.

³¹"In that day, he who is on the housetop, and his goods are in the house, let him not come down to take them away. And likewise the one who is in the field, let him not turn back. ³²Remember Lot's wife. ³³Whoever seeks to save his life will lose it, and whoever loses his life will preserve it. ³⁴I tell you, in that night there will be two men in one bed: the one will be taken and the other will be left. ³⁵Two women will be grinding together: the one will be taken and the other left. ³⁶Two men will be in the field: the one will be taken and the other left."

³⁷And they answered and said to Him, "Where, Lord?"

So He said to them, "Wherever the body is, there the eagles will be gathered together."

DEVOTIONAL

A sense of entitlement plagues our nation today. People often feel they deserve more than they have—more money, better health, a higher-paying job. The terrible consequence of entitlement is an unthankful heart. Because we have specific good things in mind we'd like to receive, we are not thankful when we receive the good things God chooses to give us. Jesus healed ten lepers, but only one of them felt the need to find Him and thank Him.

If you've put your trust in Jesus, He has healed you of the disease of sin. He has touched your life and cleansed you. Are you like the thankful leper? Too often we all forget what it cost Jesus to redeem us and are not as thankful as we should be. Take time today to thank God for His great gift of salvation and for His many other gifts in your life.

—Dr. Marty Jacumin
Bay Leaf Baptist Church, Raleigh, NC

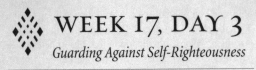

WEEK 17, DAY 3

Guarding Against Self-Righteousness

Luke 18:1–25

The Parable of the Persistent Widow

18 Then He spoke a parable to them, that men always ought to pray and not lose heart, ²saying: "There was in a certain city a judge who did not fear God nor regard man. ³Now there was a widow in that city; and she came to him, saying, 'Get justice for me from my adversary.' ⁴And he would not for a while; but afterward he said within himself, 'Though I do not fear God nor regard man, ⁵yet because this widow troubles me I will avenge her, lest by her continual coming she weary me.'"

⁶Then the Lord said, "Hear what the unjust judge said. ⁷And shall God not avenge His own elect who cry out day and night to Him, though He bears long with them? ⁸I tell you that He will avenge them speedily. Nevertheless, when the Son of Man comes, will He really find faith on the earth?"

The Parable of the Pharisee and the Tax Collector

⁹Also He spoke this parable to some who trusted in themselves that they were righteous, and despised others: ¹⁰"Two men went up to the temple to pray, one a Pharisee and the other a tax collector. ¹¹The Pharisee stood and prayed thus with himself, 'God, I thank You that I am not like other men—extortioners, unjust, adulterers, or even as this tax collector. ¹²I fast twice a week; I give tithes of all that I possess.' ¹³And the tax collector, standing afar off, would not so much as raise his eyes to heaven, but beat his breast, saying, 'God, be merciful to me a sinner!' ¹⁴I tell you, this man went down to his house justified rather than the other; for everyone who exalts himself will be humbled, and he who humbles himself will be exalted."

Jesus Blesses Little Children

¹⁵Then they also brought infants to Him that He might touch them; but when the disciples saw it, they rebuked them. ¹⁶But Jesus called them to Him and said, "Let the little children come to Me, and do not forbid them; for of such is the kingdom of God. ¹⁷Assuredly, I say to you, whoever does not receive the kingdom of God as a little child will by no means enter it."

Jesus Counsels the Rich Young Ruler

¹⁸Now a certain ruler asked Him, saying, "Good Teacher, what shall I do to inherit eternal life?"

¹⁹So Jesus said to him, "Why do you call Me good? No one is good but One, that is, God. ²⁰You know the commandments: 'Do not commit adultery,' 'Do not murder,' 'Do not steal,' 'Do not bear false witness,' 'Honor your father and your mother.'"

²¹And he said, "All these things I have kept from my youth."

²²So when Jesus heard these things, He said to him, "You still lack one thing. Sell all that you have and distribute to the poor, and you will have treasure in heaven; and come, follow Me."

²³But when he heard this, he became very sorrowful, for he was very rich.

With God All Things Are Possible

²⁴And when Jesus saw that he became very sorrowful, He said, "How hard it is for those who have riches to enter the kingdom of God! ²⁵For it is easier for a camel to go through the eye of a needle than for a rich man to enter the kingdom of God."

DEVOTIONAL

When we read about the life of Jesus, it is clear that the Pharisees hated Him and sought every opportunity to criticize Him and stop His ministry. Their hatred grew to the point where they no longer simply wanted to stop His teachings—they desired to kill Him.

It's easy for us as believers to have disdain for the Pharisees. We place ourselves on the side of Jesus and presume we would have had nothing to do with the bloodthirsty religious leaders. But we need to examine our hearts consistently as we walk with Jesus. If we're not careful, we can be judgmental toward other believers, simply because we don't agree with the way they do things, and wind up having hearts that look more like the Pharisees than we'd expect.

Jesus taught a parable about a Pharisee and a tax collector who were praying in the temple. The tax collector confessed his sins before God and cried out for forgiveness. The Pharisee never confessed his sins; He only boasted about his religious credentials and thanked God that he was more pious than the sinful men around him.

Don't let yourself fall into the sin of self-righteousness. Focus on your own life and the sins you need to confess more than the sins of those around you.

—Dr. Marty Jacumin
Bay Leaf Baptist Church, Raleigh, NC

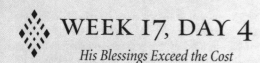

WEEK 17, DAY 4

His Blessings Exceed the Cost

Luke 18:26–19:10

And those who heard it said, "Who then can be saved?"

27But He said, "The things which are impossible with men are possible with God."

28Then Peter said, "See, we have left all and followed You."

29So He said to them, "Assuredly, I say to you, there is no one who has left house or parents or brothers or wife or children, for the sake of the kingdom of God, 30who shall not receive many times more in this present time, and in the age to come eternal life."

Jesus a Third Time Predicts His Death and Resurrection

31Then He took the twelve aside and said to them, "Behold, we are going up to Jerusalem, and all things that are written by the prophets concerning the Son of Man will be accomplished. 32For He will be delivered to the Gentiles and will be mocked and insulted and spit upon. 33They will scourge Him and kill Him. And the third day He will rise again."

34But they understood none of these things; this saying was hidden from them, and they did not know the things which were spoken.

A Blind Man Receives His Sight

35Then it happened, as He was coming near Jericho, that a certain blind man sat by the road begging. 36And hearing a multitude passing by, he asked what it meant. 37So they told him that Jesus of Nazareth was passing by. 38And he cried out, saying, "Jesus, Son of David, have mercy on me!"

39Then those who went before warned him that he should be quiet; but he cried out all the more, "Son of David, have mercy on me!"

40So Jesus stood still and commanded him to be brought to Him. And when he had come near, He asked him, 41saying, "What do you want Me to do for you?"

He said, "Lord, that I may receive my sight."

42Then Jesus said to him, "Receive your sight; your faith has made you well." 43And immediately he received his sight, and followed Him, glorifying God. And all the people, when they saw it, gave praise to God.

Jesus Comes to Zacchaeus' House

19Then Jesus entered and passed through Jericho. 2Now behold, there was a man named Zacchaeus who was a chief tax collector, and he was rich. 3And he sought to see who Jesus was, but could not because of the crowd, for he was of short stature. 4So he ran ahead and climbed up into a sycamore tree to see Him, for He was going to pass that way. 5And when Jesus came to the place, He looked up and saw him, and said to him, "Zacchaeus, make haste and come down, for today I must stay at your house." 6So he made haste and came down, and received Him joyfully. 7But when they saw it, they all complained, saying, "He has gone to be a guest with a man who is a sinner."

8Then Zacchaeus stood and said to the Lord, "Look, Lord, I give half of my goods to the poor; and if I have taken anything from anyone by false accusation, I restore fourfold."

9And Jesus said to him, "Today salvation has come to this house, because he also is a son of Abraham; 10for the Son of Man has come to seek and to save that which was lost."

DEVOTIONAL

During the current economic recession, gas and food costs have increased while savings and retirement accounts have been depleted. Most of us have been forced to change the way we live our lives, examining every expense to decide what is a necessity and what is not. We have been forced to count the cost of every choice.

We do not have to pay money to come to faith in Christ, but, according to God's Word, following Christ comes with a cost. It may cost us financial opportunities, relationships, or popularity. In some places, following Christ may even cost a person his or her life.

In our reading for today, Peter told Jesus that he and the other disciples had left everything to follow Him. They had counted the cost and forsaken every hindrance. Jesus said that whatever His faithful followers give up for the sake of the kingdom of God pales in comparison to the blessings God will pour out on them.

Let's choose to follow Christ today, confident in His promise that His blessings will exceed the cost!

—Dr. Marty Jacumin
Bay Leaf Baptist Church, Raleigh, NC

WEEK 17, DAY 5

The One True King

Luke 19:11–40

The Parable of the Minas

Now as they heard these things, He spoke another parable, because He was near Jerusalem and because they thought the kingdom of God would appear immediately. 12Therefore He said: "A certain nobleman went into a far country to receive for himself a kingdom and to return. 13So he called ten of his servants, delivered to them ten minas, and said to them, 'Do business till I come.' 14But his citizens hated him, and sent a delegation after him, saying, 'We will not have this man to reign over us.'

15"And so it was that when he returned, having received the kingdom, he then commanded these servants, to whom he had given the money, to be called to him, that he might know how much every man had gained by trading. 16Then came the first, saying, 'Master, your mina has earned ten minas.' 17And he said to him, 'Well done, good servant; because you were faithful in a very little, have authority over ten cities.' 18And the second came, saying, 'Master, your mina has earned five minas.' 19Likewise he said to him, 'You also be over five cities.'

20"Then another came, saying, 'Master, here is your mina, which I have kept put away in a handkerchief. 21For I feared you, because you are an austere man. You collect what you did not deposit, and reap what you did not sow.' 22And he said to him, 'Out of your own mouth I will judge you, you wicked servant. You knew that I was an austere man, collecting what I did not deposit and reaping what I did not sow. 23Why then did you not put my money in the bank, that at my coming I might have collected it with interest?'

24"And he said to those who stood by, 'Take the mina from him, and give it to him who has ten minas.' 25(But they said to him, 'Master, he has ten minas.') 26'For I say to you, that to everyone who has will be given; and from him who does not have, even what he has will be taken away from him. 27But bring here those enemies of mine, who did not want me to reign over them, and slay them before me.'"

The Triumphal Entry

28When He had said this, He went on ahead, going up to Jerusalem. 29And it came to pass, when He drew near to Bethphage and Bethany, at the mountain called Olivet, that He sent two of His disciples, 30saying, "Go into the village opposite you, where as you enter you will find a colt tied, on which no one has ever sat. Loose it and bring it here. 31And if anyone asks you, 'Why are you loosing it?' thus you shall say to him, 'Because the Lord has need of it.'"

32So those who were sent went their way and found it just as He had said to them. 33But as they were loosing the colt, the owners of it said to them, "Why are you loosing the colt?"

34And they said, "The Lord has need of him." 35Then they brought him to Jesus. And they threw their own clothes on the colt, and they set Jesus on him. 36And as He went, many spread their clothes on the road.

37Then, as He was now drawing near the descent of the Mount of Olives, the whole multitude of the disciples began to rejoice and praise God with a loud voice for all the mighty works they had seen, 38saying:

> "'Blessed is the King who comes in the name
>   of the Lord!'
> Peace in heaven and glory in the highest!"

39And some of the Pharisees called to Him from the crowd, "Teacher, rebuke Your disciples."

40But He answered and said to them, "I tell you that if these should keep silent, the stones would immediately cry out."

DEVOTIONAL

Most Americans have not witnessed the pomp and circumstance of a traveling monarch. American politicians often travel with an entourage of security and assistants, but royal family members usually travel with great pageantry that is worthy of their position.

When Jesus entered Jerusalem on the day we now celebrate as Palm Sunday, He was treated like a king. He traveled into the city on the back of a young donkey while the people laid down their coats, waved palm branches, and cried out praises to God. Of all the kings who ever walked on the earth, Jesus is the One who deserved all the praise He received, because as He entered the city, He knew He was heading to the cross to fulfill God's redemption plan.

Jesus is the one true King who is worthy of our praise and adoration, and He is the one true God who is worthy of our worship and complete allegiance. Live like He is your King today!

—Dr. Marty Jacumin
Bay Leaf Baptist Church, Raleigh, NC

WEEK 17, DAY 6

Grieving over What Grieves God

Luke 19:41–20:19

Jesus Weeps over Jerusalem

Now as He drew near, He saw the city and wept over it, 42saying, "If you had known, even you, especially in this your day, the things that make for your peace! But now they are hidden from your eyes. 43For days will come upon you when your enemies will build an embankment around you, surround you and close you in on every side, 44and level you, and your children within you, to the ground; and they will not leave in you one stone upon another, because you did not know the time of your visitation."

Jesus Cleanses the Temple

45Then He went into the temple and began to drive out those who bought and sold in it, 46saying to them, "It is written, 'My house is a house of prayer,' but you have made it a 'den of thieves.'"

47And He was teaching daily in the temple. But the chief priests, the scribes, and the leaders of the people sought to destroy Him, 48and were unable to do anything; for all the people were very attentive to hear Him.

Jesus' Authority Questioned

20 Now it happened on one of those days, as He taught the people in the temple and preached the gospel, that the chief priests and the scribes, together with the elders, confronted Him 2and spoke to Him, saying, "Tell us, by what authority are You doing these things? Or who is he who gave You this authority?"

3But He answered and said to them, "I also will ask you one thing, and answer Me: 4The baptism of John—was it from heaven or from men?"

5And they reasoned among themselves, saying, "If we say, 'From heaven,' He will say, 'Why then did you not believe him?' 6But if we say, 'From men,' all the people will stone us, for they are persuaded that John was a prophet." 7So they answered that they did not know where it was from.

8And Jesus said to them, "Neither will I tell you by what authority I do these things."

The Parable of the Wicked Vinedressers

9Then He began to tell the people this parable: "A certain man planted a vineyard, leased it to vinedressers, and went into a far country for a long time. 10Now at vintage-time he sent a servant to the vinedressers, that they might give him some of the fruit of the vineyard. But the vinedressers beat him and sent him away empty-handed. 11Again he sent another servant; and they beat him also, treated him shamefully, and sent him away empty-handed. 12And again he sent a third; and they wounded him also and cast him out.

13"Then the owner of the vineyard said, 'What shall I do? I will send my beloved son. Probably they will respect him when they see him.' 14But when the vinedressers saw him, they reasoned among themselves, saying, 'This is the heir. Come, let us kill him, that the inheritance may be ours.' 15So they cast him out of the vineyard and killed him. Therefore what will the owner of the vineyard do to them? 16He will come and destroy those vinedressers and give the vineyard to others."

And when they heard it they said, "Certainly not!"

17Then He looked at them and said, "What then is this that is written:

'The stone which the builders rejected
Has become the chief cornerstone'?

18Whoever falls on that stone will be broken; but on whomever it falls, it will grind him to powder."

19And the chief priests and the scribes that very hour sought to lay hands on Him, but they feared the people—for they knew He had spoken this parable against them.

DEVOTIONAL

What upsets you? Perhaps it's when you are cut off in traffic or when someone says something unkind to you. Maybe it's when your favorite team loses a game. We often get the most upset over relatively trivial things.

In Luke 19:41, Jesus was upset about something. Luke says Jesus wept over Jerusalem. It grieved Him that the Jewish people would face judgment because of their rejection of Him. In Acts 17, Paul was extremely upset when he saw all the gods worshiped in Athens while the one true God was rejected. Can you relate with either of these experiences?

As Christians, we should grieve over the things that grieve the heart of God. When was the last time you were moved to tears over the sin in your own life, or deeply upset about sin in the lives of others? Ask God to show you what grieves His heart and to make your heart like His.

—Dr. Marty Jacumin
Bay Leaf Baptist Church, Raleigh, NC

WEEK 17, DAY 7

What are some things in which you tend to trust instead of Jesus?

_____

_____

_____

_____

_____

_____

_____

_____

_____

_____

_____

_____

What has following Jesus cost you?

_____

_____

_____

_____

_____

_____

_____

_____

_____

WEEK 18, DAY 1

Receiving God's Truth

Luke 20:20–47

The Pharisees: Is It Lawful to Pay Taxes to Caesar?

So they watched Him, and sent spies who pretended to be righteous, that they might seize on His words, in order to deliver Him to the power and the authority of the governor. [21]Then they asked Him, saying, "Teacher, we know that You say and teach rightly, and You do not show personal favoritism, but teach the way of God in truth: [22]Is it lawful for us to pay taxes to Caesar or not?"

[23]But He perceived their craftiness, and said to them, "Why do you test Me? [24]Show Me a denarius. Whose image and inscription does it have?"

They answered and said, "Caesar's."

[25]And He said to them, "Render therefore to Caesar the things that are Caesar's, and to God the things that are God's."

[26]But they could not catch Him in His words in the presence of the people. And they marveled at His answer and kept silent.

The Sadducees: What About the Resurrection?

[27]Then some of the Sadducees, who deny that there is a resurrection, came to Him and asked Him, [28]saying: "Teacher, Moses wrote to us that if a man's brother dies, having a wife, and he dies without children, his brother should take his wife and raise up offspring for his brother. [29]Now there were seven brothers. And the first took a wife, and died without children. [30]And the second took her as wife, and he died childless. [31]Then the third took her, and in like manner the seven also; and they left no children, and died. [32]Last of all the woman died also. [33]Therefore, in the resurrection, whose wife does she become? For all seven had her as wife."

[34]Jesus answered and said to them, "The sons of this age marry and are given in marriage. [35]But those who are counted worthy to attain that age, and the resurrection from the dead, neither marry nor are given in marriage; [36]nor can they die anymore, for they are equal to the angels and are sons of God, being sons of the resurrection. [37]But even Moses showed in the burning bush passage that the dead are raised, when he called the Lord 'the God of Abraham, the God of Isaac, and the God of Jacob.' [38]For He is not the God of the dead but of the living, for all live to Him."

[39]Then some of the scribes answered and said, "Teacher, You have spoken well." [40]But after that they dared not question Him anymore.

Jesus: How Can David Call His Descendant Lord?

[41]And He said to them, "How can they say that the Christ is the Son of David? [42]Now David himself said in the book of Psalms:

'The LORD said to my Lord,
"Sit at My right hand,
[43]   Till I make Your enemies Your footstool."'

[44]Therefore David calls Him 'Lord'; how is He then his Son?"

Beware of the Scribes

[45]Then, in the hearing of all the people, He said to His disciples, [46]"Beware of the scribes, who desire to go around in long robes, love greetings in the marketplaces, the best seats in the synagogues, and the best places at feasts, [47]who devour widows' houses, and for a pretense make long prayers. These will receive greater condemnation."

DEVOTIONAL

Comedian W. C. Fields was known for being an atheist who was critical of Christianity. When a friend once caught him reading the Bible, Fields said he was "looking for a loophole."[6]

People frequently came to Jesus to ask Him questions. There are two kinds of questions: honest and dishonest. Sometimes people honestly wanted to know who Jesus was and what it meant to follow Him. For honest seekers, He gave simple, clear answers. Others were only looking for some excuse not to believe in Him, some loophole in His claims. Those cynics only got caught in their own trap.

Are you open to the truth? Search your heart to see if any preconceptions not founded in the truth of God's Word are holding you back. Jesus is the Way, the Truth, and the Life, and He wants to reveal more of Himself to you. Approach Him with a spirit of trust and submission. Read His Word with a heart that is willing to listen and believe, and allow it to be the only authority for your beliefs and behavior.

—Dr. Michael Cloer
Englewood Baptist Church, Rocky Mount, NC

WEEK 18, DAY 2

Our Redeemer Is Coming

Luke 21:1–28

The Widow's Two Mites

21 And He looked up and saw the rich putting their gifts into the treasury, 2and He saw also a certain poor widow putting in two mites. 3So He said, "Truly I say to you that this poor widow has put in more than all; 4for all these out of their abundance have put in offerings for God, but she out of her poverty put in all the livelihood that she had."

Jesus Predicts the Destruction of the Temple

5Then, as some spoke of the temple, how it was adorned with beautiful stones and donations, He said, 6"These things which you see—the days will come in which not one stone shall be left upon another that shall not be thrown down."

The Signs of the Times and the End of the Age

7So they asked Him, saying, "Teacher, but when will these things be? And what sign will there be when these things are about to take place?"

8And He said: "Take heed that you not be deceived. For many will come in My name, saying, 'I am He,' and, 'The time has drawn near.' Therefore do not go after them. 9But when you hear of wars and commotions, do not be terrified; for these things must come to pass first, but the end will not come immediately."

10Then He said to them, "Nation will rise against nation, and kingdom against kingdom. 11And there will be great earthquakes in various places, and famines and pestilences; and there will be fearful sights and great signs from heaven. 12But before all these things, they will lay their hands on you and persecute you, delivering you up to the synagogues and prisons. You will be brought before kings and rulers for My name's sake. 13But it will turn out for you as an occasion for testimony. 14Therefore settle it in your hearts not to meditate beforehand on what you will answer; 15for I will give you a mouth and wisdom which all your adversaries will not be able to contradict or resist. 16You will be betrayed even by parents and brothers, relatives and friends; and they will put some of you to death. 17And you will be hated by all for My name's sake. 18But not a hair of your head shall be lost. 19By your patience possess your souls.

The Destruction of Jerusalem

20"But when you see Jerusalem surrounded by armies, then know that its desolation is near. 21Then let those who are in Judea flee to the mountains, let those who are in the midst of her depart, and let not those who are in the country enter her. 22For these are the days of vengeance, that all things which are written may be fulfilled. 23But woe to those who are pregnant and to those who are nursing babies in those days! For there will be great distress in the land and wrath upon this people. 24And they will fall by the edge of the sword, and be led away captive into all nations. And Jerusalem will be trampled by Gentiles until the times of the Gentiles are fulfilled.

The Coming of the Son of Man

25"And there will be signs in the sun, in the moon, and in the stars; and on the earth distress of nations, with perplexity, the sea and the waves roaring; 26men's hearts failing them from fear and the expectation of those things which are coming on the earth, for the powers of the heavens will be shaken. 27Then they will see the Son of Man coming in a cloud with power and great glory. 28Now when these things begin to happen, look up and lift up your heads, because your redemption draws near."

DEVOTIONAL

*I*t's been said that it's always darkest just before dawn. One does not have to be a Bible scholar or historian to know that this world is becoming darker by the hour. Every day we hear of wars, famines, earthquakes, diseases—exactly what Jesus said would happen.

In today's news we see Jerusalem being encircled by hostile nations, like a pack of wolves surrounding a little lamb. This city, divinely ordained as the capital of Israel and the Jewish people, is being terrorized by Gentiles. Today, Muslims occupy the most important piece of ground on the earth, the Temple Mount, and vow never to relinquish control. Jesus told us to expect this darkness until the last Gentile who is going to be saved is saved, and He returns to take up His bride.

Do not be discouraged or hang your head when you watch the news. Instead, look up and lift your head (Luke 21:28)—Jesus may come at any time. Things are looking gloriously dark . . . our Redeemer is coming!

—Dr. Michael Cloer
Englewood Baptist Church, Rocky Mount, NC

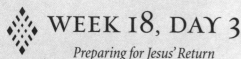

WEEK 18, DAY 3

Preparing for Jesus' Return

Luke 21:29–22:20

The Parable of the Fig Tree

Then He spoke to them a parable: "Look at the fig tree, and all the trees. ³⁰When they are already budding, you see and know for yourselves that summer is now near. ³¹So you also, when you see these things happening, know that the kingdom of God is near. ³²Assuredly, I say to you, this generation will by no means pass away till all things take place. ³³Heaven and earth will pass away, but My words will by no means pass away.

The Importance of Watching

³⁴"But take heed to yourselves, lest your hearts be weighed down with carousing, drunkenness, and cares of this life, and that Day come on you unexpectedly. ³⁵For it will come as a snare on all those who dwell on the face of the whole earth. ³⁶Watch therefore, and pray always that you may be counted worthy to escape all these things that will come to pass, and to stand before the Son of Man."

³⁷And in the daytime He was teaching in the temple, but at night He went out and stayed on the mountain called Olivet. ³⁸Then early in the morning all the people came to Him in the temple to hear Him.

The Plot to Kill Jesus

22 Now the Feast of Unleavened Bread drew near, which is called Passover. ²And the chief priests and the scribes sought how they might kill Him, for they feared the people.

³Then Satan entered Judas, surnamed Iscariot, who was numbered among the twelve. ⁴So he went his way and conferred with the chief priests and captains, how he might betray Him to them. ⁵And they were glad, and agreed to give him money. ⁶So he promised and sought opportunity to betray Him to them in the absence of the multitude.

Jesus and His Disciples Prepare the Passover

⁷Then came the Day of Unleavened Bread, when the Passover must be killed. ⁸And He sent Peter and John, saying, "Go and prepare the Passover for us, that we may eat." ⁹So they said to Him, "Where do You want us to prepare?" ¹⁰And He said to them, "Behold, when you have entered the city, a man will meet you carrying a pitcher of water; follow him into the house which he enters. ¹¹Then you shall say to the master of the house, 'The Teacher says to you, "Where is the guest room where I may eat the Passover with My disciples?" ' ¹²Then he will show you a large, furnished upper room; there make ready."

¹³So they went and found it just as He had said to them, and they prepared the Passover.

Jesus Institutes the Lord's Supper

¹⁴When the hour had come, He sat down, and the twelve apostles with Him. ¹⁵Then He said to them, "With fervent desire I have desired to eat this Passover with you before I suffer; ¹⁶for I say to you, I will no longer eat of it until it is fulfilled in the kingdom of God."

¹⁷Then He took the cup, and gave thanks, and said, "Take this and divide it among yourselves; ¹⁸for I say to you, I will not drink of the fruit of the vine until the kingdom of God comes."

¹⁹And He took bread, gave thanks and broke it, and gave it to them, saying, "This is My body which is given for you; do this in remembrance of Me."

²⁰Likewise He also took the cup after supper, saying, "This cup is the new covenant in My blood, which is shed for you."

DEVOTIONAL

*O*ur Lord commanded us to prepare for His Second Coming and warned us to be guarded against the schemes of the Enemy. The devil can use the cares, comforts, conveniences, companions, and the carousing of this life as bait for his traps. When we become so preoccupied with the events of this world, we've walked into his trap without realizing it. When we're preoccupied, we are not earnestly preparing for Jesus' return.

If all the signs point to the imminent return of Jesus Christ, what are we to do until He returns? First, we are to be careful to avoid all snares. "Take heed to yourselves," Jesus said, before describing people with hearts weighed down with the things of earthly life (Luke 21:34). Second, we are to be watchful, just like watchmen on the walls who constantly look for both their enemy and the return of their king. Third, we are to be continually prayerful. Fourth, we are to be worshipful, keeping our focus not on ourselves, but on Him.

Are you preoccupied with the immediate, or are you earnestly preparing for your King?

—Dr. Michael Cloer
Englewood Baptist Church, Rocky Mount, NC

WEEK 18, DAY 4

The Cost of Obedience

Luke 22:21–53

"But behold, the hand of My betrayer is with Me on the table. 22And truly the Son of Man goes as it has been determined, but woe to that man by whom He is betrayed!"

23Then they began to question among themselves, which of them it was who would do this thing.

The Disciples Argue About Greatness

24Now there was also a dispute among them, as to which of them should be considered the greatest. 25And He said to them, "The kings of the Gentiles exercise lordship over them, and those who exercise authority over them are called 'benefactors.' 26But not so among you; on the contrary, he who is greatest among you, let him be as the younger, and he who governs as he who serves. 27For who is greater, he who sits at the table, or he who serves? Is it not he who sits at the table? Yet I am among you as the One who serves.

28"But you are those who have continued with Me in My trials. 29And I bestow upon you a kingdom, just as My Father bestowed one upon Me, 30that you may eat and drink at My table in My kingdom, and sit on thrones judging the twelve tribes of Israel."

Jesus Predicts Peter's Denial

31And the Lord said, "Simon, Simon! Indeed, Satan has asked for you, that he may sift you as wheat. 32But I have prayed for you, that your faith should not fail; and when you have returned to Me, strengthen your brethren."

33But he said to Him, "Lord, I am ready to go with You, both to prison and to death."

34Then He said, "I tell you, Peter, the rooster shall not crow this day before you will deny three times that you know Me."

Supplies for the Road

35And He said to them, "When I sent you without money bag, knapsack, and sandals, did you lack anything?"

So they said, "Nothing."

36Then He said to them, "But now, he who has a money bag, let him take it, and likewise a knapsack; and he who has no sword, let him sell his garment and buy one. 37For I say to you that this which is written must still be accomplished in Me: 'And He was numbered with the transgressors.' For the things concerning Me have an end."

38So they said, "Lord, look, here are two swords." And He said to them, "It is enough."

The Prayer in the Garden

39Coming out, He went to the Mount of Olives, as He was accustomed, and His disciples also followed Him. 40When He came to the place, He said to them, "Pray that you may not enter into temptation."

41And He was withdrawn from them about a stone's throw, and He knelt down and prayed, 42saying, "Father, if it is Your will, take this cup away from Me; nevertheless not My will, but Yours, be done." 43Then an angel appeared to Him from heaven, strengthening Him. 44And being in agony, He prayed more earnestly. Then His sweat became like great drops of blood falling down to the ground.

45When He rose up from prayer, and had come to His disciples, He found them sleeping from sorrow. 46Then He said to them, "Why do you sleep? Rise and pray, lest you enter into temptation."

Betrayal and Arrest in Gethsemane

47And while He was still speaking, behold, a multitude; and he who was called Judas, one of the twelve, went before them and drew near to Jesus to kiss Him. 48But Jesus said to him, "Judas, are you betraying the Son of Man with a kiss?"

49When those around Him saw what was going to happen, they said to Him, "Lord, shall we strike with the sword?" 50And one of them struck the servant of the high priest and cut off his right ear.

51But Jesus answered and said, "Permit even this." And He touched his ear and healed him.

52Then Jesus said to the chief priests, captains of the temple, and the elders who had come to Him, "Have you come out, as against a robber, with swords and clubs? 53When I was with you daily in the temple, you did not try to seize Me. But this is your hour, and the power of darkness."

DEVOTIONAL

Following Jesus may cost you emotionally, financially, socially, and physically. You'll sometimes face a crisis of obedience. But God will help you. Like Peter, be willing to do anything and go anywhere for Jesus, even if that means death (Luke 22:33). Express your feelings to God and receive His comfort. Then do what He tells you to do.

—Dr. Michael Cloer
Englewood Baptist Church, Rocky Mount, NC

WEEK 18, DAY 5

Stay Close to Jesus

Luke 22:54–23:12

Peter Denies Jesus, and Weeps Bitterly

Having arrested Him, they led *Him* and brought Him into the high priest's house. But Peter followed at a distance. ⁵⁵Now when they had kindled a fire in the midst of the courtyard and sat down together, Peter sat among them. ⁵⁶And a certain servant girl, seeing him as he sat by the fire, looked intently at him and said, "This man was also with Him."

⁵⁷But he denied Him, saying, "Woman, I do not know Him."

⁵⁸And after a little while another saw him and said, "You also are of them."

But Peter said, "Man, I am not!"

⁵⁹Then after about an hour had passed, another confidently affirmed, saying, "Surely this fellow also was with Him, for he is a Galilean."

⁶⁰But Peter said, "Man, I do not know what you are saying!"

Immediately, while he was still speaking, the rooster crowed. ⁶¹And the Lord turned and looked at Peter. Then Peter remembered the word of the Lord, how He had said to him, "Before the rooster crows, you will deny Me three times." ⁶²So Peter went out and wept bitterly.

Jesus Mocked and Beaten

⁶³Now the men who held Jesus mocked Him and beat Him. ⁶⁴And having blindfolded Him, they struck Him on the face and asked Him, saying, "Prophesy! Who is the one who struck You?" ⁶⁵And many other things they blasphemously spoke against Him.

Jesus Faces the Sanhedrin

⁶⁶As soon as it was day, the elders of the people, both chief priests and scribes, came together and led Him into their council, saying, ⁶⁷"If You are the Christ, tell us."

But He said to them, "If I tell you, you will by no means believe. ⁶⁸And if I also ask you, you will by no means answer Me or let *Me* go. ⁶⁹Hereafter the Son of Man will sit on the right hand of the power of God."

⁷⁰Then they all said, "Are You then the Son of God?"

So He said to them, "You rightly say that I am."

⁷¹And they said, "What further testimony do we need? For we have heard it ourselves from His own mouth."

Jesus Handed Over to Pontius Pilate

23 Then the whole multitude of them arose and led Him to Pilate. ²And they began to accuse Him, saying, "We found this fellow perverting the nation, and forbidding to pay taxes to Caesar, saying that He Himself is Christ, a King."

³Then Pilate asked Him, saying, "Are You the King of the Jews?"

He answered him and said, "It is as you say."

⁴So Pilate said to the chief priests and the crowd, "I find no fault in this Man."

⁵But they were the more fierce, saying, "He stirs up the people, teaching throughout all Judea, beginning from Galilee to this place."

Jesus Faces Herod

⁶When Pilate heard of Galilee, he asked if the Man were a Galilean. ⁷And as soon as he knew that He belonged to Herod's jurisdiction, he sent Him to Herod, who was also in Jerusalem at that time. ⁸Now when Herod saw Jesus, he was exceedingly glad; for he had desired for a long time to see Him, because he had heard many things about Him, and he hoped to see some miracle done by Him. ⁹Then he questioned Him with many words, but He answered him nothing. ¹⁰And the chief priests and scribes stood and vehemently accused Him. ¹¹Then Herod, with his men of war, treated Him with contempt and mocked Him, arrayed Him in a gorgeous robe, and sent Him back to Pilate. ¹²That very day Pilate and Herod became friends with each other, for previously they had been at enmity with each other.

DEVOTIONAL

In one night, Peter went from exhibiting furious loyalty to Jesus to denying he even knew Him. How could a rugged fisherman cut an ear off a Roman soldier and then be such a coward in front of a teenage servant in a matter of hours?

Peter experienced the power of enjoying Jesus' presence. As long as Peter was with Jesus, he was bold and faithful. Left on his own, he compromised. Learn to enjoy abiding with Jesus. Stay close to Him daily through personal devotions, worship, Bible study, and continual prayer. Any of us are capable of denying Jesus when we try to stand alone. Stay close to Him.

—Dr. Michael Cloer
Englewood Baptist Church, Rocky Mount, NC

WEEK 18, DAY 6

Jesus Took Our Punishment

Luke 23:13–43

Taking the Place of Barabbas

Then Pilate, when he had called together the chief priests, the rulers, and the people, 14said to them, "You have brought this Man to me, as one who misleads the people. And indeed, having examined Him in your presence, I have found no fault in this Man concerning those things of which you accuse Him; 15no, neither did Herod, for I sent you back to him; and indeed nothing deserving of death has been done by Him. 16I will therefore chastise Him and release Him" 17(for it was necessary for him to release one to them at the feast).

18And they all cried out at once, saying, "Away with this Man, and release to us Barabbas"— 19who had been thrown into prison for a certain rebellion made in the city, and for murder.

20Pilate, therefore, wishing to release Jesus, again called out to them. 21But they shouted, saying, "Crucify Him, crucify Him!"

22Then he said to them the third time, "Why, what evil has He done? I have found no reason for death in Him. I will therefore chastise Him and let Him go."

23But they were insistent, demanding with loud voices that He be crucified. And the voices of these men and of the chief priests prevailed. 24So Pilate gave sentence that it should be as they requested. 25And he released to them the one they requested, who for rebellion and murder had been thrown into prison; but he delivered Jesus to their will.

The King on a Cross

26Now as they led Him away, they laid hold of a certain man, Simon a Cyrenian, who was coming from the country, and on him they laid the cross that he might bear it after Jesus.

27And a great multitude of the people followed Him, and women who also mourned and lamented Him. 28But Jesus, turning to them, said, "Daughters of Jerusalem, do not weep for Me, but weep for yourselves and for your children. 29For indeed the days are coming in which they will say, 'Blessed *are* the barren, wombs that never bore, and breasts which never nursed!' 30Then they will begin 'to say to the mountains, "Fall on us!" and to the hills, "Cover us!" ' 31For if they do these things in the green wood, what will be done in the dry?"

32There were also two others, criminals, led with Him to be put to death. 33And when they had come to the place called Calvary, there they crucified Him, and the criminals, one on the right hand and the other on the left. 34Then Jesus said, "Father, forgive them, for they do not know what they do." And they divided His garments and cast lots. 35And the people stood looking on. But even the rulers with them sneered, saying, "He saved others; let Him save Himself if He is the Christ, the chosen of God."

36The soldiers also mocked Him, coming and offering Him sour wine, 37and saying, "If You are the King of the Jews, save Yourself."

38And an inscription also was written over Him in letters of Greek, Latin, and Hebrew: THIS IS THE KING OF THE JEWS.

39Then one of the criminals who were hanged blasphemed Him, saying, "If You are the Christ, save Yourself and us."

40But the other, answering, rebuked him, saying, "Do you not even fear God, seeing you are under the same condemnation? 41And we indeed justly, for we receive the due reward of our deeds; but this Man has done nothing wrong." 42Then he said to Jesus, "Lord, remember me when You come into Your kingdom."

43And Jesus said to him, "Assuredly, I say to you, today you will be with Me in Paradise."

DEVOTIONAL

Before you condemn Barabbas, think about how you compare to him. Yes, he was a rebel, but so are we. All of us are like sheep; we wander and go our own way, doing our own thing, being our own boss (Isaiah 53:6). We're rebels.

Yes, Barabbas was a murderer. But consider this: for whose sins did Jesus die? Our sins were the nails that held Him on the cross. Our hard hearts were the hammers. All of us are guilty, just like Barabbas.

The good news is that, like Barabbas, all of us can accept the payment and freedom Jesus died to give us. Here was a guilty man who deserved the full punishment of the law, and yet an innocent man died in his place and took his punishment. Why? What had he done—and what have we done—to deserve such love? Nothing.

Today, be grateful for grace!

—Dr. Michael Cloer
Englewood Baptist Church, Rocky Mount, NC

WEEK 18, DAY 7

Can you give an effective answer that clarifies what you believe and why you believe it and that confronts any opposing belief? What can you do to develop a strong offense without being offensive?

_____

_____

_____

_____

_____

_____

_____

_____

_____

_____

_____

If you were Barabbas and someone paid your debt, assumed your punishment, and set you free, what would you do to show your gratefulness to your substitute?

_____

_____

_____

_____

_____

_____

_____

_____

_____

WEEK 19, DAY 1

*Hide God's Word
in Your Heart*

Luke 23:44–24:17

Jesus Dies on the Cross

Now it was about the sixth hour, and there was darkness over all the earth until the ninth hour. 45Then the sun was darkened, and the veil of the temple was torn in two. 46And when Jesus had cried out with a loud voice, He said, "Father, 'into Your hands I commit My spirit.'" Having said this, He breathed His last.

47So when the centurion saw what had happened, he glorified God, saying, "Certainly this was a righteous Man!"

48And the whole crowd who came together to that sight, seeing what had been done, beat their breasts and returned. 49But all His acquaintances, and the women who followed Him from Galilee, stood at a distance, watching these things.

Jesus Buried in Joseph's Tomb

50Now behold, there was a man named Joseph, a council member, a good and just man. 51He had not consented to their decision and deed. He was from Arimathea, a city of the Jews, who himself was also waiting for the kingdom of God. 52This man went to Pilate and asked for the body of Jesus. 53Then he took it down, wrapped it in linen, and laid it in a tomb that was hewn out of the rock, where no one had ever lain before. 54That day was the Preparation, and the Sabbath drew near.

55And the women who had come with Him from Galilee followed after, and they observed the tomb and how His body was laid. 56Then they returned and prepared spices and fragrant oils. And they rested on the Sabbath according to the commandment.

He Is Risen

24 Now on the first day of the week, very early in the morning, they, and certain other women with them, came to the tomb bringing the spices which they had prepared. 2But they found the stone rolled away from the tomb. 3Then they went in and did not find the body of the Lord Jesus. 4And it happened, as they were greatly perplexed about this, that behold, two men stood by them in shining garments. 5Then, as they were afraid and bowed their faces

to the earth, they said to them, "Why do you seek the living among the dead? 6He is not here, but is risen! Remember how He spoke to you when He was still in Galilee, 7saying, 'The Son of Man must be delivered into the hands of sinful men, and be crucified, and the third day rise again.'"

8And they remembered His words. 9Then they returned from the tomb and told all these things to the eleven and to all the rest. 10It was Mary Magdalene, Joanna, Mary the mother of James, and the other women with them, who told these things to the apostles. 11And their words seemed to them like idle tales, and they did not believe them. 12But Peter arose and ran to the tomb; and stooping down, he saw the linen cloths lying by themselves; and he departed, marveling to himself at what had happened.

The Road to Emmaus

13Now behold, two of them were traveling that same day to a village called Emmaus, which was seven miles from Jerusalem. 14And they talked together of all these things which had happened. 15So it was, while they conversed and reasoned, that Jesus Himself drew near and went with them. 16But their eyes were restrained, so that they did not know Him.

17And He said to them, "What kind of conversation is this that you have with one another as you walk and are sad?"

DEVOTIONAL

Handling major disappointments is usually overwhelming and difficult to navigate. Imagine what it must have been like for Jesus' disciples to watch Jesus on the cross. For three years they had pinned their hopes on the fact that Jesus would be there for them, and then they helplessly watched Him be brutally beaten, crucified, and buried. All their prayers felt futile. All their hopes and dreams were buried in the grave with Jesus.

Hopelessness, despair, and confusion clouded the disciples' understanding of Jesus' ministry among them. All that was left for them was the task of honoring His body with embalmment. When they discovered He had been resurrected, the disciples "remembered His words" (Luke 24:8)—they remembered He had promised to rise from the dead!

Hide the Word of God in your heart so that when the exigencies of life occur, they will not overcome you. And remember Jesus' words: "I will never leave you nor forsake you" (Hebrews 13:5).

—Michael Whitson
First Baptist Church, Indian Trail, NC

WEEK 19, DAY 2

The Peace and Power of Christ

Luke 24:18–53

Then the one whose name was Cleopas answered and said to Him, "Are You the only stranger in Jerusalem, and have You not known the things which happened there in these days?"

¹⁹And He said to them, "What things?"

So they said to Him, "The things concerning Jesus of Nazareth, who was a Prophet mighty in deed and word before God and all the people, ²⁰and how the chief priests and our rulers delivered Him to be condemned to death, and crucified Him. ²¹But we were hoping that it was He who was going to redeem Israel. Indeed, besides all this, today is the third day since these things happened. ²²Yes, and certain women of our company, who arrived at the tomb early, astonished us. ²³When they did not find His body, they came saying that they had also seen a vision of angels who said He was alive. ²⁴And certain of those who were with us went to the tomb and found it just as the women had said; but Him they did not see."

²⁵Then He said to them, "O foolish ones, and slow of heart to believe in all that the prophets have spoken! ²⁶Ought not the Christ to have suffered these things and to enter into His glory?" ²⁷And beginning at Moses and all the Prophets, He expounded to them in all the Scriptures the things concerning Himself.

The Disciples' Eyes Opened

²⁸Then they drew near to the village where they were going, and He indicated that He would have gone farther. ²⁹But they constrained Him, saying, "Abide with us, for it is toward evening, and the day is far spent." And He went in to stay with them.

³⁰Now it came to pass, as He sat at the table with them, that He took bread, blessed and broke it, and gave it to them. ³¹Then their eyes were opened and they knew Him; and He vanished from their sight.

³²And they said to one another, "Did not our heart burn within us while He talked with us on the road, and while He opened the Scriptures to us?" ³³So they rose up that very hour and returned to Jerusalem, and found the eleven and those who were with them gathered together, ³⁴saying, "The Lord is risen indeed, and has appeared to Simon!" ³⁵And they told about the things that had happened on the road, and how He was known to them in the breaking of bread.

Jesus Appears to His Disciples

³⁶Now as they said these things, Jesus Himself stood in the midst of them, and said to them, "Peace to you." ³⁷But they were terrified and frightened, and supposed they had seen a spirit. ³⁸And He said to them, "Why are you troubled? And why do doubts arise in your hearts? ³⁹Behold My hands and My feet, that it is I Myself. Handle Me and see, for a spirit does not have flesh and bones as you see I have."

⁴⁰When He had said this, He showed them His hands and His feet. ⁴¹But while they still did not believe for joy, and marveled, He said to them, "Have you any food here?" ⁴²So they gave Him a piece of a broiled fish and some honeycomb. ⁴³And He took it and ate in their presence.

The Scriptures Opened

⁴⁴Then He said to them, "These are the words which I spoke to you while I was still with you, that all things must be fulfilled which were written in the Law of Moses and the Prophets and the Psalms concerning Me." ⁴⁵And He opened their understanding, that they might comprehend the Scriptures.

⁴⁶Then He said to them, "Thus it is written, and thus it was necessary for the Christ to suffer and to rise from the dead the third day, ⁴⁷and that repentance and remission of sins should be preached in His name to all nations, beginning at Jerusalem. ⁴⁸And you are witnesses of these things. ⁴⁹Behold, I send the Promise of My Father upon you; but tarry in the city of Jerusalem until you are endued with power from on high."

The Ascension

⁵⁰And He led them out as far as Bethany, and He lifted up His hands and blessed them. ⁵¹Now it came to pass, while He blessed them, that He was parted from them and carried up into heaven. ⁵²And they worshiped Him, and returned to Jerusalem with great joy, ⁵³and were continually in the temple praising and blessing God. Amen.

DEVOTIONAL

In the midst of one of the disciples' greatest trials, Christ said to them, "Peace to you" (Luke 24:36). He also promised He would provide the power they needed to have victory and to be His witnesses in the world. Is your heart troubled? Allow Jesus' peace and power to reign in you. Trust Him to lead you to victory, and then share it with others.

—Michael Whitson
First Baptist Church, Indian Trail, NC

WEEK 19, DAY 3

*Finding the Miraculous
in the Familiar*

John 1:1–28

The Eternal Word

1 In the beginning was the Word, and the Word was with God, and the Word was God. ²He was in the beginning with God. ³All things were made through Him, and without Him nothing was made that was made. ⁴In Him was life, and the life was the light of men. ⁵And the light shines in the darkness, and the darkness did not comprehend it.

John's Witness: The True Light

⁶There was a man sent from God, whose name was John. ⁷This man came for a witness, to bear witness of the Light, that all through him might believe. ⁸He was not that Light, but was sent to bear witness of that Light. ⁹That was the true Light which gives light to every man coming into the world.

¹⁰He was in the world, and the world was made through Him, and the world did not know Him. ¹¹He came to His own, and His own did not receive Him. ¹²But as many as received Him, to them He gave the right to become children of God, to those who believe in His name: ¹³who were born, not of blood, nor of the will of the flesh, nor of the will of man, but of God.

The Word Becomes Flesh

¹⁴And the Word became flesh and dwelt among us, and we beheld His glory, the glory as of the only begotten of the Father, full of grace and truth.

¹⁵John bore witness of Him and cried out, saying, "This was He of whom I said, 'He who comes after me is preferred before me, for He was before me.'"

¹⁶And of His fullness we have all received, and grace for grace. ¹⁷For the law was given through Moses, but grace and truth came through Jesus Christ. ¹⁸No one has seen God at any time. The only begotten Son, who is in the bosom of the Father, He has declared Him.

A Voice in the Wilderness

¹⁹Now this is the testimony of John, when the Jews sent priests and Levites from Jerusalem to ask him, "Who are you?"

²⁰He confessed, and did not deny, but confessed, "I am not the Christ."

²¹And they asked him, "What then? Are you Elijah?" He said, "I am not."

"Are you the Prophet?"

And he answered, "No."

²²Then they said to him, "Who are you, that we may give an answer to those who sent us? What do you say about yourself?"

²³He said: "I am

'The voice of one crying in the wilderness:
"Make straight the way of the Lord,"'

as the prophet Isaiah said."

²⁴Now those who were sent were from the Pharisees. ²⁵And they asked him, saying, "Why then do you baptize if you are not the Christ, nor Elijah, nor the Prophet?"

²⁶John answered them, saying, "I baptize with water, but there stands One among you whom you do not know. ²⁷It is He who, coming after me, is preferred before me, whose sandal strap I am not worthy to loose."

²⁸These things were done in Bethabara beyond the Jordan, where John was baptizing.

DEVOTIONAL

*P*eople from earlier generations would've found it amazing to be able to text someone across the globe in a second, video chat, or have handheld computers. Today, those things are so common, they usually go unnoticed. We are no longer amazed by the technology that surrounds us. Familiarity certainly has a way of breeding contempt.

The message that God wrapped Himself up in human flesh to live among us and to die in our place is over two thousand years old. That familiarity, along with a culture that drowns out the true Christmas message with marketing schemes and spending sprees, makes it so that we must be careful not to lose our sense of wonder that the miraculous occurred. Jesus came to earth and fulfilled God's plan to redeem sinners!

Don't let familiarity with the Christmas story or a materialistic culture keep you from putting your attention on Christ and helping others do the same. Instead of going on a shopping spree, offer God a heart full of worship and adoration. Stay focused on celebrating the miraculous incarnation of Christ and the great love of God!

—Michael Whitson
First Baptist Church, Indian Trail, NC

WEEK 19, DAY 4

"Come and See"

John 1:29–51

The Lamb of God

The next day John saw Jesus coming toward him, and said, "Behold! The Lamb of God who takes away the sin of the world! 30This is He of whom I said, 'After me comes a Man who is preferred before me, for He was before me.' 31I did not know Him; but that He should be revealed to Israel, therefore I came baptizing with water."

32And John bore witness, saying, "I saw the Spirit descending from heaven like a dove, and He remained upon Him. 33I did not know Him, but He who sent me to baptize with water said to me, 'Upon whom you see the Spirit descending, and remaining on Him, this is He who baptizes with the Holy Spirit.' 34And I have seen and testified that this is the Son of God."

The First Disciples

35Again, the next day, John stood with two of his disciples. 36And looking at Jesus as He walked, he said, "Behold the Lamb of God!"

37The two disciples heard him speak, and they followed Jesus. 38Then Jesus turned, and seeing them following, said to them, "What do you seek?"

They said to Him, "Rabbi" (which is to say, when translated, Teacher), "where are You staying?"

39He said to them, "Come and see." They came and saw where He was staying, and remained with Him that day (now it was about the tenth hour).

40One of the two who heard John speak, and followed Him, was Andrew, Simon Peter's brother. 41He first found his own brother Simon, and said to him, "We have found the Messiah" (which is translated, the Christ). 42And he brought him to Jesus.

Now when Jesus looked at him, He said, "You are Simon the son of Jonah. You shall be called Cephas" (which is translated, A Stone).

Philip and Nathanael

43The following day Jesus wanted to go to Galilee, and He found Philip and said to him, "Follow Me." 44Now Philip was from Bethsaida, the city of Andrew and Peter. 45Philip found Nathanael and said to him, "We have found Him of whom Moses in the law, and also the prophets, wrote—Jesus of Nazareth, the son of Joseph."

46And Nathanael said to him, "Can anything good come out of Nazareth?"

Philip said to him, "Come and see."

47Jesus saw Nathanael coming toward Him, and said of him, "Behold, an Israelite indeed, in whom is no deceit!"

48Nathanael said to Him, "How do You know me?"

Jesus answered and said to him, "Before Philip called you, when you were under the fig tree, I saw you."

49Nathanael answered and said to Him, "Rabbi, You are the Son of God! You are the King of Israel!"

50Jesus answered and said to him, "Because I said to you, 'I saw you under the fig tree,' do you believe? You will see greater things than these." 51And He said to him, "Most assuredly, I say to you, hereafter you shall see heaven open, and the angels of God ascending and descending upon the Son of Man."

DEVOTIONAL

It didn't take long for the first disciples to discover that the very Messiah the world had been waiting for had finally come. Jesus, the Christ, was on the scene, and He had reached out to them. Shortly after Jesus called them and they began to follow Him, these men wanted others to do the same. Philip started with His family, telling his little brother to "come and see" Jesus (John 1:46).

The disciples had a front-row seat to all of Jesus' good works and teachings. Jesus told Nathanael he would get to see miraculous things take place because of his trust and faith. Jesus promised we would see even greater things happen than the people of His day did. If we are not seeing these great things, could it be because we don't ask? Or could it be that we're not coming close enough to Jesus?

While He walked this earth, Jesus was always beckoning people to spend some time with Him, and He's still beckoning today. Accept His invitation. Extend it to others. Spending time with Jesus and growing closer to Him opens the door for Him to do amazing things through you—things you can see! Don't wait until you get to heaven to have your eyes opened to all you could have seen here on earth. Follow Him now, and you will see!

—Michael Whitson
First Baptist Church, Indian Trail, NC

WEEK 19, DAY 5

Jesus' First Miracle

John 2:1–25

Water Turned to Wine

2 On the third day there was a wedding in Cana of Galilee, and the mother of Jesus was there. 2Now both Jesus and His disciples were invited to the wedding. 3And when they ran out of wine, the mother of Jesus said to Him, "They have no wine."

4Jesus said to her, "Woman, what does your concern have to do with Me? My hour has not yet come."

5His mother said to the servants, "Whatever He says to you, do it."

6Now there were set there six waterpots of stone, according to the manner of purification of the Jews, containing twenty or thirty gallons apiece. 7Jesus said to them, "Fill the waterpots with water." And they filled them up to the brim. 8And He said to them, "Draw some out now, and take it to the master of the feast." And they took it. 9When the master of the feast had tasted the water that was made wine, and did not know where it came from (but the servants who had drawn the water knew), the master of the feast called the bridegroom. 10And he said to him, "Every man at the beginning sets out the good wine, and when the guests have well drunk, then the inferior. You have kept the good wine until now!"

11This beginning of signs Jesus did in Cana of Galilee, and manifested His glory; and His disciples believed in Him.

12After this He went down to Capernaum, He, His mother, His brothers, and His disciples; and they did not stay there many days.

Jesus Cleanses the Temple

13Now the Passover of the Jews was at hand, and Jesus went up to Jerusalem. 14And He found in the temple those who sold oxen and sheep and doves, and the money changers doing business. 15When He had made a whip of cords, He drove them all out of the temple, with the sheep and the oxen, and poured out the changers' money and overturned the tables. 16And He said to those who sold doves, "Take these things away! Do not make My Father's house a house of merchandise!" 17Then His disciples remembered that it was written, "Zeal for Your house has eaten Me up."

18So the Jews answered and said to Him, "What sign do You show to us, since You do these things?"

19Jesus answered and said to them, "Destroy this temple, and in three days I will raise it up."

20Then the Jews said, "It has taken forty-six years to build this temple, and will You raise it up in three days?"

21But He was speaking of the temple of His body. 22Therefore, when He had risen from the dead, His disciples remembered that He had said this to them; and they believed the Scripture and the word which Jesus had said.

The Discerner of Hearts

23Now when He was in Jerusalem at the Passover, during the feast, many believed in His name when they saw the signs which He did. 24But Jesus did not commit Himself to them, because He knew all men, 25and had no need that anyone should testify of man, for He knew what was in man.

DEVOTIONAL

*T*his first recorded miracle of Jesus is one of the most talked-about passages in the Bible. Turning water into wine was nothing but a preview of what would take place three years later, when Christ would once again turn hopelessness into victory through His resurrection.

The Word says that Jesus came to seek and to save (Luke 19:10), and this event is a great picture of that. The worst thing that could have happened on this couple's special day would have been to run out of refreshments. Can you imagine how that would have marred their big day and the memory of it? Turning the water to wine saved the family from embarrassment and years of ridicule. Christ not only saved them from despair, but He also completely satisfied the demands. The master of the feast was impressed, thinking the bridegroom had saved the best for last. It was a testimony that Jesus satisfies, one which has been echoed throughout the ages.

Through this miracle Jesus revealed that He is the God of the universe and that He reigns over all. Praise God that He reveals Himself to us, saves us from despair, and brings us new life! Praise Him that He is a God who gives beauty for ashes, joy for mourning, and a garment of praise for the spirit of heaviness (Isaiah 61:3). Open your heart to the One who lovingly seeks, saves, and transforms.

—Michael Whitson
First Baptist Church, Indian Trail, NC

WEEK 19, DAY 6

Pointing Others to Christ

John 3:1–30

The New Birth

3 There was a man of the Pharisees named Nicodemus, a ruler of the Jews. 2This man came to Jesus by night and said to Him, "Rabbi, we know that You are a teacher come from God; for no one can do these signs that You do unless God is with him."

3Jesus answered and said to him, "Most assuredly, I say to you, unless one is born again, he cannot see the kingdom of God."

4Nicodemus said to Him, "How can a man be born when he is old? Can he enter a second time into his mother's womb and be born?"

5Jesus answered, "Most assuredly, I say to you, unless one is born of water and the Spirit, he cannot enter the kingdom of God. 6That which is born of the flesh is flesh, and that which is born of the Spirit is spirit. 7Do not marvel that I said to you, 'You must be born again.' 8The wind blows where it wishes, and you hear the sound of it, but cannot tell where it comes from and where it goes. So is everyone who is born of the Spirit."

9Nicodemus answered and said to Him, "How can these things be?"

10Jesus answered and said to him, "Are you the teacher of Israel, and do not know these things? 11Most assuredly, I say to you, We speak what We know and testify what We have seen, and you do not receive Our witness. 12If I have told you earthly things and you do not believe, how will you believe if I tell you heavenly things? 13No one has ascended to heaven but He who came down from heaven, that is, the Son of Man who is in heaven. 14And as Moses lifted up the serpent in the wilderness, even so must the Son of Man be lifted up, 15that whoever believes in Him should not perish but have eternal life. 16For God so loved the world that He gave His only begotten Son, that whoever believes in Him should not perish but have everlasting life. 17For God did not send His Son into the world to condemn the world, but that the world through Him might be saved.

18"He who believes in Him is not condemned; but he who does not believe is condemned already, because he has not believed in the name of the only begotten Son of God. 19And this is the condemnation, that the light has come into the world, and men loved darkness rather than light, because their deeds were evil. 20For everyone practicing evil hates the light and does not come to the light, lest his deeds should be exposed. 21But he who does the truth comes to the light, that his deeds may be clearly seen, that they have been done in God."

John the Baptist Exalts Christ

22After these things Jesus and His disciples came into the land of Judea, and there He remained with them and baptized. 23Now John also was baptizing in Aenon near Salim, because there was much water there. And they came and were baptized. 24For John had not yet been thrown into prison.

25Then there arose a dispute between some of John's disciples and the Jews about purification. 26And they came to John and said to him, "Rabbi, He who was with you beyond the Jordan, to whom you have testified—behold, He is baptizing, and all are coming to Him!"

27John answered and said, "A man can receive nothing unless it has been given to him from heaven. 28You yourselves bear me witness, that I said, 'I am not the Christ,' but, 'I have been sent before Him.' 29He who has the bride is the bridegroom; but the friend of the bridegroom, who stands and hears him, rejoices greatly because of the bridegroom's voice. Therefore this joy of mine is fulfilled. 30He must increase, but I must decrease."

DEVOTIONAL

*W*e need more people like John the Baptist today. If you study his life, you will discover that no matter where he was, whether he was preaching to the great congregations that followed him to his wilderness pulpit or in a dungeon awaiting his impending death, his message was still the same: "Get to Jesus, for He alone can meet the needs of your life." There was no doubt, insecurity, or jealousy about his role as the forerunner of Christ. He knew what it was to die to self so Christ could be exalted. Even Christ Himself said there was no greater prophet than John the Baptist (Luke 7:28).

We need more people who are constantly pointing others to Jesus. His last command to His disciples was to bear witness to Him. In our service to Christ, it is never about us; it's about Him. Like John the Baptist, may we never seek to steal Jesus' glory.

—Michael Whitson
First Baptist Church, Indian Trail, NC

WEEK 19, DAY 7

Jesus was God in the flesh, and He willingly laid down His life for all of humanity so that "whoever believes in Him should not perish but have everlasting life" (John 3:16). When did that become a life-changing reality for you and lead you to repentance?

_____

_____

_____

_____

_____

_____

_____

_____

_____

_____

After the resurrection of Christ, true believers were compelled to tell others about Him. Is Christ so real to you, and your new birth in Him so obvious, that you are compelled to tell others?

_____

_____

_____

_____

_____

_____

_____

_____

_____

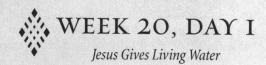

WEEK 20, DAY 1

Jesus Gives Living Water

John 3:31–4:26

"He who comes from above is above all; he who is of the earth is earthly and speaks of the earth. He who comes from heaven is above all. ³²And what He has seen and heard, that He testifies; and no one receives His testimony. ³³He who has received His testimony has certified that God is true. ³⁴For He whom God has sent speaks the words of God, for God does not give the Spirit by measure. ³⁵The Father loves the Son, and has given all things into His hand. ³⁶He who believes in the Son has everlasting life; and he who does not believe the Son shall not see life, but the wrath of God abides on him."

A Samaritan Woman Meets Her Messiah

4 Therefore, when the Lord knew that the Pharisees had heard that Jesus made and baptized more disciples than John ²(though Jesus Himself did not baptize, but His disciples), ³He left Judea and departed again to Galilee. ⁴But He needed to go through Samaria.

⁵So He came to a city of Samaria which is called Sychar, near the plot of ground that Jacob gave to his son Joseph. ⁶Now Jacob's well was there. Jesus therefore, being wearied from His journey, sat thus by the well. It was about the sixth hour.

⁷A woman of Samaria came to draw water. Jesus said to her, "Give Me a drink." ⁸For His disciples had gone away into the city to buy food.

⁹Then the woman of Samaria said to Him, "How is it that You, being a Jew, ask a drink from me, a Samaritan woman?" For Jews have no dealings with Samaritans.

¹⁰Jesus answered and said to her, "If you knew the gift of God, and who it is who says to you, 'Give Me a drink,' you would have asked Him, and He would have given you living water."

¹¹The woman said to Him, "Sir, You have nothing to draw with, and the well is deep. Where then do You get that living water? ¹²Are You greater than our father Jacob, who gave us the well, and drank from it himself, as well as his sons and his livestock?"

¹³Jesus answered and said to her, "Whoever drinks of this water will thirst again, ¹⁴but whoever drinks of the water that I shall give him will never thirst. But the water that I shall give him will become in him a fountain of water springing up into everlasting life."

¹⁵The woman said to Him, "Sir, give me this water, that I may not thirst, nor come here to draw."

¹⁶Jesus said to her, "Go, call your husband, and come here."

¹⁷The woman answered and said, "I have no husband."

Jesus said to her, "You have well said, 'I have no husband,' ¹⁸for you have had five husbands, and the one whom you now have is not your husband; in that you spoke truly."

¹⁹The woman said to Him, "Sir, I perceive that You are a prophet. ²⁰Our fathers worshiped on this mountain, and you Jews say that in Jerusalem is the place where one ought to worship."

²¹Jesus said to her, "Woman, believe Me, the hour is coming when you will neither on this mountain, nor in Jerusalem, worship the Father. ²²You worship what you do not know; we know what we worship, for salvation is of the Jews. ²³But the hour is coming, and now is, when the true worshipers will worship the Father in spirit and truth; for the Father is seeking such to worship Him. ²⁴God is Spirit, and those who worship Him must worship in spirit and truth."

²⁵The woman said to Him, "I know that Messiah is coming" (who is called Christ). "When He comes, He will tell us all things."

²⁶Jesus said to her, "I who speak to you am He."

DEVOTIONAL

Do you live like Jesus is above all else in your life? When He is, your thirsts change. His living water fills your every longing. Do you thirst for more in your life—more love, more attention, more satisfaction, more pleasure, more stuff? When He is above all, you simply thirst for more of Him.

This is not our natural inclination. We want what our human nature wants, and we meet our needs according to our abilities. But when we want what He wants, He meets our needs according to His riches. Usually, we have to try it our way and fail before we truly trust Him. In Jeremiah 2:13, the Lord spoke of His people leaving Him, "the fountain of living waters," and turning to their own sources for fulfillment—"broken cisterns that can hold no water."

History is full of men and women who resisted God's invitation to be above all else in their lives. God desires to meet us in our places of greatest resistance in order to demonstrate His plan for greater assistance, but we must trust the One who is above all!

—Paul Purvis
First Baptist Church, Temple Terrace, FL

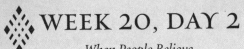

WEEK 20, DAY 2

When People Believe,
God Does Great Things

John 4:27–54

The Whitened Harvest

And at this point His disciples came, and they marveled that He talked with a woman; yet no one said, "What do You seek?" or, "Why are You talking with her?"

28The woman then left her waterpot, went her way into the city, and said to the men, 29"Come, see a Man who told me all things that I ever did. Could this be the Christ?" 30Then they went out of the city and came to Him.

31In the meantime His disciples urged Him, saying, "Rabbi, eat."

32But He said to them, "I have food to eat of which you do not know."

33Therefore the disciples said to one another, "Has anyone brought Him anything to eat?"

34Jesus said to them, "My food is to do the will of Him who sent Me, and to finish His work. 35Do you not say, 'There are still four months and then comes the harvest'? Behold, I say to you, lift up your eyes and look at the fields, for they are already white for harvest! 36And he who reaps receives wages, and gathers fruit for eternal life, that both he who sows and he who reaps may rejoice together. 37For in this the saying is true: 'One sows and another reaps.' 38I sent you to reap that for which you have not labored; others have labored, and you have entered into their labors."

The Savior of the World

39And many of the Samaritans of that city believed in Him because of the word of the woman who testified, "He told me all that I ever did." 40So when the Samaritans had come to Him, they urged Him to stay with them; and He stayed there two days. 41And many more believed because of His own word.

42Then they said to the woman, "Now we believe, not because of what you said, for we ourselves have heard Him and we know that this is indeed the Christ, the Savior of the world."

Welcome at Galilee

43Now after the two days He departed from there and went to Galilee. 44For Jesus Himself testified that a prophet has no honor in his own country. 45So when He came to Galilee, the Galileans received Him, having seen all the things He did in Jerusalem at the feast; for they also had gone to the feast.

A Nobleman's Son Healed

46So Jesus came again to Cana of Galilee where He had made the water wine. And there was a certain nobleman whose son was sick at Capernaum. 47When he heard that Jesus had come out of Judea into Galilee, he went to Him and implored Him to come down and heal his son, for he was at the point of death. 48Then Jesus said to him, "Unless you people see signs and wonders, you will by no means believe."

49The nobleman said to Him, "Sir, come down before my child dies!"

50Jesus said to him, "Go your way; your son lives." So the man believed the word that Jesus spoke to him, and he went his way. 51And as he was now going down, his servants met him and told him, saying, "Your son lives!"

52Then he inquired of them the hour when he got better. And they said to him, "Yesterday at the seventh hour the fever left him." 53So the father knew that it was at the same hour in which Jesus said to him, "Your son lives." And he himself believed, and his whole household.

54This again is the second sign Jesus did when He had come out of Judea into Galilee.

DEVOTIONAL

What must you leave in order to achieve God's best for your life? The woman at the well left her water pot so that she might become a witness to the miracle of God's life-changing power. She left the very thing God had used as a tool to introduce her to her Savior so she could introduce others to Him. Sometimes we must walk away from the things that have been important to us in order to accomplish what is important to God.

Walking away from something familiar always requires faith. It took great faith for Abraham to leave everything and set out for the land God promised to show him (Hebrews 11:8). You too must step out in faith into unknown territory if you expect to accomplish the great things God has planned for you.

The faith to step out and accomplish something great for God comes from the awareness of the great thing He has already accomplished in you. Step out of your comfort and into His control.

—Paul Purvis
First Baptist Church, Temple Terrace, FL

WEEK 20, DAY 3

God's Healing Touch

John 5:1–30

A Man Healed at the Pool of Bethesda

5 After this there was a feast of the Jews, and Jesus went up to Jerusalem. ²Now there is in Jerusalem by the Sheep Gate a pool, which is called in Hebrew, Bethesda, having five porches. ³In these lay a great multitude of sick people, blind, lame, paralyzed, waiting for the moving of the water. ⁴For an angel went down at a certain time into the pool and stirred up the water; then whoever stepped in first, after the stirring of the water, was made well of whatever disease he had. ⁵Now a certain man was there who had an infirmity thirty-eight years. ⁶When Jesus saw him lying there, and knew that he already had been in that condition a long time, He said to him, "Do you want to be made well?"

⁷The sick man answered Him, "Sir, I have no man to put me into the pool when the water is stirred up; but while I am coming, another steps down before me."

⁸Jesus said to him, "Rise, take up your bed and walk." ⁹And immediately the man was made well, took up his bed, and walked.

And that day was the Sabbath. ¹⁰The Jews therefore said to him who was cured, "It is the Sabbath; it is not lawful for you to carry your bed."

¹¹He answered them, "He who made me well said to me, 'Take up your bed and walk.'"

¹²Then they asked him, "Who is the Man who said to you, 'Take up your bed and walk'?" ¹³But the one who was healed did not know who it was, for Jesus had withdrawn, a multitude being in that place. ¹⁴Afterward Jesus found him in the temple, and said to him, "See, you have been made well. Sin no more, lest a worse thing come upon you."

¹⁵The man departed and told the Jews that it was Jesus who had made him well.

Honor the Father and the Son

¹⁶For this reason the Jews persecuted Jesus, and sought to kill Him, because He had done these things on the Sabbath. ¹⁷But Jesus answered them, "My Father has been working until now, and I have been working." ¹⁸Therefore the Jews sought all the more to kill Him, because He not only broke the Sabbath, but also said that God was His Father, making Himself equal with God. ¹⁹Then Jesus answered and said to them, "Most assuredly, I say to you,

the Son can do nothing of Himself, but what He sees the Father do; for whatever He does, the Son also does in like manner. ²⁰For the Father loves the Son, and shows Him all things that He Himself does; and He will show Him greater works than these, that you may marvel. ²¹For as the Father raises the dead and gives life to them, even so the Son gives life to whom He will. ²²For the Father judges no one, but has committed all judgment to the Son, ²³that all should honor the Son just as they honor the Father. He who does not honor the Son does not honor the Father who sent Him.

Life and Judgment Are Through the Son

²⁴"Most assuredly, I say to you, he who hears My word and believes in Him who sent Me has everlasting life, and shall not come into judgment, but has passed from death into life. ²⁵Most assuredly, I say to you, the hour is coming, and now is, when the dead will hear the voice of the Son of God; and those who hear will live. ²⁶For as the Father has life in Himself, so He has granted the Son to have life in Himself, ²⁷and has given Him authority to execute judgment also, because He is the Son of Man. ²⁸Do not marvel at this; for the hour is coming in which all who are in the graves will hear His voice ²⁹and come forth—those who have done good, to the resurrection of life, and those who have done evil, to the resurrection of condemnation. ³⁰I can of Myself do nothing. As I hear, I judge; and My judgment is righteous, because I do not seek My own will but the will of the Father who sent Me."

DEVOTIONAL

Jesus constantly encountered people in need, and on some occasions, their needs resulted from their sins. We don't know if that was the case for the man in John 5, but we do know that the brokenness of this world is a result of sin. Our unexpected circumstances, unexplained illnesses, unresolved relationships, unforgettable tragedies, and unrelenting pain all come back to the reality of sin. The only antidote for the sickness of sin is the healing touch of Jesus Christ. Only Jesus can make us well as we put our faith in Him.

Today, give Jesus praise because He healed us from the disease of sin through His work on the cross, and because He "heals the brokenhearted and binds up their wounds" (Psalm 147:3). Thank God for His healing touch in your life.

—Paul Purvis
First Baptist Church, Temple Terrace, FL

WEEK 20, DAY 4

Jesus Is Worthy of Your Trust

John 5:31–6:14

The Fourfold Witness

"If I bear witness of Myself, My witness is not true. ³²There is another who bears witness of Me, and I know that the witness which He witnesses of Me is true. ³³You have sent to John, and he has borne witness to the truth. ³⁴Yet I do not receive testimony from man, but I say these things that you may be saved. ³⁵He was the burning and shining lamp, and you were willing for a time to rejoice in his light. ³⁶But I have a greater witness than John's; for the works which the Father has given Me to finish—the very works that I do—bear witness of Me, that the Father has sent Me. ³⁷And the Father Himself, who sent Me, has testified of Me. You have neither heard His voice at any time, nor seen His form. ³⁸But you do not have His word abiding in you, because whom He sent, Him you do not believe. ³⁹You search the Scriptures, for in them you think you have eternal life; and these are they which testify of Me. ⁴⁰But you are not willing to come to Me that you may have life.

⁴¹"I do not receive honor from men. ⁴²But I know you, that you do not have the love of God in you. ⁴³I have come in My Father's name, and you do not receive Me; if another comes in his own name, him you will receive. ⁴⁴How can you believe, who receive honor from one another, and do not seek the honor that comes from the only God? ⁴⁵Do not think that I shall accuse you to the Father; there is one who accuses you—Moses, in whom you trust. ⁴⁶For if you believed Moses, you would believe Me; for he wrote about Me. ⁴⁷But if you do not believe his writings, how will you believe My words?"

Feeding the Five Thousand

6 After these things Jesus went over the Sea of Galilee, which is the Sea of Tiberias. ²Then a great multitude followed Him, because they saw His signs which He performed on those who were diseased. ³And Jesus went up on the mountain, and there He sat with His disciples. ⁴Now the Passover, a feast of the Jews, was near. ⁵Then Jesus lifted up His eyes, and seeing a great multitude coming toward Him, He said to Philip, "Where shall we buy bread, that these may eat?" ⁶But this He said to test him, for He Himself knew what He would do.

⁷Philip answered Him, "Two hundred denarii worth of bread is not sufficient for them, that every one of them may have a little."

⁸One of His disciples, Andrew, Simon Peter's brother, said to Him, ⁹"There is a lad here who has five barley loaves and two small fish, but what are they among so many?"

¹⁰Then Jesus said, "Make the people sit down." Now there was much grass in the place. So the men sat down, in number about five thousand. ¹¹And Jesus took the loaves, and when He had given thanks He distributed them to the disciples, and the disciples to those sitting down; and likewise of the fish, as much as they wanted. ¹²So when they were filled, He said to His disciples, "Gather up the fragments that remain, so that nothing is lost." ¹³Therefore they gathered them up, and filled twelve baskets with the fragments of the five barley loaves which were left over by those who had eaten. ¹⁴Then those men, when they had seen the sign that Jesus did, said, "This is truly the Prophet who is to come into the world."

DEVOTIONAL

What will it take for you to believe? For some people, no amount of evidence will lead to belief. Jesus repeatedly found Himself defending and discussing His deity with the Jewish religious leaders of His day. On the occasion recorded in John 5:1–15, He offered several reasons they should believe He was the Son of God. The religious leaders merely wanted to debate doctrine, but Jesus pointed them to the truth. Unfortunately, they still rejected Him.

For others, evidence of God's provision yields faith. Jesus' miraculous feeding of the five thousand in John 6 occurred in the presence of those following Jesus "because they saw His signs" (v. 2). Even those closest to Him, the disciples, did not naturally assume He would meet the great need of the crowd's hunger through His mighty power. The ensuing miracle prompted both the disciples and those in the crowd to trust Him more.

It is interesting to note that Jesus tested His disciples (John 6:6). God already has a plan in place for every situation we face, but He earnestly desires that we too trust His sovereign abilities. Jesus is willing to defend His deity, demonstrate His power, and even display His miraculous provision, but in the end, He demands—and deserves—your trust in Him simply for who He is.

—Paul Purvis
First Baptist Church, Temple Terrace, FL

WEEK 20, DAY 5

Believe in the God of Miracles

John 6:15–40

Jesus Walks on the Sea

Therefore when Jesus perceived that they were about to come and take Him by force to make Him king, He departed again to the mountain by Himself alone.

16Now when evening came, His disciples went down to the sea, 17got into the boat, and went over the sea toward Capernaum. And it was already dark, and Jesus had not come to them. 18Then the sea arose because a great wind was blowing. 19So when they had rowed about three or four miles, they saw Jesus walking on the sea and drawing near the boat; and they were afraid. 20But He said to them, "It is I; do not be afraid." 21Then they willingly received Him into the boat, and immediately the boat was at the land where they were going.

The Bread from Heaven

22On the following day, when the people who were standing on the other side of the sea saw that there was no other boat there, except that one which His disciples had entered, and that Jesus had not entered the boat with His disciples, but His disciples had gone away alone— 23however, other boats came from Tiberias, near the place where they ate bread after the Lord had given thanks— 24when the people therefore saw that Jesus was not there, nor His disciples, they also got into boats and came to Capernaum, seeking Jesus. 25And when they found Him on the other side of the sea, they said to Him, "Rabbi, when did You come here?"

26Jesus answered them and said, "Most assuredly, I say to you, you seek Me, not because you saw the signs, but because you ate of the loaves and were filled. 27Do not labor for the food which perishes, but for the food which endures to everlasting life, which the Son of Man will give you, because God the Father has set His seal on Him."

28Then they said to Him, "What shall we do, that we may work the works of God?"

29Jesus answered and said to them, "This is the work of God, that you believe in Him whom He sent."

30Therefore they said to Him, "What sign will You perform then, that we may see it and believe You? What work will You do? 31Our fathers ate the manna in the desert; as it is written, 'He gave them bread from heaven to eat.'"

32Then Jesus said to them, "Most assuredly, I say to you, Moses did not give you the bread from heaven, but My Father gives you the true bread from heaven. 33For the bread of God is He who comes down from heaven and gives life to the world."

34Then they said to Him, "Lord, give us this bread always."

35And Jesus said to them, "I am the bread of life. He who comes to Me shall never hunger, and he who believes in Me shall never thirst. 36But I said to you that you have seen Me and yet do not believe. 37All that the Father gives Me will come to Me, and the one who comes to Me I will by no means cast out. 38For I have come down from heaven, not to do My own will, but the will of Him who sent Me. 39This is the will of the Father who sent Me, that of all He has given Me I should lose nothing, but should raise it up at the last day. 40And this is the will of Him who sent Me, that everyone who sees the Son and believes in Him may have everlasting life; and I will raise him up at the last day."

DEVOTIONAL

God promised He will never leave us (Hebrews 13:5), but He never promised to fulfill our desires the way we expect Him to. Unfortunately, our tendency is to long for His power and look past His presence.

Jesus reprimanded His followers for seeking Him only because of the miracle He demonstrated during the feeding of the five thousand. They were amazed by the power of the sign, but they failed to see the purpose behind the sign. While God constantly works for our good, He also always works for His glory. He wants the adoration that is due Him, the adoration we can offer.

We desire to live in the constant supply of His provisions, but He desires that we understand He **is** our constant supply (John 6:34–35). Jesus promised all of our needs will be met in Him, but we must first come to Him. He is enough. Remember this simple, oft quoted phrase: Jesus + Nothing = Everything.

Jesus said, "This is the work of God, that you believe in Him whom He sent" (John 6:29). Beware of becoming so focused on what God does that you fail to see Him for who He is. It is important to believe God does miracles, but it is essential to believe in the God of miracles.

Thank God today for glimpses of His mighty power, and then determine to bask in His amazing presence.

—Paul Purvis
First Baptist Church, Temple Terrace, FL

WEEK 20, DAY 6

Keep Walking with Jesus

John 6:41–71

Rejected by His Own

The Jews then complained about Him, because He said, "I am the bread which came down from heaven." 42And they said, "Is not this Jesus, the son of Joseph, whose father and mother we know? How is it then that He says, 'I have come down from heaven'?"

43Jesus therefore answered and said to them, "Do not murmur among yourselves. 44No one can come to Me unless the Father who sent Me draws him; and I will raise him up at the last day. 45It is written in the prophets, 'And they shall all be taught by God.' Therefore everyone who has heard and learned from the Father comes to Me. 46Not that anyone has seen the Father, except He who is from God; He has seen the Father. 47Most assuredly, I say to you, he who believes in Me has everlasting life. 48I am the bread of life. 49Your fathers ate the manna in the wilderness, and are dead. 50This is the bread which comes down from heaven, that one may eat of it and not die. 51I am the living bread which came down from heaven. If anyone eats of this bread, he will live forever; and the bread that I shall give is My flesh, which I shall give for the life of the world."

52The Jews therefore quarreled among themselves, saying, "How can this Man give us His flesh to eat?"

53Then Jesus said to them, "Most assuredly, I say to you, unless you eat the flesh of the Son of Man and drink His blood, you have no life in you. 54Whoever eats My flesh and drinks My blood has eternal life, and I will raise him up at the last day. 55For My flesh is food indeed, and My blood is drink indeed. 56He who eats My flesh and drinks My blood abides in Me, and I in him. 57As the living Father sent Me, and I live because of the Father, so he who feeds on Me will live because of Me. 58This is the bread which came down from heaven—not as your fathers ate the manna, and are dead. He who eats this bread will live forever."

59These things He said in the synagogue as He taught in Capernaum.

Many Disciples Turn Away

60Therefore many of His disciples, when they heard this, said, "This is a hard saying; who can understand it?" 61When Jesus knew in Himself that His disciples complained about this, He said to them, "Does this offend you? 62What then if you should see the Son of Man ascend where He was before? 63It is the Spirit who gives life; the flesh profits nothing. The words that I speak to you are spirit, and they are life. 64But there are some of you who do not believe." For Jesus knew from the beginning who they were who did not believe, and who would betray Him. 65And He said, "Therefore I have said to you that no one can come to Me unless it has been granted to him by My Father."

66From that time many of His disciples went back and walked with Him no more. 67Then Jesus said to the twelve, "Do you also want to go away?"

68But Simon Peter answered Him, "Lord, to whom shall we go? You have the words of eternal life. 69Also we have come to believe and know that You are the Christ, the Son of the living God."

70Jesus answered them, "Did I not choose you, the twelve, and one of you is a devil?" 71He spoke of Judas Iscariot, the son of Simon, for it was he who would betray Him, being one of the twelve.

DEVOTIONAL

Will you walk in the dark with Jesus, or will you walk in the light alone? In this life you will face questions. Before that time comes, you must answer this question: "Will I press on, even if I don't have answers?"

Ponder these words from John 6: "Many of His disciples went back and walked with Him no more" (v. 66). Why would people who had previously chosen to follow Jesus, seen His miracles, and experienced the life-changing power of His message choose to leave Him? To put it simply, they didn't understand.

Often in life, unanswered questions become the impetus for falling away. But as Christ followers, unanswered questions should lead us to take steps of faith that forge our relationship with God. Your questions do not intimidate God—He is bigger than your biggest questions. But you must decide if you are willing to follow without having all the answers.

Choosing to follow Jesus means finding the answer to the question, "Who is He?" When you find that answer, you discover that the answer to "Why am I hurting?" is not that important, because you would rather walk in the dark with Jesus than walk in the light alone.

—Paul Purvis
First Baptist Church, Temple Terrace, FL

WEEK 20, DAY 7

For what are you hungering and thirsting that is not of God? What changes need to take place in your life in order for you to pursue Him more passionately?

_____

_____

_____

_____

_____

_____

_____

_____

_____

_____

In what areas of your life do you need to step out in faith? What doubts, questions, and fears do you need to place in the hands of God?

_____

_____

_____

_____

_____

_____

_____

_____

_____

_____

WEEK 21, DAY 1

Share the Truth in Love

John 7:1–31

Jesus' Brothers Disbelieve

7After these things Jesus walked in Galilee; for He did not want to walk in Judea, because the Jews sought to kill Him. 2Now the Jews' Feast of Tabernacles was at hand. 3His brothers therefore said to Him, "Depart from here and go into Judea, that Your disciples also may see the works that You are doing. 4For no one does anything in secret while he himself seeks to be known openly. If You do these things, show Yourself to the world." 5For even His brothers did not believe in Him.

6Then Jesus said to them, "My time has not yet come, but your time is always ready. 7The world cannot hate you, but it hates Me because I testify of it that its works are evil. 8You go up to this feast. I am not yet going up to this feast, for My time has not yet fully come." 9When He had said these things to them, He remained in Galilee.

The Heavenly Scholar

10But when His brothers had gone up, then He also went up to the feast, not openly, but as it were in secret. 11Then the Jews sought Him at the feast, and said, "Where is He?" 12And there was much complaining among the people concerning Him. Some said, "He is good"; others said, "No, on the contrary, He deceives the people." 13However, no one spoke openly of Him for fear of the Jews.

14Now about the middle of the feast Jesus went up into the temple and taught. 15And the Jews marveled, saying, "How does this Man know letters, having never studied?"

16Jesus answered them and said, "My doctrine is not Mine, but His who sent Me. 17If anyone wills to do His will, he shall know concerning the doctrine, whether it is from God or whether I speak on My own authority. 18He who speaks from himself seeks his own glory; but He who seeks the glory of the One who sent Him is true, and no unrighteousness is in Him. 19Did not Moses give you the law, yet none of you keeps the law? Why do you seek to kill Me?"

20The people answered and said, "You have a demon. Who is seeking to kill You?"

21Jesus answered and said to them, "I did one work, and you all marvel. 22Moses therefore gave you circumcision (not that it is from Moses, but from the fathers), and you circumcise a man on the Sabbath. 23If a man receives circumcision on the Sabbath, so that the law of Moses should not be broken, are you angry with Me because I made a man completely well on the Sabbath? 24Do not judge according to appearance, but judge with righteous judgment."

Could This Be the Christ?

25Now some of them from Jerusalem said, "Is this not He whom they seek to kill? 26But look! He speaks boldly, and they say nothing to Him. Do the rulers know indeed that this is truly the Christ? 27However, we know where this Man is from; but when the Christ comes, no one knows where He is from."

28Then Jesus cried out, as He taught in the temple, saying, "You both know Me, and you know where I am from; and I have not come of Myself, but He who sent Me is true, whom you do not know. 29But I know Him, for I am from Him, and He sent Me."

30Therefore they sought to take Him; but no one laid a hand on Him, because His hour had not yet come. 31And many of the people believed in Him, and said, "When the Christ comes, will He do more signs than these which this Man has done?"

DEVOTIONAL

Sadly, people's memories are often dependent on their wills. Peter spoke of those who "willfully forget" God's works (2 Peter 3:5). There are thousands of people in the present day who are just as blind as the Jews were. They shut their eyes to the plainest facts and doctrines of Christianity. We point them to Christ, to the Person they need to be saved from their sins, but they do not believe what they do not like. It is a willful ignorance. They refuse to listen, read, contemplate, and seek sincerely for truth. Jeremiah described foolish people as those "who have eyes and see not, and who have ears and hear not" (Jeremiah 5:21).

Sinful people don't want to hear about their sinfulness. They hated Jesus because He told the truth. They hate Christ's followers for the same reason. But that does not change the fact that we are called to love our neighbors and to share God's truth. Be prayerful, asking for opportunities to reach people. Be bold, knowing you can help others be set free by the truth. Be like Jesus. Share the truth in love.

—Dr. Rob Zinn
Immanuel Baptist Church, Highland, CA

WEEK 21, DAY 2

Everyone Has Sinned

John 7:32–8:11

Jesus and the Religious Leaders

The Pharisees heard the crowd murmuring these things concerning Him, and the Pharisees and the chief priests sent officers to take Him. ³³Then Jesus said to them, "I shall be with you a little while longer, and then I go to Him who sent Me. ³⁴You will seek Me and not find Me, and where I am you cannot come."

³⁵Then the Jews said among themselves, "Where does He intend to go that we shall not find Him? Does He intend to go to the Dispersion among the Greeks and teach the Greeks? ³⁶What is this thing that He said, 'You will seek Me and not find Me, and where I am you cannot come'?"

The Promise of the Holy Spirit

³⁷On the last day, that great day of the feast, Jesus stood and cried out, saying, "If anyone thirsts, let him come to Me and drink. ³⁸He who believes in Me, as the Scripture has said, out of his heart will flow rivers of living water." ³⁹But this He spoke concerning the Spirit, whom those believing in Him would receive; for the Holy Spirit was not yet given, because Jesus was not yet glorified.

Who Is He?

⁴⁰Therefore many from the crowd, when they heard this saying, said, "Truly this is the Prophet." ⁴¹Others said, "This is the Christ."

But some said, "Will the Christ come out of Galilee? ⁴²Has not the Scripture said that the Christ comes from the seed of David and from the town of Bethlehem, where David was?" ⁴³So there was a division among the people because of Him. ⁴⁴Now some of them wanted to take Him, but no one laid hands on Him.

Rejected by the Authorities

⁴⁵Then the officers came to the chief priests and Pharisees, who said to them, "Why have you not brought Him?"

⁴⁶The officers answered, "No man ever spoke like this Man!"

⁴⁷Then the Pharisees answered them, "Are you also deceived? ⁴⁸Have any of the rulers or the Pharisees believed in Him? ⁴⁹But this crowd that does not know the law is accursed."

⁵⁰Nicodemus (he who came to Jesus by night, being one of them) said to them, ⁵¹"Does our law judge a man before it hears him and knows what he is doing?"

⁵²They answered and said to him, "Are you also from Galilee? Search and look, for no prophet has arisen out of Galilee."

An Adulteress Faces the Light of the World

⁵³And everyone went to his own house.

8 But Jesus went to the Mount of Olives. ²Now early in the morning He came again into the temple, and all the people came to Him; and He sat down and taught them. ³Then the scribes and Pharisees brought to Him a woman caught in adultery. And when they had set her in the midst, ⁴they said to Him, "Teacher, this woman was caught in adultery, in the very act. ⁵Now Moses, in the law, commanded us that such should be stoned. But what do You say?" ⁶This they said, testing Him, that they might have something of which to accuse Him. But Jesus stooped down and wrote on the ground with His finger, as though He did not hear.

⁷So when they continued asking Him, He raised Himself up and said to them, "He who is without sin among you, let him throw a stone at her first." ⁸And again He stooped down and wrote on the ground. ⁹Then those who heard it, being convicted by their conscience, went out one by one, beginning with the oldest even to the last. And Jesus was left alone, and the woman standing in the midst. ¹⁰When Jesus had raised Himself up and saw no one but the woman, He said to her, "Woman, where are those accusers of yours? Has no one condemned you?"

¹¹She said, "No one, Lord."

And Jesus said to her, "Neither do I condemn you; go and sin no more."

DEVOTIONAL

A re you like the Pharisees who judged and condemned others, forgetting that they themselves were sinners? Or are you like Jesus, compassionate and forgiving? It is easy to be judgmental, but the truth is no one is perfect! All have sinned. All of us need God's grace and forgiveness.

Jesus saw the hypocrisy of those who wanted to stone the adulterous woman. He forgave her and gave her a second chance, telling her to leave her life of sin. We are not called to overlook or minimize sin; it's okay to call a sin a sin, just as Jesus did. However, you must also remember what God has done for you and show love and compassion to others.

—Dr. Rob Zinn
Immanuel Baptist Church, Highland, CA

WEEK 21, DAY 3

Our Father Wants Relationship

John 8:12–41

Then Jesus spoke to them again, saying, "I am the light of the world. He who follows Me shall not walk in darkness, but have the light of life."

Jesus Defends His Self-Witness

¹³The Pharisees therefore said to Him, "You bear witness of Yourself; Your witness is not true."

¹⁴Jesus answered and said to them, "Even if I bear witness of Myself, My witness is true, for I know where I came from and where I am going; but you do not know where I come from and where I am going. ¹⁵You judge according to the flesh; I judge no one. ¹⁶And yet if I do judge, My judgment is true; for I am not alone, but I am with the Father who sent Me. ¹⁷It is also written in your law that the testimony of two men is true. ¹⁸I am One who bears witness of Myself, and the Father who sent Me bears witness of Me."

¹⁹Then they said to Him, "Where is Your Father?"

Jesus answered, "You know neither Me nor My Father. If you had known Me, you would have known My Father also."

²⁰These words Jesus spoke in the treasury, as He taught in the temple; and no one laid hands on Him, for His hour had not yet come.

Jesus Predicts His Departure

²¹Then Jesus said to them again, "I am going away, and you will seek Me, and will die in your sin. Where I go you cannot come."

²²So the Jews said, "Will He kill Himself, because He says, 'Where I go you cannot come'?"

²³And He said to them, "You are from beneath; I am from above. You are of this world; I am not of this world. ²⁴Therefore I said to you that you will die in your sins; for if you do not believe that I am He, you will die in your sins."

²⁵Then they said to Him, "Who are You?"

And Jesus said to them, "Just what I have been saying to you from the beginning. ²⁶I have many things to say and to judge concerning you; but He who sent Me is true; and I speak to the world those things which I heard from Him."

²⁷They did not understand that He spoke to them of the Father.

²⁸Then Jesus said to them, "When you lift up the Son of Man, then you will know that I am He, and that I do nothing of Myself; but as My Father taught Me, I speak these things. ²⁹And He who sent Me is with Me. The Father has not left Me alone, for I always do those things that please Him." ³⁰As He spoke these words, many believed in Him.

The Truth Shall Make You Free

³¹Then Jesus said to those Jews who believed Him, "If you abide in My word, you are My disciples indeed. ³²And you shall know the truth, and the truth shall make you free."

³³They answered Him, "We are Abraham's descendants, and have never been in bondage to anyone. How can You say, 'You will be made free'?"

³⁴Jesus answered them, "Most assuredly, I say to you, whoever commits sin is a slave of sin. ³⁵And a slave does not abide in the house forever, but a son abides forever. ³⁶Therefore if the Son makes you free, you shall be free indeed.

Abraham's Seed and Satan's

³⁷"I know that you are Abraham's descendants, but you seek to kill Me, because My word has no place in you. ³⁸I speak what I have seen with My Father, and you do what you have seen with your father."

³⁹They answered and said to Him, "Abraham is our father."

Jesus said to them, "If you were Abraham's children, you would do the works of Abraham. ⁴⁰But now you seek to kill Me, a Man who has told you the truth which I heard from God. Abraham did not do this. ⁴¹You do the deeds of your father."

Then they said to Him, "We were not born of fornication; we have one Father—God."

DEVOTIONAL

Do you have a religion or a relationship? Religion involves working your way to God. But Christ is the only way to the Father, and He came to reveal the Father's love. It is likely that God's favorite name for Himself is Father. What does every father want? A family—relationships with those He loves. While God is everyone's Creator, He's not everyone's Father. Jesus knows His Father and has an eternal relationship with Him. Do you? To know the Father, you have to know the Son. Come close to the Father through the Son today.

—Dr. Rob Zinn
Immanuel Baptist Church, Highland, CA

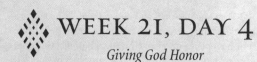

WEEK 21, DAY 4

Giving God Honor

John 8:42–9:12

Jesus said to them, "If God were your Father, you would love Me, for I proceeded forth and came from God; nor have I come of Myself, but He sent Me. ⁴³Why do you not understand My speech? Because you are not able to listen to My word. ⁴⁴You are of your father the devil, and the desires of your father you want to do. He was a murderer from the beginning, and does not stand in the truth, because there is no truth in him. When he speaks a lie, he speaks from his own resources, for he is a liar and the father of it. ⁴⁵But because I tell the truth, you do not believe Me. ⁴⁶Which of you convicts Me of sin? And if I tell the truth, why do you not believe Me? ⁴⁷He who is of God hears God's words; therefore you do not hear, because you are not of God."

Before Abraham Was, I AM

⁴⁸Then the Jews answered and said to Him, "Do we not say rightly that You are a Samaritan and have a demon?"

⁴⁹Jesus answered, "I do not have a demon; but I honor My Father, and you dishonor Me. ⁵⁰And I do not seek My own glory; there is One who seeks and judges. ⁵¹Most assuredly, I say to you, if anyone keeps My word he shall never see death."

⁵²Then the Jews said to Him, "Now we know that You have a demon! Abraham is dead, and the prophets; and You say, 'If anyone keeps My word he shall never taste death.' ⁵³Are You greater than our father Abraham, who is dead? And the prophets are dead. Who do You make Yourself out to be?"

⁵⁴Jesus answered, "If I honor Myself, My honor is nothing. It is My Father who honors Me, of whom you say that He is your God. ⁵⁵Yet you have not known Him, but I know Him. And if I say, 'I do not know Him,' I shall be a liar like you; but I do know Him and keep His word. ⁵⁶Your father Abraham rejoiced to see My day, and he saw it and was glad."

⁵⁷Then the Jews said to Him, "You are not yet fifty years old, and have You seen Abraham?"

⁵⁸Jesus said to them, "Most assuredly, I say to you, before Abraham was, I AM."

⁵⁹Then they took up stones to throw at Him; but Jesus hid Himself and went out of the temple, going through the midst of them, and so passed by.

A Man Born Blind Receives Sight

9Now as Jesus passed by, He saw a man who was blind from birth. ²And His disciples asked Him, saying, "Rabbi, who sinned, this man or his parents, that he was born blind?"

³Jesus answered, "Neither this man nor his parents sinned, but that the works of God should be revealed in him. ⁴I must work the works of Him who sent Me while it is day; the night is coming when no one can work. ⁵As long as I am in the world, I am the light of the world."

⁶When He had said these things, He spat on the ground and made clay with the saliva; and He anointed the eyes of the blind man with the clay. ⁷And He said to him, "Go, wash in the pool of Siloam" (which is translated, Sent). So he went and washed, and came back seeing.

⁸Therefore the neighbors and those who previously had seen that he was blind said, "Is not this he who sat and begged?"

⁹Some said, "This is he." Others said, "He is like him."

He said, "I am he."

¹⁰Therefore they said to him, "How were your eyes opened?"

¹¹He answered and said, "A Man called Jesus made clay and anointed my eyes and said to me, 'Go to the pool of Siloam and wash.' So I went and washed, and I received sight."

¹²Then they said to him, "Where is He?"

He said, "I do not know."

DEVOTIONAL

In John 8, the Jews slandered and accused our Lord of being a Samaritan with a demon. Jesus denied their accusation and added, "I honor My Father" (v. 49). What does it mean to honor God? The rest of the chapter gives us four answers. First, it means speaking the truth. The world will slander and deceive, but we who honor God will speak the truth in love. Second, it means obeying God. We are called to please Him, not ourselves. Third, it means glorifying God by the way we live. It is not about us; it is all about Him. Fourth, it means honoring God by loving His Son. Jesus said in John 5:23, "He who does not honor the Son does not honor the Father who sent Him." The more we love, follow, and obey Jesus, the more we bring honor to God. And if you love Him, you will want to spend time with Him and talk to Him.

How can you speak truth, obey and glorify God, and express love to Jesus today?

—Dr. Rob Zinn
Immanuel Baptist Church, Highland, CA

WEEK 21, DAY 5

Jesus Opens Our Eyes

John 9:13–41

The Pharisees Excommunicate the Healed Man

They brought him who formerly was blind to the Pharisees. ¹⁴Now it was a Sabbath when Jesus made the clay and opened his eyes. ¹⁵Then the Pharisees also asked him again how he had received his sight. He said to them, "He put clay on my eyes, and I washed, and I see."

¹⁶Therefore some of the Pharisees said, "This Man is not from God, because He does not keep the Sabbath."

Others said, "How can a man who is a sinner do such signs?" And there was a division among them.

¹⁷They said to the blind man again, "What do you say about Him because He opened your eyes?"

He said, "He is a prophet."

¹⁸But the Jews did not believe concerning him, that he had been blind and received his sight, until they called the parents of him who had received his sight. ¹⁹And they asked them, saying, "Is this your son, who you say was born blind? How then does he now see?"

²⁰His parents answered them and said, "We know that this is our son, and that he was born blind; ²¹but by what means he now sees we do not know, or who opened his eyes we do not know. He is of age; ask him. He will speak for himself." ²²His parents said these things because they feared the Jews, for the Jews had agreed already that if anyone confessed that He was Christ, he would be put out of the synagogue. ²³Therefore his parents said, "He is of age; ask him."

²⁴So they again called the man who was blind, and said to him, "Give God the glory! We know that this Man is a sinner."

²⁵He answered and said, "Whether He is a sinner or not I do not know. One thing I know: that though I was blind, now I see."

²⁶Then they said to him again, "What did He do to you? How did He open your eyes?"

²⁷He answered them, "I told you already, and you did not listen. Why do you want to hear it again? Do you also want to become His disciples?"

²⁸Then they reviled him and said, "You are His disciple, but we are Moses' disciples. ²⁹We know that God spoke to Moses; as for this fellow, we do not know where He is from."

³⁰The man answered and said to them, "Why, this is a marvelous thing, that you do not know where He is from; yet He has opened my eyes! ³¹Now we know that God does not hear sinners; but if anyone is a worshiper of God and does His will, He hears him. ³²Since the world began it has been unheard of that anyone opened the eyes of one who was born blind. ³³If this Man were not from God, He could do nothing."

³⁴They answered and said to him, "You were completely born in sins, and are you teaching us?" And they cast him out.

True Vision and True Blindness

³⁵Jesus heard that they had cast him out; and when He had found him, He said to him, "Do you believe in the Son of God?"

³⁶He answered and said, "Who is He, Lord, that I may believe in Him?"

³⁷And Jesus said to him, "You have both seen Him and it is He who is talking with you."

³⁸Then he said, "Lord, I believe!" And he worshiped Him.

³⁹And Jesus said, "For judgment I have come into this world, that those who do not see may see, and that those who see may be made blind."

⁴⁰Then some of the Pharisees who were with Him heard these words, and said to Him, "Are we blind also?"

⁴¹Jesus said to them, "If you were blind, you would have no sin; but now you say, 'We see.' Therefore your sin remains."

DEVOTIONAL

The religious leaders acknowledged Jesus' miracle of giving sight to a man born blind, but they still refused to believe in Jesus. They were like skeptical folks today who refuse to face the facts about Jesus—that He is Lord and that He saves and gives sight to anyone who will repent and receive Him as their Savior.

The man who had been given sight stuck to his testimony, telling the Pharisees, "He has opened my eyes! . . . If this Man were not from God, He could do nothing" (John 9:30, 33). He experienced Jesus, professed belief in Him as the Son of God, and worshiped Him (v. 38).

People can deny the Bible, the church, or religion, but they can't deny your testimony. Tell them what you know! Find someone to reach out to today. Someone will listen.

—Dr. Rob Zinn
Immanuel Baptist Church, Highland, CA

WEEK 21, DAY 6

Jesus Is Our Caring Shepherd

John 10:1–33

Jesus the True Shepherd

10 "Most assuredly, I say to you, he who does not enter the sheepfold by the door, but climbs up some other way, the same is a thief and a robber. 2But he who enters by the door is the shepherd of the sheep. 3To him the doorkeeper opens, and the sheep hear his voice; and he calls his own sheep by name and leads them out. 4And when he brings out his own sheep, he goes before them; and the sheep follow him, for they know his voice. 5Yet they will by no means follow a stranger, but will flee from him, for they do not know the voice of strangers." 6Jesus used this illustration, but they did not understand the things which He spoke to them.

Jesus the Good Shepherd

7Then Jesus said to them again, "Most assuredly, I say to you, I am the door of the sheep. 8All who ever came before Me are thieves and robbers, but the sheep did not hear them. 9I am the door. If anyone enters by Me, he will be saved, and will go in and out and find pasture. 10The thief does not come except to steal, and to kill, and to destroy. I have come that they may have life, and that they may have it more abundantly.

11"I am the good shepherd. The good shepherd gives His life for the sheep. 12But a hireling, he who is not the shepherd, one who does not own the sheep, sees the wolf coming and leaves the sheep and flees; and the wolf catches the sheep and scatters them. 13The hireling flees because he is a hireling and does not care about the sheep. 14I am the good shepherd; and I know My sheep, and am known by My own. 15As the Father knows Me, even so I know the Father; and I lay down My life for the sheep. 16And other sheep I have which are not of this fold; them also I must bring, and they will hear My voice; and there will be one flock and one shepherd.

17"Therefore My Father loves Me, because I lay down My life that I may take it again. 18No one takes it from Me, but I lay it down of Myself. I have power to lay it down, and I have power to take it again. This command I have received from My Father."

19Therefore there was a division again among the Jews because of these sayings. 20And many of them said, "He has a demon and is mad. Why do you listen to Him?"

21Others said, "These are not the words of one who has a demon. Can a demon open the eyes of the blind?"

The Shepherd Knows His Sheep

22Now it was the Feast of Dedication in Jerusalem, and it was winter. 23And Jesus walked in the temple, in Solomon's porch. 24Then the Jews surrounded Him and said to Him, "How long do You keep us in doubt? If You are the Christ, tell us plainly."

25Jesus answered them, "I told you, and you do not believe. The works that I do in My Father's name, they bear witness of Me. 26But you do not believe, because you are not of My sheep, as I said to you. 27My sheep hear My voice, and I know them, and they follow Me. 28And I give them eternal life, and they shall never perish; neither shall anyone snatch them out of My hand. 29My Father, who has given them to Me, is greater than all; and no one is able to snatch them out of My Father's hand. 30I and My Father are one."

Renewed Efforts to Stone Jesus

31Then the Jews took up stones again to stone Him. 32Jesus answered them, "Many good works I have shown you from My Father. For which of those works do you stone Me?"

33The Jews answered Him, saying, "For a good work we do not stone You, but for blasphemy, and because You, being a Man, make Yourself God."

DEVOTIONAL

*J*esus is our Good Shepherd. Old Testament shepherds pointed to the True Shepherd who was to come. There was Abel the righteous shepherd, Jacob the resourceful shepherd, Moses the returning shepherd, and David the royal shepherd. All of these men were partial types of Jesus, but He is the perfect, authentic Shepherd, in a class by Himself, preeminent above all others.

He is the Door of the sheep. It is through Him one finds salvation, security, and a place to rest. He is the Defender of the sheep. He will never leave us or forsake us. He is faithful to His sheep. They know Him, and He knows every one of them by name. He knows all about them—where they live, when they became His, their personalities, and their peculiarities. He is committed to His sheep. He lays down His life for them.

Don't forget that your Good Shepherd is with you. Take comfort in His loving presence and be encouraged by His powerful promises.

—Dr. Rob Zinn
Immanuel Baptist Church, Highland, CA

WEEK 21, DAY 7

What does being forgiven mean to you?

_____

_____

_____

_____

_____

_____

_____

_____

_____

_____

_____

_____

What has Jesus done for you? Write a brief version of your testimony.

_____

_____

_____

_____

_____

_____

_____

_____

_____

WEEK 22, DAY 1

The Great I AM

John 10:34–11:27

Jesus answered them, "Is it not written in your law, 'I said, "You are gods"'? 35If He called them gods, to whom the word of God came (and the Scripture cannot be broken), 36do you say of Him whom the Father sanctified and sent into the world, 'You are blaspheming,' because I said, 'I am the Son of God'? 37If I do not do the works of My Father, do not believe Me; 38but if I do, though you do not believe Me, believe the works, that you may know and believe that the Father *is* in Me, and I in Him." 39Therefore they sought again to seize Him, but He escaped out of their hand.

The Believers Beyond Jordan

40And He went away again beyond the Jordan to the place where John was baptizing at first, and there He stayed. 41Then many came to Him and said, "John performed no sign, but all the things that John spoke about this Man were true." 42And many believed in Him there.

The Death of Lazarus

11 Now a certain man was sick, Lazarus of Bethany, the town of Mary and her sister Martha. 2It was that Mary who anointed the Lord with fragrant oil and wiped His feet with her hair, whose brother Lazarus was sick. 3Therefore the sisters sent to Him, saying, "Lord, behold, he whom You love is sick."

4When Jesus heard that, He said, "This sickness is not unto death, but for the glory of God, that the Son of God may be glorified through it."

5Now Jesus loved Martha and her sister and Lazarus. 6So, when He heard that he was sick, He stayed two more days in the place where He was. 7Then after this He said to the disciples, "Let us go to Judea again."

8The disciples said to Him, "Rabbi, lately the Jews sought to stone You, and are You going there again?"

9Jesus answered, "Are there not twelve hours in the day? If anyone walks in the day, he does not stumble, because he sees the light of this world. 10But if one walks in the night, he stumbles, because the light is not in him." 11These things He said, and after that He said to them, "Our friend Lazarus sleeps, but I go that I may wake him up."

12Then His disciples said, "Lord, if he sleeps he will get well." 13However, Jesus spoke of his death, but they thought that He was speaking about taking rest in sleep.

14Then Jesus said to them plainly, "Lazarus is dead. 15And I am glad for your sakes that I was not there, that you may believe. Nevertheless let us go to him."

16Then Thomas, who is called the Twin, said to his fellow disciples, "Let us also go, that we may die with Him."

I Am the Resurrection and the Life

17So when Jesus came, He found that he had already been in the tomb four days. 18Now Bethany was near Jerusalem, about two miles away. 19And many of the Jews had joined the women around Martha and Mary, to comfort them concerning their brother.

20Then Martha, as soon as she heard that Jesus was coming, went and met Him, but Mary was sitting in the house. 21Now Martha said to Jesus, "Lord, if You had been here, my brother would not have died. 22But even now I know that whatever You ask of God, God will give You."

23Jesus said to her, "Your brother will rise again."

24Martha said to Him, "I know that he will rise again in the resurrection at the last day."

25Jesus said to her, "I am the resurrection and the life. He who believes in Me, though he may die, he shall live. 26And whoever lives and believes in Me shall never die. Do you believe this?"

27She said to Him, "Yes, Lord, I believe that You are the Christ, the Son of God, who is to come into the world."

DEVOTIONAL

When God revealed His identity to Moses, He used the words, "I AM," meaning He is the One who is and always will be. When Moses asked God how he could reassure the Israelites, the people he was seeking to deliver from Egypt, that God had truly sent him, God instructed him to say, "I AM has sent me to you" (Exodus 3:14).

When Jesus said, "I am the resurrection and the life," He was reassuring Martha He was indeed God in the flesh (John 11:25). He was also saying He is the only way to resurrection and eternal life. He is all you need in this life and the next. He is not the "I was" or the "I have been." He is the present tense "I AM"!

Jesus said, "Whoever lives and believes in Me shall never die" (John 11:26). The promise is limited to those who will believe. Today, if you believe in Jesus, the One who is and always will be, praise Him for such a promise—the dead shall live again!

—Roy Mack
Pinecrest Baptist Church, McDonough, GA

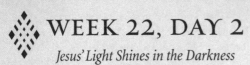

WEEK 22, DAY 2

Jesus' Light Shines in the Darkness

John 11:28–57

Jesus and Death, the Last Enemy

And when she had said these things, she went her way and secretly called Mary her sister, saying, "The Teacher has come and is calling for you." 29As soon as she heard that, she arose quickly and came to Him. 30Now Jesus had not yet come into the town, but was in the place where Martha met Him. 31Then the Jews who were with her in the house, and comforting her, when they saw that Mary rose up quickly and went out, followed her, saying, "She is going to the tomb to weep there."

32Then, when Mary came where Jesus was, and saw Him, she fell down at His feet, saying to Him, "Lord, if You had been here, my brother would not have died."

33Therefore, when Jesus saw her weeping, and the Jews who came with her weeping, He groaned in the spirit and was troubled. 34And He said, "Where have you laid him?"

They said to Him, "Lord, come and see."

35Jesus wept. 36Then the Jews said, "See how He loved him!"

37And some of them said, "Could not this Man, who opened the eyes of the blind, also have kept this man from dying?"

Lazarus Raised from the Dead

38Then Jesus, again groaning in Himself, came to the tomb. It was a cave, and a stone lay against it. 39Jesus said, "Take away the stone." Martha, the sister of him who was dead, said to Him, "Lord, by this time there is a stench, for he has been dead four days."

40Jesus said to her, "Did I not say to you that if you would believe you would see the glory of God?" 41Then they took away the stone from the place where the dead man was lying. And Jesus lifted up His eyes and said, "Father, I thank You that You have heard Me. 42And I know that You always hear Me, but because of the people who are standing by I said this, that they may believe that You sent Me." 43Now when He had said these things, He cried with a loud voice, "Lazarus, come forth!" 44And he who had died came out bound hand and foot with graveclothes, and his face was wrapped with a cloth. Jesus said to them, "Loose him, and let him go."

The Plot to Kill Jesus

45Then many of the Jews who had come to Mary, and had seen the things Jesus did, believed in Him. 46But some of them went away to the Pharisees and told them the things Jesus did. 47Then the chief priests and the Pharisees gathered a council and said, "What shall we do? For this Man works many signs. 48If we let Him alone like this, everyone will believe in Him, and the Romans will come and take away both our place and nation."

49And one of them, Caiaphas, being high priest that year, said to them, "You know nothing at all, 50nor do you consider that it is expedient for us that one man should die for the people, and not that the whole nation should perish." 51Now this he did not say on his own authority; but being high priest that year he prophesied that Jesus would die for the nation, 52and not for that nation only, but also that He would gather together in one the children of God who were scattered abroad.

53Then, from that day on, they plotted to put Him to death. 54Therefore Jesus no longer walked openly among the Jews, but went from there into the country near the wilderness, to a city called Ephraim, and there remained with His disciples.

55And the Passover of the Jews was near, and many went from the country up to Jerusalem before the Passover, to purify themselves. 56Then they sought Jesus, and spoke among themselves as they stood in the temple, "What do you think—that He will not come to the feast?" 57Now both the chief priests and the Pharisees had given a command, that if anyone knew where He was, he should report it, that they might seize Him.

DEVOTIONAL

Lazarus was raised from the dead, yet many still refused to see and believe. So it is with Jesus. John spoke of this reality earlier in his Gospel: "The light shines in the darkness, and the darkness did not comprehend it" (1:5). No one is as blind as those who refuse to see. Those who do not look at the Son and believe in Him have hearts that are darkened. The light is revealed to them—it's all around them—but they do not see the One who is light.

Today, make choices that will keep you walking in the light with Jesus. And pray that the unbelieving people in your life will no longer walk in darkness, but put their faith in Jesus and have the light of life (John 8:12).

—Roy Mack
Pinecrest Baptist Church, McDonough, GA

WEEK 22, DAY 3

The Bread of Life

John 12:1–26

The Anointing at Bethany

12 Then, six days before the Passover, Jesus came to Bethany, where Lazarus was who had been dead, whom He had raised from the dead. ²There they made Him a supper; and Martha served, but Lazarus was one of those who sat at the table with Him. ³Then Mary took a pound of very costly oil of spikenard, anointed the feet of Jesus, and wiped His feet with her hair. And the house was filled with the fragrance of the oil.

⁴But one of His disciples, Judas Iscariot, Simon's son, who would betray Him, said, ⁵"Why was this fragrant oil not sold for three hundred denarii and given to the poor?" ⁶This he said, not that he cared for the poor, but because he was a thief, and had the money box; and he used to take what was put in it.

⁷But Jesus said, "Let her alone; she has kept this for the day of My burial. ⁸For the poor you have with you always, but Me you do not have always."

The Plot to Kill Lazarus

⁹Now a great many of the Jews knew that He was there; and they came, not for Jesus' sake only, but that they might also see Lazarus, whom He had raised from the dead. ¹⁰But the chief priests plotted to put Lazarus to death also, ¹¹because on account of him many of the Jews went away and believed in Jesus.

The Triumphal Entry

¹²The next day a great multitude that had come to the feast, when they heard that Jesus was coming to Jerusalem, ¹³took branches of palm trees and went out to meet Him, and cried out:

"Hosanna!
'Blessed is He who comes in the name of
    the Lord!'
The King of Israel!"

¹⁴Then Jesus, when He had found a young donkey, sat on it; as it is written:

15 "Fear not, daughter of Zion;
    Behold, your King is coming,
    Sitting on a donkey's colt."

¹⁶His disciples did not understand these things at first; but when Jesus was glorified, then they remembered that these things were written about Him and that they had done these things to Him.

¹⁷Therefore the people, who were with Him when He called Lazarus out of his tomb and raised him from the dead, bore witness. ¹⁸For this reason the people also met Him, because they heard that He had done this sign. ¹⁹The Pharisees therefore said among themselves, "You see that you are accomplishing nothing. Look, the world has gone after Him!"

The Fruitful Grain of Wheat

²⁰Now there were certain Greeks among those who came up to worship at the feast. ²¹Then they came to Philip, who was from Bethsaida of Galilee, and asked him, saying, "Sir, we wish to see Jesus."

²²Philip came and told Andrew, and in turn Andrew and Philip told Jesus.

²³But Jesus answered them, saying, "The hour has come that the Son of Man should be glorified. ²⁴Most assuredly, I say to you, unless a grain of wheat falls into the ground and dies, it remains alone; but if it dies, it produces much grain. ²⁵He who loves his life will lose it, and he who hates his life in this world will keep it for eternal life. ²⁶If anyone serves Me, let him follow Me; and where I am, there My servant will be also. If anyone serves Me, him My Father will honor."

DEVOTIONAL

D *uring the Feast of Unleavened Bread, the Jews stop to thank God for giving them food from the earth. They thank Him for the wheat and barley that produced the bread. They also pray, "Give us life out of the earth, the grain and the harvest we need in order to live." At sundown on the day Jesus died on the cross for our sins, the Feast of Unleavened Bread began. As people were praying their prayer of thanks, the Bread of Life was on the cross. Prior to His death, Jesus said, "Unless a grain of wheat falls into the ground and dies, it remains alone; but if it dies, it produces much grain" (John 12:24). Jesus was killed and planted into the ground, but He would soon rise from the grave, giving life to all those who put their trust in Him and taste His goodness. Let the way you live show that you've received the Bread of Life, and give Him thanks!*

—Roy Mack
Pinecrest Baptist Church, McDonough, GA

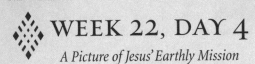

WEEK 22, DAY 4

A Picture of Jesus' Earthly Mission

John 12:27–13:4

Jesus Predicts His Death on the Cross

"Now My soul is troubled, and what shall I say? 'Father, save Me from this hour'? But for this purpose I came to this hour. 28Father, glorify Your name."

Then a voice came from heaven, saying, "I have both glorified it and will glorify it again."

29Therefore the people who stood by and heard it said that it had thundered. Others said, "An angel has spoken to Him."

30Jesus answered and said, "This voice did not come because of Me, but for your sake. 31Now is the judgment of this world; now the ruler of this world will be cast out. 32And I, if I am lifted up from the earth, will draw all peoples to Myself." 33This He said, signifying by what death He would die.

34The people answered Him, "We have heard from the law that the Christ remains forever; and how can You say, 'The Son of Man must be lifted up'? Who is this Son of Man?"

35Then Jesus said to them, "A little while longer the light is with you. Walk while you have the light, lest darkness overtake you; he who walks in darkness does not know where he is going. 36While you have the light, believe in the light, that you may become sons of light." These things Jesus spoke, and departed, and was hidden from them.

Who Has Believed Our Report?

37But although He had done so many signs before them, they did not believe in Him, 38that the word of Isaiah the prophet might be fulfilled, which he spoke:

"Lord, who has believed our report?
And to whom has the arm of the Lord been
    revealed?"

39Therefore they could not believe, because Isaiah said again:

40 "He has blinded their eyes and hardened
        their hearts,
    Lest they should see with their eyes,
    Lest they should understand with their hearts
        and turn,
    So that I should heal them."

41These things Isaiah said when he saw His glory and spoke of Him.

Walk in the Light

42Nevertheless even among the rulers many believed in Him, but because of the Pharisees they did not confess Him, lest they should be put out of the synagogue; 43for they loved the praise of men more than the praise of God.

44Then Jesus cried out and said, "He who believes in Me, believes not in Me but in Him who sent Me. 45And he who sees Me sees Him who sent Me. 46I have come as a light into the world, that whoever believes in Me should not abide in darkness. 47And if anyone hears My words and does not believe, I do not judge him; for I did not come to judge the world but to save the world. 48He who rejects Me, and does not receive My words, has that which judges him—the word that I have spoken will judge him in the last day. 49For I have not spoken on My own authority; but the Father who sent Me gave Me a command, what I should say and what I should speak. 50And I know that His command is everlasting life. Therefore, whatever I speak, just as the Father has told Me, so I speak."

Jesus Washes the Disciples' Feet

13Now before the Feast of the Passover, when Jesus knew that His hour had come that He should depart from this world to the Father, having loved His own who were in the world, He loved them to the end.

2And supper being ended, the devil having already put it into the heart of Judas Iscariot, Simon's son, to betray Him, 3Jesus, knowing that the Father had given all things into His hands, and that He had come from God and was going to God, 4rose from supper and laid aside His garments, took a towel and girded Himself.

DEVOTIONAL

In the Upper Room we see a picture of Jesus' earthly mission. John 13:4 says that after eating, He "rose from supper," just as He'd stepped away from His heavenly throne. It says He "laid aside His garments," just as He'd laid aside His deity. He girded himself with a towel, just as He'd taken the form of a servant. He poured water in a basin, just as He'd later pour out His blood on the cross. He washed the disciples' feet, and He washes us from our sins through His finished work at Calvary.

Continue Jesus' mission by serving others and telling them how He cleanses us from sin.

—Roy Mack
Pinecrest Baptist Church, McDonough, GA

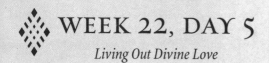

WEEK 22, DAY 5

Living Out Divine Love

John 13:5–35

After that, He poured water into a basin and began to wash the disciples' feet, and to wipe them with the towel with which He was girded. 6Then He came to Simon Peter. And Peter said to Him, "Lord, are You washing my feet?"

7Jesus answered and said to him, "What I am doing you do not understand now, but you will know after this."

8Peter said to Him, "You shall never wash my feet!"

Jesus answered him, "If I do not wash you, you have no part with Me."

9Simon Peter said to Him, "Lord, not my feet only, but also my hands and my head!"

10Jesus said to him, "He who is bathed needs only to wash his feet, but is completely clean; and you are clean, but not all of you." 11For He knew who would betray Him; therefore He said, "You are not all clean."

12So when He had washed their feet, taken His garments, and sat down again, He said to them, "Do you know what I have done to you? 13You call Me Teacher and Lord, and you say well, for so I am. 14If I then, your Lord and Teacher, have washed your feet, you also ought to wash one another's feet. 15For I have given you an example, that you should do as I have done to you. 16Most assuredly, I say to you, a servant is not greater than his master; nor is he who is sent greater than he who sent him. 17If you know these things, blessed are you if you do them.

Jesus Identifies His Betrayer

18"I do not speak concerning all of you. I know whom I have chosen; but that the Scripture may be fulfilled, 'He who eats bread with Me has lifted up his heel against Me.' 19Now I tell you before it comes, that when it does come to pass, you may believe that I am He. 20Most assuredly, I say to you, he who receives whomever I send receives Me; and he who receives Me receives Him who sent Me."

21When Jesus had said these things, He was troubled in spirit, and testified and said, "Most assuredly, I say to you, one of you will betray Me." 22Then the disciples looked at one another, perplexed about whom He spoke. 23Now there was leaning on Jesus' bosom one of His disciples, whom Jesus loved. 24Simon Peter therefore motioned to him to ask who it was of whom He spoke. 25Then, leaning back on Jesus' breast, he said to Him, "Lord, who is it?"

26Jesus answered, "It is he to whom I shall give a piece of bread when I have dipped it." And having dipped the bread, He gave it to Judas Iscariot, the son of Simon. 27Now after the piece of bread, Satan entered him. Then Jesus said to him, "What you do, do quickly." 28But no one at the table knew for what reason He said this to him. 29For some thought, because Judas had the money box, that Jesus had said to him, "Buy those things we need for the feast," or that he should give something to the poor.

30Having received the piece of bread, he then went out immediately. And it was night.

The New Commandment

31So, when he had gone out, Jesus said, "Now the Son of Man is glorified, and God is glorified in Him. 32If God is glorified in Him, God will also glorify Him in Himself, and glorify Him immediately. 33Little children, I shall be with you a little while longer. You will seek Me; and as I said to the Jews, 'Where I am going, you cannot come,' so now I say to you. 34A new commandment I give to you, that you love one another; as I have loved you, that you also love one another. 35By this all will know that you are My disciples, if you have love for one another."

DEVOTIONAL

The nature of any animal dictates the behavior of the animal. Geese fly south, bears hibernate, salmon swim upstream, woodpeckers peck, hogs wallow, dogs bark. What do Christians do? They love. It is the hallmark of a Christian. It is evidence of the new nature in us—a divine nature.

Love is an action word, and Christians ought to be known for their love in action. In John 13, we see love serving, comforting, and reaching out to an enemy. We also see love obeying the will of the Father. Another action of love is giving. "God so loved the world that He gave" His Son (John 3:16). You can give without loving, but you cannot love without giving. Ministry is giving yourself away, and true love always ministers; that is the divine nature.

By loving others with God's love, we demonstrate to a lost world what it means to be a follower of Jesus Christ. "By this all will know that you are My disciples, if you have love for one another" (John 13:35). How will you make loving others a priority today?

—Roy Mack
Pinecrest Baptist Church, McDonough, GA

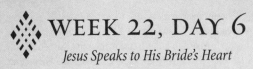

WEEK 22, DAY 6

Jesus Speaks to His Bride's Heart

John 13:36–14:24

Jesus Predicts Peter's Denial

Simon Peter said to Him, "Lord, where are You going?" Jesus answered him, "Where I am going you cannot follow Me now, but you shall follow Me afterward."

37Peter said to Him, "Lord, why can I not follow You now? I will lay down my life for Your sake."

38Jesus answered him, "Will you lay down your life for My sake? Most assuredly, I say to you, the rooster shall not crow till you have denied Me three times.

The Way, the Truth, and the Life

14 "Let not your heart be troubled; you believe in God, believe also in Me. 2In My Father's house are many mansions; if it were not so, I would have told you. I go to prepare a place for you. 3And if I go and prepare a place for you, I will come again and receive you to Myself; that where I am, there you may be also. 4And where I go you know, and the way you know."

5Thomas said to Him, "Lord, we do not know where You are going, and how can we know the way?"

6Jesus said to him, "I am the way, the truth, and the life. No one comes to the Father except through Me.

The Father Revealed

7"If you had known Me, you would have known My Father also; and from now on you know Him and have seen Him."

8Philip said to Him, "Lord, show us the Father, and it is sufficient for us."

9Jesus said to him, "Have I been with you so long, and yet you have not known Me, Philip? He who has seen Me has seen the Father; so how can you say, 'Show us the Father'? 10Do you not believe that I am in the Father, and the Father in Me? The words that I speak to you I do not speak on My own authority; but the Father who dwells in Me does the works. 11Believe Me that I am in the Father and the Father in Me, or else believe Me for the sake of the works themselves.

The Answered Prayer

12"Most assuredly, I say to you, he who believes in Me, the works that I do he will do also; and greater works than these he will do, because I go to My Father. 13And whatever you ask in My name, that I will do, that the Father may be glorified in the Son. 14If you ask anything in My name, I will do it.

Jesus Promises Another Helper

15"If you love Me, keep My commandments. 16And I will pray the Father, and He will give you another Helper, that He may abide with you forever— 17the Spirit of truth, whom the world cannot receive, because it neither sees Him nor knows Him; but you know Him, for He dwells with you and will be in you. 18I will not leave you orphans; I will come to you.

Indwelling of the Father and the Son

19"A little while longer and the world will see Me no more, but you will see Me. Because I live, you will live also. 20At that day you will know that I am in My Father, and you in Me, and I in you. 21He who has My commandments and keeps them, it is he who loves Me. And he who loves Me will be loved by My Father, and I will love him and manifest Myself to him."

22Judas (not Iscariot) said to Him, "Lord, how is it that You will manifest Yourself to us, and not to the world?"

23Jesus answered and said to him, "If anyone loves Me, he will keep My word; and My Father will love him, and We will come to him and make Our home with him. 24He who does not love Me does not keep My words; and the word which you hear is not Mine but the Father's who sent Me."

DEVOTIONAL

The hearts of the disciples were heavy as Jesus talked about going away. As the room grew silent, Jesus comforted them. He was like a man leaving His fiancée and promising to return. The bride-to-be was deeply saddened, but Jesus, the loving Bridegroom, spoke to His bride's heart: "I go to prepare a place for you" (John 14:2). He was saying, "I am building a home for us to live in together, and I will come for you." He also said He would send her another Helper, a Comforter. Jesus promised the Holy Spirit would come and speak to her heart every day, reminding her of His love and showing her His promises.

As the bride of Christ, treasure Jesus' words of love, and express love back to Him by doing His will and keeping His commandments.

—Roy Mack
Pinecrest Baptist Church, McDonough, GA

WEEK 22, DAY 7

In what practical ways can you die to self or lose your life to serve others in Jesus' name?

How is your love for God demonstrated by your actions?

WEEK 23, DAY 1

Abide in Christ

John 14:25–15:27

The Gift of His Peace

"These things I have spoken to you while being present with you. 26But the Helper, the Holy Spirit, whom the Father will send in My name, He will teach you all things, and bring to your remembrance all things that I said to you. 27Peace I leave with you, My peace I give to you; not as the world gives do I give to you. Let not your heart be troubled, neither let it be afraid. 28You have heard Me say to you, 'I am going away and coming back to you.' If you loved Me, you would rejoice because I said, 'I am going to the Father,' for My Father is greater than I.

29"And now I have told you before it comes, that when it does come to pass, you may believe. 30I will no longer talk much with you, for the ruler of this world is coming, and he has nothing in Me. 31But that the world may know that I love the Father, and as the Father gave Me commandment, so I do. Arise, let us go from here.

The True Vine

15 "I am the true vine, and My Father is the vine-dresser. 2Every branch in Me that does not bear fruit He takes away; and every branch that bears fruit He prunes, that it may bear more fruit. 3You are already clean because of the word which I have spoken to you. 4Abide in Me, and I in you. As the branch cannot bear fruit of itself, unless it abides in the vine, neither can you, unless you abide in Me.

5"I am the vine, you are the branches. He who abides in Me, and I in him, bears much fruit; for without Me you can do nothing. 6If anyone does not abide in Me, he is cast out as a branch and is withered; and they gather them and throw them into the fire, and they are burned. 7If you abide in Me, and My words abide in you, you will ask what you desire, and it shall be done for you. 8By this My Father is glorified, that you bear much fruit; so you will be My disciples.

Love and Joy Perfected

9"As the Father loved Me, I also have loved you; abide in My love. 10If you keep My commandments, you will abide in My love, just as I have kept My Father's commandments and abide in His love.

11"These things I have spoken to you, that My joy may remain in you, and that your joy may be full. 12This is My commandment, that you love one another as I have loved you. 13Greater love has no one than this, than to lay down one's life for his friends. 14You are My friends if you do whatever I command you. 15No longer do I call you servants, for a servant does not know what his master is doing; but I have called you friends, for all things that I heard from My Father I have made known to you. 16You did not choose Me, but I chose you and appointed you that you should go and bear fruit, and that your fruit should remain, that whatever you ask the Father in My name He may give you. 17These things I command you, that you love one another.

The World's Hatred

18"If the world hates you, you know that it hated Me before it hated you. 19If you were of the world, the world would love its own. Yet because you are not of the world, but I chose you out of the world, therefore the world hates you. 20Remember the word that I said to you, 'A servant is not greater than his master.' If they persecuted Me, they will also persecute you. If they kept My word, they will keep yours also. 21But all these things they will do to you for My name's sake, because they do not know Him who sent Me. 22If I had not come and spoken to them, they would have no sin, but now they have no excuse for their sin. 23He who hates Me hates My Father also. 24If I had not done among them the works which no one else did, they would have no sin; but now they have seen and also hated both Me and My Father. 25But this happened that the word might be fulfilled which is written in their law, 'They hated Me without a cause.'

The Coming Rejection

26"But when the Helper comes, whom I shall send to you from the Father, the Spirit of truth who proceeds from the Father, He will testify of Me. 27And you also will bear witness, because you have been with Me from the beginning."

DEVOTIONAL

Jesus used a simple analogy to help His followers understand how to flourish spiritually: we must be in union with Him as a branch stays connected to a vine (John 15:1–8). In nature, a disconnected branch will never grow or bear fruit, but a connected branch almost always will. Branches must stay linked to the vine as their source of life. In the same way, believers must abide in Christ to experience His life. Today, abide in Christ by crying out to Him in prayer, listening to Him speak through Scripture, and obeying Him by faith.

—Dr. Stephen Rummage
Bell Shoals Baptist Church, Brandon, FL

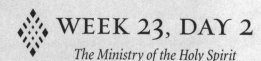

WEEK 23, DAY 2

The Ministry of the Holy Spirit

John 16:1–28

16 "These things I have spoken to you, that you should not be made to stumble. ²They will put you out of the synagogues; yes, the time is coming that whoever kills you will think that he offers God service. ³And these things they will do to you because they have not known the Father nor Me. ⁴But these things I have told you, that when the time comes, you may remember that I told you of them.

"And these things I did not say to you at the beginning, because I was with you.

The Work of the Holy Spirit

⁵"But now I go away to Him who sent Me, and none of you asks Me, 'Where are You going?' ⁶But because I have said these things to you, sorrow has filled your heart. ⁷Nevertheless I tell you the truth. It is to your advantage that I go away; for if I do not go away, the Helper will not come to you; but if I depart, I will send Him to you. ⁸And when He has come, He will convict the world of sin, and of righteousness, and of judgment: ⁹of sin, because they do not believe in Me; ¹⁰of righteousness, because I go to My Father and you see Me no more; ¹¹of judgment, because the ruler of this world is judged.

¹²"I still have many things to say to you, but you cannot bear them now. ¹³However, when He, the Spirit of truth, has come, He will guide you into all truth; for He will not speak on His own authority, but whatever He hears He will speak; and He will tell you things to come. ¹⁴He will glorify Me, for He will take of what is Mine and declare it to you. ¹⁵All things that the Father has are Mine. Therefore I said that He will take of Mine and declare it to you.

Sorrow Will Turn to Joy

¹⁶"A little while, and you will not see Me; and again a little while, and you will see Me, because I go to the Father."

¹⁷Then some of His disciples said among themselves, "What is this that He says to us, 'A little while, and you will not see Me; and again a little while, and you will see Me'; and, 'because I go to the Father'?" ¹⁸They said therefore, "What is this that He says, 'A little while'? We do not know what He is saying."

¹⁹Now Jesus knew that they desired to ask Him, and He said to them, "Are you inquiring among yourselves about what I said, 'A little while, and you will not see Me;

and again a little while, and you will see Me'? ²⁰Most assuredly, I say to you that you will weep and lament, but the world will rejoice; and you will be sorrowful, but your sorrow will be turned into joy. ²¹A woman, when she is in labor, has sorrow because her hour has come; but as soon as she has given birth to the child, she no longer remembers the anguish, for joy that a human being has been born into the world. ²²Therefore you now have sorrow; but I will see you again and your heart will rejoice, and your joy no one will take from you.

²³"And in that day you will ask Me nothing. Most assuredly, I say to you, whatever you ask the Father in My name He will give you. ²⁴Until now you have asked nothing in My name. Ask, and you will receive, that your joy may be full.

Jesus Christ Has Overcome the World

²⁵"These things I have spoken to you in figurative language; but the time is coming when I will no longer speak to you in figurative language, but I will tell you plainly about the Father. ²⁶In that day you will ask in My name, and I do not say to you that I shall pray the Father for you; ²⁷for the Father Himself loves you, because you have loved Me, and have believed that I came forth from God. ²⁸I came forth from the Father and have come into the world. Again, I leave the world and go to the Father."

DEVOTIONAL

*A*s *Jesus prepared to leave His followers physically, they were filled with despair. However, He promised to give them an even greater resource, His Holy Spirit. In John 16:5–15, Jesus described the ministry of the Holy Spirit in three essential ways.*

First, the Holy Spirit comforts. Jesus called Him "the Helper" (John 16:7), which comes from a Greek term that means "to comfort or encourage." Because the Spirit lives in us, He encourages our spiritual lives.

Next, the Spirit convicts (John 16:8). This is the work of the Spirit among those who do not know Christ. He shows lost people the reality of their sin and impending judgment, as well as their need to believe on Jesus.

Third, the Holy Spirit counsels. Jesus promised His disciples that the Spirit would guide them into all truth (John 16:13). The Holy Spirit is working today to help you understand God's Word and empower you to live for the Lord.

—Dr. Stephen Rummage
Bell Shoals Baptist Church, Brandon, FL

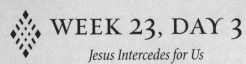

WEEK 23, DAY 3

Jesus Intercedes for Us

John 16:29–17:19

His disciples said to Him, "See, now You are speaking plainly, and using no figure of speech! 30Now we are sure that You know all things, and have no need that anyone should question You. By this we believe that You came forth from God."

31Jesus answered them, "Do you now believe? 32Indeed the hour is coming, yes, has now come, that you will be scattered, each to his own, and will leave Me alone. And yet I am not alone, because the Father is with Me. 33These things I have spoken to you, that in Me you may have peace. In the world you will have tribulation; but be of good cheer, I have overcome the world."

Jesus Prays for Himself

17 Jesus spoke these words, lifted up His eyes to heaven, and said: "Father, the hour has come. Glorify Your Son, that Your Son also may glorify You, 2as You have given Him authority over all flesh, that He should give eternal life to as many as You have given Him. 3And this is eternal life, that they may know You, the only true God, and Jesus Christ whom You have sent. 4I have glorified You on the earth. I have finished the work which You have given Me to do. 5And now, O Father, glorify Me together with Yourself, with the glory which I had with You before the world was.

Jesus Prays for His Disciples

6"I have manifested Your name to the men whom You have given Me out of the world. They were Yours, You gave them to Me, and they have kept Your word. 7Now they have known that all things which You have given Me are from You. 8For I have given to them the words which You have given Me; and they have received them, and have known surely that I came forth from You; and they have believed that You sent Me.

9"I pray for them. I do not pray for the world but for those whom You have given Me, for they are Yours. 10And all Mine are Yours, and Yours are Mine, and I am glorified in them. 11Now I am no longer in the world, but these are in the world, and I come to You. Holy Father, keep through Your name those whom You have given Me, that they may be one as We are. 12While I was with them in the world, I kept them in Your name. Those whom You gave Me I have kept; and none of them is lost except the son of perdition, that the Scripture might be fulfilled. 13But now I come to You, and these things I speak in the world, that they may have My joy fulfilled in themselves. 14I have given them Your word; and the world has hated them because they are not of the world, just as I am not of the world. 15I do not pray that You should take them out of the world, but that You should keep them from the evil one. 16They are not of the world, just as I am not of the world. 17Sanctify them by Your truth. Your word is truth. 18As You sent Me into the world, I also have sent them into the world. 19And for their sakes I sanctify Myself, that they also may be sanctified by the truth."

DEVOTIONAL

"How can I pray for you?" It's one of the kindest questions one person can ask another. The night before He was crucified, the Lord Jesus prayed what has been called the greatest prayer recorded in Scripture. This "High Priestly Prayer" of Christ in John 17 is one of intercession, as the Lord prayed first for Himself and then for His current and future disciples.

At the heart of this prayer, we can see several ways that Jesus prayed for His followers. He prayed for our unity, asking the Father that His disciples would be "one" as He and the Father are one (John 17:11). While the world often tells us we must compromise convictions in order to achieve unity, the Father and Son share a unity based on perfect truth. So should our unity be based on the truth of Jesus and His Word.

Jesus also prayed for our joy, asking for His joy to be fulfilled in us (John 17:13). The language the Lord used here suggests the beautiful image of a cup being filled to its very brim with spiritual and heavenly bliss. Whatever happens, we can have an overflowing joy through Jesus.

Next, Jesus prayed for our protection "from the evil one" (John 17:15). The Lord asked not for His followers to be evacuated from the dangers of Satan and his schemes, but rather that the Father would guard us and keep us from harm as we live for Christ.

Finally, Jesus prayed for our holiness. He asked the Father to sanctify His followers through His Word, which is truth (John 17:17).

Today, you can live with the confidence that Jesus never stops interceding for you in the presence of the Father.

—Dr. Stephen Rummage
Bell Shoals Baptist Church, Brandon, FL

WEEK 23, DAY 4

The Great Power of Jesus

John 17:20–18:18

Jesus Prays for All Believers

"I do not pray for these alone, but also for those who will believe in Me through their word; 21that they all may be one, as You, Father, are in Me, and I in You; that they also may be one in Us, that the world may believe that You sent Me. 22And the glory which You gave Me I have given them, that they may be one just as We are one: 23I in them, and You in Me; that they may be made perfect in one, and that the world may know that You have sent Me, and have loved them as You have loved Me.

24"Father, I desire that they also whom You gave Me may be with Me where I am, that they may behold My glory which You have given Me; for You loved Me before the foundation of the world. 25O righteous Father! The world has not known You, but I have known You; and these have known that You sent Me. 26And I have declared to them Your name, and will declare it, that the love with which You loved Me may be in them, and I in them."

Betrayal and Arrest in Gethsemane

18When Jesus had spoken these words, He went out with His disciples over the Brook Kidron, where there was a garden, which He and His disciples entered. 2And Judas, who betrayed Him, also knew the place; for Jesus often met there with His disciples. 3Then Judas, having received a detachment of troops, and officers from the chief priests and Pharisees, came there with lanterns, torches, and weapons. 4Jesus therefore, knowing all things that would come upon Him, went forward and said to them, "Whom are you seeking?"

5They answered Him, "Jesus of Nazareth."

Jesus said to them, "I am He." And Judas, who betrayed Him, also stood with them. 6Now when He said to them, "I am He," they drew back and fell to the ground.

7Then He asked them again, "Whom are you seeking?" And they said, "Jesus of Nazareth."

8Jesus answered, "I have told you that I am He. Therefore, if you seek Me, let these go their way," 9that the saying might be fulfilled which He spoke, "Of those whom You gave Me I have lost none."

10Then Simon Peter, having a sword, drew it and struck the high priest's servant, and cut off his right ear. The servant's name was Malchus.

11So Jesus said to Peter, "Put your sword into the sheath. Shall I not drink the cup which My Father has given Me?"

Before the High Priest

12Then the detachment of troops and the captain and the officers of the Jews arrested Jesus and bound Him. 13And they led Him away to Annas first, for he was the father-in-law of Caiaphas who was high priest that year. 14Now it was Caiaphas who advised the Jews that it was expedient that one man should die for the people.

Peter Denies Jesus

15And Simon Peter followed Jesus, and so did another disciple. Now that disciple was known to the high priest, and went with Jesus into the courtyard of the high priest. 16But Peter stood at the door outside. Then the other disciple, who was known to the high priest, went out and spoke to her who kept the door, and brought Peter in. 17Then the servant girl who kept the door said to Peter, "You are not also one of this Man's disciples, are you?"

He said, "I am not."

18Now the servants and officers who had made a fire of coals stood there, for it was cold, and they warmed themselves. And Peter stood with them and warmed himself.

DEVOTIONAL

*A*ll four Gospels tell about Jesus' arrest in Gethsemane, but John alone described one extraordinary event that occurred there. The soldiers and religious leaders came to the garden demanding to see Jesus of Nazareth, and, as recorded in the original language of the New Testament, Jesus replied with three words: "I am He." Amazingly, these simple words from the Lord's lips forced the arresting detachment to fall helplessly to the ground. Why? Because His captors were face-to-face with Christ's majesty and deity, and they could not stand. God's covenant name, which He revealed to Moses at the burning bush, is: "I AM WHO I AM" (Exodus 3:14). It is this wonderful title that Jesus, the eternal Son of God, claimed for Himself in the presence of His enemies.

You can take courage that Jesus, the great I AM, has the power to subdue all the powers of darkness, fear, and spiritual opposition, no matter what your circumstances are!

—Dr. Stephen Rummage
Bell Shoals Baptist Church, Brandon, FL

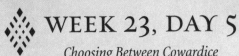

WEEK 23, DAY 5

*Choosing Between Cowardice
and Obedience*

John 18:19–19:3

Jesus Questioned by the High Priest

The high priest then asked Jesus about His disciples and His doctrine.

20Jesus answered him, "I spoke openly to the world. I always taught in synagogues and in the temple, where the Jews always meet, and in secret I have said nothing. 21Why do you ask Me? Ask those who have heard Me what I said to them. Indeed they know what I said."

22And when He had said these things, one of the officers who stood by struck Jesus with the palm of his hand, saying, "Do You answer the high priest like that?"

23Jesus answered him, "If I have spoken evil, bear witness of the evil; but if well, why do you strike Me?"

24Then Annas sent Him bound to Caiaphas the high priest.

Peter Denies Twice More

25Now Simon Peter stood and warmed himself. Therefore they said to him, "You are not also one of His disciples, are you?"

He denied it and said, "I am not!"

26One of the servants of the high priest, a relative of him whose ear Peter cut off, said, "Did I not see you in the garden with Him?" 27Peter then denied again; and immediately a rooster crowed.

In Pilate's Court

28Then they led Jesus from Caiaphas to the Praetorium, and it was early morning. But they themselves did not go into the Praetorium, lest they should be defiled, but that they might eat the Passover. 29Pilate then went out to them and said, "What accusation do you bring against this Man?"

30They answered and said to him, "If He were not an evildoer, we would not have delivered Him up to you."

31Then Pilate said to them, "You take Him and judge Him according to your law."

Therefore the Jews said to him, "It is not lawful for us to put anyone to death," 32that the saying of Jesus might be fulfilled which He spoke, signifying by what death He would die.

33Then Pilate entered the Praetorium again, called Jesus, and said to Him, "Are You the King of the Jews?"

34Jesus answered him, "Are you speaking for yourself about this, or did others tell you this concerning Me?"

35Pilate answered, "Am I a Jew? Your own nation and the chief priests have delivered You to me. What have You done?"

36Jesus answered, "My kingdom is not of this world. If My kingdom were of this world, My servants would fight, so that I should not be delivered to the Jews; but now My kingdom is not from here."

37Pilate therefore said to Him, "Are You a king then?"

Jesus answered, "You say rightly that I am a king. For this cause I was born, and for this cause I have come into the world, that I should bear witness to the truth. Everyone who is of the truth hears My voice."

38Pilate said to Him, "What is truth?" And when he had said this, he went out again to the Jews, and said to them, "I find no fault in Him at all.

Taking the Place of Barabbas

39"But you have a custom that I should release someone to you at the Passover. Do you therefore want me to release to you the King of the Jews?"

40Then they all cried again, saying, "Not this Man, but Barabbas!" Now Barabbas was a robber.

The Soldiers Mock Jesus

19 So then Pilate took Jesus and scourged Him. 2And the soldiers twisted a crown of thorns and put it on His head, and they put on Him a purple robe. 3Then they said, "Hail, King of the Jews!" And they struck Him with their hands.

DEVOTIONAL

Perhaps the most heartbreaking thing about tragic characters is their unfulfilled potential. Such was the case of the Roman procurator named Pilate. This powerful man, who was no doubt trained for leadership in the best of the Roman tradition, found himself incapable of doing what he knew was right as Jesus stood before him. Pilate recognized Jesus was innocent, yet he delivered the Lord to death anyway. Why did he cave in to his own cowardice? We can see two major reasons: First, Pilate valued expediency above truth (John 18:38). Second, he feared people more than God (18:40–19:1). Resist the temptation to be pragmatic or popular instead of obeying God.

—Dr. Stephen Rummage
Bell Shoals Baptist Church, Brandon, FL

WEEK 23, DAY 6

Staying Near the Cross

John 19:4–27

Pilate then went out again, and said to them, "Behold, I am bringing Him out to you, that you may know that I find no fault in Him."

Pilate's Decision

⁵Then Jesus came out, wearing the crown of thorns and the purple robe. And Pilate said to them, "Behold the Man!"

⁶Therefore, when the chief priests and officers saw Him, they cried out, saying, "Crucify Him, crucify Him!"

Pilate said to them, "You take Him and crucify Him, for I find no fault in Him."

⁷The Jews answered him, "We have a law, and according to our law He ought to die, because He made Himself the Son of God."

⁸Therefore, when Pilate heard that saying, he was the more afraid, ⁹and went again into the Praetorium, and said to Jesus, "Where are You from?" But Jesus gave him no answer.

¹⁰Then Pilate said to Him, "Are You not speaking to me? Do You not know that I have power to crucify You, and power to release You?"

¹¹Jesus answered, "You could have no power at all against Me unless it had been given you from above. Therefore the one who delivered Me to you has the greater sin."

¹²From then on Pilate sought to release Him, but the Jews cried out, saying, "If you let this Man go, you are not Caesar's friend. Whoever makes himself a king speaks against Caesar."

¹³When Pilate therefore heard that saying, he brought Jesus out and sat down in the judgment seat in a place that is called The Pavement, but in Hebrew, Gabbatha. ¹⁴Now it was the Preparation Day of the Passover, and about the sixth hour. And he said to the Jews, "Behold your King!"

¹⁵But they cried out, "Away with Him, away with Him! Crucify Him!"

Pilate said to them, "Shall I crucify your King?"

The chief priests answered, "We have no king but Caesar!"

¹⁶Then he delivered Him to them to be crucified. So they took Jesus and led Him away.

The King on a Cross

¹⁷And He, bearing His cross, went out to a place called the Place of a Skull, which is called in Hebrew, Golgotha, ¹⁸where they crucified Him, and two others with Him, one on either side, and Jesus in the center. ¹⁹Now Pilate wrote a title and put it on the cross. And the writing was:

JESUS OF NAZARETH, THE KING OF THE JEWS.

²⁰Then many of the Jews read this title, for the place where Jesus was crucified was near the city; and it was written in Hebrew, Greek, and Latin.

²¹Therefore the chief priests of the Jews said to Pilate, "Do not write, 'The King of the Jews,' but, 'He said, "I am the King of the Jews."'"

²²Pilate answered, "What I have written, I have written."

²³Then the soldiers, when they had crucified Jesus, took His garments and made four parts, to each soldier a part, and also the tunic. Now the tunic was without seam, woven from the top in one piece. ²⁴They said therefore among themselves, "Let us not tear it, but cast lots for it, whose it shall be," that the Scripture might be fulfilled which says:

"They divided My garments among them,
And for My clothing they cast lots."

Therefore the soldiers did these things.

Behold Your Mother

²⁵Now there stood by the cross of Jesus His mother, and His mother's sister, Mary the wife of Clopas, and Mary Magdalene. ²⁶When Jesus therefore saw His mother, and the disciple whom He loved standing by, He said to His mother, "Woman, behold your son!" ²⁷Then He said to the disciple, "Behold your mother!" And from that hour that disciple took her to his own home.

DEVOTIONAL

Guilt by association is not just a recent phenomenon. It was a reality in Jesus' day as well. Lingering close to one who was crucified carried the risk of abuse, ridicule, harassment, and even condemnation and death. But there are times you simply do not leave those you love. So, near the cross of Jesus, a small group of four women and one man remained, bound by love to risk staying by His side. Today, Jesus calls you to remain near His cross.

—Dr. Stephen Rummage
Bell Shoals Baptist Church, Brandon, FL

WEEK 23, DAY 7

What areas of your life do you need to adjust in order to abide in Jesus? List any barriers that are keeping you from obedience and fruitfulness as you seek to follow Him.

_____

_____

_____

_____

_____

_____

_____

_____

_____

_____

_____

_____

How do you experience the presence and strength of the Holy Spirit in your everyday routine? Where is He leading you? What does He desire to empower you to be and do?

_____

_____

_____

_____

_____

_____

_____

_____

_____

_____

WEEK 24, DAY I

The "Done Plan" of Salvation

John 19:28–20:10

It Is Finished

After this, Jesus, knowing that all things were now accomplished, that the Scripture might be fulfilled, said, "I thirst!" 29Now a vessel full of sour wine was sitting there; and they filled a sponge with sour wine, put it on hyssop, and put it to His mouth. 30So when Jesus had received the sour wine, He said, "It is finished!" And bowing His head, He gave up His spirit.

Jesus' Side Is Pierced

31Therefore, because it was the Preparation Day, that the bodies should not remain on the cross on the Sabbath (for that Sabbath was a high day), the Jews asked Pilate that their legs might be broken, and that they might be taken away. 32Then the soldiers came and broke the legs of the first and of the other who was crucified with Him. 33But when they came to Jesus and saw that He was already dead, they did not break His legs. 34But one of the soldiers pierced His side with a spear, and immediately blood and water came out. 35And he who has seen has testified, and his testimony is true; and he knows that he is telling the truth, so that you may believe. 36For these things were done that the Scripture should be fulfilled, "Not one of His bones shall be broken." 37And again another Scripture says, "They shall look on Him whom they pierced."

Jesus Buried in Joseph's Tomb

38After this, Joseph of Arimathea, being a disciple of Jesus, but secretly, for fear of the Jews, asked Pilate that he might take away the body of Jesus; and Pilate gave him permission. So he came and took the body of Jesus. 39And Nicodemus, who at first came to Jesus by night, also came, bringing a mixture of myrrh and aloes, about a hundred pounds. 40Then they took the body of Jesus, and bound it in strips of linen with the spices, as the custom of the Jews is to bury. 41Now in the place where He was crucified there was a garden, and in the garden a new tomb in which no one had yet been laid. 42So there they laid Jesus, because of the Jews' Preparation Day, for the tomb was nearby.

The Empty Tomb

20 Now on the first day of the week Mary Magdalene went to the tomb early, while it was still dark, and saw that the stone had been taken away from the tomb. 2Then she ran and came to Simon Peter, and to the other disciple, whom Jesus loved, and said to them, "They have taken away the Lord out of the tomb, and we do not know where they have laid Him."

3Peter therefore went out, and the other disciple, and were going to the tomb. 4So they both ran together, and the other disciple outran Peter and came to the tomb first. 5And he, stooping down and looking in, saw the linen cloths lying there; yet he did not go in. 6Then Simon Peter came, following him, and went into the tomb; and he saw the linen cloths lying there, 7and the handkerchief that had been around His head, not lying with the linen cloths, but folded together in a place by itself. 8Then the other disciple, who came to the tomb first, went in also; and he saw and believed. 9For as yet they did not know the Scripture, that He must rise again from the dead. 10Then the disciples went away again to their own homes.

DEVOTIONAL

There are two ways people look at salvation. One is a "do plan," and the other is a "done plan." Those who select the "do plan" focus on earning God's favor. The "done plan" is found in today's reading. On the cross Jesus said, "It is finished!" (John 19:30). The work was done; the salvation was complete. In His death, Jesus atoned for our sin.

We must never fall into thinking we have in any way earned our salvation. Paul stated clearly, "By grace you have been saved through faith, and that not of yourselves; it is the gift of God, not of works, lest anyone should boast" (Ephesians 2:8–9). We've received a gift—the best gift imaginable—not because of our "do plan," but because of Jesus' work on the cross in God's "done plan." The gift reflects the goodness of the Giver, not the worthiness of the recipients.

The resurrection of Jesus Christ is the cornerstone of Christianity. Christians cannot explain the resurrection . . . but the resurrection certainly explains Christians. It defines us. If Jesus is not risen, we should tear up our Bibles, fire the pastor, and sell the church buildings (1 Corinthians 15:17). If Jesus is risen, we must proclaim it loud and clear—and He is!

Declare the cross as the power of God for salvation. He died for you and saved you! Embrace it. Declare it.

—Dr. Ted Traylor
Olive Baptist Church, Pensacola, FL

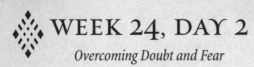

WEEK 24, DAY 2

Overcoming Doubt and Fear

John 20:11–31

Mary Magdalene Sees the Risen Lord

But Mary stood outside by the tomb weeping, and as she wept she stooped down and looked into the tomb. ¹²And she saw two angels in white sitting, one at the head and the other at the feet, where the body of Jesus had lain. ¹³Then they said to her, "Woman, why are you weeping?"

She said to them, "Because they have taken away my Lord, and I do not know where they have laid Him."

¹⁴Now when she had said this, she turned around and saw Jesus standing there, and did not know that it was Jesus. ¹⁵Jesus said to her, "Woman, why are you weeping? Whom are you seeking?"

She, supposing Him to be the gardener, said to Him, "Sir, if You have carried Him away, tell me where You have laid Him, and I will take Him away."

¹⁶Jesus said to her, "Mary!"

She turned and said to Him, "Rabboni!" (which is to say, Teacher).

¹⁷Jesus said to her, "Do not cling to Me, for I have not yet ascended to My Father; but go to My brethren and say to them, 'I am ascending to My Father and your Father, and to My God and your God.'"

¹⁸Mary Magdalene came and told the disciples that she had seen the Lord, and that He had spoken these things to her.

The Apostles Commissioned

¹⁹Then, the same day at evening, being the first day of the week, when the doors were shut where the disciples were assembled, for fear of the Jews, Jesus came and stood in the midst, and said to them, "Peace be with you." ²⁰When He had said this, He showed them His hands and His side. Then the disciples were glad when they saw the Lord.

²¹So Jesus said to them again, "Peace to you! As the Father has sent Me, I also send you." ²²And when He had said this, He breathed on them, and said to them, "Receive the Holy Spirit. ²³If you forgive the sins of any, they are forgiven them; if you retain the *sins* of any, they are retained."

Seeing and Believing

²⁴Now Thomas, called the Twin, one of the twelve, was not with them when Jesus came. ²⁵The other disciples therefore said to him, "We have seen the Lord."

So he said to them, "Unless I see in His hands the print of the nails, and put my finger into the print of the nails, and put my hand into His side, I will not believe."

²⁶And after eight days His disciples were again inside, and Thomas with them. Jesus came, the doors being shut, and stood in the midst, and said, "Peace to you!" ²⁷Then He said to Thomas, "Reach your finger here, and look at My hands; and reach your hand here, and put it into My side. Do not be unbelieving, but believing."

²⁸And Thomas answered and said to Him, "My Lord and my God!"

²⁹Jesus said to him, "Thomas, because you have seen Me, you have believed. Blessed are those who have not seen and yet have believed."

That You May Believe

³⁰And truly Jesus did many other signs in the presence of His disciples, which are not written in this book; ³¹but these are written that you may believe that Jesus is the Christ, the Son of God, and that believing you may have life in His name.

DEVOTIONAL

*T*homas wanted to see Jesus' wounds for himself before he would believe Jesus had risen. After eight days of doubting, he saw Jesus and declared, "My Lord and my God!" (John 20:28). But the Lord calls us to be more trusting of Him. We are to walk not by sight but by faith. We are blessed when we believe without having seen.

Doubt is often born in fear. Maybe you fear rejection or not being loved. Maybe you fear poverty, poor health, or death. While suffering is part of life on earth, God is able to meet your needs and carry you through every hardship you'll ever face. He tells His people not to fear. In a dangerous storm, Jesus told His disciples not to be afraid—He, the Almighty, was with them. Jesus also said, "In Me you may have peace. In the world you will have tribulation; but be of good cheer, I have overcome the world" (John 16:33). Fear not! Jesus is alive!

Honor the Lord by trusting His love and power. Build your faith and be led to worship by reading His Word. Find peace in His promises and praise Him with your life.

—Dr. Ted Traylor
Olive Baptist Church, Pensacola, FL

WEEK 24, DAY 3

God's Word Gives Us Truth to Believe

John 21:1–25

Breakfast by the Sea

21 After these things Jesus showed Himself again to the disciples at the Sea of Tiberias, and in this way He showed Himself: ²Simon Peter, Thomas called the Twin, Nathanael of Cana in Galilee, the sons of Zebedee, and two others of His disciples were together. ³Simon Peter said to them, "I am going fishing."

They said to him, "We are going with you also." They went out and immediately got into the boat, and that night they caught nothing. ⁴But when the morning had now come, Jesus stood on the shore; yet the disciples did not know that it was Jesus. ⁵Then Jesus said to them, "Children, have you any food?"

They answered Him, "No."

⁶And He said to them, "Cast the net on the right side of the boat, and you will find some." So they cast, and now they were not able to draw it in because of the multitude of fish.

⁷Therefore that disciple whom Jesus loved said to Peter, "It is the Lord!" Now when Simon Peter heard that it was the Lord, he put on his outer garment (for he had removed it), and plunged into the sea. ⁸But the other disciples came in the little boat (for they were not far from land, but about two hundred cubits), dragging the net with fish. ⁹Then, as soon as they had come to land, they saw a fire of coals there, and fish laid on it, and bread. ¹⁰Jesus said to them, "Bring some of the fish which you have just caught."

¹¹Simon Peter went up and dragged the net to land, full of large fish, one hundred and fifty-three; and although there were so many, the net was not broken. ¹²Jesus said to them, "Come and eat breakfast." Yet none of the disciples dared ask Him, "Who are You?"—knowing that it was the Lord. ¹³Jesus then came and took the bread and gave it to them, and likewise the fish.

¹⁴This is now the third time Jesus showed Himself to His disciples after He was raised from the dead.

Jesus Restores Peter

¹⁵So when they had eaten breakfast, Jesus said to Simon Peter, "Simon, son of Jonah, do you love Me more than these?"

He said to Him, "Yes, Lord; You know that I love You."

He said to him, "Feed My lambs."

¹⁶He said to him again a second time, "Simon, son of Jonah, do you love Me?"

He said to Him, "Yes, Lord; You know that I love You."

He said to him, "Tend My sheep."

¹⁷He said to him the third time, "Simon, son of Jonah, do you love Me?" Peter was grieved because He said to him the third time, "Do you love Me?"

And he said to Him, "Lord, You know all things; You know that I love You."

Jesus said to him, "Feed My sheep. ¹⁸Most assuredly, I say to you, when you were younger, you girded yourself and walked where you wished; but when you are old, you will stretch out your hands, and another will gird you and carry you where you do not wish." ¹⁹This He spoke, signifying by what death he would glorify God. And when He had spoken this, He said to him, "Follow Me."

The Beloved Disciple and His Book

²⁰Then Peter, turning around, saw the disciple whom Jesus loved following, who also had leaned on His breast at the supper, and said, "Lord, who is the one who betrays You?" ²¹Peter, seeing him, said to Jesus, "But Lord, what about this man?"

²²Jesus said to him, "If I will that he remain till I come, what is that to you? You follow Me."

²³Then this saying went out among the brethren that this disciple would not die. Yet Jesus did not say to him that he would not die, but, "If I will that he remain till I come, what is that to you?"

²⁴This is the disciple who testifies of these things, and wrote these things; and we know that his testimony is true.

²⁵And there are also many other things that Jesus did, which if they were written one by one, I suppose that even the world itself could not contain the books that would be written. Amen.

DEVOTIONAL

The four gospels tell the story of Jesus. As John indicated in the closing sentences of chapters 20 and 21, however, not all of Jesus' activity was recorded. The accounts we have received were written so that we may believe Jesus is the Son of God and have life in His name (John 20:31). Divine inspiration gave us what we need to know about Jesus. The Bible is a perfect Book about a perfect Savior. Read it. Meditate on it. Be inspired by it. Ask the Holy Spirit to lead you in understanding the truth of God. And look forward to the day when we will learn the rest of the story in heaven.

—Dr. Ted Traylor
Olive Baptist Church, Pensacola, FL

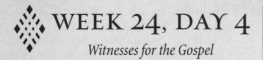

WEEK 24, DAY 4

Witnesses for the Gospel

Acts 1:1–26

Prologue

1 The former account I made, O Theophilus, of all that Jesus began both to do and teach, ²until the day in which He was taken up, after He through the Holy Spirit had given commandments to the apostles whom He had chosen, ³to whom He also presented Himself alive after His suffering by many infallible proofs, being seen by them during forty days and speaking of the things pertaining to the kingdom of God.

The Holy Spirit Promised

⁴And being assembled together with them, He commanded them not to depart from Jerusalem, but to wait for the Promise of the Father, "which," He said, "you have heard from Me; ⁵for John truly baptized with water, but you shall be baptized with the Holy Spirit not many days from now." ⁶Therefore, when they had come together, they asked Him, saying, "Lord, will You at this time restore the kingdom to Israel?" ⁷And He said to them, "It is not for you to know times or seasons which the Father has put in His own authority. ⁸But you shall receive power when the Holy Spirit has come upon you; and you shall be witnesses to Me in Jerusalem, and in all Judea and Samaria, and to the end of the earth."

Jesus Ascends to Heaven

⁹Now when He had spoken these things, while they watched, He was taken up, and a cloud received Him out of their sight. ¹⁰And while they looked steadfastly toward heaven as He went up, behold, two men stood by them in white apparel, ¹¹who also said, "Men of Galilee, why do you stand gazing up into heaven? This same Jesus, who was taken up from you into heaven, will so come in like manner as you saw Him go into heaven."

The Upper Room Prayer Meeting

¹²Then they returned to Jerusalem from the mount called Olivet, which is near Jerusalem, a Sabbath day's journey. ¹³And when they had entered, they went up into the upper room where they were staying: Peter, James, John, and Andrew; Philip and Thomas; Bartholomew and Matthew; James the son of Alphaeus and Simon the Zealot; and Judas the son of James. ¹⁴These all continued with one accord in prayer and supplication, with the women and Mary the mother of Jesus, and with His brothers.

Matthias Chosen

¹⁵And in those days Peter stood up in the midst of the disciples (altogether the number of names was about a hundred and twenty), and said, ¹⁶"Men and brethren, this Scripture had to be fulfilled, which the Holy Spirit spoke before by the mouth of David concerning Judas, who became a guide to those who arrested Jesus; ¹⁷for he was numbered with us and obtained a part in this ministry."

¹⁸(Now this man purchased a field with the wages of iniquity; and falling headlong, he burst open in the middle and all his entrails gushed out. ¹⁹And it became known to all those dwelling in Jerusalem; so that field is called in their own language, Akel Dama, that is, Field of Blood.)

²⁰"For it is written in the book of Psalms:

'Let his dwelling place be desolate,
 And let no one live in it';

and,

'Let another take his office.'

²¹"Therefore, of these men who have accompanied us all the time that the Lord Jesus went in and out among us, ²²beginning from the baptism of John to that day when He was taken up from us, one of these must become a witness with us of His resurrection."

²³And they proposed two: Joseph called Barsabas, who was surnamed Justus, and Matthias. ²⁴And they prayed and said, "You, O Lord, who know the hearts of all, show which of these two You have chosen ²⁵to take part in this ministry and apostleship from which Judas by transgression fell, that he might go to his own place." ²⁶And they cast their lots, and the lot fell on Matthias. And he was numbered with the eleven apostles.

DEVOTIONAL

A cts 1:8 speaks of the power and plan of the Holy Spirit in mission work. As you are filled with the Spirit, you become a witness for the gospel. The geographical outline of Jerusalem, Judea, Samaria, and the world suggests we are to be active in each simultaneously—we have neighbors, regions, and people groups to give witness to. The church must have all of these targets on her radar. Begin where you are. Witness today.

—Dr. Ted Traylor
Olive Baptist Church, Pensacola, FL

WEEK 24, DAY 5

God's Spirit Fills His People

Acts 2:1–28

Coming of the Holy Spirit

2 When the Day of Pentecost had fully come, they were all with one accord in one place. ²And suddenly there came a sound from heaven, as of a rushing mighty wind, and it filled the whole house where they were sitting. ³Then there appeared to them divided tongues, as of fire, and one sat upon each of them. ⁴And they were all filled with the Holy Spirit and began to speak with other tongues, as the Spirit gave them utterance.

The Crowd's Response

⁵And there were dwelling in Jerusalem Jews, devout men, from every nation under heaven. ⁶And when this sound occurred, the multitude came together, and were confused, because everyone heard them speak in his own language. ⁷Then they were all amazed and marveled, saying to one another, "Look, are not all these who speak Galileans? ⁸And how is it that we hear, each in our own language in which we were born? ⁹Parthians and Medes and Elamites, those dwelling in Mesopotamia, Judea and Cappadocia, Pontus and Asia, ¹⁰Phrygia and Pamphylia, Egypt and the parts of Libya adjoining Cyrene, visitors from Rome, both Jews and proselytes, ¹¹Cretans and Arabs—we hear them speaking in our own tongues the wonderful works of God." ¹²So they were all amazed and perplexed, saying to one another, "Whatever could this mean?"

¹³Others mocking said, "They are full of new wine."

Peter's Sermon

¹⁴But Peter, standing up with the eleven, raised his voice and said to them, "Men of Judea and all who dwell in Jerusalem, let this be known to you, and heed my words. ¹⁵For these are not drunk, as you suppose, since it is only the third hour of the day. ¹⁶But this is what was spoken by the prophet Joel:

17 'And it shall come to pass in the last days,
    says God,
    That I will pour out of My Spirit on all flesh;
    Your sons and your daughters shall prophesy,
    Your young men shall see visions,
    Your old men shall dream dreams.

18 And on My menservants and on My
        maidservants
    I will pour out My Spirit in those days;
    And they shall prophesy.

19 I will show wonders in heaven above
    And signs in the earth beneath:
    Blood and fire and vapor of smoke.

20 The sun shall be turned into darkness,
    And the moon into blood,
    Before the coming of the great and awesome
        day of the LORD.

21 And it shall come to pass
    That whoever calls on the name of the LORD
    Shall be saved.'

²²"Men of Israel, hear these words: Jesus of Nazareth, a Man attested by God to you by miracles, wonders, and signs which God did through Him in your midst, as you yourselves also know— ²³Him, being delivered by the determined purpose and foreknowledge of God, you have taken by lawless hands, have crucified, and put to death; ²⁴whom God raised up, having loosed the pains of death, because it was not possible that He should be held by it. ²⁵For David says concerning Him:

'I foresaw the LORD always before my face,
    For He is at my right hand, that I may not
        be shaken.

26 Therefore my heart rejoiced, and my tongue
        was glad;
    Moreover my flesh also will rest in hope.

27 For You will not leave my soul in Hades,
    Nor will You allow Your Holy One to see
        corruption.

28 You have made known to me the ways of life;
    You will make me full of joy in Your presence.'"

DEVOTIONAL

*P*entecost ushered in a new era for the church. As believers, each of us is to be continually filled with the Holy Spirit. How does this happen?

First, present your body to Christ as a living sacrifice (Romans 12:1–2). Second, ask for the fullness. "Ask, and it will be given to you" (Luke 11:9). Third, be obedient to Jesus' commands (Acts 5:32). And fourth, have faith that God will fill you (Galatians 3:2). Be faithful in these things, and God will make known to you the ways of life and the fullness of joy.

—Dr. Ted Traylor
Olive Baptist Church, Pensacola, FL

WEEK 24, DAY 6

Repentance Leads to Transformation

Acts 2:29–3:10

"Men and brethren, let me speak freely to you of the patriarch David, that he is both dead and buried, and his tomb is with us to this day. 30Therefore, being a prophet, and knowing that God had sworn with an oath to him that of the fruit of his body, according to the flesh, He would raise up the Christ to sit on his throne, 31he, foreseeing this, spoke concerning the resurrection of the Christ, that His soul was not left in Hades, nor did His flesh see corruption. 32This Jesus God has raised up, of which we are all witnesses. 33Therefore being exalted to the right hand of God, and having received from the Father the promise of the Holy Spirit, He poured out this which you now see and hear.

34"For David did not ascend into the heavens, but he says himself:

'The LORD said to my Lord,
"Sit at My right hand,
35 Till I make Your enemies Your footstool." '

36"Therefore let all the house of Israel know assuredly that God has made this Jesus, whom you crucified, both Lord and Christ."

37Now when they heard this, they were cut to the heart, and said to Peter and the rest of the apostles, "Men and brethren, what shall we do?"

38Then Peter said to them, "Repent, and let every one of you be baptized in the name of Jesus Christ for the remission of sins; and you shall receive the gift of the Holy Spirit. 39For the promise is to you and to your children, and to all who are afar off, as many as the Lord our God will call."

A Vital Church Grows

40And with many other words he testified and exhorted them, saying, "Be saved from this perverse generation." 41Then those who gladly received his word were baptized; and that day about three thousand souls were added to them. 42And they continued steadfastly in the apostles' doctrine and fellowship, in the breaking of bread, and in prayers. 43Then fear came upon every soul, and many wonders and signs were done through the apostles. 44Now all who believed were together, and had all things in common, 45and sold their possessions and goods, and divided them among all, as anyone had need.

46So continuing daily with one accord in the temple, and breaking bread from house to house, they ate their food with gladness and simplicity of heart, 47praising God and having favor with all the people. And the Lord added to the church daily those who were being saved.

A Lame Man Healed

3 Now Peter and John went up together to the temple at the hour of prayer, the ninth hour. 2And a certain man lame from his mother's womb was carried, whom they laid daily at the gate of the temple which is called Beautiful, to ask alms from those who entered the temple; 3who, seeing Peter and John about to go into the temple, asked for alms. 4And fixing his eyes on him, with John, Peter said, "Look at us." 5So he gave them his attention, expecting to receive something from them. 6Then Peter said, "Silver and gold I do not have, but what I do have I give you: In the name of Jesus Christ of Nazareth, rise up and walk." 7And he took him by the right hand and lifted him up, and immediately his feet and ankle bones received strength. 8So he, leaping up, stood and walked and entered the temple with them—walking, leaping, and praising God. 9And all the people saw him walking and praising God. 10Then they knew that it was he who sat begging alms at the Beautiful Gate of the temple; and they were filled with wonder and amazement at what had happened to him.

DEVOTIONAL

There is a key element to Christianity found in Acts 2:38, and many in the church today have lost sight of it. It's the word repent, *and we need to reclaim it. When people turn from sin and pursue God, a wonderful transformation occurs. A perverse generation can be changed and made holy.*

When repentance occurs, it is followed by fruit. It strengthens fellowship and brings unity to the body of Christ. When we are repentant, our hearts are full of humility, joy, and sincerity. Generosity abounds and praise rises to the Lord. The lost are drawn to Jesus, and we have exciting opportunities for evangelism.

Search your heart. Is there any rebellion against God there? Don't let a lack of repentance build barriers in your relationship with Him and keep you from His blessings.

—Dr. Ted Traylor
Olive Baptist Church, Pensacola, FL

WEEK 24, DAY 7

What actions are you taking to be a witness to your neighbors, your region, or a people group?

_____
_____
_____
_____
_____
_____
_____
_____
_____
_____
_____

What stands between you and a Spirit-filled life?

_____
_____
_____
_____
_____
_____
_____
_____
_____
_____

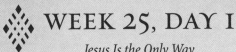

WEEK 25, DAY I

Jesus Is the Only Way to Salvation

Acts 3:11—4:12

Preaching in Solomon's Portico

Now as the lame man who was healed held on to Peter and John, all the people ran together to them in the porch which is called Solomon's, greatly amazed. 12So when Peter saw it, he responded to the people: "Men of Israel, why do you marvel at this? Or why look so intently at us, as though by our own power or godliness we had made this man walk? 13The God of Abraham, Isaac, and Jacob, the God of our fathers, glorified His Servant Jesus, whom you delivered up and denied in the presence of Pilate, when he was determined to let Him go. 14But you denied the Holy One and the Just, and asked for a murderer to be granted to you, 15and killed the Prince of life, whom God raised from the dead, of which we are witnesses. 16And His name, through faith in His name, has made this man strong, whom you see and know. Yes, the faith which comes through Him has given him this perfect soundness in the presence of you all.

17"Yet now, brethren, I know that you did it in ignorance, as did also your rulers. 18But those things which God foretold by the mouth of all His prophets, that the Christ would suffer, He has thus fulfilled. 19Repent therefore and be converted, that your sins may be blotted out, so that times of refreshing may come from the presence of the Lord, 20and that He may send Jesus Christ, who was preached to you before, 21whom heaven must receive until the times of restoration of all things, which God has spoken by the mouth of all His holy prophets since the world began. 22For Moses truly said to the fathers, 'The LORD your God will raise up for you a Prophet like me from your brethren. Him you shall hear in all things, whatever He says to you. 23And it shall be that every soul who will not hear that Prophet shall be utterly destroyed from among the people.' 24Yes, and all the prophets, from Samuel and those who follow, as many as have spoken, have also foretold these days. 25You are sons of the prophets, and of the covenant which God made with our fathers, saying to Abraham, 'And in your seed all the families of the earth shall be blessed.' 26To you first, God, having raised up His Servant Jesus, sent Him to bless you, in turning away every one of you from your iniquities."

Peter and John Arrested

4 Now as they spoke to the people, the priests, the captain of the temple, and the Sadducees came upon them, 2being greatly disturbed that they taught the people and preached in Jesus the resurrection from the dead. 3And they laid hands on them, and put them in custody until the next day, for it was already evening. 4However, many of those who heard the word believed; and the number of the men came to be about five thousand.

Addressing the Sanhedrin

5And it came to pass, on the next day, that their rulers, elders, and scribes, 6as well as Annas the high priest, Caiaphas, John, and Alexander, and as many as were of the family of the high priest, were gathered together at Jerusalem. 7And when they had set them in the midst, they asked, "By what power or by what name have you done this?"

8Then Peter, filled with the Holy Spirit, said to them, "Rulers of the people and elders of Israel: 9If we this day are judged for a good deed done to a helpless man, by what means he has been made well, 10let it be known to you all, and to all the people of Israel, that by the name of Jesus Christ of Nazareth, whom you crucified, whom God raised from the dead, by Him this man stands here before you whole. 11This is the 'stone which was rejected by you builders, which has become the chief cornerstone.' 12Nor is there salvation in any other, for there is no other name under heaven given among men by which we must be saved."

DEVOTIONAL

Peter was the first to preach in Jesus' name on the day of Pentecost, and He preached twice. While the Holy Spirit set the stage for the fireworks in the first sermon, Peter and John's healing of a crippled man drew the crowd for his second message. Both times Peter spoke, his subject was the same: people can be saved by grace through faith alone. Jesus is the only way to heaven.

Jesus' very name means "the Lord is salvation." An angel of the Lord told Joseph to name Him Jesus, "for He will save His people from their sins" (Matthew 1:21).

Because there is salvation in no one else, we must preach Jesus as dying men to dying people. Spread Peter's message that Jesus Christ is the only hope for the world.

—Tim Anderson
Clements Baptist Church, Athens, AL

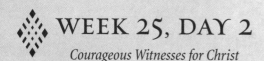

WEEK 25, DAY 2

Courageous Witnesses for Christ

Acts 4:13–37

The Name of Jesus Forbidden

Now when they saw the boldness of Peter and John, and perceived that they were uneducated and untrained men, they marveled. And they realized that they had been with Jesus. 14And seeing the man who had been healed standing with them, they could say nothing against it. 15But when they had commanded them to go aside out of the council, they conferred among themselves, 16saying, "What shall we do to these men? For, indeed, that a notable miracle has been done through them is evident to all who dwell in Jerusalem, and we cannot deny it. 17But so that it spreads no further among the people, let us severely threaten them, that from now on they speak to no man in this name."

18So they called them and commanded them not to speak at all nor teach in the name of Jesus. 19But Peter and John answered and said to them, "Whether it is right in the sight of God to listen to you more than to God, you judge. 20For we cannot but speak the things which we have seen and heard." 21So when they had further threatened them, they let them go, finding no way of punishing them, because of the people, since they all glorified God for what had been done. 22For the man was over forty years old on whom this miracle of healing had been performed.

Prayer for Boldness

23And being let go, they went to their own companions and reported all that the chief priests and elders had said to them. 24So when they heard that, they raised their voice to God with one accord and said: "Lord, You are God, who made heaven and earth and the sea, and all that is in them, 25who by the mouth of Your servant David have said:

'Why did the nations rage,
And the people plot vain things?
26 The kings of the earth took their stand,
And the rulers were gathered together
Against the LORD and against His Christ.'

27"For truly against Your holy Servant Jesus, whom You anointed, both Herod and Pontius Pilate, with the Gentiles and the people of Israel, were gathered together 28to do whatever Your hand and Your purpose determined before to be done. 29Now, Lord, look on their threats, and grant to Your servants that with all boldness they may speak Your word, 30by stretching out Your hand to heal, and that signs and wonders may be done through the name of Your holy Servant Jesus."

31And when they had prayed, the place where they were assembled together was shaken; and they were all filled with the Holy Spirit, and they spoke the word of God with boldness.

Sharing in All Things

32Now the multitude of those who believed were of one heart and one soul; neither did anyone say that any of the things he possessed was his own, but they had all things in common. 33And with great power the apostles gave witness to the resurrection of the Lord Jesus. And great grace was upon them all. 34Nor was there anyone among them who lacked; for all who were possessors of lands or houses sold them, and brought the proceeds of the things that were sold, 35and laid them at the apostles' feet; and they distributed to each as anyone had need.

36And Joses, who was also named Barnabas by the apostles (which is translated Son of Encouragement), a Levite of the country of Cyprus, 37having land, sold it, and brought the money and laid it at the apostles' feet.

DEVOTIONAL

The great need of the hour is courage to preach the truth at all costs. When Peter and John refused to compromise their message, what was the result of their witness? Men and women glorified God! Today is not the day to keep quiet about the good news of Jesus Christ.

The uniqueness of Jesus is the cause of all Christian martyrdom. It is senseless to die for one faith if another faith will lead you to God. Developing courage to speak of Jesus' uniqueness does not require more education, but a genuine experience with Jesus that leads us to say, "I cannot help but speak what I have seen and heard." Mere education never made a timid man bold. Courage only comes from spending time with the living God.

May we never fear those who can kill the body, but solely fear the One who can destroy both body and soul in hell (Matthew 10:28). May God grant us this courage.

—Tim Anderson
Clements Baptist Church, Athens, AL

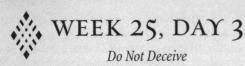

WEEK 25, DAY 3

Do Not Deceive

Acts 5:1–21

Lying to the Holy Spirit

5But a certain man named Ananias, with Sapphira his wife, sold a possession. 2And he kept back part of the proceeds, his wife also being aware of it, and brought a certain part and laid it at the apostles' feet. 3But Peter said, "Ananias, why has Satan filled your heart to lie to the Holy Spirit and keep back part of the price of the land for yourself? 4While it remained, was it not your own? And after it was sold, was it not in your own control? Why have you conceived this thing in your heart? You have not lied to men but to God."

5Then Ananias, hearing these words, fell down and breathed his last. So great fear came upon all those who heard these things. 6And the young men arose and wrapped him up, carried him out, and buried him.

7Now it was about three hours later when his wife came in, not knowing what had happened. 8And Peter answered her, "Tell me whether you sold the land for so much?"

She said, "Yes, for so much."

9Then Peter said to her, "How is it that you have agreed together to test the Spirit of the Lord? Look, the feet of those who have buried your husband are at the door, and they will carry you out." 10Then immediately she fell down at his feet and breathed her last. And the young men came in and found her dead, and carrying her out, buried her by her husband. 11So great fear came upon all the church and upon all who heard these things.

Continuing Power in the Church

12And through the hands of the apostles many signs and wonders were done among the people. And they were all with one accord in Solomon's Porch. 13Yet none of the rest dared join them, but the people esteemed them highly. 14And believers were increasingly added to the Lord, multitudes of both men and women, 15so that they brought the sick out into the streets and laid them on beds and couches, that at least the shadow of Peter passing by might fall on some of them. 16Also a multitude gathered from the surrounding cities to Jerusalem, bringing sick people and those who were tormented by unclean spirits, and they were all healed.

Imprisoned Apostles Freed

17Then the high priest rose up, and all those who were with him (which is the sect of the Sadducees), and they were filled with indignation, 18and laid their hands on the apostles and put them in the common prison. 19But at night an angel of the Lord opened the prison doors and brought them out, and said, 20"Go, stand in the temple and speak to the people all the words of this life."

21And when they heard that, they entered the temple early in the morning and taught. But the high priest and those with him came and called the council together, with all the elders of the children of Israel, and sent to the prison to have them brought.

DEVOTIONAL

*A*nanias and Sapphira lacked what we all should strive to have: personal integrity and a desire for God to remove selfishness from our lives. Sadly, they instead set out to deliberately deceive Peter and the other apostles. They pretended to have a great love for God and then lied about their generous financial gift to the church. What did it cost them? Their lives!

We may not necessarily lie about our giving, but we do lie about other things. We often pretend to be devoted to God just to impress our family and friends. Ananias committed this sin unto death.

The truth is that the spirit of Ananias and Sapphira is still alive in the church today. If Christians today were judged by the motives of the heart as Ananias and Sapphira were, the average church would probably lose a majority of her members. When we sing, teach, or play instruments, are we truly doing it all to God's glory? We go to church and convince ourselves that grace means tolerance and that trying to deceive God and others isn't a big deal.

When God taught the church a great lesson that day, fear gripped the church. What we need today is another awakening of the fear of God. Ananias and Sapphira wanted acceptance so much that they became pretenders. When they did, they allowed Satan, and not the Holy Spirit, to fill their hearts. The Holy Spirit never promotes deception. In fact, He promotes love and truth. In the name of Jesus, let's covet truth.

—Tim Anderson
Clements Baptist Church, Athens, AL

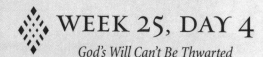

WEEK 25, DAY 4

God's Will Can't Be Thwarted

Acts 5:22–6:7

Apostles on Trial Again

But when the officers came and did not find them in the prison, they returned and reported, 23saying, "Indeed we found the prison shut securely, and the guards standing outside before the doors; but when we opened them, we found no one inside!" 24Now when the high priest, the captain of the temple, and the chief priests heard these things, they wondered what the outcome would be. 25So one came and told them, saying, "Look, the men whom you put in prison are standing in the temple and teaching the people!"

26Then the captain went with the officers and brought them without violence, for they feared the people, lest they should be stoned. 27And when they had brought them, they set them before the council. And the high priest asked them, 28saying, "Did we not strictly command you not to teach in this name? And look, you have filled Jerusalem with your doctrine, and intend to bring this Man's blood on us!"

29But Peter and the other apostles answered and said: "We ought to obey God rather than men. 30The God of our fathers raised up Jesus whom you murdered by hanging on a tree. 31Him God has exalted to His right hand to be Prince and Savior, to give repentance to Israel and forgiveness of sins. 32And we are His witnesses to these things, and so also is the Holy Spirit whom God has given to those who obey Him."

Gamaliel's Advice

33When they heard this, they were furious and plotted to kill them. 34Then one in the council stood up, a Pharisee named Gamaliel, a teacher of the law held in respect by all the people, and commanded them to put the apostles outside for a little while. 35And he said to them: "Men of Israel, take heed to yourselves what you intend to do regarding these men. 36For some time ago Theudas rose up, claiming to be somebody. A number of men, about four hundred, joined him. He was slain, and all who obeyed him were scattered and came to nothing. 37After this man, Judas of Galilee rose up in the days of the census, and drew away many people after him. He also perished, and all who obeyed him were dispersed. 38And now I say

to you, keep away from these men and let them alone; for if this plan or this work is of men, it will come to nothing; 39but if it is of God, you cannot overthrow it—lest you even be found to fight against God."

40And they agreed with him, and when they had called for the apostles and beaten them, they commanded that they should not speak in the name of Jesus, and let them go. 41So they departed from the presence of the council, rejoicing that they were counted worthy to suffer shame for His name. 42And daily in the temple, and in every house, they did not cease teaching and preaching Jesus as the Christ.

Seven Chosen to Serve

6Now in those days, when the number of the disciples was multiplying, there arose a complaint against the Hebrews by the Hellenists, because their widows were neglected in the daily distribution. 2Then the twelve summoned the multitude of the disciples and said, "It is not desirable that we should leave the word of God and serve tables. 3Therefore, brethren, seek out from among you seven men of good reputation, full of the Holy Spirit and wisdom, whom we may appoint over this business; 4but we will give ourselves continually to prayer and to the ministry of the word."

5And the saying pleased the whole multitude. And they chose Stephen, a man full of faith and the Holy Spirit, and Philip, Prochorus, Nicanor, Timon, Parmenas, and Nicolas, a proselyte from Antioch, 6whom they set before the apostles; and when they had prayed, they laid hands on them.

7Then the word of God spread, and the number of the disciples multiplied greatly in Jerusalem, and a great many of the priests were obedient to the faith.

DEVOTIONAL

Cults, false religions, and false prophets abound today. Often they grow faster than the true church does. However, the idea that whatever succeeds in life is always the will of God is simply false. Similarly, Gamaliel believed things that are not of God must fail. The problem with this thinking is that it doesn't consider the sinful depravity of humanity and the presence of satanic opposition in the world. Mark Twain once said, "A lie can travel halfway around the world while the truth is putting on its shoes."[7] No doubt truth will win out, but in the meantime, Satan seeks people to devour like a roaring lion (1 Peter 5:8). Fight his falsehoods by spreading God's truth!

—Tim Anderson
Clements Baptist Church, Athens, AL

WEEK 25, DAY 5

*Tell the Nations
What God Has Done*

Acts 6:8–7:16

Stephen Accused of Blasphemy

And Stephen, full of faith and power, did great wonders and signs among the people. ⁹Then there arose some from what is called the Synagogue of the Freedmen (Cyrenians, Alexandrians, and those from Cilicia and Asia), disputing with Stephen. ¹⁰And they were not able to resist the wisdom and the Spirit by which he spoke. ¹¹Then they secretly induced men to say, "We have heard him speak blasphemous words against Moses and God." ¹²And they stirred up the people, the elders, and the scribes; and they came upon him, seized him, and brought him to the council. ¹³They also set up false witnesses who said, "This man does not cease to speak blasphemous words against this holy place and the law; ¹⁴for we have heard him say that this Jesus of Nazareth will destroy this place and change the customs which Moses delivered to us." ¹⁵And all who sat in the council, looking steadfastly at him, saw his face as the face of an angel.

Stephen's Address: The Call of Abraham

Then the high priest said, "Are these things so?"
²And he said, "Brethren and fathers, listen: The God of glory appeared to our father Abraham when he was in Mesopotamia, before he dwelt in Haran, ³and said to him, 'Get out of your country and from your relatives, and come to a land that I will show you.' ⁴Then he came out of the land of the Chaldeans and dwelt in Haran. And from there, when his father was dead, He moved him to this land in which you now dwell. ⁵And God gave him no inheritance in it, not even enough to set his foot on. But even when Abraham had no child, He promised to give it to him for a possession, and to his descendants after him. ⁶But God spoke in this way: that his descendants would dwell in a foreign land, and that they would bring them into bondage and oppress them four hundred years. ⁷'And the nation to whom they will be in bondage I will judge,' said God, 'and after that they shall come out and serve Me in this place.' ⁸Then He gave him the covenant of circumcision; and so Abraham begot Isaac and circumcised him on the eighth day; and Isaac begot Jacob, and Jacob begot the twelve patriarchs.

The Patriarchs in Egypt

⁹"And the patriarchs, becoming envious, sold Joseph into Egypt. But God was with him ¹⁰and delivered him out of all his troubles, and gave him favor and wisdom in the presence of Pharaoh, king of Egypt; and he made him governor over Egypt and all his house. ¹¹Now a famine and great trouble came over all the land of Egypt and Canaan, and our fathers found no sustenance. ¹²But when Jacob heard that there was grain in Egypt, he sent out our fathers first. ¹³And the second time Joseph was made known to his brothers, and Joseph's family became known to the Pharaoh. ¹⁴Then Joseph sent and called his father Jacob and all his relatives to him, seventy-five people. ¹⁵So Jacob went down to Egypt; and he died, he and our fathers. ¹⁶And they were carried back to Shechem and laid in the tomb that Abraham bought for a sum of money from the sons of Hamor, the father of Shechem."

DEVOTIONAL

Telling the nations what God has done is a thousand times more important than American football. Yet you'll hear people talk about football more than they talk about the gospel. Of course, who doesn't love football? It's a great sport! But the truth is, the gospel should be our life.

After a fast and furious start and tremendous growth, the early church began experiencing growing pains. The widows were being neglected, there were new members who needed discipling, and the leaders simply had difficulty reaching out to everyone (Acts 6:1). They handled the problem in a godly manner, setting an example for us to follow: they concentrated on the Word of God. Ministers today should also choose the "plan and neglect" method of ministry—plan to neglect everything until the gospel is complete!

Every church has its share of problems, including either growing problems or dying problems. Problems of all kinds give us the opportunity to examine our ministry and our lives so we can make necessary adjustments. Success can spoil us into thinking we need not make any changes, but anything that does not get evaluated gets stale. Let's follow the early church and "give ourselves continually to prayer and to the ministry of the word" (Acts 6:4). Let's make spreading the gospel our priority.

—Tim Anderson
Clements Baptist Church, Athens, AL

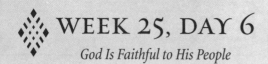

WEEK 25, DAY 6

God Is Faithful to His People

Acts 7:17–41

God Delivers Israel by Moses

"But when the time of the promise drew near which God had sworn to Abraham, the people grew and multiplied in Egypt 18till another king arose who did not know Joseph. 19This man dealt treacherously with our people, and oppressed our forefathers, making them expose their babies, so that they might not live. 20At this time Moses was born, and was well pleasing to God; and he was brought up in his father's house for three months. 21But when he was set out, Pharaoh's daughter took him away and brought him up as her own son. 22And Moses was learned in all the wisdom of the Egyptians, and was mighty in words and deeds.

23"Now when he was forty years old, it came into his heart to visit his brethren, the children of Israel. 24And seeing one of them suffer wrong, he defended and avenged him who was oppressed, and struck down the Egyptian. 25For he supposed that his brethren would have understood that God would deliver them by his hand, but they did not understand. 26And the next day he appeared to two of them as they were fighting, and tried to reconcile them, saying, 'Men, you are brethren; why do you wrong one another?' 27But he who did his neighbor wrong pushed him away, saying, 'Who made you a ruler and a judge over us? 28Do you want to kill me as you did the Egyptian yesterday?' 29Then, at this saying, Moses fled and became a dweller in the land of Midian, where he had two sons.

30"And when forty years had passed, an Angel of the Lord appeared to him in a flame of fire in a bush, in the wilderness of Mount Sinai. 31When Moses saw it, he marveled at the sight; and as he drew near to observe, the voice of the Lord came to him, 32saying, 'I am the God of your fathers—the God of Abraham, the God of Isaac, and the God of Jacob.' And Moses trembled and dared not look. 33Then the LORD said to him, "Take your sandals off your feet, for the place where you stand is holy ground. 34I have surely seen the oppression of My people who are in Egypt; I have heard their groaning and have come down to deliver them. And now come, I will send you to Egypt."'

35"This Moses whom they rejected, saying, 'Who made you a ruler and a judge?' is the one God sent to be a ruler and a deliverer by the hand of the Angel who appeared to him in the bush. 36He brought them out, after he had shown wonders and signs in the land of Egypt, and in the Red Sea, and in the wilderness forty years.

Israel Rebels Against God

37"This is that Moses who said to the children of Israel, 'The LORD your God will raise up for you a Prophet like me from your brethren. Him you shall hear.' 38This is he who was in the congregation in the wilderness with the Angel who spoke to him on Mount Sinai, and with our fathers, the one who received the living oracles to give to us, 39whom our fathers would not obey, but rejected. And in their hearts they turned back to Egypt, 40saying to Aaron, 'Make us gods to go before us; as for this Moses who brought us out of the land of Egypt, we do not know what has become of him.' 41And they made a calf in those days, offered sacrifices to the idol, and rejoiced in the works of their own hands."

DEVOTIONAL

Stephen was a very spiritual man. He was full of the Holy Spirit and full of grace, faith, and power. His critics "were not able to resist the wisdom and the Spirit by which he spoke" (Acts 6:10). Yet after his testimony there came a brutal attack. He was accused of speaking blasphemous words against Moses and God.

When Stephen gave his defense, he told a short version of Israel's history. He referred to the people of Israel as a stiff-necked people who always resisted the Holy Spirit (Acts 7:51). Throughout Israel's history, God worked on Israel's behalf again and again with repeated acts of mercy and long-suffering. But the Israelites repeatedly hardened their hearts toward God.

Stephen's message ministers to us in at least two ways: it serves as both an encouragement and a warning. Contrary to today's popular opinion, God is not eager to punish. He is eager to forgive our sins, and He shows faithfulness to thousands! He warns us, however, that one day His patience will come to an end, and we will be handed over to face the consequences of our sin.

Give God praise for His faithfulness. Soften your heart toward Him in humble repentance and obedience, and encourage others to do the same.

—Tim Anderson
Clements Baptist Church, Athens, AL

WEEK 25, DAY 7

It is a human tendency to avoid responsibility. It seems that nothing is anybody's fault anymore. The only sin that can be forgiven, however, is the sin we own. Owning our sin and our choices is a very humbling experience, but it is the only way back to God. What sins do you need to acknowledge in order to receive God's forgiveness and full pardon?

_____

_____

_____

_____

_____

_____

_____

_____

_____

_____

_____

The Bible often warns about judging others. It is easy to quickly point fingers at friends, while allowing the plank to remain in our own eye. It takes divine wisdom to maintain balance between biblical discernment and critical judgment. Nothing good comes from blame. Whom do you need to stop judging and extend grace to today?

_____

_____

_____

_____

_____

_____

_____

_____

_____

WEEK 26, DAY 1

Seeing and Sharing the Truth of Jesus

Acts 7:42–8:3

"Then God turned and gave them up to worship the host of heaven, as it is written in the book of the Prophets:

'Did you offer Me slaughtered animals and
    sacrifices during forty years in the wilderness,
O house of Israel?
43 You also took up the tabernacle of Moloch,
    And the star of your god Remphan,
    Images which you made to worship;
    And I will carry you away beyond Babylon.'

God's True Tabernacle

44"Our fathers had the tabernacle of witness in the wilderness, as He appointed, instructing Moses to make it according to the pattern that he had seen, 45which our fathers, having received it in turn, also brought with Joshua into the land possessed by the Gentiles, whom God drove out before the face of our fathers until the days of David, 46who found favor before God and asked to find a dwelling for the God of Jacob. 47But Solomon built Him a house.

48"However, the Most High does not dwell in temples made with hands, as the prophet says:

49 'Heaven is My throne,
    And earth is My footstool.
    What house will you build for Me? says the LORD,
    Or what is the place of My rest?
50   Has My hand not made all these things?'

Israel Resists the Holy Spirit

51"You stiff-necked and uncircumcised in heart and ears! You always resist the Holy Spirit; as your fathers did, so do you. 52Which of the prophets did your fathers not persecute? And they killed those who foretold the coming of the Just One, of whom you now have become the betrayers and murderers, 53who have received the law by the direction of angels and have not kept it."

Stephen the Martyr

54When they heard these things they were cut to the heart, and they gnashed at him with their teeth. 55But he, being full of the Holy Spirit, gazed into heaven and saw the glory of God, and Jesus standing at the right hand of God, 56and said, "Look! I see the heavens opened and the Son of Man standing at the right hand of God!"

57Then they cried out with a loud voice, stopped their ears, and ran at him with one accord; 58and they cast him out of the city and stoned him. And the witnesses laid down their clothes at the feet of a young man named Saul. 59And they stoned Stephen as he was calling on God and saying, "Lord Jesus, receive my spirit." 60Then he knelt down and cried out with a loud voice, "Lord, do not charge them with this sin." And when he had said this, he fell asleep.

Saul Persecutes the Church

8 Now Saul was consenting to his death. At that time a great persecution arose against the church which was at Jerusalem; and they were all scattered throughout the regions of Judea and Samaria, except the apostles. 2And devout men carried Stephen to his burial, and made great lamentation over him.

3As for Saul, he made havoc of the church, entering every house, and dragging off men and women, committing them to prison.

DEVOTIONAL

Why is it that two people can look at the same sight and see different things? Why is it one sees something while the other doesn't? Stephen saw the truth about Jesus. He knew Jesus was the Christ, sent from God to save us from our sins, the fulfillment to all prophecy and the hope of all humanity. And so he told others the truth about Jesus. But sadly, they did not see. The very truth that liberates one angers another. The truth that frees is also the truth that convicts. Having been exposed by the light of the gospel in Stephen's message, the religious establishment lashed out. They picked up stones and silenced Stephen, but they did not silence his message.

A religious leader named Saul, who zealously persecuted the church, consented to Stephen's death. He had not yet seen what Stephen had seen, but that would change in time. A blinding light would knock him off his horse, and his eyes would be opened. You never know who will put their faith in Jesus! The believer's job is to share the truth. Some will respond in faith and some will not, but the truth is the truth just the sanee. Share it.

—Dr. Willy Rice
Calvary Baptist Church, Clearwater, FL

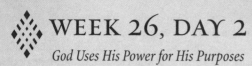

WEEK 26, DAY 2

God Uses His Power for His Purposes

Acts 8:4–25

Christ Is Preached in Samaria

Therefore those who were scattered went everywhere preaching the word. 5Then Philip went down to the city of Samaria and preached Christ to them. 6And the multitudes with one accord heeded the things spoken by Philip, hearing and seeing the miracles which he did. 7For unclean spirits, crying with a loud voice, came out of many who were possessed; and many who were paralyzed and lame were healed. 8And there was great joy in that city.

The Sorcerer's Profession of Faith

9But there was a certain man called Simon, who previously practiced sorcery in the city and astonished the people of Samaria, claiming that he was someone great, 10to whom they all gave heed, from the least to the greatest, saying, "This man is the great power of God." 11And they heeded him because he had astonished them with his sorceries for a long time. 12But when they believed Philip as he preached the things concerning the kingdom of God and the name of Jesus Christ, both men and women were baptized. 13Then Simon himself also believed; and when he was baptized he continued with Philip, and was amazed, seeing the miracles and signs which were done.

The Sorcerer's Sin

14Now when the apostles who were at Jerusalem heard that Samaria had received the word of God, they sent Peter and John to them, 15who, when they had come down, prayed for them that they might receive the Holy Spirit. 16For as yet He had fallen upon none of them. They had only been baptized in the name of the Lord Jesus. 17Then they laid hands on them, and they received the Holy Spirit.

18And when Simon saw that through the laying on of the apostles' hands the Holy Spirit was given, he offered them money, 19saying, "Give me this power also, that anyone on whom I lay hands may receive the Holy Spirit."

20But Peter said to him, "Your money perish with you, because you thought that the gift of God could be purchased with money! 21You have neither part nor portion in this matter, for your heart is not right in the sight of God. 22Repent therefore of this your wickedness, and pray God if perhaps the thought of your heart may be forgiven you. 23For I see that you are poisoned by bitterness and bound by iniquity."

24Then Simon answered and said, "Pray to the Lord for me, that none of the things which you have spoken may come upon me."

25So when they had testified and preached the word of the Lord, they returned to Jerusalem, preaching the gospel in many villages of the Samaritans.

DEVOTIONAL

The power of the apostles was unmistakable and undeniable. God's own Spirit had empowered these preachers of the gospel, and their words and deeds carried power. God worked through them to accomplish many mighty miracles and to bring the gospel message to those who had never heard.

Simon saw their power, and he wanted it. He was a mystic who practiced some type of witchcraft, and he seemed to know the real thing when he saw it. Simon believed and was baptized, but he still didn't fully understand. He was seeking God, but his heart was not right before Him. Simon wanted the power for the sake of the power, perhaps only for what it could do for him. Bible students can argue the authenticity of his conversion, but no one can doubt the depth of his confusion. He wanted to "buy" this spiritual power—as if the Holy Spirit was a trick to be learned (like most of his sorcery) or a skill to be nurtured. Peter called him out on it. God's Spirit cannot be bought or earned—it is His gift to us that comes by grace through faith in Christ alone.

You can't buy your way into heaven, and you can't buy God's power on the open market. There will always be those who confuse the gospel with worldly power. There will always be those who have suspect motives or warped views of God. There will always be those who are motivated by pride and jealousy. We must practice discernment. We should be wary of any ministry that exalts individuals instead of God. We must also check our own motives. Do we serve God to impress people or to please God? Humble yourself before the Lord, submit to His purposes, and use His power to do His will.

—Dr. Willy Rice
Calvary Baptist Church, Clearwater, FL

WEEK 26, DAY 3

Reach Out to Those
Who Are Searching

Acts 8:26–9:9

Christ Is Preached to an Ethiopian

Now an angel of the Lord spoke to Philip, saying, "Arise and go toward the south along the road which goes down from Jerusalem to Gaza." This is desert. 27So he arose and went. And behold, a man of Ethiopia, a eunuch of great authority under Candace the queen of the Ethiopians, who had charge of all her treasury, and had come to Jerusalem to worship, 28was returning. And sitting in his chariot, he was reading Isaiah the prophet. 29Then the Spirit said to Philip, "Go near and overtake this chariot."

30So Philip ran to him, and heard him reading the prophet Isaiah, and said, "Do you understand what you are reading?"

31And he said, "How can I, unless someone guides me?" And he asked Philip to come up and sit with him. 32The place in the Scripture which he read was this:

"He was led as a sheep to the slaughter;
And as a lamb before its shearer is silent,
So He opened not His mouth.
33　In His humiliation His justice was taken away,
And who will declare His generation?
For His life is taken from the earth."

34So the eunuch answered Philip and said, "I ask you, of whom does the prophet say this, of himself or of some other man?" 35Then Philip opened his mouth, and beginning at this Scripture, preached Jesus to him. 36Now as they went down the road, they came to some water. And the eunuch said, "See, here is water. What hinders me from being baptized?"

37Then Philip said, "If you believe with all your heart, you may."

And he answered and said, "I believe that Jesus Christ is the Son of God."

38So he commanded the chariot to stand still. And both Philip and the eunuch went down into the water, and he baptized him. 39Now when they came up out of the water, the Spirit of the Lord caught Philip away, so that the eunuch saw him no more; and he went on his way rejoicing. 40But Philip was found at Azotus. And passing through, he preached in all the cities till he came to Caesarea.

The Damascus Road: Saul Converted

9Then Saul, still breathing threats and murder against the disciples of the Lord, went to the high priest 2and asked letters from him to the synagogues of Damascus, so that if he found any who were of the Way, whether men or women, he might bring them bound to Jerusalem.

3As he journeyed he came near Damascus, and suddenly a light shone around him from heaven. 4Then he fell to the ground, and heard a voice saying to him, "Saul, Saul, why are you persecuting Me?"

5And he said, "Who are You, Lord?"

Then the Lord said, "I am Jesus, whom you are persecuting. It is hard for you to kick against the goads."

6So he, trembling and astonished, said, "Lord, what do You want me to do?"

Then the Lord said to him, "Arise and go into the city, and you will be told what you must do."

7And the men who journeyed with him stood speechless, hearing a voice but seeing no one. 8Then Saul arose from the ground, and when his eyes were opened he saw no one. But they led him by the hand and brought him into Damascus. 9And he was three days without sight, and neither ate nor drank.

DEVOTIONAL

It is a long way from Ethiopia to Jerusalem, but the African official in Acts 8 had made the trek. It was not a political meeting but a spiritual search that had launched him on this journey. He had come looking for answers—for God. As he was heading home, he was still searching. Apparently the religious traditions and temple grandeur had not been enough to satisfy his soul. In God's providential timing, Philip came onto the scene while this man was reading Isaiah. Philip was there as God's messenger to point the way to Jesus. He was faithful to go out of his way to get near this searcher and speak truth to him.

Who do you know that may be searching? You never know what may be going on in someone's life when you feel the prompting of God's Spirit to go to that person and share the truth about Jesus. Philip was busy, but he wasn't too busy to follow God's prompting and share the greatest message in the world. Don't be too busy to help someone find his or her way to God. There is someone waiting for you.

—Dr. Willy Rice
Calvary Baptist Church, Clearwater, FL

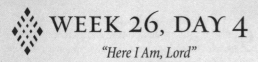

WEEK 26, DAY 4

"Here I Am, Lord"

Acts 9:10–35

Ananias Baptizes Saul

Now there was a certain disciple at Damascus named Ananias; and to him the Lord said in a vision, "Ananias." And he said, "Here I am, Lord."

11So the Lord said to him, "Arise and go to the street called Straight, and inquire at the house of Judas for one called Saul of Tarsus, for behold, he is praying. 12And in a vision he has seen a man named Ananias coming in and putting his hand on him, so that he might receive his sight."

13Then Ananias answered, "Lord, I have heard from many about this man, how much harm he has done to Your saints in Jerusalem. 14And here he has authority from the chief priests to bind all who call on Your name."

15But the Lord said to him, "Go, for he is a chosen vessel of Mine to bear My name before Gentiles, kings, and the children of Israel. 16For I will show him how many things he must suffer for My name's sake."

17And Ananias went his way and entered the house; and laying his hands on him he said, "Brother Saul, the Lord Jesus, who appeared to you on the road as you came, has sent me that you may receive your sight and be filled with the Holy Spirit." 18Immediately there fell from his eyes something like scales, and he received his sight at once; and he arose and was baptized.

19So when he had received food, he was strengthened. Then Saul spent some days with the disciples at Damascus.

Saul Preaches Christ

20Immediately he preached the Christ in the synagogues, that He is the Son of God.

21Then all who heard were amazed, and said, "Is this not he who destroyed those who called on this name in Jerusalem, and has come here for that purpose, so that he might bring them bound to the chief priests?"

22But Saul increased all the more in strength, and confounded the Jews who dwelt in Damascus, proving that this Jesus is the Christ.

Saul Escapes Death

23Now after many days were past, the Jews plotted to kill him. 24But their plot became known to Saul. And they watched the gates day and night, to kill him. 25Then the disciples took him by night and let him down through the wall in a large basket.

Saul at Jerusalem

26And when Saul had come to Jerusalem, he tried to join the disciples; but they were all afraid of him, and did not believe that he was a disciple. 27But Barnabas took him and brought him to the apostles. And he declared to them how he had seen the Lord on the road, and that He had spoken to him, and how he had preached boldly at Damascus in the name of Jesus. 28So he was with them at Jerusalem, coming in and going out. 29And he spoke boldly in the name of the Lord Jesus and disputed against the Hellenists, but they attempted to kill him. 30When the brethren found out, they brought him down to Caesarea and sent him out to Tarsus.

The Church Prospers

31Then the churches throughout all Judea, Galilee, and Samaria had peace and were edified. And walking in the fear of the Lord and in the comfort of the Holy Spirit, they were multiplied.

Aeneas Healed

32Now it came to pass, as Peter went through all parts of the country, that he also came down to the saints who dwelt in Lydda. 33There he found a certain man named Aeneas, who had been bedridden eight years and was paralyzed. 34And Peter said to him, "Aeneas, Jesus the Christ heals you. Arise and make your bed." Then he arose immediately. 35So all who dwelt at Lydda and Sharon saw him and turned to the Lord.

DEVOTIONAL

Ananias is a name many forget, but few forget the name of Paul. He was the great apostle, the prolific evangelist, the gifted author, the mighty preacher. And yet you might have never heard of Paul if a man named Ananias hadn't answered God's call with four simple words: "Here I am, Lord" (Acts 9:10). He was a servant ready to obey his Lord. He listened and responded, Paul believed, and the world was changed.

What is God calling you to do? What miracle is waiting on the other side of your obedience? Four words can change your life: "Here I am, Lord." Just say them. Then follow through.

—Dr. Willy Rice
Calvary Baptist Church, Clearwater, FL

WEEK 26, DAY 5

God Hears and Answers Prayers

Acts 9:36–10:23a

Dorcas Restored to Life

At Joppa there was a certain disciple named Tabitha, which is translated Dorcas. This woman was full of good works and charitable deeds which she did. 37But it happened in those days that she became sick and died. When they had washed her, they laid her in an upper room. 38And since Lydda was near Joppa, and the disciples had heard that Peter was there, they sent two men to him, imploring him not to delay in coming to them. 39Then Peter arose and went with them. When he had come, they brought him to the upper room. And all the widows stood by him weeping, showing the tunics and garments which Dorcas had made while she was with them. 40But Peter put them all out, and knelt down and prayed. And turning to the body he said, "Tabitha, arise." And she opened her eyes, and when she saw Peter she sat up. 41Then he gave her his hand and lifted her up; and when he had called the saints and widows, he presented her alive. 42And it became known throughout all Joppa, and many believed on the Lord. 43So it was that he stayed many days in Joppa with Simon, a tanner.

Cornelius Sends a Delegation

10 There was a certain man in Caesarea called Cornelius, a centurion of what was called the Italian Regiment, 2a devout man and one who feared God with all his household, who gave alms generously to the people, and prayed to God always. 3About the ninth hour of the day he saw clearly in a vision an angel of God coming in and saying to him, "Cornelius!"

4And when he observed him, he was afraid, and said, "What is it, lord?"

So he said to him, "Your prayers and your alms have come up for a memorial before God. 5Now send men to Joppa, and send for Simon whose surname is Peter. 6He is lodging with Simon, a tanner, whose house is by the sea. He will tell you what you must do." 7And when the angel who spoke to him had departed, Cornelius called two of his household servants and a devout soldier from among those who waited on him continually. 8So when he had explained all these things to them, he sent them to Joppa.

Peter's Vision

9The next day, as they went on their journey and drew near the city, Peter went up on the housetop to pray, about the sixth hour. 10Then he became very hungry and wanted to eat; but while they made ready, he fell into a trance 11and saw heaven opened and an object like a great sheet bound at the four corners, descending to him and let down to the earth. 12In it were all kinds of four-footed animals of the earth, wild beasts, creeping things, and birds of the air. 13And a voice came to him, "Rise, Peter; kill and eat."

14But Peter said, "Not so, Lord! For I have never eaten anything common or unclean."

15And a voice spoke to him again the second time, "What God has cleansed you must not call common." 16This was done three times. And the object was taken up into heaven again.

Summoned to Caesarea

17Now while Peter wondered within himself what this vision which he had seen meant, behold, the men who had been sent from Cornelius had made inquiry for Simon's house, and stood before the gate. 18And they called and asked whether Simon, whose surname was Peter, was lodging there.

19While Peter thought about the vision, the Spirit said to him, "Behold, three men are seeking you. 20Arise therefore, go down and go with them, doubting nothing; for I have sent them."

21Then Peter went down to the men who had been sent to him from Cornelius, and said, "Yes, I am he whom you seek. For what reason have you come?"

22And they said, "Cornelius the centurion, a just man, one who fears God and has a good reputation among all the nation of the Jews, was divinely instructed by a holy angel to summon you to his house, and to hear words from you." 23Then he invited them in and lodged them.

DEVOTIONAL

When you pray, mighty things happen. When Peter prayed, one of the mightiest miracles in the Bible took place—Tabitha came back to life. Cornelius sought God in prayer, and God heard and provided a messenger to bring the good news. One received physical life; the other received spiritual life. James 4:2 says we do not have because we do not ask. What are you believing God for that seems impossible? Ask Him to do what only He can do.

—Dr. Willy Rice
Calvary Baptist Church, Clearwater, FL

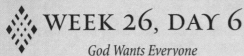

WEEK 26, DAY 6

God Wants Everyone to Hear the Good News

Acts 10:23b–48

On the next day Peter went away with them, and some brethren from Joppa accompanied him.

Peter Meets Cornelius

24And the following day they entered Caesarea. Now Cornelius was waiting for them, and had called together his relatives and close friends. 25As Peter was coming in, Cornelius met him and fell down at his feet and worshiped him. 26But Peter lifted him up, saying, "Stand up; I myself am also a man." 27And as he talked with him, he went in and found many who had come together. 28Then he said to them, "You know how unlawful it is for a Jewish man to keep company with or go to one of another nation. But God has shown me that I should not call any man common or unclean. 29Therefore I came without objection as soon as I was sent for. I ask, then, for what reason have you sent for me?"

30So Cornelius said, "Four days ago I was fasting until this hour; and at the ninth hour I prayed in my house, and behold, a man stood before me in bright clothing, 31and said, 'Cornelius, your prayer has been heard, and your alms are remembered in the sight of God. 32Send therefore to Joppa and call Simon here, whose surname is Peter. He is lodging in the house of Simon, a tanner, by the sea. When he comes, he will speak to you.' 33So I sent to you immediately, and you have done well to come. Now therefore, we are all present before God, to hear all the things commanded you by God."

Preaching to Cornelius' Household

34Then Peter opened his mouth and said: "In truth I perceive that God shows no partiality. 35But in every nation whoever fears Him and works righteousness is accepted by Him. 36The word which God sent to the children of Israel, preaching peace through Jesus Christ—He is Lord of all— 37that word you know, which was proclaimed throughout all Judea, and began from Galilee after the baptism which John preached: 38how God anointed Jesus of Nazareth with the Holy Spirit and with power, who went about doing good and healing all who were oppressed by the devil, for God was with Him. 39And

we are witnesses of all things which He did both in the land of the Jews and in Jerusalem, whom they killed by hanging on a tree. 40Him God raised up on the third day, and showed Him openly, 41not to all the people, but to witnesses chosen before by God, even to us who ate and drank with Him after He arose from the dead. 42And He commanded us to preach to the people, and to testify that it is He who was ordained by God to be Judge of the living and the dead. 43To Him all the prophets witness that, through His name, whoever believes in Him will receive remission of sins."

The Holy Spirit Falls on the Gentiles

44While Peter was still speaking these words, the Holy Spirit fell upon all those who heard the word. 45And those of the circumcision who believed were astonished, as many as came with Peter, because the gift of the Holy Spirit had been poured out on the Gentiles also. 46For they heard them speak with tongues and magnify God.

Then Peter answered, 47"Can anyone forbid water, that these should not be baptized who have received the Holy Spirit just as we have?" 48And he commanded them to be baptized in the name of the Lord. Then they asked him to stay a few days.

DEVOTIONAL

Peter had a vision. A vision can be as simple as a new insight or a truth revealed. Peter saw animals clean and unclean, and he heard the command to kill and eat. It wasn't really a vision about the menu; it was a vision about ministry. God challenged Peter's beliefs about people. God cares about everyone, Jews and Gentiles, and God wants everyone to hear the good news of grace and be saved.

After Peter had the vision, there was a knock at the door. If God shows you a new truth, you had better believe He will also bring a new opportunity! Peter answered the knock, responded to the call, and carried the message to Cornelius's household. They heard and believed, and the church grew exponentially. It happened because one man saw that God cares about everyone. He answered the knock at the door and faithfully carried the message to those who needed to hear it.

Peter's ideas about ministry needed to be corrected, and sometimes ours do too. Who do you sometimes see as unclean, beyond hope, and not your responsibility? God says, "Go." Go and love everyone. Go and share the good news.

—Dr. Willy Rice
Calvary Baptist Church, Clearwater, FL

WEEK 26, DAY 7

Who is waiting on the other side of your obedience? Who in your life needs to hear the good news? List their names, and pray that God will use you to influence them.

_____

_____

_____

_____

_____

_____

_____

_____

_____

_____

We all have blind spots that God needs to correct, just as Peter had a blind spot toward Gentiles that God needed to correct. God sends insights to heal our blindness. What might your blind spots be? How is God calling you to branch out and minister to others in new ways?

_____

_____

_____

_____

_____

_____

_____

_____

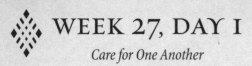

WEEK 27, DAY 1

Care for One Another

Acts 11:1–30

Peter Defends God's Grace

11 Now the apostles and brethren who were in Judea heard that the Gentiles had also received the word of God. ²And when Peter came up to Jerusalem, those of the circumcision contended with him, ³saying, "You went in to uncircumcised men and ate with them!"

⁴But Peter explained it to them in order from the beginning, saying: ⁵"I was in the city of Joppa praying; and in a trance I saw a vision, an object descending like a great sheet, let down from heaven by four corners; and it came to me. ⁶When I observed it intently and considered, I saw four-footed animals of the earth, wild beasts, creeping things, and birds of the air. ⁷And I heard a voice saying to me, 'Rise, Peter; kill and eat.' ⁸But I said, 'Not so, Lord! For nothing common or unclean has at any time entered my mouth.' ⁹But the voice answered me again from heaven, 'What God has cleansed you must not call common.' ¹⁰Now this was done three times, and all were drawn up again into heaven. ¹¹At that very moment, three men stood before the house where I was, having been sent to me from Caesarea. ¹²Then the Spirit told me to go with them, doubting nothing. Moreover these six brethren accompanied me, and we entered the man's house. ¹³And he told us how he had seen an angel standing in his house, who said to him, 'Send men to Joppa, and call for Simon whose surname is Peter, ¹⁴who will tell you words by which you and all your household will be saved.' ¹⁵And as I began to speak, the Holy Spirit fell upon them, as upon us at the beginning. ¹⁶Then I remembered the word of the Lord, how He said, 'John indeed baptized with water, but you shall be baptized with the Holy Spirit.' ¹⁷If therefore God gave them the same gift as He gave us when we believed on the Lord Jesus Christ, who was I that I could withstand God?"

¹⁸When they heard these things they became silent; and they glorified God, saying, "Then God has also granted to the Gentiles repentance to life."

Barnabas and Saul at Antioch

¹⁹Now those who were scattered after the persecution that arose over Stephen traveled as far as Phoenicia, Cyprus, and Antioch, preaching the word to no one but the Jews only. ²⁰But some of them were men from Cyprus and Cyrene, who, when they had come to Antioch, spoke to the Hellenists, preaching the Lord Jesus. ²¹And the hand of the Lord was with them, and a great number believed and turned to the Lord.

²²Then news of these things came to the ears of the church in Jerusalem, and they sent out Barnabas to go as far as Antioch. ²³When he came and had seen the grace of God, he was glad, and encouraged them all that with purpose of heart they should continue with the Lord. ²⁴For he was a good man, full of the Holy Spirit and of faith. And a great many people were added to the Lord.

²⁵Then Barnabas departed for Tarsus to seek Saul. ²⁶And when he had found him, he brought him to Antioch. So it was that for a whole year they assembled with the church and taught a great many people. And the disciples were first called Christians in Antioch.

Relief to Judea

²⁷And in these days prophets came from Jerusalem to Antioch. ²⁸Then one of them, named Agabus, stood up and showed by the Spirit that there was going to be a great famine throughout all the world, which also happened in the days of Claudius Caesar. ²⁹Then the disciples, each according to his ability, determined to send relief to the brethren dwelling in Judea. ³⁰This they also did, and sent it to the elders by the hands of Barnabas and Saul.

DEVOTIONAL

*T*here are two marks of genuine believers revealed in Acts 11. First, we see that God's people are marked by grace (vv. 1–18). Peter defends God's grace and tells the Jews that grace has been extended to the Gentiles. This reminds us that spiritual rescue has been extended to all through Christ's atoning work on the cross. As one pastor said, "It is not race, face, or place that earns favor in God's sight. It is only grace!"

Second, we see that God's people are marked by generosity (Acts 11:27–30). When there was a severe famine in Judea, Gentile believers in Antioch sent aid to the Jewish believers in their time of great need. This is what genuine believers do—they care for others during times of distress.

Is there someone you can extend grace to today? Who would be blessed by your generosity? Look for ways you can take care of people and reflect the nature of the God you worship.

—Dr. Jim Perdue
Second Baptist Church, Warner Robins, GA

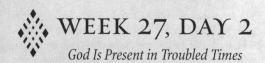

WEEK 27, DAY 2

God Is Present in Troubled Times

Acts 12:1–24

Herod's Violence to the Church

12 Now about that time Herod the king stretched out his hand to harass some from the church. ²Then he killed James the brother of John with the sword. ³And because he saw that it pleased the Jews, he proceeded further to seize Peter also. Now it was during the Days of Unleavened Bread. ⁴So when he had arrested him, he put him in prison, and delivered him to four squads of soldiers to keep him, intending to bring him before the people after Passover.

Peter Freed from Prison

⁵Peter was therefore kept in prison, but constant prayer was offered to God for him by the church. ⁶And when Herod was about to bring him out, that night Peter was sleeping, bound with two chains between two soldiers; and the guards before the door were keeping the prison. ⁷Now behold, an angel of the Lord stood by him, and a light shone in the prison; and he struck Peter on the side and raised him up, saying, "Arise quickly!" And his chains fell off his hands. ⁸Then the angel said to him, "Gird yourself and tie on your sandals"; and so he did. And he said to him, "Put on your garment and follow me." ⁹So he went out and followed him, and did not know that what was done by the angel was real, but thought he was seeing a vision. ¹⁰When they were past the first and the second guard posts, they came to the iron gate that leads to the city, which opened to them of its own accord; and they went out and went down one street, and immediately the angel departed from him.

¹¹And when Peter had come to himself, he said, "Now I know for certain that the Lord has sent His angel, and has delivered me from the hand of Herod and from all the expectation of the Jewish people."

¹²So, when he had considered this, he came to the house of Mary, the mother of John whose surname was Mark, where many were gathered together praying. ¹³And as Peter knocked at the door of the gate, a girl named Rhoda came to answer. ¹⁴When she recognized Peter's voice, because of her gladness she did not open the gate, but ran in and announced that Peter stood before the gate. ¹⁵But they said to her, "You are beside yourself!" Yet she kept insisting that it was so. So they said, "It is his angel."

¹⁶Now Peter continued knocking; and when they opened the door and saw him, they were astonished. ¹⁷But motioning to them with his hand to keep silent, he declared to them how the Lord had brought him out of the prison. And he said, "Go, tell these things to James and to the brethren." And he departed and went to another place.

¹⁸Then, as soon as it was day, there was no small stir among the soldiers about what had become of Peter. ¹⁹But when Herod had searched for him and not found him, he examined the guards and commanded that they should be put to death.

And he went down from Judea to Caesarea, and stayed there.

Herod's Violent Death

²⁰Now Herod had been very angry with the people of Tyre and Sidon; but they came to him with one accord, and having made Blastus the king's personal aide their friend, they asked for peace, because their country was supplied with food by the king's country.

²¹So on a set day Herod, arrayed in royal apparel, sat on his throne and gave an oration to them. ²²And the people kept shouting, "The voice of a god and not of a man!" ²³Then immediately an angel of the Lord struck him, because he did not give glory to God. And he was eaten by worms and died.

²⁴But the word of God grew and multiplied.

DEVOTIONAL

*W*hoever said the Christian life is free from trouble is probably not a Christian! Being a Christian does not guarantee a problem-free existence. In fact, the exact opposite is true. Jesus promised His followers would have trouble in this world (John 16:33). He also told His disciples, "If they persecuted Me, they will also persecute you" (15:20).

Acts 12 records a remarkable story of God's miraculous intervention to free the apostle Peter from prison. In this case, God answered the fervent prayers of His people and delivered His servant from suffering and harm. But remember, God has not promised He will always deliver us from pain and sorrow. However, He has promised He will be with us in times of trouble. Sometimes He bails us out; sometimes He doesn't. We are not the ones who decide—He is!

Whatever your situation, draw near to God in prayer. Cast your cares on Him, and keep trusting His wisdom and relying on Him.

—Dr. Jim Perdue
Second Baptist Church, Warner Robins, GA

WEEK 27, DAY 3

*God's Miracles Can Lead
Us Toward Faith*

Acts 12:25–13:25

Barnabas and Saul Appointed

And Barnabas and Saul returned from Jerusalem when they had fulfilled their ministry, and they also took with them John whose surname was Mark.

13 Now in the church that was at Antioch there were certain prophets and teachers: Barnabas, Simeon who was called Niger, Lucius of Cyrene, Manaen who had been brought up with Herod the tetrarch, and Saul. 2As they ministered to the Lord and fasted, the Holy Spirit said, "Now separate to Me Barnabas and Saul for the work to which I have called them." 3Then, having fasted and prayed, and laid hands on them, they sent them away.

Preaching in Cyprus

4So, being sent out by the Holy Spirit, they went down to Seleucia, and from there they sailed to Cyprus. 5And when they arrived in Salamis, they preached the word of God in the synagogues of the Jews. They also had John as their assistant.

6Now when they had gone through the island to Paphos, they found a certain sorcerer, a false prophet, a Jew whose name was Bar-Jesus, 7who was with the proconsul, Sergius Paulus, an intelligent man. This man called for Barnabas and Saul and sought to hear the word of God. 8But Elymas the sorcerer (for so his name is translated) withstood them, seeking to turn the proconsul away from the faith. 9Then Saul, who also is called Paul, filled with the Holy Spirit, looked intently at him 10and said, "O full of all deceit and all fraud, you son of the devil, you enemy of all righteousness, will you not cease perverting the straight ways of the Lord? 11And now, indeed, the hand of the Lord is upon you, and you shall be blind, not seeing the sun for a time."

And immediately a dark mist fell on him, and he went around seeking someone to lead him by the hand. 12Then the proconsul believed, when he saw what had been done, being astonished at the teaching of the Lord.

At Antioch in Pisidia

13Now when Paul and his party set sail from Paphos, they came to Perga in Pamphylia; and John, departing from them, returned to Jerusalem. 14But when they departed from Perga, they came to Antioch in Pisidia, and went into the synagogue on the Sabbath day and sat down. 15And after the reading of the Law and the Prophets, the rulers of the synagogue sent to them, saying, "Men and brethren, if you have any word of exhortation for the people, say on."

16Then Paul stood up, and motioning with his hand said, "Men of Israel, and you who fear God, listen: 17The God of this people Israel chose our fathers, and exalted the people when they dwelt as strangers in the land of Egypt, and with an uplifted arm He brought them out of it. 18Now for a time of about forty years He put up with their ways in the wilderness. 19And when He had destroyed seven nations in the land of Canaan, He distributed their land to them by allotment.

20"After that He gave them judges for about four hundred and fifty years, until Samuel the prophet. 21And afterward they asked for a king; so God gave them Saul the son of Kish, a man of the tribe of Benjamin, for forty years. 22And when He had removed him, He raised up for them David as king, to whom also He gave testimony and said, 'I have found David the son of Jesse, a man after My own heart, who will do all My will.' 23From this man's seed, according to the promise, God raised up for Israel a Savior—Jesus— 24after John had first preached, before His coming, the baptism of repentance to all the people of Israel. 25And as John was finishing his course, he said, 'Who do you think I am? I am not He. But behold, there comes One after me, the sandals of whose feet I am not worthy to loose.'"

DEVOTIONAL

Today is Independence Day. It is a day marked on our calendars each year to celebrate and commemorate our nation's freedom. This day is a reminder of a greater reality—we experience freedom because of the sacrifice of so many people. In Acts 12–13 we see God performing miracles through Paul and Barnabas. These miracles led others to faith in Jesus Christ.

Today there is often much confusion about miracles. But if you pay very close attention to the New Testament and to the miracles of Christ you will notice something important. The miracles of Christ and of the apostles always supported the message of the gospel. Miracles were never intended to be simply entertainment. Let the miracles of the New Testament be a reminder to you of a greater reality—Jesus Christ is the Son of God, the Savior and Lord of all.

—Dr. Jim Perdue
Second Baptist Church, Warner Robins, GA

WEEK 27, DAY 4

The Saved Are Glad and Glorify God

Acts 13:26–52

"Men and brethren, sons of the family of Abraham, and those among you who fear God, to you the word of this salvation has been sent. 27For those who dwell in Jerusalem, and their rulers, because they did not know Him, nor even the voices of the Prophets which are read every Sabbath, have fulfilled them in condemning Him. 28And though they found no cause for death in Him, they asked Pilate that He should be put to death. 29Now when they had fulfilled all that was written concerning Him, they took Him down from the tree and laid Him in a tomb. 30But God raised Him from the dead. 31He was seen for many days by those who came up with Him from Galilee to Jerusalem, who are His witnesses to the people. 32And we declare to you glad tidings—that promise which was made to the fathers. 33God has fulfilled this for us their children, in that He has raised up Jesus. As it is also written in the second Psalm:

'You are My Son,
 Today I have begotten You.'

34And that He raised Him from the dead, no more to return to corruption, He has spoken thus:

'I will give you the sure mercies of David.'

35Therefore He also says in another Psalm:

'You will not allow Your Holy One to see corruption.'

36"For David, after he had served his own generation by the will of God, fell asleep, was buried with his fathers, and saw corruption; 37but He whom God raised up saw no corruption. 38Therefore let it be known to you, brethren, that through this Man is preached to you the forgiveness of sins; 39and by Him everyone who believes is justified from all things from which you could not be justified by the law of Moses. 40Beware therefore, lest what has been spoken in the prophets come upon you:

41 'Behold, you despisers,
   Marvel and perish!
   For I work a work in your days,
   A work which you will by no means believe,
   Though one were to declare it to you.'"

Blessing and Conflict at Antioch

42So when the Jews went out of the synagogue, the Gentiles begged that these words might be preached to them the next Sabbath. 43Now when the congregation had broken up, many of the Jews and devout proselytes followed Paul and Barnabas, who, speaking to them, persuaded them to continue in the grace of God.

44On the next Sabbath almost the whole city came together to hear the word of God. 45But when the Jews saw the multitudes, they were filled with envy; and contradicting and blaspheming, they opposed the things spoken by Paul. 46Then Paul and Barnabas grew bold and said, "It was necessary that the word of God should be spoken to you first; but since you reject it, and judge yourselves unworthy of everlasting life, behold, we turn to the Gentiles. 47For so the Lord has commanded us:

'I have set you as a light to the Gentiles,
  That you should be for salvation to the ends of
    the earth.'"

48Now when the Gentiles heard this, they were glad and glorified the word of the Lord. And as many as had been appointed to eternal life believed.

49And the word of the Lord was being spread throughout all the region. 50But the Jews stirred up the devout and prominent women and the chief men of the city, raised up persecution against Paul and Barnabas, and expelled them from their region. 51But they shook off the dust from their feet against them, and came to Iconium. 52And the disciples were filled with joy and with the Holy Spirit.

DEVOTIONAL

Read Acts 13:48 again. The Bible says the Gentiles who trusted Christ for salvation were glad. Here, that word means more than being happy. The word is used in other passages to describe a positive outlook one has even in the midst of persecution and suffering (for example, 2 Corinthians 6:10). That's much more substantial than superficial emotion. Acts 13:48 also says the Gentiles "glorified the word of the Lord." These are the responses of people who have been saved by God's grace.

Did you respond similarly when you first put your faith in Christ? Do you still give God thanks for His salvation at this point in your journey with Him? Pause to recall His great acts of grace in your life, and praise Him for them! Let your heart develop deeper gladness in Him and a stronger desire to glorify Him every day.

—Dr. Jim Perdue
Second Baptist Church, Warner Robins, GA

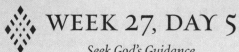

WEEK 27, DAY 5

Seek God's Guidance

Acts 14:1–28

At Iconium

14 Now it happened in Iconium that they went together to the synagogue of the Jews, and so spoke that a great multitude both of the Jews and of the Greeks believed. 2But the unbelieving Jews stirred up the Gentiles and poisoned their minds against the brethren. 3Therefore they stayed there a long time, speaking boldly in the Lord, who was bearing witness to the word of His grace, granting signs and wonders to be done by their hands.

4But the multitude of the city was divided: part sided with the Jews, and part with the apostles. 5And when a violent attempt was made by both the Gentiles and Jews, with their rulers, to abuse and stone them, 6they became aware of it and fled to Lystra and Derbe, cities of Lycaonia, and to the surrounding region. 7And they were preaching the gospel there.

Idolatry at Lystra

8And in Lystra a certain man without strength in his feet was sitting, a cripple from his mother's womb, who had never walked. 9This man heard Paul speaking. Paul, observing him intently and seeing that he had faith to be healed, 10said with a loud voice, "Stand up straight on your feet!" And he leaped and walked. 11Now when the people saw what Paul had done, they raised their voices, saying in the Lycaonian language, "The gods have come down to us in the likeness of men!" 12And Barnabas they called Zeus, and Paul, Hermes, because he was the chief speaker. 13Then the priest of Zeus, whose temple was in front of their city, brought oxen and garlands to the gates, intending to sacrifice with the multitudes.

14But when the apostles Barnabas and Paul heard this, they tore their clothes and ran in among the multitude, crying out 15and saying, "Men, why are you doing these things? We also are men with the same nature as you, and preach to you that you should turn from these useless things to the living God, who made the heaven, the earth, the sea, and all things that are in them, 16who in bygone generations allowed all nations to walk in their own ways. 17Nevertheless He did not leave Himself without witness, in that He did good, gave us rain from heaven and fruitful seasons, filling our hearts with food and gladness." 18And with these sayings they could scarcely restrain the multitudes from sacrificing to them.

Stoning, Escape to Derbe

19Then Jews from Antioch and Iconium came there; and having persuaded the multitudes, they stoned Paul and dragged him out of the city, supposing him to be dead. 20However, when the disciples gathered around him, he rose up and went into the city. And the next day he departed with Barnabas to Derbe.

Strengthening the Converts

21And when they had preached the gospel to that city and made many disciples, they returned to Lystra, Iconium, and Antioch, 22strengthening the souls of the disciples, exhorting them to continue in the faith, and saying, "We must through many tribulations enter the kingdom of God." 23So when they had appointed elders in every church, and prayed with fasting, they commended them to the Lord in whom they had believed. 24And after they had passed through Pisidia, they came to Pamphylia. 25Now when they had preached the word in Perga, they went down to Attalia. 26From there they sailed to Antioch, where they had been commended to the grace of God for the work which they had completed.

27Now when they had come and gathered the church together, they reported all that God had done with them, and that He had opened the door of faith to the Gentiles. 28So they stayed there a long time with the disciples.

DEVOTIONAL

*M*ost people don't like to ask for directions. With today's technology, they never have to.

The book of Acts records the journey of the early church and its members. In chapter 14 alone, we see division (vv. 1–7), confusion (vv. 8–17), persecution (verses 19–20), and tribulation (vv. 21–28). But through it all, God was leading His people. We can clearly see Him direct the journey of Paul and Barnabas.

This chapter reminds us of the importance of following God's will every day of our lives. The Holy Spirit reveals God's will to believers through prayer, Bible study, circumstances, and the advice of godly people. The next time you decide to go somewhere, make sure to ask God for directions. He wants to lead you every step of the way!

—Dr. Jim Perdue
Second Baptist Church, Warner Robins, GA

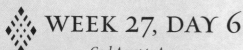

WEEK 27, DAY 6

God Accepts Anyone Who Comes to Him

Acts 15:1–21

Conflict over Circumcision

15 And certain men came down from Judea and taught the brethren, "Unless you are circumcised according to the custom of Moses, you cannot be saved." ²Therefore, when Paul and Barnabas had no small dissension and dispute with them, they determined that Paul and Barnabas and certain others of them should go up to Jerusalem, to the apostles and elders, about this question.

³So, being sent on their way by the church, they passed through Phoenicia and Samaria, describing the conversion of the Gentiles; and they caused great joy to all the brethren. ⁴And when they had come to Jerusalem, they were received by the church and the apostles and the elders; and they reported all things that God had done with them. ⁵But some of the sect of the Pharisees who believed rose up, saying, "It is necessary to circumcise them, and to command them to keep the law of Moses."

The Jerusalem Council

⁶Now the apostles and elders came together to consider this matter. ⁷And when there had been much dispute, Peter rose up and said to them: "Men and brethren, you know that a good while ago God chose among us, that by my mouth the Gentiles should hear the word of the gospel and believe. ⁸So God, who knows the heart, acknowledged them by giving them the Holy Spirit, just as He did to us, ⁹and made no distinction between us and them, purifying their hearts by faith. ¹⁰Now therefore, why do you test God by putting a yoke on the neck of the disciples which neither our fathers nor we were able to bear? ¹¹But we believe that through the grace of the Lord Jesus Christ we shall be saved in the same manner as they."

¹²Then all the multitude kept silent and listened to Barnabas and Paul declaring how many miracles and wonders God had worked through them among the Gentiles. ¹³And after they had become silent, James answered, saying, "Men and brethren, listen to me: ¹⁴Simon has declared how God at the first visited the Gentiles to take out of them a people for His name. ¹⁵And with this the words of the prophets agree, just as it is written:

¹⁶ 'After this I will return

And will rebuild the tabernacle of David, which
   has fallen down;
I will rebuild its ruins,
And I will set it up;
¹⁷ So that the rest of mankind may seek the LORD,
Even all the Gentiles who are called by My name,
Says the LORD who does all these things.'

¹⁸"Known to God from eternity are all His works. ¹⁹Therefore I judge that we should not trouble those from among the Gentiles who are turning to God, ²⁰but that we write to them to abstain from things polluted by idols, from sexual immorality, from things strangled, and from blood. ²¹For Moses has had throughout many generations those who preach him in every city, being read in the synagogues every Sabbath."

DEVOTIONAL

*C*an you think of a time when you found out that you'd been accepted to a school or offered a job you'd been excited about? In that moment, you were thrilled! After putting in the necessary time and effort to become a candidate they were looking for and completing the application process, you finally met your goal. What a great feeling!

Did you know God has an acceptance policy too? His is much simpler. There is only one condition: you must come to the cross in repentance and faith, completely trusting in the finished work of Christ for salvation. That's right—no complicated application process, no weighted system to evaluate grades, no required work experience—simply grace.

Acts 15 reminds us that our salvation is not based on our ability to fulfill the law. The Judaizers taught that one must keep the Law of Moses and be circumcised in addition to having faith in Christ. But this is completely contrary to grace. Grace teaches that God accepts anyone who comes to Him in repentance and faith.

Jesus accused the Pharisees of cleaning the outside of the cup while ignoring the inside (Luke 11:39), which is exactly what legalism does. It focuses only on external activities while ignoring the attitude of the heart. In the end, we should all know we are incapable of fulfilling the law, and this should make us desperate for God's grace. Embrace this reality today and humble yourself at the feet of Jesus.

—Dr. Jim Perdue
Second Baptist Church, Warner Robins, GA

WEEK 27, DAY 7

How has your salvation and God's transforming work in your heart led you to become a source of grace and generosity to others?

_____

_____

_____

_____

_____

_____

_____

_____

_____

_____

_____

_____

Describe a specific time in your life when you clearly understood and followed God's will. How did you discover it?

_____

_____

_____

_____

_____

_____

_____

_____

_____

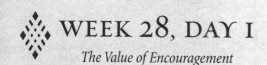

WEEK 28, DAY 1

The Value of Encouragement

Acts 15:22–16:5

The Jerusalem Decree

Then it pleased the apostles and elders, with the whole church, to send chosen men of their own company to Antioch with Paul and Barnabas, namely, Judas who was also named Barsabas, and Silas, leading men among the brethren.

23They wrote this letter by them:

The apostles, the elders, and the brethren,

To the brethren who are of the Gentiles in Antioch, Syria, and Cilicia:

Greetings.

24 Since we have heard that some who went out from us have troubled you with words, unsettling your souls, saying, "You must be circumcised and keep the law"—to whom we gave no such commandment—25it seemed good to us, being assembled with one accord, to send chosen men to you with our beloved Barnabas and Paul, 26men who have risked their lives for the name of our Lord Jesus Christ. 27We have therefore sent Judas and Silas, who will also report the same things by word of mouth. 28For it seemed good to the Holy Spirit, and to us, to lay upon you no greater burden than these necessary things: 29that you abstain from things offered to idols, from blood, from things strangled, and from sexual immorality. If you keep yourselves from these, you will do well.

Farewell.

Continuing Ministry in Syria

30So when they were sent off, they came to Antioch; and when they had gathered the multitude together, they delivered the letter. 31When they had read it, they rejoiced over its encouragement. 32Now Judas and Silas, themselves being prophets also, exhorted and strengthened the brethren with many words. 33And after they had stayed there for a time, they were sent back with greetings from the brethren to the apostles.

34However, it seemed good to Silas to remain there. 35Paul and Barnabas also remained in Antioch, teaching and preaching the word of the Lord, with many others also.

Division over John Mark

36Then after some days Paul said to Barnabas, "Let us now go back and visit our brethren in every city where we have preached the word of the Lord, and see how they are doing." 37Now Barnabas was determined to take with them John called Mark. 38But Paul insisted that they should not take with them the one who had departed from them in Pamphylia, and had not gone with them to the work. 39Then the contention became so sharp that they parted from one another. And so Barnabas took Mark and sailed to Cyprus; 40but Paul chose Silas and departed, being commended by the brethren to the grace of God. 41And he went through Syria and Cilicia, strengthening the churches.

Timothy Joins Paul and Silas

16Then he came to Derbe and Lystra. And behold, a certain disciple was there, named Timothy, the son of a certain Jewish woman who believed, but his father was Greek. 2He was well spoken of by the brethren who were at Lystra and Iconium. 3Paul wanted to have him go on with him. And he took him and circumcised him because of the Jews who were in that region, for they all knew that his father was Greek. 4And as they went through the cities, they delivered to them the decrees to keep, which were determined by the apostles and elders at Jerusalem. 5So the churches were strengthened in the faith, and increased in number daily.

DEVOTIONAL

Think about the people who lift your spirit. More than likely, they are encouragers. These people lift up, appreciate, and affirm others. Barnabas was an encourager. The six times he is mentioned in Scripture, he is cheering on others. And we can see the results—he changed the trajectory of people's lives. Paul and John Mark, for example, were both grateful for how Barnabas believed in them when no one else wanted to take a chance.

What about you? Whom do you need to encourage? Whom do you need to take under your wings and develop? People need encouragement. The voice of affirmation and appreciation is clearly distinguished over the endless noise of critics and cynics. Don't underestimate the power of your encouragement to others! Do it today!

—Dr. Richard Mark Lee
First Baptist Church, McKinney, TX

WEEK 28, DAY 2

Invest in the Growth of Others

Acts 16:6–34

The Macedonian Call

Now when they had gone through Phrygia and the region of Galatia, they were forbidden by the Holy Spirit to preach the word in Asia. 7After they had come to Mysia, they tried to go into Bithynia, but the Spirit did not permit them. 8So passing by Mysia, they came down to Troas. 9And a vision appeared to Paul in the night. A man of Macedonia stood and pleaded with him, saying, "Come over to Macedonia and help us." 10Now after he had seen the vision, immediately we sought to go to Macedonia, concluding that the Lord had called us to preach the gospel to them.

Lydia Baptized at Philippi

11Therefore, sailing from Troas, we ran a straight course to Samothrace, and the next day came to Neapolis, 12and from there to Philippi, which is the foremost city of that part of Macedonia, a colony. And we were staying in that city for some days. 13And on the Sabbath day we went out of the city to the riverside, where prayer was customarily made; and we sat down and spoke to the women who met there. 14Now a certain woman named Lydia heard us. She was a seller of purple from the city of Thyatira, who worshiped God. The Lord opened her heart to heed the things spoken by Paul. 15And when she and her household were baptized, she begged us, saying, "If you have judged me to be faithful to the Lord, come to my house and stay." So she persuaded us.

Paul and Silas Imprisoned

16Now it happened, as we went to prayer, that a certain slave girl possessed with a spirit of divination met us, who brought her masters much profit by fortune-telling. 17This girl followed Paul and us, and cried out, saying, "These men are the servants of the Most High God, who proclaim to us the way of salvation." 18And this she did for many days.

But Paul, greatly annoyed, turned and said to the spirit, "I command you in the name of Jesus Christ to come out of her." And he came out that very hour. 19But when her masters saw that their hope of profit was gone, they seized Paul and Silas and dragged them into the marketplace to the authorities.

20And they brought them to the magistrates, and said, "These men, being Jews, exceedingly trouble our city; 21and they teach customs which are not lawful for us, being Romans, to receive or observe." 22Then the multitude rose up together against them; and the magistrates tore off their clothes and commanded them to be beaten with rods. 23And when they had laid many stripes on them, they threw them into prison, commanding the jailer to keep them securely. 24Having received such a charge, he put them into the inner prison and fastened their feet in the stocks.

The Philippian Jailer Saved

25But at midnight Paul and Silas were praying and singing hymns to God, and the prisoners were listening to them. 26Suddenly there was a great earthquake, so that the foundations of the prison were shaken; and immediately all the doors were opened and everyone's chains were loosed. 27And the keeper of the prison, awaking from sleep and seeing the prison doors open, supposing the prisoners had fled, drew his sword and was about to kill himself. 28But Paul called with a loud voice, saying, "Do yourself no harm, for we are all here."

29Then he called for a light, ran in, and fell down trembling before Paul and Silas. 30And he brought them out and said, "Sirs, what must I do to be saved?"

31So they said, "Believe on the Lord Jesus Christ, and you will be saved, you and your household." 32Then they spoke the word of the Lord to him and to all who were in his house. 33And he took them the same hour of the night and washed their stripes. And immediately he and all his family were baptized. 34Now when he had brought them into his house, he set food before them; and he rejoiced, having believed in God with all his household.

DEVOTIONAL

*L*eading others to grow in Christ is more than a program of study or scheduled activity. Real life change happens in the teachable moments that aren't always planned.

Paul and Silas habitually took extra time to invest in others (Acts 16:15, 28). They didn't run when they had the chance—they stayed! Similarly, your investment in others will create life change all around you. Take time to slow down and live in the present. When you live like Jesus in close relationship with others, people can see, hear, and experience the new life Christ offers. Listen and watch for the interruptions that may lead to teachable moments and real life change!

—Dr. Richard Mark Lee
First Baptist Church, McKinney, TX

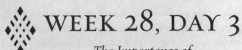

WEEK 28, DAY 3

The Importance of Knowing God's Word

Acts 16:35–17:15

Paul Refuses to Depart Secretly

And when it was day, the magistrates sent the officers, saying, "Let those men go."

36So the keeper of the prison reported these words to Paul, saying, "The magistrates have sent to let you go. Now therefore depart, and go in peace."

37But Paul said to them, "They have beaten us openly, uncondemned Romans, and have thrown us into prison. And now do they put us out secretly? No indeed! Let them come themselves and get us out."

38And the officers told these words to the magistrates, and they were afraid when they heard that they were Romans. 39Then they came and pleaded with them and brought them out, and asked them to depart from the city. 40So they went out of the prison and entered the house of Lydia; and when they had seen the brethren, they encouraged them and departed.

Preaching Christ at Thessalonica

17Now when they had passed through Amphipolis and Apollonia, they came to Thessalonica, where there was a synagogue of the Jews. 2Then Paul, as his custom was, went in to them, and for three Sabbaths reasoned with them from the Scriptures, 3explaining and demonstrating that the Christ had to suffer and rise again from the dead, and saying, "This Jesus whom I preach to you is the Christ." 4And some of them were persuaded; and a great multitude of the devout Greeks, and not a few of the leading women, joined Paul and Silas.

Assault on Jason's House

5But the Jews who were not persuaded, becoming envious, took some of the evil men from the marketplace, and gathering a mob, set all the city in an uproar and attacked the house of Jason, and sought to bring them out to the people. 6But when they did not find them, they dragged Jason and some brethren to the rulers of the city, crying out, "These who have turned the world upside down have come here too. 7Jason has harbored them, and these are all acting contrary to the decrees of Caesar, saying there is another king—Jesus." 8And they troubled the crowd and the rulers of the city when they heard these things. 9So when they had taken security from Jason and the rest, they let them go.

Ministering at Berea

10Then the brethren immediately sent Paul and Silas away by night to Berea. When they arrived, they went into the synagogue of the Jews. 11These were more fair-minded than those in Thessalonica, in that they received the word with all readiness, and searched the Scriptures daily to find out whether these things were so. 12Therefore many of them believed, and also not a few of the Greeks, prominent women as well as men. 13But when the Jews from Thessalonica learned that the word of God was preached by Paul at Berea, they came there also and stirred up the crowds. 14Then immediately the brethren sent Paul away, to go to the sea; but both Silas and Timothy remained there. 15So those who conducted Paul brought him to Athens; and receiving a command for Silas and Timothy to come to him with all speed, they departed.

DEVOTIONAL

There's a big difference between sorting through spam and sorting through personal e-mail. Communication from someone you know means more. God's Word is His letter, His text, His communication with you that should be cherished until you are with Him for eternity.

In Acts 17:11, Paul and Silas led Jews in Berea through a process of spiritual growth. They taught, explained, and demonstrated the Word to the Jews, and the Jews received it "with all readiness." Likewise, we should approach our personal time of Bible study with readiness to hear and receive from God. The Jews searched the Scriptures "to find out whether these things were so." Similarly, we need to know what Scripture says, because it helps us to discern truth in the midst of a pluralistic society. It is also critical to search the Scriptures for ourselves and not just accept everything that people may tell us about what the Bible does or does not say.

God's Word is also our weapon of choice, both on the offense and the defense in our spiritual lives. Jesus quoted Scripture when He dealt with temptation, doubt, and discouragement. He set an example for us to follow.

The more we get into God's Word, the more it gets into us, and the more we allow the Spirit of God to speak to us when we need Him most. Let's keep reading, meditating on, and living out God's Word. Let's allow His truth to change us from the inside out.

—Dr. Richard Mark Lee
First Baptist Church, McKinney, TX

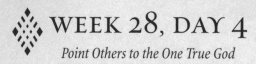

WEEK 28, DAY 4

Point Others to the One True God

Acts 17:16–18:4

The Philosophers at Athens

Now while Paul waited for them at Athens, his spirit was provoked within him when he saw that the city was given over to idols. 17Therefore he reasoned in the synagogue with the Jews and with the Gentile worshipers, and in the marketplace daily with those who happened to be there. 18Then certain Epicurean and Stoic philosophers encountered him. And some said, "What does this babbler want to say?"

Others said, "He seems to be a proclaimer of foreign gods," because he preached to them Jesus and the resurrection.

19And they took him and brought him to the Areopagus, saying, "May we know what this new doctrine is of which you speak? 20For you are bringing some strange things to our ears. Therefore we want to know what these things mean." 21For all the Athenians and the foreigners who were there spent their time in nothing else but either to tell or to hear some new thing.

Addressing the Areopagus

22Then Paul stood in the midst of the Areopagus and said, "Men of Athens, I perceive that in all things you are very religious; 23for as I was passing through and considering the objects of your worship, I even found an altar with this inscription:

TO THE UNKNOWN GOD.

Therefore, the One whom you worship without knowing, Him I proclaim to you: 24God, who made the world and everything in it, since He is Lord of heaven and earth, does not dwell in temples made with hands. 25Nor is He worshiped with men's hands, as though He needed anything, since He gives to all life, breath, and all things. 26And He has made from one blood every nation of men to dwell on all the face of the earth, and has determined their preappointed times and the boundaries of their dwellings, 27so that they should seek the Lord, in the hope that they might grope for Him and find Him, though He is not far from each one of us; 28for in Him we live and move and have our being, as also some of your own poets have said, 'For we are also His offspring.' 29Therefore, since we are the offspring of God, we ought not to think that the Divine Nature is like gold or silver or stone, something shaped by art and man's devising. 30Truly, these times of ignorance God overlooked, but now commands all men everywhere to repent, 31because He has appointed a day on which He will judge the world in righteousness by the Man whom He has ordained. He has given assurance of this to all by raising Him from the dead."

32And when they heard of the resurrection of the dead, some mocked, while others said, "We will hear you again on this matter." 33So Paul departed from among them. 34However, some men joined him and believed, among them Dionysius the Areopagite, a woman named Damaris, and others with them.

Ministering at Corinth

18After these things Paul departed from Athens and went to Corinth. 2And he found a certain Jew named Aquila, born in Pontus, who had recently come from Italy with his wife Priscilla (because Claudius had commanded all the Jews to depart from Rome); and he came to them. 3So, because he was of the same trade, he stayed with them and worked; for by occupation they were tentmakers. 4And he reasoned in the synagogue every Sabbath, and persuaded both Jews and Greeks.

DEVOTIONAL

There are many similarities to the spiritual climate of Acts 17 and our culture today. People are searching. Culture has crafted a god of its own making. Let's call it the American Jesus, which is not defined by Christianity but by a blending of various beliefs, thoughts, and desires. Similar to the epicurean and stoic philosophers of Paul's day, the American Jesus says you can have it your way: pleasure and the absence of pain and disturbance. But that is not the message from the God of the Bible.

Just like Paul, we must tell others about the one true God, the One who is above all others. "The Unknown God" can in fact be known, and Jesus is the way to Him (Acts 17:23–24). There is no other life-giving message than the gospel of Jesus Christ as it is revealed in Scripture. Everything people are searching for can be found in a vibrant relationship with Jesus Christ, the Son of God. Just like the early believers, we too must share and declare the one true God. Live out the gospel today, not only in word but also in action.

—Dr. Richard Mark Lee
First Baptist Church, McKinney, TX

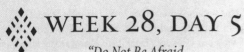

WEEK 28, DAY 5

"Do Not Be Afraid . . . I Am with You"

Acts 18:5–28

When Silas and Timothy had come from Macedonia, Paul was compelled by the Spirit, and testified to the Jews that Jesus is the Christ. 6But when they opposed him and blasphemed, he shook his garments and said to them, "Your blood be upon your own heads; I am clean. From now on I will go to the Gentiles." 7And he departed from there and entered the house of a certain man named Justus, one who worshiped God, whose house was next door to the synagogue. 8Then Crispus, the ruler of the synagogue, believed on the Lord with all his household. And many of the Corinthians, hearing, believed and were baptized.

9Now the Lord spoke to Paul in the night by a vision, "Do not be afraid, but speak, and do not keep silent; 10for I am with you, and no one will attack you to hurt you; for I have many people in this city." 11And he continued there a year and six months, teaching the word of God among them.

12When Gallio was proconsul of Achaia, the Jews with one accord rose up against Paul and brought him to the judgment seat, 13saying, "This fellow persuades men to worship God contrary to the law."

14And when Paul was about to open his mouth, Gallio said to the Jews, "If it were a matter of wrongdoing or wicked crimes, O Jews, there would be reason why I should bear with you. 15But if it is a question of words and names and your own law, look to it yourselves; for I do not want to be a judge of such matters." 16And he drove them from the judgment seat. 17Then all the Greeks took Sosthenes, the ruler of the synagogue, and beat him before the judgment seat. But Gallio took no notice of these things.

Paul Returns to Antioch

18So Paul still remained a good while. Then he took leave of the brethren and sailed for Syria, and Priscilla and Aquila were with him. He had his hair cut off at Cenchrea, for he had taken a vow. 19And he came to Ephesus, and left them there; but he himself entered the synagogue and reasoned with the Jews. 20When they asked him to stay a longer time with them, he did not consent, 21but took leave of them, saying, "I must by all means keep this coming feast in Jerusalem; but I will return again to you, God willing." And he sailed from Ephesus.

22And when he had landed at Caesarea, and gone up and greeted the church, he went down to Antioch. 23After he had spent some time there, he departed and went over the region of Galatia and Phrygia in order, strengthening all the disciples.

Ministry of Apollos

24Now a certain Jew named Apollos, born at Alexandria, an eloquent man and mighty in the Scriptures, came to Ephesus. 25This man had been instructed in the way of the Lord; and being fervent in spirit, he spoke and taught accurately the things of the Lord, though he knew only the baptism of John. 26So he began to speak boldly in the synagogue. When Aquila and Priscilla heard him, they took him aside and explained to him the way of God more accurately. 27And when he desired to cross to Achaia, the brethren wrote, exhorting the disciples to receive him; and when he arrived, he greatly helped those who had believed through grace; 28for he vigorously refuted the Jews publicly, showing from the Scriptures that Jesus is the Christ.

DEVOTIONAL

Have you ever been paralyzed by fear? Whether it is a fear of loss, failure, rejection, ridicule, or persecution, what fear grips you?

You may have heard the acronym that fear is False Evidence Appearing Real. One of the biggest "false evidences" of fear is that you either are or will be all alone. However, the truth is that Jesus Christ is always with you. Fear is not something you just have to live with. Have you noticed how brave you can become when someone else is with you? Allow the promise of God's presence to dispel fear and drive your courage to move forward in faith.

There are nine accounts in the Gospels of Jesus saying, "Don't be afraid." Four other times, He encouraged His followers with the promise of His presence. We see the same message in today's reading when the Lord said to Paul, "Do not be afraid, but speak, and do not keep silent; for I am with you" (Acts 18:9–10).

God's presence makes all the difference. His perfect love drives out fear (1 John 4:18). Whatever God asks of you, you need not fear. He has promised you will not go alone. Focus on His presence and power to overcome your fear!

—Dr. Richard Mark Lee
First Baptist Church, McKinney, TX

WEEK 28, DAY 6

Repentance Means Abandoning Sin

Acts 19:1–22

Paul at Ephesus

19 And it happened, while Apollos was at Corinth, that Paul, having passed through the upper regions, came to Ephesus. And finding some disciples ²he said to them, "Did you receive the Holy Spirit when you believed?"

So they said to him, "We have not so much as heard whether there is a Holy Spirit."

³And he said to them, "Into what then were you baptized?"

So they said, "Into John's baptism."

⁴Then Paul said, "John indeed baptized with a baptism of repentance, saying to the people that they should believe on Him who would come after him, that is, on Christ Jesus."

⁵When they heard this, they were baptized in the name of the Lord Jesus. ⁶And when Paul had laid hands on them, the Holy Spirit came upon them, and they spoke with tongues and prophesied. ⁷Now the men were about twelve in all.

⁸And he went into the synagogue and spoke boldly for three months, reasoning and persuading concerning the things of the kingdom of God. ⁹But when some were hardened and did not believe, but spoke evil of the Way before the multitude, he departed from them and withdrew the disciples, reasoning daily in the school of Tyrannus. ¹⁰And this continued for two years, so that all who dwelt in Asia heard the word of the Lord Jesus, both Jews and Greeks.

Miracles Glorify Christ

¹¹Now God worked unusual miracles by the hands of Paul, ¹²so that even handkerchiefs or aprons were brought from his body to the sick, and the diseases left them and the evil spirits went out of them. ¹³Then some of the itinerant Jewish exorcists took it upon themselves to call the name of the Lord Jesus over those who had evil spirits, saying, "We exorcise you by the Jesus whom Paul preaches." ¹⁴Also there were seven sons of Sceva, a Jewish chief priest, who did so.

¹⁵And the evil spirit answered and said, "Jesus I know, and Paul I know; but who are you?"

¹⁶Then the man in whom the evil spirit was leaped on them, overpowered them, and prevailed against them, so that they fled out of that house naked and wounded.

¹⁷This became known both to all Jews and Greeks dwelling in Ephesus; and fear fell on them all, and the name of the Lord Jesus was magnified. ¹⁸And many who had believed came confessing and telling their deeds. ¹⁹Also, many of those who had practiced magic brought their books together and burned them in the sight of all. And they counted up the value of them, and it totaled fifty thousand pieces of silver. ²⁰So the word of the Lord grew mightily and prevailed.

The Riot at Ephesus

²¹When these things were accomplished, Paul purposed in the Spirit, when he had passed through Macedonia and Achaia, to go to Jerusalem, saying, "After I have been there, I must also see Rome." ²²So he sent into Macedonia two of those who ministered to him, Timothy and Erastus, but he himself stayed in Asia for a time.

DEVOTIONAL

So much of history, culture, and truth has been redefined to fit our comfort. We tend to focus on things that make us feel good about ourselves and discard the rest, even if what's discarded is truth. We all sin, and whether you want to call those sins mistakes, little white lies, or small slips, sin is still rebellion against God. Left unrepented, sin gradually grows and ultimately destroys people in its wake.

Repentance is a difficult word and an even more difficult practice. While confession admits wrong, repentance turns from and abandons the sinful behavior. Repentance requires both internal change and a new external practice. For example, people can confess that they need to eat right and exercise more, but until they actually do just that, there will be little improvement in their health. The same is true in dealing with sin. Confession, shame, embarrassment, or hope alone doesn't change behavior. We must take action if we want a life change.

Share your struggles with someone you can trust so that they are no longer secret. Develop new disciplines or activities to replace sin with godliness. Win the war one battle at a time. Heed the words of Proverbs 28:13, which says, "Whoever confesses and forsakes [their sin] will have mercy."

—Dr. Richard Mark Lee
First Baptist Church, McKinney, TX

WEEK 28, DAY 7

Everyone needs encouragement. How can you be like Barnabas in your circle of influence? Whom do you need to reach out to and encourage?

_____

_____

_____

_____

_____

_____

_____

_____

_____

_____

_____

_____

_____

Think back through the past six days of reading. When did you have a cause for pause? Reflect, remember, and respond. Is there an area in your life where you need to repent? What habits do you need to abandon and replace?

_____

_____

_____

_____

_____

_____

_____

_____

_____

_____

WEEK 29, DAY 1

Vengeance Is the Lord's

Acts 19:23–20:6

And about that time there arose a great commotion about the Way. ²⁴For a certain man named Demetrius, a silversmith, who made silver shrines of Diana, brought no small profit to the craftsmen. ²⁵He called them together with the workers of similar occupation, and said: "Men, you know that we have our prosperity by this trade. ²⁶Moreover you see and hear that not only at Ephesus, but throughout almost all Asia, this Paul has persuaded and turned away many people, saying that they are not gods which are made with hands. ²⁷So not only is this trade of ours in danger of falling into disrepute, but also the temple of the great goddess Diana may be despised and her magnificence destroyed, whom all Asia and the world worship."

²⁸Now when they heard this, they were full of wrath and cried out, saying, "Great is Diana of the Ephesians!" ²⁹So the whole city was filled with confusion, and rushed into the theater with one accord, having seized Gaius and Aristarchus, Macedonians, Paul's travel companions. ³⁰And when Paul wanted to go in to the people, the disciples would not allow him. ³¹Then some of the officials of Asia, who were his friends, sent to him pleading that he would not venture into the theater. ³²Some therefore cried one thing and some another, for the assembly was confused, and most of them did not know why they had come together. ³³And they drew Alexander out of the multitude, the Jews putting him forward. And Alexander motioned with his hand, and wanted to make his defense to the people. ³⁴But when they found out that he was a Jew, all with one voice cried out for about two hours, "Great is Diana of the Ephesians!"

³⁵And when the city clerk had quieted the crowd, he said: "Men of Ephesus, what man is there who does not know that the city of the Ephesians is temple guardian of the great goddess Diana, and of the image which fell down from Zeus? ³⁶Therefore, since these things cannot be denied, you ought to be quiet and do nothing rashly. ³⁷For you have brought these men here who are neither robbers of temples nor blasphemers of your goddess. ³⁸Therefore, if Demetrius and his fellow craftsmen have a case against anyone, the courts are open and there are proconsuls. Let them bring charges against one another. ³⁹But if you have any other inquiry to make, it shall be determined in the lawful assembly. ⁴⁰For we are in danger of being called in question for today's uproar, there being no reason which we may give to account for this disorderly gathering." ⁴¹And when he had said these things, he dismissed the assembly.

Journeys in Greece

20 After the uproar had ceased, Paul called the disciples to himself, embraced them, and departed to go to Macedonia. ²Now when he had gone over that region and encouraged them with many words, he came to Greece ³and stayed three months. And when the Jews plotted against him as he was about to sail to Syria, he decided to return through Macedonia. ⁴And Sopater of Berea accompanied him to Asia—also Aristarchus and Secundus of the Thessalonians, and Gaius of Derbe, and Timothy, and Tychicus and Trophimus of Asia. ⁵These men, going ahead, waited for us at Troas. ⁶But we sailed away from Philippi after the Days of Unleavened Bread, and in five days joined them at Troas, where we stayed seven days.

DEVOTIONAL

Few of us have ever been attacked by a mob like Alexander in Acts 19. However, it is very likely you've experienced a relational conflict and have even felt attacked by those you love and trust.

When conflict arises, it is best to reconcile peaceably if we can. If we cannot, however, we should never seek revenge. Hebrews 12:14–15 says we should "pursue peace with all people," helping them experience the grace of God. We should not allow "any root of bitterness" to spring up and cause trouble, because "by this many become defiled." An angry, bitter attitude bent on "getting even" will hurt us and negatively affect our relationships.

When we seek revenge or even aggressively defend ourselves at the expense of others, we demonstrate a lack of faith in God. Romans 12:19 teaches us not to avenge ourselves, but to leave that up to our Father. God came to Alexander's rescue, and He will defeat your enemies as well. God is able to defend you and will eventually make all things right. Resist revengeful impulses and honor God by recognizing that it is His prerogative to punish sin and His pleasure to protect and defend you.

—Dr. Dwayne Mercer
First Baptist Church, Oviedo, FL

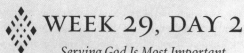

WEEK 29, DAY 2

Serving God Is Most Important

Acts 20:7–38

Ministering at Troas

Now on the first day of the week, when the disciples came together to break bread, Paul, ready to depart the next day, spoke to them and continued his message until midnight. 8There were many lamps in the upper room where they were gathered together. 9And in a window sat a certain young man named Eutychus, who was sinking into a deep sleep. He was overcome by sleep; and as Paul continued speaking, he fell down from the third story and was taken up dead. 10But Paul went down, fell on him, and embracing him said, "Do not trouble yourselves, for his life is in him." 11Now when he had come up, had broken bread and eaten, and talked a long while, even till daybreak, he departed. 12And they brought the young man in alive, and they were not a little comforted.

From Troas to Miletus

13Then we went ahead to the ship and sailed to Assos, there intending to take Paul on board; for so he had given orders, intending himself to go on foot. 14And when he met us at Assos, we took him on board and came to Mitylene. 15We sailed from there, and the next *day* came opposite Chios. The following *day* we arrived at Samos and stayed at Trogyllium. The next *day* we came to Miletus. 16For Paul had decided to sail past Ephesus, so that he would not have to spend time in Asia; for he was hurrying to be at Jerusalem, if possible, on the Day of Pentecost.

The Ephesian Elders Exhorted

17From Miletus he sent to Ephesus and called for the elders of the church. 18And when they had come to him, he said to them: "You know, from the first day that I came to Asia, in what manner I always lived among you, 19serving the Lord with all humility, with many tears and trials which happened to me by the plotting of the Jews; 20how I kept back nothing that was helpful, but proclaimed it to you, and taught you publicly and from house to house, 21testifying to Jews, and also to Greeks, repentance toward God and faith toward our Lord Jesus Christ. 22And see, now I go bound in the spirit to Jerusalem, not knowing the things that will happen to me there, 23except that the Holy Spirit testifies in every city, saying that chains and tribulations await me. 24But none of these things move me; nor do I count my life dear to myself, so that I may finish my race with joy, and the ministry which I received from the Lord Jesus, to testify to the gospel of the grace of God.

25"And indeed, now I know that you all, among whom I have gone preaching the kingdom of God, will see my face no more. 26Therefore I testify to you this day that I am innocent of the blood of all men. 27For I have not shunned to declare to you the whole counsel of God. 28Therefore take heed to yourselves and to all the flock, among which the Holy Spirit has made you overseers, to shepherd the church of God which He purchased with His own blood. 29For I know this, that after my departure savage wolves will come in among you, not sparing the flock. 30Also from among yourselves men will rise up, speaking perverse things, to draw away the disciples after themselves. 31Therefore watch, and remember that for three years I did not cease to warn everyone night and day with tears.

32"So now, brethren, I commend you to God and to the word of His grace, which is able to build you up and give you an inheritance among all those who are sanctified. 33I have coveted no one's silver or gold or apparel. 34Yes, you yourselves know that these hands have provided for my necessities, and for those who were with me. 35I have shown you in every way, by laboring like this, that you must support the weak. And remember the words of the Lord Jesus, that He said, 'It is more blessed to give than to receive.'"

36And when he had said these things, he knelt down and prayed with them all. 37Then they all wept freely, and fell on Paul's neck and kissed him, 38sorrowing most of all for the words which he spoke, that they would see his face no more. And they accompanied him to the ship.

DEVOTIONAL

We can see the heart of Paul very clearly in this passage. Out of necessity he had to leave the church he loved in order to take the gospel to those who had never heard.

Paul poured out his life with all humility to testify to the gospel of grace (Acts 20:19). Why the dedication? Why the passion? Perhaps it was because he never got over his salvation. The same humility that brought him to the foot of the cross on the Damascus Road compelled him to stay near that cross, embrace the gospel (20:20), and finish well (2 Timothy 4:7). He said, "God forbid that I should boast except in the cross of our Lord Jesus Christ" (Galatians 6:14).

What about you? Where is your passion? Find it at the foot of the cross.

—Dr. Dwayne Mercer
First Baptist Church, Oviedo, FL

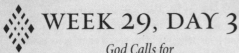

WEEK 29, DAY 3

God Calls for Uncompromising Faithfulness

Acts 21:1–25

Warnings on the Journey to Jerusalem

21 Now it came to pass, that when we had departed from them and set sail, running a straight course we came to Cos, the following day to Rhodes, and from there to Patara. ²And finding a ship sailing over to Phoenicia, we went aboard and set sail. ³When we had sighted Cyprus, we passed it on the left, sailed to Syria, and landed at Tyre; for there the ship was to unload her cargo. ⁴And finding disciples, we stayed there seven days. They told Paul through the Spirit not to go up to Jerusalem. ⁵When we had come to the end of those days, we departed and went on our way; and they all accompanied us, with wives and children, till we were out of the city. And we knelt down on the shore and prayed. ⁶When we had taken our leave of one another, we boarded the ship, and they returned home.

⁷And when we had finished our voyage from Tyre, we came to Ptolemais, greeted the brethren, and stayed with them one day. ⁸On the next day we who were Paul's companions departed and came to Caesarea, and entered the house of Philip the evangelist, who was one of the seven, and stayed with him. ⁹Now this man had four virgin daughters who prophesied. ¹⁰And as we stayed many days, a certain prophet named Agabus came down from Judea. ¹¹When he had come to us, he took Paul's belt, bound his own hands and feet, and said, "Thus says the Holy Spirit, 'So shall the Jews at Jerusalem bind the man who owns this belt, and deliver him into the hands of the Gentiles.'"

¹²Now when we heard these things, both we and those from that place pleaded with him not to go up to Jerusalem. ¹³Then Paul answered, "What do you mean by weeping and breaking my heart? For I am ready not only to be bound, but also to die at Jerusalem for the name of the Lord Jesus." ¹⁴So when he would not be persuaded, we ceased, saying, "The will of the Lord be done."

Paul Urged to Make Peace

¹⁵And after those days we packed and went up to Jerusalem. ¹⁶Also some of the disciples from Caesarea went with us and brought with them a certain Mnason of Cyprus, an early disciple, with whom we were to lodge.

¹⁷And when we had come to Jerusalem, the brethren received us gladly. ¹⁸On the following day Paul went in with us to James, and all the elders were present. ¹⁹When he had greeted them, he told in detail those things which God had done among the Gentiles through his ministry. ²⁰And when they heard it, they glorified the Lord. And they said to him, "You see, brother, how many myriads of Jews there are who have believed, and they are all zealous for the law; ²¹but they have been informed about you that you teach all the Jews who are among the Gentiles to forsake Moses, saying that they ought not to circumcise their children nor to walk according to the customs. ²²What then? The assembly must certainly meet, for they will hear that you have come. ²³Therefore do what we tell you: We have four men who have taken a vow. ²⁴Take them and be purified with them, and pay their expenses so that they may shave their heads, and that all may know that those things of which they were informed concerning you are nothing, but that you yourself also walk orderly and keep the law. ²⁵But concerning the Gentiles who believe, we have written and decided that they should observe no such thing, except that they should keep themselves from things offered to idols, from blood, from things strangled, and from sexual immorality."

DEVOTIONAL

In Acts 21, it appeared that Paul would be arrested and put to death in Jerusalem. Death would not in fact come to Paul at that time, but the journey and outlook for Paul was similar to Jesus'—a Jewish plot to accuse the righteous, a handing over of the accused to Gentiles, a prediction of his suffering. Also, as in the Garden of Gethsemane, we see a strong resolution to do the will of God regardless of the consequences. Paul said, "I am ready not only to be bound, but also to die at Jerusalem for the name of the Lord Jesus" (Acts 21:13).

What courage and faithfulness Paul displayed! What is the secret? Faithfulness grows out of our faith. We move away from our sinful inclination to demand our own will, and we take on Jesus' heart. We desire God's will most. This is the resolution that sets us free. The key to Paul's courage is that he had already resolved in his heart that without reservation God's will had to be done in his life.

What about you? The essence of receiving salvation and belonging to God is surrendering your will to Him. It's exchanging gods—Jehovah God instead of you. When we live this, we begin to realize we can trust His will just as we trust His heart.

—Dr. Dwayne Mercer
First Baptist Church, Oviedo, FL

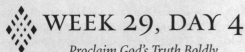

WEEK 29, DAY 4

Proclaim God's Truth Boldly

Acts 21:26–22:5

Arrested in the Temple

Then Paul took the men, and the next day, having been purified with them, entered the temple to announce the expiration of the days of purification, at which time an offering should be made for each one of them.

27Now when the seven days were almost ended, the Jews from Asia, seeing him in the temple, stirred up the whole crowd and laid hands on him, 28crying out, "Men of Israel, help! This is the man who teaches all men everywhere against the people, the law, and this place; and furthermore he also brought Greeks into the temple and has defiled this holy place." 29(For they had previously seen Trophimus the Ephesian with him in the city, whom they supposed that Paul had brought into the temple.)

30And all the city was disturbed; and the people ran together, seized Paul, and dragged him out of the temple; and immediately the doors were shut. 31Now as they were seeking to kill him, news came to the commander of the garrison that all Jerusalem was in an uproar. 32He immediately took soldiers and centurions, and ran down to them. And when they saw the commander and the soldiers, they stopped beating Paul. 33Then the commander came near and took him, and commanded him to be bound with two chains; and he asked who he was and what he had done. 34And some among the multitude cried one thing and some another.

So when he could not ascertain the truth because of the tumult, he commanded him to be taken into the barracks. 35When he reached the stairs, he had to be carried by the soldiers because of the violence of the mob. 36For the multitude of the people followed after, crying out, "Away with him!"

Addressing the Jerusalem Mob

37Then as Paul was about to be led into the barracks, he said to the commander, "May I speak to you?"

He replied, "Can you speak Greek? 38Are you not the Egyptian who some time ago stirred up a rebellion and led the four thousand assassins out into the wilderness?"

39But Paul said, "I am a Jew from Tarsus, in Cilicia, a citizen of no mean city; and I implore you, permit me to speak to the people."

40So when he had given him permission, Paul stood on the stairs and motioned with his hand to the people. And when there was a great silence, he spoke to them in the Hebrew language, saying,

22 "Brethren and fathers, hear my defense before you now." 2And when they heard that he spoke to them in the Hebrew language, they kept all the more silent.

Then he said: 3"I am indeed a Jew, born in Tarsus of Cilicia, but brought up in this city at the feet of Gamaliel, taught according to the strictness of our fathers' law, and was zealous toward God as you all are today. 4I persecuted this Way to the death, binding and delivering into prisons both men and women, 5as also the high priest bears me witness, and all the council of the elders, from whom I also received letters to the brethren, and went to Damascus to bring in chains even those who were there to Jerusalem to be punished."

DEVOTIONAL

As we serve the Lord, we are often misunderstood, both by believers and unbelievers alike. When Paul entered Jerusalem, he did so with Gentile companions whom he had led to faith in Christ. Some assumptions were made, wrong reports spread throughout the town, and then the gossip blossomed into accusations that Paul was bringing Gentiles into the holy place of the temple. It simply was not true. But the damage was already done—the rumor led to an emotional upheaval and the Jews demanding Paul's death!

Paul's heart was in the right place. He was trying to reach the Gentiles with the gospel while not offending the Jews. However, just as in the case of Christ, he was misunderstood in his ministry. How did Paul respond to being attacked? Did he respond in anger or shrink away to pout about getting his feelings hurt? No, Paul's answer to this conflict was to proclaim the gospel boldly! Scripture tells us the hearts and minds of unbelievers can be blinded to the truth (2 Corinthians 4:4), so like Paul, we need to remember that even when the world misunderstands us, our mandate to share the good news remains the same. We need to love people as Jesus loves them.

When you are misunderstood, try not to take the insults personally. Find common ground with others, as Paul did, and show people the love of Christ by sharing Jesus and His Word—even in the face of mistreatment.

—Dr. Dwayne Mercer
First Baptist Church, Oviedo, FL

WEEK 29, DAY 5

God Has Plans for You

Acts 22:6–29

"Now it happened, as I journeyed and came near Damascus at about noon, suddenly a great light from heaven shone around me. 7And I fell to the ground and heard a voice saying to me, 'Saul, Saul, why are you persecuting Me?' 8So I answered, 'Who are You, Lord?' And He said to me, 'I am Jesus of Nazareth, whom you are persecuting.'

9"And those who were with me indeed saw the light and were afraid, but they did not hear the voice of Him who spoke to me. 10So I said, 'What shall I do, Lord?' And the Lord said to me, 'Arise and go into Damascus, and there you will be told all things which are appointed for you to do.' 11And since I could not see for the glory of that light, being led by the hand of those who were with me, I came into Damascus.

12"Then a certain Ananias, a devout man according to the law, having a good testimony with all the Jews who dwelt there, 13came to me; and he stood and said to me, 'Brother Saul, receive your sight.' And at that same hour I looked up at him. 14Then he said, 'The God of our fathers has chosen you that you should know His will, and see the Just One, and hear the voice of His mouth. 15For you will be His witness to all men of what you have seen and heard. 16And now why are you waiting? Arise and be baptized, and wash away your sins, calling on the name of the Lord.'

17"Now it happened, when I returned to Jerusalem and was praying in the temple, that I was in a trance 18and saw Him saying to me, 'Make haste and get out of Jerusalem quickly, for they will not receive your testimony concerning Me.' 19So I said, 'Lord, they know that in every synagogue I imprisoned and beat those who believe on You. 20And when the blood of Your martyr Stephen was shed, I also was standing by consenting to his death, and guarding the clothes of those who were killing him.' 21Then He said to me, 'Depart, for I will send you far from here to the Gentiles.'"

Paul's Roman Citizenship

22And they listened to him until this word, and then they raised their voices and said, "Away with such a fellow from the earth, for he is not fit to live!" 23Then, as they cried out and tore off their clothes and threw dust into the air, 24the commander ordered him to be brought into the barracks, and said that he should be examined under scourging, so that he might know why they shouted so against him. 25And as they bound him with thongs, Paul said to the centurion who stood by, "Is it lawful for you to scourge a man who is a Roman, and uncondemned?"

26When the centurion heard that, he went and told the commander, saying, "Take care what you do, for this man is a Roman."

27Then the commander came and said to him, "Tell me, are you a Roman?"

He said, "Yes."

28The commander answered, "With a large sum I obtained this citizenship."

And Paul said, "But I was born a citizen."

29Then immediately those who were about to examine him withdrew from him; and the commander was also afraid after he found out that he was a Roman, and because he had bound him.

DEVOTIONAL

Jeremiah 29:11 tells us, "I know the thoughts that I think toward you, says the Lord, thoughts of peace and not of evil, to give you a future and a hope." God has a plan for every believer.

God's plan for Paul was that of a pioneer missionary to the Gentiles. Paul revealed his witness of Christ to those who wanted to take his life (Acts 22:6–21). As he shared his dramatic conversion story and God-given mission to spread the gospel, one would expect a happy ending—that his listeners would repent and give their hearts to Christ. However, it was not a happy ending, and although Paul's audience did not believe his message, he was responsible only for delivering the good news. His job was to be a missionary, and he left the results of his seed-sowing up to God.

God has a personal plan for you, just as He did for Paul, and He expects you only to take on the role He's called you to. Your plan looks different from everyone else's because we all have a niche in which we best bring glory to God. He has given us talents, gifts, experiences, and burdens that point the way to His special will for our lives. We need to set aside preconceived ideas and traditions to embrace His plan for us.

Ask God to reveal to you more of His plan for your life. Like Paul, offer yourself to God for His purposes and be willing to be faithful, even in difficult situations.

—Dr. Dwayne Mercer
First Baptist Church, Oviedo, FL

WEEK 29, DAY 6

God Stands by His Own

Acts 22:30–23:22

The Sanhedrin Divided

The next day, because he wanted to know for certain why he was accused by the Jews, he released him from his bonds, and commanded the chief priests and all their council to appear, and brought Paul down and set him before them.

23 Then Paul, looking earnestly at the council, said, "Men and brethren, I have lived in all good conscience before God until this day." 2And the high priest Ananias commanded those who stood by him to strike him on the mouth. 3Then Paul said to him, "God will strike you, you whitewashed wall! For you sit to judge me according to the law, and do you command me to be struck contrary to the law?"

4And those who stood by said, "Do you revile God's high priest?"

5Then Paul said, "I did not know, brethren, that he was the high priest; for it is written, 'You shall not speak evil of a ruler of your people.'"

6But when Paul perceived that one part were Sadducees and the other Pharisees, he cried out in the council, "Men and brethren, I am a Pharisee, the son of a Pharisee; concerning the hope and resurrection of the dead I am being judged!"

7And when he had said this, a dissension arose between the Pharisees and the Sadducees; and the assembly was divided. 8For Sadducees say that there is no resurrection—and no angel or spirit; but the Pharisees confess both. 9Then there arose a loud outcry. And the scribes of the Pharisees' party arose and protested, saying, "We find no evil in this man; but if a spirit or an angel has spoken to him, let us not fight against God."

10Now when there arose a great dissension, the commander, fearing lest Paul might be pulled to pieces by them, commanded the soldiers to go down and take him by force from among them, and bring him into the barracks.

The Plot Against Paul

11But the following night the Lord stood by him and said, "Be of good cheer, Paul; for as you have testified for Me in Jerusalem, so you must also bear witness at Rome."

12And when it was day, some of the Jews banded together and bound themselves under an oath, saying that they would neither eat nor drink till they had killed Paul. 13Now there were more than forty who had formed this conspiracy. 14They came to the chief priests and elders, and said, "We have bound ourselves under a great oath that we will eat nothing until we have killed Paul. 15Now you, therefore, together with the council, suggest to the commander that he be brought down to you tomorrow, as though you were going to make further inquiries concerning him; but we are ready to kill him before he comes near."

16So when Paul's sister's son heard of their ambush, he went and entered the barracks and told Paul. 17Then Paul called one of the centurions to him and said, "Take this young man to the commander, for he has something to tell him." 18So he took him and brought him to the commander and said, "Paul the prisoner called me to him and asked me to bring this young man to you. He has something to say to you."

19Then the commander took him by the hand, went aside, and asked privately, "What is it that you have to tell me?"

20And he said, "The Jews have agreed to ask that you bring Paul down to the council tomorrow, as though they were going to inquire more fully about him. 21But do not yield to them, for more than forty of them lie in wait for him, men who have bound themselves by an oath that they will neither eat nor drink till they have killed him; and now they are ready, waiting for the promise from you."

22So the commander let the young man depart, and commanded him, "Tell no one that you have revealed these things to me."

DEVOTIONAL

In his quest to discourage and even destroy the people of God, Satan often uses people. Ironically, most of those involved in this endeavor believe they are doing the Lord's work. Such was the case of the forty who wanted to take Paul's life. God, however, had other plans for Paul's continued ministry. God came to Paul's rescue and protected his life until his work was finished.

God stands by you. As long as you are in His will, nothing can happen to you unless God wills it to happen. You can be confident that "He who has begun a good work in you will complete it until the day of Jesus Christ" (Philippians 1:6). Get in God's will. It's the safest place on earth.

—Dr. Dwayne Mercer
First Baptist Church, Oviedo, FL

WEEK 29, DAY 7

Who in your life has offended you? Was it a mistake on their part, a consequence of their selfishness, or a personal attack? Think through the steps you need to take to forgive them.

_____

_____

_____

_____

_____

_____

_____

_____

_____

_____

Have you "gotten over" your salvation? What do you need to do to bring yourself back to the humility of the cross (Revelation 2:2–5)?

_____

_____

_____

_____

_____

_____

_____

_____

WEEK 30, DAY 1

Godly Love Leads to Doing Right

Acts 23:23–24:16

Sent to Felix

And he called for two centurions, saying, "Prepare two hundred soldiers, seventy horsemen, and two hundred spearmen to go to Caesarea at the third hour of the night; 24and provide mounts to set Paul on, and bring him safely to Felix the governor." 25He wrote a letter in the following manner:

26 Claudius Lysias,

To the most excellent governor Felix:

Greetings.

27 This man was seized by the Jews and was about to be killed by them. Coming with the troops I rescued him, having learned that he was a Roman. 28And when I wanted to know the reason they accused him, I brought him before their council. 29I found out that he was accused concerning questions of their law, but had nothing charged against him deserving of death or chains. 30And when it was told me that the Jews lay in wait for the man, I sent him immediately to you, and also commanded his accusers to state before you the charges against him.

Farewell.

31Then the soldiers, as they were commanded, took Paul and brought him by night to Antipatris. 32The next day they left the horsemen to go on with him, and returned to the barracks. 33When they came to Caesarea and had delivered the letter to the governor, they also presented Paul to him. 34And when the governor had read it, he asked what province he was from. And when he understood that he was from Cilicia, 35he said, "I will hear you when your accusers also have come." And he commanded him to be kept in Herod's Praetorium.

Accused of Sedition

24 Now after five days Ananias the high priest came down with the elders and a certain orator named Tertullus. These gave evidence to the governor against Paul. 2And when he was called upon, Tertullus began his accusation, saying: "Seeing that through you we enjoy great peace, and prosperity is being brought to this nation by your foresight, 3we accept it always and in all places, most noble Felix, with all thankfulness. 4Nevertheless, not to be tedious to you any further, I beg you to hear, by your courtesy, a few words from us. 5For we have found this man a plague, a creator of dissension among all the Jews throughout the world, and a ringleader of the sect of the Nazarenes. 6He even tried to profane the temple, and we seized him, and wanted to judge him according to our law. 7But the commander Lysias came by and with great violence took him out of our hands, 8commanding his accusers to come to you. By examining him yourself you may ascertain all these things of which we accuse him." 9And the Jews also assented, maintaining that these things were so.

The Defense Before Felix

10Then Paul, after the governor had nodded to him to speak, answered: "Inasmuch as I know that you have been for many years a judge of this nation, I do the more cheerfully answer for myself, 11because you may ascertain that it is no more than twelve days since I went up to Jerusalem to worship. 12And they neither found me in the temple disputing with anyone nor inciting the crowd, either in the synagogues or in the city. 13Nor can they prove the things of which they now accuse me. 14But this I confess to you, that according to the Way which they call a sect, so I worship the God of my fathers, believing all things which are written in the Law and in the Prophets. 15I have hope in God, which they themselves also accept, that there will be a resurrection of the dead, both of the just and the unjust. 16This being so, I myself always strive to have a conscience without offense toward God and men."

DEVOTIONAL

*P*aul said he always strived "to have a conscience without offense toward God and men" (Acts 24:16). His resolve to obey God and reach people for Him was fueled by passionate love and a deep desire to see others come to know Jesus and His mighty love for them. Paul understood that action fueled by godly love led him to do what was right in God's eyes.

Jesus said to love others as you love yourself (Matthew 22:39). Could your motives withstand the "love for others" test? As you receive more of God's love and allow Him to fill your heart with His love, they will. Throughout your day, check yourself: are your actions fueled by godly love?

—Tim DeTellis
New Missions, Orlando, FL

WEEK 30, DAY 2

The Righteous Need Not Fear God's Judgment

Acts 24:17–25:12

"Now after many years I came to bring alms and offerings to my nation, [18]in the midst of which some Jews from Asia found me purified in the temple, neither with a mob nor with tumult. [19]They ought to have been here before you to object if they had anything against me. [20]Or else let those who are here themselves say if they found any wrongdoing in me while I stood before the council, [21]unless it is for this one statement which I cried out, standing among them, 'Concerning the resurrection of the dead I am being judged by you this day.'"

Felix Procrastinates

[22]But when Felix heard these things, having more accurate knowledge of the Way, he adjourned the proceedings and said, "When Lysias the commander comes down, I will make a decision on your case." [23]So he commanded the centurion to keep Paul and to let him have liberty, and told him not to forbid any of his friends to provide for or visit him.

[24]And after some days, when Felix came with his wife Drusilla, who was Jewish, he sent for Paul and heard him concerning the faith in Christ. [25]Now as he reasoned about righteousness, self-control, and the judgment to come, Felix was afraid and answered, "Go away for now; when I have a convenient time I will call for you." [26]Meanwhile he also hoped that money would be given him by Paul, that he might release him. Therefore he sent for him more often and conversed with him.

[27]But after two years Porcius Festus succeeded Felix; and Felix, wanting to do the Jews a favor, left Paul bound.

Paul Appeals to Caesar

25 Now when Festus had come to the province, after three days he went up from Caesarea to Jerusalem. [2]Then the high priest and the chief men of the Jews informed him against Paul; and they petitioned him, [3]asking a favor against him, that he would summon him to Jerusalem—while they lay in ambush along the road to kill him. [4]But Festus answered that Paul should be kept at Caesarea, and that he himself was going there shortly. [5]"Therefore," he said, "let those who have authority among you go down with me and accuse this man, to see if there is any fault in him."

[6]And when he had remained among them more than ten days, he went down to Caesarea. And the next day, sitting on the judgment seat, he commanded Paul to be brought. [7]When he had come, the Jews who had come down from Jerusalem stood about and laid many serious complaints against Paul, which they could not prove, [8]while he answered for himself, "Neither against the law of the Jews, nor against the temple, nor against Caesar have I offended in anything at all."

[9]But Festus, wanting to do the Jews a favor, answered Paul and said, "Are you willing to go up to Jerusalem and there be judged before me concerning these things?"

[10]So Paul said, "I stand at Caesar's judgment seat, where I ought to be judged. To the Jews I have done no wrong, as you very well know. [11]For if I am an offender, or have committed anything deserving of death, I do not object to dying; but if there is nothing in these things of which these men accuse me, no one can deliver me to them. I appeal to Caesar."

[12]Then Festus, when he had conferred with the council, answered, "You have appealed to Caesar? To Caesar you shall go!"

DEVOTIONAL

Paul knew he could stand before God and men with a clear conscience. He was unafraid of both God's and Caesar's judgment (Acts 25:10–11). Paul had long been faithful in loving God and loving his enemies, and he knew God's abiding love stood as a shield for him against the weapons of his enemies.

Scripture declares the righteous will have boldness in the day of judgment because "love has been perfected" among them and "perfect love casts out fear" (1 John 4:17–18). This truth is what emboldened Paul as he stood before the rulers of the world and proclaimed the gospel of Jesus Christ. Fearlessly, Paul stood his ground, secure in God's perfect love.

The unrighteous, however, are not in the same position. They have never embraced God's perfect love, and therefore do not dwell in His presence under the shadow of His protective wings. Their fear of judgment arises out of their sense of insecurity and a lack of confidence in their future. Intercede for them today, asking God to draw them unto Himself in love. And thank God for His protecting love by following Paul's example of faithfulness and trust in God.

—Tim DeTellis
New Missions, Orlando, FL

WEEK 30, DAY 3

The Testimony of a Blameless Life

Acts 25:13–26:8

Paul Before Agrippa

A nd after some days King Agrippa and Bernice came to Caesarea to greet Festus. 14When they had been there many days, Festus laid Paul's case before the king, saying: "There is a certain man left a prisoner by Felix, 15about whom the chief priests and the elders of the Jews informed me, when I was in Jerusalem, asking for a judgment against him. 16To them I answered, 'It is not the custom of the Romans to deliver any man to destruction before the accused meets the accusers face to face, and has opportunity to answer for himself concerning the charge against him.' 17Therefore when they had come together, without any delay, the next day I sat on the judgment seat and commanded the man to be brought in. 18When the accusers stood up, they brought no accusation against him of such things as I supposed, 19but had some questions against him about their own religion and about a certain Jesus, who had died, whom Paul affirmed to be alive. 20And because I was uncertain of such questions, I asked whether he was willing to go to Jerusalem and there be judged concerning these matters. 21But when Paul appealed to be reserved for the decision of Augustus, I commanded him to be kept till I could send him to Caesar."

22Then Agrippa said to Festus, "I also would like to hear the man myself."

"Tomorrow," he said, "you shall hear him."

23So the next day, when Agrippa and Bernice had come with great pomp, and had entered the auditorium with the commanders and the prominent men of the city, at Festus' command Paul was brought in. 24And Festus said: "King Agrippa and all the men who are here present with us, you see this man about whom the whole assembly of the Jews petitioned me, both at Jerusalem and here, crying out that he was not fit to live any longer. 25But when I found that he had committed nothing deserving of death, and that he himself had appealed to Augustus, I decided to send him. 26I have nothing certain to write to my lord concerning him. Therefore I have brought him out before you, and especially before you, King Agrippa, so that after the examination has taken place I may have something to write. 27For it seems to me unreasonable to send a prisoner and not to specify the charges against him."

Paul's Early Life

26 Then Agrippa said to Paul, "You are permitted to speak for yourself."

So Paul stretched out his hand and answered for himself: 2"I think myself happy, King Agrippa, because today I shall answer for myself before you concerning all the things of which I am accused by the Jews, 3especially because you are expert in all customs and questions which have to do with the Jews. Therefore I beg you to hear me patiently.

4"My manner of life from my youth, which was spent from the beginning among my own nation at Jerusalem, all the Jews know. 5They knew me from the first, if they were willing to testify, that according to the strictest sect of our religion I lived a Pharisee. 6And now I stand and am judged for the hope of the promise made by God to our fathers. 7To this promise our twelve tribes, earnestly serving God night and day, hope to attain. For this hope's sake, King Agrippa, I am accused by the Jews. 8Why should it be thought incredible by you that God raises the dead?"

DEVOTIONAL

I n Acts 26:4–7, we read the beginning of Paul's testimony to King Agrippa. Throughout his early years in life, back when his name was still Saul, Paul devoted himself to what he thought was God's plan for him—living as a strict Pharisee—until one day when he was traveling on the road to Damascus. That encounter with the risen Lord Jesus turned Saul's world upside down and placed him on a path that was completely different from anything he had ever dreamed it would be.

Like Paul, you have the opportunity to become a witness of God's love. As you take hold of Him and He renews you from the inside out, you will become a living testimony of a blameless life. A clear conscience, a pure heart, and a willing spirit are hallmarks of a blameless life. You will be able to grow and mature into this kind of living as you surrender your heart to God and lean into the embrace of His love.

We cannot remain the same after an encounter with the Holy One. Seek Him daily and allow Him to mold you into the image of Christ. Meditate on things that are praiseworthy and of good report (Philippians 4:8). Focus on Jesus Christ and on His purposes and plans. When you do, you will be a powerful witness for Christ and your life will rise above reproach.

—Tim DeTellis
New Missions, Orlando, FL

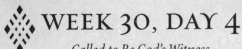

WEEK 30, DAY 4

Called to Be God's Witness

Acts 26:9–32

"Indeed, I myself thought I must do many things contrary to the name of Jesus of Nazareth. ¹⁰This I also did in Jerusalem, and many of the saints I shut up in prison, having received authority from the chief priests; and when they were put to death, I cast my vote against them. ¹¹And I punished them often in every synagogue and compelled them to blaspheme; and being exceedingly enraged against them, I persecuted them even to foreign cities.

Paul Recounts His Conversion

¹²"While thus occupied, as I journeyed to Damascus with authority and commission from the chief priests, ¹³at midday, O king, along the road I saw a light from heaven, brighter than the sun, shining around me and those who journeyed with me. ¹⁴And when we all had fallen to the ground, I heard a voice speaking to me and saying in the Hebrew language, 'Saul, Saul, why are you persecuting Me? It is hard for you to kick against the goads.' ¹⁵So I said, 'Who are You, Lord?' And He said, 'I am Jesus, whom you are persecuting. ¹⁶But rise and stand on your feet; for I have appeared to you for this purpose, to make you a minister and a witness both of the things which you have seen and of the things which I will yet reveal to you. ¹⁷I will deliver you from the Jewish people, as well as from the Gentiles, to whom I now send you, ¹⁸to open their eyes, in order to turn them from darkness to light, and from the power of Satan to God, that they may receive forgiveness of sins and an inheritance among those who are sanctified by faith in Me.'

Paul's Post-Conversion Life

¹⁹"Therefore, King Agrippa, I was not disobedient to the heavenly vision, ²⁰but declared first to those in Damascus and in Jerusalem, and throughout all the region of Judea, and then to the Gentiles, that they should repent, turn to God, and do works befitting repentance. ²¹For these reasons the Jews seized me in the temple and tried to kill me. ²²Therefore, having obtained help from God, to this day I stand, witnessing both to small and great, saying no other things than those which the prophets and Moses said would come— ²³that the Christ would suffer, that He would be the first to rise from the dead, and would proclaim light to the Jewish people and to the Gentiles."

Agrippa Parries Paul's Challenge

²⁴Now as he thus made his defense, Festus said with a loud voice, "Paul, you are beside yourself! Much learning is driving you mad!"

²⁵But he said, "I am not mad, most noble Festus, but speak the words of truth and reason. ²⁶For the king, before whom I also speak freely, knows these things; for I am convinced that none of these things escapes his attention, since this thing was not done in a corner. ²⁷King Agrippa, do you believe the prophets? I know that you do believe."

²⁸Then Agrippa said to Paul, "You almost persuade me to become a Christian."

²⁹And Paul said, "I would to God that not only you, but also all who hear me today, might become both almost and altogether such as I am, except for these chains."

³⁰When he had said these things, the king stood up, as well as the governor and Bernice and those who sat with them; ³¹and when they had gone aside, they talked among themselves, saying, "This man is doing nothing deserving of death or chains."

³²Then Agrippa said to Festus, "This man might have been set free if he had not appealed to Caesar."

DEVOTIONAL

While he was on his way to Damascus to persecute Christians, Saul learned of God's plan for his life through an encounter with the risen Christ. As a Pharisee, Saul thought he had already figured out what his role was in Israel—a defender of the Torah and an executor of God's judgment. But that was not to be. God even changed Saul's name to prove it! Do you have your life figured out? If so, you may be ripe for a "Damascus Road" experience of your own!

When God calls and you answer, new insights, visions, and experiences will become more commonplace. God's call will always take you beyond your comfort zone and into the vast unexplored reaches of His grace and mercy. The truth is you are called to be God's witness, just like Paul. Your response to God's call may look different than Paul's, but it is just as real. You can reach people others cannot, go places others cannot, and do things others cannot.

Hear God calling to you today. Ask Him to show you how you can reach people within your sphere of influence for Him. Wherever you are, be a witness for Him!

—Tim DeTellis
New Missions, Orlando, FL

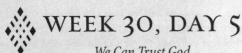

WEEK 30, DAY 5

We Can Trust God
to Keep His Promises

Acts 27:1–26

The Voyage to Rome Begins

27 And when it was decided that we should sail to Italy, they delivered Paul and some other prisoners to one named Julius, a centurion of the Augustan Regiment. ²So, entering a ship of Adramyttium, we put to sea, meaning to sail along the coasts of Asia. Aristarchus, a Macedonian of Thessalonica, was with us. ³And the next day we landed at Sidon. And Julius treated Paul kindly and gave him liberty to go to his friends and receive care. ⁴When we had put to sea from there, we sailed under the shelter of Cyprus, because the winds were contrary. ⁵And when we had sailed over the sea which is off Cilicia and Pamphylia, we came to Myra, a city of Lycia. ⁶There the centurion found an Alexandrian ship sailing to Italy, and he put us on board.

⁷When we had sailed slowly many days, and arrived with difficulty off Cnidus, the wind not permitting us to proceed, we sailed under the shelter of Crete off Salmone. ⁸Passing it with difficulty, we came to a place called Fair Havens, near the city of Lasea.

Paul's Warning Ignored

⁹Now when much time had been spent, and sailing was now dangerous because the Fast was already over, Paul advised them, ¹⁰saying, "Men, I perceive that this voyage will end with disaster and much loss, not only of the cargo and ship, but also our lives." ¹¹Nevertheless the centurion was more persuaded by the helmsman and the owner of the ship than by the things spoken by Paul. ¹²And because the harbor was not suitable to winter in, the majority advised to set sail from there also, if by any means they could reach Phoenix, a harbor of Crete opening toward the southwest and northwest, and winter there.

In the Tempest

¹³When the south wind blew softly, supposing that they had obtained their desire, putting out to sea, they sailed close by Crete. ¹⁴But not long after, a tempestuous head wind arose, called Euroclydon. ¹⁵So when the ship was caught, and could not head into the wind, we let her drive. ¹⁶And running under the shelter of an island called Clauda, we secured the skiff with difficulty. ¹⁷When they had taken it on board, they used cables to undergird the ship; and fearing lest they should run aground on the Syrtis Sands, they struck sail and so were driven. ¹⁸And because we were exceedingly tempest-tossed, the next day they lightened the ship. ¹⁹On the third day we threw the ship's tackle overboard with our own hands. ²⁰Now when neither sun nor stars appeared for many days, and no small tempest beat on us, all hope that we would be saved was finally given up.

²¹But after long abstinence from food, then Paul stood in the midst of them and said, "Men, you should have listened to me, and not have sailed from Crete and incurred this disaster and loss. ²²And now I urge you to take heart, for there will be no loss of life among you, but only of the ship. ²³For there stood by me this night an angel of the God to whom I belong and whom I serve, ²⁴saying, 'Do not be afraid, Paul; you must be brought before Caesar; and indeed God has granted you all those who sail with you.' ²⁵Therefore take heart, men, for I believe God that it will be just as it was told me. ²⁶However, we must run aground on a certain island."

DEVOTIONAL

*T*he lives of all of the passengers on the ship in Acts 27 seemed to be in great danger. In such a severe storm, the ship's destruction seemed inevitable. Paul, however, knew something the others did not: everyone would remain safe. An angel of God had told him the night before that although the ship would run aground, there would be no loss of life.

God's Word is filled with promises. Whether you're looking at His words about salvation and eternal life or His assurance that all your needs will be met by His riches in glory, you can see proof that God is mindful of you (John 3:16–17; Philippians 4:19). The key is to believe that what God says is true! Most Christians believe God will provide for others in need, but question whether He will provide for them when they are in need.

Paul had no doubts about what the angel said. He trusted God's promise of safety. Will you do the same with the promises God has made to you? It is time to step up and believe God's Word concerning you. It is time to realize He knows your needs and He cares for you as much as He cares for others. Now is the time to trust God and His promises.

—Tim DeTellis
New Missions, Orlando, FL

WEEK 30, DAY 6

God Uses Us to Accomplish His Purposes

Acts 27:27–28:10

Now when the fourteenth night had come, as we were driven up and down in the Adriatic Sea, about midnight the sailors sensed that they were drawing near some land. ²⁸And they took soundings and found it to be twenty fathoms; and when they had gone a little farther, they took soundings again and found it to be fifteen fathoms. ²⁹Then, fearing lest we should run aground on the rocks, they dropped four anchors from the stern, and prayed for day to come. ³⁰And as the sailors were seeking to escape from the ship, when they had let down the skiff into the sea, under pretense of putting out anchors from the prow, ³¹Paul said to the centurion and the soldiers, "Unless these men stay in the ship, you cannot be saved." ³²Then the soldiers cut away the ropes of the skiff and let it fall off.

³³And as day was about to dawn, Paul implored them all to take food, saying, "Today is the fourteenth day you have waited and continued without food, and eaten nothing. ³⁴Therefore I urge you to take nourishment, for this is for your survival, since not a hair will fall from the head of any of you." ³⁵And when he had said these things, he took bread and gave thanks to God in the presence of them all; and when he had broken it he began to eat. ³⁶Then they were all encouraged, and also took food themselves. ³⁷And in all we were two hundred and seventy-six persons on the ship. ³⁸So when they had eaten enough, they lightened the ship and threw out the wheat into the sea.

Shipwrecked on Malta

³⁹When it was day, they did not recognize the land; but they observed a bay with a beach, onto which they planned to run the ship if possible. ⁴⁰And they let go the anchors and left them in the sea, meanwhile loosing the rudder ropes; and they hoisted the mainsail to the wind and made for shore. ⁴¹But striking a place where two seas met, they ran the ship aground; and the prow stuck fast and remained immovable, but the stern was being broken up by the violence of the waves.

⁴²And the soldiers' plan was to kill the prisoners, lest any of them should swim away and escape. ⁴³But the centurion, wanting to save Paul, kept them from their purpose, and commanded that those who could swim should jump overboard first and get to land, ⁴⁴and the rest, some on boards and some on parts of the ship. And so it was that they all escaped safely to land.

Paul's Ministry on Malta

28 Now when they had escaped, they then found out that the island was called Malta. ²And the natives showed us unusual kindness; for they kindled a fire and made us all welcome, because of the rain that was falling and because of the cold. ³But when Paul had gathered a bundle of sticks and laid them on the fire, a viper came out because of the heat, and fastened on his hand. ⁴So when the natives saw the creature hanging from his hand, they said to one another, "No doubt this man is a murderer, whom, though he has escaped the sea, yet justice does not allow to live." ⁵But he shook off the creature into the fire and suffered no harm. ⁶However, they were expecting that he would swell up or suddenly fall down dead. But after they had looked for a long time and saw no harm come to him, they changed their minds and said that he was a god.

⁷In that region there was an estate of the leading citizen of the island, whose name was Publius, who received us and entertained us courteously for three days. ⁸And it happened that the father of Publius lay sick of a fever and dysentery. Paul went in to him and prayed, and he laid his hands on him and healed him. ⁹So when this was done, the rest of those on the island who had diseases also came and were healed. ¹⁰They also honored us in many ways; and when we departed, they provided such things as were necessary.

DEVOTIONAL

God's purposes are greater than we can imagine, yet He chooses to work in and through us to accomplish them. As we participate with Him, amazing things begin to happen around us as He brings to pass that which He desires.

God has saved you "for such a time as this" (Esther 4:14). He has gifted you especially for His work at this point in history. Your perspective on life is unique and significant, and He wants to use you to carry out His will at this hour.

Will you allow God to work through you? His promises are sure, His faithfulness is unquestionable, and His love is undeniable. You can be a historymaker as you partner with God in this great adventure. Submit yourself to His purposes today.

—Tim DeTellis
New Missions, Orlando, FL

WEEK 30, DAY 7

How does God's love move through you to reach others?

_____
_____
_____
_____
_____
_____
_____
_____
_____
_____
_____
_____
_____
_____
_____

Will you become an instrument in God's hand to accomplish His purposes at this hour?

_____
_____
_____
_____
_____
_____
_____
_____
_____
_____
_____
_____

WEEK 31, DAY 1

Share God's Story with Others

Acts 28:11–31

Arrival at Rome

After three months we sailed in an Alexandrian ship whose figurehead was the Twin Brothers, which had wintered at the island. 12And landing at Syracuse, we stayed three days. 13From there we circled round and reached Rhegium. And after one day the south wind blew; and the next day we came to Puteoli, 14where we found brethren, and were invited to stay with them seven days. And so we went toward Rome. 15And from there, when the brethren heard about us, they came to meet us as far as Appii Forum and Three Inns. When Paul saw them, he thanked God and took courage.

16Now when we came to Rome, the centurion delivered the prisoners to the captain of the guard; but Paul was permitted to dwell by himself with the soldier who guarded him.

Paul's Ministry at Rome

17And it came to pass after three days that Paul called the leaders of the Jews together. So when they had come together, he said to them: "Men and brethren, though I have done nothing against our people or the customs of our fathers, yet I was delivered as a prisoner from Jerusalem into the hands of the Romans, 18who, when they had examined me, wanted to let me go, because there was no cause for putting me to death. 19But when the Jews spoke against it, I was compelled to appeal to Caesar, not that I had anything of which to accuse my nation. 20For this reason therefore I have called for you, to see you and speak with you, because for the hope of Israel I am bound with this chain."

21Then they said to him, "We neither received letters from Judea concerning you, nor have any of the brethren who came reported or spoken any evil of you. 22But we desire to hear from you what you think; for concerning this sect, we know that it is spoken against everywhere."

23So when they had appointed him a day, many came to him at his lodging, to whom he explained and solemnly testified of the kingdom of God, persuading them concerning Jesus from both the Law of Moses and the Prophets, from morning till evening. 24And some were persuaded by the things which were spoken, and some disbelieved. 25So when they did not agree among themselves, they departed after Paul had said one word: "The Holy Spirit spoke rightly through Isaiah the prophet to our fathers, 26saying,

'Go to this people and say:
"Hearing you will hear, and shall not understand;
And seeing you will see, and not perceive;
27 For the hearts of this people have grown dull.
Their ears are hard of hearing,
And their eyes they have closed,
Lest they should see with their eyes and hear with their ears,
Lest they should understand with their hearts and turn,
So that I should heal them."'

28"Therefore let it be known to you that the salvation of God has been sent to the Gentiles, and they will hear it!" 29And when he had said these words, the Jews departed and had a great dispute among themselves.

30Then Paul dwelt two whole years in his own rented house, and received all who came to him, 31preaching the kingdom of God and teaching the things which concern the Lord Jesus Christ with all confidence, no one forbidding him.

DEVOTIONAL

As Christians, we often spend much of our time going out and looking for people to share the gospel with. This is indeed a good thing, but we need to remain sensitive to the Spirit of God and to the individuals He places right in front of us for that very purpose. We might be walking right past the people God has brought to us while we're busy looking for someone to share with. Have you ever been guilty of missing a blessing that is right in front of you?

Just as Paul shared Christ with everyone God brought into his life (Acts 28:30–31), be sensitive to the people God places in your life today. Keep looking for opportunities to share, but don't miss the moments God's already ordained that will unfold right before your eyes. Those God moments may sneak up on you when you least expect them!

God has a story He wants you to share with others. The destination of that story has no limits and is not for your choosing. Share it with someone who is in your path today.

—Scott Cannon
Pump Springs Baptist, Harrogate, TN

WEEK 31, DAY 2

Give Glory to God

Romans 1:1–27

Greeting

1 Paul, a bondservant of Jesus Christ, called to be an apostle, separated to the gospel of God ²which He promised before through His prophets in the Holy Scriptures, ³concerning His Son Jesus Christ our Lord, who was born of the seed of David according to the flesh, ⁴and declared to be the Son of God with power according to the Spirit of holiness, by the resurrection from the dead. ⁵Through Him we have received grace and apostleship for obedience to the faith among all nations for His name, ⁶among whom you also are the called of Jesus Christ;

⁷To all who are in Rome, beloved of God, called to be saints:

Grace to you and peace from God our Father and the Lord Jesus Christ.

Desire to Visit Rome

⁸First, I thank my God through Jesus Christ for you all, that your faith is spoken of throughout the whole world. ⁹For God is my witness, whom I serve with my spirit in the gospel of His Son, that without ceasing I make mention of you always in my prayers, ¹⁰making request if, by some means, now at last I may find a way in the will of God to come to you. ¹¹For I long to see you, that I may impart to you some spiritual gift, so that you may be established— ¹²that is, that I may be encouraged together with you by the mutual faith both of you and me.

¹³Now I do not want you to be unaware, brethren, that I often planned to come to you (but was hindered until now), that I might have some fruit among you also, just as among the other Gentiles. ¹⁴I am a debtor both to Greeks and to barbarians, both to wise and to unwise. ¹⁵So, as much as is in me, I am ready to preach the gospel to you who are in Rome also.

The Just Live by Faith

¹⁶For I am not ashamed of the gospel of Christ, for it is the power of God to salvation for everyone who believes, for the Jew first and also for the Greek. ¹⁷For in it the righteousness of God is revealed from faith to faith; as it is written, "The just shall live by faith."

God's Wrath on Unrighteousness

¹⁸For the wrath of God is revealed from heaven against all ungodliness and unrighteousness of men, who suppress the truth in unrighteousness, ¹⁹because what may be known of God is manifest in them, for God has shown it to them. ²⁰For since the creation of the world His invisible attributes are clearly seen, being understood by the things that are made, even His eternal power and Godhead, so that they are without excuse, ²¹because, although they knew God, they did not glorify Him as God, nor were thankful, but became futile in their thoughts, and their foolish hearts were darkened. ²²Professing to be wise, they became fools, ²³and changed the glory of the incorruptible God into an image made like corruptible man—and birds and four-footed animals and creeping things.

²⁴Therefore God also gave them up to uncleanness, in the lusts of their hearts, to dishonor their bodies among themselves, ²⁵who exchanged the truth of God for the lie, and worshiped and served the creature rather than the Creator, who is blessed forever. Amen.

²⁶For this reason God gave them up to vile passions. For even their women exchanged the natural use for what is against nature. ²⁷Likewise also the men, leaving the natural use of the woman, burned in their lust for one another, men with men committing what is shameful, and receiving in themselves the penalty of their error which was due.

DEVOTIONAL

I t's been said that darkness is the absence of light. If God's people would let their light shine brighter in this world, there would be less darkness to prevail. After all, Jesus told His followers, "You are the light of the world. . . . Let your light so shine before men, that they may see your good works and glorify your Father in heaven" (Matthew 5:14, 16). However, many Christians seem ashamed to take a stand and tell others about God's beauty and majesty.

All of creation was designed to bring God glory (Romans 1:20). We must let the light of Christ shine through us, as it does throughout all creation. There has never been a greater need for the children of God to stand up with the rest of creation and proclaim the good news.

Don't be ashamed to live for Christ today. Stand tall! Be bold! Remember that you were created to be an expression of God to a world that He loves, a world that desperately needs Him.

—Scott Cannon
Pump Springs Baptist, Harrogate, TN

WEEK 31, DAY 3

God Holds Us Accountable

Romans 1:28–2:16

And even as they did not like to retain God in their knowledge, God gave them over to a debased mind, to do those things which are not fitting; 29being filled with all unrighteousness, sexual immorality, wickedness, covetousness, maliciousness; full of envy, murder, strife, deceit, evil-mindedness; they are whisperers, 30backbiters, haters of God, violent, proud, boasters, inventors of evil things, disobedient to parents, 31undiscerning, untrustworthy, unloving, unforgiving, unmerciful; 32who, knowing the righteous judgment of God, that those who practice such things are deserving of death, not only do the same but also approve of those who practice them.

God's Righteous Judgment

2 Therefore you are inexcusable, O man, whoever you are who judge, for in whatever you judge another you condemn yourself; for you who judge practice the same things. 2But we know that the judgment of God is according to truth against those who practice such things. 3And do you think this, O man, you who judge those practicing such things, and doing the same, that you will escape the judgment of God? 4Or do you despise the riches of His goodness, forbearance, and longsuffering, not knowing that the goodness of God leads you to repentance? 5But in accordance with your hardness and your impenitent heart you are treasuring up for yourself wrath in the day of wrath and revelation of the righteous judgment of God, 6who "will render to each one according to his deeds": 7eternal life to those who by patient continuance in doing good seek for glory, honor, and immortality; 8but to those who are self-seeking and do not obey the truth, but obey unrighteousness—indignation and wrath, 9tribulation and anguish, on every soul of man who does evil, of the Jew first and also of the Greek; 10but glory, honor, and peace to everyone who works what is good, to the Jew first and also to the Greek. 11For there is no partiality with God.

12For as many as have sinned without law will also perish without law, and as many as have sinned in the law will be judged by the law 13(for not the hearers of the law are just in the sight of God, but the doers of the law will be justified; 14for when Gentiles, who do not have the law, by nature do the things in the law, these, although not having the law, are a law to themselves, 15who show the work of the law written in their hearts, their conscience also bearing witness, and between themselves their thoughts accusing or else excusing them) 16in the day when God will judge the secrets of men by Jesus Christ, according to my gospel.

DEVOTIONAL

We are quick to condemn others for grievous acts of unrighteousness, even while we have our own sinful practices and strongholds. Jesus exposed this human tendency when He asked, "Why do you look at the speck in your brother's eye, but do not consider the plank in your own eye?" (Matthew 7:3).

Each of us is accountable to God for our lives—public and private. God knows our secrets. Sin can be fun for a moment, but it never goes unpunished. It is foolish to take sin lightly (Proverbs 14:9). And as Christians, we have no excuse for sin in our lives—we know better!

If you're resisting repentance, consider the words of Galatians 6:7: "Do not be deceived, God is not mocked; for whatever a man sows, that he will also reap." Your sin will be found out. God already knows about it, and He's waiting for you to agree with Him about what He already knows. It's better for us to deal with our sins with God in private now, confessing them and receiving forgiveness, than to wait until God confronts us as Judge. But either way, God will hold us responsible for our sins.

What sin do you need to repent of today? Maybe you need to ask God to give you awareness of your sin. Whatever sin God reveals to you, admit it to Him. Allow Him to cleanse you. David gave us a model of a prayer of repentance in Psalm 51. He said, "I acknowledge my transgressions . . . against You, You only, have I sinned, and done this evil in Your sight" (verses 3–4). He asked God to have mercy on him according to His lovingkindness, to blot out his sins, and to wash him thoroughly.

It doesn't matter what your sins are—God is merciful and will bless your obedience and repentance. You can trust God to be who He says He is. He is waiting on you to come to Him so He can start the process of forgiveness, healing, and redirection!

—Scott Cannon
Pump Springs Baptist, Harrogate, TN

WEEK 31, DAY 4

God Wants Us to Change Our Hearts and Lives

Romans 2:17–3:18

The Jews Guilty as the Gentiles

Indeed you are called a Jew, and rest on the law, and make your boast in God, 18and know His will, and approve the things that are excellent, being instructed out of the law, 19and are confident that you yourself are a guide to the blind, a light to those who are in darkness, 20an instructor of the foolish, a teacher of babes, having the form of knowledge and truth in the law. 21You, therefore, who teach another, do you not teach yourself? You who preach that a man should not steal, do you steal? 22You who say, "Do not commit adultery," do you commit adultery? You who abhor idols, do you rob temples? 23You who make your boast in the law, do you dishonor God through breaking the law? 24For "the name of God is blasphemed among the Gentiles because of you," as it is written.

Circumcision of No Avail

25For circumcision is indeed profitable if you keep the law; but if you are a breaker of the law, your circumcision has become uncircumcision. 26Therefore, if an uncircumcised man keeps the righteous requirements of the law, will not his uncircumcision be counted as circumcision? 27And will not the physically uncircumcised, if he fulfills the law, judge you who, even with your written code and circumcision, are a transgressor of the law? 28For he is not a Jew who is one outwardly, nor is circumcision that which is outward in the flesh; 29but he is a Jew who is one inwardly; and circumcision is that of the heart, in the Spirit, not in the letter; whose praise is not from men but from God.

God's Judgment Defended

3 What advantage then has the Jew, or what is the profit of circumcision? 2Much in every way! Chiefly because to them were committed the oracles of God. 3For what if some did not believe? Will their unbelief make the faithfulness of God without effect? 4Certainly not! Indeed, let God be true but every man a liar. As it is written:

"That You may be justified in Your words,
And may overcome when You are judged."

5But if our unrighteousness demonstrates the righteousness of God, what shall we say? Is God unjust who inflicts wrath? (I speak as a man.) 6Certainly not! For then how will God judge the world?

7For if the truth of God has increased through my lie to His glory, why am I also still judged as a sinner? 8And why not say, "Let us do evil that good may come"?—as we are slanderously reported and as some affirm that we say. Their condemnation is just.

All Have Sinned

9What then? Are we better than they? Not at all. For we have previously charged both Jews and Greeks that they are all under sin.

10As it is written:

"There is none righteous, no, not one;
11 There is none who understands;
There is none who seeks after God.
12 They have all turned aside;
They have together become unprofitable;
There is none who does good, no, not one."
13 "Their throat is an open tomb;
With their tongues they have practiced deceit";
"The poison of asps is under their lips";
14 "Whose mouth is full of cursing and bitterness."
15 "Their feet are swift to shed blood;
16 Destruction and misery are in their ways;
17 And the way of peace they have not known."
18 "There is no fear of God before their eyes."

DEVOTIONAL

We live in a world that puts a tremendous emphasis on outward appearance. But when we follow the world and put so much focus on what we look like—what clothes we wear, what hairstyle we have, how much we weigh—we forget what matters most. How are our hearts? How are we living?

God certainly looks at our hearts (1 Samuel 16:7). He judges them, He sees the problem, and He calls our problem sin. But He loves us and wants to make us holy.

Spend time evaluating your heart today. Ask God to help you see your life as He does. God is more concerned with the "inner you" than He is with the "outer you." Who you are on the inside will be lived out for all to see. Are there aspects of the "outer you" that need to change to match the "inner you"? Don't let the world distract you from letting God cleanse your heart and lead your steps today.

—Scott Cannon
Pump Springs Baptist, Harrogate, TN

WEEK 31, DAY 5

Faith in God Is Our Salvation

Romans 3:19–4:12

Now we know that whatever the law says, it says to those who are under the law, that every mouth may be stopped, and all the world may become guilty before God. 20Therefore by the deeds of the law no flesh will be justified in His sight, for by the law *is* the knowledge of sin.

God's Righteousness Through Faith

21But now the righteousness of God apart from the law is revealed, being witnessed by the Law and the Prophets, 22even the righteousness of God, through faith in Jesus Christ, to all and on all who believe. For there is no difference; 23for all have sinned and fall short of the glory of God, 24being justified freely by His grace through the redemption that is in Christ Jesus, 25whom God set forth as a propitiation by His blood, through faith, to demonstrate His righteousness, because in His forbearance God had passed over the sins that were previously committed, 26to demonstrate at the present time His righteousness, that He might be just and the justifier of the one who has faith in Jesus.

Boasting Excluded

27Where is boasting then? It is excluded. By what law? Of works? No, but by the law of faith. 28Therefore we conclude that a man is justified by faith apart from the deeds of the law. 29Or is He the God of the Jews only? Is He not also the God of the Gentiles? Yes, of the Gentiles also, 30since there is one God who will justify the circumcised by faith and the uncircumcised through faith. 31Do we then make void the law through faith? Certainly not! On the contrary, we establish the law.

Abraham Justified by Faith

4What then shall we say that Abraham our father has found according to the flesh? 2For if Abraham was justified by works, he has something to boast about, but not before God. 3For what does the Scripture say? "Abraham believed God, and it was accounted to him for righteousness." 4Now to him who works, the wages are not counted as grace but as debt.

David Celebrates the Same Truth

5But to him who does not work but believes on Him who justifies the ungodly, his faith is accounted for righteousness, 6just as David also describes the blessedness of the man to whom God imputes righteousness apart from works:

7 "Blessed are those whose lawless deeds are
forgiven,
And whose sins are covered;
8 Blessed is the man to whom the LORD shall not
impute sin."

Abraham Justified Before Circumcision

9Does this blessedness then come upon the circumcised only, or upon the uncircumcised also? For we say that faith was accounted to Abraham for righteousness. 10How then was it accounted? While he was circumcised, or uncircumcised? Not while circumcised, but while uncircumcised. 11And he received the sign of circumcision, a seal of the righteousness of the faith which he had while still uncircumcised, that he might be the father of all those who believe, though they are uncircumcised, that righteousness might be imputed to them also, 12and the father of circumcision to those who not only are of the circumcision, but who also walk in the steps of the faith which our father Abraham had while still uncircumcised.

DEVOTIONAL

Romans 3:23 says we all have a problem that must be addressed: we were born sinful and separated from a holy God. This holy God longs for a relationship with us, but our sin stands in the way. It robs us from having fellowship with Him and prevents us from ever living up to God's standard. On our own, we'll always fall short of the mark.

It doesn't matter how good you are. It doesn't matter if you can point to grand achievements in life or if your name is written on a church membership. You cannot work hard enough to earn salvation—so quit trying! Fellowship with God is made possible only through a relationship with His Son, Jesus Christ. He gives you the gift of salvation when you place your faith in Jesus Christ alone.

Do you need to turn from sin and self in repentance? Will you turn to Christ in faith and trust Him as Savior? If you already have, give thanks to God and share your faith with someone today.

—Scott Cannon
Pump Springs Baptist, Harrogate, TN

WEEK 31, DAY 6

God Has Great Love for Us

Romans 4:13–5:11

The Promise Granted Through Faith

For the promise that he would be the heir of the world was not to Abraham or to his seed through the law, but through the righteousness of faith. [14]For if those who are of the law are heirs, faith is made void and the promise made of no effect, [15]because the law brings about wrath; for where there is no law there is no transgression.

[16]Therefore it is of faith that it might be according to grace, so that the promise might be sure to all the seed, not only to those who are of the law, but also to those who are of the faith of Abraham, who is the father of us all [17](as it is written, "I have made you a father of many nations") in the presence of Him whom he believed—God, who gives life to the dead and calls those things which do not exist as though they did; [18]who, contrary to hope, in hope believed, so that he became the father of many nations, according to what was spoken, "So shall your descendants be." [19]And not being weak in faith, he did not consider his own body, already dead (since he was about a hundred years old), and the deadness of Sarah's womb. [20]He did not waver at the promise of God through unbelief, but was strengthened in faith, giving glory to God, [21]and being fully convinced that what He had promised He was also able to perform. [22]And therefore "it was accounted to him for righteousness."

[23]Now it was not written for his sake alone that it was imputed to him, [24]but also for us. It shall be imputed to us who believe in Him who raised up Jesus our Lord from the dead, [25]who was delivered up because of our offenses, and was raised because of our justification.

Faith Triumphs in Trouble

5 Therefore, having been justified by faith, we have peace with God through our Lord Jesus Christ, [2]through whom also we have access by faith into this grace in which we stand, and rejoice in hope of the glory of God. [3]And not only that, but we also glory in tribulations, knowing that tribulation produces perseverance; [4]and perseverance, character; and character, hope. [5]Now hope does not disappoint, because the love of God has been poured out in our hearts by the Holy Spirit who was given to us.

Christ in Our Place

[6]For when we were still without strength, in due time Christ died for the ungodly. [7]For scarcely for a righteous man will one die; yet perhaps for a good man someone would even dare to die. [8]But God demonstrates His own love toward us, in that while we were still sinners, Christ died for us. [9]Much more then, having now been justified by His blood, we shall be saved from wrath through Him. [10]For if when we were enemies we were reconciled to God through the death of His Son, much more, having been reconciled, we shall be saved by His life. [11]And not only that, but we also rejoice in God through our Lord Jesus Christ, through whom we have now received the reconciliation.

DEVOTIONAL

We do not deserve the love of the heavenly Father. He simply chooses to love us in spite of our selfishness and sinfulness. John 3:16, one of the greatest verses in the Word of God, states that "God so loved the world that He gave His only begotten Son, that whosoever believes in Him should not perish but have everlasting life." Is there any greater proof of His love for us?

God knew we could do nothing on our own to save ourselves, so He came to our rescue. He sent the one and only lifeline that could save us, His Son, Jesus Christ. His love is greater than we could ever imagine!

God never wavers in showing us His love—it is unfailing and eternal. He is indeed faithful! Even today, God is pursuing you with His love. Ask Him to help you receive it. Look around you and consider your life situation. What are evidences of God's love for you this very moment?

First John 4:19 says, "We love Him because He first loved us." The Father longs for us to give Him our love in return, and there are so many ways we can do it. We love Him when we put faith in His Son, spend time with Him, grow to know Him better, honor Him in obedience, and love and bless others in service—and that's just to name a few!

David wrote, "Because your lovingkindness is better than life, my lips shall praise You" (Psalm 63:3). Fill in the second part of that sentence your own way today with a heart full of love for and gratitude to God!

—Scott Cannon
Pump Springs Baptist, Harrogate, TN

WEEK 31, DAY 7

In what ways did you bring God glory and honor this week? Were there any missed opportunities?

_____

_____

_____

_____

_____

_____

_____

_____

_____

_____

_____

_____

What personal sin did you come face-to-face with this week? Did you confess that sin, or continue in disobedience? How have you seen God show His love to you recently?

_____

_____

_____

_____

_____

_____

_____

_____

_____

_____

WEEK 32, DAY 1

Christ Frees Us from the Power of Sin

Romans 5:12–6:14

Death in Adam, Life in Christ

Therefore, just as through one man sin entered the world, and death through sin, and thus death spread to all men, because all sinned— 13(For until the law sin was in the world, but sin is not imputed when there is no law. 14Nevertheless death reigned from Adam to Moses, even over those who had not sinned according to the likeness of the transgression of Adam, who is a type of Him who was to come. 15But the free gift is not like the offense. For if by the one man's offense many died, much more the grace of God and the gift by the grace of the one Man, Jesus Christ, abounded to many. 16And the gift is not like that which came through the one who sinned. For the judgment which came from one offense resulted in condemnation, but the free gift which came from many offenses resulted in justification. 17For if by the one man's offense death reigned through the one, much more those who receive abundance of grace and of the gift of righteousness will reign in life through the One, Jesus Christ.)

18Therefore, as through one man's offense judgment came to all men, resulting in condemnation, even so through one Man's righteous act the free gift came to all men, resulting in justification of life. 19For as by one man's disobedience many were made sinners, so also by one Man's obedience many will be made righteous.

20Moreover the law entered that the offense might abound. But where sin abounded, grace abounded much more, 21so that as sin reigned in death, even so grace might reign through righteousness to eternal life through Jesus Christ our Lord.

Dead to Sin, Alive to God

6What shall we say then? Shall we continue in sin that grace may abound? 2Certainly not! How shall we who died to sin live any longer in it? 3Or do you not know that as many of us as were baptized into Christ Jesus were baptized into His death? 4Therefore we were buried with Him through baptism into death, that just as Christ was raised from the dead by the glory of the Father, even so we also should walk in newness of life. 5For if we have been united together in the likeness of His death, certainly we also shall be in the likeness of His resurrection, 6knowing this, that our old man was crucified with Him, that the body of sin might be done away with, that we should no longer be slaves of sin. 7For he who has died has been freed from sin. 8Now if we died with Christ, we believe that we shall also live with Him, 9knowing that Christ, having been raised from the dead, dies no more. Death no longer has dominion over Him. 10For the death that He died, He died to sin once for all; but the life that He lives, He lives to God. 11Likewise you also, reckon yourselves to be dead indeed to sin, but alive to God in Christ Jesus our Lord.

12Therefore do not let sin reign in your mortal body, that you should obey it in its lusts. 13And do not present your members as instruments of unrighteousness to sin, but present yourselves to God as being alive from the dead, and your members as instruments of righteousness to God. 14For sin shall not have dominion over you, for you are not under law but under grace.

DEVOTIONAL

Today's passage describes in detail a marvelous truth: as Christ followers we are dead to sin (Romans 6:11). In Adam, all people are sinners; in Christ, they are saints. In Adam's family, death reigns; in Christ's family, deliverance reigns. We all know sin has no power over someone who is dead. Sin and temptation can show up, but the dead man will never give in.

When you became a Christ follower, sin lost its power over you the same way it loses its power over someone who has died. You can still sin, but you don't have to—you're not a slave to it anymore. Sin has lost its power over you. Why? Because you are aligned and identified with Christ. You were buried with Him and raised with Him. You share in His victory and are freed from sin!

Whenever you choose to give in to sin and temptation, you are rejecting the freedom Christ purchased for you at Calvary. Remember Paul's clear teaching in Romans 6:1–2 that those who are dead to sin should not live in it any longer. You are called to choose the way of God daily, to "walk in newness of life" and consider yourself "dead indeed to sin, but alive to God in Christ Jesus our Lord" (Romans 6:4, 11). Ask the Holy Spirit to fill you, rule in you, and guide you in living out who you are in Christ!

—Chris Dixon
Liberty Baptist Church, Dublin, GA

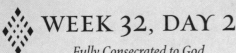

WEEK 32, DAY 2

Fully Consecrated to God

Romans 6:15–7:12

From Slaves of Sin to Slaves of God

What then? Shall we sin because we are not under law but under grace? Certainly not! 16Do you not know that to whom you present yourselves slaves to obey, you are that one's slaves whom you obey, whether of sin leading to death, or of obedience leading to righteousness? 17But God be thanked that though you were slaves of sin, yet you obeyed from the heart that form of doctrine to which you were delivered. 18And having been set free from sin, you became slaves of righteousness. 19I speak in human terms because of the weakness of your flesh. For just as you presented your members as slaves of uncleanness, and of lawlessness leading to more lawlessness, so now present your members as slaves of righteousness for holiness.

20For when you were slaves of sin, you were free in regard to righteousness. 21What fruit did you have then in the things of which you are now ashamed? For the end of those things is death. 22But now having been set free from sin, and having become slaves of God, you have your fruit to holiness, and the end, everlasting life. 23For the wages of sin is death, but the gift of God is eternal life in Christ Jesus our Lord.

Freed from the Law

7 Or do you not know, brethren (for I speak to those who know the law), that the law has dominion over a man as long as he lives? 2For the woman who has a husband is bound by the law to her husband as long as he lives. But if the husband dies, she is released from the law of her husband. 3So then if, while her husband lives, she marries another man, she will be called an adulteress; but if her husband dies, she is free from that law, so that she is no adulteress, though she has married another man. 4Therefore, my brethren, you also have become dead to the law through the body of Christ, that you may be married to another—to Him who was raised from the dead, that we should bear fruit to God. 5For when we were in the flesh, the sinful passions which were aroused by the law were at work in our members to bear fruit to death. 6But now we have been delivered from the law, having died to what we were held by, so that we should serve in the newness of the Spirit and not in the oldness of the letter.

Sin's Advantage in the Law

7What shall we say then? Is the law sin? Certainly not! On the contrary, I would not have known sin except through the law. For I would not have known covetousness unless the law had said, "You shall not covet." 8But sin, taking opportunity by the commandment, produced in me all manner of evil desire. For apart from the law sin was dead. 9I was alive once without the law, but when the commandment came, sin revived and I died. 10And the commandment, which was to bring life, I found to bring death. 11For sin, taking occasion by the commandment, deceived me, and by it killed me. 12Therefore the law is holy, and the commandment holy and just and good.

DEVOTIONAL

Dwight L. Moody was one of the most effective Christian evangelists in American history. Early in Moody's Christian life, he encountered Henry Varley, a British evangelist who challenged him with the words that have often been attributed to Moody. In a conversation following an evening of evangelistic meetings, Varley said to Moody, "The world has yet to see what God will do with and for and through and in and by the man who is fully and wholly consecrated to Him." Moody said Varley's statement pierced his heart and spoke to his soul. He thought to himself, "It lies with the man himself whether he will or will not make that entire and full consecration. I will try my uttermost to be that man."8 It became his life aim.

Paul called believers to live with the same commitment to God. He said Christ followers have been "set free from sin" and have become "slaves of righteousness" (Romans 6:18). When we recognize that every part of our lives and all we are belongs to Him, we begin living God's way. Our part is to understand we are stewards of all He has entrusted to us. Every dream, desire, plan, and material resource must be presented to Him daily as an act of surrender and worship.

Welcome God's reign in your heart today. Pray, "Search me, O God, and know my heart . . . lead me in the way everlasting" (Psalm 139:23–24). Examine every area of your life today, and allow God to show you how He would have you commit each area to Him.

—Chris Dixon
Liberty Baptist Church, Dublin, GA

WEEK 32, DAY 3

Be Ready to Obey

Romans 7:13–8:17

Law Cannot Save from Sin

Has then what is good become death to me? Certainly not! But sin, that it might appear sin, was producing death in me through what is good, so that sin through the commandment might become exceedingly sinful. 14For we know that the law is spiritual, but I am carnal, sold under sin. 15For what I am doing, I do not understand. For what I will to do, that I do not practice; but what I hate, that I do. 16If, then, I do what I will not to do, I agree with the law that it is good. 17But now, it is no longer I who do it, but sin that dwells in me. 18For I know that in me (that is, in my flesh) nothing good dwells; for to will is present with me, but how to perform what is good I do not find. 19For the good that I will to do, I do not do; but the evil I will not to do, that I practice. 20Now if I do what I will not to do, it is no longer I who do it, but sin that dwells in me.

21I find then a law, that evil is present with me, the one who wills to do good. 22For I delight in the law of God according to the inward man. 23But I see another law in my members, warring against the law of my mind, and bringing me into captivity to the law of sin which is in my members. 24O wretched man that I am! Who will deliver me from this body of death? 25I thank God—through Jesus Christ our Lord!

So then, with the mind I myself serve the law of God, but with the flesh the law of sin.

Free from Indwelling Sin

8 There is therefore now no condemnation to those who are in Christ Jesus, who do not walk according to the flesh, but according to the Spirit. 2For the law of the Spirit of life in Christ Jesus has made me free from the law of sin and death. 3For what the law could not do in that it was weak through the flesh, God did by sending His own Son in the likeness of sinful flesh, on account of sin: He condemned sin in the flesh, 4that the righteous requirement of the law might be fulfilled in us who do not walk according to the flesh but according to the Spirit. 5For those who live according to the flesh set their minds on the things of the flesh, but those who live according to the Spirit, the things of the Spirit. 6For to be carnally minded is death, but to be spiritually minded is life and peace. 7Because the carnal mind is enmity against God; for it is not subject to the law of God, nor indeed can be. 8So then, those who are in the flesh cannot please God.

9But you are not in the flesh but in the Spirit, if indeed the Spirit of God dwells in you. Now if anyone does not have the Spirit of Christ, he is not His. 10And if Christ is in you, the body is dead because of sin, but the Spirit is life because of righteousness. 11But if the Spirit of Him who raised Jesus from the dead dwells in you, He who raised Christ from the dead will also give life to your mortal bodies through His Spirit who dwells in you.

Sonship Through the Spirit

12Therefore, brethren, we are debtors—not to the flesh, to live according to the flesh. 13For if you live according to the flesh you will die; but if by the Spirit you put to death the deeds of the body, you will live. 14For as many as are led by the Spirit of God, these are sons of God. 15For you did not receive the spirit of bondage again to fear, but you received the Spirit of adoption by whom we cry out, "Abba, Father." 16The Spirit Himself bears witness with our spirit that we are children of God, 17and if children, then heirs—heirs of God and joint heirs with Christ, if indeed we suffer with Him, that we may also be glorified together.

DEVOTIONAL

You have probably heard the phrase "It's better to ask forgiveness than permission." Essentially it means someone is saying, "I've already decided what I want to do, and I'm not really open to finding out why it's not a good idea."

When we listen to teaching from Scripture, it's easy to rationalize why a particular verse or message does not apply to our personal situations. We are hesitant to be completely ready to obey God in whatever He says. We are quick to see God as a cosmic killjoy or to think He cannot relate to our day and age. As prevalent as this attitude is, even among Christ followers, nothing could be further from the truth.

You cannot possibly imagine all God has in store for you when you trust in Him (Ephesians 3:20). Take Paul's advice in Romans 8:5 and set your mind on the things of the Spirit. Ask God daily, "What shall I do, Lord?"

—Chris Dixon
Liberty Baptist Church, Dublin, GA

WEEK 32, DAY 4

Proof of God's Love

Romans 8:18–39

From Suffering to Glory

For I consider that the sufferings of this present time are not worthy to be compared with the glory which shall be revealed in us. 19For the earnest expectation of the creation eagerly waits for the revealing of the sons of God. 20For the creation was subjected to futility, not willingly, but because of Him who subjected it in hope; 21because the creation itself also will be delivered from the bondage of corruption into the glorious liberty of the children of God. 22For we know that the whole creation groans and labors with birth pangs together until now. 23Not only that, but we also who have the firstfruits of the Spirit, even we ourselves groan within ourselves, eagerly waiting for the adoption, the redemption of our body. 24For we were saved in this hope, but hope that is seen is not hope; for why does one still hope for what he sees? 25But if we hope for what we do not see, we eagerly wait for it with perseverance.

26Likewise the Spirit also helps in our weaknesses. For we do not know what we should pray for as we ought, but the Spirit Himself makes intercession for us with groanings which cannot be uttered. 27Now He who searches the hearts knows what the mind of the Spirit is, because He makes intercession for the saints according to the will of God.

28And we know that all things work together for good to those who love God, to those who are the called according to His purpose. 29For whom He foreknew, He also predestined to be conformed to the image of His Son, that He might be the firstborn among many brethren. 30Moreover whom He predestined, these He also called; whom He called, these He also justified; and whom He justified, these He also glorified.

God's Everlasting Love

31What then shall we say to these things? If God is for us, who can be against us? 32He who did not spare His own Son, but delivered Him up for us all, how shall He not with Him also freely give us all things? 33Who shall bring a charge against God's elect? It is God who justifies. 34Who is he who condemns? It is Christ who died, and furthermore is also risen, who is even at the right hand of God, who also makes intercession for us. 35Who shall separate us from the love of Christ? Shall tribulation, or distress, or persecution, or famine, or nakedness, or peril, or sword? 36As it is written:

> "For Your sake we are killed all day long;
> We are accounted as sheep for the slaughter."

37Yet in all these things we are more than conquerors through Him who loved us. 38For I am persuaded that neither death nor life, nor angels nor principalities nor powers, nor things present nor things to come, 39nor height nor depth, nor any other created thing, shall be able to separate us from the love of God which is in Christ Jesus our Lord.

DEVOTIONAL

Oh, how God loves His people! And His love is not only declared but also demonstrated. When it comes to love, talk is cheap. People can say they love you, but before you believe it, you have to ask, "Where is the proof? How can I know this person truly loves me?" God has given us His Son as proof of His love. Allowing His Son to die on the cross was His way of demonstrating to us beyond a shadow of a doubt that He loves us.

There are certain things that happen in life that can make us doubt God's love. We experience pain and begin to ask, "How could a loving God allow this to happen to us?" Always remember this: the cross trumps everything. God promised us we would never be separated from His love, but He did not say we would never face difficulties or challenges. There are a lot of things in life you may doubt, but you can never look at the cross of Jesus Christ and doubt God loves you.

True love does not just say, "I love you"; true love is always expressed visibly. True love is something you can see, not just something you can feel. Jesus Christ hanging on the cross is God's love for everyone to see. If you will allow the death of Jesus on the cross to forever settle any questions you might have about God's love, you will approach any challenge with a newfound confidence. Let the fact that God dealt with your greatest problem—sin—serve as evidence to you that there is no challenge He cannot overcome. We are more than conquerors through Him who loves us (Romans 8:37)!

—Chris Dixon
Liberty Baptist Church, Dublin, GA

WEEK 32, DAY 5

Trust the Character of God

Romans 9:1–29

Israel's Rejection of Christ

9 I tell the truth in Christ, I am not lying, my conscience also bearing me witness in the Holy Spirit, 2that I have great sorrow and continual grief in my heart. 3For I could wish that I myself were accursed from Christ for my brethren, my countrymen according to the flesh, 4who are Israelites, to whom pertain the adoption, the glory, the covenants, the giving of the law, the service of God, and the promises; 5of whom are the fathers and from whom, according to the flesh, Christ came, who is over all, the eternally blessed God. Amen.

Israel's Rejection and God's Purpose

6But it is not that the word of God has taken no effect. For they are not all Israel who are of Israel, 7nor are they all children because they are the seed of Abraham; but, "In Isaac your seed shall be called." 8That is, those who are the children of the flesh, these are not the children of God; but the children of the promise are counted as the seed. 9For this is the word of promise: "At this time I will come and Sarah shall have a son."

10And not only this, but when Rebecca also had conceived by one man, even by our father Isaac 11(for the children not yet being born, nor having done any good or evil, that the purpose of God according to election might stand, not of works but of Him who calls), 12it was said to her, "The older shall serve the younger." 13As it is written, "Jacob I have loved, but Esau I have hated."

Israel's Rejection and God's Justice

14What shall we say then? *Is there* unrighteousness with God? Certainly not! 15For He says to Moses, "I will have mercy on whomever I will have mercy, and I will have compassion on whomever I will have compassion." 16So then it is not of him who wills, nor of him who runs, but of God who shows mercy. 17For the Scripture says to the Pharaoh, "For this very purpose I have raised you up, that I may show My power in you, and that My name may be declared in all the earth." 18Therefore He has mercy on whom He wills, and whom He wills He hardens.

19You will say to me then, "Why does He still find fault? For who has resisted His will?" 20But indeed, O man, who are you to reply against God? Will the thing formed say to him who formed it, "Why have you made me like this?" 21Does not the potter have power over the clay, from the same lump to make one vessel for honor and another for dishonor?

22What if God, wanting to show His wrath and to make His power known, endured with much longsuffering the vessels of wrath prepared for destruction, 23and that He might make known the riches of His glory on the vessels of mercy, which He had prepared beforehand for glory, 24even us whom He called, not of the Jews only, but also of the Gentiles?

25As He says also in Hosea:

> "I will call them My people, who were not
>   My people,
> And her beloved, who was not beloved."
> 26 "And it shall come to pass in the place where it
>   was said to them,
> 'You are not My people,'
> There they shall be called sons of the living
>   God."

27Isaiah also cries out concerning Israel:

> "Though the number of the children of Israel be
>   as the sand of the sea,
> The remnant will be saved.
> 28 For He will finish the work and cut it short in
>   righteousness,
> Because the LORD will make a short work upon
>   the earth."

29And as Isaiah said before:

> "Unless the LORD of Sabaoth had left us a seed,
> We would have become like Sodom,
> And we would have been made like Gomorrah."

DEVOTIONAL

W e've all had unmet hopes, and as a result, felt that God is unfair. But the truth is that God is just and loving. He wants us to succeed in life, but He wants our attention to be on the right avenue, not the distractions. Our hope must be in the Lord, not our expectations. To get over disappointments remember God's mercy—what He has done for you and saved you from. Let Scripture remind you that your knowledge and experience does not compare to His. Surrender to the God and become His clay, allowing Him to mold and shape you, for He is trustworthy.

—Chris Dixon
Liberty Baptist Church, Dublin, GA

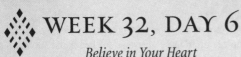

WEEK 32, DAY 6

Believe in Your Heart

Romans 9:30–10:21

Present Condition of Israel

What shall we say then? That Gentiles, who did not pursue righteousness, have attained to righteousness, even the righteousness of faith; 31but Israel, pursuing the law of righteousness, has not attained to the law of righteousness. 32Why? Because they did not seek it by faith, but as it were, by the works of the law. For they stumbled at that stumbling stone. 33As it is written:

"Behold, I lay in Zion a stumbling stone and rock
   of offense,
And whoever believes on Him will not be put
   to shame."

Israel Needs the Gospel

10Brethren, my heart's desire and prayer to God for Israel is that they may be saved. 2For I bear them witness that they have a zeal for God, but not according to knowledge. 3For they being ignorant of God's righteousness, and seeking to establish their own righteousness, have not submitted to the righteousness of God. 4For Christ is the end of the law for righteousness to everyone who believes.

5For Moses writes about the righteousness which is of the law, "The man who does those things shall live by them." 6But the righteousness of faith speaks in this way, "Do not say in your heart, 'Who will ascend into heaven?'" (that is, to bring Christ down from above) 7or, " 'Who will descend into the abyss?'" (that is, to bring Christ up from the dead). 8But what does it say? "The word is near you, in your mouth and in your heart" (that is, the word of faith which we preach): 9that if you confess with your mouth the Lord Jesus and believe in your heart that God has raised Him from the dead, you will be saved. 10For with the heart one believes unto righteousness, and with the mouth confession is made unto salvation. 11For the Scripture says, "Whoever believes on Him will not be put to shame." 12For there is no distinction between Jew and Greek, for the same Lord over all is rich to all who call upon Him. 13For "whoever calls on the name of the LORD shall be saved."

Israel Rejects the Gospel

14How then shall they call on Him in whom they have not believed? And how shall they believe in Him of whom they have not heard? And how shall they hear without a preacher? 15And how shall they preach unless they are sent? As it is written:

"How beautiful are the feet of those who preach
      the gospel of peace,
   Who bring glad tidings of good things!"

16But they have not all obeyed the gospel. For Isaiah says, "LORD, who has believed our report?" 17So then faith comes by hearing, and hearing by the word of God.

18But I say, have they not heard? Yes indeed:

"Their sound has gone out to all the earth,
   And their words to the ends of the world."

19But I say, did Israel not know? First Moses says:

"I will provoke you to jealousy by those who are
      not a nation,
   I will move you to anger by a foolish nation."

20But Isaiah is very bold and says:

"I was found by those who did not seek Me;
   I was made manifest to those who did not ask
      for Me."

21But to Israel he says:

"All day long I have stretched out My hands
   To a disobedient and contrary people."

DEVOTIONAL

On the cross, Jesus wrote the payment check for our sins. At the empty tomb, God cashed that check and gave a receipt that said, "Paid in full." You may read those words and think, I believe that. *But where do you believe it? In your head, or in your heart?*

Romans 10:9 says that those who confess faith in Christ and believe in their hearts that Jesus rose again will be saved. Real belief is not in the head, but in the heart. The Jews considered the heart to be the core of the soul, the center of what a person really is. You can believe in your head everything you want to believe about Jesus Christ, but your life will never be changed until you believe it in your heart.

—Chris Dixon
Liberty Baptist Church, Dublin, GA

WEEK 32, DAY 7

What are some areas of your life you need to surrender to Jesus Christ?

_____

_____

_____

_____

_____

_____

_____

_____

_____

_____

_____

Are your expectations and disappointments distracting you from God's perfect plan for your life? If so, make a list of things that are distracting you and place them under God's authority in prayer.

_____

_____

_____

_____

_____

_____

_____

_____

WEEK 33, DAY I

God's Mercy and Kindness

Romans 11:1–21

Israel's Rejection Not Total

11 I say then, has God cast away His people? Certainly not! For I also am an Israelite, of the seed of Abraham, of the tribe of Benjamin. [2]God has not cast away His people whom He foreknew. Or do you not know what the Scripture says of Elijah, how he pleads with God against Israel, saying, [3]"LORD, they have killed Your prophets and torn down Your altars, and I alone am left, and they seek my life"? [4]But what does the divine response say to him? "I have reserved for Myself seven thousand men who have not bowed the knee to Baal." [5]Even so then, at this present time there is a remnant according to the election of grace. [6]And if by grace, then it is no longer of works; otherwise grace is no longer grace. But if it is of works, it is no longer grace; otherwise work is no longer work.

[7]What then? Israel has not obtained what it seeks; but the elect have obtained it, and the rest were blinded. [8]Just as it is written:

"God has given them a spirit of stupor,
Eyes that they should not see
And ears that they should not hear,
To this very day."

[9]And David says:

"Let their table become a snare and a trap,
A stumbling block and a recompense to them.
[10] Let their eyes be darkened, so that they do
not see,
And bow down their back always."

Israel's Rejection Not Final

[11]I say then, have they stumbled that they should fall? Certainly not! But through their fall, to provoke them to jealousy, salvation has come to the Gentiles. [12]Now if their fall is riches for the world, and their failure riches for the Gentiles, how much more their fullness!

[13]For I speak to you Gentiles; inasmuch as I am an apostle to the Gentiles, I magnify my ministry, [14]if by any means I may provoke to jealousy those who are my flesh and save some of them. [15]For if their being cast away is the reconciling of the world, what will their acceptance be but life from the dead?

[16]For if the firstfruit is holy, the lump is also holy; and if the root is holy, so are the branches. [17]And if some of the branches were broken off, and you, being a wild olive tree, were grafted in among them, and with them became a partaker of the root and fatness of the olive tree, [18]do not boast against the branches. But if you do boast, remember that you do not support the root, but the root supports you.

[19]You will say then, "Branches were broken off that I might be grafted in." [20]Well said. Because of unbelief they were broken off, and you stand by faith. Do not be haughty, but fear. [21]For if God did not spare the natural branches, He may not spare you either.

DEVOTIONAL

God chose the nation of Israel to be a visible manifestation of His mercy and kindness. They were to be a light to the nations of the world. God loved the people of Israel and blessed them in many ways. Yet, as a nation, Israel turned away from God. We see this over and over in the Old Testament. They often forsook the Lord and worshiped pagan deities. They rejected the warnings of God's prophets and profaned God's name. The ultimate sin of Israel was the rejection of Jesus Christ as the Messiah.

Amazingly, God never turned away from Israel. There has always been a remnant of Jews who have trusted in Jesus Christ as their Lord and Savior, and God has welcomed them into His family. There are more Jews coming to Christ today than at any other time in recorded history.

When Israel turned away from God, He stretched His hand out to the Gentile world. They were not the original vine, but in His great love, He grafted them in. Those of us who are Gentile believers in Jesus must never give way to a spirit of pride. Our being in the family of God has nothing to do with who we are or what we are; it is all because of His mercy and kindness. As the old hymn declares, "Nothing in my hand I bring; simply to Thy cross I cling."

Today, all Christians, whether Jewish or Gentile, are to be His light in a dark world. With great humility, our lives should show forth His mercy and kindness to a world that so desperately needs to know Jesus. Let your light shine for His glory!

—Dr. Bob Pitman
Bob Pitman Ministries, Muscle Shoals, AL

WEEK 33, DAY 2

Make Your Life a Sacrifice of Obedience

Romans 11:22–12:8

Therefore consider the goodness and severity of God: on those who fell, severity; but toward you, goodness, if you continue in His goodness. Otherwise you also will be cut off. ²³And they also, if they do not continue in unbelief, will be grafted in, for God is able to graft them in again. ²⁴For if you were cut out of the olive tree which is wild by nature, and were grafted contrary to nature into a cultivated olive tree, how much more will these, who are natural branches, be grafted into their own olive tree?

²⁵For I do not desire, brethren, that you should be ignorant of this mystery, lest you should be wise in your own opinion, that blindness in part has happened to Israel until the fullness of the Gentiles has come in. ²⁶And so all Israel will be saved, as it is written:

> "The Deliverer will come out of Zion,
>   And He will turn away ungodliness from Jacob;
> ²⁷ For this is My covenant with them,
>   When I take away their sins."

²⁸Concerning the gospel they are enemies for your sake, but concerning the election they are beloved for the sake of the fathers. ²⁹For the gifts and the calling of God are irrevocable. ³⁰For as you were once disobedient to God, yet have now obtained mercy through their disobedience, ³¹even so these also have now been disobedient, that through the mercy shown you they also may obtain mercy. ³²For God has committed them all to disobedience, that He might have mercy on all.

³³Oh, the depth of the riches both of the wisdom and knowledge of God! How unsearchable are His judgments and His ways past finding out!

³⁴ "For who has known the mind of the LORD?
  Or who has become His counselor?"
³⁵ "Or who has first given to Him
  And it shall be repaid to him?"

³⁶For of Him and through Him and to Him are all things, to whom be glory forever. Amen.

Living Sacrifices to God

12I beseech you therefore, brethren, by the mercies of God, that you present your bodies a living sacrifice, holy, acceptable to God, which is your reasonable service. ²And do not be conformed to this world, but be transformed by the renewing of your mind, that you may prove what is that good and acceptable and perfect will of God.

Serve God with Spiritual Gifts

³For I say, through the grace given to me, to everyone who is among you, not to think of himself more highly than he ought to think, but to think soberly, as God has dealt to each one a measure of faith. ⁴For as we have many members in one body, but all the members do not have the same function, ⁵so we, being many, are one body in Christ, and individually members of one another. ⁶Having then gifts differing according to the grace that is given to us, let us use them: if prophecy, let us prophesy in proportion to our faith; ⁷or ministry, let us use it in our ministering; he who teaches, in teaching; ⁸he who exhorts, in exhortation; he who gives, with liberality; he who leads, with diligence; he who shows mercy, with cheerfulness.

DEVOTIONAL

What a mighty God we serve! He knows the end from the beginning. In fact, He has determined the end from the beginning!

The destiny of this world is not in the hands of any human government, but in the hands of God. No earthly king, president, prime minister, or emperor will be in charge at the end. Jesus Christ will return from heaven someday, and He will be in charge. He will rule as the King of kings and the Lord of lords. Every knee will bow before Him, and every tongue will confess Him as Lord.

Our future is not hidden in a dark mist; it has been clearly revealed. "The Deliverer will come" (Romans 11:26). One day He's coming. O glorious day!

Until He returns, those of us who know Him are called to present ourselves as living sacrifices. That is really an oxymoron. A sacrifice is something that has been slain as an offering to God. As living sacrifices we are dead and alive at the same time. We are dead to the world, the flesh, and the devil, but we are alive to Jesus Christ and His will for us.

Finding God's will is life's highest accomplishment; following God's will is life's highest fulfillment. His will is not a miserable, meaningless existence. His will is good, acceptable, and perfect. It is the place where we experience His provision and protection. Seek to know and do His will.

—Dr. Bob Pitman
Bob Pitman Ministries, Muscle Shoals, AL

WEEK 33, DAY 3

Real Christian Love

Romans 12:9–13:14

Behave Like a Christian

Let love be without hypocrisy. Abhor what is evil. Cling to what is good. [10]Be kindly affectionate to one another with brotherly love, in honor giving preference to one another; [11]not lagging in diligence, fervent in spirit, serving the Lord; [12]rejoicing in hope, patient in tribulation, continuing steadfastly in prayer; [13]distributing to the needs of the saints, given to hospitality.

[14]Bless those who persecute you; bless and do not curse. [15]Rejoice with those who rejoice, and weep with those who weep. [16]Be of the same mind toward one another. Do not set your mind on high things, but associate with the humble. Do not be wise in your own opinion.

[17]Repay no one evil for evil. Have regard for good things in the sight of all men. [18]If it is possible, as much as depends on you, live peaceably with all men. [19]Beloved, do not avenge yourselves, but rather give place to wrath; for it is written, "Vengeance is Mine, I will repay," says the Lord. [20]Therefore

"If your enemy is hungry, feed him;
If he is thirsty, give him a drink;
For in so doing you will heap coals of fire on
his head."

[21]Do not be overcome by evil, but overcome evil with good.

Submit to Government

13 Let every soul be subject to the governing authorities. For there is no authority except from God, and the authorities that exist are appointed by God. [2]Therefore whoever resists the authority resists the ordinance of God, and those who resist will bring judgment on themselves. [3]For rulers are not a terror to good works, but to evil. Do you want to be unafraid of the authority? Do what is good, and you will have praise from the same. [4]For he is God's minister to you for good. But if you do evil, be afraid; for he does not bear the sword in vain; for he is God's minister, an avenger to execute wrath on him who practices evil. [5]Therefore you must be subject, not only because of wrath but also for conscience' sake. [6]For because of this you also pay taxes, for they are God's ministers attending continually to this very thing. [7]Render therefore to all their due: taxes to whom taxes are due, customs to whom customs, fear to whom fear, honor to whom honor.

Love Your Neighbor

[8]Owe no one anything except to love one another, for he who loves another has fulfilled the law. [9]For the commandments, "You shall not commit adultery," "You shall not murder," "You shall not steal," "You shall not bear false witness," "You shall not covet," and if there is any other commandment, are all summed up in this saying, namely, "You shall love your neighbor as yourself." [10]Love does no harm to a neighbor; therefore love is the fulfillment of the law.

Put on Christ

[11]And do this, knowing the time, that now it is high time to awake out of sleep; for now our salvation is nearer than when we first believed. [12]The night is far spent, the day is at hand. Therefore let us cast off the works of darkness, and let us put on the armor of light. [13]Let us walk properly, as in the day, not in revelry and drunkenness, not in lewdness and lust, not in strife and envy. [14]But put on the Lord Jesus Christ, and make no provision for the flesh, to fulfill its lusts.

DEVOTIONAL

The word love is such an overused word in our culture. We say we love the Lord, we love our families, we love football, we love our dogs and cats, we love to go fishing with worms, and we love pizza. We use the same word to describe our affection for God, our affection for sports, and our affection for food.

Real love is not a superficial emotion; it is an act of the will. We love those whom we choose to love. It is often sacrificial and is always Christlike. You are never more like Jesus than when you are loving.

Christian love is never passive, but active. It is not just something we say; it is something we do! It involves giving, praying, respecting, obeying, serving, and forgiving.

We are to manifest Christian love to our families, our neighbors, our leaders, and our brothers and sisters in Christ. Through love we keep the commandments, we honor the Lord, we bless the lives of others, and we even make life better for ourselves.

Love someone today in Jesus' name!

—Dr. Bob Pitman
Bob Pitman Ministries, Muscle Shoals, AL

WEEK 33, DAY 4

Live in a Way That Pleases God

Romans 14:1–15:3

The Law of Liberty

14 Receive one who is weak in the faith, but not to disputes over doubtful things. ²For one believes he may eat all things, but he who is weak eats only vegetables. ³Let not him who eats despise him who does not eat, and let not him who does not eat judge him who eats; for God has received him. ⁴Who are you to judge another's servant? To his own master he stands or falls. Indeed, he will be made to stand, for God is able to make him stand.

⁵One person esteems one day above another; another esteems every day alike. Let each be fully convinced in his own mind. ⁶He who observes the day, observes it to the Lord; and he who does not observe the day, to the Lord he does not observe it. He who eats, eats to the Lord, for he gives God thanks; and he who does not eat, to the Lord he does not eat, and gives God thanks. ⁷For none of us lives to himself, and no one dies to himself. ⁸For if we live, we live to the Lord; and if we die, we die to the Lord. Therefore, whether we live or die, we are the Lord's. ⁹For to this end Christ died and rose and lived again, that He might be Lord of both the dead and the living. ¹⁰But why do you judge your brother? Or why do you show contempt for your brother? For we shall all stand before the judgment seat of Christ. ¹¹For it is written:

"As I live, says the LORD,
Every knee shall bow to Me,
And every tongue shall confess to God."

¹²So then each of us shall give account of himself to God. ¹³Therefore let us not judge one another anymore, but rather resolve this, not to put a stumbling block or a cause to fall in our brother's way.

The Law of Love

¹⁴I know and am convinced by the Lord Jesus that there is nothing unclean of itself; but to him who considers anything to be unclean, to him it is unclean. ¹⁵Yet if your brother is grieved because of your food, you are no longer walking in love. Do not destroy with your food the one for whom Christ died. ¹⁶Therefore do not let your good be spoken of as evil; ¹⁷for the kingdom of God is not eating and drinking, but righteousness and peace and joy in the Holy Spirit. ¹⁸For he who serves Christ in these things is acceptable to God and approved by men.

¹⁹Therefore let us pursue the things which make for peace and the things by which one may edify another. ²⁰Do not destroy the work of God for the sake of food. All things indeed are pure, but it is evil for the man who eats with offense. ²¹It is good neither to eat meat nor drink wine nor do anything by which your brother stumbles or is offended or is made weak. ²²Do you have faith? Have it to yourself before God. Happy is he who does not condemn himself in what he approves. ²³But he who doubts is condemned if he eats, because he does not eat from faith; for whatever is not from faith is sin.

Bearing Others' Burdens

15 We then who are strong ought to bear with the scruples of the weak, and not to please ourselves. ²Let each of us please his neighbor for his good, leading to edification. ³For even Christ did not please Himself; but as it is written, "The reproaches of those who reproached You fell on Me."

DEVOTIONAL

*L*ife would be much simpler if everyone believed the same things, thought the same thoughts, and acted in the same ways. It would also be much duller.

Every person who has truly been saved is a member of the family of God. All Christians are brothers and sisters in Christ. However, not all Christians live at the same spiritual maturity level. Some Christians still struggle with legalism, while others are still seeking the full meaning of the grace-filled life.

Paul said, "We then who are strong ought to bear with the scruples of the weak, and not to please ourselves" (Romans 15:1). Many believers don't know whether they belong in the weak or strong category. Many forget there is a difference between personal preference, personal conviction, and absolute truth. Too many Christians argue about things that have nothing to do with biblical truth. They fuss about things that are only preferences or personal convictions. Satan loves it when we do that.

As brothers and sisters in God's family, our chief aim should be to live in a way that brings honor to Him. We must not waste our lives criticizing others. Let us determine to please the Lord in all we do and leave the judging to Him.

—Dr. Bob Pitman
Bob Pitman Ministries, Muscle Shoals, AL

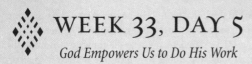

WEEK 33, DAY 5

God Empowers Us to Do His Work

Romans 15:4–29

For whatever things were written before were written for our learning, that we through the patience and comfort of the Scriptures might have hope. ⁵Now may the God of patience and comfort grant you to be like-minded toward one another, according to Christ Jesus, ⁶that you may with one mind and one mouth glorify the God and Father of our Lord Jesus Christ.

Glorify God Together

⁷Therefore receive one another, just as Christ also received us, to the glory of God. ⁸Now I say that Jesus Christ has become a servant to the circumcision for the truth of God, to confirm the promises made to the fathers, 9and that the Gentiles might glorify God for His mercy, as it is written:

"For this reason I will confess to You among the
    Gentiles,
And sing to Your name."

¹⁰And again he says:

"Rejoice, O Gentiles, with His people!"

¹¹And again:

"Praise the LORD, all you Gentiles!
Laud Him, all you peoples!"

¹²And again, Isaiah says:

"There shall be a root of Jesse;
And He who shall rise to reign over the Gentiles,
In Him the Gentiles shall hope."

¹³Now may the God of hope fill you with all joy and peace in believing, that you may abound in hope by the power of the Holy Spirit.

From Jerusalem to Illyricum

¹⁴Now I myself am confident concerning you, my brethren, that you also are full of goodness, filled with all knowledge, able also to admonish one another. ¹⁵Nevertheless, brethren, I have written more boldly to you on some points, as reminding you, because of the grace given to me by God, ¹⁶that I might be a minister of Jesus Christ to the Gentiles, ministering the gospel of God, that the offering of the Gentiles might be acceptable, sanctified by the Holy Spirit. ¹⁷Therefore I have reason to glory in Christ Jesus in the things which pertain to God. ¹⁸For I will not dare to speak of any of those things which Christ has not accomplished through me, in word and deed, to make the Gentiles obedient— ¹⁹in mighty signs and wonders, by the power of the Spirit of God, so that from Jerusalem and round about to Illyricum I have fully preached the gospel of Christ. ²⁰And so I have made it my aim to preach the gospel, not where Christ was named, lest I should build on another man's foundation, ²¹but as it is written:

"To whom He was not announced, they shall see;
And those who have not heard shall understand."

Plan to Visit Rome

²²For this reason I also have been much hindered from coming to you. ²³But now no longer having a place in these parts, and having a great desire these many years to come to you, ²⁴whenever I journey to Spain, I shall come to you. For I hope to see you on my journey, and to be helped on my way there by you, if first I may enjoy your company for a while. ²⁵But now I am going to Jerusalem to minister to the saints. ²⁶For it pleased those from Macedonia and Achaia to make a certain contribution for the poor among the saints who are in Jerusalem. ²⁷It pleased them indeed, and they are their debtors. For if the Gentiles have been partakers of their spiritual things, their duty is also to minister to them in material things. ²⁸Therefore, when I have performed this and have sealed to them this fruit, I shall go by way of you to Spain. ²⁹But I know that when I come to you, I shall come in the fullness of the blessing of the gospel of Christ.

DEVOTIONAL

There is more to the Christian life than fun, food, and fellowship. There is a message to proclaim and a ministry to perform. There are lost people to be won and saved people to be discipled. This is the work of the church, and it is the work of every believer.

However, we do not do God's work in the power of the flesh. We do the work of the Lord in the power of the Holy Spirit. The Holy Spirit takes the emphasis away from us and puts it all on Christ. He turns confusion into purpose and frustration into victory. Allow Him to be your source of strength, and your life and ministry will be affirmed with joy, peace, and hope.

—Dr. Bob Pitman
Bob Pitman Ministries, Muscle Shoals, AL

WEEK 33, DAY 6

Watch Out for False Prophets

Romans 15:30–16:27

Now I beg you, brethren, through the Lord Jesus Christ, and through the love of the Spirit, that you strive together with me in prayers to God for me, 31that I may be delivered from those in Judea who do not believe, and that my service for Jerusalem may be acceptable to the saints, 32that I may come to you with joy by the will of God, and may be refreshed together with you. 33Now the God of peace be with you all. Amen.

Sister Phoebe Commended

16 I commend to you Phoebe our sister, who is a servant of the church in Cenchrea, 2that you may receive her in the Lord in a manner worthy of the saints, and assist her in whatever business she has need of you; for indeed she has been a helper of many and of myself also.

Greeting Roman Saints

3Greet Priscilla and Aquila, my fellow workers in Christ Jesus, 4who risked their own necks for my life, to whom not only I give thanks, but also all the churches of the Gentiles. 5Likewise greet the church that is in their house.

Greet my beloved Epaenetus, who is the firstfruits of Achaia to Christ. 6Greet Mary, who labored much for us. 7Greet Andronicus and Junia, my countrymen and my fellow prisoners, who are of note among the apostles, who also were in Christ before me.

8Greet Amplias, my beloved in the Lord. 9Greet Urbanus, our fellow worker in Christ, and Stachys, my beloved. 10Greet Apelles, approved in Christ. Greet those who are of the household of Aristobulus. 11Greet Herodion, my countryman. Greet those who are of the household of Narcissus who are in the Lord.

12Greet Tryphena and Tryphosa, who have labored in the Lord. Greet the beloved Persis, who labored much in the Lord. 13Greet Rufus, chosen in the Lord, and his mother and mine. 14Greet Asyncritus, Phlegon, Hermas, Patrobas, Hermes, and the brethren who are with them. 15Greet Philologus and Julia, Nereus and his sister, and Olympas, and all the saints who are with them.

16Greet one another with a holy kiss. The churches of Christ greet you.

Avoid Divisive Persons

17Now I urge you, brethren, note those who cause divisions and offenses, contrary to the doctrine which you learned, and avoid them. 18For those who are such do not serve our Lord Jesus Christ, but their own belly, and by smooth words and flattering speech deceive the hearts of the simple. 19For your obedience has become known to all. Therefore I am glad on your behalf; but I want you to be wise in what is good, and simple concerning evil. 20And the God of peace will crush Satan under your feet shortly.

The grace of our Lord Jesus Christ be with you. Amen.

Greetings from Paul's Friends

21Timothy, my fellow worker, and Lucius, Jason, and Sosipater, my countrymen, greet you.

22I, Tertius, who wrote this epistle, greet you in the Lord.

23Gaius, my host and the host of the whole church, greets you. Erastus, the treasurer of the city, greets you, and Quartus, a brother. 24The grace of our Lord Jesus Christ be with you all. Amen.

Benediction

25Now to Him who is able to establish you according to my gospel and the preaching of Jesus Christ, according to the revelation of the mystery kept secret since the world began 26but now made manifest, and by the prophetic Scriptures made known to all nations, according to the commandment of the everlasting God, for obedience to the faith— 27to God, alone wise, be glory through Jesus Christ forever. Amen.

DEVOTIONAL

Paul closed the book of Romans by giving special mention to those believers who had faithfully served the Lord Jesus. Effective Christianity is never the work of just one person or just one church. We are all in this together!

He also gave a word of warning concerning false prophets. They are motivated by selfish ambitions. They divide the body of Christ and dishonor the Lord Himself. They substitute vain philosophy for doctrinal truth.

Work together with your fellow believers, and be swift to hear, but be sure you are listening to the right voices!

—Dr. Bob Pitman
Bob Pitman Ministries, Muscle Shoals, AL

WEEK 33, DAY 7

How can you let the love of Jesus Christ shine forth in your life among those you see each day?

_____
_____
_____
_____
_____
_____
_____
_____
_____
_____
_____
_____
_____
_____

What things in your life hinder you from knowing and doing God's will?

_____
_____
_____
_____
_____
_____
_____
_____
_____
_____

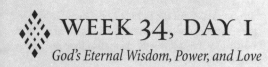

WEEK 34, DAY I

God's Eternal Wisdom, Power, and Love

1 Corinthians 1:1–25

Greeting

1 Paul, called to be an apostle of Jesus Christ through the will of God, and Sosthenes our brother,

2To the church of God which is at Corinth, to those who are sanctified in Christ Jesus, called to be saints, with all who in every place call on the name of Jesus Christ our Lord, both theirs and ours:

3Grace to you and peace from God our Father and the Lord Jesus Christ.

Spiritual Gifts at Corinth

4I thank my God always concerning you for the grace of God which was given to you by Christ Jesus, 5that you were enriched in everything by Him in all utterance and all knowledge, 6even as the testimony of Christ was confirmed in you, 7so that you come short in no gift, eagerly waiting for the revelation of our Lord Jesus Christ, 8who will also confirm you to the end, that you may be blameless in the day of our Lord Jesus Christ. 9God is faithful, by whom you were called into the fellowship of His Son, Jesus Christ our Lord.

Sectarianism Is Sin

10Now I plead with you, brethren, by the name of our Lord Jesus Christ, that you all speak the same thing, and that there be no divisions among you, but that you be perfectly joined together in the same mind and in the same judgment. 11For it has been declared to me concerning you, my brethren, by those of Chloe's household, that there are contentions among you. 12Now I say this, that each of you says, "I am of Paul," or "I am of Apollos," or "I am of Cephas," or "I am of Christ." 13Is Christ divided? Was Paul crucified for you? Or were you baptized in the name of Paul?

14I thank God that I baptized none of you except Crispus and Gaius, 15lest anyone should say that I had baptized in my own name. 16Yes, I also baptized the household of Stephanas. Besides, I do not know whether I baptized any other. 17For Christ did not send me to baptize, but to preach the gospel, not with wisdom of words, lest the cross of Christ should be made of no effect.

Christ the Power and Wisdom of God

18For the message of the cross is foolishness to those who are perishing, but to us who are being saved it is the power of God. 19For it is written:

"I will destroy the wisdom of the wise,
  And bring to nothing the understanding of the
    prudent."

20Where is the wise? Where is the scribe? Where is the disputer of this age? Has not God made foolish the wisdom of this world? 21For since, in the wisdom of God, the world through wisdom did not know God, it pleased God through the foolishness of the message preached to save those who believe. 22For Jews request a sign, and Greeks seek after wisdom; 23but we preach Christ crucified, to the Jews a stumbling block and to the Greeks foolishness, 24but to those who are called, both Jews and Greeks, Christ the power of God and the wisdom of God. 25Because the foolishness of God is wiser than men, and the weakness of God is stronger than men.

DEVOTIONAL

G odless philosophies and worldly traditions have taken many forms throughout the ages. What people consider to be true one year is invariably refuted and rejected the next. But the eternal God and His truth do not change like the theories and philosophies of humans. Malachi 3:6 says, "I am the Lord, I do not change." Do you know why that is such a powerful statement? Because His attributes do not change. The same God who loved you enough to put His Son on the cross two thousand years ago still loves you with that same love today!

When you are troubled and facing difficulties in life, turn to God. You don't have to worry about catching God in a bad mood or about whether He will respond to you in anger or disgust. No, the God of love does not change. You can count on Him to be the one constant in your life. You can always rely on His powerful presence. He will help you, heal you, and deliver you through the problems of life. God's wisdom and strength is beyond human comprehension (1 Corinthians 1:25)! Only when you come to the end of yourself and turn to God will you experience the power of God to save and deliver you.

—Rusty Womack
Lost Mountain Baptist Church, Powder Springs, GA

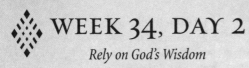

WEEK 34, DAY 2

Rely on God's Wisdom

1 Corinthians 1:26–2:16

Glory Only in the Lord

For you see your calling, brethren, that not many wise according to the flesh, not many mighty, not many noble, are called. 27But God has chosen the foolish things of the world to put to shame the wise, and God has chosen the weak things of the world to put to shame the things which are mighty; 28and the base things of the world and the things which are despised God has chosen, and the things which are not, to bring to nothing the things that are, 29that no flesh should glory in His presence. 30But of Him you are in Christ Jesus, who became for us wisdom from God—and righteousness and sanctification and redemption— 31that, as it is written, "He who glories, let him glory in the LORD."

Christ Crucified

2And I, brethren, when I came to you, did not come with excellence of speech or of wisdom declaring to you the testimony of God. 2For I determined not to know anything among you except Jesus Christ and Him crucified. 3I was with you in weakness, in fear, and in much trembling. 4And my speech and my preaching were not with persuasive words of human wisdom, but in demonstration of the Spirit and of power, 5that your faith should not be in the wisdom of men but in the power of God.

Spiritual Wisdom

6However, we speak wisdom among those who are mature, yet not the wisdom of this age, nor of the rulers of this age, who are coming to nothing. 7But we speak the wisdom of God in a mystery, the hidden wisdom which God ordained before the ages for our glory, 8which none of the rulers of this age knew; for had they known, they would not have crucified the Lord of glory.

9But as it is written:

"Eye has not seen, nor ear heard,
  Nor have entered into the heart of man
  The things which God has prepared for those
    who love Him."

10But God has revealed them to us through His Spirit. For the Spirit searches all things, yes, the deep things of God. 11For what man knows the things of a man except the spirit of the man which is in him? Even so no one knows the things of God except the Spirit of God. 12Now we have received, not the spirit of the world, but the Spirit who is from God, that we might know the things that have been freely given to us by God.

13These things we also speak, not in words which man's wisdom teaches but which the Holy Spirit teaches, comparing spiritual things with spiritual. 14But the natural man does not receive the things of the Spirit of God, for they are foolishness to him; nor can he know them, because they are spiritually discerned. 15But he who is spiritual judges all things, yet he himself is rightly judged by no one. 16For "who has known the mind of the LORD that he may instruct Him?" But we have the mind of Christ.

DEVOTIONAL

There are many churches today that base their operations on human traditions rather than biblical teaching. It's sad but true that some sermons and ministry programs are most likely not at all what God had in mind for His church. Christians are choosing human wisdom over God's wisdom, and that is exactly what Paul warned believers about in 1 Corinthians 2.

Paul told the Corinthians that when he preached, he did not rely on "persuasive words of human wisdom" (1 Corinthians 2:4). Paul was a very capable individual, and he could have put his trust in his own cleverness and strong communication skills as he served God. Instead, he put his trust in God's message and God's power. His confidence was in knowing what message God wanted him to preach: salvation through Jesus Christ. He said his preaching demonstrated the power of the Holy Spirit so that people's faith would be in the power of God (vv. 4–5).

Paul's preaching pricked and penetrated human hearts, causing people to cry out, "What must I do to be saved?" (Acts 16:30). Paul's secret was prayer. Prayerless preaching yields no power. We must rely on the Spirit of God to do the work of God.

For your ministry and your daily life, are you trusting in God's wisdom or in human wisdom? Like Paul, join God's agenda for His work instead of making your own. Jesus taught His disciples that their first calling was to "be with Him" (Mark 3:14). Simply by being with Him, they would know what to say (1 Corinthians 2:14). Answer Jesus' call to be with Him, and follow His lead today.

—Rusty Womack
Lost Mountain Baptist Church, Powder Springs, GA

WEEK 34, DAY 3

Christ Is the Cornerstone

1 Corinthians 3:1–4:5

Sectarianism Is Carnal

3 And I, brethren, could not speak to you as to spiritual people but as to carnal, as to babes in Christ. ²I fed you with milk and not with solid food; for until now you were not able to receive it, and even now you are still not able; ³for you are still carnal. For where there are envy, strife, and divisions among you, are you not carnal and behaving like mere men? ⁴For when one says, "I am of Paul," and another, "I am of Apollos," are you not carnal?

Watering, Working, Warning

⁵Who then is Paul, and who *is* Apollos, but ministers through whom you believed, as the Lord gave to each one? ⁶I planted, Apollos watered, but God gave the increase. ⁷So then neither he who plants is anything, nor he who waters, but God who gives the increase. ⁸Now he who plants and he who waters are one, and each one will receive his own reward according to his own labor.

⁹For we are God's fellow workers; you are God's field, you are God's building. ¹⁰According to the grace of God which was given to me, as a wise master builder I have laid the foundation, and another builds on it. But let each one take heed how he builds on it. ¹¹For no other foundation can anyone lay than that which is laid, which is Jesus Christ. ¹²Now if anyone builds on this foundation with gold, silver, precious stones, wood, hay, straw, ¹³each one's work will become clear; for the Day will declare it, because it will be revealed by fire; and the fire will test each one's work, of what sort it is. ¹⁴If anyone's work which he has built on it endures, he will receive a reward. ¹⁵If anyone's work is burned, he will suffer loss; but he himself will be saved, yet so as through fire.

¹⁶Do you not know that you are the temple of God and that the Spirit of God dwells in you? ¹⁷If anyone defiles the temple of God, God will destroy him. For the temple of God is holy, which temple you are.

Avoid Worldly Wisdom

¹⁸Let no one deceive himself. If anyone among you seems to be wise in this age, let him become a fool that he may become wise. ¹⁹For the wisdom of this world is foolishness with God. For it is written, "He catches the wise in their own craftiness"; ²⁰and again, "The LORD knows the thoughts of the wise, that they are futile." ²¹Therefore let no one boast in men. For all things are yours: ²²whether Paul or Apollos or Cephas, or the world or life or death, or things present or things to come—all are yours. ²³And you are Christ's, and Christ is God's.

Stewards of the Mysteries of God

4 Let a man so consider us, as servants of Christ and stewards of the mysteries of God. ²Moreover it is required in stewards that one be found faithful. ³But with me it is a very small thing that I should be judged by you or by a human court. In fact, I do not even judge myself. ⁴For I know of nothing against myself, yet I am not justified by this; but He who judges me is the Lord. ⁵Therefore judge nothing before the time, until the Lord comes, who will both bring to light the hidden things of darkness and reveal the counsels of the hearts. Then each one's praise will come from God.

DEVOTIONAL

A hundred years from now, many things will be far less important to you than they are today—your meticulously groomed lawn, the amount of money in your IRA, the make and model of your car, or who won the World Series, Super Bowl, or Masters tournament.

Now, there's nothing wrong with any of these things, but it's important to answer this question: what in your life today will remain when the mountains have crumbled, the stars have fallen from the sky, and a new heaven and a new earth are created?

Wood, hay, and stumble will all go up in flames someday (1 Corinthians 3:12–13). Those three things are an analogy for temporary things we worry over, get stressed out about, and work for tirelessly—they are all going to dissolve. Many people are giving their lives to things that will not last, things that have no eternal value.

What are you living for that will last? What are you working for that will remain? Is your portfolio eternal? Paul said, "If anyone's work which he has built on it endures, he will receive a reward" (1 Corinthians 3:14). When we look back on this life with heavenly eyes, things are going to look much differently than they do now, so begin today to build for eternity with Jesus as your cornerstone.

—Rusty Womack
Lost Mountain Baptist Church, Powder Springs, GA

WEEK 34, DAY 4

God Will Not Tolerate Sin

1 Corinthians 4:6–5:8

Fools for Christ's Sake

Now these things, brethren, I have figuratively transferred to myself and Apollos for your sakes, that you may learn in us not to think beyond what is written, that none of you may be puffed up on behalf of one against the other. 7For who makes you differ from another? And what do you have that you did not receive? Now if you did indeed receive it, why do you boast as if you had not received it?

8You are already full! You are already rich! You have reigned as kings without us—and indeed I could wish you did reign, that we also might reign with you! 9For I think that God has displayed us, the apostles, last, as men condemned to death; for we have been made a spectacle to the world, both to angels and to men. 10We are fools for Christ's sake, but you are wise in Christ! We are weak, but you are strong! You are distinguished, but we are dishonored! 11To the present hour we both hunger and thirst, and we are poorly clothed, and beaten, and homeless. 12And we labor, working with our own hands. Being reviled, we bless; being persecuted, we endure; 13being defamed, we entreat. We have been made as the filth of the world, the offscouring of all things until now.

Paul's Paternal Care

14I do not write these things to shame you, but as my beloved children I warn you. 15For though you might have ten thousand instructors in Christ, yet you do not have many fathers; for in Christ Jesus I have begotten you through the gospel. 16Therefore I urge you, imitate me. 17For this reason I have sent Timothy to you, who is my beloved and faithful son in the Lord, who will remind you of my ways in Christ, as I teach everywhere in every church.

18Now some are puffed up, as though I were not coming to you. 19But I will come to you shortly, if the Lord wills, and I will know, not the word of those who are puffed up, but the power. 20For the kingdom of God is not in word but in power. 21What do you want? Shall I come to you with a rod, or in love and a spirit of gentleness?

Immorality Defiles the Church

5 It is actually reported that there is sexual immorality among you, and such sexual immorality as is not even named among the Gentiles—that a man has his father's wife! 2And you are puffed up, and have not rather mourned, that he who has done this deed might be taken away from among you. 3For I indeed, as absent in body but present in spirit, have already judged (as though I were present) him who has so done this deed. 4In the name of our Lord Jesus Christ, when you are gathered together, along with my spirit, with the power of our Lord Jesus Christ, 5deliver such a one to Satan for the destruction of the flesh, that his spirit may be saved in the day of the Lord Jesus.

6Your glorying *is* not good. Do you not know that a little leaven leavens the whole lump? 7Therefore purge out the old leaven, that you may be a new lump, since you truly are unleavened. For indeed Christ, our Passover, was sacrificed for us. 8Therefore let us keep the feast, not with old leaven, nor with the leaven of malice and wickedness, but with the unleavened bread of sincerity and truth.

DEVOTIONAL

People have the idea today that it is okay to live in immorality and that God is going to overlook their "little" indiscretions. But Scripture tells us, "Do not be deceived, God is not mocked; for whatever a man sows, that he will also reap" (Galatians 6:7). God doesn't miss one single beat of our lives. He is the righteous judge, and He will judge accordingly.

Does that mean that if you have done anything immoral that you can't be saved? No! First Corinthians 6:11 speaks to Christians with dark pasts, saying that unbelieving sinners will not inherit the kingdom of God, "but you were washed, but you were sanctified, but you were justified in the name of the Lord Jesus and by the Spirit of our God." Hallelujah! Praise Jesus!

There is no sin so awful that the blood of Christ cannot cleanse it. He makes the dirtiest sinner clean. God will not tolerate sin in your life because He is holy and because of the great sacrifice Jesus Christ made for you on the cross. If there is an area of unconfessed sin in your life, He will deal with you personally, persistently, and powerfully until you put it out of your life (1 Corinthians 5:13).

Your sin may not be mentioned here on this page, but sin is sin. If left alone, sin will cost you more than you want to pay, take you further than you want to go, and keep you longer than you want to stay. Deal with sin today!

—Rusty Womack
Lost Mountain Baptist Church, Powder Springs, GA

WEEK 34, DAY 5

Honor God with Your Body

1 Corinthians 5:9–6:20

Immorality Must Be Judged

Iwrote to you in my epistle not to keep company with sexually immoral people. [10]Yet I certainly did not mean with the sexually immoral people of this world, or with the covetous, or extortioners, or idolaters, since then you would need to go out of the world. [11]But now I have written to you not to keep company with anyone named a brother, who is sexually immoral, or covetous, or an idolater, or a reviler, or a drunkard, or an extortioner—not even to eat with such a person.

[12]For what have I to do with judging those also who are outside? Do you not judge those who are inside? [13]But those who are outside God judges. Therefore "put away from yourselves the evil person."

Do Not Sue the Brethren

6Dare any of you, having a matter against another, go to law before the unrighteous, and not before the saints? [2]Do you not know that the saints will judge the world? And if the world will be judged by you, are you unworthy to judge the smallest matters? [3]Do you not know that we shall judge angels? How much more, things that pertain to this life? [4]If then you have judgments concerning things pertaining to this life, do you appoint those who are least esteemed by the church to judge? [5]I say this to your shame. Is it so, that there is not a wise man among you, not even one, who will be able to judge between his brethren? [6]But brother goes to law against brother, and that before unbelievers!

[7]Now therefore, it is already an utter failure for you that you go to law against one another. Why do you not rather accept wrong? Why do you not rather let yourselves be cheated? [8]No, you yourselves do wrong and cheat, and you do these things to your brethren! [9]Do you not know that the unrighteous will not inherit the kingdom of God? Do not be deceived. Neither fornicators, nor idolaters, nor adulterers, nor homosexuals, nor sodomites, [10]nor thieves, nor covetous, nor drunkards, nor revilers, nor extortioners will inherit the kingdom of God. [11]And such were some of you. But you were washed, but you were sanctified, but you were justified in the name of the Lord Jesus and by the Spirit of our God.

Glorify God in Body and Spirit

[12]All things are lawful for me, but all things are not helpful. All things are lawful for me, but I will not be brought under the power of any. [13]Foods for the stomach and the stomach for foods, but God will destroy both it and them. Now the body is not for sexual immorality but for the Lord, and the Lord for the body. [14]And God both raised up the Lord and will also raise us up by His power.

[15]Do you not know that your bodies are members of Christ? Shall I then take the members of Christ and make them members of a harlot? Certainly not! [16]Or do you not know that he who is joined to a harlot is one body with her? For "the two," He says, "shall become one flesh." [17]But he who is joined to the Lord is one spirit with Him.

[18]Flee sexual immorality. Every sin that a man does is outside the body, but he who commits sexual immorality sins against his own body. [19]Or do you not know that your body is the temple of the Holy Spirit who is in you, whom you have from God, and you are not your own? [20]For you were bought at a price; therefore glorify God in your body and in your spirit, which are God's.

DEVOTIONAL

The sin of immorality is not a sin we are told to fight in the Bible—it is a sin we are told to flee from (2 Timothy 2:22). God tells us to get out of every compromising situation. Remember what Joseph did when Potiphar's wife approached him (Genesis 39:7–12)? In a word, he fled. Joseph got out of that compromising situation as fast as he could!

We live in a society of moral relativism, but Scripture reminds us that God indeed judges immoral behavior (1 Corinthians 5:9–13; Hebrews 13:4). Proverbs 6:32–33 offer strong words regarding sexual immorality: "Whoever commits adultery . . . destroys his own soul. Wounds and dishonor he will get, and his reproach will not be wiped away."

If there is someone in your office who flirts with you inappropriately, it would be better for you to quit your job than to remain in the office. Lose your job and keep your integrity! If someone who is married begins to communicate with you in a suggestive way, lose the relationship instead of your reputation. If you find yourself in any kind of compromising situation, don't see how close you can come to it—see how far you can get away from it. Honor God with your body and with your life!

—Rusty Womack
Lost Mountain Baptist Church, Powder Springs, GA

WEEK 34, DAY 6

Marriage Is a Gift from God

1 Corinthians 7:1–24

Principles of Marriage

7Now concerning the things of which you wrote to me: It is good for a man not to touch a woman. ²Nevertheless, because of sexual immorality, let each man have his own wife, and let each woman have her own husband. ³Let the husband render to his wife the affection due her, and likewise also the wife to her husband. ⁴The wife does not have authority over her own body, but the husband does. And likewise the husband does not have authority over his own body, but the wife does. ⁵Do not deprive one another except with consent for a time, that you may give yourselves to fasting and prayer; and come together again so that Satan does not tempt you because of your lack of self-control. ⁶But I say this as a concession, not as a commandment. ⁷For I wish that all men were even as I myself. But each one has his own gift from God, one in this manner and another in that.

⁸But I say to the unmarried and to the widows: It is good for them if they remain even as I am; ⁹but if they cannot exercise self-control, let them marry. For it is better to marry than to burn with passion.

Keep Your Marriage Vows

¹⁰Now to the married I command, yet not I but the Lord: A wife is not to depart from her husband. ¹¹But even if she does depart, let her remain unmarried or be reconciled to her husband. And a husband is not to divorce his wife.

¹²But to the rest I, not the Lord, say: If any brother has a wife who does not believe, and she is willing to live with him, let him not divorce her. ¹³And a woman who has a husband who does not believe, if he is willing to live with her, let her not divorce him. ¹⁴For the unbelieving husband is sanctified by the wife, and the unbelieving wife is sanctified by the husband; otherwise your children would be unclean, but now they are holy. ¹⁵But if the unbeliever departs, let him depart; a brother or a sister is not under bondage in such cases. But God has called us to peace. ¹⁶For how do you know, O wife, whether you will save your husband? Or how do you know, O husband, whether you will save your wife?

Live as You Are Called

¹⁷But as God has distributed to each one, as the Lord has called each one, so let him walk. And so I ordain in all the churches. ¹⁸Was anyone called while circumcised? Let him not become uncircumcised. Was anyone called while uncircumcised? Let him not be circumcised. ¹⁹Circumcision is nothing and uncircumcision is nothing, but keeping the commandments of God is what matters. ²⁰Let each one remain in the same calling in which he was called. ²¹Were you called while a slave? Do not be concerned about it; but if you can be made free, rather use it. ²²For he who is called in the Lord while a slave is the Lord's freedman. Likewise he who is called while free is Christ's slave. ²³You were bought at a price; do not become slaves of men. ²⁴Brethren, let each one remain with God in that state in which he was called.

DEVOTIONAL

Perhaps you've heard that the divorce rate of second marriages is much higher than in first marriages, and that it increases with every remarriage after. Why? Because very few people correct the problems that led to the first divorce. Our society has made it too easy for people to get a divorce, but divorce papers will never completely undo what God has done, because it is nearly impossible for couples to completely separate emotionally.

God says that marriage is two individuals becoming one flesh (Genesis 2:24). Marriage is like supergluing two pieces of cardboard together. If you tear them apart, pieces of one will be permanently attached to the other, and you'll make a mess in the process. People cannot be divorced without leaving a part of themselves with their former mate and carrying a part of their former mate with them.

First Corinthians 7:10–11 clearly teaches Christians not to divorce one another. It is always too soon to quit a marriage—it is a gift from God!

If you are divorced today and have not remarried, do everything you can to reconcile with your first spouse, or remain unmarried (1 Corinthians 7:11). If you have remarried, then stay that way. A second divorce is not going to correct the mistake you made with the first one. Just be sure that you and your spouse love Jesus Christ more than each other. A marriage without Jesus is like a ship without a rudder. You may move forward, but you won't be able to sail around the storms of life.

—Rusty Womack
Lost Mountain Baptist Church, Powder Springs, GA

WEEK 34, DAY 7

Are you spending unhurried time with God? Why or why not? Read Jeremiah 23, Mark 3:13–15, and 1 Corinthians 2:4–5, and list the benefits of being in God's presence.

_____

_____

_____

_____

_____

_____

_____

_____

_____

_____

_____

Are you happy in your marriage or relationship? Is it glorifying to God? Why or why not? What do you need to work on to take your relationship to the next level?

_____

_____

_____

_____

_____

_____

_____

_____

_____

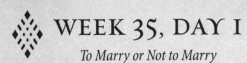

WEEK 35, DAY I

To Marry or Not to Marry

1 Corinthians 7:25–8:8

To the Unmarried and Widows

Now concerning virgins: I have no commandment from the Lord; yet I give judgment as one whom the Lord in His mercy has made trustworthy. 26I suppose therefore that this is good because of the present distress—that it is good for a man to remain as he is: 27Are you bound to a wife? Do not seek to be loosed. Are you loosed from a wife? Do not seek a wife. 28But even if you do marry, you have not sinned; and if a virgin marries, she has not sinned. Nevertheless such will have trouble in the flesh, but I would spare you.

29But this I say, brethren, the time is short, so that from now on even those who have wives should be as though they had none, 30those who weep as though they did not weep, those who rejoice as though they did not rejoice, those who buy as though they did not possess, 31and those who use this world as not misusing it. For the form of this world is passing away.

32But I want you to be without care. He who is unmarried cares for the things of the Lord—how he may please the Lord. 33But he who is married cares about the things of the world—how he may please his wife. 34There is a difference between a wife and a virgin. The unmarried woman cares about the things of the Lord, that she may be holy both in body and in spirit. But she who is married cares about the things of the world—how she may please her husband. 35And this I say for your own profit, not that I may put a leash on you, but for what is proper, and that you may serve the Lord without distraction.

36But if any man thinks he is behaving improperly toward his virgin, if she is past the flower of youth, and thus it must be, let him do what he wishes. He does not sin; let them marry. 37Nevertheless he who stands steadfast in his heart, having no necessity, but has power over his own will, and has so determined in his heart that he will keep his virgin, does well. 38So then he who gives her in marriage does well, but he who does not give her in marriage does better.

39A wife is bound by law as long as her husband lives; but if her husband dies, she is at liberty to be married to whom she wishes, only in the Lord. 40But she is happier if she remains as she is, according to my judgment—and I think I also have the Spirit of God.

Be Sensitive to Conscience

8 Now concerning things offered to idols: We know that we all have knowledge. Knowledge puffs up, but love edifies. 2And if anyone thinks that he knows anything, he knows nothing yet as he ought to know. 3But if anyone loves God, this one is known by Him.

4Therefore concerning the eating of things offered to idols, we know that an idol is nothing in the world, and that there is no other God but one. 5For even if there are so-called gods, whether in heaven or on earth (as there are many gods and many lords), 6yet for us there is one God, the Father, of whom are all things, and we for Him; and one Lord Jesus Christ, through whom are all things, and through whom we live.

7However, there is not in everyone that knowledge; for some, with consciousness of the idol, until now eat it as a thing offered to an idol; and their conscience, being weak, is defiled. 8But food does not commend us to God; for neither if we eat are we the better, nor if we do not eat are we the worse.

DEVOTIONAL

The two most important decisions in life are how we respond to Jesus and who—or if—we marry. Both are lifelong commitments and should be taken seriously!

The Bible addresses the real issues of life. Paul encouraged both the married and unmarried to remain as they are (1 Corinthians 7:26). Salvation does not alter our marital status. Marriage is an earthly arrangement that will not continue in heaven (Matthew 22:30). Therefore, Paul was concerned about the cares brought on by an earthly agreement that causes a believer to focus on pleasing his or her spouse instead of pleasing the Lord (1 Corinthians 7:32–35). But he gave no commandment to remain single.

In today's church culture we often think everyone should be married. It is not unusual to find self-appointed matchmakers in the pews attempting to connect single friends. Neither Paul nor Jesus taught that marriage or singleness was above the other. In fact, both commended singleness (Matthew 19:10–12).

Thank God for addressing the issues of life in His Word, and make sure your views of marriage and singleness line up with His.

—Allan Taylor, Minister of Education
First Baptist Church, Woodstock, GA

WEEK 35, DAY 2

Putting Others in Our Community First

1 Corinthians 8:9–9:23

But beware lest somehow this liberty of yours become a stumbling block to those who are weak. 10For if anyone sees you who have knowledge eating in an idol's temple, will not the conscience of him who is weak be emboldened to eat those things offered to idols? 11And because of your knowledge shall the weak brother perish, for whom Christ died? 12But when you thus sin against the brethren, and wound their weak conscience, you sin against Christ. 13Therefore, if food makes my brother stumble, I will never again eat meat, lest I make my brother stumble.

A Pattern of Self-Denial

9Am I not an apostle? Am I not free? Have I not seen Jesus Christ our Lord? Are you not my work in the Lord? 2If I am not an apostle to others, yet doubtless I am to you. For you are the seal of my apostleship in the Lord.

3My defense to those who examine me is this: 4Do we have no right to eat and drink? 5Do we have no right to take along a believing wife, as do also the other apostles, the brothers of the Lord, and Cephas? 6Or is it only Barnabas and I who have no right to refrain from working? 7Who ever goes to war at his own expense? Who plants a vineyard and does not eat of its fruit? Or who tends a flock and does not drink of the milk of the flock?

8Do I say these things as a mere man? Or does not the law say the same also? 9For it is written in the law of Moses, "You shall not muzzle an ox while it treads out the grain." Is it oxen God is concerned about? 10Or does He say it altogether for our sakes? For our sakes, no doubt, this is written, that he who plows should plow in hope, and he who threshes in hope should be partaker of his hope. 11If we have sown spiritual things for you, is it a great thing if we reap your material things? 12If others are partakers of this right over you, are we not even more?

Nevertheless we have not used this right, but endure all things lest we hinder the gospel of Christ. 13Do you not know that those who minister the holy things eat of the things of the temple, and those who serve at the altar partake of the offerings of the altar? 14Even so the Lord has commanded that those who preach the gospel should live from the gospel.

15But I have used none of these things, nor have I written these things that it should be done so to me; for it would be better for me to die than that anyone should make my boasting void. 16For if I preach the gospel, I have nothing to boast of, for necessity is laid upon me; yes, woe is me if I do not preach the gospel! 17For if I do this willingly, I have a reward; but if against my will, I have been entrusted with a stewardship. 18What is my reward then? That when I preach the gospel, I may present the gospel of Christ without charge, that I may not abuse my authority in the gospel.

Serving All Men

19For though I am free from all men, I have made myself a servant to all, that I might win the more; 20and to the Jews I became as a Jew, that I might win Jews; to those who are under the law, as under the law, that I might win those who are under the law; 21to those who are without law, as without law (not being without law toward God, but under law toward Christ), that I might win those who are without law; 22to the weak I became as weak, that I might win the weak. I have become all things to all men, that I might by all means save some. 23Now this I do for the gospel's sake, that I may be partaker of it with you.

DEVOTIONAL

We are so self-absorbed that we often see the effects of our sin on ourselves but fail to see it on others. In the Christian life, we are to be our brother's keeper. We must not just live to ourselves; we have to consider how our actions and attitudes affect others. This is one of the most glaring yet overlooked problems in the Christian community today. If we truly practice the second greatest commandment, to love our neighbors as ourselves, then how can we be content to ignore becoming a stumbling block to others for whom Christ died?

Paul stated that some Christians were offended by other believers eating meat offered to idols. Today, many believers are offended by those who drink alcohol. Many Christian social drinkers make their case as to why it is permissible, but Paul clearly stated, "When you thus sin against the brethren . . . you sin against Christ" (1 Corinthians 8:12). What a strong indictment! Paul would not even take a minister's salary so as not to offend anyone "for the gospel's sake" (9:23). Neither should we offend others for the gospel's sake!

Be careful not to be a stumbling block or offense to others today.

—Allan Taylor, Minister of Education
First Baptist Church, Woodstock, GA

WEEK 35, DAY 3

Stand Firm Against Temptation

1 Corinthians 9:24–10:22

Striving for a Crown

Do you not know that those who run in a race all run, but one receives the prize? Run in such a way that you may obtain it. ²⁵And everyone who competes for the prize is temperate in all things. Now they do it to obtain a perishable crown, but we for an imperishable crown. ²⁶Therefore I run thus: not with uncertainty. Thus I fight: not as one who beats the air. ²⁷But I discipline my body and bring it into subjection, lest, when I have preached to others, I myself should become disqualified.

Old Testament Examples

10Moreover, brethren, I do not want you to be unaware that all our fathers were under the cloud, all passed through the sea, ²all were baptized into Moses in the cloud and in the sea, ³all ate the same spiritual food, ⁴and all drank the same spiritual drink. For they drank of that spiritual Rock that followed them, and that Rock was Christ. ⁵But with most of them God was not well pleased, for their bodies were scattered in the wilderness.

⁶Now these things became our examples, to the intent that we should not lust after evil things as they also lusted. ⁷And do not become idolaters as were some of them. As it is written, "The people sat down to eat and drink, and rose up to play." ⁸Nor let us commit sexual immorality, as some of them did, and in one day twenty-three thousand fell; ⁹nor let us tempt Christ, as some of them also tempted, and were destroyed by serpents; ¹⁰nor complain, as some of them also complained, and were destroyed by the destroyer. ¹¹Now all these things happened to them as examples, and they were written for our admonition, upon whom the ends of the ages have come.

¹²Therefore let him who thinks he stands take heed lest he fall. ¹³No temptation has overtaken you except such as is common to man; but God is faithful, who will not allow you to be tempted beyond what you are able, but with the temptation will also make the way of escape, that you may be able to bear it.

Flee from Idolatry

¹⁴Therefore, my beloved, flee from idolatry. ¹⁵I speak as to wise men; judge for yourselves what I say. ¹⁶The cup of blessing which we bless, is it not the communion of the blood of Christ? The bread which we break, is it not the communion of the body of Christ? ¹⁷For we, though many, are one bread and one body; for we all partake of that one bread.

¹⁸Observe Israel after the flesh: Are not those who eat of the sacrifices partakers of the altar? ¹⁹What am I saying then? That an idol is anything, or what is offered to idols is anything? ²⁰Rather, that the things which the Gentiles sacrifice they sacrifice to demons and not to God, and I do not want you to have fellowship with demons. ²¹You cannot drink the cup of the Lord and the cup of demons; you cannot partake of the Lord's table and of the table of demons. ²²Or do we provoke the Lord to jealousy? Are we stronger than He?

DEVOTIONAL

Discipline *is perhaps the most hated word in the Christian vocabulary. Many of us are not disciplined in our business deals, entertainment, or language. We all want our ticket to heaven stamped, but we don't want to be bothered with Christian disciplines while on our journey there.*

Discipline is an inside job—it cannot be done by proxy. Only you can discipline yourself! D. L. Moody once said, "The Bible will keep you from sin, or sin will keep you from the Bible."⁹ That statement is an encouragement to be disciplined in Bible reading, and it's true of other spiritual disciplines as well. "Prayer will keep you from sin, or sin will keep you from prayer." "A Bible-preaching church will keep you from sin, or sin will keep you from a Bible-preaching church."

We do not want to follow the example of the Israelites, with whom "God was not well pleased" (1 Corinthians 10:5). They were idolaters, adulterers, tempters, and complainers. They did not heed Moses' commands not to do evil in God's sight. Paul said we are all *both capable of sin and of escaping sin (vv. 12–13). You can fall, but you don't have to! You can be a victim of sin, or you can be a victor over sin! It takes discipline, it takes saying no to the flesh, and it takes relying on the help of the Holy Spirit.*

Like Paul, discipline your body and your spirit, bring them into subjection, and be temperate in all things.

—Allan Taylor, Minister of Education
First Baptist Church, Woodstock, GA

WEEK 35, DAY 4
Honor God by Honoring Others

1 Corinthians 10:23–11:22

All to the Glory of God

All things are lawful for me, but not all things are helpful; all things are lawful for me, but not all things edify. ²⁴Let no one seek his own, but each one the other's well-being.

²⁵Eat whatever is sold in the meat market, asking no questions for conscience' sake; ²⁶for "the earth is the LORD's, and all its fullness."

²⁷If any of those who do not believe invites you to dinner, and you desire to go, eat whatever is set before you, asking no question for conscience' sake. ²⁸But if anyone says to you, "This was offered to idols," do not eat it for the sake of the one who told you, and for conscience' sake; for "the earth is the LORD's, and all its fullness." ²⁹"Conscience," I say, not your own, but that of the other. For why is my liberty judged by another man's conscience? ³⁰But if I partake with thanks, why am I evil spoken of for the food over which I give thanks?

³¹Therefore, whether you eat or drink, or whatever you do, do all to the glory of God. ³²Give no offense, either to the Jews or to the Greeks or to the church of God, ³³just as I also please all men in all things, not seeking my own profit, but the profit of many, that they may be saved.

11 Imitate me, just as I also imitate Christ.

Head Coverings

²Now I praise you, brethren, that you remember me in all things and keep the traditions just as I delivered them to you. ³But I want you to know that the head of every man is Christ, the head of woman is man, and the head of Christ is God. ⁴Every man praying or prophesying, having his head covered, dishonors his head. ⁵But every woman who prays or prophesies with her head uncovered dishonors her head, for that is one and the same as if her head were shaved. ⁶For if a woman is not covered, let her also be shorn. But if it is shameful for a woman to be shorn or shaved, let her be covered. ⁷For a man indeed ought not to cover his head, since he is the image and glory of God; but woman is the glory of man. ⁸For man is not from woman, but woman from man. ⁹Nor was man created for the woman, but woman for the man. ¹⁰For this reason the woman ought to have a symbol of authority on her head, because of the angels. ¹¹Nevertheless, neither is man independent of woman, nor woman independent of man, in the Lord. ¹²For as woman came from man, even so man also comes through woman; but all things are from God.

¹³Judge among yourselves. Is it proper for a woman to pray to God with her head uncovered? ¹⁴Does not even nature itself teach you that if a man has long hair, it is a dishonor to him? ¹⁵But if a woman has long hair, it is a glory to her; for her hair is given to her for a covering. ¹⁶But if anyone seems to be contentious, we have no such custom, nor do the churches of God.

Conduct at the Lord's Supper

¹⁷Now in giving these instructions I do not praise you, since you come together not for the better but for the worse. ¹⁸For first of all, when you come together as a church, I hear that there are divisions among you, and in part I believe it. ¹⁹For there must also be factions among you, that those who are approved may be recognized among you. ²⁰Therefore when you come together in one place, it is not to eat the Lord's Supper. ²¹For in eating, each one takes his own supper ahead of others; and one is hungry and another is drunk. ²²What! Do you not have houses to eat and drink in? Or do you despise the church of God and shame those who have nothing? What shall I say to you? Shall I praise you in this? I do not praise you.

DEVOTIONAL

In this passage we see three ways we can honor God. First, we honor God by not offending others. Many do things they know are offensive to others because they don't think others should find them offensive. But Paul commanded, "Let no one seek his own, but each one the other's well-being" (1 Corinthians 10:24). We do affect others and must not exercise our Christian liberties to the demise of others. Paul also said we should not do anything that makes a fellow believer weak or stumble, for "none of us lives to himself, and no one dies to himself" (Romans 14:7, 21).

Second, we honor God by submitting to others. Ephesians 5:21 echoes this command, saying we should do so out of reverence for Christ and in fear of God.

Third, we honor God by preferring others. Paul reprimanded the Corinthian believers for dividing into cliques, eating at different times, and refusing to share with the poor when they gathered to celebrate the Lord's Supper.

In honoring others, we honor Christ. How will you do that today?

—Allan Taylor, Minister of Education
First Baptist Church, Woodstock, GA

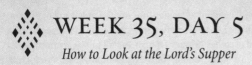

WEEK 35, DAY 5

How to Look at the Lord's Supper

1 Corinthians 11:23–12:11

Institution of the Lord's Supper

For I received from the Lord that which I also delivered to you: that the Lord Jesus on the same night in which He was betrayed took bread; 24and when He had given thanks, He broke it and said, "Take, eat; this is My body which is broken for you; do this in remembrance of Me." 25In the same manner He also took the cup after supper, saying, "This cup is the new covenant in My blood. This do, as often as you drink it, in remembrance of Me."

26For as often as you eat this bread and drink this cup, you proclaim the Lord's death till He comes.

Examine Yourself

27Therefore whoever eats this bread or drinks this cup of the Lord in an unworthy manner will be guilty of the body and blood of the Lord. 28But let a man examine himself, and so let him eat of the bread and drink of the cup. 29For he who eats and drinks in an unworthy manner eats and drinks judgment to himself, not discerning the Lord's body. 30For this reason many are weak and sick among you, and many sleep. 31For if we would judge ourselves, we would not be judged. 32But when we are judged, we are chastened by the Lord, that we may not be condemned with the world.

33Therefore, my brethren, when you come together to eat, wait for one another. 34But if anyone is hungry, let him eat at home, lest you come together for judgment. And the rest I will set in order when I come.

Spiritual Gifts: Unity in Diversity

12 Now concerning spiritual gifts, brethren, I do not want you to be ignorant: 2You know that you were Gentiles, carried away to these dumb idols, however you were led. 3Therefore I make known to you that no one speaking by the Spirit of God calls Jesus accursed, and no one can say that Jesus is Lord except by the Holy Spirit.

4There are diversities of gifts, but the same Spirit. 5There are differences of ministries, but the same Lord. 6And there are diversities of activities, but it is the same God who works all in all. 7But the manifestation of the Spirit is given to each one for the profit of all: 8for to one is given the word of wisdom through the Spirit, to another the word of knowledge through the same Spirit, 9to another faith by the same Spirit, to another gifts of healings by the same Spirit, 10to another the working of miracles, to another prophecy, to another discerning of spirits, to another different kinds of tongues, to another the interpretation of tongues. 11But one and the same Spirit works all these things, distributing to each one individually as He wills.

DEVOTIONAL

Jesus instituted the Lord's Supper with His disciples the night before His crucifixion. The bread represents His body, which was broken for us. It bore our griefs, carried our sorrows, was smitten by God, and was wounded for our transgressions (Isaiah 53:4–5). The juice represents Jesus' blood, which was shed for us. His sacrifice was necessary for the forgiveness of our sins because "without shedding of blood there is no remission" (Hebrews 9:22).

There are three aspects of the Lord's Supper. First, there is a backward look. Jesus said, "Do this in remembrance of Me" (1 Corinthians 11:24). Reading the Gospel accounts of His crucifixion before we take the Lord's Supper helps us remember all Jesus went through to pay the price for our sins and demonstrate His great love for us.

Second, there is a forward look. Jesus said, "As often as you eat this bread and drink this cup, you proclaim the Lord's death till He comes" (1 Corinthians 11:26). Praise God, Jesus is coming again! At the Lord's table, we pause to remember His promised return.

Third, there is an inward look. Paul said we should examine and judge ourselves. Why? So we do not partake of the Lord's body and blood in an unworthy manner. The Lord chastened those who did; some became sick and weak, and some even died (1 Corinthians 11:30). We must not come to the Lord's table flippantly! We must not eat of the ordinance of the Lord's Supper with known, unconfessed sin in our lives.

Don't forget to take a backward, forward, and inward look the next time you take part in the Lord's Supper. Doing so will help you be mindful of all Jesus has done for us in the past and all He has promised to His followers in the future.

—Allan Taylor, Minister of Education
First Baptist Church, Woodstock, GA

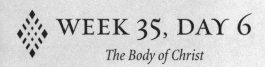

WEEK 35, DAY 6

The Body of Christ

1 Corinthians 12:12–13:13

Unity and Diversity in One Body

For as the body is one and has many members, but all the members of that one body, being many, are one body, so also is Christ. 13For by one Spirit we were all baptized into one body—whether Jews or Greeks, whether slaves or free—and have all been made to drink into one Spirit. 14For in fact the body is not one member but many.

15If the foot should say, "Because I am not a hand, I am not of the body," is it therefore not of the body? 16And if the ear should say, "Because I am not an eye, I am not of the body," is it therefore not of the body? 17If the whole body were an eye, where would be the hearing? If the whole were hearing, where would be the smelling? 18But now God has set the members, each one of them, in the body just as He pleased. 19And if they were all one member, where would the body be?

20But now indeed there are many members, yet one body. 21And the eye cannot say to the hand, "I have no need of you"; nor again the head to the feet, "I have no need of you." 22No, much rather, those members of the body which seem to be weaker are necessary. 23And those members of the body which we think to be less honorable, on these we bestow greater honor; and our unpresentable parts have greater modesty, 24but our presentable parts have no need. But God composed the body, having given greater honor to that part which lacks it, 25that there should be no schism in the body, but that the members should have the same care for one another. 26And if one member suffers, all the members suffer with it; or if one member is honored, all the members rejoice with it.

27Now you are the body of Christ, and members individually. 28And God has appointed these in the church: first apostles, second prophets, third teachers, after that miracles, then gifts of healings, helps, administrations, varieties of tongues. 29Are all apostles? Are all prophets? Are all teachers? Are all workers of miracles? 30Do all have gifts of healings? Do all speak with tongues? Do all interpret? 31But earnestly desire the best gifts. And yet I show you a more excellent way.

The Greatest Gift

13Though I speak with the tongues of men and of angels, but have not love, I have become sounding brass or a clanging cymbal. 2And though I have the gift of prophecy, and understand all mysteries and all knowledge, and though I have all faith, so that I could remove mountains, but have not love, I am nothing. 3And though I bestow all my goods to feed the poor, and though I give my body to be burned, but have not love, it profits me nothing.

4Love suffers long and is kind; love does not envy; love does not parade itself, is not puffed up; 5does not behave rudely, does not seek its own, is not provoked, thinks no evil; 6does not rejoice in iniquity, but rejoices in the truth; 7bears all things, believes all things, hopes all things, endures all things.

8Love never fails. But whether there are prophecies, they will fail; whether there are tongues, they will cease; whether there is knowledge, it will vanish away. 9For we know in part and we prophesy in part. 10But when that which is perfect has come, then that which is in part will be done away.

11When I was a child, I spoke as a child, I understood as a child, I thought as a child; but when I became a man, I put away childish things. 12For now we see in a mirror, dimly, but then face to face. Now I know in part, but then I shall know just as I also am known.

13And now abide faith, hope, love, these three; but the greatest of these is love.

DEVOTIONAL

There are three vital aspects of the body of Christ. First, there is unity in the body. Jesus prayed we would be one as Jesus is one with the Father (John 17:20–21). Wow! That is a lot of oneness! God the Father answered Jesus' prayer by sending the Holy Spirit to make us one. Paul said "the body is one" and "by one Spirit we were all baptized into one body" (1 Corinthians 12:12–13).

Second, there is diversity in the body. We are not all the same. The Holy Spirit has gifted us differently for various tasks and ministries within the body. This passage reminds us that each "body part" is necessary and contributes a function important to the working of the body.

Third, there is maturity in the body. Your spiritual giftedness is of no value if it is not exercised with love. The fruit of the Spirit is more important than the gifts of the Spirit!

Do your part in honoring God's design for the body of Christ. Seek unity with others, respect others' spiritual gifts, and do all things in love.

—Allan Taylor, Minister of Education
First Baptist Church, Woodstock, GA

WEEK 35, DAY 7

Do you think of others and how your attitudes and actions may affect them? What do you need to consider changing so you do not offend others?

_____

_____

_____

_____

_____

_____

_____

_____

_____

_____

_____

_____

What are your spiritual gifts? How are you using them to build up others?

_____

_____

_____

_____

_____

_____

_____

_____

_____

WEEK 36, DAY 1

Spiritual Gifts

1 Corinthians 14:1–25

Prophecy and Tongues

14 Pursue love, and desire spiritual gifts, but especially that you may prophesy. ²For he who speaks in a tongue does not speak to men but to God, for no one understands him; however, in the spirit he speaks mysteries. ³But he who prophesies speaks edification and exhortation and comfort to men. ⁴He who speaks in a tongue edifies himself, but he who prophesies edifies the church. ⁵I wish you all spoke with tongues, but even more that you prophesied; for he who prophesies is greater than he who speaks with tongues, unless indeed he interprets, that the church may receive edification.

Tongues Must Be Interpreted

⁶But now, brethren, if I come to you speaking with tongues, what shall I profit you unless I speak to you either by revelation, by knowledge, by prophesying, or by teaching? ⁷Even things without life, whether flute or harp, when they make a sound, unless they make a distinction in the sounds, how will it be known what is piped or played? ⁸For if the trumpet makes an uncertain sound, who will prepare for battle? ⁹So likewise you, unless you utter by the tongue words easy to understand, how will it be known what is spoken? For you will be speaking into the air. ¹⁰There are, it may be, so many kinds of languages in the world, and none of them is without significance. ¹¹Therefore, if I do not know the meaning of the language, I shall be a foreigner to him who speaks, and he who speaks will be a foreigner to me. ¹²Even so you, since you are zealous for spiritual gifts, let it be for the edification of the church that you seek to excel.

¹³Therefore let him who speaks in a tongue pray that he may interpret. ¹⁴For if I pray in a tongue, my spirit prays, but my understanding is unfruitful. ¹⁵What is the conclusion then? I will pray with the spirit, and I will also pray with the understanding. I will sing with the spirit, and I will also sing with the understanding. ¹⁶Otherwise, if you bless with the spirit, how will he who occupies the place of the uninformed say "Amen" at your giving of thanks, since he does not understand what you say? ¹⁷For you indeed give thanks well, but the other is not edified. ¹⁸I thank my God I speak with tongues more than you all; ¹⁹yet in the church I would rather speak five words with my understanding, that I may teach others also, than ten thousand words in a tongue.

Tongues a Sign to Unbelievers

²⁰Brethren, do not be children in understanding; however, in malice be babes, but in understanding be mature. ²¹In the law it is written:

"With men of other tongues and other lips
I will speak to this people;
And yet, for all that, they will not hear Me,"

says the Lord. ²²Therefore tongues are for a sign, not to those who believe but to unbelievers; but prophesying is not for unbelievers but for those who believe. ²³Therefore if the whole church comes together in one place, and all speak with tongues, and there come in those who are uninformed or unbelievers, will they not say that you are out of your mind? ²⁴But if all prophesy, and an unbeliever or an uninformed person comes in, he is convinced by all, he is convicted by all. ²⁵And thus the secrets of his heart are revealed; and so, falling down on his face, he will worship God and report that God is truly among you.

DEVOTIONAL

Spiritual gifts are the supernatural tools God gives to every believer. When these miraculous gifts are coordinated to complement each other, they build up the church, the individual Christian, and even unreached people! How is that possible? Spiritual gifts edify the church.

The word *edify*, used in 1 Corinthians 14:3–5, 12, comes from two Greek words that literally mean "to build the house." Some gifts build up the individual (v. 4), some build up the church (verses 4, 5), and some help to evangelize the lost (vv. 24–25).

If you hired a carpenter, a painter, an electrician, and a plumber to work on your house, all of them would use different tools and do different jobs, but in the end, the finished product would be home improvement. Spiritual gifts are just like that. Even though our tools and our tasks differ, the church is edified through the exercise of spiritual gifts.

Are you taking part in what God is doing in and through the body of Christ? Look around you for needs to meet, and offer your spiritual gifts to build up others. Ask God to guide you and use you for His purposes.

—Dr. J. Kie Bowman
Hyde Park Baptist Church, Austin, TX

WEEK 36, DAY 2

The Essentials of the Christian Faith

1 Corinthians 14:26–15:11

Order in Church Meetings

How is it then, brethren? Whenever you come together, each of you has a psalm, has a teaching, has a tongue, has a revelation, has an interpretation. Let all things be done for edification. 27If anyone speaks in a tongue, let there be two or at the most three, each in turn, and let one interpret. 28But if there is no interpreter, let him keep silent in church, and let him speak to himself and to God. 29Let two or three prophets speak, and let the others judge. 30But if anything is revealed to another who sits by, let the first keep silent. 31For you can all prophesy one by one, that all may learn and all may be encouraged. 32And the spirits of the prophets are subject to the prophets. 33For God is not the author of confusion but of peace, as in all the churches of the saints.

34Let your women keep silent in the churches, for they are not permitted to speak; but they are to be submissive, as the law also says. 35And if they want to learn something, let them ask their own husbands at home; for it is shameful for women to speak in church.

36Or did the word of God come originally from you? Or was it you only that it reached? 37If anyone thinks himself to be a prophet or spiritual, let him acknowledge that the things which I write to you are the commandments of the Lord. 38But if anyone is ignorant, let him be ignorant.

39Therefore, brethren, desire earnestly to prophesy, and do not forbid to speak with tongues. 40Let all things be done decently and in order.

The Risen Christ, Faith's Reality

15 Moreover, brethren, I declare to you the gospel which I preached to you, which also you received and in which you stand, 2by which also you are saved, if you hold fast that word which I preached to you—unless you believed in vain.

3For I delivered to you first of all that which I also received: that Christ died for our sins according to the Scriptures, 4and that He was buried, and that He rose again the third day according to the Scriptures, 5and that He was seen by Cephas, then by the twelve. 6After that He was seen by over five hundred brethren at once, of whom the greater part remain to the present, but some have fallen asleep. 7After that He was seen by James, then by all the apostles. 8Then last of all He was seen by me also, as by one born out of due time.

9For I am the least of the apostles, who am not worthy to be called an apostle, because I persecuted the church of God. 10But by the grace of God I am what I am, and His grace toward me was not in vain; but I labored more abundantly than they all, yet not I, but the grace of God which was with me. 11Therefore, whether it was I or they, so we preach and so you believed.

DEVOTIONAL

After encouraging an orderly manner of teaching God's Word and utilizing spiritual gifts (1 Corinthians 14:26–40), Paul moved on to discuss the core truths of the church: "that Christ died for our sins according to the Scriptures, and that He was buried, and that He rose again the third day according to the Scriptures" (15:3–4). The cross and the resurrection of Jesus are the central themes of our Christian message! It is the truth by which we are saved and upon which we stand (verses 1, 2).

Fortunately, the message of the cross is not subject to the changing moods of culture, which come and go with the seasons. Instead, the gospel, revealed in the written Word of God, needs no editorial adaptation from generation to generation and will never be shaken by the ebb and flow of popular opinion. Paul received the good news as it was and passed it on to others "according to the Scriptures" (1 Corinthians 15:4). Thank God our gospel does not change!

A woman who was getting older and forgetful once asked her grandson to help her find a Sears catalog—not from the current time, but from thirty years earlier. She wanted something that the store no longer carried, and she wanted to pay the prices from decades ago. In her confusion, she mistakenly assumed that the old catalogs, like her memories, were frozen in time. Of course it doesn't work that way in our earthly economy, but in a way, it does work that way in God's. You see, the price for our sin was set long ago, a price we could never pay on our own, and the glorious truth is that it has already been paid! The unchanging truth of the gospel is that all we have to do is accept the free gift Jesus offers. Hold fast to God's unchanging truth today!

—Dr. J. Kie Bowman
Hyde Park Baptist Church, Austin, TX

WEEK 36, DAY 3

In Christ We Will Rise

1 Corinthians 15:12–49

The Risen Christ, Our Hope

Now if Christ is preached that He has been raised from the dead, how do some among you say that there is no resurrection of the dead? 13But if there is no resurrection of the dead, then Christ is not risen. 14And if Christ is not risen, then our preaching is empty and your faith is also empty. 15Yes, and we are found false witnesses of God, because we have testified of God that He raised up Christ, whom He did not raise up—if in fact the dead do not rise. 16For if the dead do not rise, then Christ is not risen. 17And if Christ is not risen, your faith is futile; you are still in your sins! 18Then also those who have fallen asleep in Christ have perished. 19If in this life only we have hope in Christ, we are of all men the most pitiable.

The Last Enemy Destroyed

20But now Christ is risen from the dead, and has become the firstfruits of those who have fallen asleep. 21For since by man came death, by Man also came the resurrection of the dead. 22For as in Adam all die, even so in Christ all shall be made alive. 23But each one in his own order: Christ the firstfruits, afterward those who are Christ's at His coming. 24Then comes the end, when He delivers the kingdom to God the Father, when He puts an end to all rule and all authority and power. 25For He must reign till He has put all enemies under His feet. 26The last enemy that will be destroyed is death. 27For "He has put all things under His feet." But when He says "all things are put under Him," it is evident that He who put all things under Him is excepted. 28Now when all things are made subject to Him, then the Son Himself will also be subject to Him who put all things under Him, that God may be all in all.

Effects of Denying the Resurrection

29Otherwise, what will they do who are baptized for the dead, if the dead do not rise at all? Why then are they baptized for the dead? 30And why do we stand in jeopardy every hour? 31I affirm, by the boasting in you which I have in Christ Jesus our Lord, I die daily. 32If, in the manner of men, I have fought with beasts at Ephesus, what advantage is it to me? If the dead do not rise, "Let us eat and drink, for tomorrow we die!"

33Do not be deceived: "Evil company corrupts good habits." 34Awake to righteousness, and do not sin; for some do not have the knowledge of God. I speak this to your shame.

A Glorious Body

35But someone will say, "How are the dead raised up? And with what body do they come?" 36Foolish one, what you sow is not made alive unless it dies. 37And what you sow, you do not sow that body that shall be, but mere grain—perhaps wheat or some other grain. 38But God gives it a body as He pleases, and to each seed its own body.

39All flesh is not the same flesh, but there is one kind of flesh of men, another flesh of animals, another of fish, and another of birds.

40There are also celestial bodies and terrestrial bodies; but the glory of the celestial is one, and the glory of the terrestrial is another. 41There is one glory of the sun, another glory of the moon, and another glory of the stars; for one star differs from another star in glory.

42So also is the resurrection of the dead. The body is sown in corruption, it is raised in incorruption. 43It is sown in dishonor, it is raised in glory. It is sown in weakness, it is raised in power. 44It is sown a natural body, it is raised a spiritual body. There is a natural body, and there is a spiritual body. 45And so it is written, "The first man Adam became a living being." The last Adam became a life-giving spirit.

46However, the spiritual is not first, but the natural, and afterward the spiritual. 47The first man was of the earth, made of dust; the second Man is the Lord from heaven. 48As was the man of dust, so also are those who are made of dust; and as is the heavenly Man, so also are those who are heavenly. 49And as we have borne the image of the man of dust, we shall also bear the image of the heavenly Man.

DEVOTIONAL

In one sense, every day is Easter for Christians, because Jesus is alive! His resurrection is the assurance of our own. In fact, it could be said that the resurrection of Jesus is the death of death.

America has been engaged in a battle against terrorism for years, and the struggle continues. It feels at times as if we will never see the end of our enemy's hatred toward our nation. Each of us, however, has a far worse enemy than a terrorist. Death is the "last enemy" of every human being, but the resurrection of Jesus has destroyed forever the power of that foe (1 Corinthians 15:25–26). In Christ we will rise!

—Dr. J. Kie Bowman
Hyde Park Baptist Church, Austin, TX

WEEK 36, DAY 4

Be Prepared for Opposition

1 Corinthians 15:50–16:24

Our Final Victory

Now this I say, brethren, that flesh and blood cannot inherit the kingdom of God; nor does corruption inherit incorruption. 51Behold, I tell you a mystery: We shall not all sleep, but we shall all be changed— 52in a moment, in the twinkling of an eye, at the last trumpet. For the trumpet will sound, and the dead will be raised incorruptible, and we shall be changed. 53For this corruptible must put on incorruption, and this mortal must put on immortality. 54So when this corruptible has put on incorruption, and this mortal has put on immortality, then shall be brought to pass the saying that is written: "Death is swallowed up in victory."

55 "O Death, where is your sting?
O Hades, where is your victory?"

56The sting of death is sin, and the strength of sin is the law. 57But thanks be to God, who gives us the victory through our Lord Jesus Christ.

58Therefore, my beloved brethren, be steadfast, immovable, always abounding in the work of the Lord, knowing that your labor is not in vain in the Lord.

Collection for the Saints

16 Now concerning the collection for the saints, as I have given orders to the churches of Galatia, so you must do also: 2On the first day of the week let each one of you lay something aside, storing up as he may prosper, that there be no collections when I come. 3And when I come, whomever you approve by your letters I will send to bear your gift to Jerusalem. 4But if it is fitting that I go also, they will go with me.

Personal Plans

5Now I will come to you when I pass through Macedonia (for I am passing through Macedonia). 6And it may be that I will remain, or even spend the winter with you, that you may send me on my journey, wherever I go. 7For I do not wish to see you now on the way; but I hope to stay a while with you, if the Lord permits.

8But I will tarry in Ephesus until Pentecost. 9For a great and effective door has opened to me, and there are many adversaries.

10And if Timothy comes, see that he may be with you without fear; for he does the work of the Lord, as I also do. 11Therefore let no one despise him. But send him on his journey in peace, that he may come to me; for I am waiting for him with the brethren.

12Now concerning our brother Apollos, I strongly urged him to come to you with the brethren, but he was quite unwilling to come at this time; however, he will come when he has a convenient time.

Final Exhortations

13Watch, stand fast in the faith, be brave, be strong. 14Let all that you do be done with love.

15I urge you, brethren—you know the household of Stephanas, that it is the firstfruits of Achaia, and that they have devoted themselves to the ministry of the saints— 16that you also submit to such, and to everyone who works and labors with us.

17I am glad about the coming of Stephanas, Fortunatus, and Achaicus, for what was lacking on your part they supplied. 18For they refreshed my spirit and yours. Therefore acknowledge such men.

Greetings and a Solemn Farewell

19The churches of Asia greet you. Aquila and Priscilla greet you heartily in the Lord, with the church that is in their house. 20All the brethren greet you.

Greet one another with a holy kiss.

21The salutation with my own hand—Paul's.

22If anyone does not love the Lord Jesus Christ, let him be accursed. O Lord, come!

23The grace of our Lord Jesus Christ be with you. 24My love be with you all in Christ Jesus. Amen.

DEVOTIONAL

The old song says, "Nobody knows the trouble I've seen. Nobody knows my sorrow." While it may be true that each of us feels our own personal suffering in a way others cannot, we each face trouble. Paul knew his share. He said, "There are many adversaries" (1 Corinthians 16:9). The word adversaries comes from a root word that means "to be put up against"—in opposition. We can expect difficulties, but we can also expect God's grace! With the Spirit's help, respond to the troubles of life with faith, courage, strength, and love (verses 13–14).

—Dr. J. Kie Bowman
Hyde Park Baptist Church, Austin, TX

WEEK 36, DAY 5

When Troubles Come, Trust

2 Corinthians 1:1–17

Greeting

1 Paul, an apostle of Jesus Christ by the will of God, and Timothy our brother,

To the church of God which is at Corinth, with all the saints who are in all Achaia:

²Grace to you and peace from God our Father and the Lord Jesus Christ.

Comfort in Suffering

³Blessed be the God and Father of our Lord Jesus Christ, the Father of mercies and God of all comfort, ⁴who comforts us in all our tribulation, that we may be able to comfort those who are in any trouble, with the comfort with which we ourselves are comforted by God. ⁵For as the sufferings of Christ abound in us, so our consolation also abounds through Christ. ⁶Now if we are afflicted, it is for your consolation and salvation, which is effective for enduring the same sufferings which we also suffer. Or if we are comforted, it is for your consolation and salvation. ⁷And our hope for you is steadfast, because we know that as you are partakers of the sufferings, so also you will partake of the consolation.

Delivered from Suffering

⁸For we do not want you to be ignorant, brethren, of our trouble which came to us in Asia: that we were burdened beyond measure, above strength, so that we despaired even of life. ⁹Yes, we had the sentence of death in ourselves, that we should not trust in ourselves but in God who raises the dead, ¹⁰who delivered us from so great a death, and does deliver us; in whom we trust that He will still deliver us, ¹¹you also helping together in prayer for us, that thanks may be given by many persons on our behalf for the gift granted to us through many.

Paul's Sincerity

¹²For our boasting is this: the testimony of our conscience that we conducted ourselves in the world in simplicity and godly sincerity, not with fleshly wisdom but by the grace of God, and more abundantly toward you. ¹³For we are not writing any other things to you than what you read or understand. Now I trust you will understand, even to the end ¹⁴(as also you have understood us in part), that we are your boast as you also are ours, in the day of the Lord Jesus.

Sparing the Church

¹⁵And in this confidence I intended to come to you before, that you might have a second benefit— ¹⁶to pass by way of you to Macedonia, to come again from Macedonia to you, and be helped by you on my way to Judea. ¹⁷Therefore, when I was planning this, did I do it lightly? Or the things I plan, do I plan according to the flesh, that with me there should be Yes, Yes, and No, No?

DEVOTIONAL

*J*oseph Parker, a famous British pastor, once offered good advice to other preachers: "Preach to the suffering, and you will never lack a congregation. There is a broken heart in every pew."¹⁰ That statement was true when he said it, and it is true today. People hurt.

Paul described God as the "God of all comfort, who comforts us in all our tribulation" (2 Corinthians 1:3–4). We have a compassionate, loving, heavenly Father. The word comfort occurs five times in verses 3–4 and comes from the same word Jesus used to describe the Holy Spirit! The word literally means "one who is called along beside." The God of the universe Himself helps us shoulder life's hurts. He stands near as one called along beside us. Isn't that incredible?

We will all need comfort at various points in our journey—"tribulation" and "trouble" are expected in life (2 Corinthians 1:4). Those two words, while translated differently in the English text, are merely a repetition of the same Greek word, meaning "external pressures." Paul experienced those external pressures when he was "burdened beyond measure, above strength" and "despaired even of life" (v. 8). It was in the midst of his troubles that he was reminded to "trust" in God, "who raises the dead" (v. 9)!

What external pressures are you experiencing right now? Perhaps you're dealing with difficulties that seem beyond your capacity to endure another moment. You are not alone in your pain. The almighty God is near—right alongside you, in fact. He is comforting you. Trust Him to deliver you (2 Corinthians 1:10). He will do it.

—Dr. J. Kie Bowman
Hyde Park Baptist Church, Austin, TX

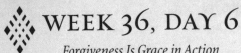

WEEK 36, DAY 6

Forgiveness Is Grace in Action

2 Corinthians 1:18–3:3

But as God is faithful, our word to you was not Yes and No. 19For the Son of God, Jesus Christ, who was preached among you by us—by me, Silvanus, and Timothy—was not Yes and No, but in Him was Yes. 20For all the promises of God in Him are Yes, and in Him Amen, to the glory of God through us. 21Now He who establishes us with you in Christ and has anointed us is God, 22who also has sealed us and given us the Spirit in our hearts as a guarantee.

23Moreover I call God as witness against my soul, that to spare you I came no more to Corinth. 24Not that we have dominion over your faith, but are fellow workers for your joy; for by faith you stand.

But I determined this within myself, that I would not come again to you in sorrow. 2For if I make you sorrowful, then who is he who makes me glad but the one who is made sorrowful by me?

Forgive the Offender

3And I wrote this very thing to you, lest, when I came, I should have sorrow over those from whom I ought to have joy, having confidence in you all that my joy is the joy of you all. 4For out of much affliction and anguish of heart I wrote to you, with many tears, not that you should be grieved, but that you might know the love which I have so abundantly for you.

5But if anyone has caused grief, he has not grieved me, but all of you to some extent—not to be too severe. 6This punishment which was inflicted by the majority is sufficient for such a man, 7so that, on the contrary, you ought rather to forgive and comfort him, lest perhaps such a one be swallowed up with too much sorrow. 8Therefore I urge you to reaffirm your love to him. 9For to this end I also wrote, that I might put you to the test, whether you are obedient in all things. 10Now whom you forgive anything, I also forgive. For if indeed I have forgiven anything, I have forgiven that one for your sakes in the presence of Christ, 11lest Satan should take advantage of us; for we are not ignorant of his devices.

Triumph in Christ

12Furthermore, when I came to Troas to preach Christ's gospel, and a door was opened to me by the Lord,

13I had no rest in my spirit, because I did not find Titus my brother; but taking my leave of them, I departed for Macedonia.

14Now thanks be to God who always leads us in triumph in Christ, and through us diffuses the fragrance of His knowledge in every place. 15For we are to God the fragrance of Christ among those who are being saved and among those who are perishing. 16To the one we are the aroma of death leading to death, and to the other aroma of life leading to life. And who is sufficient for these things? 17For we are not, as so many, peddling the word of God; but as of sincerity, but as from God, we speak in the sight of God in Christ.

Christ's Epistle

Do we begin again to commend ourselves? Or do we need, as some others, epistles of commendation to you or letters of commendation from you? 2You are our epistle written in our hearts, known and read by all men; 3clearly you are an epistle of Christ, ministered by us, written not with ink but by the Spirit of the living God, not on tablets of stone but on tablets of flesh, that is, of the heart.

DEVOTIONAL

Anyone who has been part of a church knows that problems can occur, even in the Lord's family. The church at Corinth had its share of troubles. They argued among themselves, criticized leadership, got drunk during church fellowships, and engaged in scandalous sexual immorality. As a church of new Christians living in a pagan metropolitan city, maintaining a pure Christian witness was always a challenge. It always is.

One of their church conflicts involved the church rebuking or punishing one of the members (2 Corinthians 2:5–6). It might have been the immoral man of 1 Corinthians 5, although Paul did not say for certain. What he did say informs us today. Even when someone is clearly guilty, if they repent and demonstrate godly sorrow, it is time to forgive (vv. 6–7)!

The word forgive *used in verses 7 and 10 is a verb form of the word usually translated "grace" in the New Testament. In other words, forgiveness is grace in action! When we forgive, we are "doing" grace.*

In what area of your life do you need to "act out" grace? Whom do you need to forgive? Pour out the grace you have received from the Lord to everyone in your life.

—Dr. J. Kie Bowman
Hyde Park Baptist Church, Austin, TX

WEEK 36, DAY 7

How have you identified and specifically used your spiritual gifts to build up the body of Christ?

_____

_____

_____

_____

_____

_____

_____

_____

_____

_____

_____

_____

As a believer whose comfort is in God, have you ever sought another source of comfort? What was the long-term result of that decision?

_____

_____

_____

_____

_____

_____

_____

_____

_____

WEEK 37, DAY I

Persevere in Christ

2 Corinthians 3:4–4:15

The Spirit, Not the Letter

And we have such trust through Christ toward God. 5Not that we are sufficient of ourselves to think of anything as being from ourselves, but our sufficiency is from God, 6who also made us sufficient as ministers of the new covenant, not of the letter but of the Spirit; for the letter kills, but the Spirit gives life.

Glory of the New Covenant

7But if the ministry of death, written and engraved on stones, was glorious, so that the children of Israel could not look steadily at the face of Moses because of the glory of his countenance, which glory was passing away, 8how will the ministry of the Spirit not be more glorious? 9For if the ministry of condemnation had glory, the ministry of righteousness exceeds much more in glory. 10For even what was made glorious had no glory in this respect, because of the glory that excels. 11For if what is passing away was glorious, what remains is much more glorious.

12Therefore, since we have such hope, we use great boldness of speech— 13unlike Moses, who put a veil over his face so that the children of Israel could not look steadily at the end of what was passing away. 14But their minds were blinded. For until this day the same veil remains unlifted in the reading of the Old Testament, because the veil is taken away in Christ. 15But even to this day, when Moses is read, a veil lies on their heart. 16Nevertheless when one turns to the Lord, the veil is taken away. 17Now the Lord is the Spirit; and where the Spirit of the Lord is, there is liberty. 18But we all, with unveiled face, beholding as in a mirror the glory of the Lord, are being transformed into the same image from glory to glory, just as by the Spirit of the Lord.

The Light of Christ's Gospel

Therefore, since we have this ministry, as we have received mercy, we do not lose heart. 2But we have renounced the hidden things of shame, not walking in craftiness nor handling the word of God deceitfully, but by manifestation of the truth commending ourselves to every man's conscience in the sight of God. 3But even if our gospel is veiled, it is veiled to those who are perishing, 4whose minds the god of this age has blinded, who do not believe, lest the light of the gospel of the glory of Christ, who is the image of God, should shine on them. 5For we do not preach ourselves, but Christ Jesus the Lord, and ourselves your bondservants for Jesus' sake. 6For it is the God who commanded light to shine out of darkness, who has shone in our hearts to give the light of the knowledge of the glory of God in the face of Jesus Christ.

Cast Down but Unconquered

7But we have this treasure in earthen vessels, that the excellence of the power may be of God and not of us. 8We are hard-pressed on every side, yet not crushed; we are perplexed, but not in despair; 9persecuted, but not forsaken; struck down, but not destroyed— 10always carrying about in the body the dying of the Lord Jesus, that the life of Jesus also may be manifested in our body. 11For we who live are always delivered to death for Jesus' sake, that the life of Jesus also may be manifested in our mortal flesh. 12So then death is working in us, but life in you.

13And since we have the same spirit of faith, according to what is written, "I believed and therefore I spoke," we also believe and therefore speak, 14knowing that He who raised up the Lord Jesus will also raise us up with Jesus, and will present us with you. 15For all things are for your sakes, that grace, having spread through the many, may cause thanksgiving to abound to the glory of God.

DEVOTIONAL

In spite of tremendous obstacles and difficulties, Paul did not lose heart. He kept believing and speaking the truth of God. His example of courage and perseverance motivates us to give our all for Christ.

Another person God has used to inspire many is Andy Andrews. Andy experienced some very challenging times as a young man. When he was nineteen years old, both his mother and father died. His life spiraled downward, and he ended up being homeless. But through the encouragement of others, Andy pressed forward in life. God has richly blessed him and given him a platform to speak to millions. The New York Times *called him one of the most influential people in America, four US presidents have invited him to speak, and every minute, one of his many books is purchased!*

Remember who you are in Christ and persist. If you do, one day many will render thanksgiving to God because of your faithful service.

—Dr. Danny Forshee
Great Hills Baptist Church, Austin, TX

WEEK 37, DAY 2

The Righteous Will Receive Eternal Glory

2 Corinthians 4:16–6:2

Seeing the Invisible

Therefore we do not lose heart. Even though our outward man is perishing, yet the inward man is being renewed day by day. ¹⁷For our light affliction, which is but for a moment, is working for us a far more exceeding and eternal weight of glory, ¹⁸while we do not look at the things which are seen, but at the things which are not seen. For the things which are seen are temporary, but the things which are not seen are eternal.

Assurance of the Resurrection

5 For we know that if our earthly house, this tent, is destroyed, we have a building from God, a house not made with hands, eternal in the heavens. ²For in this we groan, earnestly desiring to be clothed with our habitation which is from heaven, ³if indeed, having been clothed, we shall not be found naked. ⁴For we who are in this tent groan, being burdened, not because we want to be unclothed, but further clothed, that mortality may be swallowed up by life. ⁵Now He who has prepared us for this very thing is God, who also has given us the Spirit as a guarantee.

⁶So we are always confident, knowing that while we are at home in the body we are absent from the Lord. ⁷For we walk by faith, not by sight. ⁸We are confident, yes, well pleased rather to be absent from the body and to be present with the Lord.

The Judgment Seat of Christ

⁹Therefore we make it our aim, whether present or absent, to be well pleasing to Him. ¹⁰For we must all appear before the judgment seat of Christ, that each one may receive the things done in the body, according to what he has done, whether good or bad. ¹¹Knowing, therefore, the terror of the Lord, we persuade men; but we are well known to God, and I also trust are well known in your consciences.

Be Reconciled to God

¹²For we do not commend ourselves again to you, but give you opportunity to boast on our behalf, that you may have an answer for those who boast in appearance and not in heart. ¹³For if we are beside ourselves, it is for God; or if we are of sound mind, it is for you. ¹⁴For the love of Christ compels us, because we judge thus: that if One died for all, then all died; ¹⁵and He died for all, that those who live should live no longer for themselves, but for Him who died for them and rose again.

¹⁶Therefore, from now on, we regard no one according to the flesh. Even though we have known Christ according to the flesh, yet now we know Him thus no longer. ¹⁷Therefore, if anyone is in Christ, he is a new creation; old things have passed away; behold, all things have become new. ¹⁸Now all things are of God, who has reconciled us to Himself through Jesus Christ, and has given us the ministry of reconciliation, ¹⁹that is, that God was in Christ reconciling the world to Himself, not imputing their trespasses to them, and has committed to us the word of reconciliation.

²⁰Now then, we are ambassadors for Christ, as though God were pleading through us: we implore you on Christ's behalf, be reconciled to God. ²¹For He made Him who knew no sin to be sin for us, that we might become the righteousness of God in Him.

Marks of the Ministry

6 We then, as workers together with Him also plead with you not to receive the grace of God in vain. ²For He says:

"In an acceptable time I have heard you,
    And in the day of salvation I have helped you."

Behold, now is the accepted time; behold, now is the day of salvation.

DEVOTIONAL

The only way to live the Christian life is the same way we began it—by faith. It has been said that our faith reaches into the eternal but often denies the daily. At the end of 2 Corinthians 4, Paul admonishes us to remember that our eternal home is in heaven and our security is in Christ. The Holy Spirit lives within us as the divine guarantee. As we look to a greater day with God in eternity, we can endure the temporary hardships of life on earth and not lose heart.

God does not take us to heaven the very moment we receive Christ because He has work for us to do during our earthly sojourn. The greatest work for which He has saved us is to point others to Christ. Live by faith today—give yourself to God's work, and look forward to heaven!

—Dr. Danny Forshee
Great Hills Baptist Church, Austin, TX

WEEK 37, DAY 3

Persisting in Service to God

2 Corinthians 6:3–7:7

We give no offense in anything, that our ministry may not be blamed. 4But in all things we commend ourselves as ministers of God: in much patience, in tribulations, in needs, in distresses, 5in stripes, in imprisonments, in tumults, in labors, in sleeplessness, in fastings; 6by purity, by knowledge, by longsuffering, by kindness, by the Holy Spirit, by sincere love, 7by the word of truth, by the power of God, by the armor of righteousness on the right hand and on the left, 8by honor and dishonor, by evil report and good report; as deceivers, and yet true; 9as unknown, and yet well known; as dying, and behold we live; as chastened, and yet not killed; 10as sorrowful, yet always rejoicing; as poor, yet making many rich; as having nothing, and yet possessing all things.

Be Holy

11O Corinthians! We have spoken openly to you, our heart is wide open. 12You are not restricted by us, but you are restricted by your own affections. 13Now in return for the same (I speak as to children), you also be open.

14Do not be unequally yoked together with unbelievers. For what fellowship has righteousness with lawlessness? And what communion has light with darkness? 15And what accord has Christ with Belial? Or what part has a believer with an unbeliever? 16And what agreement has the temple of God with idols? For you are the temple of the living God. As God has said:

"I will dwell in them
And walk among them.
I will be their God,
And they shall be My people."

17Therefore

"Come out from among them
And be separate, says the Lord.
Do not touch what is unclean,
And I will receive you."

18 "I will be a Father to you,
And you shall be My sons and daughters,
Says the Lord Almighty."

7Therefore, having these promises, beloved, let us cleanse ourselves from all filthiness of the flesh and spirit, perfecting holiness in the fear of God.

The Corinthians' Repentance

2Open your hearts to us. We have wronged no one, we have corrupted no one, we have cheated no one. 3I do not say this to condemn; for I have said before that you are in our hearts, to die together and to live together. 4Great is my boldness of speech toward you, great is my boasting on your behalf. I am filled with comfort. I am exceedingly joyful in all our tribulation.

5For indeed, when we came to Macedonia, our bodies had no rest, but we were troubled on every side. Outside were conflicts, inside were fears. 6Nevertheless God, who comforts the downcast, comforted us by the coming of Titus, 7and not only by his coming, but also by the consolation with which he was comforted in you, when he told us of your earnest desire, your mourning, your zeal for me, so that I rejoiced even more.

DEVOTIONAL

The story of Adoniram and Ann "Nancy" Judson, the first missionaries sent from America, is one of remarkable commitment and sacrifice. They labored in Burma for six years before they saw their first convert. After nine years of service, there was a grand total of only eighteen Burmese converts. It seems it would have been easy to get discouraged. But they persisted, and through many dangers, toils, and snares, God used them powerfully to establish a strong Christian witness and presence in Burma.

In 1824, Adoniram was falsely accused of being a spy and placed in a horrible prison. Nancy pled for his release and provided basic necessities for him. While suffering in prison, Adoniram wrote these words: "It is possible my life will be spared; if so, with what ardor shall I pursue my work! If not—His will be done. The door will be open for others who will do the work better."11

Second Corinthians is Paul's most biographical epistle in the New Testament. He shared his heart with the church at Corinth, telling them how God gave him joy in the midst of his trials and used men like Titus to boost his lagging spirit.

Are you distressed in your service to God? May He send people who will refresh your spirit. In the meantime, be faithful. Be holy. Persevere!

—Dr. Danny Forshee
Great Hills Baptist Church, Austin, TX

WEEK 37, DAY 4

Keep Trusting and Living for God

2 Corinthians 7:8–8:15

For even if I made you sorry with my letter, I do not regret it; though I did regret it. For I perceive that the same epistle made you sorry, though only for a while. 9Now I rejoice, not that you were made sorry, but that your sorrow led to repentance. For you were made sorry in a godly manner, that you might suffer loss from us in nothing. 10For godly sorrow produces repentance leading to salvation, not to be regretted; but the sorrow of the world produces death. 11For observe this very thing, that you sorrowed in a godly manner: What diligence it produced in you, what clearing of yourselves, what indignation, what fear, what vehement desire, what zeal, what vindication! In all things you proved yourselves to be clear in this matter. 12Therefore, although I wrote to you, I did not do it for the sake of him who had done the wrong, nor for the sake of him who suffered wrong, but that our care for you in the sight of God might appear to you.

The Joy of Titus

13Therefore we have been comforted in your comfort. And we rejoiced exceedingly more for the joy of Titus, because his spirit has been refreshed by you all. 14For if in anything I have boasted to him about you, I am not ashamed. But as we spoke all things to you in truth, even so our boasting to Titus was found true. 15And his affections are greater for you as he remembers the obedience of you all, how with fear and trembling you received him. 16Therefore I rejoice that I have confidence in you in everything.

Excel in Giving

8 Moreover, brethren, we make known to you the grace of God bestowed on the churches of Macedonia: 2that in a great trial of affliction the abundance of their joy and their deep poverty abounded in the riches of their liberality. 3For I bear witness that according to their ability, yes, and beyond their ability, they were freely willing, 4imploring us with much urgency that we would receive the gift and the fellowship of the ministering to the saints. 5And not only as we had hoped, but they first gave themselves to the Lord, and then to us by the will of God. 6So we urged Titus, that as he had begun, so he would also complete this grace in you as well. 7But as you abound in everything—in faith, in speech, in knowledge, in all diligence, and in your love for us—see that you abound in this grace also.

Christ Our Pattern

8I speak not by commandment, but I am testing the sincerity of your love by the diligence of others. 9For you know the grace of our Lord Jesus Christ, that though He was rich, yet for your sakes He became poor, that you through His poverty might become rich.

10And in this I give advice: It is to your advantage not only to be doing what you began and were desiring to do a year ago; 11but now you also must complete the doing of it; that as there was a readiness to desire it, so there also may be a completion out of what you have. 12For if there is first a willing mind, it is accepted according to what one has, and not according to what he does not have.

13For I do not mean that others should be eased and you burdened; 14but by an equality, that now at this time your abundance may supply their lack, that their abundance also may supply your lack—that there may be equality. 15As it is written, "He who gathered much had nothing left over, and he who gathered little had no lack."

DEVOTIONAL

Felix is a man in his eighties who lives a radiant life for Christ. He's worked hard throughout his life and also endured great hardships. When he and his wife were in their midtwenties, just ten days after their first child was born, his wife died from a blood clot. It was a devastating time for Felix, but he continued to trust God and live for Him. God later blessed him with a new wife, and they have been married for fifty-six years. Looking back at his life, Felix says, "God has been very good to me." He is grateful, generous, and a blessing to those around him.

Similarly, Paul praised the Macedonians because despite a "trial of great affliction the abundance of their joy and their deep poverty abounded in the riches of their liberality" (2 Corinthians 8:2). Like Felix, the Macedonians knew great hardships, but that didn't make them bitter or stingy—not with their joy, their money, or their service.

Whatever comes your way, keep choosing to trust God and live for Him. Ask God to help you live in His grace, lead you to love and build up others, give generously, and persevere—even through the hard times.

—Dr. Danny Forshee
Great Hills Baptist Church, Austin, TX

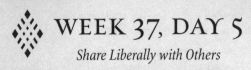

WEEK 37, DAY 5

Share Liberally with Others

2 Corinthians 8:16–9:15

Collection for the Judean Saints

But thanks be to God who puts the same earnest care for you into the heart of Titus. 16For he not only accepted the exhortation, but being more diligent, he went to you of his own accord. 18And we have sent with him the brother whose praise is in the gospel throughout all the churches, 19and not only that, but who was also chosen by the churches to travel with us with this gift, which is administered by us to the glory of the Lord Himself and to show your ready mind, 20avoiding this: that anyone should blame us in this lavish gift which is administered by us— 21providing honorable things, not only in the sight of the Lord, but also in the sight of men.

22And we have sent with them our brother whom we have often proved diligent in many things, but now much more diligent, because of the great confidence which we have in you. 23If anyone inquires about Titus, he is my partner and fellow worker concerning you. Or if our brethren are inquired about, they are messengers of the churches, the glory of Christ. 24Therefore show to them, and before the churches, the proof of your love and of our boasting on your behalf.

Administering the Gift

9 Now concerning the ministering to the saints, it is superfluous for me to write to you; 2for I know your willingness, about which I boast of you to the Macedonians, that Achaia was ready a year ago; and your zeal has stirred up the majority. 3Yet I have sent the brethren, lest our boasting of you should be in vain in this respect, that, as I said, you may be ready; 4lest if some Macedonians come with me and find you unprepared, we (not to mention you!) should be ashamed of this confident boasting. 5Therefore I thought it necessary to exhort the brethren to go to you ahead of time, and prepare your generous gift beforehand, which you had previously promised, that it may be ready as a matter of generosity and not as a grudging obligation.

The Cheerful Giver

6But this I say: He who sows sparingly will also reap sparingly, and he who sows bountifully will also reap bountifully. 7So let each one give as he purposes in his heart, not grudgingly or of necessity; for God loves a cheerful giver. 8And God is able to make all grace abound toward you, that you, always having all sufficiency in all things, may have an abundance for every good work. 9As it is written:

> "He has dispersed abroad,
> He has given to the poor;
> His righteousness endures forever."

10Now may He who supplies seed to the sower, and bread for food, supply and multiply the seed you have sown and increase the fruits of your righteousness, 11while you are enriched in everything for all liberality, which causes thanksgiving through us to God. 12For the administration of this service not only supplies the needs of the saints, but also is abounding through many thanksgivings to God, 13while, through the proof of this ministry, they glorify God for the obedience of your confession to the gospel of Christ, and for your liberal sharing with them and all men, 14and by their prayer for you, who long for you because of the exceeding grace of God in you. 15Thanks be to God for His indescribable gift!

DEVOTIONAL

Ten-year-old Anna understands much about giving to God. She was once saving money to buy a camera, but then one day she and her mom came across a request in the mail for money to purchase Bibles. Anna didn't like the fact that many people did not have a copy of God's Word. She asked her parents for more odd jobs around the house so she could earn more money.

After saving forty dollars, she told her parents she felt that people needed Bibles more than she needed a new digital camera! When her dad asked her if she was sure she wanted to do this, her response was priceless: "Of course, Dad. Isn't that what it means to be a Christian?"[12]

According to today's text, Paul would certainly agree that generosity should characterize all of Christ's followers. We are most like God when we give our money and time for the blessing and benefit of others. A stingy Christian is an oxymoron! "So let each one give as he purposes in his heart, not grudgingly or of necessity; for God loves a cheerful giver" (2 Corinthians 9:7). It's not hard to find a need or a worthy cause, so give with joyful generosity today!

—Dr. Danny Forshee
Great Hills Baptist Church, Austin, TX

WEEK 37, DAY 6

Encourage Spiritual Leaders

2 Corinthians 10:1–11:4

The Spiritual War

10 Now I, Paul, myself am pleading with you by the meekness and gentleness of Christ—who in presence am lowly among you, but being absent am bold toward you. ²But I beg you that when I am present I may not be bold with that confidence by which I intend to be bold against some, who think of us as if we walked according to the flesh. ³For though we walk in the flesh, we do not war according to the flesh. ⁴For the weapons of our warfare are not carnal but mighty in God for pulling down strongholds, ⁵casting down arguments and every high thing that exalts itself against the knowledge of God, bringing every thought into captivity to the obedience of Christ, ⁶and being ready to punish all disobedience when your obedience is fulfilled.

Reality of Paul's Authority

⁷Do you look at things according to the outward appearance? If anyone is convinced in himself that he is Christ's, let him again consider this in himself, that just as he is Christ's, even so we are Christ's. ⁸For even if I should boast somewhat more about our authority, which the Lord gave us for edification and not for your destruction, I shall not be ashamed— ⁹lest I seem to terrify you by letters. ¹⁰"For his letters," they say, "are weighty and powerful, but his bodily presence is weak, and his speech contemptible." ¹¹Let such a person consider this, that what we are in word by letters when we are absent, such we will also be in deed when we are present.

Limits of Paul's Authority

¹²For we dare not class ourselves or compare ourselves with those who commend themselves. But they, measuring themselves by themselves, and comparing themselves among themselves, are not wise. ¹³We, however, will not boast beyond measure, but within the limits of the sphere which God appointed us—a sphere which especially includes you. ¹⁴For we are not overextending ourselves (as though our authority did not extend to you), for it was to you that we came with the gospel of Christ; ¹⁵not boasting of things beyond measure, that is, in other men's labors, but having hope, that as your faith is increased, we shall be greatly enlarged by you in our sphere, ¹⁶to preach the gospel in the regions beyond you, and not to boast in another man's sphere of accomplishment.

¹⁷But "he who glories, let him glory in the LORD." ¹⁸For not he who commends himself is approved, but whom the Lord commends.

Concern for Their Faithfulness

11 Oh, that you would bear with me in a little folly—and indeed you do bear with me. ²For I am jealous for you with godly jealousy. For I have betrothed you to one husband, that I may present you as a chaste virgin to Christ. ³But I fear, lest somehow, as the serpent deceived Eve by his craftiness, so your minds may be corrupted from the simplicity that is in Christ. ⁴For if he who comes preaches another Jesus whom we have not preached, or if you receive a different spirit which you have not received, or a different gospel which you have not accepted—you may well put up with it!

DEVOTIONAL

There were people in Corinth who greatly opposed Paul. They criticized him, calling his physical appearance weak and his speech contemptible (literally, "to despise utterly"). Rest assured that when there are harsh criticisms and verbal attacks within the local church, Satan is behind them.

Paul gave a defense of his ministry to the Corinthian church and then went on to challenge their mind-set and discernment. He was concerned about their shallowness as they focused so much on the outward, about their tendency to be overly critical, and about their susceptibility to false prophets, who came preaching another Jesus and promoting a different spirit and gospel.

If you have a pastor who walks with God, preaches the Scriptures, and loves his family, then do all you can to encourage him—there is no doubt that Satan hates him and has a bull's-eye on him. The statistics of struggling pastors are alarming: Fifteen hundred pastors leave the ministry every month due to moral failure, burnout, or strife in their churches. Fifty percent of pastors' marriages do not last, and eighty percent feel discouraged in their role as pastor.¹³ Refuse to let your pastor become another statistic. Pray for him and continually encourage him.

—Dr. Danny Forshee
Great Hills Baptist Church, Austin, TX

WEEK 37, DAY 7

What are some ways you can become more generous and gracious in the giving of your money and time for the work of Christ?

_____

_____

_____

_____

_____

_____

_____

_____

_____

_____

_____

_____

What can you do today to encourage the pastors in your church who, like Paul of old, faithfully serve you and preach the Scriptures?

_____

_____

_____

_____

_____

_____

_____

_____

_____

_____

_____

WEEK 38, DAY 1

Be a Genuine Servant of the Gospel

2 Corinthians 11:5–33

Paul and False Apostles

For I consider that I am not at all inferior to the most eminent apostles. ⁶Even though I am untrained in speech, yet I am not in knowledge. But we have been thoroughly manifested among you in all things.

⁷Did I commit sin in humbling myself that you might be exalted, because I preached the gospel of God to you free of charge? ⁸I robbed other churches, taking wages from them to minister to you. ⁹And when I was present with you, and in need, I was a burden to no one, for what I lacked the brethren who came from Macedonia supplied. And in everything I kept myself from being burdensome to you, and so I will keep myself. ¹⁰As the truth of Christ is in me, no one shall stop me from this boasting in the regions of Achaia. ¹¹Why? Because I do not love you? God knows!

¹²But what I do, I will also continue to do, that I may cut off the opportunity from those who desire an opportunity to be regarded just as we are in the things of which they boast. ¹³For such are false apostles, deceitful workers, transforming themselves into apostles of Christ. ¹⁴And no wonder! For Satan himself transforms himself into an angel of light. ¹⁵Therefore it is no great thing if his ministers also transform themselves into ministers of righteousness, whose end will be according to their works.

Reluctant Boasting

¹⁶I say again, let no one think me a fool. If otherwise, at least receive me as a fool, that I also may boast a little. ¹⁷What I speak, I speak not according to the Lord, but as it were, foolishly, in this confidence of boasting. ¹⁸Seeing that many boast according to the flesh, I also will boast. ¹⁹For you put up with fools gladly, since you yourselves are wise! ²⁰For you put up with it if one brings you into bondage, if one devours you, if one takes from you, if one exalts himself, if one strikes you on the face. ²¹To our shame I say that we were too weak for that! But in whatever anyone is bold—I speak foolishly—I am bold also.

Suffering for Christ

²²Are they Hebrews? So am I. Are they Israelites? So am I. Are they the seed of Abraham? So am I. ²³Are they ministers of Christ?—I speak as a fool—I am more: in labors more abundant, in stripes above measure, in prisons more frequently, in deaths often. ²⁴From the Jews five times I received forty stripes minus one. ²⁵Three times I was beaten with rods; once I was stoned; three times I was shipwrecked; a night and a day I have been in the deep; ²⁶in journeys often, in perils of waters, in perils of robbers, in perils of my own countrymen, in perils of the Gentiles, in perils in the city, in perils in the wilderness, in perils in the sea, in perils among false brethren; ²⁷in weariness and toil, in sleeplessness often, in hunger and thirst, in fastings often, in cold and nakedness— ²⁸besides the other things, what comes upon me daily: my deep concern for all the churches. ²⁹Who is weak, and I am not weak? Who is made to stumble, and I do not burn with indignation?

³⁰If I must boast, I will boast in the things which concern my infirmity. ³¹The God and Father of our Lord Jesus Christ, who is blessed forever, knows that I am not lying. ³²In Damascus the governor, under Aretas the king, was guarding the city of the Damascenes with a garrison, desiring to arrest me; ³³but I was let down in a basket through a window in the wall, and escaped from his hands.

DEVOTIONAL

As it was in the time of Paul, so it is in our time—deceitful workers abound. There are those who, in the name of the gospel, use their ministry vocation to build personal empires and maintain exorbitant lifestyles. There are others who so desire fame or a privileged position that they will compromise personal integrity and the integrity of the gospel for that end. As Paul concludes, these are indeed deceitful workers who are energized by Satan himself, and it is important that the people of God use discernment in choosing and following leaders.

In contrast to these deceitful workers, Paul gladly boasted about the transforming power of the love of Jesus and reluctantly boasted about his own role in living it out. His words in 2 Corinthians 11 provide an important reminder: those with a genuine faith and sacrificial love for Jesus will demonstrate them in both their words and their deeds. Paul's life was a living sacrifice, and he demonstrated his willingness to traverse any height or depth to make known the beautiful gospel of Jesus, regardless of the cost. Are we willing to do the same? The world we live in desperately needs those kinds of Christians. How can you demonstrate your genuine faith and sacrificial love for Jesus?

—Dr. Jerry Gillis
The Chapel at Crosspoint, Getzville, NY

WEEK 38, DAY 2

Our Surrender Brings God's Strength

2 Corinthians 12:1–13:4

The Vision of Paradise

12 It is doubtless not profitable for me to boast. I will come to visions and revelations of the Lord: ²I know a man in Christ who fourteen years ago—whether in the body I do not know, or whether out of the body I do not know, God knows—such a one was caught up to the third heaven. ³And I know such a man—whether in the body or out of the body I do not know, God knows— ⁴how he was caught up into Paradise and heard inexpressible words, which it is not lawful for a man to utter. ⁵Of such a one I will boast; yet of myself I will not boast, except in my infirmities. ⁶For though I might desire to boast, I will not be a fool; for I will speak the truth. But I refrain, lest anyone should think of me above what he sees me to be or hears from me.

The Thorn in the Flesh

⁷And lest I should be exalted above measure by the abundance of the revelations, a thorn in the flesh was given to me, a messenger of Satan to buffet me, lest I be exalted above measure. ⁸Concerning this thing I pleaded with the Lord three times that it might depart from me. ⁹And He said to me, "My grace is sufficient for you, for My strength is made perfect in weakness." Therefore most gladly I will rather boast in my infirmities, that the power of Christ may rest upon me. ¹⁰Therefore I take pleasure in infirmities, in reproaches, in needs, in persecutions, in distresses, for Christ's sake. For when I am weak, then I am strong.

Signs of an Apostle

¹¹I have become a fool in boasting; you have compelled me. For I ought to have been commended by you; for in nothing was I behind the most eminent apostles, though I am nothing. ¹²Truly the signs of an apostle were accomplished among you with all perseverance, in signs and wonders and mighty deeds. ¹³For what is it in which you were inferior to other churches, except that I myself was not burdensome to you? Forgive me this wrong!

Love for the Church

¹⁴Now for the third time I am ready to come to you. And I will not be burdensome to you; for I do not seek yours, but you. For the children ought not to lay up for the parents, but the parents for the children. ¹⁵And I will very gladly spend and be spent for your souls; though the more abundantly I love you, the less I am loved.

¹⁶But be that as it may, I did not burden you. Nevertheless, being crafty, I caught you by cunning! ¹⁷Did I take advantage of you by any of those whom I sent to you? ¹⁸I urged Titus, and sent our brother with him. Did Titus take advantage of you? Did we not walk in the same spirit? Did we not walk in the same steps?

¹⁹Again, do you think that we excuse ourselves to you? We speak before God in Christ. But we do all things, beloved, for your edification. ²⁰For I fear lest, when I come, I shall not find you such as I wish, and that I shall be found by you such as you do not wish; lest there be contentions, jealousies, outbursts of wrath, selfish ambitions, backbitings, whisperings, conceits, tumults; ²¹lest, when I come again, my God will humble me among you, and I shall mourn for many who have sinned before and have not repented of the uncleanness, fornication, and lewdness which they have practiced.

Coming with Authority

13 This will be the third time I am coming to you. "By the mouth of two or three witnesses every word shall be established." ²I have told you before, and foretell as if I were present the second time, and now being absent I write to those who have sinned before, and to all the rest, that if I come again I will not spare— ³since you seek a proof of Christ speaking in me, who is not weak toward you, but mighty in you. ⁴For though He was crucified in weakness, yet He lives by the power of God. For we also are weak in Him, but we shall live with Him by the power of God toward you.

DEVOTIONAL

Though weakness seems to be the antithesis of strength, it is not so in the kingdom of God. God uses the weak things of the world to shame the wise, and He manifests His grace to the world through those weak enough to depend on Him. Looking at it the other way around, it is when we think we are strong that we are our weakest, because true strength only comes through surrendered dependence on Jesus. Today, turn from the temptation to be self-reliant and embrace a life of surrender so His grace may be seen in you.

—Dr. Jerry Gillis
The Chapel at Crosspoint, Getzville, NY

WEEK 38, DAY 3

The Pure Gospel

2 Corinthians 13:5–Galatians 1:17

Examine yourselves as to whether you are in the faith. Test yourselves. Do you not know yourselves, that Jesus Christ is in you?—unless indeed you are disqualified. 6But I trust that you will know that we are not disqualified.

Paul Prefers Gentleness

7Now I pray to God that you do no evil, not that we should appear approved, but that you should do what is honorable, though we may seem disqualified. 8For we can do nothing against the truth, but for the truth. 9For we are glad when we are weak and you are strong. And this also we pray, that you may be made complete. 10Therefore I write these things being absent, lest being present I should use sharpness, according to the authority which the Lord has given me for edification and not for destruction.

Greetings and Benediction

11Finally, brethren, farewell. Become complete. Be of good comfort, be of one mind, live in peace; and the God of love and peace will be with you.

12Greet one another with a holy kiss.

13All the saints greet you.

14The grace of the Lord Jesus Christ, and the love of God, and the communion of the Holy Spirit be with you all. Amen.

Greeting

1 Paul, an apostle (not from men nor through man, but through Jesus Christ and God the Father who raised Him from the dead), 2and all the brethren who are with me,

To the churches of Galatia:

3Grace to you and peace from God the Father and our Lord Jesus Christ, 4who gave Himself for our sins, that He might deliver us from this present evil age, according to the will of our God and Father, 5to whom be glory forever and ever. Amen.

Only One Gospel

6I marvel that you are turning away so soon from Him who called you in the grace of Christ, to a different gospel, 7which is not another; but there are some who trouble you and want to pervert the gospel of Christ. 8But even if we, or an angel from heaven, preach any other gospel to you than what we have preached to you, let him be accursed.

9As we have said before, so now I say again, if anyone preaches any other gospel to you than what you have received, let him be accursed.

10For do I now persuade men, or God? Or do I seek to please men? For if I still pleased men, I would not be a bondservant of Christ.

Call to Apostleship

11But I make known to you, brethren, that the gospel which was preached by me is not according to man. 12For I neither received it from man, nor was I taught it, but it came through the revelation of Jesus Christ.

13For you have heard of my former conduct in Judaism, how I persecuted the church of God beyond measure and tried to destroy it. 14And I advanced in Judaism beyond many of my contemporaries in my own nation, being more exceedingly zealous for the traditions of my fathers.

15But when it pleased God, who separated me from my mother's womb and called me through His grace, 16to reveal His Son in me, that I might preach Him among the Gentiles, I did not immediately confer with flesh and blood, 17nor did I go up to Jerusalem to those who were apostles before me; but I went to Arabia, and returned again to Damascus.

DEVOTIONAL

Whether Paul was in Corinth or Galatia, he was concerned about people understanding the truth of the gospel. In Galatia, there were some agitators who perverted the true gospel Paul had deposited among them, saying that people needed to add the requirements of the law to their faith in Jesus. Paul understood so well that Jesus was the fulfillment of the law and that the pure gospel was about putting faith in Jesus alone, that Paul actually was bold enough to say that anyone who taught otherwise—whether human or angel—should be accursed (Galatians 1:8).

This should sober us. If the Galatians could be confused about the gospel that easily, modern believers could be too. There is no end to the list of add-ons we use to prop up our faith or to try to justify ourselves in the sight of God. But God is not impressed with us. He is impressed with Jesus. The pure gospel is the message that God welcomes us into relationship with Himself through our faith in Jesus alone—not based upon the works we have done to impress Him.

Are you putting your faith in add-ons or in Christ alone?

—Dr. Jerry Gillis
The Chapel at Crosspoint, Getzville, NY

WEEK 38, DAY 4

Build Your Faith in Jesus

Galatians 1:18–2:21

Contacts at Jerusalem

Then after three years I went up to Jerusalem to see Peter, and remained with him fifteen days. 19But I saw none of the other apostles except James, the Lord's brother. 20(Now concerning the things which I write to you, indeed, before God, I do not lie.)

21Afterward I went into the regions of Syria and Cilicia. 22And I was unknown by face to the churches of Judea which were in Christ. 23But they were hearing only, "He who formerly persecuted us now preaches the faith which he once tried to destroy." 24And they glorified God in me.

Defending the Gospel

2 Then after fourteen years I went up again to Jerusalem with Barnabas, and also took Titus with me. 2And I went up by revelation, and communicated to them that gospel which I preach among the Gentiles, but privately to those who were of reputation, lest by any means I might run, or had run, in vain. 3Yet not even Titus who was with me, being a Greek, was compelled to be circumcised. 4And this occurred because of false brethren secretly brought in (who came in by stealth to spy out our liberty which we have in Christ Jesus, that they might bring us into bondage), 5to whom we did not yield submission even for an hour, that the truth of the gospel might continue with you.

6But from those who seemed to be something—whatever they were, it makes no difference to me; God shows personal favoritism to no man—for those who seemed to be something added nothing to me. 7But on the contrary, when they saw that the gospel for the uncircumcised had been committed to me, as the gospel for the circumcised was to Peter 8(for He who worked effectively in Peter for the apostleship to the circumcised also worked effectively in me toward the Gentiles), 9and when James, Cephas, and John, who seemed to be pillars, perceived the grace that had been given to me, they gave me and Barnabas the right hand of fellowship, that we should go to the Gentiles and they to the circumcised. 10They desired only that we should remember the poor, the very thing which I also was eager to do.

No Return to the Law

11Now when Peter had come to Antioch, I withstood him to his face, because he was to be blamed; 12for before certain men came from James, he would eat with the Gentiles; but when they came, he withdrew and separated himself, fearing those who were of the circumcision. 13And the rest of the Jews also played the hypocrite with him, so that even Barnabas was carried away with their hypocrisy.

14But when I saw that they were not straightforward about the truth of the gospel, I said to Peter before them all, "If you, being a Jew, live in the manner of Gentiles and not as the Jews, why do you compel Gentiles to live as Jews? 15We who are Jews by nature, and not sinners of the Gentiles, 16knowing that a man is not justified by the works of the law but by faith in Jesus Christ, even we have believed in Christ Jesus, that we might be justified by faith in Christ and not by the works of the law; for by the works of the law no flesh shall be justified.

17"But if, while we seek to be justified by Christ, we ourselves also are found sinners, is Christ therefore a minister of sin? Certainly not! 18For if I build again those things which I destroyed, I make myself a transgressor. 19For I through the law died to the law that I might live to God. 20I have been crucified with Christ; it is no longer I who live, but Christ lives in me; and the life which I now live in the flesh I live by faith in the Son of God, who loved me and gave Himself for me. 21I do not set aside the grace of God; for if righteousness comes through the law, then Christ died in vain."

DEVOTIONAL

It is possible for any believer, even someone as strong and faithful as Peter was, to fall prey to undercutting the gospel. Paul had to correct his fellow apostle because Peter had fallen back into the pressure of religion and keeping the law. By God's grace, Peter responded to this correction and returned to living out the true gospel, salvation by faith in Jesus alone—not the law.

We, too, can live by faith in other things, even religious things. Though disciplines like reading Scripture, praying, serving, and sharing our story of grace are all godly practices, they alone cannot justify us before God—only Jesus can. We should use every spiritual practice at our disposal, but we must be careful not to trust in those practices as an end in themselves. They are a vehicle that moves us toward our true goal—building our faith in the Faithful One. Keep the growth of your faith relationship with Jesus your goal.

—Dr. Jerry Gillis
The Chapel at Crosspoint, Getzville, NY

WEEK 38, DAY 5

Roadblocks to Freedom

Galatians 3:1–20

Justification by Faith

3 O foolish Galatians! Who has bewitched you that you should not obey the truth, before whose eyes Jesus Christ was clearly portrayed among you as crucified? ²This only I want to learn from you: Did you receive the Spirit by the works of the law, or by the hearing of faith? ³Are you so foolish? Having begun in the Spirit, are you now being made perfect by the flesh? ⁴Have you suffered so many things in vain—if indeed it was in vain?

⁵Therefore He who supplies the Spirit to you and works miracles among you, does He do it by the works of the law, or by the hearing of faith?— ⁶just as Abraham "believed God, and it was accounted to him for righteousness." ⁷Therefore know that only those who are of faith are sons of Abraham. ⁸And the Scripture, foreseeing that God would justify the Gentiles by faith, preached the gospel to Abraham beforehand, saying, "In you all the nations shall be blessed." ⁹So then those who are of faith are blessed with believing Abraham.

The Law Brings a Curse

¹⁰For as many as are of the works of the law are under the curse; for it is written, "Cursed is everyone who does not continue in all things which are written in the book of the law, to do them." ¹¹But that no one is justified by the law in the sight of God is evident, for "the just shall live by faith." ¹²Yet the law is not of faith, but "the man who does them shall live by them."

¹³Christ has redeemed us from the curse of the law, having become a curse for us (for it is written, "Cursed is everyone who hangs on a tree"), ¹⁴that the blessing of Abraham might come upon the Gentiles in Christ Jesus, that we might receive the promise of the Spirit through faith.

The Changeless Promise

¹⁵Brethren, I speak in the manner of men: Though it is only a man's covenant, yet if it is confirmed, no one annuls or adds to it. ¹⁶Now to Abraham and his Seed were the promises made. He does not say, "And to seeds," as of many, but as of one, "And to your Seed," who is Christ. ¹⁷And this I say, that the law, which was four hundred and thirty years later, cannot annul the covenant that was confirmed before by God in Christ, that it should make the promise of no effect. ¹⁸For if the inheritance is of the law, it is no longer of promise; but God gave it to Abraham by promise.

Purpose of the Law

¹⁹What purpose then does the law serve? It was added because of transgressions, till the Seed should come to whom the promise was made; and it was appointed through angels by the hand of a mediator. ²⁰Now a mediator does not mediate for one only, but God is one.

DEVOTIONAL

O *ne of the world's largest traffic jams occurred in Beijing, China, in the summer of 2010. It was over sixty miles long and lasted for ten days! There was virtually no way out of it, and some small businesses actually sprung up to sell products to those who were stuck in it.*

In effect, this is how Paul illustrated the law in today's text. After humanity plunged into sin, God made a covenant with Abraham that all the nations would be blessed through him. Israel, coming from Abraham, would be that vehicle of God's blessing to the world. But Israel wrecked. The law God gave them to point them to faith in Him became a substitute for that faith. It created a roadblock, a traffic jam, that slowed the redemption story from making its way to all the nations. But the law served a purpose—like a signpost, it pointed to saving faith. It shut off every other alternative to being justified in the sight of God except by faith, the very thing to which it pointed.

Because of the crucifixion and resurrection of Jesus, God opened the roadway wide again. Jesus fulfilled the promise to Abraham and gave those who have faith in Him the ability to live in the Spirit. And living in the Spirit allows us to live in freedom.

Freedom in Jesus is a core truth we need to embrace in our day, but it is possible to put up roadblocks to freedom in our own lives, just like they did in Galatia. Maybe we walk by the flesh instead of walking by the Spirit. Maybe we emphasize what we do for Jesus more than who we are in Jesus. Maybe we forget the gospel means Jesus became a curse for us through His death on the cross. To live freely is to live now like we did when we first believed—by the power of the Spirit. Do you need to remove any roadblocks to freedom in Christ today? Live in the freedom Christ died to give us!

—Dr. Jerry Gillis
The Chapel at Crosspoint, Getzville, NY

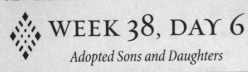

WEEK 38, DAY 6

Adopted Sons and Daughters

Galatians 3:21–4:20

Is the law then against the promises of God? Certainly not! For if there had been a law given which could have given life, truly righteousness would have been by the law. 22But the Scripture has confined all under sin, that the promise by faith in Jesus Christ might be given to those who believe. 23But before faith came, we were kept under guard by the law, kept for the faith which would afterward be revealed. 24Therefore the law was our tutor to bring us to Christ, that we might be justified by faith. 25But after faith has come, we are no longer under a tutor.

Sons and Heirs

26For you are all sons of God through faith in Christ Jesus. 27For as many of you as were baptized into Christ have put on Christ. 28There is neither Jew nor Greek, there is neither slave nor free, there is neither male nor female; for you are all one in Christ Jesus. 29And if you are Christ's, then you are Abraham's seed, and heirs according to the promise. 4Now I say that the heir, as long as he is a child, does not differ at all from a slave, though he is master of all, 2but is under guardians and stewards until the time appointed by the father. 3Even so we, when we were children, were in bondage under the elements of the world. 4But when the fullness of the time had come, God sent forth His Son, born of a woman, born under the law, 5to redeem those who were under the law, that we might receive the adoption as sons.

6And because you are sons, God has sent forth the Spirit of His Son into your hearts, crying out, "Abba, Father!" 7Therefore you are no longer a slave but a son, and if a son, then an heir of God through Christ.

Fears for the Church

8But then, indeed, when you did not know God, you served those which by nature are not gods. 9But now after you have known God, or rather are known by God, how is it that you turn again to the weak and beggarly elements, to which you desire again to be in bondage? 10You observe days and months and seasons and years. 11I am afraid for you, lest I have labored for you in vain.

12Brethren, I urge you to become like me, for I became like you. You have not injured me at all. 13You know that because of physical infirmity I preached the gospel to you at the first. 14And my trial which was in my flesh you did not despise or reject, but you received me as an angel of God, even as Christ Jesus. 15What then was the blessing you enjoyed? For I bear you witness that, if possible, you would have plucked out your own eyes and given them to me. 16Have I therefore become your enemy because I tell you the truth?

17They zealously court you, but for no good; yes, they want to exclude you, that you may be zealous for them. 18But it is good to be zealous in a good thing always, and not only when I am present with you. 19My little children, for whom I labor in birth again until Christ is formed in you, 20I would like to be present with you now and to change my tone; for I have doubts about you.

DEVOTIONAL

Faith in Jesus brings us to a place the law was never intended to take us—the place of being sons and daughters of God. Paul said that under the law, people are slaves, but through faith in Jesus, those slaves become sons and daughters. This new identity comes through the process of adoption.

Biological children are a blessing from the Lord, but there is something unique about a child who has been adopted. Often, these children have a spotted past and a questionable future. But in love, someone seeks them out, pays whatever cost is necessary to bring them home, and cares for them in a way they have never experienced. The beauty of the gospel is that God loved us so much He sent His Son to seek us out, rescue us by paying the cost of our sins with His own blood, and bring us home to be reconciled to our Father, where we will enjoy His care in this life and the life to come. We have also been given a deposit that guarantees our inheritance—the Holy Spirit living in our hearts, who causes us to lovingly cry out in praise, "Daddy!"

To be placed in such a loving family could never come by the acts of the law; it could only come through the faithfulness of Jesus on our behalf. That is why the law must stand to the side and simply applaud when this occurs, because this is what the law was leading us toward.

If you've put your faith in Jesus, give God thanks today that you are no longer a slave to the law. Praise your Father as an adopted child who lives freely in His kingdom!

—Dr. Jerry Gillis
The Chapel at Crosspoint, Getzville, NY

WEEK 38, DAY 7

Are you putting your trust or faith in anything other than Jesus, even if it is a good thing? What steps do you need to take so you can learn to trust Jesus in all things and with all things?

_____

_____

_____

_____

_____

_____

_____

_____

_____

_____

_____

_____

You were made to be free in Jesus. What are some of the roadblocks in your life that keep you from living in the freedom Jesus desires for you? What will you do when you identify those roadblocks?

_____

_____

_____

_____

_____

_____

_____

_____

_____

_____

WEEK 39, DAY I

Avoiding Harmful Extremes

Galatians 4:21–5:15

Two Covenants

Tell me, you who desire to be under the law, do you not hear the law? 22For it is written that Abraham had two sons: the one by a bondwoman, the other by a freewoman. 23But he who was of the bondwoman was born according to the flesh, and he of the freewoman through promise, 24which things are symbolic. For these are the two covenants: the one from Mount Sinai which gives birth to bondage, which is Hagar— 25for this Hagar is Mount Sinai in Arabia, and corresponds to Jerusalem which now is, and is in bondage with her children— 26but the Jerusalem above is free, which is the mother of us all. 27For it is written:

> "Rejoice, O barren,
> You who do not bear!
> Break forth and shout,
> You who are not in labor!
> For the desolate has many more children
> Than she who has a husband."

28Now we, brethren, as Isaac was, are children of promise. 29But, as he who was born according to the flesh then persecuted him who was born according to the Spirit, even so it is now. 30Nevertheless what does the Scripture say? "Cast out the bondwoman and her son, for the son of the bondwoman shall not be heir with the son of the freewoman." 31So then, brethren, we are not children of the bondwoman but of the free.

Christian Liberty

5 Stand fast therefore in the liberty by which Christ has made us free, and do not be entangled again with a yoke of bondage. 2Indeed I, Paul, say to you that if you become circumcised, Christ will profit you nothing. 3And I testify again to every man who becomes circumcised that he is a debtor to keep the whole law. 4You have become estranged from Christ, you who attempt to be justified by law; you have fallen from grace. 5For we through the Spirit eagerly wait for the hope of righteousness by faith. 6For in Christ Jesus neither circumcision nor uncircumcision avails anything, but faith working through love.

Love Fulfills the Law

7You ran well. Who hindered you from obeying the truth? 8This persuasion does not come from Him who calls you. 9A little leaven leavens the whole lump. 10I have confidence in you, in the Lord, that you will have no other mind; but he who troubles you shall bear his judgment, whoever he is.

11And I, brethren, if I still preach circumcision, why do I still suffer persecution? Then the offense of the cross has ceased. 12I could wish that those who trouble you would even cut themselves off!

13For you, brethren, have been called to liberty; only do not use liberty as an opportunity for the flesh, but through love serve one another. 14For all the law is fulfilled in one word, even in this: "You shall love your neighbor as yourself." 15But if you bite and devour one another, beware lest you be consumed by one another!

DEVOTIONAL

Two extremes that must be avoided in the Christian life are addressed in our text for today. The first extreme is legalism. Redemption is not the result of performing religious rituals and ceremonies. Sanctification is not the result of traditionalism. Adhering to codes of personal conviction (not based on Scripture) and ethics of human expectation is not the way to regeneration and a God-pleasing life. Faith in Christ's redemptive work is the only way to salvation.

If we neglect faith and return to a system of rules and regulations to please God, we will rob ourselves of joy, hinder our ability to love God, and taint the gospel. If we entrap ourselves in legalism, we will take credit for our own righteousness. Instead, we must realize our righteousness only comes through the grace of God and the exercise of faith. We must realize how much we have been forgiven and how little we deserve it. When we do, we will fuel our love for God.

A second extreme is licentiousness. Misguided Christians use their freedom as an excuse to sin. We are saved to be holy and to serve God and others, not to indulge ourselves. A proper understanding of this text results in a fulfilled and effective life.

Today, trust in Christ instead of your own rule-keeping, and give yourself to holiness and service instead of sinful self-indulgence.

—Mike Orr
First Baptist Church, Chipley, FL

WEEK 39, DAY 2

We Harvest What We Plant

Galatians 5:16–6:18

Walking in the Spirit

I say then: Walk in the Spirit, and you shall not fulfill the lust of the flesh. 17For the flesh lusts against the Spirit, and the Spirit against the flesh; and these are contrary to one another, so that you do not do the things that you wish. 18But if you are led by the Spirit, you are not under the law.

19Now the works of the flesh are evident, which are: adultery, fornication, uncleanness, lewdness, 20idolatry, sorcery, hatred, contentions, jealousies, outbursts of wrath, selfish ambitions, dissensions, heresies, 21envy, murders, drunkenness, revelries, and the like; of which I tell you beforehand, just as I also told you in time past, that those who practice such things will not inherit the kingdom of God.

22But the fruit of the Spirit is love, joy, peace, longsuffering, kindness, goodness, faithfulness, 23gentleness, self-control. Against such there is no law. 24And those who are Christ's have crucified the flesh with its passions and desires. 25If we live in the Spirit, let us also walk in the Spirit. 26Let us not become conceited, provoking one another, envying one another.

Bear and Share the Burdens

6 Brethren, if a man is overtaken in any trespass, you who are spiritual restore such a one in a spirit of gentleness, considering yourself lest you also be tempted. 2Bear one another's burdens, and so fulfill the law of Christ. 3For if anyone thinks himself to be something, when he is nothing, he deceives himself. 4But let each one examine his own work, and then he will have rejoicing in himself alone, and not in another. 5For each one shall bear his own load.

Be Generous and Do Good

6Let him who is taught the word share in all good things with him who teaches.

7Do not be deceived, God is not mocked; for whatever a man sows, that he will also reap. 8For he who sows to his flesh will of the flesh reap corruption, but he who sows to the Spirit will of the Spirit reap everlasting life. 9And let us not grow weary while doing good, for in due season we shall reap if we do not lose heart. 10Therefore, as we have opportunity, let us do good to all, especially to those who are of the household of faith.

Glory Only in the Cross

11See with what large letters I have written to you with my own hand! 12As many as desire to make a good showing in the flesh, these would compel you to be circumcised, only that they may not suffer persecution for the cross of Christ. 13For not even those who are circumcised keep the law, but they desire to have you circumcised that they may boast in your flesh. 14But God forbid that I should boast except in the cross of our Lord Jesus Christ, by whom the world has been crucified to me, and I to the world. 15For in Christ Jesus neither circumcision nor uncircumcision avails anything, but a new creation.

Blessing and a Plea

16And as many as walk according to this rule, peace and mercy be upon them, and upon the Israel of God.

17From now on let no one trouble me, for I bear in my body the marks of the Lord Jesus.

18Brethren, the grace of our Lord Jesus Christ be with your spirit. Amen.

DEVOTIONAL

Anyone who has gardened or farmed knows that the law of the harvest is constant. When you plant squash, you harvest squash. When you plant beans, you harvest beans.

Our lives are the same way. Our actions and behaviors are like seeds planted, and one day we will reap what we sow. All the decisions we make and behaviors we choose today will bring consequences tomorrow. If we choose to ignore the principles of God and follow human desires, we will ultimately reap the consequences of that type of life. Many of the hardships we experience are the results of our own decisions. We are quick to blame God for our troubles, when the fact is, we are often to blame.

Praise God that He is gracious toward us! We must be grateful for God's mercy and forgiveness but also understand that we are accountable for our actions. If we ignore God's purpose and plan, we will eventually lose our reward when we stand before Jesus.

You can look forward to a joyful harvest by surrendering to the Holy Spirit. Sow seeds of obedience every day. In time, you will reap a great harvest, one that blesses you and glorifies God.

—Mike Orr
First Baptist Church, Chipley, FL

WEEK 39, DAY 3

The Importance of Praying
for One Another

Ephesians 1:1–2:3

Greeting

1 Paul, an apostle of Jesus Christ by the will of God,

To the saints who are in Ephesus, and faithful in Christ Jesus:

²Grace to you and peace from God our Father and the Lord Jesus Christ.

Redemption in Christ

³Blessed be the God and Father of our Lord Jesus Christ, who has blessed us with every spiritual blessing in the heavenly places in Christ, ⁴just as He chose us in Him before the foundation of the world, that we should be holy and without blame before Him in love, ⁵having predestined us to adoption as sons by Jesus Christ to Himself, according to the good pleasure of His will, ⁶to the praise of the glory of His grace, by which He made us accepted in the Beloved.

⁷In Him we have redemption through His blood, the forgiveness of sins, according to the riches of His grace ⁸which He made to abound toward us in all wisdom and prudence, ⁹having made known to us the mystery of His will, according to His good pleasure which He purposed in Himself, ¹⁰that in the dispensation of the fullness of the times He might gather together in one all things in Christ, both which are in heaven and which are on earth—in Him. ¹¹In Him also we have obtained an inheritance, being predestined according to the purpose of Him who works all things according to the counsel of His will, ¹²that we who first trusted in Christ should be to the praise of His glory.

¹³In Him you also trusted, after you heard the word of truth, the gospel of your salvation; in whom also, having believed, you were sealed with the Holy Spirit of promise, ¹⁴who is the guarantee of our inheritance until the redemption of the purchased possession, to the praise of His glory.

Prayer for Spiritual Wisdom

¹⁵Therefore I also, after I heard of your faith in the Lord Jesus and your love for all the saints, ¹⁶do not cease to give thanks for you, making mention of you in my prayers: ¹⁷that the God of our Lord Jesus Christ, the Father of glory, may give to you the spirit of wisdom and revelation in the knowledge of Him, ¹⁸the eyes of your understanding being enlightened; that you may know what is the hope of His calling, what are the riches of the glory of His inheritance in the saints, ¹⁹and what is the exceeding greatness of His power toward us who believe, according to the working of His mighty power ²⁰which He worked in Christ when He raised Him from the dead and seated Him at His right hand in the heavenly places, ²¹far above all principality and power and might and dominion, and every name that is named, not only in this age but also in that which is to come.

²²And He put all things under His feet, and gave Him to be head over all things to the church, ²³which is His body, the fullness of Him who fills all in all.

By Grace Through Faith

2 And you He made alive, who were dead in trespasses and sins, ²in which you once walked according to the course of this world, according to the prince of the power of the air, the spirit who now works in the sons of disobedience, ³among whom also we all once conducted ourselves in the lusts of our flesh, fulfilling the desires of the flesh and of the mind, and were by nature children of wrath, just as the others.

DEVOTIONAL

You are precious to God. He chose you to be His very own. When you truly believe that about yourself, you should also recognize other people's value as a result. One way to acknowledge the value of others is to pray for them.

The lack of intercession among believers is one of the weaknesses of the church today. Remembering how valuable our brothers and sisters in Christ are should motivate us to love them by praying for them. Intercession will strengthen them and help them grow in faithfulness—and being others-focused will certainly bless us as well.

Try following Paul's example of intercession for the Ephesians. Pray for a realization of the hope of our salvation (Ephesians 1:18). Pray that we as Christians will understand how blessed we are to be saved and understand how to live once we are saved. And pray for an awareness of God's power, which overwhelms the forces of evil, that is available to all of us (v. 19). Start interceding today!

—Mike Orr
First Baptist Church, Chipley, FL

WEEK 39, DAY 4

God Gives Mercy and Grace

Ephesians 2:4–3:7

But God, who is rich in mercy, because of His great love with which He loved us, [5]even when we were dead in trespasses, made us alive together with Christ (by grace you have been saved), [6]and raised us up together, and made us sit together in the heavenly places in Christ Jesus, [7]that in the ages to come He might show the exceeding riches of His grace in His kindness toward us in Christ Jesus. [8]For by grace you have been saved through faith, and that not of yourselves; it is the gift of God, [9]not of works, lest anyone should boast. [10]For we are His workmanship, created in Christ Jesus for good works, which God prepared beforehand that we should walk in them.

Brought Near by His Blood

[11]Therefore remember that you, once Gentiles in the flesh—who are called Uncircumcision by what is called the Circumcision made in the flesh by hands— [12]that at that time you were without Christ, being aliens from the commonwealth of Israel and strangers from the covenants of promise, having no hope and without God in the world. [13]But now in Christ Jesus you who once were far off have been brought near by the blood of Christ.

Christ Our Peace

[14]For He Himself is our peace, who has made both one, and has broken down the middle wall of separation, [15]having abolished in His flesh the enmity, that is, the law of commandments contained in ordinances, so as to create in Himself one new man from the two, thus making peace, [16]and that He might reconcile them both to God in one body through the cross, thereby putting to death the enmity. [17]And He came and preached peace to you who were afar off and to those who were near. [18]For through Him we both have access by one Spirit to the Father.

Christ Our Cornerstone

[19]Now, therefore, you are no longer strangers and foreigners, but fellow citizens with the saints and members of the household of God, [20]having been built on the foundation of the apostles and prophets, Jesus Christ Himself being the chief cornerstone, [21]in whom the whole building, being fitted together, grows into a holy temple in the Lord, [22]in whom you also are being built together for a dwelling place of God in the Spirit.

The Mystery Revealed

3 For this reason I, Paul, the prisoner of Christ Jesus for you Gentiles— [2]if indeed you have heard of the dispensation of the grace of God which was given to me for you, [3]how that by revelation He made known to me the mystery (as I have briefly written already, [4]by which, when you read, you may understand my knowledge in the mystery of Christ), [5]which in other ages was not made known to the sons of men, as it has now been revealed by the Spirit to His holy apostles and prophets: [6]that the Gentiles should be fellow heirs, of the same body, and partakers of His promise in Christ through the gospel, [7]of which I became a minister according to the gift of the grace of God given to me by the effective working of His power.

DEVOTIONAL

Scripture says we "all have sinned and fall short of the glory of God," and that the "wages of sin is death" (Romans 3:23; 6:23). Ephesians echoes that by saying that without Christ, we were "dead in trespasses and sins" and "by nature children of wrath" (2:1, 3). We know that something dead cannot bring itself to life, but praise God that by His grace, He makes the spiritually dead spiritually alive!

When we put our faith in Christ for salvation, God "made us alive together with Christ" (Ephesians 2:5). We are united with Christ, and we share in His resurrected life and heavenly glory. We are no longer slaves to our sinful nature, we are enabled to do good works, and we are destined for heaven. God didn't just leave us in our helpless state, even though we were His enemies—He saved us and poured blessings on us. What mercy! How can this be? "Because of His great love with which He loved us" (v. 4).

God is the epitome of love. He possesses and practices a love that is beyond human comprehension, and His great love results in giving us mercy. We did not earn or deserve salvation; He took the initiative to save us because of who He is.

We are examples of God's mercy. May we not forget the state from which we have been redeemed, and may we bring Him glory for His work of salvation. Praise God today that He is holy, loving, and merciful!

—Mike Orr
First Baptist Church, Chipley, FL

WEEK 39, DAY 5

The Vastness of Christ's Love

Ephesians 3:8–4:16

Purpose of the Mystery

To me, who am less than the least of all the saints, this grace was given, that I should preach among the Gentiles the unsearchable riches of Christ, 9and to make all see what is the fellowship of the mystery, which from the beginning of the ages has been hidden in God who created all things through Jesus Christ; 10to the intent that now the manifold wisdom of God might be made known by the church to the principalities and powers in the heavenly places, 11according to the eternal purpose which He accomplished in Christ Jesus our Lord, 12in whom we have boldness and access with confidence through faith in Him. 13Therefore I ask that you do not lose heart at my tribulations for you, which is your glory.

Appreciation of the Mystery

14For this reason I bow my knees to the Father of our Lord Jesus Christ, 15from whom the whole family in heaven and earth is named, 16that He would grant you, according to the riches of His glory, to be strengthened with might through His Spirit in the inner man, 17that Christ may dwell in your hearts through faith; that you, being rooted and grounded in love, 18may be able to comprehend with all the saints what is the width and length and depth and height— 19to know the love of Christ which passes knowledge; that you may be filled with all the fullness of God.

20Now to Him who is able to do exceedingly abundantly above all that we ask or think, according to the power that works in us, 21to Him be glory in the church by Christ Jesus to all generations, forever and ever. Amen.

Walk in Unity

4 I, therefore, the prisoner of the Lord, beseech you to walk worthy of the calling with which you were called, 2with all lowliness and gentleness, with longsuffering, bearing with one another in love, 3endeavoring to keep the unity of the Spirit in the bond of peace. 4There is one body and one Spirit, just as you were called in one hope of your calling; 5one Lord, one faith, one baptism; 6one God and Father of all, who is above all, and through all, and in you all.

Spiritual Gifts

7But to each one of us grace was given according to the measure of Christ's gift. 8Therefore He says:

"When He ascended on high,
He led captivity captive,
And gave gifts to men."

9(Now this, "He ascended"—what does it mean but that He also first descended into the lower parts of the earth? 10He who descended is also the One who ascended far above all the heavens, that He might fill all things.)

11And He Himself gave some to be apostles, some prophets, some evangelists, and some pastors and teachers, 12for the equipping of the saints for the work of ministry, for the edifying of the body of Christ, 13till we all come to the unity of the faith and of the knowledge of the Son of God, to a perfect man, to the measure of the stature of the fullness of Christ; 14that we should no longer be children, tossed to and fro and carried about with every wind of doctrine, by the trickery of men, in the cunning craftiness of deceitful plotting, 15but, speaking the truth in love, may grow up in all things into Him who is the head—Christ— 16from whom the whole body, joined and knit together by what every joint supplies, according to the effective working by which every part does its share, causes growth of the body for the edifying of itself in love.

DEVOTIONAL

The power of God and understanding Christ's love is necessary for spiritual maturity.

Paul prayed that God would enable believers "to comprehend" and "know the love of Christ which passes knowledge" (Ephesians 3:18–19). We need the Holy Spirit to help us grasp the vastness of God's love. God extends His love through Christ to all of humanity. He reaches down to sinners and lifts them to heavenly places.

The ability to grasp Christ's love results in being "filled with all the fullness of God" (Ephesians 3:19). In other words, the Spirit enlightens us and empowers us to grow into the image of Christ.

Pray that you would mature spiritually by understanding God's love for you in Christ more deeply. Ask God to help you conform to Christ's image and imitate Him daily.

—Mike Orr
First Baptist Church, Chipley, FL

WEEK 39, DAY 6

Guard Against Greed

Ephesians 4:17–5:14

The New Man

This I say, therefore, and testify in the Lord, that you should no longer walk as the rest of the Gentiles walk, in the futility of their mind, 18having their understanding darkened, being alienated from the life of God, because of the ignorance that is in them, because of the blindness of their heart; 19who, being past feeling, have given themselves over to lewdness, to work all uncleanness with greediness.

20But you have not so learned Christ, 21if indeed you have heard Him and have been taught by Him, as the truth is in Jesus: 22that you put off, concerning your former conduct, the old man which grows corrupt according to the deceitful lusts, 23and be renewed in the spirit of your mind, 24and that you put on the new man which was created according to God, in true righteousness and holiness.

Do Not Grieve the Spirit

25Therefore, putting away lying, "Let each one of you speak truth with his neighbor," for we are members of one another. 26"Be angry, and do not sin": do not let the sun go down on your wrath, 27nor give place to the devil. 28Let him who stole steal no longer, but rather let him labor, working with his hands what is good, that he may have something to give him who has need. 29Let no corrupt word proceed out of your mouth, but what is good for necessary edification, that it may impart grace to the hearers. 30And do not grieve the Holy Spirit of God, by whom you were sealed for the day of redemption. 31Let all bitterness, wrath, anger, clamor, and evil speaking be put away from you, with all malice. 32And be kind to one another, tenderhearted, forgiving one another, even as God in Christ forgave you.

Walk in Love

5 Therefore be imitators of God as dear children. 2And walk in love, as Christ also has loved us and given Himself for us, an offering and a sacrifice to God for a sweet-smelling aroma.

3But fornication and all uncleanness or covetousness, let it not even be named among you, as is fitting for saints; 4neither filthiness, nor foolish talking, nor coarse jesting, which are not fitting, but rather giving of thanks. 5For this you know, that no fornicator, unclean person, nor covetous man, who is an idolater, has any inheritance in the kingdom of Christ and God. 6Let no one deceive you with empty words, for because of these things the wrath of God comes upon the sons of disobedience. 7Therefore do not be partakers with them.

Walk in Light

8For you were once darkness, but now *you are* light in the Lord. Walk as children of light 9(for the fruit of the Spirit is in all goodness, righteousness, and truth), 10finding out what is acceptable to the Lord. 11And have no fellowship with the unfruitful works of darkness, but rather expose them. 12For it is shameful even to speak of those things which are done by them in secret. 13But all things that are exposed are made manifest by the light, for whatever makes manifest is light. 14Therefore He says:

"Awake, you who sleep,
Arise from the dead,
And Christ will give you light."

DEVOTIONAL

The first three chapters of Ephesians address the doctrine of salvation, while the final three discuss how we are to live once we are saved—the practical matters of the Christian life.

Life for those who are regenerated is vastly different from those who are not. The saved and the lost are characterized by different motives and behaviors. Two similar characteristics that often dominate the spiritually dead are greed and covetousness. Both are given as descriptors of the unregenerate in Ephesians (4:19; 5:5). We must not allow these sins to creep back into our lives once we are saved.

Our culture feeds the sinful desires that result in greed and covetousness. Our society has convinced us we deserve more money and possessions. Unfortunately, even some Christian ministries today base their teaching on claims that God desires us to have more material wealth. As a result, many Christians find themselves trapped in idolatrous behaviors. Idolatry is placing anything above God and His will for us.

The almighty God can help us overcome these sinful desires. The key for us is to maintain submission to Jesus daily. The result is contentment in Christ.

—Mike Orr
First Baptist Church, Chipley, FL

WEEK 39, DAY 7

What are some of the characteristics that describe Christ's love?

_____

_____

_____

_____

_____

_____

_____

_____

_____

_____

_____

_____

What are some of the ways in which understanding Christ's love will make you more like Him?

_____

_____

_____

_____

_____

_____

_____

_____

_____

_____

WEEK 40, DAY I
Spirit-Filled Relating

Ephesians 5:15–6:4

Walk in Wisdom

See then that you walk circumspectly, not as fools but as wise, ¹⁶redeeming the time, because the days are evil.

¹⁷Therefore do not be unwise, but understand what the will of the Lord is. ¹⁸And do not be drunk with wine, in which is dissipation; but be filled with the Spirit, ¹⁹speaking to one another in psalms and hymns and spiritual songs, singing and making melody in your heart to the Lord, ²⁰giving thanks always for all things to God the Father in the name of our Lord Jesus Christ, ²¹submitting to one another in the fear of God.

Marriage—Christ and the Church

²²Wives, submit to your own husbands, as to the Lord. ²³For the husband is head of the wife, as also Christ is head of the church; and He is the Savior of the body. ²⁴Therefore, just as the church is subject to Christ, so let the wives be to their own husbands in everything.

²⁵Husbands, love your wives, just as Christ also loved the church and gave Himself for her, ²⁶that He might sanctify and cleanse her with the washing of water by the word, ²⁷that He might present her to Himself a glorious church, not having spot or wrinkle or any such thing, but that she should be holy and without blemish. ²⁸So husbands ought to love their own wives as their own bodies; he who loves his wife loves himself. ²⁹For no one ever hated his own flesh, but nourishes and cherishes it, just as the Lord does the church. ³⁰For we are members of His body, of His flesh and of His bones. ³¹"For this reason a man shall leave his father and mother and be joined to his wife, and the two shall become one flesh." ³²This is a great mystery, but I speak concerning Christ and the church. ³³Nevertheless let each one of you in particular so love his own wife as himself, and let the wife see that she respects her husband.

Children and Parents

6 Children, obey your parents in the Lord, for this is right. ²"Honor your father and mother," which is the first commandment with promise: ³"that it may be well with you and you may live long on the earth."

⁴And you, fathers, do not provoke your children to wrath, but bring them up in the training and admonition of the Lord.

When Christians read about submission in this passage, many associate it with sexism and inequality. In this age of liberation, submission is a very unpopular idea, even in the church. Unfortunately too many Christians have followed the world's example and adopted self-fulfillment as the greatest goal of marriage, promoting personal pleasure rather than a mutual commitment to sacrificial love. Biblical submission, however, is not about forced inequality—it is about loving respect and recognition of God's order of authority.

Ephesians 5:18 says we are called to "be filled with the Spirit." This is never more necessary than in family relationships. It is impossible to obey God's commands without His power. A wife must ask, "Do I love my husband enough to live for him?" A husband must ask, "Do I love my wife enough to die for her?" Both involve initial submission to the Lord. After all, Paul's verb concerning the fullness of the Spirit is in the plural, so it can be translated "all of you be filled." That means men, women, and children—all of us—are to be filled.

While submission literally refers to rank and authority, it also implies ordered, voluntary recognition of equality. What woman would not want to respect a Spirit-filled man who loves her as Christ loved the church? What child would not want to learn from a parent who has the wisdom of God?

As you seek to live in the fullness of the Spirit, sincerely progress through these steps on a daily basis: realize your need, repent of sin, relinquish to Christ's lordship, identify with His death and resurrection, and request His control.

As you aim to submit to the Lord and love your family members well, remember that giving God glory through living out His will is more important than defending your personal rights and feelings (Ephesians 5:17). The Christian life is about selflessness, not self-indulgence. It's about putting others first, not yourself.

Ask God every day to help you live a life of love and service, like Jesus, and to cherish and nourish your spouse and your children, those precious people with whom He has blessed you.

—Dr. Hayes Wicker
First Baptist Church, Naples, FL

WEEK 40, DAY 2

Fighting from Victory

Ephesians 6:5–24

Bondservants and Masters

Bondservants, be obedient to those who are your masters according to the flesh, with fear and trembling, in sincerity of heart, as to Christ; ⁶not with eyeservice, as men-pleasers, but as bondservants of Christ, doing the will of God from the heart, ⁷with goodwill doing service, as to the Lord, and not to men, ⁸knowing that whatever good anyone does, he will receive the same from the Lord, whether he is a slave or free.

⁹And you, masters, do the same things to them, giving up threatening, knowing that your own Master also is in heaven, and there is no partiality with Him.

The Whole Armor of God

¹⁰Finally, my brethren, be strong in the Lord and in the power of His might. ¹¹Put on the whole armor of God, that you may be able to stand against the wiles of the devil. ¹²For we do not wrestle against flesh and blood, but against principalities, against powers, against the rulers of the darkness of this age, against spiritual hosts of wickedness in the heavenly places. ¹³Therefore take up the whole armor of God, that you may be able to withstand in the evil day, and having done all, to stand.

¹⁴Stand therefore, having girded your waist with truth, having put on the breastplate of righteousness, ¹⁵and having shod your feet with the preparation of the gospel of peace; ¹⁶above all, taking the shield of faith with which you will be able to quench all the fiery darts of the wicked one. ¹⁷And take the helmet of salvation, and the sword of the Spirit, which is the word of God; ¹⁸praying always with all prayer and supplication in the Spirit, being watchful to this end with all perseverance and supplication for all the saints— ¹⁹and for me, that utterance may be given to me, that I may open my mouth boldly to make known the mystery of the gospel, ²⁰for which I am an ambassador in chains; that in it I may speak boldly, as I ought to speak.

A Gracious Greeting

²¹But that you also may know my affairs *and* how I am doing, Tychicus, a beloved brother and faithful minister in the Lord, will make all things known to you; ²²whom I have sent to you for this very purpose, that you may know our affairs, and that he may comfort your hearts.

²³Peace to the brethren, and love with faith, from God the Father and the Lord Jesus Christ. ²⁴Grace be with all those who love our Lord Jesus Christ in sincerity. Amen.

DEVOTIONAL

Christians face an invisible, powerful, and spiritual Enemy who will stop at nothing to outwit, outgun, and outlast us. However, as military strategists put it, "It is a winnable war." We fight not for but from victory. Satan has us in the crosshairs of his scope, but we have "the whole armor of God" (Ephesians 6:11). Our armor may not be seen by people, but it is feared by demons.

When Paul said, "We do not wrestle against flesh and blood, but against principalities" (Ephesians 6:12), he used the word we. It's not just some Christians—all of us are in the battle. Many new Christians notice that the problems in their lives intensify as soon as they turn to Christ. That is not a coincidence. Satan strikes out at us with "wiles," or schemes (v. 11). As the accuser, he develops guilt and doubt in our hearts. He lies to us. As the tempter, he tries to lead us astray and into sin. As the adversary, he opposes all that we do for God.

In a battle or war, there's always something at stake, and it's no different with spiritual warfare. In ancient Greek contests, the eyes of whoever lost the battle were gouged out, but our spiritual battle is even more intense than that! Winning or losing this battle will determine not only our spiritual eyesight but also the eternal fate of human souls— our family, church, and nation. We are fighting in hand-to-hand, heart-to-heart combat. We are not victims but victors through Christ.

We don't seek just to be winners in a contest but also prayer warriors and soul winners (Ephesians 6:18–20). Do you know someone who is in the heat of battle? Spend time praying for that person today.

Also, stand your ground so you can speak the Word today. Make yourself available to God, and be willing to open your mouth and boldly share God's saving grace with someone (Ephesians 6:19). You can trust He will use you if you are willing.

Always be confident as you wrestle in spiritual warfare. Our Enemy is powerful, but our God is greater (1 John 4:4)!.

—Dr. Hayes Wicker
First Baptist Church, Naples, FL

WEEK 40, DAY 3

A Journey of Joy

Philippians 1:1–2:4

Greeting

1 Paul and Timothy, bondservants of Jesus Christ,

To all the saints in Christ Jesus who are in Philippi, with the bishops and deacons:

²Grace to you and peace from God our Father and the Lord Jesus Christ.

Thankfulness and Prayer

³I thank my God upon every remembrance of you, ⁴always in every prayer of mine making request for you all with joy, ⁵for your fellowship in the gospel from the first day until now, ⁶being confident of this very thing, that He who has begun a good work in you will complete it until the day of Jesus Christ; ⁷just as it is right for me to think this of you all, because I have you in my heart, inasmuch as both in my chains and in the defense and confirmation of the gospel, you all are partakers with me of grace. ⁸For God is my witness, how greatly I long for you all with the affection of Jesus Christ.

⁹And this I pray, that your love may abound still more and more in knowledge and all discernment, ¹⁰that you may approve the things that are excellent, that you may be sincere and without offense till the day of Christ, ¹¹being filled with the fruits of righteousness which are by Jesus Christ, to the glory and praise of God.

Christ Is Preached

¹²But I want you to know, brethren, that the things which happened to me have actually turned out for the furtherance of the gospel, ¹³so that it has become evident to the whole palace guard, and to all the rest, that my chains are in Christ; ¹⁴and most of the brethren in the Lord, having become confident by my chains, are much more bold to speak the word without fear.

¹⁵Some indeed preach Christ even from envy and strife, and some also from goodwill: ¹⁶The former preach Christ from selfish ambition, not sincerely, supposing to add affliction to my chains; ¹⁷but the latter out of love, knowing that I am appointed for the defense of the gospel. ¹⁸What then? Only that in every way, whether in pretense or in truth, Christ is preached; and in this I rejoice, yes, and will rejoice.

To Live Is Christ

¹⁹For I know that this will turn out for my deliverance through your prayer and the supply of the Spirit of Jesus Christ, ²⁰according to my earnest expectation and hope that in nothing I shall be ashamed, but with all boldness, as always, so now also Christ will be magnified in my body, whether by life or by death. ²¹For to me, to live is Christ, and to die is gain. ²²But if I live on in the flesh, this will mean fruit from my labor; yet what I shall choose I cannot tell. ²³For I am hard-pressed between the two, having a desire to depart and be with Christ, which is far better. ²⁴Nevertheless to remain in the flesh is more needful for you. ²⁵And being confident of this, I know that I shall remain and continue with you all for your progress and joy of faith, ²⁶that your rejoicing for me may be more abundant in Jesus Christ by my coming to you again.

Striving and Suffering for Christ

²⁷Only let your conduct be worthy of the gospel of Christ, so that whether I come and see you or am absent, I may hear of your affairs, that you stand fast in one spirit, with one mind striving together for the faith of the gospel, ²⁸and not in any way terrified by your adversaries, which is to them a proof of perdition, but to you of salvation, and that from God. ²⁹For to you it has been granted on behalf of Christ, not only to believe in Him, but also to suffer for His sake, ³⁰having the same conflict which you saw in me and now hear is in me.

Unity Through Humility

2 Therefore if there is any consolation in Christ, if any comfort of love, if any fellowship of the Spirit, if any affection and mercy, ²fulfill my joy by being like-minded, having the same love, being of one accord, of one mind. ³Let nothing be done through selfish ambition or conceit, but in lowliness of mind let each esteem others better than himself. ⁴Let each of you look out not only for his own interests, but also for the interests of others.

DEVOTIONAL

The Lord's work in our lives is for our good and His glory, and it is constant in the midst of pain and chains. He keeps us secure and makes us holy. Today, figuratively hang this sign over your life: "God at work." Rejoice that you are on a journey of growth and fruitfulness and that God will finish what He's started!

—Dr. Hayes Wicker
First Baptist Church, Naples, FL

WEEK 40, DAY 4

The Victory of Our Exalted Lord

Philippians 2:5–30

The Humbled and Exalted Christ

Let this mind be in you which was also in Christ Jesus, ⁶who, being in the form of God, did not consider it robbery to be equal with God, ⁷but made Himself of no reputation, taking the form of a bondservant, and coming in the likeness of men. ⁸And being found in appearance as a man, He humbled Himself and became obedient to the point of death, even the death of the cross. ⁹Therefore God also has highly exalted Him and given Him the name which is above every name, ¹⁰that at the name of Jesus every knee should bow, of those in heaven, and of those on earth, and of those under the earth, ¹¹and that every tongue should confess that Jesus Christ is Lord, to the glory of God the Father.

Light Bearers

¹²Therefore, my beloved, as you have always obeyed, not as in my presence only, but now much more in my absence, work out your own salvation with fear and trembling; ¹³for it is God who works in you both to will and to do for His good pleasure.

¹⁴Do all things without complaining and disputing, ¹⁵that you may become blameless and harmless, children of God without fault in the midst of a crooked and perverse generation, among whom you shine as lights in the world, ¹⁶holding fast the word of life, so that I may rejoice in the day of Christ that I have not run in vain or labored in vain.

¹⁷Yes, and if I am being poured out as a drink offering on the sacrifice and service of your faith, I am glad and rejoice with you all. ¹⁸For the same reason you also be glad and rejoice with me.

Timothy Commended

¹⁹But I trust in the Lord Jesus to send Timothy to you shortly, that I also may be encouraged when I know your state. ²⁰For I have no one like-minded, who will sincerely care for your state. ²¹For all seek their own, not the things which are of Christ Jesus. ²²But you know his proven character, that as a son with his father he served with me in the gospel. ²³Therefore I hope to send him at once, as soon as I see how it goes with me. ²⁴But I trust in the Lord that I myself shall also come shortly.

Epaphroditus Praised

²⁵Yet I considered it necessary to send to you Epaphroditus, my brother, fellow worker, and fellow soldier, but your messenger and the one who ministered to my need; ²⁶since he was longing for you all, and was distressed because you had heard that he was sick. ²⁷For indeed he was sick almost unto death; but God had mercy on him, and not only on him but on me also, lest I should have sorrow upon sorrow. ²⁸Therefore I sent him the more eagerly, that when you see him again you may rejoice, and I may be less sorrowful. ²⁹Receive him therefore in the Lord with all gladness, and hold such men in esteem; ³⁰because for the work of Christ he came close to death, not regarding his life, to supply what was lacking in your service toward me.

DEVOTIONAL

As Jesus died on the cross, it looked like the Champion of Eternal Life had been knocked down and out. Satan danced around the ring with fists raised in mock triumph. But then Christ rose from the dead!

The word resurrection *comes from a Greek word meaning "to cause to stand up." After Jesus had taken Satan's best shots and there was a count of three, He was "highly exalted" and, you could say, given the title of the Undisputed Heavyweight Champion of the World (Philippians 2:9–11)! He made death a revolving door. The word* exalt *means "to lift above and beyond." Jesus is in a different league from anyone or anything. He is our Lord and our God, and one day every contender and dictator will bow before Him and recognize that fact.*

Our Lord Jesus has given us so much in this life and beyond. We have His salvation and the knowledge that He is at work in us (Philippians 2:12–13). We can face life's challenges with the help of the Holy Spirit. We have the hope of heaven and abundant joy today because we have a relationship with God the Father through Christ the Son.

Today, let your exalted Lord reign in you. As you do, He will help you turn complaining into praising (Philippians 2:14). You will be able to shine and not whine (v. 15). You will be able to have victory, even in the midst of persecution and sickness (vv. 17, 27). Nothing will be able to tyrannize, traumatize, or paralyze you when you stand in His victory. So "holding fast the word of life" (v. 16), lift up the name of Jesus through your obedience.

—Dr. Hayes Wicker
First Baptist Church, Naples, FL

WEEK 40, DAY 5

Press Toward the Goal

Philippians 3:1–21

All for Christ

3 Finally, my brethren, rejoice in the Lord. For me to write the same things to you is not tedious, but for you it is safe.

²Beware of dogs, beware of evil workers, beware of the mutilation! ³For we are the circumcision, who worship God in the Spirit, rejoice in Christ Jesus, and have no confidence in the flesh, ⁴though I also might have confidence in the flesh. If anyone else thinks he may have confidence in the flesh, I more so: ⁵circumcised the eighth day, of the stock of Israel, of the tribe of Benjamin, a Hebrew of the Hebrews; concerning the law, a Pharisee; ⁶concerning zeal, persecuting the church; concerning the righteousness which is in the law, blameless.

⁷But what things were gain to me, these I have counted loss for Christ. ⁸Yet indeed I also count all things loss for the excellence of the knowledge of Christ Jesus my Lord, for whom I have suffered the loss of all things, and count them as rubbish, that I may gain Christ ⁹and be found in Him, not having my own righteousness, which is from the law, but that which is through faith in Christ, the righteousness which is from God by faith; ¹⁰that I may know Him and the power of His resurrection, and the fellowship of His sufferings, being conformed to His death, ¹¹if, by any means, I may attain to the resurrection from the dead.

Pressing Toward the Goal

¹²Not that I have already attained, or am already perfected; but I press on, that I may lay hold of that for which Christ Jesus has also laid hold of me. ¹³Brethren, I do not count myself to have apprehended; but one thing I do, forgetting those things which are behind and reaching forward to those things which are ahead, ¹⁴I press toward the goal for the prize of the upward call of God in Christ Jesus.

¹⁵Therefore let us, as many as are mature, have this mind; and if in anything you think otherwise, God will reveal even this to you. ¹⁶Nevertheless, to the degree that we have already attained, let us walk by the same rule, let us be of the same mind.

Our Citizenship in Heaven

¹⁷Brethren, join in following my example, and note those who so walk, as you have us for a pattern. ¹⁸For many walk, of whom I have told you often, and now tell you even weeping, that they are the enemies of the cross of Christ: ¹⁹whose end is destruction, whose god is their belly, and whose glory is in their shame—who set their mind on earthly things. ²⁰For our citizenship is in heaven, from which we also eagerly wait for the Savior, the Lord Jesus Christ, ²¹who will transform our lowly body that it may be conformed to His glorious body, according to the working by which He is able even to subdue all things to Himself.

DEVOTIONAL

I n our culture, "loser" is one of the worst slurs. There is even a hand sign to designate such! Pro athletes say they fear having people say of them, "This guy has potential." When scouts and coaches say that, they are essentially saying that they're not sure an athlete has "arrived"—or ever will.

However, all Christians are people of truly great potential. We have been drafted onto God's team, and our team is destined to win (Philippians 3:7–11). We aren't losers because we haven't yet arrived—real losers are the ones playing for the wrong team.

Now that we're on God's team, He doesn't want us sitting on the sidelines. He wants us to get out on the field and in the game. And once we're in the game, we need to be ready to stay in it like it's a marathon. We are to be constantly pressing on and moving forward toward the goal.

Our objective is to know Christ, become like Him, and fulfill His will for us on earth. Like Paul, we "lay hold of" the reality and resources of Christ (Philippians 3:12). That phrase in the original language means "to seize or take possession" and has the idea of tackling or forcing someone down. Jesus caught Paul and stopped him dead in his tracks. He was saved by grace and tackled by truth. When that happens in us, God bestows on us great potential and sets us on a path of sanctification and fruitfulness, with the ultimate prize awaiting us in heaven (vv. 14, 20–21).

Let Paul's words in Philippians 3:8–11 motivate you as you press on—everything he experienced in life seemed worthless compared to the great worth of knowing Christ. You are pursuing the most valuable goal in the world in this game. So carry the ball. March down the field. No pain, no gain. You could . . . go . . . all . . . the . . . way!

—Dr. Hayes Wicker
First Baptist Church, Naples, FL

WEEK 40, DAY 6

God's Answer for Worry

Philippians 4:1–23

4 Therefore, my beloved and longed-for brethren, my joy and crown, so stand fast in the Lord, beloved.

Be United, Joyful, and in Prayer

2I implore Euodia and I implore Syntyche to be of the same mind in the Lord. 3And I urge you also, true companion, help these women who labored with me in the gospel, with Clement also, and the rest of my fellow workers, whose names are in the Book of Life.

4Rejoice in the Lord always. Again I will say, rejoice! 5Let your gentleness be known to all men. The Lord is at hand.

6Be anxious for nothing, but in everything by prayer and supplication, with thanksgiving, let your requests be made known to God; 7and the peace of God, which surpasses all understanding, will guard your hearts and minds through Christ Jesus.

Meditate on These Things

8Finally, brethren, whatever things are true, whatever things are noble, whatever things are just, whatever things are pure, whatever things are lovely, whatever things are of good report, if there is any virtue and if there is anything praiseworthy—meditate on these things. 9The things which you learned and received and heard and saw in me, these do, and the God of peace will be with you.

Philippian Generosity

10But I rejoiced in the Lord greatly that now at last your care for me has flourished again; though you surely did care, but you lacked opportunity. 11Not that I speak in regard to need, for I have learned in whatever state I am, to be content: 12I know how to be abased, and I know how to abound. Everywhere and in all things I have learned both to be full and to be hungry, both to abound and to suffer need. 13I can do all things through Christ who strengthens me.

14Nevertheless you have done well that you shared in my distress. 15Now you Philippians know also that in the beginning of the gospel, when I departed from Macedonia, no church shared with me concerning giving and receiving but you only. 16For even in Thessalonica you sent aid once and again for my necessities. 17Not that I seek the gift, but I seek the fruit that abounds to your account. 18Indeed I have all and abound. I am full, having received from Epaphroditus the things sent from you, a sweet-smelling aroma, an acceptable sacrifice, well pleasing to God. 19And my God shall supply all your need according to His riches in glory by Christ Jesus. 20Now to our God and Father be glory forever and ever. Amen.

Greeting and Blessing

21Greet every saint in Christ Jesus. The brethren who are with me greet you. 22All the saints greet you, but especially those who are of Caesar's household.

23The grace of our Lord Jesus Christ be with you all. Amen.

DEVOTIONAL

The word worry *comes from an old word meaning "to choke or strangle." The more you fret, the more you feel cut off from the peace and presence of God. But God can help us not to be consumed by our anxiety, and He tells us what we can do to receive His help in Philippians 4:6–7.*

Verse 6 says, in direct contrast to being anxious, that you are to be in prayer, which can be defined as "adoration of God." Instead of pouting, praise Him. Instead of worrying, confess that your feelings are unconscious blasphemy against God's caring character. Prayer speaks of being in the sphere of God's presence. He is with you wherever you go and in whatever you encounter, no matter how you feel. Talk to Him now.

Next, make supplication to Him by asking for help in specific areas of life. After each daily devotion or quiet time, you should leave having asked a certain thing of God and expecting His answer. It may be go (yes), no, or slow (wait awhile). Be sure to tack on a "PS" to every petition with your thanksgiving, as Philippians 4:6 says. We are often quick to ask but slow to appreciate how God has answered prayers in the past.

Only when you have done all these things will His peace guard your heart and flood your life with joy, contentment, strength, and provision (Philippians 4:7, 10–11, 13, 17).

God is calling you to direct your mind toward Him and to dwell on what is true, noble, just, pure, lovely, of good report, and praiseworthy (Philippians 4:8). Replace your worries with worship!

—Dr. Hayes Wicker
First Baptist Church, Naples, FL

WEEK 40, DAY 7

How are you loving your family as Christ loved the church? How are you failing and succeeding in nourishing and cherishing them?

_____

_____

_____

_____

_____

_____

_____

_____

_____

_____

_____

_____

If your daily thoughts were projected onto a giant screen, would they be characterized by praise and praying, or complaining and criticizing? Prayer or worry?

_____

_____

_____

_____

_____

_____

_____

_____

_____

WEEK 41, DAY 1

The Preeminence of Christ

Colossians 1:1–23

Greeting

1 Paul, an apostle of Jesus Christ by the will of God, and Timothy our brother,

2To the saints and faithful brethren in Christ who are in Colosse:

Grace to you and peace from God our Father and the Lord Jesus Christ.

Their Faith in Christ

3We give thanks to the God and Father of our Lord Jesus Christ, praying always for you, 4since we heard of your faith in Christ Jesus and of your love for all the saints; 5because of the hope which is laid up for you in heaven, of which you heard before in the word of the truth of the gospel, 6which has come to you, as it has also in all the world, and is bringing forth fruit, as it is also among you since the day you heard and knew the grace of God in truth; 7as you also learned from Epaphras, our dear fellow servant, who is a faithful minister of Christ on your behalf, 8who also declared to us your love in the Spirit.

Preeminence of Christ

9For this reason we also, since the day we heard it, do not cease to pray for you, and to ask that you may be filled with the knowledge of His will in all wisdom and spiritual understanding; 10that you may walk worthy of the Lord, fully pleasing Him, being fruitful in every good work and increasing in the knowledge of God; 11strengthened with all might, according to His glorious power, for all patience and longsuffering with joy; 12giving thanks to the Father who has qualified us to be partakers of the inheritance of the saints in the light. 13He has delivered us from the power of darkness and conveyed us into the kingdom of the Son of His love, 14in whom we have redemption through His blood, the forgiveness of sins.

15He is the image of the invisible God, the firstborn over all creation. 16For by Him all things were created that are in heaven and that are on earth, visible and invisible, whether thrones or dominions or principalities or powers. All things were created through Him and for Him. 17And He is before all things, and in Him all things consist.

18And He is the head of the body, the church, who is the beginning, the firstborn from the dead, that in all things He may have the preeminence.

Reconciled in Christ

19For it pleased the Father that in Him all the fullness should dwell, 20and by Him to reconcile all things to Himself, by Him, whether things on earth or things in heaven, having made peace through the blood of His cross.

21And you, who once were alienated and enemies in your mind by wicked works, yet now He has reconciled 22in the body of His flesh through death, to present you holy, and blameless, and above reproach in His sight— 23if indeed you continue in the faith, grounded and steadfast, and are not moved away from the hope of the gospel which you heard, which was preached to every creature under heaven, of which I, Paul, became a minister.

DEVOTIONAL

It is always a special honor when someone prays for us. In today's text, Paul prayed for the Colossians to have spiritual stamina, asking that they would walk worthy of the Lord, fully please Him, and bear fruit in every good work. He prayed they would grow in the knowledge of God, endure everything with longsuffering and joy, and give thanks to the Father.

How is this kind of life even possible for mere mortals? Paul indicated they would need to remember that Christ is preeminent in all things. The word preeminence *can be defined as "a high status importance owing to marked superiority," or "having paramount rank." Christ is superior to all things in history. Everything both visible and invisible was created by Him and for Him. He is before all things, and He is the glue that holds this universe together. The great temptation for the Colossians was the same as it is for us today. We live in a multicultural world where we are constantly feeling the pressure not only to respect the religion of others but to consider it equal with the Christian faith. But the gospel does not allow for that, because the gospel declares Christ alone is to be preeminent in our lives.*

It is possible for you to possess the spiritual stamina Paul prayed the Colossians would have, but only when you trust in Christ for all things. Take your stand in Him and cling to Him as your hope. No other is His equal, so crown Him as the Superior One in your heart and be faithful to Him alone.

—Rick White
The People's Church, Franklin, TN

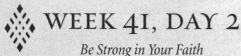

WEEK 41, DAY 2

Be Strong in Your Faith

Colossians 1:24–2:15

Sacrificial Service for Christ

I now rejoice in my sufferings for you, and fill up in my flesh what is lacking in the afflictions of Christ, for the sake of His body, which is the church, 25of which I became a minister according to the stewardship from God which was given to me for you, to fulfill the word of God, 26the mystery which has been hidden from ages and from generations, but now has been revealed to His saints. 27To them God willed to make known what are the riches of the glory of this mystery among the Gentiles: which is Christ in you, the hope of glory. 28Him we preach, warning every man and teaching every man in all wisdom, that we may present every man perfect in Christ Jesus. 29To this end I also labor, striving according to His working which works in me mightily.

Not Philosophy but Christ

2 For I want you to know what a great conflict I have for you and those in Laodicea, and for as many as have not seen my face in the flesh, 2that their hearts may be encouraged, being knit together in love, and attaining to all riches of the full assurance of understanding, to the knowledge of the mystery of God, both of the Father and of Christ, 3in whom are hidden all the treasures of wisdom and knowledge.

4Now this I say lest anyone should deceive you with persuasive words. 5For though I am absent in the flesh, yet I am with you in spirit, rejoicing to see your good order and the steadfastness of your faith in Christ.

6As you therefore have received Christ Jesus the Lord, so walk in Him, 7rooted and built up in Him and established in the faith, as you have been taught, abounding in it with thanksgiving.

8Beware lest anyone cheat you through philosophy and empty deceit, according to the tradition of men, according to the basic principles of the world, and not according to Christ. 9For in Him dwells all the fullness of the Godhead bodily; 10and you are complete in Him, who is the head of all principality and power.

Not Legalism but Christ

11In Him you were also circumcised with the circumcision made without hands, by putting off the body of the sins of the flesh, by the circumcision of Christ, 12buried with Him in baptism, in which you also were raised with Him through faith in the working of God, who raised Him from the dead. 13And you, being dead in your trespasses and the uncircumcision of your flesh, He has made alive together with Him, having forgiven you all trespasses, 14having wiped out the handwriting of requirements that was against us, which was contrary to us. And He has taken it out of the way, having nailed it to the cross. 15Having disarmed principalities and powers, He made a public spectacle of them, triumphing over them in it.

DEVOTIONAL

We all admire strong faith. We all find it inspiring. We really do desire it, but the question is, how do we acquire it? Most of us have been influenced by someone whose faith seemed to be head and shoulders above our own. Perhaps it has even caused us to question the validity of our own faith, or has motivated us in a positive way to pursue our personal journey of faith.

How can we live out the admonition of Paul to walk in Christ, being rooted, built up, and established in the faith (Colossians 2:6–7)? It all goes back to our understanding of those important words in Colossians 1: "Christ in you, the hope of glory" (v. 27). This is one of the great truths in all of Scripture. Christ's presence in His people is the bedrock of living a life of faith. His presence in us means we are strengthened by certain attributes of God now living in us. The Bible teaches us God is love, God is light, and God is life. Think about that for a moment. Christ is in us, and so the love, light, and life of God is also in us. Your faith can be strong when you start living out the truth of "Christ in you, the hope of glory."

Saint Irenaeus once declared, "The glory of God is man fully alive." You can only be fully alive when you believe, understand, and begin to live out the implications of Christ being in you. Your faith is only as strong as the One who is the object of your faith. Paul said that in Christ "dwells all the fullness of the Godhead" and that we are "complete in Him, who is the head of all principality and power" (Colossians 2:9–10).

Be strong in your faith by understanding who Christ is, who you are in Him, and what you have in Him.

—Rick White
The People's Church, Franklin, TN

WEEK 41, DAY 3

Put Away All Evil

Colossians 2:16–3:17

So let no one judge you in food or in drink, or regarding a festival or a new moon or sabbaths, 17which are a shadow of things to come, but the substance is of Christ. 18Let no one cheat you of your reward, taking delight in false humility and worship of angels, intruding into those things which he has not seen, vainly puffed up by his fleshly mind, 19and not holding fast to the Head, from whom all the body, nourished and knit together by joints and ligaments, grows with the increase that is from God.

20Therefore, if you died with Christ from the basic principles of the world, why, as though living in the world, do you subject yourselves to regulations— 21"Do not touch, do not taste, do not handle," 22which all concern things which perish with the using—according to the commandments and doctrines of men? 23These things indeed have an appearance of wisdom in self-imposed religion, false humility, and neglect of the body, but are of no value against the indulgence of the flesh.

Not Carnality but Christ

3 If then you were raised with Christ, seek those things which are above, where Christ is, sitting at the right hand of God. 2Set your mind on things above, not on things on the earth. 3For you died, and your life is hidden with Christ in God. 4When Christ who is our life appears, then you also will appear with Him in glory.

5Therefore put to death your members which are on the earth: fornication, uncleanness, passion, evil desire, and covetousness, which is idolatry. 6Because of these things the wrath of God is coming upon the sons of disobedience, 7in which you yourselves once walked when you lived in them.

8But now you yourselves are to put off all these: anger, wrath, malice, blasphemy, filthy language out of your mouth. 9Do not lie to one another, since you have put off the old man with his deeds, 10and have put on the new man who is renewed in knowledge according to the image of Him who created him, 11where there is neither Greek nor Jew, circumcised nor uncircumcised, barbarian, Scythian, slave nor free, but Christ is all and in all.

Character of the New Man

12Therefore, as the elect of God, holy and beloved, put on tender mercies, kindness, humility, meekness, longsuffering; 13bearing with one another, and forgiving one another, if anyone has a complaint against another; even as Christ forgave you, so you also must do. 14But above all these things put on love, which is the bond of perfection. 15And let the peace of God rule in your hearts, to which also you were called in one body; and be thankful. 16Let the word of Christ dwell in you richly in all wisdom, teaching and admonishing one another in psalms and hymns and spiritual songs, singing with grace in your hearts to the Lord. 17And whatever you do in word or deed, do all in the name of the Lord Jesus, giving thanks to God the Father through Him.

DEVOTIONAL

Putting our belongings away is an important lesson we learn early in life. When we fail to do so, we end up living in chaotic and confusing environments. The same kind of principle applies to our spiritual lives today. Once we come to faith in Jesus Christ and call Him Lord of our lives, there are certain attitudes and behaviors we must put away, and if we do not, we will most assuredly live in total chaos and confusion.

Paul gave two lists of five sins. The first list deals with sexual purity (Colossians 3:5), and the second deals with attitudes and speech (v. 8). All of these sins are connected to our former way of life. Many of us are familiar with the traps of sexual sins and the devastation they bring, whether we've experienced it personally or seen it in the lives of others. Paul said sexual impurity in any form—from adultery to pornography—must be put away.

The second list is about the misuse of anger and letting strong emotions lead us to use filthy language that is inconsistent with our new life in Christ. We are told to put to death, put off, and put away the old way of life and to put on the "new man"—our new nature in Christ (Colossians 3:10).

Look at the contrast of the things we are to put on in Colossians 3:12–14. The old life leads to chaos, while the new life leads to personal peace. The peace of God will rule in our hearts, helping us to live in a way that is pleasing to God. Whatever we do, we are to do it with a view of bringing honor to God. Before you start the day, put away old things and put on new things you know are pleasing to God.

—Rick White
The People's Church, Franklin, TN

WEEK 41, DAY 4

Honoring the People in Your Life

Colossians 3:18–4:18

The Christian Home

Wives, submit to your own husbands, as is fitting in the Lord.

19Husbands, love your wives and do not be bitter toward them.

20Children, obey your parents in all things, for this is well pleasing to the Lord.

21Fathers, do not provoke your children, lest they become discouraged.

22Bondservants, obey in all things your masters according to the flesh, not with eyeservice, as men-pleasers, but in sincerity of heart, fearing God. 23And whatever you do, do it heartily, as to the Lord and not to men, 24knowing that from the Lord you will receive the reward of the inheritance; for you serve the Lord Christ. 25But he who does wrong will be repaid for what he has done, and there is no partiality.

4 Masters, give your bondservants what is just and fair, knowing that you also have a Master in heaven.

Christian Graces

2Continue earnestly in prayer, being vigilant in it with thanksgiving; 3meanwhile praying also for us, that God would open to us a door for the word, to speak the mystery of Christ, for which I am also in chains, 4that I may make it manifest, as I ought to speak.

5Walk in wisdom toward those who are outside, redeeming the time. 6Let your speech always be with grace, seasoned with salt, that you may know how you ought to answer each one.

Final Greetings

7Tychicus, a beloved brother, faithful minister, and fellow servant in the Lord, will tell you all the news about me. 8I am sending him to you for this very purpose, that he may know your circumstances and comfort your hearts, 9with Onesimus, a faithful and beloved brother, who is one of you. They will make known to you all things which are happening here.

10Aristarchus my fellow prisoner greets you, with Mark the cousin of Barnabas (about whom you received instructions: if he comes to you, welcome him), 11and Jesus who is called Justus. These are my only fellow workers for the kingdom of God who are of the circumcision; they have proved to be a comfort to me.

12Epaphras, who is one of you, a bondservant of Christ, greets you, always laboring fervently for you in prayers, that you may stand perfect and complete in all the will of God. 13For I bear him witness that he has a great zeal for you, and those who are in Laodicea, and those in Hierapolis. 14Luke the beloved physician and Demas greet you. 15Greet the brethren who are in Laodicea, and Nymphas and the church that is in his house.

Closing Exhortations and Blessing

16Now when this epistle is read among you, see that it is read also in the church of the Laodiceans, and that you likewise read the epistle from Laodicea. 17And say to Archippus, "Take heed to the ministry which you have received in the Lord, that you may fulfill it."

18This salutation by my own hand—Paul. Remember my chains. Grace be with you. Amen.

DEVOTIONAL

Today's passage teaches us how to walk wisely in all of our relationships. Instructions are given to wives, husbands, children, fathers, servants, and masters. There are even words of instruction about how to treat those who are outside the faith.

We live in a world that values the youth culture and increasingly seems to be devaluing older members of society. Scripture teaches us to obey our parents and honor them because it is pleasing to the Lord (Colossians 3:20). Sometimes we apply a scripture like this to the days when we were living in the household of our parents and think once we leave their care we no longer have any responsibility.

However, honoring our parents is a lifelong responsibility. It is beautiful when Christians live out their faith by serving parents who are growing older, experiencing poor health, and approaching death. In a world with diminishing moral fiber, we need more men and women demonstrating their faith by caring for the ones who cared for them, even during difficult seasons of life.

How have you honored your parents lately? How will you serve and show respect for other people in your life today?

—Rick White
The People's Church, Franklin, TN

WEEK 41, DAY 5

Share God's Love

1 Thessalonians 1:1–2:16

Greeting

1 Paul, Silvanus, and Timothy,

To the church of the Thessalonians in God the Father and the Lord Jesus Christ:

Grace to you and peace from God our Father and the Lord Jesus Christ.

Their Good Example

2We give thanks to God always for you all, making mention of you in our prayers, 3remembering without ceasing your work of faith, labor of love, and patience of hope in our Lord Jesus Christ in the sight of our God and Father, 4knowing, beloved brethren, your election by God. 5For our gospel did not come to you in word only, but also in power, and in the Holy Spirit and in much assurance, as you know what kind of men we were among you for your sake.

6And you became followers of us and of the Lord, having received the word in much affliction, with joy of the Holy Spirit, 7so that you became examples to all in Macedonia and Achaia who believe. 8For from you the word of the Lord has sounded forth, not only in Macedonia and Achaia, but also in every place. Your faith toward God has gone out, so that we do not need to say anything. 9For they themselves declare concerning us what manner of entry we had to you, and how you turned to God from idols to serve the living and true God, 10and to wait for His Son from heaven, whom He raised from the dead, even Jesus who delivers us from the wrath to come.

Paul's Conduct

2 For you yourselves know, brethren, that our coming to you was not in vain. 2But even after we had suffered before and were spitefully treated at Philippi, as you know, we were bold in our God to speak to you the gospel of God in much conflict. 3For our exhortation did not come from error or uncleanness, nor was it in deceit.

4But as we have been approved by God to be entrusted with the gospel, even so we speak, not as pleasing men, but God who tests our hearts. 5For neither at any time did we use flattering words, as you know, nor a cloak for covetousness—

God is witness. 6Nor did we seek glory from men, either from you or from others, when we might have made demands as apostles of Christ. 7But we were gentle among you, just as a nursing mother cherishes her own children. 8So, affectionately longing for you, we were well pleased to impart to you not only the gospel of God, but also our own lives, because you had become dear to us. 9For you remember, brethren, our labor and toil; for laboring night and day, that we might not be a burden to any of you, we preached to you the gospel of God.

10You are witnesses, and God also, how devoutly and justly and blamelessly we behaved ourselves among you who believe; 11as you know how we exhorted, and comforted, and charged every one of you, as a father does his own children, 12that you would walk worthy of God who calls you into His own kingdom and glory.

Their Conversion

13For this reason we also thank God without ceasing, because when you received the word of God which you heard from us, you welcomed it not as the word of men, but as it is in truth, the word of God, which also effectively works in you who believe. 14For you, brethren, became imitators of the churches of God which are in Judea in Christ Jesus. For you also suffered the same things from your own countrymen, just as they did from the Judeans, 15who killed both the Lord Jesus and their own prophets, and have persecuted us; and they do not please God and are contrary to all men, 16forbidding us to speak to the Gentiles that they may be saved, so as always to fill up the measure of their sins; but wrath has come upon them to the uttermost.

DEVOTIONAL

*I*f you were to associate one word with the apostle Paul, it might be the word gospel. Paul was so consumed with the power of the gospel that he was willing to endure enormous hardships in order to proclaim the good news to people who were far from God.

The gospel is the story of how much God loves us. Consider how the gospel has changed your life. If you have been compelled by the love of God and if your sins have been forgiven, what would you be willing to do to get that good news to other people? God loves you, and now you get to share that love with other people.

—Rick White
The People's Church, Franklin, TN

WEEK 41, DAY 6

God Requires Holy Living

1 Thessalonians 2:17–4:12

Longing to See Them

But we, brethren, having been taken away from you for a short time in presence, not in heart, endeavored more eagerly to see your face with great desire. ¹⁸Therefore we wanted to come to you—even I, Paul, time and again—but Satan hindered us. ¹⁹For what is our hope, or joy, or crown of rejoicing? Is it not even you in the presence of our Lord Jesus Christ at His coming? ²⁰For you are our glory and joy.

Concern for Their Faith

Therefore, when we could no longer endure it, we thought it good to be left in Athens alone, ²and sent Timothy, our brother and minister of God, and our fellow laborer in the gospel of Christ, to establish you and encourage you concerning your faith, ³that no one should be shaken by these afflictions; for you yourselves know that we are appointed to this. ⁴For, in fact, we told you before when we were with you that we would suffer tribulation, just as it happened, and you know. ⁵For this reason, when I could no longer endure it, I sent to know your faith, lest by some means the tempter had tempted you, and our labor might be in vain.

Encouraged by Timothy

⁶But now that Timothy has come to us from you, and brought us good news of your faith and love, and that you always have good remembrance of us, greatly desiring to see us, as we also to see you— ⁷therefore, brethren, in all our affliction and distress we were comforted concerning you by your faith. ⁸For now we live, if you stand fast in the Lord.

⁹For what thanks can we render to God for you, for all the joy with which we rejoice for your sake before our God, ¹⁰night and day praying exceedingly that we may see your face and perfect what is lacking in your faith?

Prayer for the Church

¹¹Now may our God and Father Himself, and our Lord Jesus Christ, direct our way to you. ¹²And may the Lord make you increase and abound in love to one another and to all, just as we do to you, ¹³so that He may establish your hearts blameless in holiness before our God and Father at the coming of our Lord Jesus Christ with all His saints.

Plea for Purity

Finally then, brethren, we urge and exhort in the Lord Jesus that you should abound more and more, just as you received from us how you ought to walk and to please God; ²for you know what commandments we gave you through the Lord Jesus.

³For this is the will of God, your sanctification: that you should abstain from sexual immorality; ⁴that each of you should know how to possess his own vessel in sanctification and honor, ⁵not in passion of lust, like the Gentiles who do not know God; ⁶that no one should take advantage of and defraud his brother in this matter, because the Lord is the avenger of all such, as we also forewarned you and testified. ⁷For God did not call us to uncleanness, but in holiness. ⁸Therefore he who rejects this does not reject man, but God, who has also given us His Holy Spirit.

A Brotherly and Orderly Life

⁹But concerning brotherly love you have no need that I should write to you, for you yourselves are taught by God to love one another; ¹⁰and indeed you do so toward all the brethren who are in all Macedonia. But we urge you, brethren, that you increase more and more; ¹¹that you also aspire to lead a quiet life, to mind your own business, and to work with your own hands, as we commanded you, ¹²that you may walk properly toward those who are outside, and that you may lack nothing.

DEVOTIONAL

How often do you think of the will of God? We tend to limit God's will to the big decisions of life—where we go to school, whom we marry, what occupation we choose. Sometimes we spend so much time searching for His will that we miss the obvious.

God made His will clear in 1 Thessalonians 4:3—He wants us all to be sanctified. He wants us to continue to grow up in our faith so we resemble Him more and more.

Part of growing up in Christ is learning to live in purity, especially sexual purity. We live in a society that uses sex to sell almost everything. We have to be careful not to be controlled by the world of advertising and let sex appeal draw our gazes and guide our steps. It has been a temptation for Christians from the first century to the present day to seek personal gratification apart from Christ. But God has called us to a new standard of living. Ask Him to help you grow up in your faith and live a life of purity.

—Rick White
The People's Church, Franklin, TN

WEEK 41, DAY 7

What does it mean to you personally when you read the phrase "Christ in you, the hope of glory" in Colossians 1:27?

_____

_____

_____

_____

_____

_____

_____

_____

_____

_____

How have you "grown up" in Christ in recent months? How do you think you might need to grow in holiness in the coming months? Write a prayer asking God for conviction and guidance and expressing your willingness to be sanctified.

_____

_____

_____

_____

_____

_____

_____

_____

_____

WEEK 42, DAY I

Time Is Running Out

1 Thessalonians 4:13–5:28

The Comfort of Christ's Coming

But I do not want you to be ignorant, brethren, concerning those who have fallen asleep, lest you sorrow as others who have no hope. 14For if we believe that Jesus died and rose again, even so God will bring with Him those who sleep in Jesus.

15For this we say to you by the word of the Lord, that we who are alive and remain until the coming of the Lord will by no means precede those who are asleep. 16For the Lord Himself will descend from heaven with a shout, with the voice of an archangel, and with the trumpet of God. And the dead in Christ will rise first. 17Then we who are alive and remain shall be caught up together with them in the clouds to meet the Lord in the air. And thus we shall always be with the Lord. 18Therefore comfort one another with these words.

The Day of the Lord

5 But concerning the times and the seasons, brethren, you have no need that I should write to you. 2For you yourselves know perfectly that the day of the Lord so comes as a thief in the night. 3For when they say, "Peace and safety!" then sudden destruction comes upon them, as labor pains upon a pregnant woman. And they shall not escape. 4But you, brethren, are not in darkness, so that this Day should overtake you as a thief. 5You are all sons of light and sons of the day. We are not of the night nor of darkness. 6Therefore let us not sleep, as others do, but let us watch and be sober. 7For those who sleep, sleep at night, and those who get drunk are drunk at night. 8But let us who are of the day be sober, putting on the breastplate of faith and love, and as a helmet the hope of salvation. 9For God did not appoint us to wrath, but to obtain salvation through our Lord Jesus Christ, 10who died for us, that whether we wake or sleep, we should live together with Him.

11Therefore comfort each other and edify one another, just as you also are doing.

Various Exhortations

12And we urge you, brethren, to recognize those who labor among you, and are over you in the Lord and admonish you, 13and to esteem them very highly in love for their work's sake. Be at peace among yourselves.

14Now we exhort you, brethren, warn those who are unruly, comfort the fainthearted, uphold the weak, be patient with all. 15See that no one renders evil for evil to anyone, but always pursue what is good both for yourselves and for all.

16Rejoice always, 17pray without ceasing, 18in everything give thanks; for this is the will of God in Christ Jesus for you.

19Do not quench the Spirit. 20Do not despise prophecies. 21Test all things; hold fast what is good. 22Abstain from every form of evil.

Blessing and Admonition

23Now may the God of peace Himself sanctify you completely; and may your whole spirit, soul, and body be preserved blameless at the coming of our Lord Jesus Christ. 24He who calls you is faithful, who also will do it.

25Brethren, pray for us.

26Greet all the brethren with a holy kiss.

27I charge you by the Lord that this epistle be read to all the holy brethren.

28The grace of our Lord Jesus Christ be with you. Amen.

DEVOTIONAL

Don't you love watching the final few minutes of a close football game? Many times you will see every player on the team hold up four fingers as the third quarter ends and the fourth is about to begin—it's a sign to communicate that everyone on the team realizes time is running out. Teams seem to pull out all the stops as the game comes to a close. No matter how tired the players are, they put forth maximum effort. Coaches seem to call more aggressive plays as they realize that it is now or never.

In 1 Thessalonians 4–5, Paul wrote about the certain return of Jesus Christ to end this present age. In light of the certain return of Christ, we as believers ought to live like we are in the last minutes of the fourth quarter of the game. We know time is running out. The God of the universe has revealed what will take place, and He has commanded us to be ready.

If we are ever going to live our lives on mission for Christ, now is the time. It's now or never! Figuratively, let's raise four fingers into the air to declare that we will live with focus and energy, like we are in the fourth quarter. Let's be on mission today for Christ with a renewed passion and urgency in light of His certain return.

—Brady Cooper
New Vision Baptist Church, Murfreesboro, TN

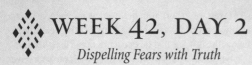

WEEK 42, DAY 2

Dispelling Fears with Truth

2 Thessalonians 1:1–2:12

Greeting

1 Paul, Silvanus, and Timothy,

To the church of the Thessalonians in God our Father and the Lord Jesus Christ:

²Grace to you and peace from God our Father and the Lord Jesus Christ.

God's Final Judgment and Glory

³We are bound to thank God always for you, brethren, as it is fitting, because your faith grows exceedingly, and the love of every one of you all abounds toward each other, ⁴so that we ourselves boast of you among the churches of God for your patience and faith in all your persecutions and tribulations that you endure, ⁵which is manifest evidence of the righteous judgment of God, that you may be counted worthy of the kingdom of God, for which you also suffer; ⁶since it is a righteous thing with God to repay with tribulation those who trouble you, ⁷and to give you who are troubled rest with us when the Lord Jesus is revealed from heaven with His mighty angels, ⁸in flaming fire taking vengeance on those who do not know God, and on those who do not obey the gospel of our Lord Jesus Christ. ⁹These shall be punished with everlasting destruction from the presence of the Lord and from the glory of His power, ¹⁰when He comes, in that Day, to be glorified in His saints and to be admired among all those who believe, because our testimony among you was believed.

¹¹Therefore we also pray always for you that our God would count you worthy of this calling, and fulfill all the good pleasure of His goodness and the work of faith with power, ¹²that the name of our Lord Jesus Christ may be glorified in you, and you in Him, according to the grace of our God and the Lord Jesus Christ.

The Great Apostasy

2 Now, brethren, concerning the coming of our Lord Jesus Christ and our gathering together to Him, we ask you, ²not to be soon shaken in mind or troubled, either by spirit or by word or by letter, as if from us, as though the day of Christ had come. ³Let no one deceive you by any means; for that Day will not come unless the falling away comes first, and the man of sin is revealed, the son of perdition, ⁴who opposes and exalts himself above all that is called God or that is worshiped, so that he sits as God in the temple of God, showing himself that he is God.

⁵Do you not remember that when I was still with you I told you these things? ⁶And now you know what is restraining, that he may be revealed in his own time. ⁷For the mystery of lawlessness is already at work; only He who now restrains will do so until He is taken out of the way. ⁸And then the lawless one will be revealed, whom the Lord will consume with the breath of His mouth and destroy with the brightness of His coming. ⁹The coming of the lawless one is according to the working of Satan, with all power, signs, and lying wonders, ¹⁰and with all unrighteous deception among those who perish, because they did not receive the love of the truth, that they might be saved. ¹¹And for this reason God will send them strong delusion, that they should believe the lie, ¹²that they all may be condemned who did not believe the truth but had pleasure in unrighteousness.

DEVOTIONAL

*I*n today's passage, Paul took the opportunity to address some concerns the Thessalonian believers had about the Second Coming of Christ. The church at Thessalonica had slipped into fear because they had believed some false information about the end times. In fact, some of them even thought they had missed the return of Christ.

We, too, can so quickly fall prey to fear in our own lives. The antidote to fear is faith, and the way God grows our faith is through a steady diet of His Word (Romans 10:17).

When you hear folks teach on the end times, much emphasis is given to the role of the Antichrist. It can generate fear in believers. The Antichrist will play a role in end time events, but not a leading role. The leading role is reserved for Christ. Paul told us in 2 Thessalonians 2:8 that Christ will overthrow the Antichrist with just "the breath of His mouth"!

What other false beliefs do you have that are generating fear? Do not be "shaken in mind or troubled," and "let no one deceive you by any means" (2 Thessalonians 2:2–3). Instead, expose those false beliefs by studying the truth of God's Word and clinging to it. When you do, those fears will be destroyed, and you will begin to live in greater levels of freedom.

—Brady Cooper
New Vision Baptist Church, Murfreesboro, TN

WEEK 42, DAY 3

Persevere in Doing Good

2 Thessalonians 2:13–3:18

Stand Fast

But we are bound to give thanks to God always for you, brethren beloved by the Lord, because God from the beginning chose you for salvation through sanctification by the Spirit and belief in the truth, 14to which He called you by our gospel, for the obtaining of the glory of our Lord Jesus Christ. 15Therefore, brethren, stand fast and hold the traditions which you were taught, whether by word or our epistle.

16Now may our Lord Jesus Christ Himself, and our God and Father, who has loved us and given us everlasting consolation and good hope by grace, 17comfort your hearts and establish you in every good word and work.

Pray for Us

3 Finally, brethren, pray for us, that the word of the Lord may run swiftly and be glorified, just as it is with you, 2and that we may be delivered from unreasonable and wicked men; for not all have faith.

3But the Lord is faithful, who will establish you and guard you from the evil one. 4And we have confidence in the Lord concerning you, both that you do and will do the things we command you.

5Now may the Lord direct your hearts into the love of God and into the patience of Christ.

Warning Against Idleness

6But we command you, brethren, in the name of our Lord Jesus Christ, that you withdraw from every brother who walks disorderly and not according to the tradition which he received from us. 7For you yourselves know how you ought to follow us, for we were not disorderly among you; 8nor did we eat anyone's bread free of charge, but worked with labor and toil night and day, that we might not be a burden to any of you, 9not because we do not have authority, but to make ourselves an example of how you should follow us.

10For even when we were with you, we commanded you this: If anyone will not work, neither shall he eat. 11For we hear that there are some who walk among you in a disorderly manner, not working at all, but are busybodies. 12Now those who are such we command and exhort through our Lord Jesus Christ that they work in quietness and eat their own bread.

13But as for you, brethren, do not grow weary in doing good. 14And if anyone does not obey our word in this epistle, note that person and do not keep company with him, that he may be ashamed. 15Yet do not count him as an enemy, but admonish him as a brother.

Benediction

16Now may the Lord of peace Himself give you peace always in every way. The Lord be with you all.

17The salutation of Paul with my own hand, which is a sign in every epistle; so I write.

18The grace of our Lord Jesus Christ be with you all. Amen.

DEVOTIONAL

Sometimes doing good begins to feel like work—hard work. We receive criticism instead of compliments. We are handed another to-do list instead of a trophy for our accomplishments. We wish we could sit this one out and let someone else carry the load. In 2 Thessalonians 3:13, Paul warned believers about this ministry fatigue, saying, "Do not grow weary in doing good." Instead of counting on our own strength and patience, we have to follow Paul's key strategies for overcoming ministry fatigue.

The first key is focusing on God and trusting Him to do the work through us. When we stop focusing on God, we rely on ourselves and grow weary. Instead, we need to "stand fast" (2 Thessalonians 2:15) and allow God to fill us with the strength we need to do His work. Isaiah 40:31 promises that "those who wait on the LORD shall renew their strength; they shall mount up with wings like eagles."

Another key is to read and study the Bible. Paul instructed believers to "hold the traditions which you were taught, whether by word or our epistle" (2 Thessalonians 2:15). Paul was referring to the Word of God. We must never forget that "all Scripture is given by inspiration of God, and is profitable for doctrine, for reproof, for correction, for instruction in righteousness, that the man of God may be complete, thoroughly equipped for every good work" (2 Timothy 3:16–17).

When you grow weary in doing good, look to God and His Word to renew your strength!

—Brady Cooper
New Vision Baptist Church, Murfreesboro, TN

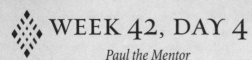

WEEK 42, DAY 4

Paul the Mentor

1 Timothy 1:1–20

Greeting

1 Paul, an apostle of Jesus Christ, by the commandment of God our Savior and the Lord Jesus Christ, our hope,

2To Timothy, a true son in the faith:

Grace, mercy, and peace from God our Father and Jesus Christ our Lord.

No Other Doctrine

3As I urged you when I went into Macedonia—remain in Ephesus that you may charge some that they teach no other doctrine, 4nor give heed to fables and endless genealogies, which cause disputes rather than godly edification which is in faith. 5Now the purpose of the commandment is love from a pure heart, from a good conscience, and from sincere faith, 6from which some, having strayed, have turned aside to idle talk, 7desiring to be teachers of the law, understanding neither what they say nor the things which they affirm.

8But we know that the law is good if one uses it lawfully, 9knowing this: that the law is not made for a righteous person, but for the lawless and insubordinate, for the ungodly and for sinners, for the unholy and profane, for murderers of fathers and murderers of mothers, for manslayers, 10for fornicators, for sodomites, for kidnappers, for liars, for perjurers, and if there is any other thing that is contrary to sound doctrine, 11according to the glorious gospel of the blessed God which was committed to my trust.

Glory to God for His Grace

12And I thank Christ Jesus our Lord who has enabled me, because He counted me faithful, putting me into the ministry, 13although I was formerly a blasphemer, a persecutor, and an insolent man; but I obtained mercy because I did it ignorantly in unbelief. 14And the grace of our Lord was exceedingly abundant, with faith and love which are in Christ Jesus. 15This is a faithful saying and worthy of all acceptance, that Christ Jesus came into the world to save sinners, of whom I am chief. 16However, for this reason I obtained mercy, that in me first Jesus Christ might show all longsuffering, as a pattern to those who are going to believe on Him for everlasting life. 17Now to the King eternal, immortal, invisible, to God who alone is wise, be honor and glory forever and ever. Amen.

Fight the Good Fight

18This charge I commit to you, son Timothy, according to the prophecies previously made concerning you, that by them you may wage the good warfare, 19having faith and a good conscience, which some having rejected, concerning the faith have suffered shipwreck, 20of whom are Hymenaeus and Alexander, whom I delivered to Satan that they may learn not to blaspheme.

DEVOTIONAL

When we think about the apostle Paul, we picture an outspoken, brave, and driven man who stood strong for Christ in spite of beatings, imprisonment, and conflict. He was the church's John Wayne. In Paul's personal letter to young Timothy, however, we discover a different picture of Paul. We see a caring mentor who shared his life with a fellow believer despite the hardships and activity in his life. Paul's letter to Timothy serves as a blueprint for us as we share our lives with others.

Paul was a transparent mentor. In 1 Timothy 1:12–17, he shared how God can use someone with an ugly past for His glory. Paul was not hiding or bragging about his past; he simply used it as an example of God's patience and grace. In Philippians 1:12, Paul wrote, "I want you to know, brethren, that the things which happened to me have actually turned out for the furtherance of the gospel."

Paul was a caring mentor. He warned Timothy to be on guard against false teachings and ideas that would lead him away from Christ. Paul understood the importance of truth. He carefully and intentionally guided Timothy to truths that bring freedom and protected him from lies that destroy.

Paul was an encouraging mentor. In 1 Timothy 1:18–19, Paul expressed his faith in Timothy to fight the good fight and remain close to God. Paul based his faith in God. We find an excellent expression of this faith in Philippians 1:6, when Paul told believers he was confident "that He who has begun a good work in you will complete it until the day of Jesus Christ."

Follow Paul's example and take time out of your hectic schedule to mentor people God has placed in your life.

—Brady Cooper
New Vision Baptist Church, Murfreesboro, TN

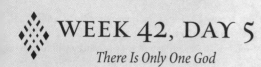

WEEK 42, DAY 5

There Is Only One God

1 Timothy 2:1–3:13

Pray for All Men

2 Therefore I exhort first of all that supplications, prayers, intercessions, and giving of thanks be made for all men, ²for kings and all who are in authority, that we may lead a quiet and peaceable life in all godliness and reverence. ³For this is good and acceptable in the sight of God our Savior, ⁴who desires all men to be saved and to come to the knowledge of the truth. ⁵For there is one God and one Mediator between God and men, the Man Christ Jesus, ⁶who gave Himself a ransom for all, to be testified in due time, ⁷for which I was appointed a preacher and an apostle—I am speaking the truth in Christ and not lying—a teacher of the Gentiles in faith and truth.

Men and Women in the Church

⁸I desire therefore that the men pray everywhere, lifting up holy hands, without wrath and doubting; ⁹in like manner also, that the women adorn themselves in modest apparel, with propriety and moderation, not with braided hair or gold or pearls or costly clothing, ¹⁰but, which is proper for women professing godliness, with good works. ¹¹Let a woman learn in silence with all submission. ¹²And I do not permit a woman to teach or to have authority over a man, but to be in silence. ¹³For Adam was formed first, then Eve. ¹⁴And Adam was not deceived, but the woman being deceived, fell into transgression. ¹⁵Nevertheless she will be saved in childbearing if they continue in faith, love, and holiness, with self-control.

Qualifications of Overseers

3 This is a faithful saying: If a man desires the position of a bishop, he desires a good work. ²A bishop then must be blameless, the husband of one wife, temperate, sober-minded, of good behavior, hospitable, able to teach; ³not given to wine, not violent, not greedy for money, but gentle, not quarrelsome, not covetous; ⁴one who rules his own house well, having his children in submission with all reverence ⁵(for if a man does not know how to rule his own house, how will he take care of the church of God?); ⁶not a novice, lest being puffed up with pride he fall into the same condemnation as the devil. ⁷Moreover he must have a good testimony among those who are outside, lest he fall into reproach and the snare of the devil.

Qualifications of Deacons

⁸Likewise deacons must be reverent, not double-tongued, not given to much wine, not greedy for money, ⁹holding the mystery of the faith with a pure conscience. ¹⁰But let these also first be tested; then let them serve as deacons, being found blameless. ¹¹Likewise, their wives must be reverent, not slanderers, temperate, faithful in all things. ¹²Let deacons be the husbands of one wife, ruling their children and their own houses well. ¹³For those who have served well as deacons obtain for themselves a good standing and great boldness in the faith which is in Christ Jesus.

DEVOTIONAL

*P*aul makes the assertion in 1 Timothy 2:5 that there is only one God. As Christians, we often take this truth for granted, but it is a foundational truth for what we believe. In this passage alone, we see several implications of that truth.

First, since there is one God, He determines how people can make their way to Him. We do not have the freedom to choose the terms of our relationship with Him. First Timothy 2:5–6 make it clear that God has provided a way for us to have a relationship with Himself through His Son, Jesus Christ. He is the only Mediator between God and man. The implication for believers is that we must share the good news of salvation in Jesus Christ and pray for the conversion of souls. There is no other way to be saved.

Second, since there is one God, we do not have the freedom to choose how we will run His church. First Timothy 2:9–3:13, a passage about men's and women's roles and church leaders, tends to be controversial. Bible-believing Christians may disagree over what the Bible means in this instance, but we do not have the freedom to ignore the Bible altogether. In other words, we are bound by God's Word. He has the right to determine the qualifications for the leaders of His church.

God's authority extends to every aspect of our lives. We are subject to His Word and His will. But this is good news: because He is a good and loving God, "His commandments are not burdensome" (1 John 5:3). Take joy in submitting yourself to the instruction and wisdom of the one true God.

—Brady Cooper
New Vision Baptist Church, Murfreesboro, TN

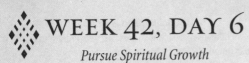

WEEK 42, DAY 6

Pursue Spiritual Growth

1 Timothy 3:14–4:16

The Great Mystery

These things I write to you, though I hope to come to you shortly; 15but if I am delayed, I write so that you may know how you ought to conduct yourself in the house of God, which is the church of the living God, the pillar and ground of the truth. 16And without controversy great is the mystery of godliness:

God was manifested in the flesh,
Justified in the Spirit,
Seen by angels,
Preached among the Gentiles,
Believed on in the world,
Received up in glory.

The Great Apostasy

4 Now the Spirit expressly says that in latter times some will depart from the faith, giving heed to deceiving spirits and doctrines of demons, 2speaking lies in hypocrisy, having their own conscience seared with a hot iron, 3forbidding to marry, and commanding to abstain from foods which God created to be received with thanksgiving by those who believe and know the truth. 4For every creature of God is good, and nothing is to be refused if it is received with thanksgiving; 5for it is sanctified by the word of God and prayer.

A Good Servant of Jesus Christ

6If you instruct the brethren in these things, you will be a good minister of Jesus Christ, nourished in the words of faith and of the good doctrine which you have carefully followed. 7But reject profane and old wives' fables, and exercise yourself toward godliness. 8For bodily exercise profits a little, but godliness is profitable for all things, having promise of the life that now is and of that which is to come. 9This is a faithful saying and worthy of all acceptance. 10For to this end we both labor and suffer reproach, because we trust in the living God, who is the Savior of all men, especially of those who believe. 11These things command and teach.

Take Heed to Your Ministry

12Let no one despise your youth, but be an example to the believers in word, in conduct, in love, in spirit, in faith, in purity. 13Till I come, give attention to reading, to exhortation, to doctrine. 14Do not neglect the gift that is in you, which was given to you by prophecy with the laying on of the hands of the eldership. 15Meditate on these things; give yourself entirely to them, that your progress may be evident to all. 16Take heed to yourself and to the doctrine. Continue in them, for in doing this you will save both yourself and those who hear you.

DEVOTIONAL

In his prime, Arnold Schwarzenegger was the greatest bodybuilder in the world, being named Mr. Universe three times and Mr. Olympia seven times. At his best, Schwarzenegger bench-pressed 440 pounds and squatted 470 pounds.

In contrast to Schwarzenegger, consider Billy Graham. Even on his best day, Graham has never come close to matching Schwarzenegger's physical prowess. However, while Schwarzenegger devoted himself to physical training as a young man, Graham devoted himself to godliness. Now in his nineties, Graham's body is weak and feeble, but his godliness far surpasses that of his youth. Schwarzenegger, on the other hand, can no longer bench-press the 440 pounds of his prime, and the older he gets, the weaker his body will become.

Paul commended to Timothy the value of exercising himself toward godliness because godliness draws us closer to God and prepares us to spend an eternity with Him. Godliness also benefits those who are around us. Paul charged Timothy to be an example "in word, in conduct, in love, in spirit, in faith, in purity" (1 Timothy 4:12). These traits are the fruit of a life devoted to godliness.

No doubt, Schwarzenegger has been an inspiration to many aspiring body builders, but in the end he will lose all that he worked so hard to achieve (Mark 8:36). On the other hand, Graham has made an eternal impact upon thousands through his ministry and his godly example, and he still looks forward to the day when his training will reap even more benefits in the life to come.

Are you following Paul's charge to Timothy? Nurture your relationship with God and pursue spiritual growth in Him. Make training in godliness your priority in life!

—Brady Cooper
New Vision Baptist Church, Murfreesboro, TN

WEEK 42, DAY 7

Every believer has been entrusted with a spiritual gift. Our spiritual gift often combines our heart, abilities, passions, and experiences. Do you have a sense of how you are gifted spiritually? How are you developing that gift? What are some ways you could deploy that gift for God's glory?

_____

_____

_____

_____

_____

_____

_____

_____

_____

A bodybuilder cannot reach his training goals without using the tools of weights, diet, and exercise. What tools has God provided to assist you in your spiritual training? Are you putting all the tools at your disposal to good use?

_____

_____

_____

_____

_____

_____

_____

WEEK 43, DAY I

Love the Family of God

1 Timothy 5:1–25

Treatment of Church Members

5 Do not rebuke an older man, but exhort him as a father, younger men as brothers, ²older women as mothers, younger women as sisters, with all purity.

Honor True Widows

³Honor widows who are really widows. ⁴But if any widow has children or grandchildren, let them first learn to show piety at home and to repay their parents; for this is good and acceptable before God. ⁵Now she who is really a widow, and left alone, trusts in God and continues in supplications and prayers night and day. ⁶But she who lives in pleasure is dead while she lives. ⁷And these things command, that they may be blameless. ⁸But if anyone does not provide for his own, and especially for those of his household, he has denied the faith and is worse than an unbeliever.

⁹Do not let a widow under sixty years old be taken into the number, and not unless she has been the wife of one man, ¹⁰well reported for good works: if she has brought up children, if she has lodged strangers, if she has washed the saints' feet, if she has relieved the afflicted, if she has diligently followed every good work.

¹¹But refuse the younger widows; for when they have begun to grow wanton against Christ, they desire to marry, ¹²having condemnation because they have cast off their first faith. ¹³And besides they learn to be idle, wandering about from house to house, and not only idle but also gossips and busybodies, saying things which they ought not. ¹⁴Therefore I desire that the younger widows marry, bear children, manage the house, give no opportunity to the adversary to speak reproachfully. ¹⁵For some have already turned aside after Satan. ¹⁶If any believing man or woman has widows, let them relieve them, and do not let the church be burdened, that it may relieve those who are really widows.

Honor the Elders

¹⁷Let the elders who rule well be counted worthy of double honor, especially those who labor in the word and doctrine. ¹⁸For the Scripture says, "You shall not muzzle an ox while it treads out the grain," and, "The laborer is worthy of his wages." ¹⁹Do not receive an accusation against an elder except from two or three witnesses. ²⁰Those who are sinning rebuke in the presence of all, that the rest also may fear.

²¹I charge you before God and the Lord Jesus Christ and the elect angels that you observe these things without prejudice, doing nothing with partiality. ²²Do not lay hands on anyone hastily, nor share in other people's sins; keep yourself pure.

²³No longer drink only water, but use a little wine for your stomach's sake and your frequent infirmities.

²⁴Some men's sins are clearly evident, preceding them to judgment, but those of some men follow later. ²⁵Likewise, the good works of some are clearly evident, and those that are otherwise cannot be hidden.

DEVOTIONAL

God's family—not a framed building—is called the church. We are an organism, not an organization. We are the bride of God's Son, Jesus Christ, and a representation of God to the world.

First John 4:8 tells us God is love, and as we show His character to the world in our relating, He wants us to treat all members of the body with love. As we read this list of dos and don'ts in 1 Timothy 5, we must keep in mind God's greatest commands to us are to love Him with all we are and to love others as ourselves. Paul gave believers practical ways to honor and serve each other in this chapter because it is so important we do it! Love, as Colossians 3:14 reminds us, is what binds the body of Christ together.

It has been said that real love heals people; everything else eventually hurts them. Do you know any hurting souls who are far from God? Give them a glimpse of God's love in all your interactions with them and pray they will come to faith in Christ and receive God's powerful, personal, agape love for them. Are you struggling in some kind of conflict with another believer? Ask God to fill your heart with His unconditional love and grace and to help you pour it out to that person. God is love, and He wants His family to be people of love.

Praise God He has given us His Love Letter, that He leads us in loving, and that He "keeps covenant and mercy for a thousand generations with those who love Him and keep His commandments" (Deuteronomy 7:9).

—Dr. Bobby Joiner
Road Chaplain for Newsong, Leesburg, GA

WEEK 43, DAY 2

A Godly Attitude

1 Timothy 6:1–21

Honor Masters

6Let as many bondservants as are under the yoke count their own masters worthy of all honor, so that the name of God and His doctrine may not be blasphemed. 2And those who have believing masters, let them not despise them because they are brethren, but rather serve them because those who are benefited are believers and beloved. Teach and exhort these things.

Error and Greed

3If anyone teaches otherwise and does not consent to wholesome words, even the words of our Lord Jesus Christ, and to the doctrine which accords with godliness, 4he is proud, knowing nothing, but is obsessed with disputes and arguments over words, from which come envy, strife, reviling, evil suspicions, 5useless wranglings of men of corrupt minds and destitute of the truth, who suppose that godliness is a means of gain. From such withdraw yourself.

6Now godliness with contentment is great gain. 7For we brought nothing into this world, and it is certain we can carry nothing out. 8And having food and clothing, with these we shall be content. 9But those who desire to be rich fall into temptation and a snare, and into many foolish and harmful lusts which drown men in destruction and perdition. 10For the love of money is a root of all kinds of evil, for which some have strayed from the faith in their greediness, and pierced themselves through with many sorrows.

The Good Confession

11But you, O man of God, flee these things and pursue righteousness, godliness, faith, love, patience, gentleness. 12Fight the good fight of faith, lay hold on eternal life, to which you were also called and have confessed the good confession in the presence of many witnesses. 13I urge you in the sight of God who gives life to all things, and before Christ Jesus who witnessed the good confession before Pontius Pilate, 14that you keep this commandment without spot, blameless until our Lord Jesus Christ's appearing, 15which He will manifest in His own time, He who is the blessed and only Potentate, the King of kings and Lord of lords, 16who alone has immortality, dwelling in unapproachable light, whom no man has seen or can see, to whom be honor and everlasting power. Amen.

Instructions to the Rich

17Command those who are rich in this present age not to be haughty, nor to trust in uncertain riches but in the living God, who gives us richly all things to enjoy. 18Let them do good, that they be rich in good works, ready to give, willing to share, 19storing up for themselves a good foundation for the time to come, that they may lay hold on eternal life.

Guard the Faith

20O Timothy! Guard what was committed to your trust, avoiding the profane and idle babblings and contradictions of what is falsely called knowledge— 21by professing it some have strayed concerning the faith.

Grace be with you. Amen.

DEVOTIONAL

In 1 Timothy 6, Paul described how believers can have godly attitudes in many areas of life, giving clear instructions of things to avoid and pursue. We are to avoid pride, excessive arguing, envy, and strife (vv. 3–5). We are to be free of the love of money and greed and be content with what God gives us (vv. 6–10). We can't take earthly riches to heaven, so the Father instructs us to send treasures ahead by investing our personal resources—time, talents, and gifts (including money)—to the cause of Christ.

Paul said, "Flee these things and pursue righteousness, godliness, faith, love, patience, gentleness. Fight the good fight of faith, lay hold on eternal life" (1 Timothy 6:11–12). We are to respect authority figures, consent to the words of Christ, and be content (vv. 1, 3, 6). We are to be motivated not by selfish gains, religious approval, or pressure from others, but by our love for God. As we aim to live a life that pleases Him, we are to study and apply God's Word and walk by the Spirit.

This humble state of godliness described in 1 Timothy 6 is the condition of soul that Jesus exhibited during His thirty-three years on earth. Imitate your Savior and Lord today. Recognize and confess your sin regularly to help you remain in this blessed state, and remember that everything you do in this godly condition and in His Holy Spirit will be blessed here and rewarded in heaven.

—Dr. Bobby Joiner
Road Chaplain for Newsong, Leesburg, GA

WEEK 43, DAY 3

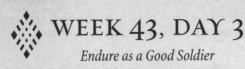

Endure as a Good Soldier

2 Timothy 1:1–2:10

Greeting

1 Paul, an apostle of Jesus Christ by the will of God, according to the promise of life which is in Christ Jesus,

2To Timothy, a beloved son:

Grace, mercy, and peace from God the Father and Christ Jesus our Lord.

Timothy's Faith and Heritage

3I thank God, whom I serve with a pure conscience, as my forefathers did, as without ceasing I remember you in my prayers night and day, 4greatly desiring to see you, being mindful of your tears, that I may be filled with joy, 5when I call to remembrance the genuine faith that is in you, which dwelt first in your grandmother Lois and your mother Eunice, and I am persuaded is in you also. 6Therefore I remind you to stir up the gift of God which is in you through the laying on of my hands. 7For God has not given us a spirit of fear, but of power and of love and of a sound mind.

Not Ashamed of the Gospel

8Therefore do not be ashamed of the testimony of our Lord, nor of me His prisoner, but share with me in the sufferings for the gospel according to the power of God, 9who has saved us and called us with a holy calling, not according to our works, but according to His own purpose and grace which was given to us in Christ Jesus before time began, 10but has now been revealed by the appearing of our Savior Jesus Christ, who has abolished death and brought life and immortality to light through the gospel, 11to which I was appointed a preacher, an apostle, and a teacher of the Gentiles. 12For this reason I also suffer these things; nevertheless I am not ashamed, for I know whom I have believed and am persuaded that He is able to keep what I have committed to Him until that Day.

Be Loyal to the Faith

13Hold fast the pattern of sound words which you have heard from me, in faith and love which are in Christ Jesus. 14That good thing which was committed to you, keep by the Holy Spirit who dwells in us.

15This you know, that all those in Asia have turned away from me, among whom are Phygellus and Hermogenes.

16The Lord grant mercy to the household of Onesiphorus, for he often refreshed me, and was not ashamed of my chain; 17but when he arrived in Rome, he sought me out very zealously and found me. 18The Lord grant to him that he may find mercy from the Lord in that Day—and you know very well how many ways he ministered to me at Ephesus.

Be Strong in Grace

2 You therefore, my son, be strong in the grace that is in Christ Jesus. 2And the things that you have heard from me among many witnesses, commit these to faithful men who will be able to teach others also. 3You therefore must endure hardship as a good soldier of Jesus Christ. 4No one engaged in warfare entangles himself with the affairs of this life, that he may please him who enlisted him as a soldier. 5And also if anyone competes in athletics, he is not crowned unless he competes according to the rules. 6The hardworking farmer must be first to partake of the crops. 7Consider what I say, and may the Lord give you understanding in all things.

8Remember that Jesus Christ, of the seed of David, was raised from the dead according to my gospel, 9for which I suffer trouble as an evildoer, even to the point of chains; but the word of God is not chained. 10Therefore I endure all things for the sake of the elect, that they also may obtain the salvation which is in Christ Jesus with eternal glory.

DEVOTIONAL

*T*imothy was facing opposition when Paul wrote to encourage him to stay the course. Paul told him to "be strong in the grace that is in Christ Jesus" and to "endure hardship as a good soldier of Jesus Christ" (2 Timothy 2:1, 3).

God doesn't want our short-term pains or gains on earth to distract us from His kingdom work and eternal rewards (2 Timothy 2:9–10). No matter how intense our earthly circumstances get, we must discipline ourselves not to get so caught up in them that we no longer focus on the will and kingdom of God. We need to view everything in life with spiritual Son-glasses and remain alert and productive soldiers for God. As we move toward spiritual victory in this invisible war, we must do so "according to the rules" (v. 5). Only the Spirit-led and Bible-obeying "heroes" will be highly decorated by God in eternity.

Whatever you're facing today, continue in obedience in His strength and for His sake.

—Dr. Bobby Joiner
Road Chaplain for Newsong, Leesburg, GA

WEEK 43, DAY 4

Live and Love According to God's Word

2 Timothy 2:11–3:11

This is a faithful saying:

For if we died with Him,
   We shall also live with Him.
12   If we endure,
   We shall also reign with Him.
   If we deny Him,
   He also will deny us.
13   If we are faithless,
   He remains faithful;
He cannot deny Himself.

Approved and Disapproved Workers

14Remind them of these things, charging them before the Lord not to strive about words to no profit, to the ruin of the hearers. 15Be diligent to present yourself approved to God, a worker who does not need to be ashamed, rightly dividing the word of truth. 16But shun profane and idle babblings, for they will increase to more ungodliness. 17And their message will spread like cancer. Hymenaeus and Philetus are of this sort, 18who have strayed concerning the truth, saying that the resurrection is already past; and they overthrow the faith of some. 19Nevertheless the solid foundation of God stands, having this seal: "The Lord knows those who are His," and, "Let everyone who names the name of Christ depart from iniquity."

20But in a great house there are not only vessels of gold and silver, but also of wood and clay, some for honor and some for dishonor. 21Therefore if anyone cleanses himself from the latter, he will be a vessel for honor, sanctified and useful for the Master, prepared for every good work. 22Flee also youthful lusts; but pursue righteousness, faith, love, peace with those who call on the Lord out of a pure heart. 23But avoid foolish and ignorant disputes, knowing that they generate strife. 24And a servant of the Lord must not quarrel but be gentle to all, able to teach, patient, 25in humility correcting those who are in opposition, if God perhaps will grant them repentance, so that they may know the truth, 26and that they may come to their senses and escape the snare of the devil, having been taken captive by him to do his will.

Perilous Times and Perilous Men

3But know this, that in the last days perilous times will come: 2For men will be lovers of themselves, lovers of money, boasters, proud, blasphemers, disobedient to parents, unthankful, unholy, 3unloving, unforgiving, slanderers, without self-control, brutal, despisers of good, 4traitors, headstrong, haughty, lovers of pleasure rather than lovers of God, 5having a form of godliness but denying its power. And from such people turn away! 6For of this sort are those who creep into households and make captives of gullible women loaded down with sins, led away by various lusts, 7always learning and never able to come to the knowledge of the truth. 8Now as Jannes and Jambres resisted Moses, so do these also resist the truth: men of corrupt minds, disapproved concerning the faith; 9but they will progress no further, for their folly will be manifest to all, as theirs also was.

The Man of God and the Word of God

10But you have carefully followed my doctrine, manner of life, purpose, faith, longsuffering, love, perseverance, 11persecutions, afflictions, which happened to me at Antioch, at Iconium, at Lystra—what persecutions I endured. And out of them all the Lord delivered me.

DEVOTIONAL

In 2 Timothy 2:15, Paul spoke of the importance of being diligent to study, understand, and honor the Word of God. In the very next chapter, we see one of the consequences of failing to do so—a disordering of our loves.

Rejecting God's Word and God's love results in the inability to love God and others properly. Those who do will love other things instead—themselves, money, pleasure—and seek to satisfy only their sensual desires (2 Timothy 3:2–5). Eventually, this lack of knowledge and practice of God's love will produce a vacuum effect in the soul that pulls in various pseudo-loves (human lusts). This vortex of evil will increase and spread like cancer to other aspects of life. If not stopped by proper spiritual application of God's Word, this evil will spread into communities, churches, and beyond.

Heed God's warning that a failure to learn His Word and to live and love according to it always results in ungodliness and selfish living. Diligently seek Him in His Word and ask Him to help you love what He loves. Spend your life loving God and others!

—Dr. Bobby Joiner
Road Chaplain for Newsong, Leesburg, GA

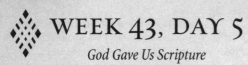

WEEK 43, DAY 5
God Gave Us Scripture

---

2 Timothy 3:12–4:22

Yes, and all who desire to live godly in Christ Jesus will suffer persecution. 13But evil men and impostors will grow worse and worse, deceiving and being deceived. 14But you must continue in the things which you have learned and been assured of, knowing from whom you have learned them, 15and that from childhood you have known the Holy Scriptures, which are able to make you wise for salvation through faith which is in Christ Jesus.

16All Scripture is given by inspiration of God, and is profitable for doctrine, for reproof, for correction, for instruction in righteousness, 17that the man of God may be complete, thoroughly equipped for every good work.

Preach the Word

4I charge you therefore before God and the Lord Jesus Christ, who will judge the living and the dead at His appearing and His kingdom: 2Preach the word! Be ready in season and out of season. Convince, rebuke, exhort, with all longsuffering and teaching. 3For the time will come when they will not endure sound doctrine, but according to their own desires, because they have itching ears, they will heap up for themselves teachers; 4and they will turn their ears away from the truth, and be turned aside to fables. 5But you be watchful in all things, endure afflictions, do the work of an evangelist, fulfill your ministry.

Paul's Valedictory

6For I am already being poured out as a drink offering, and the time of my departure is at hand. 7I have fought the good fight, I have finished the race, I have kept the faith. 8Finally, there is laid up for me the crown of righteousness, which the Lord, the righteous Judge, will give to me on that Day, and not to me only but also to all who have loved His appearing.

The Abandoned Apostle

9Be diligent to come to me quickly; 10for Demas has forsaken me, having loved this present world, and has departed for Thessalonica—Crescens for Galatia, Titus for Dalmatia. 11Only Luke is with me. Get Mark and bring him with you, for he is useful to me for ministry. 12And Tychicus I have sent to Ephesus. 13Bring the cloak that I left with Carpus at Troas when you come—and the books, especially the parchments.

14Alexander the coppersmith did me much harm. May the Lord repay him according to his works. 15You also must beware of him, for he has greatly resisted our words.

16At my first defense no one stood with me, but all forsook me. May it not be charged against them.

The Lord Is Faithful

17But the Lord stood with me and strengthened me, so that the message might be preached fully through me, and that all the Gentiles might hear. Also I was delivered out of the mouth of the lion. 18And the Lord will deliver me from every evil work and preserve me for His heavenly kingdom. To Him be glory forever and ever. Amen!

Come Before Winter

19Greet Prisca and Aquila, and the household of Onesiphorus. 20Erastus stayed in Corinth, but Trophimus I have left in Miletus sick.

21Do your utmost to come before winter.

Eubulus greets you, as well as Pudens, Linus, Claudia, and all the brethren.

Farewell

22The Lord Jesus Christ be with your spirit. Grace be with you. Amen.

DEVOTIONAL

All of Scripture is inspired by God, alive and powerful, and applicable to all believers today. It teaches us sound doctrine, leads us in righteousness, helps us mature spiritually, and equips us for good works (2 Timothy 3:16–17). God wants us to be intentional about getting to know Him more and becoming more like Him by studying His Word. He wants us to be able to explain its truths to others at any point in time, in any season (4:2; 1 Peter 3:15).

Try using the acrostic EDDY to help you draw closer to God. Come to God Early—make it the first thing you do. Read His Word Daily and Diligently. As you do, discipline yourself to say Yes—to obey His Word instead of your feelings and submit to His will instead of your own.

If you spend the rest of your days drawing close to God and obeying Him, you will be able to say with Paul, "I have fought the good fight, I have finished the race, I have kept the faith" (2 Timothy 4:7). Your daily choices reveal whether you want to "get your gold" here, or when you stand before God. Indeed, we all will stand before Him, and eternity is too long to be wrong!

—Dr. Bobby Joiner
Road Chaplain for Newsong, Leesburg, GA

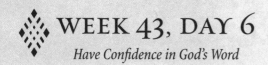

WEEK 43, DAY 6

Have Confidence in God's Word

Titus 1:1–2:8

Greeting

1 Paul, a bondservant of God and an apostle of Jesus Christ, according to the faith of God's elect and the acknowledgment of the truth which accords with godliness, ²in hope of eternal life which God, who cannot lie, promised before time began, ³but has in due time manifested His word through preaching, which was committed to me according to the commandment of God our Savior;

⁴To Titus, a true son in our common faith:

Grace, mercy, and peace from God the Father and the Lord Jesus Christ our Savior.

Qualified Elders

⁵For this reason I left you in Crete, that you should set in order the things that are lacking, and appoint elders in every city as I commanded you— ⁶if a man is blameless, the husband of one wife, having faithful children not accused of dissipation or insubordination. ⁷For a bishop must be blameless, as a steward of God, not self-willed, not quick-tempered, not given to wine, not violent, not greedy for money, ⁸but hospitable, a lover of what is good, sober-minded, just, holy, self-controlled, ⁹holding fast the faithful word as he has been taught, that he may be able, by sound doctrine, both to exhort and convict those who contradict.

The Elders' Task

¹⁰For there are many insubordinate, both idle talkers and deceivers, especially those of the circumcision, ¹¹whose mouths must be stopped, who subvert whole households, teaching things which they ought not, for the sake of dishonest gain. ¹²One of them, a prophet of their own, said, "Cretans are always liars, evil beasts, lazy gluttons." ¹³This testimony is true. Therefore rebuke them sharply, that they may be sound in the faith, ¹⁴not giving heed to Jewish fables and commandments of men who turn from the truth. ¹⁵To the pure all things are pure, but to those who are defiled and unbelieving nothing is pure; but even their mind and conscience are defiled. ¹⁶They profess to know God, but in works they deny Him, being abominable, disobedient, and disqualified for every good work.

Qualities of a Sound Church

2 But as for you, speak the things which are proper for sound doctrine: ²that the older men be sober, reverent, temperate, sound in faith, in love, in patience; ³the older women likewise, that they be reverent in behavior, not slanderers, not given to much wine, teachers of good things— ⁴that they admonish the young women to love their husbands, to love their children, ⁵to be discreet, chaste, homemakers, good, obedient to their own husbands, that the word of God may not be blasphemed.

⁶Likewise, exhort the young men to be sober-minded, ⁷in all things showing yourself to be a pattern of good works; in doctrine showing integrity, reverence, incorruptibility, ⁸sound speech that cannot be condemned, that one who is an opponent may be ashamed, having nothing evil to say of you.

DEVOTIONAL

G od's Word is the only source of truth for living and dying. Satan's simple goal is to cause us to doubt God's Word and love. He has deceived many into following leaders who claim to be God's messengers but are actually impostors who use His name to gain personal wealth and power. As we can see in today's reading, the early church had to deal with false teachers (Titus 1:10–15). Paul told Titus the deceivers "must be stopped" because they were subverting "whole households, teaching things which they ought not" (v. 11). Lies had prompted doubts and doubts turned into unbelief.

In Titus 1:2, Paul spoke of the "hope of eternal life." The Greek word for "hope" here can also be translated "confidence." God wants us to put all our confidence in Him, the Creator and Sustainer of the universe, the only wise God. He wants us to read His Love Letter daily, putting our hope in every true word and putting our faith in His power! Unless we take Him at His Word, we will lack the hope the Father desires His children to have.

Don't buy into the Enemy's lies. The Bible reveals the one true God, and He cannot lie (Titus 1:2). His love for you reaches to the heavens and was demonstrated on the cross. The only way to salvation and to a blessed life is to throw away your doubts and fully surrender and submit to Him! Resolve to live with strong, unwavering faith in God and His Word all of your days.

—Dr. Bobby Joiner
Road Chaplain for Newsong, Leesburg, GA

WEEK 43, DAY 7

In what ways do you need to rely more upon your faith in your Father's unchanging Word than in your fickle feelings?

_____

_____

_____

_____

_____

_____

_____

_____

_____

_____

_____

_____

If God called you into His physical presence today for a ten-minute review of your life, then sent you back to live another year here, what changes would you make in your daily priorities?

_____

_____

_____

_____

_____

_____

_____

_____

_____

_____

_____

_____

WEEK 44, DAY 1

God's "Big Reveal" Moments

Titus 2:9–3:15

Exhort bondservants to be obedient to their own masters, to be well pleasing in all things, not answering back, ¹⁰not pilfering, but showing all good fidelity, that they may adorn the doctrine of God our Savior in all things.

Trained by Saving Grace

¹¹For the grace of God that brings salvation has appeared to all men, ¹²teaching us that, denying ungodliness and worldly lusts, we should live soberly, righteously, and godly in the present age, ¹³looking for the blessed hope and glorious appearing of our great God and Savior Jesus Christ, ¹⁴who gave Himself for us, that He might redeem us from every lawless deed and purify for Himself His own special people, zealous for good works.

¹⁵Speak these things, exhort, and rebuke with all authority. Let no one despise you.

Graces of the Heirs of Grace

3 Remind them to be subject to rulers and authorities, to obey, to be ready for every good work, ²to speak evil of no one, to be peaceable, gentle, showing all humility to all men. ³For we ourselves were also once foolish, disobedient, deceived, serving various lusts and pleasures, living in malice and envy, hateful and hating one another. ⁴But when the kindness and the love of God our Savior toward man appeared, ⁵not by works of righteousness which we have done, but according to His mercy He saved us, through the washing of regeneration and renewing of the Holy Spirit, ⁶whom He poured out on us abundantly through Jesus Christ our Savior, ⁷that having been justified by His grace we should become heirs according to the hope of eternal life.

⁸This is a faithful saying, and these things I want you to affirm constantly, that those who have believed in God should be careful to maintain good works. These things are good and profitable to men.

Avoid Dissension

⁹But avoid foolish disputes, genealogies, contentions, and strivings about the law; for they are unprofitable and useless. ¹⁰Reject a divisive man after the first and second admonition, ¹¹knowing that such a person is warped and sinning, being self-condemned.

Final Messages

¹²When I send Artemas to you, or Tychicus, be diligent to come to me at Nicopolis, for I have decided to spend the winter there. ¹³Send Zenas the lawyer and Apollos on their journey with haste, that they may lack nothing. ¹⁴And let our people also learn to maintain good works, to meet urgent needs, that they may not be unfruitful.

Farewell

¹⁵All who are with me greet you. Greet those who love us in the faith.

Grace be with you all. Amen.

DEVOTIONAL

Have you have ever watched a home makeover TV show? The whole show builds toward a "big reveal" moment when a family in great need gets to see the finished product of their house made completely new. Watching that family discover all that has been accomplished for them is often an emotional experience. The celebration, the joy, the tears . . . what a moment!

Twice in Titus 2:9–3:15 Paul used the word appeared *(2:11; 3:4). This word comes from a Greek word that means "to show forth, exhibit, or shine the light upon" something or someone. The Bible teaches there was a specific "big reveal" moment in history when God pulled back the curtain and shined the light on His grace, kindness, and love for the world. The world experienced this moment when God took on human flesh in the Person of Jesus Christ, entered humanity, and accomplished the amazing plan of redemption for us all. And it was more than a moment. The tense of the verb* appeared *indicates the impact is still being felt today. Can you imagine the rejoicing in heaven that must have taken place as the angels finally began to understand the mystery of God's plan? The celebration, the joy, the tears . . . what a moment!*

And don't forget that Titus 2:13 reminds us there is one more "big reveal" moment coming. The One who came is coming again. We will see with our own eyes the finished work of His hands! The celebration, the joy, the tears . . . what a moment!

—Vance Pitman
Hope Baptist Church, Las Vegas, NV

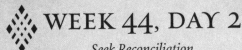

WEEK 44, DAY 2

Seek Reconciliation

Philemon 1–25

Greeting

1 Paul, a prisoner of Christ Jesus, and Timothy our brother,

To Philemon our beloved friend and fellow laborer, 2to the beloved Apphia, Archippus our fellow soldier, and to the church in your house:

3Grace to you and peace from God our Father and the Lord Jesus Christ.

Philemon's Love and Faith

4I thank my God, making mention of you always in my prayers, 5hearing of your love and faith which you have toward the Lord Jesus and toward all the saints, 6that the sharing of your faith may become effective by the acknowledgment of every good thing which is in you in Christ Jesus. 7For we have great joy and consolation in your love, because the hearts of the saints have been refreshed by you, brother.

The Plea for Onesimus

8Therefore, though I might be very bold in Christ to command you what is fitting, 9yet for love's sake I rather appeal to you—being such a one as Paul, the aged, and now also a prisoner of Jesus Christ— 10I appeal to you for my son Onesimus, whom I have begotten while in my chains, 11who once was unprofitable to you, but now is profitable to you and to me.

12I am sending him back. You therefore receive him, that is, my own heart, 13whom I wished to keep with me, that on your behalf he might minister to me in my chains for the gospel. 14But without your consent I wanted to do nothing, that your good deed might not be by compulsion, as it were, but voluntary.

15For perhaps he departed for a while for this purpose, that you might receive him forever, 16no longer as a slave but more than a slave—a beloved brother, especially to me but how much more to you, both in the flesh and in the Lord.

Philemon's Obedience Encouraged

17If then you count me as a partner, receive him as you would me. 18But if he has wronged you or owes anything, put that on my account. 19I, Paul, am writing with my own hand. I will repay—not to mention to you that you owe me even your own self besides. 20Yes, brother, let me have joy from you in the Lord; refresh my heart in the Lord.

21Having confidence in your obedience, I write to you, knowing that you will do even more than I say. 22But, meanwhile, also prepare a guest room for me, for I trust that through your prayers I shall be granted to you.

Farewell

23Epaphras, my fellow prisoner in Christ Jesus, greets you, 24as do Mark, Aristarchus, Demas, Luke, my fellow laborers.

25The grace of our Lord Jesus Christ be with your spirit. Amen.

DEVOTIONAL

*H*ave you ever heard it said that following Jesus is all about relationships? It's true. First and foremost, following Jesus is about having an intimate love relationship with God. It's not about dos and don'ts, rights and wrongs, rules and regulations; it's about the experience of knowing and loving God in a personal relationship. But following Jesus is not just about a relationship with God; it is also about relationships with others.

Because you have a relationship with God, you have a relationship with God's family, and it is impossible to be right with God and not be right with God's family. Nowhere in Scripture is this more obvious than the book of Philemon. The whole book is dedicated to reconciling one relationship. There's a lesson to be learned here: if the Spirit of God inspired an entire book of the Bible to show the importance of reconciling relationships between brothers and sisters in Christ, then we should make it a priority to examine our relationships and do everything in our power to live in right fellowship with others.

Is there any relationship in your life that needs to be reconciled? Whom do you need to go to today to seek or give forgiveness, pay back a debt, honor a commitment made, or remove an obstacle in your fellowship? Maybe God wants to use you, as He did Paul, as His instrument to bring reconciliation between others who are at odds.

The book of Philemon is a living example of Paul's instruction in Romans 12:18: "If it is possible, as much as depends on you, live peaceably with all men." Are you living this way?

—Vance Pitman
Hope Baptist Church, Las Vegas, NV

WEEK 44, DAY 3

God's Great Salvation

Hebrews 1:1–2:4

God's Supreme Revelation

1 God, who at various times and in various ways spoke in time past to the fathers by the prophets, ²has in these last days spoken to us by His Son, whom He has appointed heir of all things, through whom also He made the worlds; ³who being the brightness of His glory and the express image of His person, and upholding all things by the word of His power, when He had by Himself purged our sins, sat down at the right hand of the Majesty on high, ⁴having become so much better than the angels, as He has by inheritance obtained a more excellent name than they.

The Son Exalted Above Angels

⁵For to which of the angels did He ever say:

"You are My Son,
Today I have begotten You"?

And again:

"I will be to Him a Father,
And He shall be to Me a Son"?

⁶But when He again brings the firstborn into the world, He says:

"Let all the angels of God worship Him."

⁷And of the angels He says:

"Who makes His angels spirits
And His ministers a flame of fire."

⁸But to the Son He says:

"Your throne, O God, is forever and ever;
A scepter of righteousness is the scepter of
Your kingdom.
⁹ You have loved righteousness and hated
lawlessness;
Therefore God, Your God, has anointed You
With the oil of gladness more than Your
companions."

¹⁰And:

"You, LORD, in the beginning laid the foundation
of the earth,
And the heavens are the work of Your hands.

¹¹ They will perish, but You remain;
And they will all grow old like a garment;
¹² Like a cloak You will fold them up,
And they will be changed.
But You are the same,
And Your years will not fail."

¹³But to which of the angels has He ever said:

"Sit at My right hand,
Till I make Your enemies Your footstool"?

¹⁴Are they not all ministering spirits sent forth to minister for those who will inherit salvation?

Do Not Neglect Salvation

2 Therefore we must give the more earnest heed to the things we have heard, lest we drift away. ²For if the word spoken through angels proved steadfast, and every transgression and disobedience received a just reward, ³how shall we escape if we neglect so great a salvation, which at the first began to be spoken by the Lord, and was confirmed to us by those who heard Him, ⁴God also bearing witness both with signs and wonders, with various miracles, and gifts of the Holy Spirit, according to His own will?

DEVOTIONAL

T omorrow begins the countdown to Thanksgiving. There's so much to look forward to! The worship, the family and friends, the sports—and oh yes, the food! Of course we don't look forward to all the plans, preparations, and work that's involved in serving a meal for a crowd . . . but it's all worth it when everyone is together at the table, enjoying the feast!

Hebrews 1 reveals that in eternity past, God established a plan to deal with the problem of the sins of humanity. At the right point in time, He took on human flesh and carried out that plan. Then He "sat down at the right hand of the Majesty on high" (Hebrews 1:3). Jesus finished all the work necessary for us to know God and to be accepted by Him.

If you don't know Him today, He is inviting you into a relationship with Himself. You don't have to earn it or deserve it; He has made all the preparations and done all the work. If you do know Him, your acceptance today is not based on your performance for Christ, but your position in Christ. Welcome to the table, and enjoy the feast!

—Vance Pitman
Hope Baptist Church, Las Vegas, NV

WEEK 44, DAY 4

Jesus Makes His People Holy

Hebrews 2:5–3:6

The Son Made Lower than Angels

For He has not put the world to come, of which we speak, in subjection to angels. 6But one testified in a certain place, saying:

> "What is man that You are mindful of him,
> Or the son of man that You take care of him?
> 7   You have made him a little lower than the angels;
> You have crowned him with glory and honor,
> And set him over the works of Your hands.
> 8   You have put all things in subjection under
> his feet."

For in that He put all in subjection under him, He left nothing that is not put under him. But now we do not yet see all things put under him. 9But we see Jesus, who was made a little lower than the angels, for the suffering of death crowned with glory and honor, that He, by the grace of God, might taste death for everyone.

Bringing Many Sons to Glory

10For it was fitting for Him, for whom are all things and by whom are all things, in bringing many sons to glory, to make the captain of their salvation perfect through sufferings. 11For both He who sanctifies and those who are being sanctified are all of one, for which reason He is not ashamed to call them brethren, 12saying:

> "I will declare Your name to My brethren;
> In the midst of the assembly I will sing praise
> to You."

13And again:

> "I will put My trust in Him."

And again:

> "Here am I and the children whom God has
> given Me."

14Inasmuch then as the children have partaken of flesh and blood, He Himself likewise shared in the same, that through death He might destroy him who had the power of death, that is, the devil, 15and release those who through fear of death were all their lifetime subject to bondage. 16For indeed He does not give aid to angels, but He does give aid to the seed of Abraham. 17Therefore, in all things He had to be made like His brethren, that He might be a merciful and faithful High Priest in things pertaining to God, to make propitiation for the sins of the people. 18For in that He Himself has suffered, being tempted, He is able to aid those who are tempted.

The Son Was Faithful

3Therefore, holy brethren, partakers of the heavenly calling, consider the Apostle and High Priest of our confession, Christ Jesus, 2who was faithful to Him who appointed Him, as Moses also was faithful in all His house. 3For this One has been counted worthy of more glory than Moses, inasmuch as He who built the house has more honor than the house. 4For every house is built by someone, but He who built all things is God. 5And Moses indeed was faithful in all His house as a servant, for a testimony of those things which would be spoken afterward, 6but Christ as a Son over His own house, whose house we are if we hold fast the confidence and the rejoicing of the hope firm to the end.

DEVOTIONAL

In Hebrews 3:1, the Spirit of God inspired the writer to call believers "holy brethren." If we're honest, most of us would not look at our lives and choose "holy" as a fitting adjective. But the reality is, that's exactly the way God sees those who are in Christ Jesus.

It's not that He sees us as just "trying to be holy" or "kind of holy"; we are as holy as Jesus in His sight. It's not because we've demonstrated that kind of holiness in our lives in a practical way, but because positionally we are in Christ! That means all that He is has been imputed to us, and before God, we are as holy as we'll ever be. After ten thousand years in heaven, God will not see us positionally any more holy than we are right now. There is nothing holier than Jesus, and that's how God sees us! What amazing grace!

That same grace is enabling you to become holier in a practical sense too. Out of the overflow of intimacy with God, He changes you from the inside out. He begins to change your attitudes, actions, desires, relationships—literally every area of your life. And what comes out of your life is not a better you; it is literally Christ in you, and that is holiness! Clyde Cranford said it this way: "Holy is what we are, who we are, and what we become progressively as we pursue holiness on a daily basis."14 Move forward in your pursuit of holiness today.

—Vance Pitman
Hope Baptist Church, Las Vegas, NV

WEEK 44, DAY 5

God Desires Loving Obedience

Hebrews 3:7–4:13

Be Faithful

Therefore, as the Holy Spirit says:

"Today, if you will hear His voice,
8 Do not harden your hearts as in the rebellion,
   In the day of trial in the wilderness,
9 Where your fathers tested Me, tried Me,
   And saw My works forty years.
10 Therefore I was angry with that generation,
   And said, 'They always go astray in their heart,
   And they have not known My ways.'
11 So I swore in My wrath,
   'They shall not enter My rest.'"

12Beware, brethren, lest there be in any of you an evil heart of unbelief in departing from the living God; 13but exhort one another daily, while it is called "Today," lest any of you be hardened through the deceitfulness of sin. 14For we have become partakers of Christ if we hold the beginning of our confidence steadfast to the end, 15while it is said:

"Today, if you will hear His voice,
   Do not harden your hearts as in the rebellion."

Failure of the Wilderness Wanderers

16For who, having heard, rebelled? Indeed, was it not all who came out of Egypt, led by Moses? 17Now with whom was He angry forty years? Was it not with those who sinned, whose corpses fell in the wilderness? 18And to whom did He swear that they would not enter His rest, but to those who did not obey? 19So we see that they could not enter in because of unbelief.

The Promise of Rest

4Therefore, since a promise remains of entering His rest, let us fear lest any of you seem to have come short of it. 2For indeed the gospel was preached to us as well as to them; but the word which they heard did not profit them, not being mixed with faith in those who heard it. 3For we who have believed do enter that rest, as He has said:

"So I swore in My wrath,
   'They shall not enter My rest,'"

although the works were finished from the foundation of the world. 4For He has spoken in a certain place of the seventh day in this way: "And God rested on the seventh day from all His works"; 5and again in this place: "They shall not enter My rest."

6Since therefore it remains that some must enter it, and those to whom it was first preached did not enter because of disobedience, 7again He designates a certain day, saying in David, "Today," after such a long time, as it has been said:

"Today, if you will hear His voice,
   Do not harden your hearts."

8For if Joshua had given them rest, then He would not afterward have spoken of another day. 9There remains therefore a rest for the people of God. 10For he who has entered His rest has himself also ceased from his works as God did from His.

The Word Discovers Our Condition

11Let us therefore be diligent to enter that rest, lest anyone fall according to the same example of disobedience. 12For the word of God is living and powerful, and sharper than any two-edged sword, piercing even to the division of soul and spirit, and of joints and marrow, and is a discerner of the thoughts and intents of the heart. 13And there is no creature hidden from His sight, but all things are naked and open to the eyes of Him to whom we must give account.

DEVOTIONAL

God's greatest desire for you is not obedience, but intimacy, because obedience is the natural overflow of a heart that is in love with Jesus. Whenever we get this out of balance, we fall prey to the bondage of our flesh and miss the freedom of a relationship with God. As we seek Him daily and know Him intimately, He produces the very life of Jesus in us, which is perfectly obedient to the will of the Father.

Clearly, we are to obey God's voice, but He wants our obedience to flow out of a heart full of love and gratitude for Him. He desires obedience that is the expression of our passion for Him and the manifestation of His very life in us. Then and only then does that obedience result in the divine rest and freedom He so graciously promises.

Evaluate the source of your obedience—may it always flow from a heart that is walking intimately with the Father.

—Vance Pitman
Hope Baptist Church, Las Vegas, NV

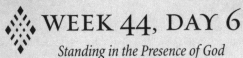

WEEK 44, DAY 6

Standing in the Presence of God

Hebrews 4:14–6:8

Our Compassionate High Priest

Seeing then that we have a great High Priest who has passed through the heavens, Jesus the Son of God, let us hold fast our confession. ¹⁵For we do not have a High Priest who cannot sympathize with our weaknesses, but was in all points tempted as we are, yet without sin. ¹⁶Let us therefore come boldly to the throne of grace, that we may obtain mercy and find grace to help in time of need.

Qualifications for High Priesthood

5 For every high priest taken from among men is appointed for men in things pertaining to God, that he may offer both gifts and sacrifices for sins. ²He can have compassion on those who are ignorant and going astray, since he himself is also subject to weakness. ³Because of this he is required as for the people, so also for himself, to offer sacrifices for sins. ⁴And no man takes this honor to himself, but he who is called by God, just as Aaron was.

A Priest Forever

⁵So also Christ did not glorify Himself to become High Priest, but it was He who said to Him:

"You are My Son,
    Today I have begotten You."

⁶As He also says in another place:

"You are a priest forever
    According to the order of Melchizedek";

⁷who, in the days of His flesh, when He had offered up prayers and supplications, with vehement cries and tears to Him who was able to save Him from death, and was heard because of His godly fear, ⁸though He was a Son, yet He learned obedience by the things which He suffered. ⁹And having been perfected, He became the author of eternal salvation to all who obey Him, ¹⁰called by God as High Priest "according to the order of Melchizedek," ¹¹of whom we have much to say, and hard to explain, since you have become dull of hearing.

Spiritual Immaturity

¹²For though by this time you ought to be teachers, you need someone to teach you again the first principles of the oracles of God; and you have come to need milk and not solid food. ¹³For everyone who partakes only of milk is unskilled in the word of righteousness, for he is a babe. ¹⁴But solid food belongs to those who are of full age, that is, those who by reason of use have their senses exercised to discern both good and evil.

The Peril of Not Progressing

6 Therefore, leaving the discussion of the elementary principles of Christ, let us go on to perfection, not laying again the foundation of repentance from dead works and of faith toward God, ²of the doctrine of baptisms, of laying on of hands, of resurrection of the dead, and of eternal judgment. ³And this we will do if God permits.

⁴For it is impossible for those who were once enlightened, and have tasted the heavenly gift, and have become partakers of the Holy Spirit, ⁵and have tasted the good word of God and the powers of the age to come, ⁶if they fall away, to renew them again to repentance, since they crucify again for themselves the Son of God, and put Him to an open shame.

⁷For the earth which drinks in the rain that often comes upon it, and bears herbs useful for those by whom it is cultivated, receives blessing from God; ⁸but if it bears thorns and briers, it is rejected and near to being cursed, whose end is to be burned.

DEVOTIONAL

*I*magine traveling to a foreign country and visiting with high-ranking government officials. You'd probably receive instructions on diplomacy and protocol, no doubt leaving you anxious about making a mistake that would create an international incident! While that kind of encounter would be an honor and privilege, it would not even compare with standing in the very presence of God, the Creator and Sustainer of all things.

It seems almost unthinkable that we could stand before God, yet Hebrews 4:16 says we can not only approach God, but do so with boldness. The Greek word translated "boldly" means "to speak freely all that one thinks or pleases." We can go right into God's presence today and share any hurt, burden, care, problem, situation, or circumstance, and find Him ready to help us. How is this possible? Because we have Someone who made it possible for us, and His name is Jesus.

Give Him thanks, and spend time in the presence of God with confidence today.

—Vance Pitman
Hope Baptist Church, Las Vegas, NV

WEEK 44, DAY 7

Are there any relationships in your life you need to attempt to reconcile today?

_____

_____

_____

_____

_____

_____

_____

_____

_____

_____

Are you genuinely seeking to live out of the overflow of a love relationship with God? Are you more focused on doing for God, or being with God?

_____

_____

_____

_____

_____

_____

_____

_____

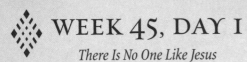

WEEK 45, DAY I

There Is No One Like Jesus

Hebrews 6:9–7:10

A Better Estimate

But, beloved, we are confident of better things concerning you, yes, things that accompany salvation, though we speak in this manner. ¹⁰For God is not unjust to forget your work and labor of love which you have shown toward His name, in that you have ministered to the saints, and do minister. ¹¹And we desire that each one of you show the same diligence to the full assurance of hope until the end, ¹²that you do not become sluggish, but imitate those who through faith and patience inherit the promises.

God's Infallible Purpose in Christ

¹³For when God made a promise to Abraham, because He could swear by no one greater, He swore by Himself, ¹⁴saying, "Surely blessing I will bless you, and multiplying I will multiply you." ¹⁵And so, after he had patiently endured, he obtained the promise. ¹⁶For men indeed swear by the greater, and an oath for confirmation is for them an end of all dispute. ¹⁷Thus God, determining to show more abundantly to the heirs of promise the immutability of His counsel, confirmed it by an oath, ¹⁸that by two immutable things, in which it is impossible for God to lie, we might have strong consolation, who have fled for refuge to lay hold of the hope set before us.

¹⁹This hope we have as an anchor of the soul, both sure and steadfast, and which enters the Presence behind the veil, ²⁰where the forerunner has entered for us, even Jesus, having become High Priest forever according to the order of Melchizedek.

The King of Righteousness

7For this Melchizedek, king of Salem, priest of the Most High God, who met Abraham returning from the slaughter of the kings and blessed him, ²to whom also Abraham gave a tenth part of all, first being translated "king of righteousness," and then also king of Salem, meaning "king of peace," ³without father, without mother, without genealogy, having neither beginning of days nor end of life, but made like the Son of God, remains a priest continually.

⁴Now consider how great this man was, to whom even the patriarch Abraham gave a tenth of the spoils. ⁵And indeed those who are of the sons of Levi, who receive the priesthood, have a commandment to receive tithes from the people according to the law, that is, from their brethren, though they have come from the loins of Abraham; ⁶but he whose genealogy is not derived from them received tithes from Abraham and blessed him who had the promises. ⁷Now beyond all contradiction the lesser is blessed by the better. ⁸Here mortal men receive tithes, but there he receives them, of whom it is witnessed that he lives. ⁹Even Levi, who receives tithes, paid tithes through Abraham, so to speak, ¹⁰for he was still in the loins of his father when Melchizedek met him.

DEVOTIONAL

There is no one like Jesus. He existed before anyone or anything else was. He is both the Sun of Righteousness and the Prince of Peace. He never lies. He holds all truth and, at the same time, is truth. He is the resurrection and the life. He is the Light of the World and the Good Shepherd. He is the Lamb of God and the One "seated at the right hand of the throne of the Majesty in the heavens" (Hebrews 8:1). Isn't He amazing? He is absolutely incomparable.

Hebrews 6:19 says He is the anchor of our souls. Just as a boat needs an anchor, we have an anchor in Jesus and the gospel He came to preach. His good news shapes our lives from the moment of conversion to the moment of His Second Coming.

How should we respond to One so incomparable in His power and goodness? We should place all we have and all we are before Him, just as Abraham did. We should honor Jesus by giving Him at least one-tenth of all He has entrusted to us in life—whatever we receive through work or as a gift. We can't forget that all we have, every good thing, comes from Jesus. Apart from Him, we are nothing and have nothing.

No matter what your life is like today, hold on to the anchor of your soul. He is there for you, even in the darkest moments of life. Run to Him. Run away from everything else. Honor Him with gifts because He is worthy—greater than everything and everyone else! Give Him your best and give Him your all. The greatest gift you can give Jesus is your life. Once He receives this from you, He receives everything.

There has never been, nor will there ever be, anyone like Jesus Christ. Hold nothing back.

—Dr. Ronnie Floyd
Cross Church, Springdale, AR

WEEK 45, DAY 2

Christ, Our Intercessor

Hebrews 7:11–8:6

Need for a New Priesthood

Therefore, if perfection were through the Levitical priesthood (for under it the people received the law), what further need was there that another priest should rise according to the order of Melchizedek, and not be called according to the order of Aaron? 12For the priesthood being changed, of necessity there is also a change of the law. 13For He of whom these things are spoken belongs to another tribe, from which no man has officiated at the altar.

14For it is evident that our Lord arose from Judah, of which tribe Moses spoke nothing concerning priesthood. 15And it is yet far more evident if, in the likeness of Melchizedek, there arises another priest 16who has come, not according to the law of a fleshly commandment, but according to the power of an endless life. 17For He testifies:

"You are a priest forever
According to the order of Melchizedek."

18For on the one hand there is an annulling of the former commandment because of its weakness and unprofitableness, 19for the law made nothing perfect; on the other hand, there is the bringing in of a better hope, through which we draw near to God.

Greatness of the New Priest

20And inasmuch as He was not made priest without an oath 21(for they have become priests without an oath, but He with an oath by Him who said to Him:

"The LORD has sworn
And will not relent,
'You are a priest forever
According to the order of Melchizedek'"),

22by so much more Jesus has become a surety of a better covenant.

23Also there were many priests, because they were prevented by death from continuing. 24But He, because He continues forever, has an unchangeable priesthood. 25Therefore He is also able to save to the uttermost those who come to God through Him, since He always lives to make intercession for them.

26For such a High Priest was fitting for us, who is holy, harmless, undefiled, separate from sinners, and has become higher than the heavens; 27who does not need daily, as those high priests, to offer up sacrifices, first for His own sins and then for the people's, for this He did once for all when He offered up Himself. 28For the law appoints as high priests men who have weakness, but the word of the oath, which came after the law, appoints the Son who has been perfected forever.

The New Priestly Service

8 Now this is the main point of the things we are saying: We have such a High Priest, who is seated at the right hand of the throne of the Majesty in the heavens, 2a Minister of the sanctuary and of the true tabernacle which the Lord erected, and not man.

3For every high priest is appointed to offer both gifts and sacrifices. Therefore it is necessary that this One also have something to offer. 4For if He were on earth, He would not be a priest, since there are priests who offer the gifts according to the law; 5who serve the copy and shadow of the heavenly things, as Moses was divinely instructed when he was about to make the tabernacle. For He said, "See that you make all things according to the pattern shown you on the mountain." 6But now He has obtained a more excellent ministry, inasmuch as He is also Mediator of a better covenant, which was established on better promises.

DEVOTIONAL

Jesus wants us to draw near to Him. His life, death, and resurrection give us a better hope (Hebrews 7:19). It's a hope that is not only better than what the world could ever give us, but it's also better than what the old covenant could give us. Jesus is the personal guarantee for us to have this better hope.

One of the great reasons we need to draw near to Jesus is that He lives to make intercession for us (Hebrews 7:25). Our Lord stands in the gap, appealing to the Father on our behalf. This Great High Priest is always praying for us.

Throughout today, and later tonight when you lay your head on your pillow, know with all confidence that Someone is praying for you. He always has your best interests at heart. His name is Jesus. Draw near to Him and thank Him for giving you a better hope and for interceding for you.

—Dr. Ronnie Floyd
Cross Church, Springdale, AR

WEEK 45, DAY 3

In the Presence of God

Hebrews 8:7–9:12

A New Covenant

For if that first covenant had been faultless, then no place would have been sought for a second. 8Because finding fault with them, He says: "Behold, the days are coming, says the LORD, when I will make a new covenant with the house of Israel and with the house of Judah— 9not according to the covenant that I made with their fathers in the day when I took them by the hand to lead them out of the land of Egypt; because they did not continue in My covenant, and I disregarded them, says the LORD. 10For this is the covenant that I will make with the house of Israel after those days, says the LORD: I will put My laws in their mind and write them on their hearts; and I will be their God, and they shall be My people. 11None of them shall teach his neighbor, and none his brother, saying, 'Know the LORD,' for all shall know Me, from the least of them to the greatest of them. 12For I will be merciful to their unrighteousness, and their sins and their lawless deeds I will remember no more."

13In that He says, "A new covenant," He has made the first obsolete. Now what is becoming obsolete and growing old is ready to vanish away.

The Earthly Sanctuary

9Then indeed, even the first covenant had ordinances of divine service and the earthly sanctuary. 2For a tabernacle was prepared: the first part, in which was the lampstand, the table, and the showbread, which is called the sanctuary; 3and behind the second veil, the part of the tabernacle which is called the Holiest of All, 4which had the golden censer and the ark of the covenant overlaid on all sides with gold, in which were the golden pot that had the manna, Aaron's rod that budded, and the tablets of the covenant; 5and above it were the cherubim of glory overshadowing the mercy seat. Of these things we cannot now speak in detail.

Limitations of the Earthly Service

6Now when these things had been thus prepared, the priests always went into the first part of the tabernacle, performing the services. 7But into the second part the high priest went alone once a year, not without blood, which he offered for himself and for the people's sins committed in ignorance; 8the Holy Spirit indicating this, that the way into the Holiest of All was not yet made manifest while the first tabernacle was still standing. 9It was symbolic for the present time in which both gifts and sacrifices are offered which cannot make him who performed the service perfect in regard to the conscience— 10concerned only with foods and drinks, various washings, and fleshly ordinances imposed until the time of reformation.

The Heavenly Sanctuary

11But Christ came as High Priest of the good things to come, with the greater and more perfect tabernacle not made with hands, that is, not of this creation. 12Not with the blood of goats and calves, but with His own blood He entered the Most Holy Place once for all, having obtained eternal redemption.

DEVOTIONAL

The book of Hebrews frequently compares Jesus' sacrifice on the cross to the Jewish sacrificial system. The old covenant's system had good intentions, but it was insufficient. That system is now obsolete (Hebrews 8:13). Why? Because Jesus provides something better—something perfect.

The old system required blood—repeated animal sacrifices—for the forgiveness of sins. The people also needed a high priest to go into the Most Holy Place, into the presence of God, to represent them before God. Jesus met the blood requirement for sin, not by offering the blood of goats and calves, but by offering His own blood for the sins of the world (Hebrews 9:12). As a result of this personal sacrifice, those who put their faith in Him no longer need a human priest to represent them before God. Jesus is the Great High Priest who never knew sin personally and came to this world in order to offer this perfect blood sacrifice for our sins.

We can now go to God anywhere, at anytime, about anything—because of the work of Christ and because of our faith in Him. We no longer need a system to take us into the presence of God. We now have a Savior who is the presence of God! Don't take this precious gift for granted. The enormous barrier of sin has been removed, and you may draw near to the living God! Speak to Jesus and listen to Him. Thank Him for His grace. Repent. Bring your burdens to Him. Delight in His presence and worship Him!

—Dr. Ronnie Floyd
Cross Church, Springdale, AR

WEEK 45, DAY 4

Jesus Reconciles Us to God

Hebrews 9:13–10:10

For if the blood of bulls and goats and the ashes of a heifer, sprinkling the unclean, sanctifies for the purifying of the flesh, 14how much more shall the blood of Christ, who through the eternal Spirit offered Himself without spot to God, cleanse your conscience from dead works to serve the living God? 15And for this reason He is the Mediator of the new covenant, by means of death, for the redemption of the transgressions under the first covenant, that those who are called may receive the promise of the eternal inheritance.

The Mediator's Death Necessary

16For where there is a testament, there must also of necessity be the death of the testator. 17For a testament is in force after men are dead, since it has no power at all while the testator lives. 18Therefore not even the first covenant was dedicated without blood. 19For when Moses had spoken every precept to all the people according to the law, he took the blood of calves and goats, with water, scarlet wool, and hyssop, and sprinkled both the book itself and all the people, 20saying, "This is the blood of the covenant which God has commanded you." 21Then likewise he sprinkled with blood both the tabernacle and all the vessels of the ministry. 22And according to the law almost all things are purified with blood, and without shedding of blood there is no remission.

Greatness of Christ's Sacrifice

23Therefore it was necessary that the copies of the things in the heavens should be purified with these, but the heavenly things themselves with better sacrifices than these. 24For Christ has not entered the holy places made with hands, which are copies of the true, but into heaven itself, now to appear in the presence of God for us; 25not that He should offer Himself often, as the high priest enters the Most Holy Place every year with blood of another— 26He then would have had to suffer often since the foundation of the world; but now, once at the end of the ages, He has appeared to put away sin by the sacrifice of Himself. 27And as it is appointed for men to die once, but after this the judgment, 28so Christ was offered once to bear the sins of many. To those who eagerly wait for Him He will appear a second time, apart from sin, for salvation.

Animal Sacrifices Insufficient

10 For the law, having a shadow of the good things to come, and not the very image of the things, can never with these same sacrifices, which they offer continually year by year, make those who approach perfect. 2For then would they not have ceased to be offered? For the worshipers, once purified, would have had no more consciousness of sins. 3But in those sacrifices there is a reminder of sins every year. 4For it is not possible that the blood of bulls and goats could take away sins.

Christ's Death Fulfills God's Will

5Therefore, when He came into the world, He said:

"Sacrifice and offering You did not desire,
    But a body You have prepared for Me.
6   In burnt offerings and sacrifices for sin
    You had no pleasure.
7   Then I said, 'Behold, I have come—
    In the volume of the book it is written of Me—
    To do Your will, O God.'"

8Previously saying, "Sacrifice and offering, burnt offerings, and offerings for sin You did not desire, nor had pleasure in them" (which are offered according to the law), 9then He said, "Behold, I have come to do Your will, O God." He takes away the first that He may establish the second. 10By that will we have been sanctified through the offering of the body of Jesus Christ once for all.

DEVOTIONAL

On the cross, Jesus did what no human could ever do— He resolved the problem of sin and reconciled fallen people with a holy God. He did what was necessary to provide forgiveness of sins when He shed His own blood. He put away sin by the sacrifice of Himself. He bore the sins of the world!

He not only made forgiveness possible, but He also provided the only way humans can get to God. Jesus is not one of many paths to God; He is the only path to God.

Jesus died for everyone, and His offering of redemption is for everyone, including you. If you're relying on religion for salvation, remember that your religion is just like the system Jesus replaced. It is dull, insufficient, and obsolete. Jesus died for you to provide you with a relationship with God, not another religious system. Praise Him because His blood makes this possible for you, and put your faith in Him alone!

—Dr. Ronnie Floyd
Cross Church, Springdale, AR

WEEK 45, DAY 5

Demonstrate Your Faith in Christ

Hebrews 10:11–39

Christ's Death Perfects the Sanctified

And every priest stands ministering daily and offering repeatedly the same sacrifices, which can never take away sins. 12But this Man, after He had offered one sacrifice for sins forever, sat down at the right hand of God, 13from that time waiting till His enemies are made His footstool. 14For by one offering He has perfected forever those who are being sanctified.

15But the Holy Spirit also witnesses to us; for after He had said before,

16"This is the covenant that I will make with them after those days, says the Lord: I will put My laws into their hearts, and in their minds I will write them," 17then He adds, "Their sins and their lawless deeds I will remember no more." 18Now where there is remission of these, there is no longer an offering for sin.

Hold Fast Your Confession

19Therefore, brethren, having boldness to enter the Holiest by the blood of Jesus, 20by a new and living way which He consecrated for us, through the veil, that is, His flesh, 21and having a High Priest over the house of God, 22let us draw near with a true heart in full assurance of faith, having our hearts sprinkled from an evil conscience and our bodies washed with pure water. 23Let us hold fast the confession of our hope without wavering, for He who promised is faithful. 24And let us consider one another in order to stir up love and good works, 25not forsaking the assembling of ourselves together, as is the manner of some, but exhorting one another, and so much the more as you see the Day approaching.

The Just Live by Faith

26For if we sin willfully after we have received the knowledge of the truth, there no longer remains a sacrifice for sins, 27but a certain fearful expectation of judgment, and fiery indignation which will devour the adversaries. 28Anyone who has rejected Moses' law dies without mercy on the testimony of two or three witnesses. 29Of how much worse punishment, do you suppose, will he be thought worthy who has trampled the Son of God underfoot, counted the blood of the covenant by which he was sanctified a common thing, and insulted the Spirit of grace? 30For we know Him who said, "Vengeance is Mine, I will repay," says the Lord. And again, "The Lord will judge His people." 31It is a fearful thing to fall into the hands of the living God.

32But recall the former days in which, after you were illuminated, you endured a great struggle with sufferings: 33partly while you were made a spectacle both by reproaches and tribulations, and partly while you became companions of those who were so treated; 34for you had compassion on me in my chains, and joyfully accepted the plundering of your goods, knowing that you have a better and an enduring possession for yourselves in heaven. 35Therefore do not cast away your confidence, which has great reward. 36For you have need of endurance, so that after you have done the will of God, you may receive the promise:

37 "For yet a little while,
   And He who is coming will come and will
      not tarry.
38 Now the just shall live by faith;
   But if anyone draws back,
   My soul has no pleasure in him."

39But we are not of those who draw back to perdition, but of those who believe to the saving of the soul.

DEVOTIONAL

Hebrews 10:19–25 *helps us understand how we can hold fast to our confession of faith in Christ: we should continually draw near to Him, confessing Him as our only hope, and consider how we can love and serve others.*

In faith, we are to come into the presence of God with boldness—not because we are boastful, but because of Jesus' blood. In faith, we are to "stir up love and good works, not forsaking the assembling of ourselves together" (Hebrews 10:24–25).

Jesus loves the church, His bride, and died for her. He gifted the Spirit to His followers, and He is coming again for us. We must not forsake His blood-bought church. We need to worship with our fellow believers weekly and encourage each other in the faith we share—and even more as we see Christ's return drawing near. We need to love and serve others in and through the body of Christ.

Today, tell Jesus you love Him and His church, and then demonstrate your faith and love in worship and service.

—Dr. Ronnie Floyd
Cross Church, Springdale, AR

WEEK 45, DAY 6

Faith Pleases God

Hebrews 11:1–22

By Faith We Understand

11 Now faith is the substance of things hoped for, the evidence of things not seen. ²For by it the elders obtained a good testimony.

³By faith we understand that the worlds were framed by the word of God, so that the things which are seen were not made of things which are visible.

Faith at the Dawn of History

⁴By faith Abel offered to God a more excellent sacrifice than Cain, through which he obtained witness that he was righteous, God testifying of his gifts; and through it he being dead still speaks.

⁵By faith Enoch was taken away so that he did not see death, "and was not found, because God had taken him"; for before he was taken he had this testimony, that he pleased God. ⁶But without faith it is impossible to please Him, for he who comes to God must believe that He is, and that He is a rewarder of those who diligently seek Him.

⁷By faith Noah, being divinely warned of things not yet seen, moved with godly fear, prepared an ark for the saving of his household, by which he condemned the world and became heir of the righteousness which is according to faith.

Faithful Abraham

⁸By faith Abraham obeyed when he was called to go out to the place which he would receive as an inheritance. And he went out, not knowing where he was going. ⁹By faith he dwelt in the land of promise as in a foreign country, dwelling in tents with Isaac and Jacob, the heirs with him of the same promise; ¹⁰for he waited for the city which has foundations, whose builder and maker is God.

¹¹By faith Sarah herself also received strength to conceive seed, and she bore a child when she was past the age, because she judged Him faithful who had promised. ¹²Therefore from one man, and him as good as dead, were born as many as the stars of the sky in multitude—innumerable as the sand which is by the seashore.

The Heavenly Hope

¹³These all died in faith, not having received the promises, but having seen them afar off were assured of them, embraced them and confessed that they were strangers and pilgrims on the earth. ¹⁴For those who say such things declare plainly that they seek a homeland. ¹⁵And truly if they had called to mind that country from which they had come out, they would have had opportunity to return. ¹⁶But now they desire a better, that is, a heavenly country. Therefore God is not ashamed to be called their God, for He has prepared a city for them.

The Faith of the Patriarchs

¹⁷By faith Abraham, when he was tested, offered up Isaac, and he who had received the promises offered up his only begotten son, ¹⁸of whom it was said, "In Isaac your seed shall be called," ¹⁹concluding that God was able to raise him up, even from the dead, from which he also received him in a figurative sense.

²⁰By faith Isaac blessed Jacob and Esau concerning things to come.

²¹By faith Jacob, when he was dying, blessed each of the sons of Joseph, and worshiped, leaning on the top of his staff.

²²By faith Joseph, when he was dying, made mention of the departure of the children of Israel, and gave instructions concerning his bones.

DEVOTIONAL

F aith occurs as an inner conviction, and it is not based on what you see, feel, or know. Hebrews 11:1 defines faith as "the substance of things hoped for, the evidence of things not seen." God calls us to rely on Him, not on our own senses. Proverbs 3:5 says, "Trust . . . understanding." And Paul told believers, "We walk by faith, not by sight" (2 Corinthians 5:7). Do you want to please God? Stop determining the course of your life by what you see or feel.

A great preacher of the past named Manley Beasley said, "Faith is believing something is so when it is not so in order for it to be so because God says it is so."¹⁵ He saw faith as a believer's sixth sense, and the sense by which God wants His people to live daily. If we just opened our spiritual eyes and took the time to see what He sees, there is no limit to what God would do with us. Great men and women of faith always see more than the human eye sees and feel more than the human heart feels.

You can become a person of great faith. Choose to walk by faith today!

—Dr. Ronnie Floyd
Cross Church, Springdale, AR

WEEK 45, DAY 7

Through your reading this week, what have you realized you need to work on personally?

_____

_____

_____

_____

_____

_____

_____

_____

_____

_____

_____

Real faith that operates with spiritual eyes and an inner spiritual conviction can only occur when we believe God is who He says He is and He can do what He says He can do. What are three areas of your life where you can walk by faith and trust God like this?

_____

_____

_____

_____

_____

_____

_____

_____

WEEK 46, DAY 1

God Corrects Those He Loves

Hebrews 11:23–12:6

The Faith of Moses

By faith Moses, when he was born, was hidden three months by his parents, because they saw he was a beautiful child; and they were not afraid of the king's command.

²⁴By faith Moses, when he became of age, refused to be called the son of Pharaoh's daughter, ²⁵choosing rather to suffer affliction with the people of God than to enjoy the passing pleasures of sin, ²⁶esteeming the reproach of Christ greater riches than the treasures in Egypt; for he looked to the reward.

²⁷By faith he forsook Egypt, not fearing the wrath of the king; for he endured as seeing Him who is invisible. ²⁸By faith he kept the Passover and the sprinkling of blood, lest he who destroyed the firstborn should touch them.

²⁹By faith they passed through the Red Sea as by dry land, whereas the Egyptians, attempting to do so, were drowned.

By Faith They Overcame

³⁰By faith the walls of Jericho fell down after they were encircled for seven days. ³¹By faith the harlot Rahab did not perish with those who did not believe, when she had received the spies with peace.

³²And what more shall I say? For the time would fail me to tell of Gideon and Barak and Samson and Jephthah, also of David and Samuel and the prophets: ³³who through faith subdued kingdoms, worked righteousness, obtained promises, stopped the mouths of lions, ³⁴quenched the violence of fire, escaped the edge of the sword, out of weakness were made strong, became valiant in battle, turned to flight the armies of the aliens. ³⁵Women received their dead raised to life again.

Others were tortured, not accepting deliverance, that they might obtain a better resurrection. ³⁶Still others had trial of mockings and scourgings, yes, and of chains and imprisonment. ³⁷They were stoned, they were sawn in two, were tempted, were slain with the sword. They wandered about in sheepskins and goatskins, being destitute, afflicted, tormented— ³⁸of whom the world was not worthy. They wandered in deserts and mountains, in dens and caves of the earth.

³⁹And all these, having obtained a good testimony through faith, did not receive the promise, ⁴⁰God having provided something better for us, that they should not be made perfect apart from us.

The Race of Faith

12 Therefore we also, since we are surrounded by so great a cloud of witnesses, let us lay aside every weight, and the sin which so easily ensnares us, and let us run with endurance the race that is set before us, ²looking unto Jesus, the author and finisher of our faith, who for the joy that was set before Him endured the cross, despising the shame, and has sat down at the right hand of the throne of God.

The Discipline of God

³For consider Him who endured such hostility from sinners against Himself, lest you become weary and discouraged in your souls. ⁴You have not yet resisted to bloodshed, striving against sin. ⁵And you have forgotten the exhortation which speaks to you as to sons:

> "My son, do not despise the chastening of
> the LORD,
> Nor be discouraged when you are rebuked
> by Him;
> ⁶ For whom the LORD loves He chastens,
> And scourges every son whom He receives."

DEVOTIONAL

The fact that God corrects His children is almost a forgotten truth among believers today. Many choose to focus only on God's loving acceptance, and as a result, they do not have a balanced, biblical view of God. They fail to acknowledge He is a holy God who hates sin and that sin is a serious matter in the life of a believer.

Numbers 32:23 says, "Be sure your sin will find you out." This statement was addressed to the children of Israel, God's chosen people. God does not ignore in His children what He does not condone in the unsaved. When God chastens us, it means He is interested in us. He teaches and helps us through His correction and chastisement. It's evidence of His love, just like parents who correct their children. When parents really love their children, they are closely involved with their lives, and discipline is a part of that involvement. Pray that you will be quick to receive God's love in all forms, even correction and discipline.

—Norman Hunt
Hopewell Baptist Church, Canton, GA

WEEK 46, DAY 2

Be All You Can Be for God

Hebrews 12:7–29

If you endure chastening, God deals with you as with sons; for what son is there whom a father does not chasten? 8But if you are without chastening, of which all have become partakers, then you are illegitimate and not sons. 9Furthermore, we have had human fathers who corrected us, and we paid them respect. Shall we not much more readily be in subjection to the Father of spirits and live? 10For they indeed for a few days chastened us as seemed best to them, but He for our profit, that we may be partakers of His holiness. 11Now no chastening seems to be joyful for the present, but painful; nevertheless, afterward it yields the peaceable fruit of righteousness to those who have been trained by it.

Renew Your Spiritual Vitality

12Therefore strengthen the hands which hang down, and the feeble knees, 13and make straight paths for your feet, so that what is lame may not be dislocated, but rather be healed.

14Pursue peace with all people, and holiness, without which no one will see the Lord: 15looking carefully lest anyone fall short of the grace of God; lest any root of bitterness springing up cause trouble, and by this many become defiled; 16lest there be any fornicator or profane person like Esau, who for one morsel of food sold his birthright. 17For you know that afterward, when he wanted to inherit the blessing, he was rejected, for he found no place for repentance, though he sought it diligently with tears.

The Glorious Company

18For you have not come to the mountain that may be touched and that burned with fire, and to blackness and darkness and tempest, 19and the sound of a trumpet and the voice of words, so that those who heard it begged that the word should not be spoken to them anymore. 20(For they could not endure what was commanded: "And if so much as a beast touches the mountain, it shall be stoned or shot with an arrow." 21And so terrifying was the sight that Moses said, "I am exceedingly afraid and trembling.")

22But you have come to Mount Zion and to the city of the living God, the heavenly Jerusalem, to an innumerable company of angels, 23to the general assembly and church of the firstborn who are registered in heaven, to God the Judge of all, to the spirits of just men made perfect, 24to Jesus the Mediator of the new covenant, and to the blood of sprinkling that speaks better things than that of Abel.

Hear the Heavenly Voice

25See that you do not refuse Him who speaks. For if they did not escape who refused Him who spoke on earth, much more shall we not escape if we turn away from Him who speaks from heaven, 26whose voice then shook the earth; but now He has promised, saying, "Yet once more I shake not only the earth, but also heaven." 27Now this, "Yet once more," indicates the removal of those things that are being shaken, as of things that are made, that the things which cannot be shaken may remain.

28Therefore, since we are receiving a kingdom which cannot be shaken, let us have grace, by which we may serve God acceptably with reverence and godly fear. 29For our God is a consuming fire.

DEVOTIONAL

The great theme of the entire letter to the Hebrews is clear in this statement: "Let us go on to perfection" (6:1). This doesn't mean we will ever arrive at sinlessness in our lives, but it does mean we are called to go on to full maturity in the Lord.

We often have to be reminded that God corrects us because He loves us. He wants what is best for our lives! The word correction *means "the whole training and education of a child." In other words, it refers to all the discipline and correction that is essential for a child to grow and become what that child is intended to be. When we fail to accept God's correction and chastisement, we fail to become all that God means for us to become by His grace. You see, there is the potential in that grace of God to provide us every power, every opportunity, and every strength necessary to grow to maturity in the Lord Jesus.*

Paul wrote, "By the grace of God I am what I am" (1 Corinthians 15:10). He was simply saying, "I am saved by the grace of God, and anything my life has become is due to the working of God's grace in my life." The whole point of God's correction in our lives is that we will not fail to become all that grace can make us.

What an honor and privilege it is to be in the family of the Lord Most High. By His grace, let's be all we can be for Him!

—Norman Hunt
Hopewell Baptist Church, Canton, GA

WEEK 46, DAY 3

Live in a Way That Pleases God

Hebrews 13:1–25

Concluding Moral Directions

13 Let brotherly love continue. ²Do not forget to entertain strangers, for by so doing some have unwittingly entertained angels. ³Remember the prisoners as if chained with them—those who are mistreated—since you yourselves are in the body also.

⁴Marriage is honorable among all, and the bed undefiled; but fornicators and adulterers God will judge.

⁵Let your conduct be without covetousness; be content with such things as you have. For He Himself has said, "I will never leave you nor forsake you." ⁶So we may boldly say:

"The LORD is my helper;
I will not fear.
What can man do to me?"

Concluding Religious Directions

⁷Remember those who rule over you, who have spoken the word of God to you, whose faith follow, considering the outcome of their conduct. ⁸Jesus Christ is the same yesterday, today, and forever. ⁹Do not be carried about with various and strange doctrines. For it is good that the heart be established by grace, not with foods which have not profited those who have been occupied with them.

¹⁰We have an altar from which those who serve the tabernacle have no right to eat. ¹¹For the bodies of those animals, whose blood is brought into the sanctuary by the high priest for sin, are burned outside the camp. ¹²Therefore Jesus also, that He might sanctify the people with His own blood, suffered outside the gate. ¹³Therefore let us go forth to Him, outside the camp, bearing His reproach. ¹⁴For here we have no continuing city, but we seek the one to come. ¹⁵Therefore by Him let us continually offer the sacrifice of praise to God, that is, the fruit of our lips, giving thanks to His name. ¹⁶But do not forget to do good and to share, for with such sacrifices God is well pleased.

¹⁷Obey those who rule over you, and be submissive, for they watch out for your souls, as those who must give account. Let them do so with joy and not with grief, for that would be unprofitable for you.

Prayer Requested

¹⁸Pray for us; for we are confident that we have a good conscience, in all things desiring to live honorably. ¹⁹But I especially urge you to do this, that I may be restored to you the sooner.

Benediction, Final Exhortation, Farewell

²⁰Now may the God of peace who brought up our Lord Jesus from the dead, that great Shepherd of the sheep, through the blood of the everlasting covenant, ²¹make you complete in every good work to do His will, working in you what is well pleasing in His sight, through Jesus Christ, to whom be glory forever and ever. Amen.

²²And I appeal to you, brethren, bear with the word of exhortation, for I have written to you in few words. ²³Know that our brother Timothy has been set free, with whom I shall see you if he comes shortly.

²⁴Greet all those who rule over you, and all the saints. Those from Italy greet you.

²⁵Grace be with you all. Amen.

DEVOTIONAL

G od calls us to live in a way that pleases Him. Paul told believers, *"Present your bodies a living sacrifice, holy, acceptable to God. . . . Do not be conformed to this world, but be transformed by the renewing of your mind, that you may prove what is that good and acceptable and perfect will of God" (Romans 12:1–2).* If we desire to be pleasing to the Lord, this must be our spiritual practice. The transforming of our lives is an inside working of the Holy Spirit.

The people who first read this letter to the Hebrews had just recently moved away from a religious system and into full salvation by faith in the Lord Jesus. These individuals had previously attempted to live their lives for God on the basis of ceremony and law. They were accustomed to thinking if they kept enough rules and rituals, somehow they were going to be pleasing to the Lord and gain favor and merit with Him. They needed to hear the truth that *"it is good that the heart be established by grace" (Hebrews 13:9).*

The grace way of living is not about trying to live the Christian life in your own strength and ability—it's about depending on Christ. In the Person of the Holy Spirit, God has come to live inside you. Now on the basis of the indwelling grace of God, you can live a life that is pleasing to God. Surrender to the Spirit, and let Him lead you in obedience and worship today.

—Norman Hunt
Hopewell Baptist Church, Canton, GA

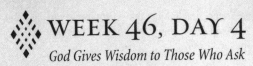

WEEK 46, DAY 4

God Gives Wisdom to Those Who Ask

James 1:1–27

Greeting to the Twelve Tribes

1 James, a bondservant of God and of the Lord Jesus Christ,

To the twelve tribes which are scattered abroad:

Greetings.

Profiting from Trials

2My brethren, count it all joy when you fall into various trials, 3knowing that the testing of your faith produces patience. 4But let patience have its perfect work, that you may be perfect and complete, lacking nothing. 5If any of you lacks wisdom, let him ask of God, who gives to all liberally and without reproach, and it will be given to him. 6But let him ask in faith, with no doubting, for he who doubts is like a wave of the sea driven and tossed by the wind. 7For let not that man suppose that he will receive anything from the Lord; 8he is a double-minded man, unstable in all his ways.

The Perspective of Rich and Poor

9Let the lowly brother glory in his exaltation, 10but the rich in his humiliation, because as a flower of the field he will pass away. 11For no sooner has the sun risen with a burning heat than it withers the grass; its flower falls, and its beautiful appearance perishes. So the rich man also will fade away in his pursuits.

Loving God Under Trials

12Blessed is the man who endures temptation; for when he has been approved, he will receive the crown of life which the Lord has promised to those who love Him. 13Let no one say when he is tempted, "I am tempted by God"; for God cannot be tempted by evil, nor does He Himself tempt anyone. 14But each one is tempted when he is drawn away by his own desires and enticed. 15Then, when desire has conceived, it gives birth to sin; and sin, when it is full-grown, brings forth death. 16Do not be deceived, my beloved brethren. 17Every good gift and every perfect gift is from above, and comes down from the Father of lights, with whom there is no variation or shadow of turning. 18Of His own will He brought us forth by the word of truth, that we might be a kind of firstfruits of His creatures.

Qualities Needed in Trials

19So then, my beloved brethren, let every man be swift to hear, slow to speak, slow to wrath; 20for the wrath of man does not produce the righteousness of God.

Doers—Not Hearers Only

21Therefore lay aside all filthiness and overflow of wickedness, and receive with meekness the implanted word, which is able to save your souls.

22But be doers of the word, and not hearers only, deceiving yourselves. 23For if anyone is a hearer of the word and not a doer, he is like a man observing his natural face in a mirror; 24for he observes himself, goes away, and immediately forgets what kind of man he was. 25But he who looks into the perfect law of liberty and continues in it, and is not a forgetful hearer but a doer of the work, this one will be blessed in what he does.

26If anyone among you thinks he is religious, and does not bridle his tongue but deceives his own heart, this one's religion is useless. 27Pure and undefiled religion before God and the Father is this: to visit orphans and widows in their trouble, and to keep oneself unspotted from the world.

DEVOTIONAL

We are living in a world where people desperately need the wisdom of God. It is God's desire that as believers we be complete, which means mature and lacking nothing (James 1:4). But if we are to be mature, we need to live according to God's wisdom.

True wisdom is a supernatural gift from God that enables you to take your own knowledge and the knowledge you gain from reading Scripture and apply it appropriately to your daily problems. If we are honest, it is not a matter of if we lack wisdom (James 1:5)—we most certainly do! We find ourselves in a hundred situations every day where we desperately need the wisdom of God.

First Timothy 1:17 refers to God as He "who alone is wise." God has cornered the market on wisdom. Whenever you lack wisdom, you must go to God to get it. Be encouraged by the fact that God "gives to all liberally and without reproach" (James 1:5)! It is the character and nature of God to give—He is just waiting for us to ask!

—Norman Hunt
Hopewell Baptist Church, Canton, GA

WEEK 46, DAY 5

Do Not Show Partiality

James 2:1–26

Beware of Personal Favoritism

2 My brethren, do not hold the faith of our Lord Jesus Christ, the Lord of glory, with partiality. ²For if there should come into your assembly a man with gold rings, in fine apparel, and there should also come in a poor man in filthy clothes, ³and you pay attention to the one wearing the fine clothes and say to him, "You sit here in a good place," and say to the poor man, "You stand there," or, "Sit here at my footstool," ⁴have you not shown partiality among yourselves, and become judges with evil thoughts?

⁵Listen, my beloved brethren: Has God not chosen the poor of this world to be rich in faith and heirs of the kingdom which He promised to those who love Him? ⁶But you have dishonored the poor man. Do not the rich oppress you and drag you into the courts? ⁷Do they not blaspheme that noble name by which you are called?

⁸If you really fulfill the royal law according to the Scripture, "You shall love your neighbor as yourself," you do well; ⁹but if you show partiality, you commit sin, and are convicted by the law as transgressors. ¹⁰For whoever shall keep the whole law, and yet stumble in one point, he is guilty of all. ¹¹For He who said, "Do not commit adultery," also said, "Do not murder." Now if you do not commit adultery, but you do murder, you have become a transgressor of the law. ¹²So speak and so do as those who will be judged by the law of liberty. ¹³For judgment is without mercy to the one who has shown no mercy. Mercy triumphs over judgment.

Faith Without Works Is Dead

¹⁴What does it profit, my brethren, if someone says he has faith but does not have works? Can faith save him? ¹⁵If a brother or sister is naked and destitute of daily food, ¹⁶and one of you says to them, "Depart in peace, be warmed and filled," but you do not give them the things which are needed for the body, what does it profit? ¹⁷Thus also faith by itself, if it does not have works, is dead.

¹⁸But someone will say, "You have faith, and I have works." Show me your faith without your works, and I will show you my faith by my works. ¹⁹You believe that there is one God. You do well. Even the demons believe—and tremble! ²⁰But do you want to know, O foolish man, that faith without works is dead? ²¹Was not Abraham our father justified by works when he offered Isaac his son on the altar? ²²Do you see that faith was working together with his works, and by works faith was made perfect? ²³And the Scripture was fulfilled which says, "Abraham believed God, and it was accounted to him for righteousness." And he was called the friend of God. ²⁴You see then that a man is justified by works, and not by faith only.

²⁵Likewise, was not Rahab the harlot also justified by works when she received the messengers and sent them out another way?

²⁶For as the body without the spirit is dead, so faith without works is dead also.

DEVOTIONAL

J ames discussed something that is absolutely incompatible with the Christian faith: the sin of partiality (2:1–13). It is essentially playing favorites or being snobby in the house of God. It is letting yourself be influenced by some kind of outward consideration rather than pausing long enough to see what's really on the inside. But if a true New Testament church understands the teachings of the Scriptures, it is a community in which everyone is someone and Jesus Christ is Lord.

Proverbs 28:21 says, "To show partiality is not good." Why? Because every person is of great worth to God. Favoritism says there are some people who are worth more than other people. Proverbs 22:2 says, "The rich and the poor have this in common, the LORD is the maker of them all."

When Jesus came into the world and died on the cross of Calvary, He died for all. Anyone who wants to be saved can be saved! It has been said that the ground is level at the foot of the cross. That is perfectly true. If we are the people of God following the Word of God, we simply must not play favorites among each other.

How could your interactions with different people within the body of Christ be described? Do you treat those who are wealthy, powerful, or nice-looking better than those who are not? Is there anyone you consider insignificant or undeserving of your attention, respect, and love? If you are guilty of showing favoritism, acknowledge it as a sin and repent of it. Ask God to put His heart in you, so that you may sincerely value and love people as He does.

—Norman Hunt
Hopewell Baptist Church, Canton, GA

 WEEK 46, DAY 6

Tame Your Tongue

James 3:1–4:10

The Untamable Tongue

3My brethren, let not many of you become teachers, knowing that we shall receive a stricter judgment. 2For we all stumble in many things. If anyone does not stumble in word, he is a perfect man, able also to bridle the whole body. 3Indeed, we put bits in horses' mouths that they may obey us, and we turn their whole body. 4Look also at ships: although they are so large and are driven by fierce winds, they are turned by a very small rudder wherever the pilot desires. 5Even so the tongue is a little member and boasts great things.

See how great a forest a little fire kindles! 6And the tongue is a fire, a world of iniquity. The tongue is so set among our members that it defiles the whole body, and sets on fire the course of nature; and it is set on fire by hell. 7For every kind of beast and bird, of reptile and creature of the sea, is tamed and has been tamed by mankind. 8But no man can tame the tongue. It is an unruly evil, full of deadly poison. 9With it we bless our God and Father, and with it we curse men, who have been made in the similitude of God. 10Out of the same mouth proceed blessing and cursing. My brethren, these things ought not to be so. 11Does a spring send forth fresh water and bitter from the same opening? 12Can a fig tree, my brethren, bear olives, or a grapevine bear figs? Thus no spring yields both salt water and fresh.

Heavenly Versus Demonic Wisdom

13Who is wise and understanding among you? Let him show by good conduct that his works are done in the meekness of wisdom. 14But if you have bitter envy and self-seeking in your hearts, do not boast and lie against the truth. 15This wisdom does not descend from above, but is earthly, sensual, demonic. 16For where envy and self-seeking exist, confusion and every evil thing are there. 17But the wisdom that is from above is first pure, then peaceable, gentle, willing to yield, full of mercy and good fruits, without partiality and without hypocrisy. 18Now the fruit of righteousness is sown in peace by those who make peace.

Pride Promotes Strife

4Where do wars and fights come from among you? Do they not come from your desires for pleasure that war in your members? 2You lust and do not have. You murder and covet and cannot obtain. You fight and war. Yet you do not have because you do not ask. 3You ask and do not receive, because you ask amiss, that you may spend it on your pleasures. 4Adulterers and adulteresses! Do you not know that friendship with the world is enmity with God? Whoever therefore wants to be a friend of the world makes himself an enemy of God. 5Or do you think that the Scripture says in vain, "The Spirit who dwells in us yearns jealously"?

6But He gives more grace. Therefore He says:

"God resists the proud,
But gives grace to the humble."

Humility Cures Worldliness

7Therefore submit to God. Resist the devil and he will flee from you. 8Draw near to God and He will draw near to you. Cleanse your hands, you sinners; and purify your hearts, you double-minded. 9Lament and mourn and weep! Let your laughter be turned to mourning and your joy to gloom. 10Humble yourselves in the sight of the Lord, and He will lift you up.

DEVOTIONAL

*M*ost of us understand how powerful the human tongue can be. Proverbs 18:21 says, "Death and life are in the power of the tongue," which tells us we can use our words for great evil or great good.

James wrote, "If anyone does not stumble in word, he is a perfect man, able also to bridle the whole body" (3:2). Most occurrences of the word perfect *in Scripture do not mean "sinless"; perfect usually means "mature." So those who do not stumble and do not offend in word are mature. James was saying that a test of spiritual maturity is the ability of a believer to control his or her tongue.*

Jesus said we are to be very careful about our words because "out of the abundance of the heart the mouth speaks" (Matthew 12:34). In other words, your words are an indication of what is in your heart.

Ask God to purify your heart and to give you self-control and wisdom as you choose your words. Heed the instructions of Ephesians 4:29: "Let no corrupt word proceed out of your mouth, but what is good for necessary edification, that it may impart grace to the hearers." Use your tongue to love, bless, and build up those around you and to honor and worship the Lord.

—Norman Hunt
Hopewell Baptist Church, Canton, GA

WEEK 46, DAY 7

Hebrews 12:6 says, "Whom the LORD loves He chastens." List some of the things God has taught you throughout your life through correction and chastisement.

_____

_____

_____

_____

_____

_____

_____

_____

_____

_____

_____

_____

Our tongues can get us into a world of trouble. What are things you personally find helpful as you work on taming your tongue and controlling your conversation?

_____

_____

_____

_____

_____

_____

_____

_____

_____

_____

WEEK 47, DAY I

God Works Through Our Prayers

James 4:11–5:20

Do Not Judge a Brother

Do not speak evil of one another, brethren. He who speaks evil of a brother and judges his brother, speaks evil of the law and judges the law. But if you judge the law, you are not a doer of the law but a judge. 12There is one Lawgiver, who is able to save and to destroy. Who are you to judge another?

Do Not Boast About Tomorrow

13Come now, you who say, "Today or tomorrow we will go to such and such a city, spend a year there, buy and sell, and make a profit"; 14whereas you do not know what will happen tomorrow. For what is your life? It is even a vapor that appears for a little time and then vanishes away. 15Instead you ought to say, "If the Lord wills, we shall live and do this or that." 16But now you boast in your arrogance. All such boasting is evil.

17Therefore, to him who knows to do good and does not do it, to him it is sin.

Rich Oppressors Will Be Judged

5Come now, you rich, weep and howl for your miseries that are coming upon you! 2Your riches are corrupted, and your garments are moth-eaten. 3Your gold and silver are corroded, and their corrosion will be a witness against you and will eat your flesh like fire. You have heaped up treasure in the last days. 4Indeed the wages of the laborers who mowed your fields, which you kept back by fraud, cry out; and the cries of the reapers have reached the ears of the Lord of Sabaoth. 5You have lived on the earth in pleasure and luxury; you have fattened your hearts as in a day of slaughter. 6You have condemned, you have murdered the just; he does not resist you.

Be Patient and Persevering

7Therefore be patient, brethren, until the coming of the Lord. See how the farmer waits for the precious fruit of the earth, waiting patiently for it until it receives the early and latter rain. 8You also be patient. Establish your hearts, for the coming of the Lord is at hand.

9Do not grumble against one another, brethren, lest you be condemned. Behold, the Judge is standing at the door! 10My brethren, take the prophets, who spoke in the name of the Lord, as an example of suffering and patience. 11Indeed we count them blessed who endure. You have heard of the perseverance of Job and seen the end intended by the Lord—that the Lord is very compassionate and merciful.

12But above all, my brethren, do not swear, either by heaven or by earth or with any other oath. But let your "Yes" be "Yes," and your "No," "No," lest you fall into judgment.

Meeting Specific Needs

13Is anyone among you suffering? Let him pray. Is anyone cheerful? Let him sing psalms. 14Is anyone among you sick? Let him call for the elders of the church, and let them pray over him, anointing him with oil in the name of the Lord. 15And the prayer of faith will save the sick, and the Lord will raise him up. And if he has committed sins, he will be forgiven. 16Confess your trespasses to one another, and pray for one another, that you may be healed. The effective, fervent prayer of a righteous man avails much. 17Elijah was a man with a nature like ours, and he prayed earnestly that it would not rain; and it did not rain on the land for three years and six months. 18And he prayed again, and the heaven gave rain, and the earth produced its fruit.

Bring Back the Erring One

19Brethren, if anyone among you wanders from the truth, and someone turns him back, 20let him know that he who turns a sinner from the error of his way will save a soul from death and cover a multitude of sins.

DEVOTIONAL

Mark Twain wrote, *"Few things are harder to put up with than the annoyance of a good example."* Elijah, the man who prayed there would be no rain for three and a half years (1 Kings 17–18) is the example James used to exhort God's people to pray. The danger in examples is that we may feel we do not measure up. But James said that *"Elijah was a man with a nature like ours"* (James 5:17). The power of Elijah's prayer did not lie in Elijah's ability, but in God's.

James repeatedly exhorted God's people to pray (1:5–6; 4:2). Effective prayers are not often flowery, but they are always fervent. God works mightily through our prayers. Call upon the resources of heaven for every problem you face today. Turn to God in prayer!

—Scott Yirka
Hibernia Baptist Church, Fleming Island, FL

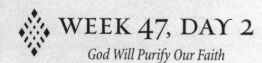

WEEK 47, DAY 2

God Will Purify Our Faith

1 Peter 1:1–21

Greeting to the Elect Pilgrims

1 Peter, an apostle of Jesus Christ,

To the pilgrims of the Dispersion in Pontus, Galatia, Cappadocia, Asia, and Bithynia, ²elect according to the fore-knowledge of God the Father, in sanctification of the Spirit, for obedience and sprinkling of the blood of Jesus Christ:

Grace to you and peace be multiplied.

A Heavenly Inheritance

³Blessed be the God and Father of our Lord Jesus Christ, who according to His abundant mercy has begotten us again to a living hope through the resurrection of Jesus Christ from the dead, ⁴to an inheritance incorruptible and undefiled and that does not fade away, reserved in heaven for you, ⁵who are kept by the power of God through faith for salvation ready to be revealed in the last time.

⁶In this you greatly rejoice, though now for a little while, if need be, you have been grieved by various trials, ⁷that the genuineness of your faith, being much more precious than gold that perishes, though it is tested by fire, may be found to praise, honor, and glory at the revelation of Jesus Christ, ⁸whom having not seen you love. Though now you do not see Him, yet believing, you rejoice with joy inexpressible and full of glory, ⁹receiving the end of your faith—the salvation of your souls.

¹⁰Of this salvation the prophets have inquired and searched carefully, who prophesied of the grace that would come to you, ¹¹searching what, or what manner of time, the Spirit of Christ who was in them was indicating when He testified beforehand the sufferings of Christ and the glories that would follow. ¹²To them it was revealed that, not to themselves, but to us they were ministering the things which now have been reported to you through those who have preached the gospel to you by the Holy Spirit sent from heaven—things which angels desire to look into.

Living Before God Our Father

¹³Therefore gird up the loins of your mind, be sober, and rest your hope fully upon the grace that is to be brought to you at the revelation of Jesus Christ; ¹⁴as obedient children, not conforming yourselves to the former lusts, as in your ignorance; ¹⁵but as He who called you is holy, you also be holy in all your conduct, ¹⁶because it is written, "Be holy, for I am holy."

¹⁷And if you call on the Father, who without partiality judges according to each one's work, conduct yourselves throughout the time of your stay here in fear; ¹⁸knowing that you were not redeemed with corruptible things, like silver or gold, from your aimless conduct received by tradition from your fathers, ¹⁹but with the precious blood of Christ, as of a lamb without blemish and without spot. ²⁰He indeed was foreordained before the foundation of the world, but was manifest in these last times for you ²¹who through Him believe in God, who raised Him from the dead and gave Him glory, so that your faith and hope are in God.

DEVOTIONAL

*T*he insane, egomaniacal, and evil Nero was rising to power in Rome, and persecution was on the horizon for the precious believers in Asia Minor to whom Peter wrote this epistle. They were unsettling times for these Christians, to say the least.

These believers could have embraced dread and been paralyzed by fear, but instead they chose to be joyful in the midst of a trial. Peter wrote, "In this you greatly rejoice, though now for a little while, if need be, you have been grieved by various trials" (1 Peter 1:6). They were fully assured that they were kept by God, and they boldly walked through dark days with faith and joy.

The trials we face are meant for a purpose. Each trial is meant to prove, purify, and perfect our faith, and knowing this purpose helps eradicate our fear. As our faith is strengthened, our joy increases (Nehemiah 8:10).

Peter used a picture from the work of a goldsmith to illustrate how God purifies our faith. Fire is how gold is put to the test. Dross is removed, making a purer gold. The goldsmith's fire is a symbol of the trials we encounter. God purifies our faith when, through trials, doubts are weakened and our assurance is strengthened. Tried and proven faith is trusted and precious faith. Gold will perish; true faith will not.

Do not fear the temporary, multifaceted, dark trials that may come into your life. They do not take God by surprise, and they are necessary for the purifying of your faith. As Peter said, "Gird up the loins of your mind, be sober, and rest your hope fully upon [His] grace" (1 Peter 1:3).

—Scott Yirka
Hibernia Baptist Church, Fleming Island, FL

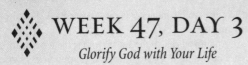

WEEK 47, DAY 3

Glorify God with Your Life

1 Peter 1:22–2:17

The Enduring Word

Since you have purified your souls in obeying the truth through the Spirit in sincere love of the brethren, love one another fervently with a pure heart, 23having been born again, not of corruptible seed but incorruptible, through the word of God which lives and abides forever, 24because

"All flesh is as grass,
And all the glory of man as the flower of the grass.
The grass withers,
And its flower falls away,
25 But the word of the LORD endures forever."

Now this is the word which by the gospel was preached to you.

2 Therefore, laying aside all malice, all deceit, hypocrisy, envy, and all evil speaking, 2as newborn babes, desire the pure milk of the word, that you may grow thereby, 3if indeed you have tasted that the Lord is gracious.

The Chosen Stone and His Chosen People

4Coming to Him as to a living stone, rejected indeed by men, but chosen by God and precious, 5you also, as living stones, are being built up a spiritual house, a holy priesthood, to offer up spiritual sacrifices acceptable to God through Jesus Christ. 6Therefore it is also contained in the Scripture,

"Behold, I lay in Zion
A chief cornerstone, elect, precious,
And he who believes on Him will by no means
be put to shame."

7Therefore, to you who believe, He is precious; but to those who are disobedient,

"The stone which the builders rejected
Has become the chief cornerstone,"

8and

"A stone of stumbling
And a rock of offense."

They stumble, being disobedient to the word, to which they also were appointed.

9But you are a chosen generation, a royal priesthood, a holy nation, His own special people, that you may proclaim the praises of Him who called you out of darkness into His marvelous light; 10who once were not a people but are now the people of God, who had not obtained mercy but now have obtained mercy.

Living Before the World

11Beloved, I beg you as sojourners and pilgrims, abstain from fleshly lusts which war against the soul, 12having your conduct honorable among the Gentiles, that when they speak against you as evildoers, they may, by your good works which they observe, glorify God in the day of visitation.

Submission to Government

13Therefore submit yourselves to every ordinance of man for the Lord's sake, whether to the king as supreme, 14or to governors, as to those who are sent by him for the punishment of evildoers and for the praise of those who do good. 15For this is the will of God, that by doing good you may put to silence the ignorance of foolish men— 16as free, yet not using liberty as a cloak for vice, but as bondservants of God. 17Honor all people. Love the brotherhood. Fear God. Honor the king.

DEVOTIONAL

It is always good to hear a sermon. But the world doesn't often get to hear one, so it needs to see the good news in believers' lives.

Jesus illustrated His teaching with the way He lived. He did not only talk about love; He loved. He did not just command forgiveness; He forgave. When His life was scrutinized, no fault was found in Him. He truly lived to the glory of the Father. Shortly before His crucifixion, Jesus said to His Father, "I have glorified You on the earth. I have finished the work which You have given Me to do" (John 17:4).

As a Christ follower, you are part of God's special envoy to this world. Paul called each believer an ambassador of Christ, a representative of Him in this world (2 Corinthians 5:20). The words of 1 Peter 2:11–17 echo an exhortation of Jesus: "Let your light so shine before men, that they may see your good works and glorify your Father in heaven" (Matthew 5:16). Today, aim to glorify God by living in a way that points the lost to Him.

—Scott Yirka
Hibernia Baptist Church, Fleming Island, FL

WEEK 47, DAY 4

Live in Peace

1 Peter 2:18–3:12

Submission to Masters

Servants, be submissive to your masters with all fear, not only to the good and gentle, but also to the harsh. 19For this is commendable, if because of conscience toward God one endures grief, suffering wrongfully. 20For what credit is it if, when you are beaten for your faults, you take it patiently? But when you do good and suffer, if you take it patiently, this is commendable before God. 21For to this you were called, because Christ also suffered for us, leaving us an example, that you should follow His steps:

22 "Who committed no sin,
Nor was deceit found in His mouth";

23who, when He was reviled, did not revile in return; when He suffered, He did not threaten, but committed Himself to Him who judges righteously; 24who Himself bore our sins in His own body on the tree, that we, having died to sins, might live for righteousness—by whose stripes you were healed. 25For you were like sheep going astray, but have now returned to the Shepherd and Overseer of your souls.

Submission to Husbands

3 Wives, likewise, be submissive to your own husbands, that even if some do not obey the word, they, without a word, may be won by the conduct of their wives, 2when they observe your chaste conduct accompanied by fear. 3Do not let your adornment be merely outward—arranging the hair, wearing gold, or putting on fine apparel— 4rather let it be the hidden person of the heart, with the incorruptible beauty of a gentle and quiet spirit, which is very precious in the sight of God. 5For in this manner, in former times, the holy women who trusted in God also adorned themselves, being submissive to their own husbands, 6as Sarah obeyed Abraham, calling him lord, whose daughters you are if you do good and are not afraid with any terror.

A Word to Husbands

7Husbands, likewise, dwell with them with understanding, giving honor to the wife, as to the weaker vessel, and as being heirs together of the grace of life, that your prayers may not be hindered.

Called to Blessing

8Finally, all of you be of one mind, having compassion for one another; love as brothers, be tenderhearted, be courteous; 9not returning evil for evil or reviling for reviling, but on the contrary blessing, knowing that you were called to this, that you may inherit a blessing. 10For

"He who would love life
And see good days,
Let him refrain his tongue from evil,
And his lips from speaking deceit.
11 Let him turn away from evil and do good;
Let him seek peace and pursue it.
12 For the eyes of the LORD are on the righteous,
And His ears are open to their prayers;
But the face of the LORD is against those who
do evil."

DEVOTIONAL

What exactly is the "good life"? Is it earning enough money to do what you want when you want? Is it getting married and settling down in the suburbs or some uptown apartment? Is it having season tickets or getting the corner office? However people define it, everyone desires the good life. The good life ceases to be good, however, when human relationships are broken. Life is about relationships, and no amount of achievement or material gain can fix broken hearts.

Peter said the good life is living at peace with people. If we love life, we will love others and seek to be at peace with them (Psalm 34:14; 1 Peter 3:11).

Paul said we should do our best to live at peace with one another (Romans 12:18), and Jesus said, "Blessed are the peacemakers" (Matthew 5:9). Living in peace means becoming a bridge-builder. The ultimate reason we are to seek reconciliation with others is that God sought reconciliation with us. By the blood of the cross, God made peace with us when we were His enemies (Colossians 1:19–20).

Today, seek to be a peacemaker and a reconciler. Be a blessing to as many people as possible, "knowing that you were called to this, that you may inherit a blessing" (1 Peter 3:9). Now that sounds like the good life!

—Scott Yirka
Hibernia Baptist Church, Fleming Island, FL

WEEK 47, DAY 5

Share Your Faith

1 Peter 3:13–4:11

Suffering for Right and Wrong

And who is he who will harm you if you become followers of what is good? [14]But even if you should suffer for righteousness' sake, you are blessed. "And do not be afraid of their threats, nor be troubled." [15]But sanctify the Lord God in your hearts, and always be ready to give a defense to everyone who asks you a reason for the hope that is in you, with meekness and fear; [16]having a good conscience, that when they defame you as evildoers, those who revile your good conduct in Christ may be ashamed. [17]For it is better, if it is the will of God, to suffer for doing good than for doing evil.

Christ's Suffering and Ours

[18]For Christ also suffered once for sins, the just for the unjust, that He might bring us to God, being put to death in the flesh but made alive by the Spirit, [19]by whom also He went and preached to the spirits in prison, [20]who formerly were disobedient, when once the Divine longsuffering waited in the days of Noah, while the ark was being prepared, in which a few, that is, eight souls, were saved through water. [21]There is also an antitype which now saves us—baptism (not the removal of the filth of the flesh, but the answer of a good conscience toward God), through the resurrection of Jesus Christ, [22]who has gone into heaven and is at the right hand of God, angels and authorities and powers having been made subject to Him. [4]Therefore, since Christ suffered for us in the flesh, arm yourselves also with the same mind, for he who has suffered in the flesh has ceased from sin, [2]that he no longer should live the rest of his time in the flesh for the lusts of men, but for the will of God. [3]For we have spent enough of our past lifetime in doing the will of the Gentiles—when we walked in lewdness, lusts, drunkenness, revelries, drinking parties, and abominable idolatries. [4]In regard to these, they think it strange that you do not run with them in the same flood of dissipation, speaking evil of you. [5]They will give an account to Him who is ready to judge the living and the dead. [6]For this reason the gospel was preached also to those who are dead, that they might be judged according to men in the flesh, but live according to God in the spirit.

Serving for God's Glory

[7]But the end of all things is at hand; therefore be serious and watchful in your prayers. [8]And above all things have fervent love for one another, for "love will cover a multitude of sins." [9]Be hospitable to one another without grumbling. [10]As each one has received a gift, minister it to one another, as good stewards of the manifold grace of God. [11]If anyone speaks, let him speak as the oracles of God. If anyone ministers, let him do it as with the ability which God supplies, that in all things God may be glorified through Jesus Christ, to whom belong the glory and the dominion forever and ever. Amen.

DEVOTIONAL

You probably have never heard of a humble Sunday school teacher named Edward Kimball. One day he visited a young shoe salesman who had been visiting his class. In the shoe stockroom, the Sunday school teacher shared the love of Christ with this young man, and Dwight Lyman Moody was saved. While you may not be familiar with Edward Kimball, you have probably heard of D. L. Moody. He was a great soul-winning layman who reached thousands for Christ.

Peter tells us to "sanctify the Lord God" in our hearts (1 Peter 3:15). He is calling us to magnify the Lord by submitting our wills to His. Soul winners don't set out to win souls, but because Christ is so precious to them, they feel they must share Him with everyone—even if it means suffering for Him.

If you sanctify the Lord God in your heart, be ready for the Holy Spirit to prompt you to share your faith. Remember that Peter said, "The end of all things is at hand" (1 Peter 4:7). Jesus is coming and we have been left here, not only to wait for our Lord, but also to help as many people get to heaven as possible. Don't let the Enemy silence you. Don't let suffering stop you. People want to experience true hope today, and you know the Source. They need to be introduced to the Savior.

You may not be like D. L. Moody, but you are a child of the living God and empowered by the same Spirit. You have a hope in you, and others need to hear about that hope. Share your faith with others today!

—Scott Yirka
Hibernia Baptist Church, Fleming Island, FL

WEEK 47, DAY 6

Give All Your Worries to God

1 Peter 4:12–5:14

Suffering for God's Glory

Beloved, do not think it strange concerning the fiery trial which is to try you, as though some strange thing happened to you; 13but rejoice to the extent that you partake of Christ's sufferings, that when His glory is revealed, you may also be glad with exceeding joy. 14If you are reproached for the name of Christ, blessed are you, for the Spirit of glory and of God rests upon you. On their part He is blasphemed, but on your part He is glorified. 15But let none of you suffer as a murderer, a thief, an evildoer, or as a busybody in other people's matters. 16Yet if anyone suffers as a Christian, let him not be ashamed, but let him glorify God in this matter.

17For the time has come for judgment to begin at the house of God; and if it begins with us first, what will be the end of those who do not obey the gospel of God? 18Now

"If the righteous one is scarcely saved,
    Where will the ungodly and the sinner appear?"

19Therefore let those who suffer according to the will of God commit their souls to Him in doing good, as to a faithful Creator.

Shepherd the Flock

5The elders who are among you I exhort, I who am a fellow elder and a witness of the sufferings of Christ, and also a partaker of the glory that will be revealed: 2Shepherd the flock of God which is among you, serving as overseers, not by compulsion but willingly, not for dishonest gain but eagerly; 3nor as being lords over those entrusted to you, but being examples to the flock; 4and when the Chief Shepherd appears, you will receive the crown of glory that does not fade away.

Submit to God, Resist the Devil

5Likewise you younger people, submit yourselves to your elders. Yes, all of you be submissive to one another, and be clothed with humility, for

"God resists the proud,
    But gives grace to the humble."

6Therefore humble yourselves under the mighty hand of God, that He may exalt you in due time, 7casting all your care upon Him, for He cares for you.

8Be sober, be vigilant; because your adversary the devil walks about like a roaring lion, seeking whom he may devour. 9Resist him, steadfast in the faith, knowing that the same sufferings are experienced by your brotherhood in the world. 10But may the God of all grace, who called us to His eternal glory by Christ Jesus, after you have suffered a while, perfect, establish, strengthen, and settle you. 11To Him be the glory and the dominion forever and ever. Amen.

Farewell and Peace

12By Silvanus, our faithful brother as I consider him, I have written to you briefly, exhorting and testifying that this is the true grace of God in which you stand.

13She who is in Babylon, elect together with you, greets you; and so does Mark my son. 14Greet one another with a kiss of love.

Peace to you all who are in Christ Jesus. Amen.

DEVOTIONAL

A woman with severe abdominal pain was taken to the hospital. An X-ray revealed something a cat could identify with—a giant hair ball made mostly of sock fibers. Why would someone eat socks? Her boyfriend said she routinely ate half an athletic sock at night to "relax."

While eating socks to calm down may not be that common, anxiety certainly is. Each day emergency rooms are visited by men and women who think they are having a heart attack or some other physical problem, and then they are diagnosed with an anxiety attack. Anxiety and worry are real problems for everyone, and the Enemy knows it.

Beware of the Adversary. He has many tools to discourage and devour. Worry is just one of them, but it is an effective weapon against us. However, our God is greater than our Enemy and our problems! He wants us to cast all of our anxieties on Him because He cares for us (1 Peter 5:7). His care for us is greater than our concern for ourselves.

Your problem may not be what you are eating, but what is eating you. Humble yourself under God's hand and ask Him for help. He gives grace to the humble, but He stiff-arms the proud. Remember that He cares for you, and put your trust in Him.

—Scott Yirka
Hibernia Baptist Church, Fleming Island, FL

WEEK 47, DAY 7

Give thanks for the prayers God has answered this week. What are you trusting God for now in prayer? Do you believe God is working even now?

_____

_____

_____

_____

_____

_____

_____

_____

_____

_____

_____

_____

_____

_____

Trials will come, and so will opportunities to share your faith through them. Who are ten people with whom you are praying you can share your faith? How can you begin the process of sharing your faith with them?

_____

_____

_____

_____

_____

_____

_____

_____

_____

_____

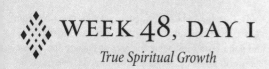

WEEK 48, DAY 1

True Spiritual Growth

2 Peter 1:1–21

Greeting the Faithful

1 Simon Peter, a bondservant and apostle of Jesus Christ,

To those who have obtained like precious faith with us by the righteousness of our God and Savior Jesus Christ:

²Grace and peace be multiplied to you in the knowledge of God and of Jesus our Lord, ³as His divine power has given to us all things that pertain to life and godliness, through the knowledge of Him who called us by glory and virtue, ⁴by which have been given to us exceedingly great and precious promises, that through these you may be partakers of the divine nature, having escaped the corruption that is in the world through lust.

Fruitful Growth in the Faith

⁵But also for this very reason, giving all diligence, add to your faith virtue, to virtue knowledge, ⁶to knowledge self-control, to self-control perseverance, to perseverance godliness, ⁷to godliness brotherly kindness, and to brotherly kindness love. ⁸For if these things are yours and abound, you will be neither barren nor unfruitful in the knowledge of our Lord Jesus Christ. ⁹For he who lacks these things is shortsighted, even to blindness, and has forgotten that he was cleansed from his old sins.

¹⁰Therefore, brethren, be even more diligent to make your call and election sure, for if you do these things you will never stumble; ¹¹for so an entrance will be supplied to you abundantly into the everlasting kingdom of our Lord and Savior Jesus Christ.

Peter's Approaching Death

¹²For this reason I will not be negligent to remind you always of these things, though you know and are established in the present truth. ¹³Yes, I think it is right, as long as I am in this tent, to stir you up by reminding you, ¹⁴knowing that shortly I must put off my tent, just as our Lord Jesus Christ showed me. ¹⁵Moreover I will be careful to ensure that you always have a reminder of these things after my decease.

The Trustworthy Prophetic Word

¹⁶For we did not follow cunningly devised fables when we made known to you the power and coming of our Lord Jesus Christ, but were eyewitnesses of His majesty. ¹⁷For He received from God the Father honor and glory when such a voice came to Him from the Excellent Glory: "This is My beloved Son, in whom I am well pleased." ¹⁸And we heard this voice which came from heaven when we were with Him on the holy mountain.

¹⁹And so we have the prophetic word confirmed, which you do well to heed as a light that shines in a dark place, until the day dawns and the morning star rises in your hearts; ²⁰knowing this first, that no prophecy of Scripture is of any private interpretation, ²¹for prophecy never came by the will of man, but holy men of God spoke as they were moved by the Holy Spirit.

DEVOTIONAL

When a person comes to faith in Christ, it is only the beginning. Conversion marks the start of spiritual life. Spiritual life, in turn, should mark the beginning of spiritual growth. As Paul said in 1 Corinthians 13:11: "When I was a child, I spoke as a child, I understood as a child, I thought as a child; but when I became a man, I put away childish things." We are to keep moving forward in our spiritual maturity.

For many, the concept of spiritual growth equates only to the acquisition of Christian knowledge. This misconception about growth leads people to believe that one's growth level is tantamount to how much they know. Growth and maturity are then tied to the number of verses memorized, books read, and Bible studies completed.

Peter's understanding of true spiritual growth was quite different and very simple; it was just becoming more like Jesus. Peter reminds us God has given us "all things that pertain to life and godliness" (2 Peter 1:3). To be precise, God has spared nothing as it relates to us progressively becoming more like Christ. What does that mean for us? It means we have no excuse for the absence of spiritual growth in our lives.

According to Peter, adding to your faith virtue, knowledge, self-control, perseverance, godliness, brotherly kindness, and love is an outline for growth (2 Peter 1:5–7). These qualities are characteristics that make us more like Jesus. This is real spiritual growth!

—Trevor Barton
Hawk Creek Church, London, KY

WEEK 48, DAY 2

God Condemns False Teachers

2 Peter 2:1–22

Destructive Doctrines

2 But there were also false prophets among the people, even as there will be false teachers among you, who will secretly bring in destructive heresies, even denying the Lord who bought them, and bring on themselves swift destruction. ²And many will follow their destructive ways, because of whom the way of truth will be blasphemed. ³By covetousness they will exploit you with deceptive words; for a long time their judgment has not been idle, and their destruction does not slumber.

Doom of False Teachers

⁴For if God did not spare the angels who sinned, but cast them down to hell and delivered them into chains of darkness, to be reserved for judgment; ⁵and did not spare the ancient world, but saved Noah, one of eight people, a preacher of righteousness, bringing in the flood on the world of the ungodly; ⁶and turning the cities of Sodom and Gomorrah into ashes, condemned them to destruction, making them an example to those who afterward would live ungodly; ⁷and delivered righteous Lot, who was oppressed by the filthy conduct of the wicked ⁸(for that righteous man, dwelling among them, tormented his righteous soul from day to day by seeing and hearing their lawless deeds)— ⁹then the Lord knows how to deliver the godly out of temptations and to reserve the unjust under punishment for the day of judgment, ¹⁰and especially those who walk according to the flesh in the lust of uncleanness and despise authority. They are presumptuous, self-willed. They are not afraid to speak evil of dignitaries, ¹¹whereas angels, who are greater in power and might, do not bring a reviling accusation against them before the Lord.

Depravity of False Teachers

¹²But these, like natural brute beasts made to be caught and destroyed, speak evil of the things they do not understand, and will utterly perish in their own corruption, ¹³and will receive the wages of unrighteousness, as those who count it pleasure to carouse in the daytime. They are spots and blemishes, carousing in their own deceptions while they feast with you, ¹⁴having eyes full of adultery and that cannot cease from sin, enticing unstable souls. They have a heart trained in covetous practices, and are accursed children. ¹⁵They have forsaken the right way and gone astray, following the way of Balaam the son of Beor, who loved the wages of unrighteousness; ¹⁶but he was rebuked for his iniquity: a dumb donkey speaking with a man's voice restrained the madness of the prophet.

¹⁷These are wells without water, clouds carried by a tempest, for whom is reserved the blackness of darkness forever.

Deceptions of False Teachers

¹⁸For when they speak great swelling words of emptiness, they allure through the lusts of the flesh, through lewdness, the ones who have actually escaped from those who live in error. ¹⁹While they promise them liberty, they themselves are slaves of corruption; for by whom a person is overcome, by him also he is brought into bondage. ²⁰For if, after they have escaped the pollutions of the world through the knowledge of the Lord and Savior Jesus Christ, they are again entangled in them and overcome, the latter end is worse for them than the beginning. ²¹For it would have been better for them not to have known the way of righteousness, than having known it, to turn from the holy commandment delivered to them. ²²But it has happened to them according to the true proverb: "A dog returns to his own vomit," and, "a sow, having washed, to her wallowing in the mire."

DEVOTIONAL

The existence of false teachers is not in doubt. Today, you can easily find someone willing to compromise the truth of God in order to draw a crowd. The same was true when Peter wrote this epistle, and he did not hold back when he wrote about them. These people are professional con artists. They lack self-control and a spine, and they would rather sell out than proclaim the truth of God. They prefer the immediate, but temporary, perks of money and popularity. Peter made a point of saying that they know the gospel about which they lie. Like any lie, it is not painted scarlet with a flashing sign.

False teachers' presence is certain, and many people will be enticed into following them. It is not a pretty picture, but God promises to dole out punishment on the unjust and to deliver His people from temptation. You can rest assured that with the firm foundation of God's unchanging Word and the guidance of the Holy Spirit, God will preserve His people to the end.

—Trevor Barton
Hawk Creek Church, London, KY

WEEK 48, DAY 3

Trust God's Promises

2 Peter 3:1–18

God's Promise Is Not Slack

3 Beloved, I now write to you this second epistle (in both of which I stir up your pure minds by way of reminder), ²that you may be mindful of the words which were spoken before by the holy prophets, and of the commandment of us, the apostles of the Lord and Savior, ³knowing this first: that scoffers will come in the last days, walking according to their own lusts, ⁴and saying, "Where is the promise of His coming? For since the fathers fell asleep, all things continue as they were from the beginning of creation." ⁵For this they willfully forget: that by the word of God the heavens were of old, and the earth standing out of water and in the water, ⁶by which the world that then existed perished, being flooded with water. ⁷But the heavens and the earth which are now preserved by the same word, are reserved for fire until the day of judgment and perdition of ungodly men.

⁸But, beloved, do not forget this one thing, that with the Lord one day is as a thousand years, and a thousand years as one day. ⁹The Lord is not slack concerning His promise, as some count slackness, but is longsuffering toward us, not willing that any should perish but that all should come to repentance.

The Day of the Lord

¹⁰But the day of the Lord will come as a thief in the night, in which the heavens will pass away with a great noise, and the elements will melt with fervent heat; both the earth and the works that are in it will be burned up. ¹¹Therefore, since all these things will be dissolved, what manner of persons ought you to be in holy conduct and godliness, ¹²looking for and hastening the coming of the day of God, because of which the heavens will be dissolved, being on fire, and the elements will melt with fervent heat? ¹³Nevertheless we, according to His promise, look for new heavens and a new earth in which righteousness dwells.

Be Steadfast

¹⁴Therefore, beloved, looking forward to these things, be diligent to be found by Him in peace, without spot and blameless; ¹⁵and consider that the longsuffering of our Lord is salvation—as also our beloved brother Paul, according to the wisdom given to him, has written to you, ¹⁶as also in all his epistles, speaking in them of these things, in which are some things hard to understand, which untaught and unstable people twist to their own destruction, as they do also the rest of the Scriptures.

¹⁷You therefore, beloved, since you know this beforehand, beware lest you also fall from your own steadfastness, being led away with the error of the wicked; ¹⁸but grow in the grace and knowledge of our Lord and Savior Jesus Christ.

To Him be the glory both now and forever. Amen.

DEVOTIONAL

*M*any of those who read Peter's letter in the first century were suffering fierce persecution. Some of them were in danger of being ostracized, imprisoned, or even put to death because of their faith. Living in a culture filled with such animosity toward Christianity understandably left some believers struggling with discouragement and disillusionment.

Seeking to prevent any further uncertainty, Peter warned believers that "scoffers will come in the last days, walking according to their own lusts, and saying, 'Where is the promise of His coming?'" (2 Peter 3:3–4). Peter knew false teachers would try to persuade discouraged believers that they were sacrificing and enduring persecution for nothing—that the hope of their calling was really a sham.

So with this in mind, Peter sought to encourage those Christians by reminding them of God's promise that Christ will one day return for His followers. Though there would be some who would dismiss this promise simply because of the apparent delay, Peter called for believers to stand strong in their faith concerning God's promise. While our Father is not bound by an earthly timetable we understand, He will never go back on His promise to return, for "the Lord is not slack concerning His promise" (2 Peter 3:8–9)!

According to Peter, the reality of Christ's future coming should motivate believers of all ages to live in a godly way and to have a joyful expectation for what is yet to come (2 Peter 3:14–15).

So even though two thousand years have passed, modern believers are to live in faith of this same promise. This faith should be so strong that it actually affects how we behave. To say it another way, our complete trust in God's promises for the future should result in present obedience. Do God's promises motivate your present behavior?

—Trevor Barton
Hawk Creek Church, London, KY

WEEK 48, DAY 4

Live in the Light

1 John 1:1–2:14

What Was Heard, Seen, and Touched

1 That which was from the beginning, which we have heard, which we have seen with our eyes, which we have looked upon, and our hands have handled, concerning the Word of life— 2the life was manifested, and we have seen, and bear witness, and declare to you that eternal life which was with the Father and was manifested to us— 3that which we have seen and heard we declare to you, that you also may have fellowship with us; and truly our fellowship is with the Father and with His Son Jesus Christ. 4And these things we write to you that your joy may be full.

Fellowship with Him and One Another

5This is the message which we have heard from Him and declare to you, that God is light and in Him is no darkness at all. 6If we say that we have fellowship with Him, and walk in darkness, we lie and do not practice the truth. 7But if we walk in the light as He is in the light, we have fellowship with one another, and the blood of Jesus Christ His Son cleanses us from all sin.

8If we say that we have no sin, we deceive ourselves, and the truth is not in us. 9If we confess our sins, He is faithful and just to forgive us our sins and to cleanse us from all unrighteousness. 10If we say that we have not sinned, we make Him a liar, and His word is not in us.

2 My little children, these things I write to you, so that you may not sin. And if anyone sins, we have an Advocate with the Father, Jesus Christ the righteous. 2And He Himself is the propitiation for our sins, and not for ours only but also for the whole world.

The Test of Knowing Him

3Now by this we know that we know Him, if we keep His commandments. 4He who says, "I know Him," and does not keep His commandments, is a liar, and the truth is not in him. 5But whoever keeps His word, truly the love of God is perfected in him. By this we know that we are in Him. 6He who says he abides in Him ought himself also to walk just as He walked.

7Brethren, I write no new commandment to you, but an old commandment which you have had from the beginning. The old commandment is the word which you heard from the beginning. 8Again, a new commandment I write to you, which thing is true in Him and in you, because the darkness is passing away, and the true light is already shining.

9He who says he is in the light, and hates his brother, is in darkness until now. 10He who loves his brother abides in the light, and there is no cause for stumbling in him. 11But he who hates his brother is in darkness and walks in darkness, and does not know where he is going, because the darkness has blinded his eyes.

Their Spiritual State

12 I write to you, little children,
  Because your sins are forgiven you for His
    name's sake.
13 I write to you, fathers,
  Because you have known Him who is from the
    beginning.
 I write to you, young men,
  Because you have overcome the wicked one.
 I write to you, little children,
  Because you have known the Father.
14 I have written to you, fathers,
  Because you have known Him who is from the
    beginning.
 I have written to you, young men,
  Because you are strong, and the word of God
    abides in you,
 And you have overcome the wicked one.

DEVOTIONAL

*J*ohn used the image of light throughout his writings to communicate multiple ideas: the coming of Jesus, the person of Jesus, the saving knowledge of Jesus, the redemption made possible by Jesus . . . all things Jesus. It is because of Jesus that our sins have been forgiven. It is by Jesus that we have been brought into a relationship with the eternal God of all creation. It is through Jesus that we can have victory over sin and death.

John called believers to walk in these truths. When we do, the world will see a people characterized by an audacious love for one another. It will see people who prize the Word of God and live obediently to the call of God. Live in the light of what Jesus has done, and you will reflect that light in a dark world.

—Trevor Barton
Hawk Creek Church, London, KY

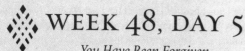

WEEK 48, DAY 5

You Have Been Forgiven

1 John 2:15–3:9

Do Not Love the World

Do not love the world or the things in the world. If anyone loves the world, the love of the Father is not in him. 16For all that is in the world—the lust of the flesh, the lust of the eyes, and the pride of life—is not of the Father but is of the world. 17And the world is passing away, and the lust of it; but he who does the will of God abides forever.

Deceptions of the Last Hour

18Little children, it is the last hour; and as you have heard that the Antichrist is coming, even now many antichrists have come, by which we know that it is the last hour. 19They went out from us, but they were not of us; for if they had been of us, they would have continued with us; but they went out that they might be made manifest, that none of them were of us.

20But you have an anointing from the Holy One, and you know all things. 21I have not written to you because you do not know the truth, but because you know it, and that no lie is of the truth.

22Who is a liar but he who denies that Jesus is the Christ? He is antichrist who denies the Father and the Son. 23Whoever denies the Son does not have the Father either; he who acknowledges the Son has the Father also.

Let Truth Abide in You

24Therefore let that abide in you which you heard from the beginning. If what you heard from the beginning abides in you, you also will abide in the Son and in the Father. 25And this is the promise that He has promised us—eternal life.

26These things I have written to you concerning those who try to deceive you. 27But the anointing which you have received from Him abides in you, and you do not need that anyone teach you; but as the same anointing teaches you concerning all things, and is true, and is not a lie, and just as it has taught you, you will abide in Him.

The Children of God

28And now, little children, abide in Him, that when He appears, we may have confidence and not be ashamed before Him at His coming. 29If you know that He is righteous, you know that everyone who practices righteousness is born of Him.

3 Behold what manner of love the Father has bestowed on us, that we should be called children of God! Therefore the world does not know us, because it did not know Him. 2Beloved, now we are children of God; and it has not yet been revealed what we shall be, but we know that when He is revealed, we shall be like Him, for we shall see Him as He is. 3And everyone who has this hope in Him purifies himself, just as He is pure.

Sin and the Child of God

4Whoever commits sin also commits lawlessness, and sin is lawlessness. 5And you know that He was manifested to take away our sins, and in Him there is no sin. 6Whoever abides in Him does not sin. Whoever sins has neither seen Him nor known Him.

7Little children, let no one deceive you. He who practices righteousness is righteous, just as He is righteous. 8He who sins is of the devil, for the devil has sinned from the beginning. For this purpose the Son of God was manifested, that He might destroy the works of the devil. 9Whoever has been born of God does not sin, for His seed remains in him; and he cannot sin, because he has been born of God.

DEVOTIONAL

Forgiveness is awesome! When God forgives us, He covers, forgets, and removes our sins from us. John reminds us that Christ came in order to "take away our sins" (1 John 3:5). His words echo John the Baptist, who said, "Behold! The Lamb of God who takes away the sin of the world!" (John 1:29). The Old Testament contains similar language in the book of Psalms: "As far as the east is from the west, so far has He removed our transgressions from us" (103:12).

The language of Scripture concerning forgiveness is powerful. The fact that God has forgiven us and taken away our sin is overwhelming. Think of it this way: every week your garbage is picked up outside your house; not once have they ever brought a piece of it back. They took it away! Forgiveness in Jesus is exactly the same. When He forgives us, He takes away the garbage of our lives, and He never brings it back. Thank Him for His amazing forgiveness today!

—Trevor Barton
Hawk Creek Church, London, KY

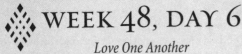

WEEK 48, DAY 6

Love One Another

1 John 3:10–4:16

The Imperative of Love

In this the children of God and the children of the devil are manifest: Whoever does not practice righteousness is not of God, nor is he who does not love his brother. 11For this is the message that you heard from the beginning, that we should love one another, 12not as Cain who was of the wicked one and murdered his brother. And why did he murder him? Because his works were evil and his brother's righteous.

13Do not marvel, my brethren, if the world hates you. 14We know that we have passed from death to life, because we love the brethren. He who does not love his brother abides in death. 15Whoever hates his brother is a murderer, and you know that no murderer has eternal life abiding in him.

The Outworking of Love

16By this we know love, because He laid down His life for us. And we also ought to lay down our lives for the brethren. 17But whoever has this world's goods, and sees his brother in need, and shuts up his heart from him, how does the love of God abide in him?

18My little children, let us not love in word or in tongue, but in deed and in truth. 19And by this we know that we are of the truth, and shall assure our hearts before Him. 20For if our heart condemns us, God is greater than our heart, and knows all things. 21Beloved, if our heart does not condemn us, we have confidence toward God. 22And whatever we ask we receive from Him, because we keep His commandments and do those things that are pleasing in His sight. 23And this is His commandment: that we should believe on the name of His Son Jesus Christ and love one another, as He gave us commandment.

The Spirit of Truth and the Spirit of Error

24Now he who keeps His commandments abides in Him, and He in him. And by this we know that He abides in us, by the Spirit whom He has given us.

4Beloved, do not believe every spirit, but test the spirits, whether they are of God; because many false prophets have gone out into the world. 2By this you know the Spirit of God: Every spirit that confesses that Jesus Christ has come in the flesh is of God, 3and every spirit that does not confess that Jesus Christ has come in the flesh is not of God. And this is the spirit of the Antichrist, which you have heard was coming, and is now already in the world.

4You are of God, little children, and have overcome them, because He who is in you is greater than he who is in the world. 5They are of the world. Therefore they speak as of the world, and the world hears them. 6We are of God. He who knows God hears us; he who is not of God does not hear us. By this we know the spirit of truth and the spirit of error.

Knowing God Through Love

7Beloved, let us love one another, for love is of God; and everyone who loves is born of God and knows God. 8He who does not love does not know God, for God is love. 9In this the love of God was manifested toward us, that God has sent His only begotten Son into the world, that we might live through Him. 10In this is love, not that we loved God, but that He loved us and sent His Son to be the propitiation for our sins. 11Beloved, if God so loved us, we also ought to love one another.

Seeing God Through Love

12No one has seen God at any time. If we love one another, God abides in us, and His love has been perfected in us. 13By this we know that we abide in Him, and He in us, because He has given us of His Spirit. 14And we have seen and testify that the Father has sent the Son as Savior of the world. 15Whoever confesses that Jesus is the Son of God, God abides in him, and he in God. 16And we have known and believed the love that God has for us. God is love, and he who abides in love abides in God, and God in him.

DEVOTIONAL

Love was a central theme of John's ministry. As an old man, he could undoubtedly be found sitting in the church, whispering to anyone who would listen, "My children, love one another." By "love" John was not referring to a warm handshake on Sunday morning. He was referring to a God kind of love that jumps out of heaven into a mortal body, hangs out with the marginal, teaches the stubborn, spares the annoying Pharisees (even though He would have been totally justified in destroying them), is beaten into a bloody mass, and hung on a tree. We can love like that only because God showed it to us first, and when we show God's love, those who are far from Him can see Him. How can you give extravagant love to others today?

—Trevor Barton
Hawk Creek Church, London, KY

WEEK 48, DAY 7

In times of persecution, what themes of Scripture do you find encouraging and helpful?

_____

_____

_____

_____

_____

_____

_____

_____

_____

_____

_____

_____

When you consider Christ's love in your life, how does it motivate and guide you in loving those around you?

_____

_____

_____

_____

_____

_____

_____

_____

_____

_____

WEEK 49, DAY 1

God Listens to Our Prayers

1 John 4:17–5:21

The Consummation of Love

Love has been perfected among us in this: that we may have boldness in the day of judgment; because as He is, so are we in this world. 18There is no fear in love; but perfect love casts out fear, because fear involves torment. But he who fears has not been made perfect in love. 19We love Him because He first loved us.

Obedience by Faith

20If someone says, "I love God," and hates his brother, he is a liar; for he who does not love his brother whom he has seen, how can he love God whom he has not seen? 21And this commandment we have from Him: that he who loves God must love his brother also.

5 Whoever believes that Jesus is the Christ is born of God, and everyone who loves Him who begot also loves him who is begotten of Him. 2By this we know that we love the children of God, when we love God and keep His commandments. 3For this is the love of God, that we keep His commandments. And His commandments are not burdensome. 4For whatever is born of God overcomes the world. And this is the victory that has overcome the world—our faith. 5Who is he who overcomes the world, but he who believes that Jesus is the Son of God?

The Certainty of God's Witness

6This is He who came by water and blood—Jesus Christ; not only by water, but by water and blood. And it is the Spirit who bears witness, because the Spirit is truth. 7For there are three that bear witness in heaven: the Father, the Word, and the Holy Spirit; and these three are one. 8And there are three that bear witness on earth: the Spirit, the water, and the blood; and these three agree as one. 9If we receive the witness of men, the witness of God is greater; for this is the witness of God which He has testified of His Son. 10He who believes in the Son of God has the witness in himself; he who does not believe God has made Him a liar, because he has not believed the testimony that God has given of His Son. 11And this is the testimony: that God has given us eternal life, and this life is in His Son. 12He who has the Son has life; he who does not have the Son of God does not have life. 13These things

I have written to you who believe in the name of the Son of God, that you may know that you have eternal life, and that you may continue to believe in the name of the Son of God.

Confidence and Compassion in Prayer

14Now this is the confidence that we have in Him, that if we ask anything according to His will, He hears us. 15And if we know that He hears us, whatever we ask, we know that we have the petitions that we have asked of Him.

16If anyone sees his brother sinning a sin which does not lead to death, he will ask, and He will give him life for those who commit sin not leading to death. There is sin leading to death. I do not say that he should pray about that. 17All unrighteousness is sin, and there is sin not leading to death.

Knowing the True—Rejecting the False

18We know that whoever is born of God does not sin; but he who has been born of God keeps himself, and the wicked one does not touch him.

19We know that we are of God, and the whole world lies under the sway of the wicked one.

20And we know that the Son of God has come and has given us an understanding, that we may know Him who is true; and we are in Him who is true, in His Son Jesus Christ. This is the true God and eternal life.

21Little children, keep yourselves from idols. Amen.

DEVOTIONAL

As a Christian you can boldly pray to God and be confident He will hear you when you pray according to His will (1 John 5:14). So how do you know God's will? You can know most of it by reading the Bible and listening to the Holy Spirit. In God's Word He has given you actions and attitudes to emulate. Take the commands and promises of God and pray them back to Him, and live your life according to them.

What about those particular situations in life that the Bible does not specifically address? With that same confidence, go to God in prayer with your requests and ask that His will be done. Acknowledge that you are sinful and limited in knowledge, and tell God you trust His sovereignty. Know that God hears your prayer, and whatever His answer is, it will be the best for you and will bring the most glory to God and His kingdom.

—Dr. Danny Wood
Shades Mountain Baptist Church, Birmingham, AL

WEEK 49, DAY 2

Live Your Faith

2 John 1–3 John 14

Greeting the Elect Lady

1 The Elder,

To the elect lady and her children, whom I love in truth, and not only I, but also all those who have known the truth, 2because of the truth which abides in us and will be with us forever:

3Grace, mercy, and peace will be with you from God the Father and from the Lord Jesus Christ, the Son of the Father, in truth and love.

Walk in Christ's Commandments

4I rejoiced greatly that I have found some of your children walking in truth, as we received commandment from the Father. 5And now I plead with you, lady, not as though I wrote a new commandment to you, but that which we have had from the beginning: that we love one another. 6This is love, that we walk according to His commandments. This is the commandment, that as you have heard from the beginning, you should walk in it.

Beware of Antichrist Deceivers

7For many deceivers have gone out into the world who do not confess Jesus Christ as coming in the flesh. This is a deceiver and an antichrist. 8Look to yourselves, that we do not lose those things we worked for, but that we may receive a full reward.

9Whoever transgresses and does not abide in the doctrine of Christ does not have God. He who abides in the doctrine of Christ has both the Father and the Son. 10If anyone comes to you and does not bring this doctrine, do not receive him into your house nor greet him; 11for he who greets him shares in his evil deeds.

John's Farewell Greeting

12Having many things to write to you, I did not wish to do so with paper and ink; but I hope to come to you and speak face to face, that our joy may be full.

13The children of your elect sister greet you. Amen.

Greeting to Gaius

1 The Elder,

To the beloved Gaius, whom I love in truth:

2Beloved, I pray that you may prosper in all things and be in health, just as your soul prospers. 3For I rejoiced greatly when brethren came and testified of the truth that is in you, just as you walk in the truth. 4I have no greater joy than to hear that my children walk in truth.

Gaius Commended for Generosity

5Beloved, you do faithfully whatever you do for the brethren and for strangers, 6who have borne witness of your love before the church. If you send them forward on their journey in a manner worthy of God, you will do well, 7because they went forth for His name's sake, taking nothing from the Gentiles. 8We therefore ought to receive such, that we may become fellow workers for the truth.

Diotrephes and Demetrius

9I wrote to the church, but Diotrephes, who loves to have the preeminence among them, does not receive us. 10Therefore, if I come, I will call to mind his deeds which he does, prating against us with malicious words. And not content with that, he himself does not receive the brethren, and forbids those who wish to, putting them out of the church.

11Beloved, do not imitate what is evil, but what is good. He who does good is of God, but he who does evil has not seen God.

12Demetrius has a good testimony from all, and from the truth itself. And we also bear witness, and you know that our testimony is true.

Farewell Greeting

13I had many things to write, but I do not wish to write to you with pen and ink; 14but I hope to see you shortly, and we shall speak face to face.

Peace to you. Our friends greet you. Greet the friends by name.

DEVOTIONAL

*T*raveling Christians who crossed paths with Gaius went back to their churches telling of his hospitality and faithfulness. His testimony spread and encouraged others. Like Gaius, stay committed to the Word, to living your faith, and to serving and encouraging others.

—Dr. Danny Wood
Shades Mountain Baptist Church, Birmingham, AL

WEEK 49, DAY 3

Contending for the Faith

Jude 1–13

Greeting to the Called

1 Jude, a bondservant of Jesus Christ, and brother of James,

To those who are called, sanctified by God the Father, and preserved in Jesus Christ:

2 Mercy, peace, and love be multiplied to you.

Contend for the Faith

3 Beloved, while I was very diligent to write to you concerning our common salvation, I found it necessary to write to you exhorting you to contend earnestly for the faith which was once for all delivered to the saints. 4 For certain men have crept in unnoticed, who long ago were marked out for this condemnation, ungodly men, who turn the grace of our God into lewdness and deny the only Lord God and our Lord Jesus Christ.

Old and New Apostates

5 But I want to remind you, though you once knew this, that the Lord, having saved the people out of the land of Egypt, afterward destroyed those who did not believe. 6 And the angels who did not keep their proper domain, but left their own abode, He has reserved in everlasting chains under darkness for the judgment of the great day; 7 as Sodom and Gomorrah, and the cities around them in a similar manner to these, having given themselves over to sexual immorality and gone after strange flesh, are set forth as an example, suffering the vengeance of eternal fire.

8 Likewise also these dreamers defile the flesh, reject authority, and speak evil of dignitaries. 9 Yet Michael the archangel, in contending with the devil, when he disputed about the body of Moses, dared not bring against him a reviling accusation, but said, "The Lord rebuke you!" 10 But these speak evil of whatever they do not know; and whatever they know naturally, like brute beasts, in these things they corrupt themselves. 11 Woe to them! For they have gone in the way of Cain, have run greedily in the error of Balaam for profit, and perished in the rebellion of Korah.

Apostates Depraved and Doomed

12 These are spots in your love feasts, while they feast with you without fear, serving only themselves. They are clouds without water, carried about by the winds; late autumn trees without fruit, twice dead, pulled up by the roots; 13 raging waves of the sea, foaming up their own shame; wandering stars for whom is reserved the blackness of darkness forever.

DEVOTIONAL

No matter which political party is in power to lead our country, we as Christians will continue to have to stand strong in our faith. We are in the midst of a clashing of worldviews and a steady degradation of society. During the time of Jude, people were experiencing an increase in sexual immorality, widespread rejection of authority, and an escalation of spiritual ignorance and arrogance. Sound familiar?

Jude challenged the believers to "contend earnestly for the faith which was once for all delivered to the saints" (Jude 3). As an athlete strenuously exerts his or her energies toward the goal, so the Christian is to actively and energetically compete for the faith. The word "faith" here describes the common body of Christian teaching. This includes the divinity of Jesus Christ, who lived a sinless life, died on the cross as the atoning sacrifice for our sins, and rose from the dead three days later to conquer sin and death. The faith also includes salvation by grace through faith, the indwelling of the Holy Spirit, and the holy lifestyle that flows from God's grace in Christ. These are the nonnegotiable fundamentals of the faith.

In today's society these fundamentals are being attacked and watered down through tolerance and political correctness. As a Christian you cannot contend and defend the faith if you do not understand and live the faith. Commit to reading and studying God's Word. Learn the essentials, and live out the expressions of the faith. Heed the words in 2 Corinthians 5:20: "We are ambassadors of Christ, as though God were pleading through us." May God use your life to be a serious contender for the faith!

—Dr. Danny Wood
Shades Mountain Baptist Church, Birmingham, AL

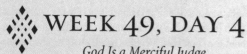

WEEK 49, DAY 4

God Is a Merciful Judge

Jude 14–25

Now Enoch, the seventh from Adam, prophesied about these men also, saying, "Behold, the Lord comes with ten thousands of His saints, [15]to execute judgment on all, to convict all who are ungodly among them of all their ungodly deeds which they have committed in an ungodly way, and of all the harsh things which ungodly sinners have spoken against Him."

Apostates Predicted

[16]These are grumblers, complainers, walking according to their own lusts; and they mouth great swelling words, flattering people to gain advantage. [17]But you, beloved, remember the words which were spoken before by the apostles of our Lord Jesus Christ: [18]how they told you that there would be mockers in the last time who would walk according to their own ungodly lusts. [19]These are sensual persons, who cause divisions, not having the Spirit.

Maintain Your Life with God

[20]But you, beloved, building yourselves up on your most holy faith, praying in the Holy Spirit, [21]keep yourselves in the love of God, looking for the mercy of our Lord Jesus Christ unto eternal life.

[22]And on some have compassion, making a distinction; [23]but others save with fear, pulling them out of the fire, hating even the garment defiled by the flesh.

Glory to God

[24] Now to Him who is able to keep you from stumbling,
And to present you faultless
Before the presence of His glory with exceeding joy,
[25] To God our Savior,
Who alone is wise,
Be glory and majesty,
Dominion and power,
Both now and forever.
Amen.

DEVOTIONAL

God is both a just judge and a merciful judge. Jude 15 affirms that no sinner will escape God's judgment—all will be judged, and all the ungodly will be convicted of all their ungodly deeds and actions. In just one verse, the word *all* is used four times to describe who and what God will judge. God has revealed His moral law, and because He is just, He must judge according to that law.

However, Jude 24 reminds us that God is a merciful judge. Those who believe in Jesus Christ will be saved and live forever. God is the One who is able to keep us as Christians from stumbling, and He will guard us so we can make it to the finish line. God is the only One who can present us to Himself as faultless and blameless at the final judgment.

Ephesians 2:4–5 says, "God, who is rich in mercy, because of His great love with which He loved us, even when we were dead in trespasses, made us alive together with Christ (by grace you have been saved)." The cross makes mercy available to us. As our forerunner and our sacrifice, Jesus has made it possible for us to stand before God without blemish, and thus be granted mercy at the judgment. Those who accept the grace gift of God now will receive God's mercy forever. Those who reject His grace gift now will be sentenced to eternal separation from God.

Divine mercy is not a temporary mood, but an attribute of God's eternal being. We can't say, "I hope God feels merciful today!" Nothing has occurred or will occur in heaven or on earth that will change the tender mercies of our God. His mercy stands forever and is available to you right now in your present situation.

The closing doxology of Jude is a picture of when we will stand in God's presence. We will see His holiness and perfection in contrast to the awfulness of our sins. We will recognize God's infinite wisdom and will fully realize the meaning of Jesus' work on the cross. We will comprehend God's mercy and lift up praises to Him for all eternity. Don't wait—wherever you are today, lift up your praises to our merciful Lord.

—Dr. Danny Wood
Shades Mountain Baptist Church, Birmingham, AL

WEEK 49, DAY 5

The First and the Last

Revelation 1:1–20

Introduction and Benediction

1 The Revelation of Jesus Christ, which God gave Him to show His servants—things which must shortly take place. And He sent and signified it by His angel to His servant John, ²who bore witness to the word of God, and to the testimony of Jesus Christ, to all things that he saw. ³Blessed is he who reads and those who hear the words of this prophecy, and keep those things which are written in it; for the time is near.

Greeting the Seven Churches

⁴John, to the seven churches which are in Asia:

Grace to you and peace from Him who is and who was and who is to come, and from the seven Spirits who are before His throne, ⁵and from Jesus Christ, the faithful witness, the firstborn from the dead, and the ruler over the kings of the earth.

To Him who loved us and washed us from our sins in His own blood, ⁶and has made us kings and priests to His God and Father, to Him be glory and dominion forever and ever. Amen.

⁷Behold, He is coming with clouds, and every eye will see Him, even they who pierced Him. And all the tribes of the earth will mourn because of Him. Even so, Amen.

⁸"I am the Alpha and the Omega, the Beginning and the End," says the Lord, "who is and who was and who is to come, the Almighty."

Vision of the Son of Man

⁹I, John, both your brother and companion in the tribulation and kingdom and patience of Jesus Christ, was on the island that is called Patmos for the word of God and for the testimony of Jesus Christ. ¹⁰I was in the Spirit on the Lord's Day, and I heard behind me a loud voice, as of a trumpet, ¹¹saying, "I am the Alpha and the Omega, the First and the Last," and, "What you see, write in a book and send it to the seven churches which are in Asia: to Ephesus, to Smyrna, to Pergamos, to Thyatira, to Sardis, to Philadelphia, and to Laodicea."

¹²Then I turned to see the voice that spoke with me. And having turned I saw seven golden lampstands, ¹³and in the midst of the seven lampstands One like the Son of Man, clothed with a garment down to the feet and girded about the chest with a golden band. ¹⁴His head and hair were white like wool, as white as snow, and His eyes like a flame of fire; ¹⁵His feet were like fine brass, as if refined in a furnace, and His voice as the sound of many waters; ¹⁶He had in His right hand seven stars, out of His mouth went a sharp two-edged sword, and His countenance was like the sun shining in its strength. ¹⁷And when I saw Him, I fell at His feet as dead. But He laid His right hand on me, saying to me, "Do not be afraid; I am the First and the Last. ¹⁸I am He who lives, and was dead, and behold, I am alive forevermore. Amen. And I have the keys of Hades and of Death. ¹⁹Write the things which you have seen, and the things which are, and the things which will take place after this. ²⁰The mystery of the seven stars which you saw in My right hand, and the seven golden lampstands: The seven stars are the angels of the seven churches, and the seven lampstands which you saw are the seven churches."

DEVOTIONAL

When Jesus referred to Himself in Revelation 1:11 as *"the Alpha and the Omega," He was saying He is the beginning and the end and everything in between. Jesus is Lord of all creation and all history. He created the world and sustains the world (Colossians 1:16–17).*

As "the First and the Last," Jesus has authority over life and death (Revelation 1:11). By dying on the cross and rising from the dead to live forevermore, Jesus was given the right to have the "keys of Hades and of Death" (v. 18).

Keys grant you access. Do you remember how excited you were when you got your first job and they gave you keys to the office? There might have been a time in your career when you were given a key that no one else had because you were the only one allowed access. Keys indicate authority, and Jesus was given the most important keys—the ones that give access to death and Hades, the realm of the dead. Jesus alone determines who will enter death and Hades, and who will come out of them.

The good news is that death does not have the last word—Jesus does! You belong to Him and He holds the keys, so you have nothing to fear in this life or in the life beyond.

—Dr. Danny Wood
Shades Mountain Baptist Church, Birmingham, AL

WEEK 49, DAY 6

Regain Your Love for Christ

Revelation 2:1–17

The Loveless Church

2 "To the angel of the church of Ephesus write,
'These things says He who holds the seven stars in His right hand, who walks in the midst of the seven golden lampstands: ²"I know your works, your labor, your patience, and that you cannot bear those who are evil. And you have tested those who say they are apostles and are not, and have found them liars; ³and you have persevered and have patience, and have labored for My name's sake and have not become weary. ⁴Nevertheless I have this against you, that you have left your first love. ⁵Remember therefore from where you have fallen; repent and do the first works, or else I will come to you quickly and remove your lampstand from its place—unless you repent. ⁶But this you have, that you hate the deeds of the Nicolaitans, which I also hate.

⁷"He who has an ear, let him hear what the Spirit says to the churches. To him who overcomes I will give to eat from the tree of life, which is in the midst of the Paradise of God." '

The Persecuted Church

⁸"And to the angel of the church in Smyrna write,
'These things says the First and the Last, who was dead, and came to life: ⁹"I know your works, tribulation, and poverty (but you are rich); and I know the blasphemy of those who say they are Jews and are not, but are a synagogue of Satan. ¹⁰Do not fear any of those things which you are about to suffer. Indeed, the devil is about to throw some of you into prison, that you may be tested, and you will have tribulation ten days. Be faithful until death, and I will give you the crown of life.

¹¹"He who has an ear, let him hear what the Spirit says to the churches. He who overcomes shall not be hurt by the second death." '

The Compromising Church

¹²"And to the angel of the church in Pergamos write,
'These things says He who has the sharp two-edged sword: ¹³"I know your works, and where you dwell, where Satan's throne is. And you hold fast to My name, and did not deny My faith even in the days in which Antipas was My faithful martyr, who was killed among you, where Satan dwells. ¹⁴But I have a few things against you, because you have there those who hold the doctrine of Balaam, who taught Balak to put a stumbling block before the children of Israel, to eat things sacrificed to idols, and to commit sexual immorality. ¹⁵Thus you also have those who hold the doctrine of the Nicolaitans, which thing I hate. ¹⁶Repent, or else I will come to you quickly and will fight against them with the sword of My mouth.

¹⁷"He who has an ear, let him hear what the Spirit says to the churches. To him who overcomes I will give some of the hidden manna to eat. And I will give him a white stone, and on the stone a new name written which no one knows except him who receives it." ' "

DEVOTIONAL

*S*ome of the greatest people to be around are newlyweds. They are so in love with each other and are wrapped up in the thrill of being married. Their love for each other is evident, and the way they fawn over each other is so sweet. Over time, however, other things will compete with the relationship. Less time and attention will be given to nurture the marriage. In some cases, where there was once closeness, there will be distance. Some will drift away from their first love.

The church at Ephesus was condemned for leaving her first love. "First love" could be both love for God and love for fellow believers. The word leaving means "to abandon; to leave behind; to go on to something else." It implies a process, even something almost imperceptible like erosion. Somehow this church that had labored for the Lord, persevered, and done good works in His name had over time lost her first love.

It is relatively easy for us to do the same and lose our love for God and for others. We can get so busy doing other things, even good things, that our loving devotion to God gets lost. Our sense of self-sufficiency grows, and our sense of needing God dwindles. We drift away from our first love.

But all hope is not lost! Jesus has told us how to regain our first love. Remember where you were to see how far you have fallen. Repent of your sinful attitude and conduct. Return to what you were doing at the beginning that nurtured your love for God and for others. Jesus wants you to return to Him!

—Dr. Danny Wood
Shades Mountain Baptist Church, Birmingham, AL

WEEK 49, DAY 7

In what arenas of your life do you have to contend for the faith? How are you preparing yourself to be an ambassador for Christ who contends for the faith?

_____

_____

_____

_____

_____

_____

_____

_____

_____

_____

Identify the time in your life when you were closest to God and in fellowship with other believers. If that is today, praise the Lord and continue growing in those relationships. If it was in the past, why are you not as close to God and to others as before? Repent of any sinful attitudes or conduct. Make a list of steps to take to move closer to your first love.

_____

_____

_____

_____

_____

_____

_____

_____

_____

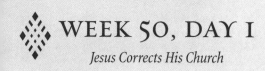

WEEK 50, DAY 1

Jesus Corrects His Church

Revelation 2:18–3:6

The Corrupt Church

"And to the angel of the church in Thyatira write, 'These things says the Son of God, who has eyes like a flame of fire, and His feet like fine brass: 19"I know your works, love, service, faith, and your patience; and as for your works, the last are more than the first. 20Nevertheless I have a few things against you, because you allow that woman Jezebel, who calls herself a prophetess, to teach and seduce My servants to commit sexual immorality and eat things sacrificed to idols. 21And I gave her time to repent of her sexual immorality, and she did not repent. 22Indeed I will cast her into a sickbed, and those who commit adultery with her into great tribulation, unless they repent of their deeds. 23I will kill her children with death, and all the churches shall know that I am He who searches the minds and hearts. And I will give to each one of you according to your works.

24"Now to you I say, and to the rest in Thyatira, as many as do not have this doctrine, who have not known the depths of Satan, as they say, I will put on you no other burden. 25But hold fast what you have till I come. 26And he who overcomes, and keeps My works until the end, to him I will give power over the nations—

27   'He shall rule them with a rod of iron;
      They shall be dashed to pieces like the potter's
         vessels'—

as I also have received from My Father; 28and I will give him the morning star.

29"He who has an ear, let him hear what the Spirit says to the churches.'"

The Dead Church

3 "And to the angel of the church in Sardis write, 'These things says He who has the seven Spirits of God and the seven stars: "I know your works, that you have a name that you are alive, but you are dead. 2"Be watchful, and strengthen the things which remain, that are ready to die, for I have not found your works perfect before God. 3Remember therefore how you have received and heard; hold fast and repent. Therefore if you will not watch, I will come upon you as a thief, and you will not know what hour I will come upon you. 4You have a few names even in Sardis who have not defiled their garments; and they shall walk with Me in white, for they are worthy. 5He who overcomes shall be clothed in white garments, and I will not blot out his name from the Book of Life; but I will confess his name before My Father and before His angels.

6"He who has an ear, let him hear what the Spirit says to the churches."'"

DEVOTIONAL

A pair of boys played in a huge backyard, running wild. With no adult supervision, their playfulness turned into mischief, and their mischief turned into foolishness and wrongdoing. Even with adult supervision—and plenty of rules—the boys kept pushing the limits, and eventually the adults strongly rebuked and disciplined them. The boys had earned it and needed it. Even though it felt harsh at the time, it helped them learn what was right and helped them grow to become better men because of it. Those adults who corrected the boys in firmness and love saved the day.

In this passage, Jesus corrected a corrupt church in Thyatira. He reminded them of His holy standards and that He expected them to be holy. He told them not to tolerate the false teachings and sinful behavior within their church. Jesus gave a harsh rebuke to Jezebel, who had a sinful lifestyle and was unrepentant, and to those under her influence. He told those who were not involved in the corruption to hold fast to what they had in Him, not to allow sin to remain in their lives, and to remain faithful.

In our first example, the adults who disciplined the young boys were aware of the boys' bad behavior before they stepped in. How much more does our heavenly Father see? He knows our every move, every thought, and every motive, and today, Jesus is calling His followers to turn away from sin and pursue holiness. Jesus "searches the minds and hearts" of His followers, and He will deal with each of us accordingly (Revelation 2:23). He wants to help us mature, walk in righteousness, and become more and more like Him. Invite His help today. Depend on His guidance, and hold firm to His life-giving principles for godliness.

—Chuck Allen
Sugar Hill Church, Sugar Hill, GA

WEEK 50, DAY 2

All In or Not In at All

Revelation 3:7–4:5

The Faithful Church

"And to the angel of the church in Philadelphia write, 'These things says He who is holy, He who is true, "He who has the key of David, He who opens and no one shuts, and shuts and no one opens": 8"I know your works. See, I have set before you an open door, and no one can shut it; for you have a little strength, have kept My word, and have not denied My name. 9Indeed I will make those of the synagogue of Satan, who say they are Jews and are not, but lie—indeed I will make them come and worship before your feet, and to know that I have loved you. 10Because you have kept My command to persevere, I also will keep you from the hour of trial which shall come upon the whole world, to test those who dwell on the earth. 11Behold, I am coming quickly! Hold fast what you have, that no one may take your crown. 12He who overcomes, I will make him a pillar in the temple of My God, and he shall go out no more. I will write on him the name of My God and the name of the city of My God, the New Jerusalem, which comes down out of heaven from My God. And I will write on him My new name.

13"He who has an ear, let him hear what the Spirit says to the churches."'

The Lukewarm Church

14"And to the angel of the church of the Laodiceans write,

'These things says the Amen, the Faithful and True Witness, the Beginning of the creation of God: 15"I know your works, that you are neither cold nor hot. I could wish you were cold or hot. 16So then, because you are lukewarm, and neither cold nor hot, I will vomit you out of My mouth. 17Because you say, 'I am rich, have become wealthy, and have need of nothing'—and do not know that you are wretched, miserable, poor, blind, and naked— 18I counsel you to buy from Me gold refined in the fire, that you may be rich; and white garments, that you may be clothed, that the shame of your nakedness may not be revealed; and anoint your eyes with eye salve, that you may see. 19As many as I love, I rebuke and chasten. Therefore be zealous and repent. 20Behold, I stand at the door and knock. If anyone hears My voice and opens the door, I will come in to him and dine with him, and he with Me. 21To him who overcomes I will grant to sit with Me on My throne, as I also overcame and sat down with My Father on His throne.

22"He who has an ear, let him hear what the Spirit says to the churches."'"

The Throne Room of Heaven

4After these things I looked, and behold, a door standing open in heaven. And the first voice which I heard was like a trumpet speaking with me, saying, "Come up here, and I will show you things which must take place after this."

2Immediately I was in the Spirit; and behold, a throne set in heaven, and One sat on the throne. 3And He who sat there was like a jasper and a sardius stone in appearance; and there was a rainbow around the throne, in appearance like an emerald. 4Around the throne were twenty-four thrones, and on the thrones I saw twenty-four elders sitting, clothed in white robes; and they had crowns of gold on their heads. 5And from the throne proceeded lightnings, thunderings, and voices. Seven lamps of fire were burning before the throne, which are the seven Spirits of God.

DEVOTIONAL

It is dangerous to make decisions based on pleasing people. When we please the person in front of us and then change directions to please the next person we encounter, we're not living according to moral convictions. We're choosing what's easy in the moment rather than being fully committed to righteousness.

Jesus' message to the Laodiceans, and to us today, is clear: make certain you are all in or not in at all (Revelation 3:16). The most dangerous position you can be in is half in and half out. When Jesus knocks on your door, He's not looking for help; He's offering help. He is offering eternity, peace, joy, hope, and love for today and forever. Our passage today assures us He is our strength, our hope, and our security.

Jesus calls us to embrace what He offers with all that we are. He calls us to die to ourselves and follow Him. As you journey through your day, be mindful that He longs for you to move away from lukewarmness and into the heat of His love. Switch your focus from your problems to His presence. Honor Him as Lord by keeping His commands and walking in the Spirit. Stop striving in your strength and watch to see what He will do in you and through you.

—Chuck Allen
Sugar Hill Church, Sugar Hill, GA

WEEK 50, DAY 3

Heaven'ly Worship

Revelation 4:6–6:2

Before the throne there was a sea of glass, like crystal. And in the midst of the throne, and around the throne, were four living creatures full of eyes in front and in back. 7The first living creature was like a lion, the second living creature like a calf, the third living creature had a face like a man, and the fourth living creature was like a flying eagle. 8The four living creatures, each having six wings, were full of eyes around and within. And they do not rest day or night, saying:

> "Holy, holy, holy,
> Lord God Almighty,
> Who was and is and is to come!"

9Whenever the living creatures give glory and honor and thanks to Him who sits on the throne, who lives forever and ever, 10the twenty-four elders fall down before Him who sits on the throne and worship Him who lives forever and ever, and cast their crowns before the throne, saying:

11 "You are worthy, O Lord,
> To receive glory and honor and power;
> For You created all things,
> And by Your will they exist and were created."

The Lamb Takes the Scroll

And I saw in the right hand of Him who sat on the throne a scroll written inside and on the back, sealed with seven seals. 2Then I saw a strong angel proclaiming with a loud voice, "Who is worthy to open the scroll and to loose its seals?" 3And no one in heaven or on the earth or under the earth was able to open the scroll, or to look at it.

4So I wept much, because no one was found worthy to open and read the scroll, or to look at it. 5But one of the elders said to me, "Do not weep. Behold, the Lion of the tribe of Judah, the Root of David, has prevailed to open the scroll and to loose its seven seals."

6And I looked, and behold, in the midst of the throne and of the four living creatures, and in the midst of the elders, stood a Lamb as though it had been slain, having seven horns and seven eyes, which are the seven Spirits of God sent out into all the earth. 7Then He came and took the scroll out of the right hand of Him who sat on the throne.

Worthy Is the Lamb

8Now when He had taken the scroll, the four living creatures and the twenty-four elders fell down before the Lamb, each having a harp, and golden bowls full of incense, which are the prayers of the saints. 9And they sang a new song, saying:

> "You are worthy to take the scroll,
> And to open its seals;
> For You were slain,
> And have redeemed us to God by Your blood
> Out of every tribe and tongue and people and nation,
10 > And have made us kings and priests to our God;
> And we shall reign on the earth."

11Then I looked, and I heard the voice of many angels around the throne, the living creatures, and the elders; and the number of them was ten thousand times ten thousand, and thousands of thousands, 12saying with a loud voice:

> "Worthy is the Lamb who was slain
> To receive power and riches and wisdom,
> And strength and honor and glory and blessing!"

13And every creature which is in heaven and on the earth and under the earth and such as are in the sea, and all that are in them, I heard saying:

> "Blessing and honor and glory and power
> Be to Him who sits on the throne,
> And to the Lamb, forever and ever!"

14Then the four living creatures said, "Amen!" And the twenty-four elders fell down and worshiped Him who lives forever and ever.

First Seal: The Conqueror

Now I saw when the Lamb opened one of the seals; and I heard one of the four living creatures saying with a voice like thunder, "Come and see." 2And I looked, and behold, a white horse. He who sat on it had a bow; and a crown was given to him, and he went out conquering and to conquer.

DEVOTIONAL

In a four-year span of his life, a Christian man buried his wife, father, and mother. As he left each graveside service, he grieved, yet he was full of joy for them. He knew they were in Glory. With all of heaven, they were praising God! May all the faithful live with hearts that cry, "Come, Lord Jesus!"

—Chuck Allen
Sugar Hill Church, Sugar Hill, GA

WEEK 50, DAY 4

A Glimpse into Eternity

Revelation 6:3–7:8

Second Seal: Conflict on Earth

When He opened the second seal, I heard the second living creature saying, "Come and see." 4Another horse, fiery red, went out. And it was granted to the one who sat on it to take peace from the earth, and that people should kill one another; and there was given to him a great sword.

Third Seal: Scarcity on Earth

5When He opened the third seal, I heard the third living creature say, "Come and see." So I looked, and behold, a black horse, and he who sat on it had a pair of scales in his hand. 6And I heard a voice in the midst of the four living creatures saying, "A quart of wheat for a denarius, and three quarts of barley for a denarius; and do not harm the oil and the wine."

Fourth Seal: Widespread Death on Earth

7When He opened the fourth seal, I heard the voice of the fourth living creature saying, "Come and see." 8So I looked, and behold, a pale horse. And the name of him who sat on it was Death, and Hades followed with him. And power was given to them over a fourth of the earth, to kill with sword, with hunger, with death, and by the beasts of the earth.

Fifth Seal: The Cry of the Martyrs

9When He opened the fifth seal, I saw under the altar the souls of those who had been slain for the word of God and for the testimony which they held. 10And they cried with a loud voice, saying, "How long, O Lord, holy and true, until You judge and avenge our blood on those who dwell on the earth?" 11Then a white robe was given to each of them; and it was said to them that they should rest a little while longer, until both the number of their fellow servants and their brethren, who would be killed as they were, was completed.

Sixth Seal: Cosmic Disturbances

12I looked when He opened the sixth seal, and behold, there was a great earthquake; and the sun became black as sackcloth of hair, and the moon became like blood. 13And the stars of heaven fell to the earth, as a fig tree drops its late figs when it is shaken by a mighty wind. 14Then the sky receded as a scroll when it is rolled up, and every mountain and island was moved out of its place. 15And the kings of the earth, the great men, the rich men, the commanders, the mighty men, every slave and every free man, hid themselves in the caves and in the rocks of the mountains, 16and said to the mountains and rocks, "Fall on us and hide us from the face of Him who sits on the throne and from the wrath of the Lamb! 17For the great day of His wrath has come, and who is able to stand?"

The Sealed of Israel

7After these things I saw four angels standing at the four corners of the earth, holding the four winds of the earth, that the wind should not blow on the earth, on the sea, or on any tree.

2Then I saw another angel ascending from the east, having the seal of the living God. And he cried with a loud voice to the four angels to whom it was granted to harm the earth and the sea,

3saying, "Do not harm the earth, the sea, or the trees till we have sealed the servants of our God on their foreheads." 4And I heard the number of those who were sealed. One hundred and forty-four thousand of all the tribes of the children of Israel were sealed:

5   of the tribe of Judah twelve thousand were sealed;
of the tribe of Reuben twelve thousand were sealed;
of the tribe of Gad twelve thousand were sealed;
6   of the tribe of Asher twelve thousand were sealed;
of the tribe of Naphtali twelve thousand were sealed;
of the tribe of Manasseh twelve thousand were sealed;
7   of the tribe of Simeon twelve thousand were sealed;
of the tribe of Levi twelve thousand were sealed;
of the tribe of Issachar twelve thousand were sealed;
8   of the tribe of Zebulun twelve thousand were sealed;
of the tribe of Joseph twelve thousand were sealed;
of the tribe of Benjamin twelve thousand were sealed.

DEVOTIONAL

As you read God's Word, you never have to wonder how this world will end. Today's passage gives you a glimpse into eternity. Go about your day with an urgency to live, love, and lead like a person who is secure in the knowledge of how this life ends and in the beauty of eternity. Give thanks that in Jesus, you are sealed in the covenant of His grace.

—Chuck Allen
Sugar Hill Church, Sugar Hill, GA

WEEK 50, DAY 5

The Almighty God Is on the Throne

Revelation 7:9–8:13

A Multitude from the Great Tribulation

After these things I looked, and behold, a great multitude which no one could number, of all nations, tribes, peoples, and tongues, standing before the throne and before the Lamb, clothed with white robes, with palm branches in their hands, 10and crying out with a loud voice, saying, "Salvation belongs to our God who sits on the throne, and to the Lamb!" 11All the angels stood around the throne and the elders and the four living creatures, and fell on their faces before the throne and worshiped God, 12saying:

"Amen! Blessing and glory and wisdom,
Thanksgiving and honor and power and might,
Be to our God forever and ever.
Amen."

13Then one of the elders answered, saying to me, "Who are these arrayed in white robes, and where did they come from?"

14And I said to him, "Sir, you know."

So he said to me, "These are the ones who come out of the great tribulation, and washed their robes and made them white in the blood of the Lamb. 15Therefore they are before the throne of God, and serve Him day and night in His temple. And He who sits on the throne will dwell among them. 16They shall neither hunger anymore nor thirst anymore; the sun shall not strike them, nor any heat; 17for the Lamb who is in the midst of the throne will shepherd them and lead them to living fountains of waters. And God will wipe away every tear from their eyes."

Seventh Seal: Prelude to the Seven Trumpets

8 When He opened the seventh seal, there was silence in heaven for about half an hour. 2And I saw the seven angels who stand before God, and to them were given seven trumpets. 3Then another angel, having a golden censer, came and stood at the altar. He was given much incense, that he should offer it with the prayers of all the saints upon the golden altar which was before the throne. 4And the smoke of the incense, with the prayers of the saints, ascended before God from the angel's hand. 5Then the angel took the censer, filled it with fire from the altar, and threw it to the earth. And there were noises, thunderings, lightnings, and an earthquake.

6So the seven angels who had the seven trumpets prepared themselves to sound.

First Trumpet: Vegetation Struck

7The first angel sounded: And hail and fire followed, mingled with blood, and they were thrown to the earth. And a third of the trees were burned up, and all green grass was burned up.

Second Trumpet: The Seas Struck

8Then the second angel sounded: And something like a great mountain burning with fire was thrown into the sea, and a third of the sea became blood. 9And a third of the living creatures in the sea died, and a third of the ships were destroyed.

Third Trumpet: The Waters Struck

10Then the third angel sounded: And a great star fell from heaven, burning like a torch, and it fell on a third of the rivers and on the springs of water. 11The name of the star is Wormwood. A third of the waters became wormwood, and many men died from the water, because it was made bitter.

Fourth Trumpet: The Heavens Struck

12Then the fourth angel sounded: And a third of the sun was struck, a third of the moon, and a third of the stars, so that a third of them were darkened. A third of the day did not shine, and likewise the night.

13And I looked, and I heard an angel flying through the midst of heaven, saying with a loud voice, "Woe, woe, woe to the inhabitants of the earth, because of the remaining blasts of the trumpet of the three angels who are about to sound!"

DEVOTIONAL

When kids play together, one might tell another, "You're not the boss of me!" Most of us don't like having a boss. But Revelation 7:9–12 depicts God on His throne in heaven, surrounded by worshipers saying that glory, wisdom, honor, and power are His forever. That puts an absolute end to all silly arguments and self-made desires. God plots our direction. Our job is to stay on the proper route planned in all that wisdom, power, and might. Today, stay on His coordinates for your life and serve Him. Be grateful He really is the Boss of your life!

—Chuck Allen
Sugar Hill Church, Sugar Hill, GA

WEEK 50, DAY 6

God Promises a Bright Future

Revelation 9:1–10:4

Fifth Trumpet: The Locusts from the Bottomless Pit

9 Then the fifth angel sounded: And I saw a star fallen from heaven to the earth. To him was given the key to the bottomless pit. ²And he opened the bottomless pit, and smoke arose out of the pit like the smoke of a great furnace. So the sun and the air were darkened because of the smoke of the pit. ³Then out of the smoke locusts came upon the earth. And to them was given power, as the scorpions of the earth have power. ⁴They were commanded not to harm the grass of the earth, or any green thing, or any tree, but only those men who do not have the seal of God on their foreheads. ⁵And they were not given authority to kill them, but to torment them for five months. Their torment was like the torment of a scorpion when it strikes a man. ⁶In those days men will seek death and will not find it; they will desire to die, and death will flee from them.

⁷The shape of the locusts was like horses prepared for battle. On their heads were crowns of something like gold, and their faces were like the faces of men. ⁸They had hair like women's hair, and their teeth were like lions' teeth. ⁹And they had breastplates like breastplates of iron, and the sound of their wings was like the sound of chariots with many horses running into battle. ¹⁰They had tails like scorpions, and there were stings in their tails. Their power was to hurt men five months. ¹¹And they had as king over them the angel of the bottomless pit, whose name in Hebrew is Abaddon, but in Greek he has the name Apollyon.

¹²One woe is past. Behold, still two more woes are coming after these things.

Sixth Trumpet: The Angels from the Euphrates

¹³Then the sixth angel sounded: And I heard a voice from the four horns of the golden altar which is before God, ¹⁴saying to the sixth angel who had the trumpet, "Release the four angels who are bound at the great river Euphrates." ¹⁵So the four angels, who had been prepared for the hour and day and month and year, were released to kill a third of mankind. ¹⁶Now the number of the army of the horsemen was two hundred million; I heard the number of them. ¹⁷And thus I saw the horses in the vision: those who sat on them had breastplates of fiery red, hyacinth blue, and sulfur yellow; and the heads of the horses were like the heads of lions; and out of their mouths came fire, smoke, and brimstone. ¹⁸By these three plagues a third of mankind was killed—by the fire and the smoke and the brimstone which came out of their mouths. ¹⁹For their power is in their mouth and in their tails; for their tails are like serpents, having heads; and with them they do harm.

²⁰But the rest of mankind, who were not killed by these plagues, did not repent of the works of their hands, that they should not worship demons, and idols of gold, silver, brass, stone, and wood, which can neither see nor hear nor walk. ²¹And they did not repent of their murders or their sorceries or their sexual immorality or their thefts.

The Mighty Angel with the Little Book

10 I saw still another mighty angel coming down from heaven, clothed with a cloud. And a rainbow was on his head, his face was like the sun, and his feet like pillars of fire. ²He had a little book open in his hand. And he set his right foot on the sea and his left foot on the land, ³and cried with a loud voice, as when a lion roars. When he cried out, seven thunders uttered their voices. ⁴Now when the seven thunders uttered their voices, I was about to write; but I heard a voice from heaven saying to me, "Seal up the things which the seven thunders uttered, and do not write them."

DEVOTIONAL

I *f you read half of a novel and then decide you're no longer interested in reading the rest of it, you may miss the very best part of the book. The ending could be amazing!*

Revelation tells us how things will end, and it will indeed be amazing. We should praise God for blessing us with a glimpse of what is to come and also remember that we still have no idea just how beautiful and majestic it will be. His ways are higher than our ways (Isaiah 55:8–9), and He has promised a future that is better than anything we could ever imagine. We simply cannot comprehend all of His glory or His promises.

Set your focus on Him today. When He is central in your mind, you will be able to view the world through the eternal perspective of His glory and promises. Rejoice in what He is doing in you and through you!

—Chuck Allen
Sugar Hill Church, Sugar Hill, GA

WEEK 50, DAY 7

Despite our culture's performance-based ideologies and self-made success stories, God calls us to abandon self-made goals and let Him have the reigns. If blessing, glory, wisdom, honor, and might are all in God, what hinders you from surrendering to Him?

_____

_____

_____

_____

_____

_____

_____

_____

_____

_____

_____

In what areas of your life might you need some course correction, as the churches in Revelation 2–3 did? List what you will surrender to God, describe how it will change the way you live, and then watch how He will work all things together for good (Romans 8:28).

_____

_____

_____

_____

_____

_____

_____

_____

WEEK 51, DAY I

Empowered to Deliver His Message

Revelation 10:5–11:14

The angel whom I saw standing on the sea and on the land raised up his hand to heaven 6and swore by Him who lives forever and ever, who created heaven and the things that are in it, the earth and the things that are in it, and the sea and the things that are in it, that there should be delay no longer, 7but in the days of the sounding of the seventh angel, when he is about to sound, the mystery of God would be finished, as He declared to His servants the prophets.

John Eats the Little Book

8Then the voice which I heard from heaven spoke to me again and said, "Go, take the little book which is open in the hand of the angel who stands on the sea and on the earth."

9So I went to the angel and said to him, "Give me the little book." And he said to me, "Take and eat it; and it will make your stomach bitter, but it will be as sweet as honey in your mouth."

10Then I took the little book out of the angel's hand and ate it, and it was as sweet as honey in my mouth. But when I had eaten it, my stomach became bitter. 11And he said to me, "You must prophesy again about many peoples, nations, tongues, and kings."

The Two Witnesses

11 Then I was given a reed like a measuring rod. And the angel stood, saying, "Rise and measure the temple of God, the altar, and those who worship there. 2But leave out the court which is outside the temple, and do not measure it, for it has been given to the Gentiles. And they will tread the holy city underfoot for forty-two months. 3And I will give power to my two witnesses, and they will prophesy one thousand two hundred and sixty days, clothed in sackcloth."

4These are the two olive trees and the two lampstands standing before the God of the earth. 5And if anyone wants to harm them, fire proceeds from their mouth and devours their enemies. And if anyone wants to harm them, he must be killed in this manner. 6These have power to shut heaven, so that no rain falls in the days of their prophecy; and they have power over waters to turn them to blood, and to strike the earth with all plagues, as often as they desire.

The Witnesses Killed

7When they finish their testimony, the beast that ascends out of the bottomless pit will make war against them, overcome them, and kill them. 8And their dead bodies will lie in the street of the great city which spiritually is called Sodom and Egypt, where also our Lord was crucified. 9Then those from the peoples, tribes, tongues, and nations will see their dead bodies three-and-a-half days, and not allow their dead bodies to be put into graves. 10And those who dwell on the earth will rejoice over them, make merry, and send gifts to one another, because these two prophets tormented those who dwell on the earth.

The Witnesses Resurrected

11Now after the three-and-a-half days the breath of life from God entered them, and they stood on their feet, and great fear fell on those who saw them. 12And they heard a loud voice from heaven saying to them, "Come up here." And they ascended to heaven in a cloud, and their enemies saw them. 13In the same hour there was a great earthquake, and a tenth of the city fell. In the earthquake seven thousand people were killed, and the rest were afraid and gave glory to the God of heaven.

14The second woe is past. Behold, the third woe is coming quickly.

DEVOTIONAL

It is the responsibility of a witness to confirm the details of a matter. Maybe you witnessed a baseball going over the fence, or you saw one automobile swipe another in a parking garage. Whatever the case, witnesses verify the truth.

It is difficult to identify the two witnesses in Revelation 11 with certainty. Our thoughts turn to Elijah and Moses with the mention of drought (1 Kings 17:1) and water turning to blood (Exodus 7:19). Furthermore, this seems possible because Jesus conversed with Moses and Elijah at the Mount of Transfiguration (Matthew 17:3). Moses represents God's Law, and Elijah represents God's Prophets. Together they witness to the greatest need in the world: humanity is hopeless without Christ (Luke 24:27).

Armed with the gospel, the church is called to be God's witness as well. Witnesses tell the truth, the whole truth, and nothing but the truth. They do not add to the story, and they do not subtract from the story. Pray that God would make us His witnesses, both in life and death!

—Jeremy Morton
Cross Point Baptist Church, Perry, GA

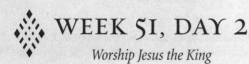

WEEK 51, DAY 2

Worship Jesus the King

Revelation 11:15–12:12

Seventh Trumpet: The Kingdom Proclaimed

Then the seventh angel sounded: And there were loud voices in heaven, saying, "The kingdoms of this world have become the kingdoms of our Lord and of His Christ, and He shall reign forever and ever!" ¹⁶And the twenty-four elders who sat before God on their thrones fell on their faces and worshiped God, ¹⁷saying:

"We give You thanks, O Lord God Almighty,
The One who is and who was and who is to come,
Because You have taken Your great power and
    reigned.
18   The nations were angry, and Your wrath has come,
And the time of the dead, that they should be judged,
And that You should reward Your servants the
        prophets and the saints,
And those who fear Your name, small and great,
And should destroy those who destroy the earth."

¹⁹Then the temple of God was opened in heaven, and the ark of His covenant was seen in His temple. And there were lightnings, noises, thunderings, an earthquake, and great hail.

The Woman, the Child, and the Dragon

12 Now a great sign appeared in heaven: a woman clothed with the sun, with the moon under her feet, and on her head a garland of twelve stars. ²Then being with child, she cried out in labor and in pain to give birth. ³And another sign appeared in heaven: behold, a great, fiery red dragon having seven heads and ten horns, and seven diadems on his heads. ⁴His tail drew a third of the stars of heaven and threw them to the earth. And the dragon stood before the woman who was ready to give birth, to devour her Child as soon as it was born. ⁵She bore a male Child who was to rule all nations with a rod of iron. And her Child was caught up to God and His throne. ⁶Then the woman fled into the wilderness, where she has a place prepared by God, that they should feed her there one thousand two hundred and sixty days.

Satan Thrown Out of Heaven

⁷And war broke out in heaven: Michael and his angels fought with the dragon; and the dragon and his angels fought, ⁸but they did not prevail, nor was a place found for them in heaven any longer. ⁹So the great dragon was cast out, that serpent of old, called the Devil and Satan, who deceives the whole world; he was cast to the earth, and his angels were cast out with him.

¹⁰Then I heard a loud voice saying in heaven, "Now salvation, and strength, and the kingdom of our God, and the power of His Christ have come, for the accuser of our brethren, who accused them before our God day and night, has been cast down. ¹¹And they overcame him by the blood of the Lamb and by the word of their testimony, and they did not love their lives to the death. ¹²Therefore rejoice, O heavens, and you who dwell in them! Woe to the inhabitants of the earth and the sea! For the devil has come down to you, having great wrath, because he knows that he has a short time."

DEVOTIONAL

There is an obvious tension in the New Testament concerning the current state of God's kingdom. On the one hand, Scripture affirms Jesus is King of the ages (1 Timothy 1:17). Even at His birth in Bethlehem, the wise men recognized Jesus as King of the Jews (Matthew 2:2). However, on the other hand, it doesn't appear Jesus is fully reigning as King because so much corruption still exists in the world. Rebellious men crucified Jesus and His apostles, and they have persecuted the church throughout history.

So is Jesus the King or not? Of course He is! But the whole world does not yet know He is. John's Revelation message lets us know that soon everyone will recognize Christ as Lord. It has been said that the kingdom of God exists where Christ is. If He lives in you, then you are in the kingdom of God. If He is present in your home and workplace, then that is kingdom territory too.

As John's Revelation continues to unfold in our present day, the cosmic battle between good and evil is nearing the boiling point. From Bethlehem to Calvary to the empty tomb to the spread of Christian missions to the nations . . . the kingdom of God is here, and it is growing. History is steadily moving to that glorious point when every knee will bow and every tongue will confess Christ is Lord of heaven and earth (Philippians 2:10–11). Bow, confess, and worship Him as your King today!

—Jeremy Morton
Cross Point Baptist Church, Perry, GA

WEEK 51, DAY 3

Be Strong in Christ

Revelation 12:13–13:18

The Woman Persecuted

Now when the dragon saw that he had been cast to the earth, he persecuted the woman who gave birth to the male Child. 14But the woman was given two wings of a great eagle, that she might fly into the wilderness to her place, where she is nourished for a time and times and half a time, from the presence of the serpent. 15So the serpent spewed water out of his mouth like a flood after the woman, that he might cause her to be carried away by the flood. 16But the earth helped the woman, and the earth opened its mouth and swallowed up the flood which the dragon had spewed out of his mouth. 17And the dragon was enraged with the woman, and he went to make war with the rest of her offspring, who keep the commandments of God and have the testimony of Jesus Christ.

The Beast from the Sea

13 Then I stood on the sand of the sea. And I saw a beast rising up out of the sea, having seven heads and ten horns, and on his horns ten crowns, and on his heads a blasphemous name. 2Now the beast which I saw was like a leopard, his feet were like the feet of a bear, and his mouth like the mouth of a lion. The dragon gave him his power, his throne, and great authority. 3And I saw one of his heads as if it had been mortally wounded, and his deadly wound was healed. And all the world marveled and followed the beast. 4So they worshiped the dragon who gave authority to the beast; and they worshiped the beast, saying, "Who is like the beast? Who is able to make war with him?"

5And he was given a mouth speaking great things and blasphemies, and he was given authority to continue for forty-two months. 6Then he opened his mouth in blasphemy against God, to blaspheme His name, His tabernacle, and those who dwell in heaven. 7It was granted to him to make war with the saints and to overcome them. And authority was given him over every tribe, tongue, and nation. 8All who dwell on the earth will worship him, whose names have not been written in the Book of Life of the Lamb slain from the foundation of the world.

9If anyone has an ear, let him hear. 10He who leads into captivity shall go into captivity; he who kills with the sword must be killed with the sword. Here is the patience and the faith of the saints.

The Beast from the Earth

11Then I saw another beast coming up out of the earth, and he had two horns like a lamb and spoke like a dragon. 12And he exercises all the authority of the first beast in his presence, and causes the earth and those who dwell in it to worship the first beast, whose deadly wound was healed. 13He performs great signs, so that he even makes fire come down from heaven on the earth in the sight of men. 14And he deceives those who dwell on the earth by those signs which he was granted to do in the sight of the beast, telling those who dwell on the earth to make an image to the beast who was wounded by the sword and lived. 15He was granted power to give breath to the image of the beast, that the image of the beast should both speak and cause as many as would not worship the image of the beast to be killed. 16He causes all, both small and great, rich and poor, free and slave, to receive a mark on their right hand or on their foreheads, 17and that no one may buy or sell except one who has the mark or the name of the beast, or the number of his name.

18Here is wisdom. Let him who has understanding calculate the number of the beast, for it is the number of a man: His number is 666.

DEVOTIONAL

Since Eden, Satan has been the ultimate deceiver. Scripture teaches that Satan has been a murderer and a liar since the beginning and that he is the father of lies (John 8:44). Though Adam was personally responsible for violating God's law, it was Satan who provided the slick, cunning bait that hooked Adam: "You will not surely die. For God knows that in the day you eat of it . . . you will be like God" (Genesis 3:4–5).

The mission of Satan might be summed up this way: he manipulates and destroys by counterfeit. John tells us Satan will continue to use this tactic until the very end. He will tell you more money will bring happiness, or a different spouse will satisfy you, or cutting corners at work will go unnoticed by the boss. Don't believe the lies! Satan places counterfeits before us to take our eyes off the only real truth the world has ever known: Jesus Christ.

Jesus is the one Person who fully withstands Satan's assault. Jesus won in the wilderness, at the cross, and through His bodily resurrection. Ask God to make you vigilant, sober, and obedient. Satan is crafty, but Christ is greater. Be strong in Him!

—Jeremy Morton
Cross Point Baptist Church, Perry, GA

WEEK 51, DAY 4

God's Presence Means Everything

Revelation 14:1–20

The Lamb and the 144,000

14 Then I looked, and behold, a Lamb standing on Mount Zion, and with Him one hundred and forty-four thousand, having His Father's name written on their foreheads. ²And I heard a voice from heaven, like the voice of many waters, and like the voice of loud thunder. And I heard the sound of harpists playing their harps. ³They sang as it were a new song before the throne, before the four living creatures, and the elders; and no one could learn that song except the hundred and forty-four thousand who were redeemed from the earth. ⁴These are the ones who were not defiled with women, for they are virgins. These are the ones who follow the Lamb wherever He goes. These were redeemed from among men, being firstfruits to God and to the Lamb.

⁵And in their mouth was found no deceit, for they are without fault before the throne of God.

The Proclamations of Three Angels

⁶Then I saw another angel flying in the midst of heaven, having the everlasting gospel to preach to those who dwell on the earth—to every nation, tribe, tongue, and people— ⁷saying with a loud voice, "Fear God and give glory to Him, for the hour of His judgment has come; and worship Him who made heaven and earth, the sea and springs of water."

⁸And another angel followed, saying, "Babylon is fallen, is fallen, that great city, because she has made all nations drink of the wine of the wrath of her fornication."

⁹Then a third angel followed them, saying with a loud voice, "If anyone worships the beast and his image, and receives his mark on his forehead or on his hand, ¹⁰he himself shall also drink of the wine of the wrath of God, which is poured out full strength into the cup of His indignation. He shall be tormented with fire and brimstone in the presence of the holy angels and in the presence of the Lamb. ¹¹And the smoke of their torment ascends forever and ever; and they have no rest day or night, who worship the beast and his image, and whoever receives the mark of his name."

¹²Here is the patience of the saints; here are those who keep the commandments of God and the faith of Jesus.

¹³Then I heard a voice from heaven saying to me, "Write: 'Blessed are the dead who die in the Lord from now on.'"

"Yes," says the Spirit, "that they may rest from their labors, and their works follow them."

Reaping the Earth's Harvest

¹⁴Then I looked, and behold, a white cloud, and on the cloud sat One like the Son of Man, having on His head a golden crown, and in His hand a sharp sickle. ¹⁵And another angel came out of the temple, crying with a loud voice to Him who sat on the cloud, "Thrust in Your sickle and reap, for the time has come for You to reap, for the harvest of the earth is ripe." ¹⁶So He who sat on the cloud thrust in His sickle on the earth, and the earth was reaped.

Reaping the Grapes of Wrath

¹⁷Then another angel came out of the temple which is in heaven, he also having a sharp sickle.

¹⁸And another angel came out from the altar, who had power over fire, and he cried with a loud cry to him who had the sharp sickle, saying, "Thrust in your sharp sickle and gather the clusters of the vine of the earth, for her grapes are fully ripe." ¹⁹So the angel thrust his sickle into the earth and gathered the vine of the earth, and threw it into the great winepress of the wrath of God. ²⁰And the winepress was trampled outside the city, and blood came out of the winepress, up to the horses' bridles, for one thousand six hundred furlongs.

DEVOTIONAL

*S*ome interpret the one hundred and forty-four thousand and John's mention of "Mount Zion" (Revelation 14:1) as a picture of believers in heaven. Others view it as Christ's followers still on the earth. Regardless of your view, this is unmistakable: the Lord is always with His children! There is never a moment in a Christian's life when he or she is unaccompanied by God. And God's presence in our lives through Christ is the key to effective, godly living.

What difference does Christ's presence make? In Revelation 14:1–5, John said those who bear the mark of Christ have a new song, they are sexually pure, and they are honest and blameless. Oh the power of a Christ-centered life! Better yet, if your life is filled with Christ's power, there is no fear in death. Verse 13 says, "Blessed are the dead who die in the Lord." God's presence means everything, in life and death. Is His presence evident in you?

—Jeremy Morton
Cross Point Baptist Church, Perry, GA

WEEK 51, DAY 5

The Wrath of God

Revelation 15:1–16:11

Prelude to the Bowl Judgments

15 Then I saw another sign in heaven, great and marvelous: seven angels having the seven last plagues, for in them the wrath of God is complete.
²And I saw something like a sea of glass mingled with fire, and those who have the victory over the beast, over his image and over his mark and over the number of his name, standing on the sea of glass, having harps of God. ³They sing the song of Moses, the servant of God, and the song of the Lamb, saying:

"Great and marvelous are Your works,
　Lord God Almighty!
Just and true are Your ways,
　O King of the saints!
⁴　Who shall not fear You, O Lord, and glorify Your
　　　name?
　For You alone are holy.
　For all nations shall come and worship before You,
　For Your judgments have been manifested."

⁵After these things I looked, and behold, the temple of the tabernacle of the testimony in heaven was opened. ⁶And out of the temple came the seven angels having the seven plagues, clothed in pure bright linen, and having their chests girded with golden bands. ⁷Then one of the four living creatures gave to the seven angels seven golden bowls full of the wrath of God who lives forever and ever. ⁸The temple was filled with smoke from the glory of God and from His power, and no one was able to enter the temple till the seven plagues of the seven angels were completed.

16 Then I heard a loud voice from the temple saying to the seven angels, "Go and pour out the bowls of the wrath of God on the earth."

First Bowl: Loathsome Sores

²So the first went and poured out his bowl upon the earth, and a foul and loathsome sore came upon the men who had the mark of the beast and those who worshiped his image.

Second Bowl: The Sea Turns to Blood

³Then the second angel poured out his bowl on the sea, and it became blood as of a dead man; and every living creature in the sea died.

Third Bowl: The Waters Turn to Blood

⁴Then the third angel poured out his bowl on the rivers and springs of water, and they became blood. ⁵And I heard the angel of the waters saying:

"You are righteous, O Lord,
　The One who is and who was and who is to be,
　Because You have judged these things.
⁶　For they have shed the blood of saints and prophets,
　And You have given them blood to drink.
　For it is their just due."

⁷And I heard another from the altar saying, "Even so, Lord God Almighty, true and righteous are Your judgments."

Fourth Bowl: Men Are Scorched

⁸Then the fourth angel poured out his bowl on the sun, and power was given to him to scorch men with fire. ⁹And men were scorched with great heat, and they blasphemed the name of God who has power over these plagues; and they did not repent and give Him glory.

Fifth Bowl: Darkness and Pain

¹⁰Then the fifth angel poured out his bowl on the throne of the beast, and his kingdom became full of darkness; and they gnawed their tongues because of the pain. ¹¹They blasphemed the God of heaven because of their pains and their sores, and did not repent of their deeds.

DEVOTIONAL

*U*nderstanding Revelation has never been an easy task. *Nevertheless, the message of Revelation is unmistakably clear: God fully and finally defeats evil through the blood of His beloved Son, Jesus Christ.*

Think about it: a violent, brutal crucifixion was required for your sin debt to be paid and for God's wrath toward sin to be satisfied. Oh the wonder of Christ's cross! The world sees a glimpse of the gravity of sin when it meditates on the savage nature of the cross.

The pictures of God's wrath in Revelation remind us that wickedness will not be tolerated forever. Should you fear judgment? If you have never trusted Christ and had your sins covered by His blood, then absolutely, be very afraid! But if your faith rests in Jesus, then fear not, for there is no condemnation for you (Romans 8:1).

—Jeremy Morton
Cross Point Baptist Church, Perry, GA

WEEK 51, DAY 6

Thrive for God's Glory

Revelation 16:12–17:8

Sixth Bowl: Euphrates Dried Up

Then the sixth angel poured out his bowl on the great river Euphrates, and its water was dried up, so that the way of the kings from the east might be prepared. ¹³And I saw three unclean spirits like frogs coming out of the mouth of the dragon, out of the mouth of the beast, and out of the mouth of the false prophet. ¹⁴For they are spirits of demons, performing signs, which go out to the kings of the earth and of the whole world, to gather them to the battle of that great day of God Almighty.

¹⁵"Behold, I am coming as a thief. Blessed is he who watches, and keeps his garments, lest he walk naked and they see his shame."

¹⁶And they gathered them together to the place called in Hebrew, Armageddon.

Seventh Bowl: The Earth Utterly Shaken

¹⁷Then the seventh angel poured out his bowl into the air, and a loud voice came out of the temple of heaven, from the throne, saying, "It is done!" ¹⁸And there were noises and thunderings and lightnings; and there was a great earthquake, such a mighty and great earthquake as had not occurred since men were on the earth. ¹⁹Now the great city was divided into three parts, and the cities of the nations fell. And great Babylon was remembered before God, to give her the cup of the wine of the fierceness of His wrath. ²⁰Then every island fled away, and the mountains were not found. ²¹And great hail from heaven fell upon men, each hailstone about the weight of a talent. Men blasphemed God because of the plague of the hail, since that plague was exceedingly great.

The Scarlet Woman and the Scarlet Beast

17 Then one of the seven angels who had the seven bowls came and talked with me, saying to me, "Come, I will show you the judgment of the great harlot who sits on many waters, ²with whom the kings of the earth committed fornication, and the inhabitants of the earth were made drunk with the wine of her fornication."

³So he carried me away in the Spirit into the wilderness. And I saw a woman sitting on a scarlet beast which was full of names of blasphemy, having seven heads and ten horns. ⁴The woman was arrayed in purple and scarlet, and adorned with gold and precious stones and pearls, having in her hand a golden cup full of abominations and the filthiness of her fornication. ⁵And on her forehead a name was written:

MYSTERY, BABYLON THE GREAT, THE MOTHER OF HARLOTS AND OF THE ABOMINATIONS OF THE EARTH.

⁶I saw the woman, drunk with the blood of the saints and with the blood of the martyrs of Jesus. And when I saw her, I marveled with great amazement.

The Meaning of the Woman and the Beast

⁷But the angel said to me, "Why did you marvel? I will tell you the mystery of the woman and of the beast that carries her, which has the seven heads and the ten horns. ⁸The beast that you saw was, and is not, and will ascend out of the bottomless pit and go to perdition. And those who dwell on the earth will marvel, whose names are not written in the Book of Life from the foundation of the world, when they see the beast that was, and is not, and yet is."

DEVOTIONAL

*B*elievers should not be gullible. Satan is committed to the full destruction of your life. Among the many lessons in Revelation, John clues us in on two of Satan's key methods for assaulting us.

First, Satan attempts to silence God's people through intimidation. The numerous references to the great Beast may indicate the Antichrist and his minions will use their authority to leverage the government's power against the church. It is sad but true; many Christians worldwide are mistreated and violently abused because of their faith. Satan wants them silenced. In some cases, he is even using political regimes to do it.

Second, Satan attempts to weaken God's people through seduction. This is a far different approach than violent persecution. Seduction occurs when God's people become distracted. Satan wants our attention on riches, popularity, or worldly models of success. Satan may even be pleased with "good things" in your life so long as God is not being glorified.

Ask God to give you a heart like His. Only God can bless you with the courage and wisdom you need to thrive for His glory.

—Jeremy Morton
Cross Point Baptist Church, Perry, GA

WEEK 51, DAY 7

You have observed in Revelation the ultimate triumph of Christ over all evil. How are you growing in spiritual victory? How is sin and evil being defeated in you?

_____

_____

_____

_____

_____

_____

_____

_____

_____

_____

_____

_____

In what way have you been persecuted for your faith? How did you respond?

_____

_____

_____

_____

_____

_____

_____

_____

WEEK 52, DAY 1

Run Away from Evil

Revelation 17:9–18:10

"Here is the mind which has wisdom: The seven heads are seven mountains on which the woman sits. 10There are also seven kings. Five have fallen, one is, and the other has not yet come. And when he comes, he must continue a short time. 11The beast that was, and is not, is himself also the eighth, and is of the seven, and is going to perdition.

12"The ten horns which you saw are ten kings who have received no kingdom as yet, but they receive authority for one hour as kings with the beast. 13These are of one mind, and they will give their power and authority to the beast. 14These will make war with the Lamb, and the Lamb will overcome them, for He is Lord of lords and King of kings; and those who are with Him are called, chosen, and faithful."

15Then he said to me, "The waters which you saw, where the harlot sits, are peoples, multitudes, nations, and tongues. 16And the ten horns which you saw on the beast, these will hate the harlot, make her desolate and naked, eat her flesh and burn her with fire. 17For God has put it into their hearts to fulfill His purpose, to be of one mind, and to give their kingdom to the beast, until the words of God are fulfilled. 18And the woman whom you saw is that great city which reigns over the kings of the earth."

The Fall of Babylon the Great

18 After these things I saw another angel coming down from heaven, having great authority, and the earth was illuminated with his glory. 2And he cried mightily with a loud voice, saying, "Babylon the great is fallen, is fallen, and has become a dwelling place of demons, a prison for every foul spirit, and a cage for every unclean and hated bird! 3For all the nations have drunk of the wine of the wrath of her fornication, the kings of the earth have committed fornication with her, and the merchants of the earth have become rich through the abundance of her luxury."

4And I heard another voice from heaven saying, "Come out of her, my people, lest you share in her sins, and lest you receive of her plagues. 5For her sins have reached to heaven, and God has remembered her iniquities. 6Render to her just as she rendered to you, and repay her double according to her works; in the cup which she has mixed, mix double for her. 7In the measure that she glorified herself and lived luxuriously, in the same measure give her torment and sorrow; for she says in her heart, 'I sit as queen, and am no widow, and will not see sorrow.' 8Therefore her plagues will come in one day—death and mourning and famine. And she will be utterly burned with fire, for strong is the Lord God who judges her.

The World Mourns Babylon's Fall

9"The kings of the earth who committed fornication and lived luxuriously with her will weep and lament for her, when they see the smoke of her burning, 10standing at a distance for fear of her torment, saying, 'Alas, alas, that great city Babylon, that mighty city! For in one hour your judgment has come.'"

DEVOTIONAL

The symbolism of the Bible can be confusing. As a result, we can get distracted by what seems hard to understand. However, is it possible that by overthinking the passage, we miss the more basic message God may have for us today?

In Revelation 18, God called His own to flee the influence of Babylon. Babylon was full of wickedness and had a defiling effect on everything it touched. Yet in spite of this reality, there were those who gladly drank of her foolishness and relished in the debauchery she had to offer. The Lord, in His great mercy, offered a loving warning: "Come out of her, my people, lest you share in her sins, and lest you receive of her plagues" (v. 4).

The sad truth is that we can be like the people described in this text. We too, tend to enjoy our secret sins—even if it includes destructive consequences (much like the plagues). The culture in which we live invites us to ignore what we know is right and join in its sin. "Eat, drink, and be merry!" is the mentality. "No worries. It's all good," we hear. However, the culture lies to us and then mocks us when we fail. God, on the other hand, loves us enough to tell us the truth.

Is there something or someplace God is calling you "out of" today? Remember, it is because of His great love for you that He calls to you. He has something so much better to offer you. Heed His call!

—Pieter Van Waarde
Woodcrest Chapel, Columbia, MO

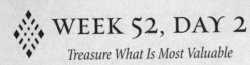

WEEK 52, DAY 2

Treasure What Is Most Valuable

Revelation 18:11–24

"And the merchants of the earth will weep and mourn over her, for no one buys their merchandise anymore: 12merchandise of gold and silver, precious stones and pearls, fine linen and purple, silk and scarlet, every kind of citron wood, every kind of object of ivory, every kind of object of most precious wood, bronze, iron, and marble; 13and cinnamon and incense, fragrant oil and frankincense, wine and oil, fine flour and wheat, cattle and sheep, horses and chariots, and bodies and souls of men. 14The fruit that your soul longed for has gone from you, and all the things which are rich and splendid have gone from you, and you shall find them no more at all. 15The merchants of these things, who became rich by her, will stand at a distance for fear of her torment, weeping and wailing, 16and saying, 'Alas, alas, that great city that was clothed in fine linen, purple, and scarlet, and adorned with gold and precious stones and pearls! 17For in one hour such great riches came to nothing.' Every shipmaster, all who travel by ship, sailors, and as many as trade on the sea, stood at a distance 18and cried out when they saw the smoke of her burning, saying, 'What is like this great city?'

19"They threw dust on their heads and cried out, weeping and wailing, and saying, 'Alas, alas, that great city, in which all who had ships on the sea became rich by her wealth! For in one hour she is made desolate.'

20"Rejoice over her, O heaven, and you holy apostles and prophets, for God has avenged you on her!"

Finality of Babylon's Fall

21Then a mighty angel took up a stone like a great millstone and threw it into the sea, saying, "Thus with violence the great city Babylon shall be thrown down, and shall not be found anymore. 22The sound of harpists, musicians, flutists, and trumpeters shall not be heard in you anymore. No craftsman of any craft shall be found in you anymore, and the sound of a millstone shall not be heard in you anymore. 23The light of a lamp shall not shine in you anymore, and the voice of bridegroom and bride shall not be heard in you anymore. For your merchants were the great men of the earth, for by your sorcery all the nations were deceived. 24And in her was found the blood of prophets and saints, and of all who were slain on the earth."

DEVOTIONAL

At first glance Revelation 18:11–24 seems like such a depressing passage to read on Christmas Day. But there is an important message here for us today. John was inspired by the Holy Spirit to write about the ultimate emptiness and shallowness of materialism. John went into considerable detail about the awe and beauty of Babylon and all that she created, and then it became clear it was ultimately all for nothing. It was burned up and lost in the end. There was no sustainable value in all her material prosperity.

Take a moment to think about the conversations that happen in our culture around Christmas. Think about the stories we hear about the shoppers fighting over the most wanted toys on Black Friday. Even in Christian circles, we can give lip service to the idea that our celebration is about the birth of Christ, while in our heart of hearts, we give priority to the material possessions we will get or give at Christmas.

Gift giving is not inherently evil. In fact, it can often be a great way to express love to those who are near and dear to us. But there is also an inherent risk with all things material. We can inadvertently treasure the gift over the Giver.

Perhaps this passage is meant to remind us that the material goods humanity generally treasures don't hold eternal value. There is a day coming when it will all be tossed into the sea. We can be as those who weep at its passing, or we can take a more proactive approach and declare that our hope and treasures lie in the things we know and have in Christ.

Paul reminds us that "we brought nothing into this world, and it is certain we can carry nothing out" (1 Timothy 6:7). And Jesus told His listeners, "Do not lay up for yourselves treasures on earth, where moth and rust destroy and where thieves break in and steal; but lay up for yourselves treasures in heaven" (Matthew 6:19–20). Is there something specific you can do today to remind yourself of this ideal?

—Pieter Van Waarde
Woodcrest Chapel, Columbia, MO

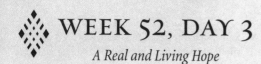

WEEK 52, DAY 3

A Real and Living Hope

Revelation 19:1–16

Heaven Exults over Babylon

19 After these things I heard a loud voice of a great multitude in heaven, saying, "Alleluia! Salvation and glory and honor and power belong to the Lord our God! 2For true and righteous are His judgments, because He has judged the great harlot who corrupted the earth with her fornication; and He has avenged on her the blood of His servants shed by her." 3Again they said, "Alleluia! Her smoke rises up forever and ever!" 4And the twenty-four elders and the four living creatures fell down and worshiped God who sat on the throne, saying, "Amen! Alleluia!" 5Then a voice came from the throne, saying, "Praise our God, all you His servants and those who fear Him, both small and great!"

6And I heard, as it were, the voice of a great multitude, as the sound of many waters and as the sound of mighty thunderings, saying, "Alleluia! For the Lord God Omnipotent reigns! 7Let us be glad and rejoice and give Him glory, for the marriage of the Lamb has come, and His wife has made herself ready." 8And to her it was granted to be arrayed in fine linen, clean and bright, for the fine linen is the righteous acts of the saints.

9Then he said to me, "Write: 'Blessed are those who are called to the marriage supper of the Lamb!'" And he said to me, "These are the true sayings of God." 10And I fell at his feet to worship him. But he said to me, "See that you do not do that! I am your fellow servant, and of your brethren who have the testimony of Jesus. Worship God! For the testimony of Jesus is the spirit of prophecy."

Christ on a White Horse

11Now I saw heaven opened, and behold, a white horse. And He who sat on him was called Faithful and True, and in righteousness He judges and makes war. 12His eyes were like a flame of fire, and on His head were many crowns. He had a name written that no one knew except Himself. 13He was clothed with a robe dipped in blood, and His name is called The Word of God. 14And the armies in heaven, clothed in fine linen, white and clean, followed Him on white horses. 15Now out of His mouth goes a sharp sword, that with it He should strike the nations. And He Himself will rule them with a rod of iron.

He Himself treads the winepress of the fierceness and wrath of Almighty God. 16And He has on His robe and on His thigh a name written:

KING OF KINGS AND LORD OF LORDS.

DEVOTIONAL

This passage provides such a stark contrast with what we just read in the previous chapter. Revelation 18 was all about the destruction of Babylon, and Revelation 19 is all about the exaltation of the Lamb. The last chapter focused on the heartache associated with putting one's hope in worldly wealth. This chapter focuses on the exhilaration associated with worshiping the King of kings and the Lord of lords.

Have you ever noticed that Scripture does not simply decry the ways of evil? The Bible isn't just a Book that teaches us about things to avoid; there is always the positive replacement. There is the admonition to abstain from that which robs us of life and the invitation to embrace the one true God, who gives us that which can only be described as abundant life. The abundant life He provides culminates in the hope that we have in and for heaven.

Unfortunately, heaven is often something extolled principally at funerals. We also tend to use it as a clichéd response to situations that are hard to explain or justify. We are apt to say, "Heaven will make all things right," simply because that allows us to sound spiritual without having to wrestle with the harder aspects of reality.

However, with that said, this vision the Lord entrusted to John is meant to provide a real and living hope for what is in store for those whose hope is in the Lord. There is a real victory awaiting us. This is not a fleeting, whimsical hope. Rather, the image of our Lord is of a mighty warrior restoring order and promising eternal life for those who will rule and reign with Him.

Are you living with this victory in mind? How would you live differently if this real and living hope were stronger in you? Dwell on what Scripture teaches is in store for God's people. Praise God for His victory and that heaven is in your future!

—Pieter Van Waarde
Woodcrest Chapel, Columbia, MO

WEEK 52, DAY 4

God's Triumph over Sin Is Complete

Revelation 19:17–20:15

The Beast and His Armies Defeated

Then I saw an angel standing in the sun; and he cried with a loud voice, saying to all the birds that fly in the midst of heaven, "Come and gather together for the supper of the great God, 18that you may eat the flesh of kings, the flesh of captains, the flesh of mighty men, the flesh of horses and of those who sit on them, and the flesh of all people, free and slave, both small and great."

19And I saw the beast, the kings of the earth, and their armies, gathered together to make war against Him who sat on the horse and against His army. 20Then the beast was captured, and with him the false prophet who worked signs in his presence, by which he deceived those who received the mark of the beast and those who worshiped his image. These two were cast alive into the lake of fire burning with brimstone. 21And the rest were killed with the sword which proceeded from the mouth of Him who sat on the horse. And all the birds were filled with their flesh.

Satan Bound 1000 Years

20Then I saw an angel coming down from heaven, having the key to the bottomless pit and a great chain in his hand. 2He laid hold of the dragon, that serpent of old, who is the Devil and Satan, and bound him for a thousand years; 3and he cast him into the bottomless pit, and shut him up, and set a seal on him, so that he should deceive the nations no more till the thousand years were finished. But after these things he must be released for a little while.

The Saints Reign with Christ 1000 Years

4And I saw thrones, and they sat on them, and judgment was committed to them. Then I saw the souls of those who had been beheaded for their witness to Jesus and for the word of God, who had not worshiped the beast or his image, and had not received his mark on their foreheads or on their hands. And they lived and reigned with Christ for a thousand years. 5But the rest of the dead did not live again until the thousand years were finished. This is the first resurrection. 6Blessed and holy is he who has part in the first resurrection. Over such the second death has no power, but they shall be priests of God and of Christ, and shall reign with Him a thousand years.

Satanic Rebellion Crushed

7Now when the thousand years have expired, Satan will be released from his prison 8and will go out to deceive the nations which are in the four corners of the earth, Gog and Magog, to gather them together to battle, whose number is as the sand of the sea. 9They went up on the breadth of the earth and surrounded the camp of the saints and the beloved city. And fire came down from God out of heaven and devoured them. 10The devil, who deceived them, was cast into the lake of fire and brimstone where the beast and the false prophet are. And they will be tormented day and night forever and ever.

The Great White Throne Judgment

11Then I saw a great white throne and Him who sat on it, from whose face the earth and the heaven fled away. And there was found no place for them. 12And I saw the dead, small and great, standing before God, and books were opened. And another book was opened, which is the Book of Life. And the dead were judged according to their works, by the things which were written in the books. 13The sea gave up the dead who were in it, and Death and Hades delivered up the dead who were in them. And they were judged, each one according to his works. 14Then Death and Hades were cast into the lake of fire. This is the second death. 15And anyone not found written in the Book of Life was cast into the lake of fire.

DEVOTIONAL

This world is not always a just place. We read stories of children starving overseas. Innocents are brutally raped. Evil perpetrators are set free. Cheaters prosper while the faithful are reviled and ridiculed.

This doesn't just happen "out there"; sometimes this is our story too. Sometimes we are the ones who are hurt and must deal with injustice. When we are the victims, it is no longer theoretical, and we can feel helpless and hopeless. We can even fall into despair and assume life will always be this way. But this passage reminds us of the truth: there is a day of justice coming! God will have the final say, and His administration is perfect and just!

Today, put your hope in the truth and in what God has said He will do. Praise God for His justice, and ask Him for strength and patience. Trust His goodness and rely on His power as you persevere.

—Pieter Van Waarde
Woodcrest Chapel, Columbia, MO

WEEK 52, DAY 5

A New and Better Day

Revelation 21:1–27

All Things Made New

21 Now I saw a new heaven and a new earth, for the first heaven and the first earth had passed away. Also there was no more sea. ²Then I, John, saw the holy city, New Jerusalem, coming down out of heaven from God, prepared as a bride adorned for her husband. ³And I heard a loud voice from heaven saying, "Behold, the tabernacle of God is with men, and He will dwell with them, and they shall be His people. God Himself will be with them and be their God. ⁴And God will wipe away every tear from their eyes; there shall be no more death, nor sorrow, nor crying. There shall be no more pain, for the former things have passed away."

⁵Then He who sat on the throne said, "Behold, I make all things new." And He said to me, "Write, for these words are true and faithful."

⁶And He said to me, "It is done! I am the Alpha and the Omega, the Beginning and the End. I will give of the fountain of the water of life freely to him who thirsts. ⁷He who overcomes shall inherit all things, and I will be his God and he shall be My son. ⁸But the cowardly, unbelieving, abominable, murderers, sexually immoral, sorcerers, idolaters, and all liars shall have their part in the lake which burns with fire and brimstone, which is the second death."

The New Jerusalem

⁹Then one of the seven angels who had the seven bowls filled with the seven last plagues came to me and talked with me, saying, "Come, I will show you the bride, the Lamb's wife." ¹⁰And he carried me away in the Spirit to a great and high mountain, and showed me the great city, the holy Jerusalem, descending out of heaven from God, ¹¹having the glory of God. Her light was like a most precious stone, like a jasper stone, clear as crystal. ¹²Also she had a great and high wall with twelve gates, and twelve angels at the gates, and names written on them, which are the names of the twelve tribes of the children of Israel: ¹³three gates on the east, three gates on the north, three gates on the south, and three gates on the west.

¹⁴Now the wall of the city had twelve foundations, and on them were the names of the twelve apostles of the Lamb. ¹⁵And he who talked with me had a gold reed to measure the city, its gates, and its wall. ¹⁶The city is laid out as a square; its length is as great as its breadth. And he measured the city with the reed: twelve thousand furlongs. Its length, breadth, and height are equal. ¹⁷Then he measured its wall: one hundred and forty-four cubits, according to the measure of a man, that is, of an angel. ¹⁸The construction of its wall was of jasper; and the city was pure gold, like clear glass. ¹⁹The foundations of the wall of the city were adorned with all kinds of precious stones: the first foundation was jasper, the second sapphire, the third chalcedony, the fourth emerald, ²⁰the fifth sardonyx, the sixth sardius, the seventh chrysolite, the eighth beryl, the ninth topaz, the tenth chrysoprase, the eleventh jacinth, and the twelfth amethyst. ²¹The twelve gates were twelve pearls: each individual gate was of one pearl. And the street of the city was pure gold, like transparent glass.

The Glory of the New Jerusalem

²²But I saw no temple in it, for the Lord God Almighty and the Lamb are its temple. ²³The city had no need of the sun or of the moon to shine in it, for the glory of God illuminated it. The Lamb is its light. ²⁴And the nations of those who are saved shall walk in its light, and the kings of the earth bring their glory and honor into it. ²⁵Its gates shall not be shut at all by day (there shall be no night there). ²⁶And they shall bring the glory and the honor of the nations into it. ²⁷But there shall by no means enter it anything that defiles, or causes an abomination or a lie, but only those who are written in the Lamb's Book of Life.

DEVOTIONAL

A brainstorming exercise that is meant to expand one's thinking about what is possible asks the question, "If your money or capacity were limitless, what would you do with your life?" When our mental and physical restraints are set aside, we can dream up some dramatic and dynamic scenarios. However, nothing we can imagine can begin to compare to what God has in mind for those who trust in Him.

The picture of a new heaven and a new earth was not given simply to encourage John in the midst of his struggles many years ago. These words were preserved in sacred texts so we might persevere and hold out hope for that new and better day coming.

Give thanks to your Father that He will accomplish great things on that new and better day, and that you will take part in it as one of His own!

—Pieter Van Waarde
Woodcrest Chapel, Columbia, MO

WEEK 52, DAY 6

Jesus Is Coming Soon

Revelation 22:1–21

The River of Life

22 And he showed me a pure river of water of life, clear as crystal, proceeding from the throne of God and of the Lamb. ²In the middle of its street, and on either side of the river, was the tree of life, which bore twelve fruits, each tree yielding its fruit every month. The leaves of the tree were for the healing of the nations. ³And there shall be no more curse, but the throne of God and of the Lamb shall be in it, and His servants shall serve Him. ⁴They shall see His face, and His name shall be on their foreheads. ⁵There shall be no night there: They need no lamp nor light of the sun, for the Lord God gives them light. And they shall reign forever and ever.

The Time Is Near

⁶Then he said to me, "These words are faithful and true." And the Lord God of the holy prophets sent His angel to show His servants the things which must shortly take place.

⁷"Behold, I am coming quickly! Blessed is he who keeps the words of the prophecy of this book."

⁸Now I, John, saw and heard these things. And when I heard and saw, I fell down to worship before the feet of the angel who showed me these things.

⁹Then he said to me, "See that you do not do that. For I am your fellow servant, and of your brethren the prophets, and of those who keep the words of this book. Worship God." ¹⁰And he said to me, "Do not seal the words of the prophecy of this book, for the time is at hand. ¹¹He who is unjust, let him be unjust still; he who is filthy, let him be filthy still; he who is righteous, let him be righteous still; he who is holy, let him be holy still."

Jesus Testifies to the Churches

¹²"And behold, I am coming quickly, and My reward is with Me, to give to every one according to his work. ¹³I am the Alpha and the Omega, the Beginning and the End, the First and the Last."

¹⁴Blessed are those who do His commandments, that they may have the right to the tree of life, and may enter through the gates into the city. ¹⁵But outside are dogs and sorcerers and sexually immoral and murderers and idolaters, and whoever loves and practices a lie.

¹⁶"I, Jesus, have sent My angel to testify to you these things in the churches. I am the Root and the Offspring of David, the Bright and Morning Star."

¹⁷And the Spirit and the bride say, "Come!" And let him who hears say, "Come!" And let him who thirsts come. Whoever desires, let him take the water of life freely.

A Warning

¹⁸For I testify to everyone who hears the words of the prophecy of this book: If anyone adds to these things, God will add to him the plagues that are written in this book; ¹⁹and if anyone takes away from the words of the book of this prophecy, God shall take away his part from the Book of Life, from the holy city, and from the things which are written in this book.

I Am Coming Quickly

²⁰He who testifies to these things says, "Surely I am coming quickly."

Amen. Even so, come, Lord Jesus!

²¹The grace of our Lord Jesus Christ be with you all. Amen.

DEVOTIONAL

Many of us make it a practice to use the end of the year as a time to reflect on where we have been and what we have done. There is much good that comes from this practice, particularly if we give God permission to speak into the process. Reflection and reevaluation are such important pieces in making resolutions. They serve as catalysts for greater fruitfulness and more deliberate effectiveness.

However, it seems that it is also wise, especially in light of the passage we have just read, to keep things in perspective of the imminent coming of Christ. We can have plans for improvements and dream dreams about what we could do, but to put off the essential and prefer the temporal is foolish.

Perhaps this is why we are given such a vivid description of Christ's return in Revelation 22. It grabs our attention and demands that we anticipate His Second Coming. Respond in obedience by praying, "Oh Lord, help me to remember! Protect me from vain planning that focuses too much on this life and leaves Your imminent return out of the picture. May all I do be done in the light of Your return. Come quickly, Lord Jesus!"

—Pieter Van Waarde
Woodcrest Chapel, Columbia, MO

WEEK 52, DAY 7

How do this week's discussions of what will happen in the future affect your life today? Are there things you need to do differently in light of what is coming?

_____

_____

_____

_____

_____

_____

_____

_____

_____

_____

Take a few moments to set some specific goals for the year ahead, taking into account the readings from this week. Remember that the objective in Bible study is not simply to add to our intellectual understanding, but rather to give God room to alter the trajectory of our lives.

_____

_____

_____

_____

_____

_____

_____

_____

_____

OUR MESSAGE TO YOU

I trust that as you come to the close of the year you now have an even greater passion for God's Word than ever before. Psalms 119, with its 176 verses, is the longest chapter in your Bible, and each section of these 176 verses are in eight-verse couplets magnifying God's Word and the God of the Word. In Psalms 119, verse 92, the Bible says that "unless Your law had been my delight, I would then have perished in my affliction." Only Heaven knows the mornings that I have gotten up and felt that if I did not hear a word from the Lord, I could not make it another day.

God's Word has not only cleansed me, but has sustained me through the years. It has taught me in many ways: how I can be cleansed; how to not wander; and how to hide the word in my heart that I might not sin. It has become my meditations, my contemplations, and my delight. God's Word has also taught me to not forget God's faithfulness, tender mercies, and goodness to me, and has reminded me that had it not been for His afflictions, I would have gone astray. I am overwhelmed when I consider the principles, as well as the promises; the rebukes, as well as the encouragement; and the comfort as well as the confrontations that I find in God's Word.

It is my prayer that as you enter the New Year, God's Word will enrich your soul, and may you say along with the Psalmist, Psalms 119, Verses 103-104, "How sweet are Your words to my taste, sweeter than honey to my mouth! Through Your precepts I get understanding: therefore I hate every false way."

Happy New Year to you! God bless you. Thank God for His dear Word.

Dr. Johnny Hunt, Senior Pastor
First Bapitst Church, Woodstock, GA

OLD TESTAMENT READING PLAN

CONTRIBUTORS

John Meador	First Baptist Church, Euless, TX	Week 12
Dr. Dwayne Mercer	First Baptist Church, Oviedo, FL	Week 29
Dr. James Merritt	Cross Pointe Church, Duluth, GA	Week 8
Jeremy Morton	Cross Point Baptist Church, Perry, GA	Week 51
Mike Orr	First Baptist Church, Chipley, FL	Week 39
Dr. Jim Perdue	Second Baptist Church, Warner Robins, GA	Week 27
Dr. Bob Pitman	Bob Pitman Ministries, Muscle Shoals, AL	Week 33
Vance Pitman	Hope Baptist Church, Las Vegas, NV	Week 44
Paul Purvis	First Baptist Church, Temple Terrace, FL	Week 20
Dr. Willy Rice	Calvary Baptist Church, Clearwater, FL	Week 26
Dr. Stephen Rummage	Bell Shoals Baptist Church, Brandon, FL	Week 23
Jeff Schreve	First Baptist Church, Texarkana, TX	Week 10
Allan Taylor	Minister of Education, FBC, Woodstock, GA	Week 35
Dr. Larry Thompson	First Baptist Church, Ft. Lauderdale, FL	Week 15
Dr. Ted Traylor	Olive Baptist Church, Pensacola, FL	Week 24
Pieter Van Waarde	Woodcrest Chapel, Columbia, MO	Week 52
Dr. Jerry Walls	Southside Baptist Church, Warner Robins, GA	Week 11
Rick White	The People's Church, Franklin, TN	Week 41
Michael Whitson	First Baptist Church, Indian Trail, NC	Week 19
Dr. Hayes Wicker	First Baptist Church, Naples, FL	Week 40
Rusty Womack	Lost Mountain Baptist Church, Powder Springs, GA	Week 34
Dr. Danny Wood	Shades Mountain Baptist Church, Birmingham, AL	Week 49
Scott Yirka	Hibernia Baptist Church, Fleming Island, FL	Week 47
Dr. Rob Zinn	Immanuel Baptist Church, Highland, CA	Week 21

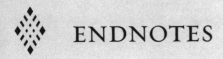

ENDNOTES

[1] Oswald Chambers, *My Utmost for His Highest* (Uhrichsville, OH: Barbour and Co., 1999), 97.

[2] Claudia Wallis, Jeanne McDowell, Alice Park, and Lisa H. Towle, "Faith and Healing," *Time*, June 24, 1996, 58-62.

[3] Quoted in Gary W. Smith, *Life Changing Thoughts* (Bloomington, IN: AuthorHouse, 2009), 304.

[4] Quoted in Edward K. Rowell, ed., *1001 Quotes, Illustrations, and Humorous Stories for Preachers, Teachers, and Writers* (Grand Rapids, MI: Baker Books, 2008), 97.

[5] T. S. Eliot, *Murder in the Cathedral* (Orlando, FL: Harcourt Brace and Co., 1963), 44.

[6] Quoted in Clifton Fadiman and André Bernard, eds., *Bartlett's Book of Anecdotes* (New York: Little, Brown and Company, 2000), 203.

[7] Quoted in Alex Ayres, ed., *The Wit and Wisdom of Mark Twain* (New York: HarperCollins, 2005), 139.

[8] See Steve Miller, *D. L. Moody on Spiritual Leadership* (Chicago: Moody Publishers, 2004), 22.

[9] Quoted in George Sweeting, *How to Begin the Christian Life* (Chicago: Moody Publishers, 1993), 17.

[10] Quoted in Edward K. Rowell, ed., *1001 Quotes, Illustrations, and Humorous Stories for Preachers, Teachers, and Writers* (Grand Rapids, MI: Baker Books, 2008), 164.

[11] See Courtney Anderson, *To the Golden Shore* (Valley Forge, PA: Judson Press, 1987), 334.

[12] Craig Groeschel, *The Christian Atheist* (Grand Rapids, MI: Zondervan, 2010), 190.

[13] Richard J. Krejcir, "Statistics on Pastors," Schaeffer Institute, accessed May 31, 2012, http://www.intothyword.org/articles_view.asp?articleid=36562&columnid.

[14] Clyde Cranford, *Because We Love Him: Embracing a Life of Holiness* (Sisters, OR: Multnomah Publishers, 2002), Google eBook, chap. 1.

[15] See Ron Owens, *Manley Beasley: Man of Faith—Instrument of Revival* (Garland, TX: CrossHouse Publishing), Kindle edition.

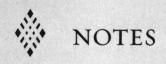

NOTES

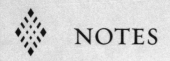

NOTES

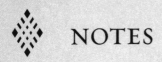

NOTES